Hawaii
a travel survival kit

Glenda Bendure
Ned Friary

P9-DCM-147

Hawaii - a travel survival kit
1st edition

Published by
Lonely Planet Publications
Head Office: PO Box 617, Hawthorn, Vic 3122, Australia
US Office: PO Box 2001A, Berkeley, CA 94702, USA

Printed by
Colorcraft Ltd, Hong Kong

Photographs by
Glenda Bendure & Ned Friary
Cover: Sunset at Keauhou Beach, Big Island, Ned Friary

Published
August 1990

Although the author and publisher have tried to make the information as accurate as possible, they accept no responsibility for any loss, injury or inconvenience sustained by any person using this book.

National Library of Australia Cataloguing in Publication Data

Bendure, Glenda
Hawaii - a travel survival kit.

Includes index.
ISBN 0 86442 089 7.

1. Hawaii – Description and travel –
1981–   – Guide-books. I. Friary, Ned.
II. Title.

919.6904

text & maps © Lonely Planet 1990
photos © photographers as indicated 1990

Glenda Bendure grew up in California's Mojave Desert. Her first trip overseas was as a high school exchange student to New Delhi in 1969. She returned to India for four months in 1972, exploring the country via third-class trains.

Ned Friary has travelled extensively throughout the USA and Central America. He studied Social Thought and Political Economy at the University of Massachusetts in Amherst and upon graduating in 1976 headed west.

They met in Santa Cruz, California, where Glenda was attending university and Ned was living on a small organic farm. In 1978, with Lonely Planet's first book *Across Asia on the Cheap* in hand, they flew to London and hit the overland trail across southern Europe, through Iran and Afghanistan, and on to India and Nepal. The next six years were spent exploring Asia and the Pacific, teaching English in Japan between jaunts.

Their first trip to Hawaii was in 1980, when they went straight from Osaka to the green lushness of Kauai, a soothing sight for concrete-weary eyes. They have returned to Hawaii many times since, often for extended stays. They're also the authors of Lonely Planet's *Micronesia – a travel survival kit*.

They live on Cape Cod in Massachusetts, where Ned is the director of a shelter for the homeless and Glenda writes a travel column for the *Cape Cod Times*.

From the Authors

Many thanks to the people who helped us on this project: Jean Greenwell of the Kona Historical Society; State Parks archaeologist Martha Yent, for assistance on historical sites throughout Hawaii; Linda Delaney from the Office of Hawaiian Affairs; Jeanne Kirby of Greenpeace; Wally Inglis, who sent us information on Hawaii's nuclear-free movement; Bill Puleloa, aquatic biologist for the Department of Land & Natural Resources; Jon Giffin of the Division of Forestry & Wildlife; Leon Bruno of the Lyman Museum in Hilo; Vonnie Lyons of the Keauhou Visitors Association; John P Lockwood, geologist at Hawaiian Volcano Observatory; the Hawaii Visitors Bureau, in particular Kenneth Johnston and Ami Gay; and Connie Wright from Destination Molokai.

Thanks to friends Richard Heinisch, Glenn Thering, Ted Brattstrom, Robert Strong, Carole Dear and Gareth Kernaghan, who hiked with us on the back trails of Molokai, the Big Island and Kauai; and also to Martha Scott, Jim & Barbara Kershner, Dick Dresie, Walter Ritte Jr, Rosemary

Smith & family, Dave Marcus, Ann Lolordo, Dan & Kathi Bennett, Ron & Kathi Driscoll and all the other helpful people we met along the way.

Lonely Planet Credits

Editors	Lindy Cameron
	Sharan Kaur
Maps	David Windle
	Glenn Beanland
•Design, Cover Design & Illustrations	Chris Lee Ack

Many thanks to Tom Smallman, Katie Cody and Lyn McGaurr for copy editing; Sharon Wertheim for indexing; Chris Lee Ack for map corrections; Ann Jeffree, Trudi Canavan and Rod Beanland for additional illustrations; Glenn Beanland for the title page; and Valerie Tellini for additional paste-up.

Thanks also to Thomas Steele for permission to use material from his book *The Hawaiian Shirt* (Thames & Hudson Ltd).

A Warning & a Request

Things change: prices go up, good places go bad, bad places go bankrupt, schedules change – nothing stays the same. If you find things better or worse, recently opened or long since closed, please write and tell us and help make the next edition better!

Your letters will be used to help update future editions and, where possible, important changes will also be included as a Stop Press section in reprints.

All information is greatly appreciated and the best letters will receive a free copy of the next edition, or any other Lonely Planet book of your choice.

Contents

MAP LEGEND

BOUNDARIES

▬·▬·▬·▬	International Boundaries
▬··▬··▬··	Internal Boundaries
·▬··▬··▬··	National Parks, Reserves
‐ ‐ ‐ ‐ ‐	The Equator
··············	The Tropics

SYMBOLS

◎ NEW DELHI	National Capital
● BOMBAY	Provincial or State Capital
● Pune	Major Town
● Barsi	Minor Town
≘	Post Office
✈	Airport
i	Tourist Information
⊖	Bus Station, Terminal
66	Highway Route Number
☾ ♁ ♁	Mosque, Church, Cathedral
∴	Temple, Ruin or Archaeological Site
⊫	Hostel
✚	Hospital
✳	Lookout
▲	Camping Areas
⌐	Picnic Areas
⌂	Hut or Chalet
▲	Mountain
⊬⊬⊬	Railway Station
⫽	Road Bridge
⊬⊬⊬	Road Rail Bridge
⊃⊂	Road Tunnel
⊬) (⊬	Railway Tunnel
⊤⊤⊤	Escarpment or Cliff
⊃	Pass
ᕙ	Ancient or Historic Wall

ROUTES

▬▬▬▬	Major Roads and Highways
‐ ‐ ‐ ‐ ‐	Unsealed Major Roads
▬▬▬	Sealed Roads
‐ ‐ ‐ ‐ ‐	Unsealed Roads, Tracks
▭▭▭	City Streets
┼┼┼┼┼┼┼┼	Railways
▬●▬	Subways
·············	Walking Tracks
‐ ‐ ‐ ‐ ‐	Ferry Routes
┼┼ ┼┼ ┼┼ ┼┼	Cable Car or Chair Lift

HYDROGRAPHIC FEATURES

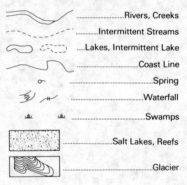

	Rivers, Creeks
	Intermittent Streams
	Lakes, Intermittent Lake
	Coast Line
↶	Spring
	Waterfall
	Swamps
	Salt Lakes, Reefs
	Glacier

OTHER FEATURES

	Parks, Gardens and National Parks
	Built Up Area
	Market Place and Pedestrian Mall
	Plaza and Town Square
	Cemetery

Note: Not all the symbols displayed above will necessarily appear in this book

Introduction

Hawaii's natural beauty is extravagantly grand. Mark Twain appropriately called Hawaii 'the loveliest fleet of islands that lies anchored in any ocean'. The islands are high and rugged. The beaches are beautiful, with sands ranging from bleached white to jet black. Most of the towns and cities are along the coast. The mountainous interiors remain largely uninhabited. They are strikingly scenic, lushly green and cut by spectacular gorges and valleys.

As one of the world's leading visitor destinations, Hawaii does have the expected mass tourism, highrise hotels and crowded beaches. But that's only one side of it.

You can also find secluded coastlines and pristine landscapes, upcountry lodges, isolated resorts, Bed & Breakfast inns and beachfront studios. And the best the islands have to offer is still free for hikers and back-country campers.

Hawaii is the world's most isolated archipelago, 2500 miles from the nearest land mass. Of the thousands of species of flora and fauna that have evolved in isolation here, over 90% exist no where else on earth.

Hawaii has the world's most active volcano (Kilauea), the largest dormant volcano (Haleakala), the highest mountain when measured from the sea floor (Mauna Kea) and the highest sea cliffs (on Molokai).

Hawaii's climate is unusually pleasant for the tropics, as near-constant trade winds prevail throughout the year. Short daytime

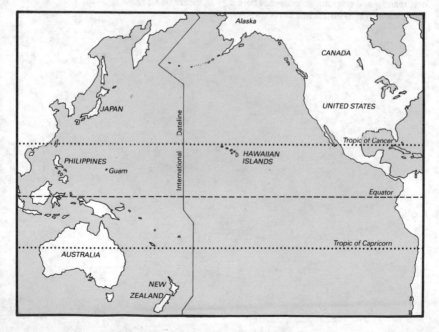

showers often accompanied by rainbows commonly fall while the sun is shining.

The islands have some of the world's top surfing and windsurfing, as well as excellent conditions for swimming, diving, snorkelling, bodysurfing and most other water sports.

Hawaii's six main islands all have lovely beaches and splendid scenery and their leeward coasts are sunny, dry and desert-like, with white sands and turquoise waters. The mountainous windward sides have tropical jungles, cascading waterfalls and pounding surf. The uplands are cool and green, with rolling pasture, small farms and ranches.

Oahu is the most crowded and developed of the islands. Waikiki still provides half the tourist accommodation in Hawaii. Honolulu has all the pluses and minuses of urban life, from congested traffic to good museums and nightlife. It has wonderful restaurants, with both inexpensive ethnic foods and gourmet cuisines. Oahu also has the best surf.

The Big Island has two things the others don't: snow and erupting volcanoes. There's room to move, with niches for cowboys, astronomers and traditional fishing villages, as well as alternative communities settling in on the side of lava flows.

Maui is the second largest and second most developed of the islands. The scenic coastal drive to Hana and the sunrise at Haleakala are two of its highlights. Maui is also the best island for watching humpback whales.

Kauai has Hawaii's greenest scenery, a deeply cut canyon resembling a mini-Grand Canyon and the famous razorback cliffs of the Na Pali Coast.

Molokai and Lanai are the smallest and the most rural, though impending resort development threatens the small-town atmosphere found on both.

Hawaii is ethnically diverse with an appealing collage of East, West and Pacific peoples and cultures. While less than 1% of the population is pure Hawaiian, almost a quarter of the islanders boast some Hawaiian ancestry and there's a resurgence of interest in traditional Hawaiian culture among islanders of all races.

Facts about the Islands

HISTORY

Hawaii is the northern point of the huge triangle of Pacific Ocean islands known as Polynesia,. The other two points are Easter Island to the south-east and New Zealand to the south-west.

The original settlers of Polynesia, which means 'many islands', apparently followed a long migratory path through South-East Asia, down through Indonesia and across Melanesia, before settling the Polynesian islands of Tonga and Samoa in about 1000 BC. Over the next 1500 years they migrated to the more distant islands of Polynesia, with Hawaii being one of the last settled.

Archaeological evidence indicates the first Polynesians arrived from the Marquesas between 500 and 700 AD. Among the links are ancient stone statues found on Hawaii's now uninhabited Necker Island which have striking similarities to those found on the Marquesas.

When the first wave of Tahitians arrived in Hawaii in about 1000 AD they apparently conquered and subjugated the Marquesans, forcing them to build their temples, irrigation ditches and fishponds.

Hawaiian legends of a tribe of little people called *menehune* may well refer to the Marquesans. The word 'menehune' is very similar to the Tahitian word for 'outcast'.

Ancient Hawaii

The earliest Hawaiians had simple animistic beliefs. Good fishing, a safe journey and a healthy child were all the result of being in tune with the spirits of nature. Their offerings to the gods were prayers and a share of the harvest.

Around the 12th century, in a later wave of migration, a powerful Tahitian *kahuna*, Paao, arrived on the Big Island. He felt the Hawaiians were too lax in their worship. He built the first *luakini* temple (Wahaula Heiau, now in Hawaii Volcanoes National Park) and introduced the offering of human sacrifice to the gods, as well as the *kapu* system of taboos which strictly regulated all social interaction.

The kapus forbade commoners from eating the same food or even walking the same ground as the *alii*, or royalty. A commoner who crossed the shadow of a king could be put to death. Women were prohibited from eating coconuts, bananas, pork and certain fish.

Paao decided that Hawaii's blue-blood was too diluted and summoned the chief Pili from Kahiki (Tahiti) to establish a new royal lineage. With Pili as chief and Paao as high priest, a new ruling house was formed. Their dynasty was to last 700 years.

King Kamehameha the Great, as well as all the Big Island chiefs, traced his lineage to Pili. Likewise, Kamehameha's *kahuna nui* (high priest) was descended from Paao.

Religion In the old Hawaiian religion there were four main gods: Ku, Lono, Kane, and Kanaloa.

Ku was the ancestor god for all generations of humankind, past, present and future. He presided over all male gods while his

Ku

wife, *Hina*, took charge of the females. When the sun rose in the morning, it was said to be Ku; when it set in the evening it was Hina. Like Yin and Yang, they were responsible for heaven and earth.

Ku had many manifestations, one as the benevolent god of fishing *Ku-ula*, (Ku of the abundant seas) and others as the god of forests and farming. People prayed to Ku when the harvest was scarce. At a time of drought or other such disaster, a temple would be built to appease Ku.

One of the most fearful of Ku's manifestations was *Kukailimoku* (Ku, the snatcher of land), the war god which Kamehameha the Great worshipped. The temples built for the worship of Kukailimoku were offered sacrifices not only of food, pigs and chickens but also human beings.

Lono was the god in charge of the elements that brought rain and an abundant harvest. He was also the god of fertility and peace. It was as Lono that the Hawaiians welcomed Captain Cook, believing the Englishman to be the god making his promised return to Kealakekua Bay on a floating island.

Kane created the first man out of the dust of the earth and breathed life into him (the Hawaiian word for man is *kane*), and it was from Kane that the Hawaiian chiefs were said to have descended.

Ku, Lono and Kane together created the earth, the moon, the stars and the ocean.

Kanaloa was a god who often struggled against Kane. When heaven and earth separated it was Kanaloa who was placed in charge of the spirits on earth. Forbidden from drinking kava, these spirits revolted and along with Kanaloa were driven to the underworld where Kanaloa became the ruler of the dead.

Below the four main gods, there were 40 lesser gods. The best known of them was *Pele*, goddess of volcanoes. Her sister *Laka* was goddess of the hula, and another sister, *Poliahu*, was the goddess of snow.

The Hawaiians had gods for all occupations and natural phenomena. There was a god for the tapa maker and a god for the canoe builder, shark gods and mountain gods.

Heiaus The remains of several heiaus, the temples of ancient Hawaii, can still be found throughout the islands. There were two basic heiau styles. One was a simple walled enclosure, the other was built of raised terraced

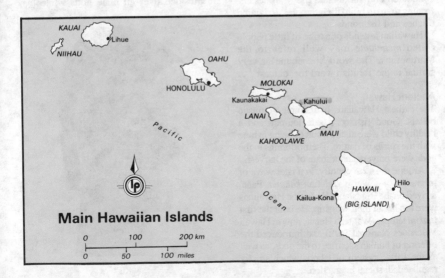

Main Hawaiian Islands

platforms, sometimes quite large. Both were constructed of lava rock.

In ancient times the heiaus had prayer towers, taboo houses and drum houses. The structures were made of ohia wood, thatched with pili grass and tied with cord from the native olona shrub. Tiki or god images called *kii*, were carved of wood and placed around the prayer towers. These days the only remains are the stone foundations.

Heiaus were most commonly dedicated to Lono, the god of harvest, or Ku, the god of war. The heiaus built in honour of Ku were called *luakini heiau* and were the only ones where human sacrifices took place.

Heiaus were built in auspicious sites, often perched on cliffs above the coast or in other places thought to have *mana*, or 'spiritual power'. When a heiau's mana was gone, it was abandoned.

Until the end of Kamehameha the Great's reign, commoners would not dare cast their shadow upon the most sacred heiaus for fear of being put to death. But by the 1820s, after Kamehameha's death and the end of the old religion, anyone could cart the rocks away to build cattle walls, roads and the like and many of the heiaus were dismantled in this way.

Petroglyphs Though the Hawaiians had no written history, they did leave petroglyphs cut into the lava. Many of these carved pictures are stylised stick figures depicting warriors with spears, barking dogs, birds, canoes and other decipherable images. Some are marks which may have recorded important events, calendars or genealogical charts.

The meanings and purposes behind Hawaiian petroglyphs are not well understood. Some may have been intentionally cryptic, while others may just be random graffiti or the carvings of a budding artist.

Most petroglyphs are found along ancient footpaths and may have been clustered at sites thought to have mana.

The Big Island has the greatest concentration of petroglyphs, with several large fields just a few minutes walk from the road.

Fishponds The Hawaiians had a well-

Petroglyph

developed aquaculture system with numerous coastal fishponds.

There were essentially two kinds of fishponds. One type was inshore and totally closed off from the sea, though generally close enough to have brackish water. These inshore ponds would be stocked with netted fry (young fish) and often had different salinity levels which the Hawaiians took advantage of by cultivating different fish in different parts of the pond.

The other kind was a shoreline fishpond, created by building a long stone wall that paralleled the beach and curved back to shore at both ends. For these walled ponds, the Hawaiians built *makaha*, or 'sluice gates', that allowed young fish to swim through but kept fattened fish from swimming back out. The fish in the pond could be easily netted at anytime.

Amaama (mullet) and *awa* (milkfish) were the two varieties most commonly raised in fishponds. Most fish were raised for the alii, not commoners.

Sports According to legend, the god Lono came down from the heavens, upon a rainbow, to a breadfruit grove above Hiilawe Falls in Waipio Valley on the Big Island. There he met Kaikilani, a beautiful female chief who was surrounded by birds. They married and moved to Kealakekua Bay.

When Lono discovered that a chief was lusting after Kaikilani, he became enraged and beat Kaikilani who, as she lay dying, professed her faithful love for Lono alone. In his grief, Lono travelled restlessly around the island challenging every man he met to a wrestling match.

After four months, Lono set sail on a canoe with a tall mast hung with sails made of finely woven Niihau mats. The huge canoe was laden with so much food that it took 40 men to carry it down to Kealakekua Bay. Lono promised to return on a floating island covered with trees and full of chickens and pigs.

The Hawaiians remembered Lono with an annual four-month festival. Each year from October to February the *makahiki* harvest festival was held, with inter-island competitions similar to the Olympics. Even during wartime, fighting would be suspended for the makahiki, so that the games and festivities dedicated to Lono could proceed.

For the makahiki, and at other times of the year as well, the Hawaiians enjoyed all sorts of competitions, from outrigger canoe racing and fishing tournaments to boxing, wrestling and foot races.

Holua, or sled racing, was ancient Hawaii's most exciting spectator sport. Racers would ride prone on narrow wooden sleds, racing at high speed down steep hills along furrows which had been covered with pili grass or ti leaves to make the surface smooth. Many of the holua slide paths were a mile or two long.

Hawaiians were heavy betters and often wagered on the holua races, as well as on foot races, surfing and many other sports.

Surfing was as big in old Hawaii as it is today. When the waves were up, everyone was out. There were royal surfing grounds and spots for commoners as well. Boards used by commoners were made of breadfruit or koa and were about six feet long. Only the alii were free to use the long *olo* boards, which were up to 16 feet in length and made of wiliwili, the lightest of native woods. The boards were highly prized possessions and

were carefully wrapped in tapa cloth and suspended from the ceilings of homes.

Other games included *ulu maika*, in which rounded stone discs were rolled between two stakes, similar to bowling, and *moa pahee*, a game using a polished wood dart.

For the more passive, there was *konane*, a strategy game similar to checkers. Indentations were carved into a stone board to hold the playing pieces which were pebbles of white coral and black lava.

Captain Cook

The Hawaiian Islands were the last of the Polynesian islands to be 'discovered' by the West. Early European explorers who entered the Pacific around the tips of either Africa or South America centred their explorations in the southern hemisphere.

Although the English were the first *known* Western explorers to set foot on Hawaiian shores, there is speculation that the Spanish, whose Manila galleons had been making annual runs between Mexico and the Philippines since 1565, may have stumbled upon Hawaii and kept the discovery a secret.

British explorer Captain James Cook spent the better part of a decade exploring and charting most of the South Pacific before chancing upon Hawaii as he sailed from Tahiti in search of a north-west passage to the Atlantic.

On 18 January 1778 Cook spotted Oahu, Kauai and Niihau. The winds favoured approaching Kauai and on 19 January Cook's ships, the *Discovery* and the *Resolution*, sailed into Kauai's Waimea Bay. Cook named the Hawaiian archipelago the Sandwich Islands in honour of the Earl of Sandwich.

Cook was surprised to find that the islanders had a strong Tahitian influence in their appearance, language and culture. They sailed out in canoes to welcome the ships and were eager to trade fish and sweet potatoes for nails. The islanders were not interested in the useless beads and trinkets used as barter elsewhere. The only thing they cared to exchange anything for was metal, which was totally absent from their islands.

After two weeks of stocking provisions

Captain Cook's Death

on Kauai and Niihau Cook's expedition continued north but, failing to find the fabled passage through the Arctic, he set sail back to Hawaii.

This time he discovered the remaining Hawaiian islands and on 17 January 1779 spotted Kealakekua Bay on the Big Island. A thousand canoes came out to greet him.

When Cook came ashore the next day he was met by the high priest and guided to a temple lined with skulls. Everywhere the English captain went people fell face down on the ground in front of him to the chant of *Lono*.

As fate would have it, Cook had landed during the makahiki, the annual festival in honour of Lono, the god of harvest. The tall masts and white sails of Cook's ships and even the way he sailed clockwise around the island all fitted the legendary descriptions of how Lono would reappear on the scene – on a floating island.

Whether the priests actually believed Cook was Lono or whether they just used his appearance to enhance their power and add a little flair to their festivities is unknown. What is clear is that Cook never realised that both of his arrivals to Hawaii had coincided with the makahiki festivals – he assumed this was the way things were in every day Hawaii.

There's little wonder Cook had a favourable impression of the islands. The islanders treated his crew with open hospitality. Hawaiian men invited the sailors to boxing matches and other competitions and the women performed dances and readily bedded down with them. For men who had just spent months roaming inhospitable frozen tundra, this was paradise indeed.

The expedition's skilled artist, John Webber, was allowed to move freely in the villages. Today his detailed drawings constitute the best visual accounts of old Hawaii.

A few weeks after their arrival the crews had restocked all the supplies needed except firewood. Rather than scour the hillsides for wood Cook directed his men to haul on board the temple railings and wooden images from the harbourside temple dedicated to Lono. As Cook had been passed off as Lono himself, the priests didn't attempt to stop them.

On 4 February the English vessels and their crews headed north out of Kealakekua Bay for Maui, but ran into a storm off the north-west coast of the Big Island where the *Resolution* broke a foremast. Uncertain of finding a safe harbour in Maui, Cook decided to go back to Kealakekua to repair the mast

- a decision which proved to be a fatal mistake.

When they arrived at Kealakekua Bay on 11 February the islanders quickly appeared with the usual provisions to barter. The ruling alii, however, seemed upset with the ships' reappearance.

Apparently the makahiki had ended and not only was Cook's timing inauspicious but so were the conditions of his return. This time he had arrived in an anti-clockwise direction and with a broken sail.

Thievery became a big problem and after a cutter was stolen, Cook ordered a blockade of the bay and then set off with a party of 11 men to the main village at the northern point of the bay. His intention was to capture the high chief Kalaniopuu and hold him until the cutter was returned. This was a tactic which Cook had used elsewhere in the Pacific and saw as reasonable diplomacy.

When one of the Hawaiian canoes tried to leave the harbour, the English sailors fired their muskets. Unknown to Cook's crew the canoe was transporting a chief, Noekema, who was killed.

In the meantime Cook had reached Kalaniopuu's house and the chief had agreed to go with him. But as they walked down to the shore, Kalaniopuu's wailing wife ran after him and the old chief suddenly balked and attempted to get away. In the midst of it all, word of Noekema's death had reached the village where a crowd quickly gathered.

Hoping to prevent bloodshed, Cook let the chief go but it became apparent that this would not be enough for the angry islanders. As Cook was walking toward his boat, he shot at one of the Hawaiians who was threatening him. The pistol misfired and the bullet bounced off the man's chest. The Hawaiians began to throw stones, and Cook's men on shore fired more shots.

Cook had always assumed, as had been the case on other Pacific islands, that to minimise trouble they could fire a few shots so the natives would run. The Hawaiians didn't know this rule.

The sailors in the boats fired a round as their captain began to retreat but before they could reload the crowd of Hawaiians moved in and Cook was struck on the head. He staggered into the shallows where the Hawaiians beat and stabbed him, passing the daggers to share in the kill. Four other sailors also died in the battle.

James Cook was intelligent, resourceful and popularly regarded as one of the greatest and most humane explorers of all time. In this freak melee on a shore of the Sandwich Islands, his last discovery, the life of the greatest explorer and navigator of the century came to a bloody end.

Cook's men went on a rampage. They burned a village, beheaded two of their victims and rowed across the bay with the heads on poles.

Eventually Kalaniopuu made a truce and returned those parts of Cook's dismembered body he was able to find. The skull was returned though it had been stripped of its skin, a common practice bestowed upon great chiefs.

Cook's remains were buried at sea in a military funeral, during which the Hawaiians placed a kapu on the bay and also held ceremonies of their own.

A week after Captain Cook's death, on 14 February, the two ships set sail landing briefly on Oahu, Kauai and Niihau before finally leaving Hawaiian waters on 15 March 1779.

Cook and his crew left the Hawaiians a costly legacy in the iron that was turned into weapons, the diseases that gained a rapid foothold and the birth of the first children of mixed-blood. The crews also returned home with charts and maps which would allow others to follow in their wake and in Britain and Europe their stories and drawings were published, stirring the public's sense of adventure.

Some of Cook's crew returned to the Pacific leading their own expeditions. Among them was Captain George Vancouver who brought the first cattle and horses to Hawaii, and the ill-fated William Bligh who captained the *Bounty*.

The effect of Western civilisation on the people of the Pacific had always been a matter of great concern to Captain James

Cook, for he knew that once the contact had been made there was no going back.

On leaving Tahiti before discovering Hawaii, Cook wrote:

I cannot avoid expressing it as my real opinion that it would have been far better for these poor people never to have known our superiority in the accommodations and arts that make life comfortable, than after once knowing it, to be abandoned in their original incapacity of improvement.

Kamehameha the Great

At the time of Cook's visit to Hawaii in 1779 the islands were divided into separate warring chiefdoms. Just over a decade later, in 1791, Kamehameha the Great, who was to become the first to unite all the Hawaiian Islands, became sole chief of the Big Island.

In 1795, after conquering Maui and Molokai, Kamehameha successfully invaded Oahu in the bloody battle of Nuuanu.

Kamehameha made two attempts to invade Kauai. In 1796 his canoes were caught in a storm at sea and forced to turn back before ever reaching the island. In 1804, while Kamehameha was in Oahu again preparing for the invasion of Kauai, his warriors were struck by a decimating outbreak of a feverish disease, probably cholera, and the invasion plans were scrapped. The luck of the roll may have been Kauai's at the time, but Kamehameha's power was too obvious to ignore, so in 1810 Kauai agreed by treaty to accept Kamehameha's suzerainty.

Despite increasing influence by foreigners throughout the 19th century, Hawaii remained an independent Polynesian kingdom until 1893.

The Sandalwood Trade

By the mid-1780s Hawaii was becoming a popular port of call for Yankee traders plying the seas between North America and China.

In the early 1790s American sea captains discovered Hawaii had great stocks of sandalwood, worth a premium in China. When they showed interest in it, Hawaiian chiefs readily began bargaining their wood away in exchange for weapons.

Kamehameha the Great

A lucrative three-way trade developed. From Hawaii the ships sailed to Canton and traded loads of sandalwood for Chinese silk and porcelain which was then carried back to New England ports and sold at high profit.

Hawaii's forests of sandalwood were so vast at this time that the Chinese name for Hawaii was *Tahn Heong Sahn* - the 'Sandalwood Mountains'.

Eventually Kamehameha put a kapu on all sandalwood forests, giving himself total control over the trade, though in the end it was the sea captains who really cashed in. Payment for the sandalwood was in overpriced goods, originally cannons and rifles, and later exotic items such as European furniture.

While Kamehameha had been careful not to use up all his forests or overburden his subjects, his successor, Liholiho, partially lifted the royal kapu, allowing island chiefs to get in on the action. The chiefs began purchasing foreign luxuries by signing promissory notes to be paid in future shipments of sandalwood.

To pay off the rising 'debts', the *makaainana* (commoners) were forced into virtual servitude. They were used like packhorses to cut and haul the wood, the sandalwood strapped to their backs with bands of ti leaves. The men who carted the wood were called *kua leho*, literally 'calloused backs' after the thick permanent layer of calluses which they developed. It was not uncommon for them to carry heavy loads 20 miles from the interior to ships waiting on the coast. Missionaries recorded seeing caravans of as many as 3000 men carting wood during the height of the trade.

After Hawaii's sandalwood forests were exhausted, Oahu's Governor Boki heard of large reserves of sandalwood in New Hebrides. On November 1829 he set off with 500 men on an ill-conceived expedition to harvest the trees. Boki's ship was lost at sea and the expedition's other ship, not too surprisingly, received a hostile welcome in New Hebrides.

In August 1830, 20 emaciated survivors sailed back into Honolulu Harbor. Boki had been a popular if troubled leader in a rapidly changing Hawaii. Hawaiians grieved in the streets of Honolulu when they heard of Boki's tragedy, and his death marked the end of the sandalwood trade.

End of the Old Religion

King Kamehameha died in 1819 at his Kamakahonu residence on the Big Island. The crown was passed to his reluctant son, Liholiho, who was proclaimed Kamehameha II. In reality the power was passed to Kaahumanu, who had been the favourite of Kamehameha's 21 wives.

Kaahumanu was an ambitious woman, determined to break down the ancient kapu system of taboos that restricted her powers. Less than six months after Kamehameha's death, Kaahumanu threw a feast for women of royalty at the sacred Kamakahonu compound. Though one of the most sacred taboos strictly forbade men from eating with women, Kaahumanu forcefully persuaded Liholiho to sit beside her and join in the meal.

It was an otherwise uneventful meal; not a single angry god manifested itself. But in that one act the old religion was cast aside, along with 600 years of taboos and restrictions. Hawaiians no longer had to fear being put to death for violating the kapus and temple smashing and idol burning immediately followed.

The chiefs and kahunas who resisted were easily squelched by Liholiho using the powerful army which Kamehameha had left behind. It was the end of an era.

Lauhala Mat Maker

Music & Dance

Perhaps nothing is more uniquely Hawaiian than the hula.

There are many different schools of hula, all very disciplined and graceful in their movements. Before Western contact students spent years training in hula schools, sometimes moving to other islands to enrol with the masters.

Most ancient hula dances expressed historical events, legendary tales and the accomplishments of the great alii. Facial expressions, hip sway and dance steps all conveyed the story. They were performed to rhythmic chants and drum beatings, serving to connect with the world of spirits. Eye movement was very important — if the story was about the sun the eyes would gaze upward, if about the netherworld they would gaze downward. One school, the *hula ohelo*, was very sensual, with movements suggesting the act of procreation. Hula dancers wore tapa cloth, not the grass skirts which were introduced from Micronesia only a hundred years ago.

The Christian missionaries thought it all too licentious for their liking and suppressed it. The hula might have been lost forever if not for King Kalakaua, the 'Merrie Monarch', who revived it in the latter half of the 19th century.

The *pahu hula*, a knee drum carved from a breadfruit or coconut log, with a sharkskin drum head, was used solely at hula performances. Other hula musical instruments include *ke laau*, sticks used to keep the beat for the dancers; *ilili*, stone castanets; *puili*, rattles made from split bamboo; and *uliuli*, gourd rattles decorated with colourful feathers.

The Hawaiians were a romantic lot. Instruments used for courting included the *ohe*, a nose flute made of bamboo, and the *ukeke*, a musical bow with a couple of strings.

The ukulele, so strongly identified with Hawaiian music, was actually derived from the braginha, an instrument introduced by Portuguese immigrants in the late 1800s.

Arts & Crafts

In ancient Hawaii, women spent much of their time beating *kapa* (tapa cloth) or preparing *lauhala* for weaving.

Tapa made from the wauke (paper mulberry tree) was the favourite. The bark was carefully stripped, then beaten with a stick. The beaters were carved with different patterns which then became the pattern of the tapa. Dyes were made from charcoal, flowers and sea urchins.

Tapa had many uses in addition to clothing, from food containers to burial shrouds.

After the missionaries introduced cotton cloth and western clothing, the art of tapa making slowly faded away. These days most of the tapa for sale in Hawaii is from Samoa, with bold designs. Hawaiian tapa was different, with more delicate patterns.

Lauhala weaving uses the leaves (*lau*) of the hala tree. Preparing the leaves for weaving is hard, messy work as there are razor-sharp spines along the leaf edges and down the centre. In old Hawaii, lauhala was woven into mats and floor coverings, but these days smaller items like hats, placemats and baskets are most common.

The Hawaiians had no pottery and made their containers using either gourds or wood. Wooden food bowls were mostly of kou or milo, two native woods which didn't leave unpleasant tastes.

Hawaii bowls were free of designs and carvings. Their beauty lay in the natural qualities of the wood and in the shape of the bowl alone. Cracked bowls were often expertly patched with dovetailed pieces of wood. Rather than decrease the value of the bowl, patching suggested heirloom status and such bowls were amongst the most highly prized.

The Hawaiians were known for their elaborate featherwork. The most impressive were the capes worn by chiefs and kings. The longer the cape, the higher the rank. Those made of the yellow feathers of the now extinct mamo bird were the most highly prized.

The mamo was a predominately black bird with a yellow upper tail. Around 80,000 mamo birds were caught to create the cape that King Kamehameha wore. It's said that bird catchers would capture the birds, pluck the desired feathers and release them unharmed. Feathers were also used to make helmets and *leis*.

The *lei palaoa*, a Hawaiian necklace traditionally worn by royalty, is made of finely braided human hair hung with a smoothly carved whale tooth pendant shaped like a curved tongue. Before foreign whalers arrived many of these pendants were made of bone.

The Missionaries

On 19 April 1820 the brig *Thaddeus* arrived from Boston with the first of the Christian missionaries to Hawaii. By a twist of fate, they landed in Kailua Bay, a stone's throw from Kamakahonu, where six months earlier Kaahumanu had feasted the overthrow of the old religion.

It was a timely arrival for the missionaries. The loss of their religion and social structure had left the Hawaiians with a spiritual void into which the Christians zealously stepped.

The *Thaddeus* carried 23 Congregationalists, the first of 12 groups to be sent in the next three decades by the New England-based American Board of Commissioners of Foreign Missions (ABCFM). Their leader was Hiram Bingham.

The missionaries befriended Hawaiian royalty and made their inroads quickly. After Queen Kaahumanu became seriously ill, Sybil Bingham nursed her back to health. Shortly after, Kaahumanu passed a law forbidding work and travel on the Sabbath.

Up until this time the Hawaiians had no written language. Using the Roman alphabet the missionaries established a written Hawaiian language that allowed them to translate the Bible. They taught the Hawaiians to read and write and established the first American high school west of the Rocky Mountains.

With encouragement from the missionaries, the Hawaiians took on Western ways, Western clothing and Western laws.

Liholiho (Kamehameha II)

With Kaahumanu holding the real power, in November 1823 a floundering Liholiho set sail for England with his favourite wife to pay a royal visit to King George – though he failed to inform anyone in England of his plans.

When Liholiho arrived unannounced in London, a misfit in Western clothing and lacking in royal etiquette, the British press roasted him with racist caricatures. He never met King George. While being prepped in the social graces for their audience with the king, Liholiho and his wife came down with measles. They died in England within a few weeks of each other, in July 1824.

The Whalers

Within a year of the missionaries' arrival, whalers began arriving in Hawaiian ports. The first were mostly New England Yankees and a sprinkling of Gay Head Indians and black men. As more ships came on line, crewmen of all nationalities roamed Hawaiian ports. Most were in their teens or twenties, ripe for adventure.

Towns sprung up with shopkeepers catering to the whalers, and saloons, brothels and hotels boomed. Honolulu and Lahaina became the main ports of call.

From 1825 to 1870 Hawaii was the whaling centre of the Pacific. It was a convenient waystation for whalers hunting both the Arctic and Japanese whaling grounds. At its peak, between 500 and 600 whaling ships were pulling into Hawaiian ports each year.

Whaling brought in big money to Hawaii and the dollars spread beyond the whaling towns. Many Maui farmers got their start supplying the whaling ships with potatoes; Big Island cattle ranches grew with the demand for beef; and even the average Hawaiian could earn a little money by turning in sailors who had jumped ship.

Hawaiians themselves made good whalers and sea captains gladly paid a $200 bond to the Hawaiian government for each 'kanaka' allowed to join their crew. Kamehameha IV set up his own fleet of whaling ships which flew under the Hawaiian flag.

Whaling in the Pacific peaked in the mid-1800s and quickly began to burn itself out. In a few short years all but the most distant whaling grounds were being depleted and whalers were forced to go farther afield to make their kills. By 1860 whale oil prices were dropping as an emerging petroleum industry was beginning to produce a less expensive fuel for lighting.

The last straw for the Pacific whaling industry came in 1871 when an early storm in the Arctic caught more than 30 ships by surprise, trapping them in ice floes above the Bering Strait. Though over 1000 seamen were rescued, half of them Hawaiian, the fleet itself was lost.

Sugar Plantations

Ko, or sugar cane, arrived in Hawaii with the early Polynesian settlers. The Hawaiians chewed the cane for its juices, but never refined sugar.

The first known attempt to produce sugar was in 1802 when a Chinese immigrant in Lanai boiled crushed sugar cane in iron pots. Other Chinese soon set up small sugar mills on the scale of neighbourhood bakeries.

In 1835 a Bostonian, William Hooper, saw a bigger opportunity in sugar and went about establishing Hawaii's first sugar plantation.

Hooper convinced Honolulu investors Ladd & Company to put up the money and worked out a deal with Kamehameha III to lease 980 acres of land on Kauai for $300. He then paid the alii for the right to use Hawaiian labourers, freeing them from their traditional work obligations.

Until the mid-1830s Hawaii was still largely feudalistic. Commoners were tied into subsistence fishing and agriculture and worked when needed for the alii. The new plantation system introduced the concept of growing crops for profit rather than subsistence. It marked the advent of capitalism and the introduction of wage labour in Hawaii.

The sugar industry emerged at the same time whalers began arriving in force. Together they formed the root of Hawaii's moneyed economy.

By the 1850s sugar plantations were established on Maui, Oahu and the Big Island, as well as Kauai.

Sugar cane, a giant grass, only flourishes with abundant water so plantations were limited to the rainier parts of Hawaii and even then were vulnerable to drought. In 1856 an 11-mile irrigation ditch was dug to bring mountain water to the Lihue cane fields on Kauai which were suffering from drought. In the 1870s the 17-mile Hamakua Ditch was dug on Maui, the first of several extensive aqueducts that would carry millions of gallons of water daily from upland rainforests to water-thirsty plantations. They turned dry central plains into drenched cane fields. Today Hawaii is still criss-crossed with hundreds of miles of working ditches and aqueducts built a century ago – as well as 180,000 acres of cane.

In addition to the irrigation systems, flumes and railroads were built to carry the sugar cane from the fields to a central mill. For over 100 years, sugar was the backbone of the Hawaiian economy.

Hawaii's Immigrants

As the sugar industry boomed, Hawaii's native population declined, largely as the result of diseases introduced by foreigners.

The plantation owners began to look overseas for a labour supply. They needed immigrants who would be accustomed to working long days in hot weather and for whom the low wages being paid would seem like an opportunity.

In 1852 they began recruiting labourers from China. In 1868 they went to Japan and in the 1870s brought in Portuguese from Madeira and the Azores. After annexation to the USA in 1898 placed restrictions on Chinese immigration, plantation owners turned to Puerto Ricans and Koreans. The Filipinos were the last group of immigrants brought in to work the fields. The first wave came in 1906, the last in 1946.

Though these six ethnic groups made up the bulk of the field hands, South Sea islanders, Scots, Scandinavians, Germans, Galicians, Spaniards and Russians all came in turn.

Each group brought its own culture, food and religion. Chinese clothing styles of the Ming Dynasty mixed with Japanese kimono and European bonnets. A dozen languages filled the air and a pidgin English developed through people's need to communicate with one another.

Conditions varied with the ethnic group and the period. At the turn of the century Japanese labourers were being paid $15 a month. After annexation, the contracts were considered indentured servitude and illegal under US law. Still, wages as low as $1 a day were common up until the 1930s.

About 350,000 immigrants came to Hawaii to work the plantations. A continuous flow of migrant workers was required to replace those who invariably found better options elsewhere. Some came for a set period to save money and return home; others worked out their contracts then moved off the plantations to settle in towns, farm their own plots or start their own businesses.

Plantation towns like Koloa, Paia and Honokaa grew up around the mills, with barber shops, fish markets, beer halls and bathhouses catering to the workers.

The major immigrant populations came to outnumber the native Hawaiians and together they created the unique blend of cultures which characterises Hawaii today.

Kamehameha III

Kamehameha III, the last son of Kamehameha the Great, ruled for 30 years from 1825 to 1854. In 1840 he introduced Hawaii's first constitution, both to protect his powers and adjust to changing times. The constitution established Hawaii's first national legislature and provided for a Supreme Court.

In addition to passing the Great Mahele land act, Kamehameha III gave all male citizens the right to vote and established religious freedom.

In 1843, George Paulet, an upstart British commander upset about a petty land deal involving a British subject, sailed into Honolulu commanding the British ship *Carysfort* and seized Oahu for six months. In that short period, he Anglicised street names, seized property and began to collect taxes.

To avoid bloodshed, Kamehameha III watched as the British flag was raised and the ship's band played 'God Save the Queen'. Queen Victoria herself wasn't flattered. After catching wind of the incident, she dispatched Admiral Richard Thomas to restore Hawaiian independence. Admiral Thomas re-raised the Hawaiian flag at the site of what is today Honolulu's Thomas Square. As the flag was raised Kamehameha III uttered the words *Ua mau ke ea o ka aina i ka pono*, meaning 'The life of the land is preserved in righteousness', which remains Hawaii's motto.

The Great Mahele

The Great Mahele of 1848 changed Hawaiian concepts of land ownership, for the first time allowing land to become a commodity which could be bought and sold.

Through this act the king, who had previously owned all the land, gave up title to the majority of it. Island chiefs were allowed to purchase some of the lands they had controlled as fiefdoms for the king. Other lands were made available to all Hawaiians, divided into farm plots called *kuleana*, each about three acres. In order to retain title, chiefs and commoners had to pay a tax and register the land.

The chiefs had the option of paying the tax in property and many did so. Commoners without land had to pay the fees. Though the act was intended to turn Hawaii into a country of small farms, in the end only a few thousand commoners carried through with the paperwork and received kuleanas.

In 1850 land purchases were opened to foreigners. Unlike the Hawaiians, the Westerners jumped at the opportunity and before the native islanders could clearly grasp the concept of private land ownership, there was little land left to own.

Within a few decades, the Westerners, who were more adept at wheeling and dealing in real estate, owned 80% of all privately held lands, with the bulk of it in huge estates. Many of the Hawaiians who had gone through the process of getting their own kuleana eventually ended up selling it to the *haoles*.

Hawaiians who had grown taro for generations became a landless people, drifting toward the larger towns.

Though commoners had no rights to the land prior to the Great Mahele, they were free to move around and work the property of any chief. In return for their personal use of the land they paid the chief in labour or with a percentage of their produce. In this way they lived off the land. After the Great Mahele, they were simply *off* the land.

Kamehameha IV

Kamehameha IV had a short and rather confusing reign (1855-1863). He tried to give his rule an element of European regality, à la Queen Victoria, and he and his consort, Queen Emma, established a Hawaiian branch of the Anglican Church of England. He also passed a law mandating all children be given a Christian name along with their Hawaiian name. The law stayed on the books until 1967.

Struggles between those wanting to strengthen the monarchy and those wishing to limit it marked the period.

Kamehameha V

Kamehameha V's (1863-1872) major accomplishment was the establishment of a controversial constitution that gave greater power to the king at the expense of elected officials. It also restricted the right to vote.

Kamehameha V, who suffered a severe bout of unrequited love, was also the last of his line. From childhood he was enraptured by Princess Bernice Pauahi who eventually turned him down, opting to marry American Charles Bishop. Jolted by the rejection, Kamehameha V never married yet he apparently also never gave up on the princess. On his death bed he offered her his kingdom but Princess Bernice passed it up.

The bachelor king left no heirs. His death in December 1872 brought an end to the Kamehameha dynasty. Future kings would be elected.

Lunalilo

King Lunalilo (1873-1874) had a short reign. His cabinet, made up largely of Americans, was instrumental in paving the way for a treaty of reciprocity with the USA.

Though the USA was the biggest market for Hawaiian sugar, US sugar tariffs ate heavily into profit margins. As a means of eliminating the tariffs, most plantation owners favoured annexation to the USA.

The American Government was cool to the idea of annexation, but it warmed to the possibility of establishing a naval base on Oahu. In 1872 General John Schofield was sent to assess Pearl Harbor's strategic value.

He was impressed with what he saw – the largest anchorage in the Pacific – and reported his enthusiasm back to Washington.

Though native Hawaiians protested in the streets and the Royal Troops even staged a little mutiny, there would eventually be a reciprocity agreement that would cede Pearl Harbor to the USA in exchange for duty-free access for Hawaiian sugar.

King Kalakaua

King David Kalakaua (1874-1891) was Hawaii's last king. Though known as the 'Merrie Monarch', he ruled in troubled times.

The first trouble he had to deal with was on election day. His contender had been the dowager Queen Emma and when the results were announced, her followers rioted in the streets. Kalakaua had to request aid from the American and British warships which were in Honolulu Harbor.

Despite the initial setback, Kalakaua went on to become a great Hawaiian revivalist. He tried to ensure some self-rule for native Hawaiians, now a minority in their own land, and he composed the national anthem *Aloha Ponoi*, which is now the state song. He also brought back the *hula*, turning around

King David Kalakaua

decades of missionary repression against the 'heathen dance'.

When he left for his first trip overseas, scores of Hawaiians came to the waterfront weeping. The last king to leave the islands, Kamehameha II, had come back in a coffin.

While in America, Kalakaua met with President Ulysses Grant and persuaded him to accept the reciprocity treaty which Congress had been resisting. Kalakaua even managed to postpone the ceding of Pearl Harbor for eight years. He returned to Hawaii a hero, to the business community for the treaty and to the Hawaiians for simply making it back alive.

Kalakaua became a world traveller, visiting India, Egypt, Europe and South-East Asia. To counter the Western powers that were gaining hold of Hawaii, he made a futile attempt to establish a Polynesian-Pacific empire. On a visit with the emperor of Japan, he even proposed a royal marriage between his niece Princess Kaiulani and a Japanese prince but the Japanese declined.

Visits with other foreign monarchs gave Kalakaua a taste for royal pageantry. He returned to build Iolani Palace for what the haole business community thought was an extravagant $360,000. He was a lavish spender who was fond of partying and throwing public luaus.

Kalakaua incurred big debts and became increasingly less popular with the sugar barons whose businesses were now the backbone of the economy. They formed the Hawaiian League in 1887 and developed their own armies which stood ready to overthrow Kalakaua. The league presented Kalakaua with a list of demands and forced him to accept a new constitution strictly limiting his powers. It also limited suffrage to property owners, which by then excluded the vast majority of Hawaiians.

On 30 July 1889, about 150 Hawaiians attempted to overthrow the constitution by occupying Iolani Palace. Called the Wilcox Rebellion after its part-Hawaiian leader, it was a confused and futile attempt and they were forced to surrender.

Kalakaua died in San Francisco in 1891.

Queen Liliuokalani

Kalakaua was succeeded by his sister, Liliuokalani, wife of Oahu's governor John Dominis.

Queen Liliuokalani (1891-1893) was even more determined than Kalakaua to strengthen the power of the monarchy. She charged that the 1887 constitution had illegally been forced upon King Kalakaua. The Hawaii Supreme Court upheld her contention.

In January 1893, as Liliuokalani was about to proclaim a new constitution to restore royal powers, a group of armed haole businessmen occupied the Supreme Court and declared the monarchy overthrown. They announced a provisional government, led by Sanford Dole, son of a pioneer missionary. Wanting to avoid bloodshed, the queen stepped down.

The provisional government immediately appealed to the USA for annexation, while the queen appealed to the USA to restore the monarchy. Timing was in the queen's favour. Democrat president Grover Cleveland had just replaced a Republican administration and his sentiments favoured the queen.

Cleveland sent an envoy, James Blount, to

Queen Liliuokalani

investigate and determine what course of action the American Government should take. In the meantime he received Queen Liluokalani's niece, Princess Kaiulani, who, at the time of the coup, had been in London being prepared for the throne. The beautiful 18-year-old princess eloquently pleaded the monarchy's case. She also made a favourable impression with the American press which already largely caricatured those in favour of the annexation as dour, greedy buffoons.

Cleveland ordered the American flag be taken down and the queen restored to her throne. The provisional government, now firmly in power, turned a deaf ear, declaring that Cleveland was meddling in 'Hawaiian' affairs.

The new government, with Dole as president, inaugurated itself as the Republic of Hawaii on 4 July 1894.

In early 1895 a group of Hawaiian royalists attempted a counter revolution that was easily squashed in a fortnight. Liliuokalani was accused of being a conspirator and placed under arrest.

To humiliate her, she was tried in her own palace and referred to only as Mrs John O Dominis. She was fined $5000 and sentenced to five years of hard labour, later reduced to nine months of house arrest at the palace.

Liliuokalani spent the rest of her life in her husband's residence, Washington Place, one block from the palace. When she died in November 1917, all of Honolulu came out for the funeral procession. To most islanders, Liliuokalani was still their queen.

Annexation

With the Spanish-American War of 1898 Americans suddenly acquired a taste for expansionism.

Not only was Hawaii gifted with Pearl Harbor, but it took on new strategic importance being midway between the USA and its newly acquired possession, the Philippines. Annexation of Hawaii passed in the US Congress on 7 July 1898. Hawaii would enter the 20th century as a territory of the USA.

In just over a century of Western contact the native Hawaiian population had been decimated by foreign diseases to which they had no immunities. It began with the venereal disease brought by Captain Cook's crew in 1778. The whalers followed with cholera and smallpox, and Chinese immigrants, who came to replace Hawaiian labourers, brought leprosy. The native Hawaiian population had been reduced from an estimated 300,000 to less than 50,000.

Descendants of the early missionaries had taken over first the land and now the government. Without ever having fought a single battle against a foreign power, Hawaiians had lost their islands to ambitious foreigners. All in all as far as the native Hawaiians were concerned, the annexation wasn't anything to celebrate.

The Chinese and Japanese were also uneasy. One of the reasons for the reluctance of the US Congress to annex Hawaii had been the racial mix of the islands' population. There were already restrictions on Chinese immigration to America, and restrictions on Japanese seemed likely to follow.

In a rush to avoid a labour shortage the sugar plantation owners quickly brought 70,000 Japanese immigrants into Hawaii. By the time the immigration wave was over the Japanese accounted for over 40% of Hawaii's population.

In the years since the reciprocity agreement, sugar production had increased tenfold. Those who ruled the land ruled the government and closer bonding with the USA didn't change the formula. In 1900 Sanford Dole was appointed the first territorial governor.

World War I

Soon after annexation, the US Navy set up a massive Pacific headquarters at Pearl Harbor and built Schofield Barracks, the largest American army base anywhere. The military became the leading sector of Oahu's economy.

The islands were relatively untouched by WW I, though the first German prisoners of war 'captured' by the USA were in Hawaii. They were escorted off the German gunboat *Grier* which had the misfortune to be docked at Honolulu Harbor when war broke out.

The war affected people in Hawaii in other ways. Heinrich Hackfeld, a German sea captain long settled in the islands, had established Hawaii's most successful merchandise stores, B F Ehler's and Company. He had also developed a real estate empire rooted in sugar, purchasing Lahaina's Pioneer Mill, among other properties. He lost it all during WW I.

Anti-German sentiments forced Hackfeld to liquidate his holdings and American Factors (Amfac) took over his properties, renaming the stores Liberty House.

Pineapple

In the early 1900s pineapple emerged as Hawaii's second major export crop. James Dole, a cousin of Sanford, purchased the island of Lanai in 1922 and turned it into the world's largest pineapple plantation. Though sugar remained king in export value, the more labour-intensive pineapple eventually surpassed it in terms of employment.

In 1936 Pan American flew the first passenger flights from the US mainland to Hawaii, an aviation milestone which ushered in the transpacific air age. Hawaii was now only hours away from the West Coast.

World War II

On 7 December 1941 a wave of Japanese bombers attacked Pearl Harbor, jolting the USA into WW II. The attack caught the American fleet totally by surprise, though there had been warnings, some of which were far from subtle.

At 6.40 am the USS *Ward* spotted a submarine conning tower approaching the entrance of Pearl Harbor. The *Ward* immediately attacked with depth charges and sank what turned out to be one of five midget Japanese submarines launched to penetrate the harbour.

At 7.02 am a radar station on the north shore of Oahu reported planes approaching. Even though they were coming from the wrong direction, they were assumed to be American planes from the mainland.

At 7.55 am Pearl Harbor was hit. Within minutes the USS *Arizona* went down in a fiery inferno, trapping 1177 men beneath the surface. Twenty other US ships were sunk or damaged, along with 347 aircraft. More than 2500 people were killed.

It wasn't until 15 minutes after the attack that American anti-aircraft guns began to shell Japanese planes. The Japanese lost 29 aircraft in the attack.

Hawaii was placed under martial law and Oahu took on the face of a military camp. Already heavily militarised, vast tracts of Hawaii's land were turned over to the US forces for expanded military bases, training and weapons testing. Some of that land would never be returned. Throughout the war, Oahu served as the command post for US Pacific operations.

Following the attack on Pearl Harbor a wave of suspicion landed on the *nissei* (people of Japanese descent) in Hawaii. Sheer numbers prevented the sort of internment practices that took place on the mainland, however, the Japanese in Hawaii were subject to interrogation and their religious and civic leaders were sent to mainland internment camps.

Japanese language schools were closed and many teachers arrested. Posters were hung in restaurants and other public places warning islanders to be careful about speaking carelessly in front of anyone of Japanese ancestry. Nissei were dismissed from posts in the Hawaiian National Guard and prevented from joining the armed services.

Eventually the US allowed these second-generation Japanese-Americans to volunteer for a segregated regiment, though they were kept on the mainland and out of action for much of the war.

During the final stages of the war, however, when fighting was at its heaviest, the nissei were given the chance to form a combat unit. Volunteers were called and more than 10,000 nissei signed up, forming two distinguished Japanese-American regiments.

The 442nd Second Regimental Combat Team was sent into action on the European

Honolulu Star-Bulletin 1st EXTRA

Evening Bulletin, Est. 1882, No. 11287
Hawaiian Star, Vol. XLVIII No. 15294

HONOLULU, TERRITORY OF HAWAII, U. S. A., SUNDAY, DECEMBER 7, 1941

★ PRICE FIVE CENTS

WAR !

(Associated Press by Transpacific Telephone)

SAN FRANCISCO, Dec. 7.—President Roosevelt announced this morning that Japanese planes had attacked Manila and Pearl Harbor.

OAHU BOMBED BY JAPANESE PLANES

SIX KNOWN DEAD, 21 INJURED, AT EMERGENCY HOSPITAL

Pearl Harbor Bombing

front and became the most decorated fighting unit in US history.

The veterans returned to Hawaii with different expectations. Many went on to college using the GI bill and today account for some of Hawaii's most influential lawyers. Among the veterans of the 442nd are Hawaii's two current US senators, Spark Matsunaga and Daniel Inouye, the latter who lost an arm in the fighting.

Unionising Hawaii

The feisty mainland-based International Longshoremen's and Warehousemen's Union (ILWU) began organising Hawaiian labour in the 1930s.

After WW II, the ILWU organised an intensive campaign against the 'Big Five' – C Brewer, Castle & Cooke, Alexander & Baldwin, Theo Davies and Amfac – Hawaii's biggest businesses and landholders, all with roots in sugar.

The ILWU's six-month waterfront strike in 1949 virtually halted all shipments to and from Hawaii. They went on to organise plantation strikes which resulted in Hawaii's sugar and pineapple workers becoming the world's highest paid.

The new union movement helped develop a political opposition to the staunchly Republican big landowners, who had maintained a stronghold on the political scene since annexation.

In the 1950s McCarthyism, the fanatical wave of anti-Communism which swept the mainland, spilled over to Hawaii. In the fallout, the leader of the ILWU in Hawaii, Jack Hall, was tried and convicted of being a Communist.

Post-War Hawaii

WW II brought Hawaii closer to the centre stage of American culture and politics.

The prospect of statehood had long been the central topic in Hawaiian political circles.

Three decades has passed since Hawaii's first delegate to the US Congress, Prince Jonah Kuhio Kalanianaole, introduced the first statehood bill in 1919. It had received a cool reception in Washington at that time and there were mixed feelings in Hawaii as well. However by the time the war was over, opinion polls showed that two out of three Hawaiian residents favoured statehood.

Still, Hawaii was too much of a melting pot for many congressmen to support statehood, particularly those from the segregated southern states. To the overwhelmingly white and largely conservative Congress, Hawaii's multi-ethnic community was too exotic and foreign to be thought of as American.

Congress was also concerned with the success of Hawaiian labour strikes and the growth of membership in the ILWU. It all combined to keep statehood at bay until the end of the 1950s.

Statehood

In March 1959 the US Congress finally passed legislation to make Hawaii a state. On 27 June a plebiscite was held in Hawaii. Over 90% of the islanders voted for statehood. The island of Niihau was the only precinct to vote against it.

On 21 August 1959, after 61 years of territorial status, Hawaii became the 50th state of the USA.

GEOLOGY

The Hawaiian Islands are the tips of massive mountains, created by a crack in the earth's mantle which has been spewing out molten rock for 25 million years. The hot spot is stationary, but the ocean floor is part of the Pacific Plate which is moving north-west at the rate of about three inches a year. (The eastern edge of this plate is California's San Andreas fault.)

As weak spots in the earth's crust pass over the hot spot, molten lava bursts through as volcanoes, building underwater mountains. Some of them finally emerge above the water as islands.

Each new volcano eventually creeps northward past the hot spot which created it.

The farther from the source, the lower the volcanic activity, until the volcano is eventually cut off completely and turns cold.

Once the lava stops it's a downhill battle. The forces of erosion – wind, rain and waves – slowly wash the mountains away. In addition, the settling of the ocean floor causes the land to gradually recede.

Thus the once mountainous Northwestern Hawaiian Islands, the oldest in the Hawaiian chain, are now low flat atolls that eventually will be totally submerged.

The Big Island, Hawaii's southernmost island, is still in the birthing process. Its most active volcano, Kilauea, is directly over the hot spot. In its latest eruptive phase, which began in 1983 and still continues, it has pumped out more than one billion cubic yards of lava, making this the largest known volcanic eruption in Hawaii.

Less than 30 miles south-east of the Big Island, a new seamount named Loihi has already built up 15,000 feet on the ocean floor. The growing mounds of lava are expected to break the ocean surface within 10,000 years. If it were to get hyperactive, it could emerge within a century or two.

In 1987 the Woods Hole Oceanographic Institute explored Loihi with *Alvin*, the same deepwater mini-sub that had discovered the *Titanic* wreck the year before. They measured Loihi's summit to be 3117 feet below the surface of the water.

Hawaii's volcanoes are shield volcanoes which form not by explosion but by a slow build-up of layer upon layer of lava. They rise from the sea with gentle slopes and a relatively smooth surface. It's only after eons of facing the elements that their surfaces become eroded. It's for this reason that the Na Pali cliffs on Kauai, the oldest of the main islands, are the most jagged in Hawaii.

Hawaii's active volcanoes are Kilauea and Mauna Loa, both on the Big Island. The Big Island's Mauna Kea and Hualalei and Maui's Haleakala are dormant, with future eruptions possible. The volcanoes on all the other Hawaiian islands are considered extinct.

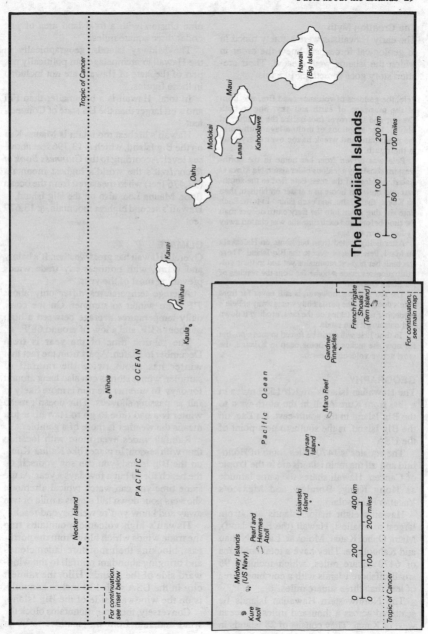

The Hawaiian Islands

The Creation Myth

The early Hawaiians were astutely tuned in to geological forces and knew the order in which the islands were created. Their creation story goes something like this:

Pele, the goddess of volcanoes and fire, was born of the marriage of earth and sky. She is both Creator and Destroyer (not unlike the Hindu god Shiva). Her eruptions of molten lava both build the mountains and wreak havoc over everything in their path.

Pele was driven from her home in the northwestern shoals by a jealous older sister, Na Maka O Kahai, goddess of the seas. Pele fled to the southeast and built her home in a crater on Niihau, then on Kauai, then Oahu, and each island in turn. Each time she dug down into the fiery earth deeper than the time before, and each time she was chased away by her sister, the sea.

After being routed from her home on Haleakala on Maui, Pele crossed over to the Big Island. There she built her highest mountains yet and in their volcanic recesses made a home far from the reaches of Na Maka O Kahai.

The sea goddess, however, is still never far from Pele's doorstep. She persistently wears away at Pele's home, her waves taking on the lava, eroding it down and crushing it into sand.

In time Pele will again be forced to move on, but for now she makes her home deep in Kilauea, the most active volcano on earth.

GEOGRAPHY

The Hawaiian Islands stretch 1523 miles in a line from Kure Atoll in the north-west to the Big Island in the south-east. Ka Lae, on the Big Island, is the southernmost point of the USA.

The equator is 1470 miles south of Honolulu and all the main islands are in the Tropic of Cancer. Hawaii shares the same latitude as Hong Kong, Bombay and Mexico's Yucatan Peninsula.

Hawaii's eight major islands are, from largest to smallest, Hawaii (the Big Island), Maui, Oahu, Kauai, Molokai, Lanai, Niihau and Kahoolawe. They have a total land area of 6470 square miles, which includes 96 small offshore islands with a combined area of less than three square miles.

The Northwestern Hawaiian Islands lie scattered across a thousand miles of ocean west of Kauai. They consist of 28 islands in nine clusters with a total land area of just under three square miles.

The Midway Islands, geographically in the Hawaiian archipelago but politically not part of the state of Hawaii, are not included in these figures.

In total, Hawaii is a bit smaller than Fiji and a bit larger than the US state of Connecticut.

Hawaii's highest mountain is Mauna Kea on the Big Island, which is 13,796 feet above sea level. According to the *Guinness Book of Records* it's the world's highest mountain (33,476 feet) when measured from the ocean floor. Mauna Loa, also on the Big Island, is Hawaii's second highest mountain, at 13,679 feet.

CLIMATE

Overall, Hawaii has great weather. It's balmy and warm, with northeasterly trade winds prevailing most of the year.

Average temperatures differ only about 7°F from winter to summer. On the coast daily temperatures average between a high of about 83°F, and a low of around 68°F.

The rainiest time of the year is from December to March. Apart from the fact that winter has about twice the rainfall of summer, winter storms can also hang around for days. In summer the rain is more likely to fall as passing showers. This doesn't mean winter is a bad time to go to Hawaii, it just means the weather is more of a gamble.

Rainfall varies even more with location than with season. In places like Kailua-Kona, on the Big Island, you can sun yourself on the beach for all but a few days a year. At the same time you can watch typical afternoon showers pour down hill slopes a mile or two away and know you're well beyond reach.

Hawaii's high volcanic mountains trap the trade winds which blow from the northeast, blocking their moisture-laden clouds and bringing abundant rainfall to the windward side of the islands. Hilo, the rainiest city in the USA with 130 inches annually, is on the windward side of the Big Island.

Conversely, the same mountains block the wind and rain from the southwesterly, or leeward side of the islands, so it's there you'll find the driest, sunniest conditions and the calmest waters. Leeward areas generally receive 10 to 25 inches of rain a year.

During kona weather the winds blow from the south, a shift from the typical north-east trades. The ocean swell pattern also changes – dive spots suddenly become surfing spots and vice versa. Kona storms usually occur in winter and are vey unpredictable.

The summits of Mauna Kea and Mauna Loa on the Big Island receive snow each winter and Haleakala on Maui also dips below freezing. The lowest temperature ever recorded on Mauna Kea, Hawaii's coldest spot, was 11°F, while the highest temperature there was 66°F.

FLORA & FAUNA

The Hawaiian island chain, which is 2500 miles from the nearest continental land mass, is one of the most remote in the world.

All living things which reached Hawaii's shores were carried across the ocean on the wind or the waves – seeds clinging to a bird's feather, a floating hala plant, or insect eggs in a piece of driftwood. Probably the first to arrive on the new volcanoes were fern and moss spores, able to drift thousands of miles in the air.

It's estimated that before human contact a new species managed to take hold only once every 100,000 years. New arrivals found specialised habitats from desert to rainforest and elevations from sea level to nearly 14,000 feet. They evolved to fit their new environment.

Over 90% of Hawaii's native flora and fauna are found nowhere else on earth. Some still resemble their ancestors. The *nene*, for instance, looks like its cousin the Canada goose, but its feet have adapted to walking on lava by losing most of their webbing. The majority of Hawaiian birds, however, have evolved so thoroughly that it's not possible to trace them to any continental ancestors.

Many of Hawaii's birds may have evolved from a single species, as is thought to have been the case with over 30 species of native honeycreeper. At the time of

Western contact, Hawaii had 70 native bird species. Of those, 24 are now extinct and an additional 30 are threatened with extinction.

Having evolved with limited competition and few predators, Hawaii's native species generally fare poorly amongst more aggressive introduced flora and fauna. They are also highly sensitive to habitat destruction.

When the first Polynesian settlers arrived, they weren't travelling light. They brought food and medicinal plants, chickens, dogs and pigs.

The pace of introducing exotic species escalated with the arrival of Westerners, starting with Captain Cook who dropped off goats and left some melon and pumpkin seeds. The next Western visitors left cattle and horses.

Prior to human contact, Hawaii had no land mammals at all except for monk seals and hoary bats. The introduction of foraging and grazing animals caught many plants by surprise. Pigs, cattle and goats devastated Hawaii's fragile ecosystems. Released songbirds and gamebirds spread avian diseases to which native Hawaiian birds had no immunity. Erosion, deforestation and thousands of introduced plants which compete with and choke out native vegetation have all taken their toll.

Today more than 25% of all endangered species in the USA are Hawaiian plants and animals. Of approximately 2400 different native plants, half are either threatened or endangered.

Hawaiian Monk Seal

The Hawaiian monk seal, so named for the cowl-like fold of skin at its neck, exists only in Hawaii. The species has remained nearly unchanged for 15 million years but is now in danger of dying out completely. Only about 1000 remain.

Hawaiian monk seals, sensitive to human disruption, breed and give birth primarily in the Northwestern Hawaiian Islands. In recent years, however, sightings of seals hauling themselves onto Kauai's beaches have increased.

Of the world's two other monk seal species, the Caribbean monk seal is already extinct and the Mediterranean monk seal also numbers only in the hundreds.

Whales & Dolphins

Whales and dolphins are marine cetaceans which means they are air breathing, warm blooded, placental mammals. Basically there are two types of whales: baleen – which include the humpback, right, fin, minke and the huge blue whale; and toothed – which includes not only pilot, killer and sperm whales but also dolphins and porpoises.

The latter variety obviously have teeth, which they use to catch and rip apart their prey. The toothless whales have rows of baleen, otherwise known as whalebone, which is a horny elastic material that hangs from the upper jaw on either side of the palate. The baleen acts as a filter to extract plankton from the water entering the whale's mouth as it swims along. (This is the same whalebone once used as stiffening in corsets.)

Several types of whales frequent Hawaiian waters, though it is the migrating humpback which everyone wants to see. Luckily for whale watchers, humpback whales are coast-huggers, preferring waters with depths of less than 600 feet.

Other migratory whales which pass by the islands on occasion include the fin whale, minke whale and right whale.

All of Hawaii's year-round resident cetaceans are toothed whales. The most common is the pilot whale, a small whale which often travels in large groups, preferring the deep offshore waters.

Others include the sperm whale, false killer whale, pigmy killer whale, beaked whale and melon-head whale.

Though it's easy to think of whales as gargantuan fish, all are red-blooded mammals which need air to breathe and which lactate and nurse their young.

Curiously, the Hawaiians seem to have paid little attention to whales. They are not seen in petroglyph drawings and there are virtually no legends about whales.

There are a few dolphins common to Hawaiian waters including the bottlenose, slender-beaked, spinner and rough-toothed varieties. The *mahimahi* or 'dolphin' that you may come across on menus in Hawaii is not the mammal but a fish.

Humpback Whales Humpbacks, once one of the most abundant of the great whales, were hunted almost to extinction and are now an endangered species. Around the turn of the century an estimated 15,000 humpbacks remained. They were still being hunted as late as 1966 when the International Whaling Commission enforced a ban.

The entire population of North Pacific humpbacks is now thought to be about 1500. More than half of those winter in Hawaii, while most of the others head for Mexico.

Humpbacks feed all summer in the plankton-rich waters off Alaska, developing a layer of blubber which sustains them through the winter. They are one of the toothless whales which gulp in huge quantities of water and then strain it back out through a filter-like baleen in their mouths, trapping krill and small fish. They can eat close to a ton of food a day.

During their romantic winter sojourn in the warm tropical waters off Hawaii they mate and give birth. The gestation period is 10 to 12 months.

Mothers stay in shallow waters once the calf is born, apparently as protection from shark attacks. At birth calves are about 12 feet long and weigh 3000 pounds. They are nursed for about six months and can put on 100 pounds a day in the first few weeks. Adults go without eating while in Hawaii.

Humpbacks are the fifth largest of the great whales. They reach lengths of 45 feet and weigh 40 to 45 tons.

Humpbacks don't arrive in Hawaii en masse, but start filtering in around November. They can be found throughout the islands, though their most popular wintering spot is the shallow waters between Maui, Lanai, Molokai and Kahoolawe. The Kona coast of the Big Island is another favoured spot, as is the Penguin Bank west of Molokai.

Whales are highly sensitive to human activity and noise and seek out quiet coastal areas. They have abandoned areas where

Top: Kaina Keana'aina Hula Troupe, Big Island
Left: Eddie Pu, ranger at Oheo Gulch, Maui
Right: Hawaiian weaving demonstration, Polynesian Cultural Center, Oahu

human activities have picked up and seem to have a particular distaste for jet skis.

Humpbacks have distinctive long white flippers and knobby heads. They're great performers, known for their acrobatic displays combining arching dives, breaching and slapping the water with their narrow flippers.

In breaching, humpbacks jump almost clear out of the water and then splash down with tremendous force.

They save the best performances for breeding time. Sometimes several bull whales will do a series of crashing breaches to gain the favour of a cow, often bashing into one another, even drawing blood, before the most impressive emerges the winner.

Humpbacks are protected by US federal law under the Marine Mammal Protection Act and the Endangered Species Act. Approaching within 100 yards of a humpback in US waters is prohibited.

The humpback whale has been designated Hawaii's official marine mammal.

Whale Songs Humpbacks are remarkable not only for their acrobatics but also for their singing. They are the only species of large whales known to do either.

Each member of the herd sings the same set of songs, in the same order. Their songs last anywhere from six to 30 minutes and evolve as the season goes on, with new phrases added and old ones dropped, so that the songs the whales sing when they arrive in Hawaii become different songs by the time they leave.

This ability to compose complex tunes is just one indicator of the humpback's highly developed intelligence.

It's thought that the humpbacks don't sing in their feeding grounds in Alaska. When they return to Hawaii six months later they recall the songs from the last season and begin where they left off. The humpback's elaborate songs include the range of frequencies audible to the human ear.

Environmental Groups
Sierra Club Legal Defense Fund The Sierra Club Legal Defense Fund is in the forefront pressing legal challenges against abuses to Hawaii's fragile environment.

In conjunction with Greenpeace, they have been challenging the state of Hawaii for allowing jet skis and parasailing in waters used by endangered humpback whales and green sea turtles.

In another challenge, they took on the National Rifle Association and the state to force the removal of introduced mouflon game sheep from the slopes of Mauna Kea on the Big Island. The sheep were found to be the primary cause for the decline of a small, native honeycreeper called the *palila*.

It was the first time that habitat destruction was successfully defined as the 'taking' (meaning killing, harming or harassing) of an endangered species under the US Endangered Species Act. The State Department of Land & Natural Resources spent a bundle to fight the Sierra Club tooth and nail but finally lost after 10 years of legal action. If you want to learn more about their present struggles, the Sierra Club Legal Defense Fund's Mid-Pacific office (tel 599-2436) is at 212 Merchant St, Suite 202, Honolulu, HI 96813.

Nature Conservancy The Nature Conservancy of Hawaii is protecting Hawaii's rarest ecosystems by buying up vast tracts of land and working out long-term stewardships with some of Hawaii's biggest landholders.

One project included purchasing the Kipahulu Valley on Maui in conjunction with the state and turning the 11,000 acres over to the federal government to become part of Haleakala National Park. The Oheo Pools south of Hana are part of this land.

On Molokai they manage the rainforest at Kamakou and Pelekunu Valley on the wet north-east coast and the windswept Moomomi dunes on the dry north-west coast.

They also manage a crater above Hanauma Bay on Oahu, the Waikamoi rainforest on Maui, a native dryland forest in Lanai and a Kauai nesting site for the *ao* (Newell's shearwater), a threatened species once thought extinct.

For more information contact the Nature Conservancy of Hawaii (tel 537-4508), 1116 Smith St, Honolulu, HI 96817.

Hawaii Greens A Hawaii branch of the Green Movement was started in 1987 with people from the University of Hawaii and is beginning to grow. This political movement started in New Zealand in the late 1970s and has since spread to many other countries.

The roots are in ecology, global responsibility and non-violence, all geared for the survival of the planet. For more information contact the Hawaii Greens (tel 524-2185), Box 61508, Honolulu, HI 96839.

GOVERNMENT

Hawaii has three levels of government: federal, state and county. The seat of state government is in Honolulu.

Hawaii has a typical state government with executive power vested in the governor. The current governor, John Waihee, is Hawaii's first governor of Hawaiian ancestry. He is a Democrat and was elected to a four-year term in 1986.

John Waihee

The state's lawmaking body is a bicameral legislature. The Senate is comprised of 25 members, elected for four-year terms from the state's 25 senatorial districts. The House of Representatives has 51 members, each elected for a two-year term.

The legislature has a typical Hawaiian casualness. The regular legislative session, which convenes on the third Wednesday of January, meets for only 60 days a year. Special sessions of up to 30 days can be convened by the governor, but otherwise that's it.

Hawaii is the only US state to have a public education system run by the state, rather than county or town education boards. Education accounts for approximately one-third of the state budget.

Unlike the mainland states, Hawaii has no municipal governments, though it is divided into four county governments. The city of Honolulu is part of Honolulu County which governs all of Oahu; Hawaii County governs the Big Island; Kauai County governs Kauai and Niihau; and Maui County governs Maui, Molokai and Lanai.

The leprosy colony of Kalaupapa on Molokai is called the 'county' of Kalawao, but it has no county government and is under the jurisdiction of the Hawaii State Department of Health.

Each county has a mayor and county council. The counties provide services, such as police and fire protection, that on the mainland are usually assigned to cities. Development issues are usually decided at county level and are the central issue of most mayoral elections.

ECONOMY

Tourism is Hawaii's largest industry and accounts for about 30% of the state's income. Hawaii gets about six million visitors a year. In total they spend about $6.6 billion in the state, but not all at the same rate. In 1987, the 3.7 million visiting Americans spent an average of $102 a day, while the 1.2 million Japanese averaged $367 a day.

The second largest sector in the economy is the US military, pumping out $2 billion annually. Agriculture is a distant third.

Sugar and pineapple, once the base of Hawaii's economy, are losing ground. Together in 1987 they accounted for $317 million in sales. Flowers and macadamia nuts brought in another $91 million.

Pakalolo is a far bigger cash crop than all other crops combined. An estimated $1.9 billion worth of marijuana was confiscated in police raids in 1987. The quantity that made it to harvest is unknown, but it's assumed that the police haul was only a fraction of the total.

Hawaii is moving to diversify its economy and one direction it's heading is into the area of high technology. The state is in the forefront of a lot of renewable energy research, including volcanic geothermal and ocean thermal energy conversion. It's also home to some of the world's top astronomy observatories, while space industry projects include 'Star Wars' laser beams and plans for a Big Island satellite launch pad. Aquaculture is another rapidly developing industry, including the raising of nori, freshwater prawns, 'Maine' lobsters and spirulina

Hawaii's former agribusiness-based economy is in the midst of change. Hawaii's 'Big Five' companies – Amfac, Castle & Cooke, C Brewer, Theo Davies and Alexander & Baldwin – all had their origins in sugar, which is on the decline. The Big Five hold on to their plantations not so much for what's being produced on them, but for the potential they hold as future golf courses and condo developments – and bit by bit they're being sold off for those purposes.

The islands are undergoing a major building boom, largely in resort developments. The construction crane is often jokingly called Hawaii's state bird.

The boom has been so rapid that island governments haven't had a chance to catch up with it. The development of the basic infrastructure, including water supplies, electricity, hospitals and schools, has lagged behind.

The cost of living is 17% higher in Honolulu than the average on the mainland. Wages are 9% lower. For those stuck in service jobs, the most rapidly growing sector of the economy, it's tough to get by.

Native Hawaiians have the lowest median family income in Hawaii and are at the bottom of most health and welfare indicators, including high school drop-out rates, suicide rates and tragic death and major disease statistics.

Hawaiian Home Lands

In 1920, under the sponsorship of Prince Jonah Kuhio Kalanianaole, who was the Territory of Hawaii's congressional delegate, the US Congress passed the Hawaiian Homes Commission Act.

The act set aside almost 200,000 acres of land for homesteading by native Hawaiians, who were by this time the most landless ethnic group in Hawaii. The land was a fraction of the 1¾ million acres of government and crown lands that America took from the Kingdom of Hawaii when it annexed the islands in 1898.

People of at least 50% Hawaiian ancestry were eligible to appply for 99-year leases at $1 a year. Originally most of the leases were for 40-acre parcels of agricultural land, though more recently residential lots as small as a quarter of an acre have been allocated.

Hawaii's prime land, already in the hands of the sugar barons, was excluded from the act. Much of what was designated for homesteading was on less hospitable turf.

Indeed the first homesteading village, at Kalanianaole on Molokai, failed when the wells drew brackish waters and destroyed newly established crops. Still many Hawaiians were able to make a go of it, settling homesteads on Oahu, the Big Island, Kauai, Maui and Molokai.

Like many acts established to help native Hawaiians, administration of the Hawaiian Home Lands has been riddled with abuse. The majority of the land has not been allocated to native Hawaiians but has been leased out to big business, ostensibly as a means of creating an income for the administration of the programme.

Parker Ranch on the Big Island has 32,845 acres of Hawaiian Home Lands under lease at $3.79 an acre. In comparison, the total homestead use by native Hawaiians on all the islands combined is only 32,713 acres.

Kekaha Sugar, an Amfac subsidiary, leases the lion's share of Kauai's 18,569 acres of Hawaiian Home Lands, while less than 5% is leased to native Hawaiians.

In the meantime, more than 19,000 homestead applicants remain on waiting lists. In Kauai, Hawaiians tired of waiting have set up an encampment at Anahola Beach Park which, though on Hawaiian Home Lands, has been used for decades by the county as a public beach park.

The mismanagement of the Hawaiian Home Lands has become a rallying issue for a number of native Hawaiian groups. One of the fastest growing, Ka Lahui Hawaii, has adopted a constitution for a Hawaiian nation within the USA, similar to that of Native Americans on the mainland who have their own tribal governments and lands. They want all the Hawaiian Home Lands, as well as the title to much of the crown land taken during annexation, turned over to native Hawaiians.

Most other native Hawaiian groups are now calling for some degree of self determination, as well as monetary reparations and an apology for the role America played in the overthrow of the monarchy.

'Agricultural' Golf Courses

In 1986 the state passed a controversial bill to allow golf courses to be built on agriculture-zoned land.

This bill has already led to the gobbling up of major tracts of farm land by Japanese developers and the eviction of small leasehold farmers. Hawaii is one of the few Pacific island chains where island-grown produce has been relatively abundant. The eviction of farmers who have been growing crops on the land for generations will no doubt make the islands more reliant on imported foods. One of the slogans of the resistance movement is: 'No can eat golf balls'.

Public sentiments are overwhelmingly in favour of repeal of the bill. On Oahu alone 35 new golf courses have been proposed since the 1986 bill was passed.

The Military Presence

Hawaii is the most militarised state in the nation. Some 3400 ships are homeported in Hawaii and 64,000 military personnel along with 70,000 dependants live on the islands.

In total, the military has a grip on 265,000 acres of Hawaiian land. The greatest holding is on Oahu, where 25% of the island is controlled by the armed forces and there are more than 100 installations, from ridgetop radar stations to Waikiki's Fort DeRussy Beach.

Oahu is the hub of the Pacific Command which directs military activities from the west coast of the USA to the east coast of Africa. The navy, which accounts for 40% of Hawaii's military presence, is centred at Pearl Harbor, home of the Pacific Fleet.

The military spends $2 billion annually in the state, pays out $500 million in contracted services and hires 21,000 civilians directly.

Hawaii's politicians, while otherwise liberal-leaning, generally embrace the military presence. The Chamber of Commerce of Hawaii even has a special military affairs council that lobbies in Washington DC to draw still more military activity to Hawaii.

All in all the military holds a lot of sway and, except for the unpopular bombing of Kahoolawe, they score well on PR work, participating in island activities that range from sporting events to the Merrie Monarch Festival on the Big Island.

Over 3000 nuclear weapons, some 10% of the US nuclear arsenal, are stockpiled in Oahu. Pearl Harbor has the most, while other nuclear weapons are based at Barbers Point navy base, Schofield Barracks army base and the Kaneohe Marine Corps Air Station.

PEOPLE

In 1987 the population of Hawaii was 1,083,000, not counting the 135,000 visitors in Hawaii on an average day. The permanent population is relatively young, with a median age of 31.

There is no ethnic majority in Hawaii: everyone belongs to a minority.

Hawaii's people are known for their racial harmony. Race is generally not a factor in marriage. Islanders have a 50/50 chance of marrying someone of a race different than their own. The result has been a unique rainbow of people and Hawaii has some of the most beautiful children anywhere.

In Hawaii, 31% of the population claims 'mixed ethnicity', and a majority of those have some Hawaiian blood.

As for the rest, haoles (Caucasians) and Japanese each account for 23% of the population, followed by Filipinos (11%), Chinese (5%), blacks, Koreans, Puerto Ricans and Samoans. There are 8100 full-blooded Hawaiians, less than 1% of the population.

For the island breakdown, 830,600 people live on Oahu, 114,400 on the Big Island, 81,100 on Maui, 47,400 on Kauai, 6700 on Molokai, 2200 on Lanai and 202 on Niihau.

CULTURE

Hawaiians listen to the same pop music and watch the same TV shows as their fellow Americans on the mainland and, just like North America, Hawaii has discos and ballroom dancing, rock bands and classical orchestras, junk food and nouvelle cuisine. The wonderful thing about Hawaii, however, is that the American influences stand beside, rather than engulf, the culture of the islands.

Not only is traditional Hawaiian culture an integral part of the social fabric, but so are the customs of the ethnically diverse immigrants who have made Hawaii their home.

Hawaii is more than just a meeting place of East and West. It is, rather, a merging of the two societies for it tends to bring out the best of both worlds, and in a more relaxed and manner than is typically found in either.

The 1970s saw the start of a Hawaiian cultural renaissance that continues today. Hawaiian language classes are thriving and there is a concerted effort to reintroduce Hawaiian words into modern speech. Hula classes concentrate more on the nuances behind hand movements and facial expressions than on the dramatic hip-shaking that sells dance shows. Many Hawaiian artists are returning to traditional mediums and themes.

The tourist centres have long been overrun with packaged Hawaiiana, from plastic leis to theme-park luaus, that seem almost a parody of island culture. But the growing interest in traditional Hawaiiana is finally having an impact on the tourist industry with displays in island hotels of native artwork and authentic performances by young hula students and contemporary musicians.

Hula

Hulu halaus (schools) have experienced an influx of new students in recent years. Some practice in public places, such as school grounds and parks. Although many of the halaus rely on tuition fees, others receive sponsorship from hotels and shopping centres and give weekly public performances in return.

There are also annual island-wide hula competitions, such as the Prince Lot Hula Festival held each July in Oahu, or the week-long Merrie Monarch Festival which begins on Easter Sunday in Hilo.

Music

Contemporary Hawaiian music gives centre stage to the guitar, most prominently the steel guitar, an instrument designed in 1889 by Joseph Kekuku, a native Hawaiian. The steel guitar is one if only two major musical instruments invented in what is now the USA. The other is the banjo. The steel guitar is usually played with slack key tunings and carries the melody throughout the song.

The ukulele, so strongly identified with Hawaiian music, was actually developed from a Portuguese instrument introduced to Hawaii in the 1800s. The word 'ukulele' is Hawaiian for 'jumping flea'.

Both the ukulele and the steel guitar were essential to the light-hearted, romantic music popularised in Hawaii from the 1930s to the 1950s. Due in part to the 'Hawaii Calls' radio show, which for more than 30 years was broadcast worldwide from the Moana Hotel in Waikiki, this music became instantly recognisable as Hawaiian, conjuring up images of beautiful hula dancers swaying under palm trees in a tropical paradise.

Hawaii has many renowned steel guitar players, including Jerry Byrd, Barney Isaacs, Benny Kalama and Ray Kane. If you want to pick up an album look for music by the late Gabby Pahinui, one of the true virtuosos.

Humuhumunukunukuapuaa

Popular contemporary Hawaiian musicians include the innovative Peter Moon Band; Keola & Kapono Band, who fuse island pop with slack key guitar; the rock band Kalapana; Cecilio & Kapono, who merge rock, folk and Hawaiian influences; and the more traditional Brothers Cazimero.

Art

Many artists draw inspiration from Hawaii's rich cultural heritage and natural beauty.

Well-known Hawaiian painter Herb Kawainui Kane creates oil paintings of the early Polynesian settlers and Kamehameha's battles. His works are mainly on display in museums and permanent gallery collections.

Rocky Kaiouliokahihikoloehu Jensen does wood sculptures and drawings of Hawaiian gods, ancient chiefs and early Hawaiians with the aim of creating sacred art in the tradition of *makaku*, or 'creative artistic mana'. Jensen is the director of Hale Naua III, the Society of Hawaiian Artists.

Pegge Hopper paints large Hawaiian women in relaxed poses using a distinctive graphic design style and bright washes of colour. Her work has been widely reproduced on posters and postcards.

James Hoyle paints Kauai's landscapes in an impressionistic style. In Maui, marine art depicting both land and underwater scenes in the same painting are all the rage, as are anything with humpback whales. The goddess Pele is a source of inspiration for many Big Island artists - some even use molten lava as a sculpting material.

Some of Hawaii's most impressive crafts are ceramics, bowls made of native woods and baskets woven of native fibres. Hawaiian quilting is another unique art form.

Official Hawaii

State flower: *pua aloalo* – hibiscus

State tree: *kukui* – candlenut tree

State bird: *nene* – Hawaiian goose

State marine mammal: humpback whale

State fish: *humuhumunukunukuapuaa* – rectangular triggerfish

State motto: *Ua mau ke ea o ka aina i ka pono* – 'The life of the land is perpetuated in righteousness'.

State song: *Hawaii Ponoi* – written by King Kalakaua; in use since Hawaii was a kingdom.

State nickname: The Aloha State

State flag: Designed for King Kamehameha I prior to 1816, it has Britain's Union Jack in the upper left hand corner. Eight stripes of red, white and blue represent the eight largest islands.

State seal: The state seal incorporates the state motto and a heraldic shield flanked by Kamehameha I on one side and the Goddess of Liberty holding the Hawaiian flag on the other. It also has taro and banana leaves, ferns, a phoenix and the statehood year of 1959.

RELIGION

Hawaii's population is religiously diverse. In addition to the standard Christian denominations, Hawaii also has about 100 Buddhist temples, numerous Shinto shrines and 23 Hindu temples. Other religious groups are Taoists, Tenrikyos, Jews and Muslims.

Christianity predominates and Catholics form the largest religious denomination in Hawaii. Strangely enough, the United Church of Christ, which includes the Congregationalists who started it all, claim only about half as many members as the Mormons and one-tenth as many as the Catholics.

Ka Molokai Makahiki Festival

HOLIDAYS & FESTIVALS

Hawaii, with its multitude of cultures and religions and good year-round weather, has a seemingly endless variety of holidays, festivals and sporting events.

For the exact dates of the following, and other events, check the local papers or contact the Hawaii Visitors Bureau. Water sports particularly are reliant on the weather and the surf, so any schedule is tentative.

State and national holidays often spawn a variety of activities on the islands. Businesses and banks are usually closed. Many attractions such as museums and gardens which are open 'daily' close on major holidays, especially Christmas, New Year's Day, Thanksgiving and Easter.

Every Friday is Aloha Friday, when even the yippies (young island professionals) shed their office suits for Hawaiian dress. It's the one day of the week when you'll definitely see *muumuus* and *holokus* on women and *aloha* shirts on men, from the governor to bank tellers to the newscasters on TV.

January

New Year's Day is a national holiday. You can find firework displays all over the place on New Year's Eve.

Martin Luther King Day is a national holiday on the third Monday.

Chinese New Year, begins at the second new moon after winter solstice, (around mid-January to early February) with lion dances and firecrackers. Honolulu's Chinatown is the hot spot. (Oahu)

The *Narcissus Festival*, part of the Chinese New Year celebrations, runs for about five weeks and includes arts and crafts, food booths, a beauty pageant and coronation ball. (Oahu)

Ka Molokai Makahiki is a modern version of the ancient makahiki festival held in Kaunakakai. The week-long celebration begins with a canoe fishing contest and includes a tournament of traditional Hawaiian games and sporting events. There's also Hawaiian music and hula. (Molokai)

February

Presidents' Day, a national holiday; the third Monday.

Cherry Blossom Festival includes a variety of Japanese cultural events from tea ceremonies to parades. Held in February and March. (Oahu)

March

Prince Kuhio Day, the 26th, is a state holiday honouring Jonah Kuhio Kalanianaole, Hawaii's first delegate to the US Congress.

Easter falls in late March or early April.

St Patrick's Day, the 17th, is celebrated with a parade down Kalakaua Ave, Waikiki. (Oahu)

The *Merrie Monarch Festival* in Hilo is Hawaii's biggest hula competition and Hawaiiana festival, named after King David Kalakaua. It starts on Easter Sunday and lasts a week. (Big Island)

May

May Day, on the 1st, is Lei Day in Hawaii. Everybody dons a lei for this one.

Lei Day in Oahu is celebrated with lei-making competitions, hula and the crowning of a lei queen.

Memorial Day, on the last Monday in the month, is a national holiday to honour war dead.

The *50th State Fair* at Aloha Stadium has livestock, commercial exhibits, food, crafts and entertainment over four weekends from late May. (Oahu).

The *Ke Ola Hou Hawaiian Spring Festival* has arts and crafts, hula and ethnic foods at Hanapepe Town Park. (Kauai)

June

Festival of the Pacific is a multicultural presentation of music, dances, sports competitions etc, held in Honolulu in late May or early June. (Oahu)

King Kamehameha Day, 11 June, is a state holiday celebrated on the day or the nearest weekend.

On Oahu the statue of Kamehameha is draped with leis. There's also a parade from downtown Honolulu to Kapiolani Park.

On Kauau there's a parade and arts and crafts displays at the Lihue and Kukui Grove shopping centres.

On Maui the day is celebrated with a parade in Lahaina and an archery tournament in Kahului. Big Island celebrations include lei draping of the King Kamehameha statue in Kapaau; a parade and celebrations in Kailua-Kona; and entertainment, crafts and food at Coconut Island in Hilo.

The *King Kamehameha Hula & Chant Competition* sees hula schools competing in one of Hawaii's biggest hula competitions. (Oahu)

July

The *Puuhonua O Honaunau Cultural Festival* is held at the 'Place of Refuge' national historical park on the weekend closest to 1 July. The festival includes a 'royal court', *hukilau*, hula, traditional craft displays and food tasting. (Big Island)

Independence Day, the 4th, is a national holiday. There's fireworks and festivities on all islands.

The *Prince Lot Hula Festival* is held at Moanalua Gardens and features hula competitions from Hawaii's major hula schools. (Oahu)

A *Ukelele Festival* is held at the Kapiolani Park Bandstand at the end of the month. (Oahu)

The *Kalua Pig Cookoff* at Kaanapali Beach has an *imu* pig roasting competition on the 4th. There's also a parade, canoe rides, crafts etc. (Maui)

The *Obon* season, held throughout July and August, is marked by Japanese bon odori dances to honour deceased ancestors. The season ends on the eve of the full moon in August with floating lantern ceremonies in the Ala Wai Canal. (Oahu)

August

Admissions Day, a state holiday on the third Friday, observes the anniversary of Hawaiian statehood.

Samoan Flag Day is celebrated at Keehi Lagoon Park in Honolulu with a parade, flag raising, music and a kava-drinking ceremony. (Oahu)

September

Aloha Week is a celebration of all things Hawaiian with parades, cultural events, contests, canoe races and Hawaiian music. Festivities are staggered throughout September and October, depending on the island. Oahu has a street fair in downtown Honolulu and a parade in Waikiki.

Labor Day is a national holiday on the first Monday.

October

Columbus Day, a national holiday on the second Monday.

November

Veterans' Day, the 11th, is a national holiday.

Thanksgiving is a national holiday on the fourth Thursday.

The *Hawaii International Film Festival*, sponsored by the East-West Center, features up to 100 films and shorts made in Pacific Rim and Asian nations. Big-time directors make guest appearances. Films are shown at nine locations in Oahu; the daily papers print the schedule. (Oahu)

The *Kona Coffee Festival*, held in Kailua-Kona, has a parade, Filipino fiesta, Japanese lantern ceremony, ethnic food, arts and crafts and a Miss Coffee beauty pageant. (Big Island)

December

Christmas Day is a national holiday. Holiday festivals, parades and craft fairs are held on all the islands throughout December.

Bodhi Day,N the Buddhist Day of Enlightenment, is celebrated with ceremonies at Buddhist temples.

Sporting Events

January

Hula Bowl is the classic East/West college all-star football game held at Aloha Stadium, usually on the first or second Saturday of the year. (Oahu)

The *Race Fest Hawaii Formula 40 World Cup* has catamaran and trimaran races at Ala Wai Yacht Harbor. (Oahu)

International Bodyboard Championships Some of the world's top bodyboarders hit the Banzai Pipeline's huge waves early in the month. (Oahu)

The *Kilauea Volcano Wilderness Marathon and Rim Runs* (mid-month) at Hawaii Volcanoes National Park are a 10-mile run around the rim of Kilauea, a 5½-mile race into Kilauea Iki crater and a 26.2-mile marathon through the Kau Desert. Runs are limited to 200 to 500 people. Kilauea Visitor Center has all the info. (Big Island)

February

Aloha Run is an annual 8.2-mile fun run from Aloha Tower to Aloha Stadium held on Presidents' Day. It attracts about 30,000 runners. (Oahu)

The *Hawaiian Open Golf Tournament* at Waialae Country Club is Hawaii's biggest, with a $750,000 purse. (Oahu)

The *LPGA Women's Kemper Open Golf Tournament*, held at Princeville, is Hawaii's biggest international golf tourney for women. (Kauai)

March

Buffalo's Big Board Surfing Classic held at Makaha Beach is a surf contest using old-time 12-foot longboards. Held first two weekends.(Oahu)

Hawaii's Celebration of Kites is a weekend festival at Kapiolani Park. It includes stunt championships by the pros, with colourful kites dancing against the backdrop of Diamond Head. (Oahu)

The *Makapuu Bodysurfing Championships* is an international event held at Makapuu Beach. (Oahu)

Kona Stampede is two days of *paniolo* rodeo events at the Honaunau Arena. (Big Island)

The *Hawaii Ski Cup* and *Mauna Kea Ski Meet* are ski races down Mauna Kea – snow permitting. (Big Island)

April

Marui/O'Neill Invitational is an international windsurfing competition held at Hookipa Beach early in the month. (Oahu)

The *International Pro Rodeo Championships* are held at Aloha Stadium. Rodeo riders from Australia, Canada, New Zealand and the USA, including Hawaiian paniolos, meet to compete. (Oahu)

The *Carole Kai International Bed Race and Parade* is an offbeat wheeled bed race at Kapiolani Park, preceded by a parade down Waikiki's Kalakaua Ave. This is a charity fund raiser. (Oahu)

May

The *Kanaka Ikaika Molokai to Oahu Kayak Race* is a 32-mile kayak/surfski race, in mid-May, across the treacherous Kaiwi Channel, from Kaluakoi Resort, Molokai to Koko Marina, Oahu.

The *Keauhou-Kona Triathlon* is a half-Ironman with a mere 56-mile bike race and 13-mile run starting at Keauhou Bay. (Big Island)

Western Week in Honokaa includes a rodeo and parade, followed by a big hoe-down and some corny stuff like a Saloon Girl contest. (Big Island)

June

The *TDK/Gotcha Pro Surf Championships* are held at Sandy Beach Park. It's a week of board surfing, bodysurfing and bikini contests. (Oahu)

July

On odd-numbered years sailboats in the *Transpacific Yacht Race* leave Los Angeles on the 4 July weekend and arrive in Honolulu 10 to 14 days later. The race has been held since the turn of the century. (Oahu)

Makawao Statewide Rodeo is an old-fashioned Fourth of July rodeo in Makawao's cowboy country. (Maui)

Parker Ranch Rodeo is held at Paniolo Park in Waimea on 4 July. (Big Island)

The *Hawaiian International Billfish Tournament* is the world's number one marlin tournament. It lasts a week, is held in Kailua-Kona and begins in late July or early August. (Big Island)

August

The *Haleakala Run to the Sun* is a 36-mile run to the top of Haleakala, beginning at dawn in Kahului. It's held late in the month. (Maui)

September

The *Maui Channel Relay Swim* is a nine-mile six-person swim from Lanai to Lahaina in Maui.

Cycle to the Sun is a 38-mile bicycle race from sea-level Paia to the summit of Haleakala Crater. (Maui)

The *Hana Relay* is an end-of-month 54-mile relay run from Kahului to Hana. (Maui)

Na Wahine O Ke Kai, Hawaii's major annual women's outrigger canoe race, from Hale O Lono Harbor on Molokai to Waikiki's Fort DeRussy on Oahu.

The *Wailea Speed Crossing* is a windsurfing race (in early September) across the channel from Wailea on Maui to Kaunakakai on Molokai.

October

The *Aloha Classic* wave sailing championships at Hookipa Beach, near the end of the month, has top international windsurfing action. (Maui)

The *Bankoh Molokai Hoe* is Hawaii's major men's outrigger canoe race. It starts after sunrise from Hale O Lono Harbor on Molokai and finishes at Fort DeRussy Beach on Oahu about five hours later. Teams from Australia, Tahiti, Germany and the US mainland join the Hawaiians in this annual competition which was first held in 1952.

The *Ironman Triathlon* is considered by many the ultimate endurance race. This is the triathlon that started it all. The 2.4-mile swim, 112-mile bike race and 26.2-mile marathon begins and ends at Kailua Pier. (Big Island)

December

The *Honolulu Marathon*, Hawaii's biggest, is run early in the month along a 26-mile course from the Aloha Tower to Kapiolani Park. (Oahu)

The *Aloha Bowl* is the big collegiate football game held at Aloha Stadium on Christmas Day. (Oahu)

The *Triple Crown of Surfing* covers three events that draw the world's top surfers to the Oahu's North Shore: the Hard Rock Cafe World Cup of Surfing, the Marui Pipeline Masters and the Billabong Pro & Sunset Beach Women's Pro. Purses go as high as $100,000. The events run throughout December, with the exact dates and locations depending on when and where the surf's up.

LANGUAGE

English is the unifying language of the Hawaiian islands. It's liberally peppered with Hawaiian phrases, pidgin slang and loan words from Hawaii's many immigrants.

It's not uncommon to hear islanders speaking in other languages. The main language spoken in one out of every four homes is a mother tongue other than English.

The Hawaiian language is closely related to other Polynesian languages. It is melodic, full of vowels and repeated syllables, and phonetically simple.

Some 85% of all place names in Hawaii are in Hawaiian. Often they have interesting translations and stories behind them.

The Hawaiians had no written language until the 1820s when Christian missionaries arrived and wrote down the spoken language in roman letters.

Pronunciation

The written Hawaiian language has just 12 letters. Pronunciation is easy and there are few consonant clusters.

Vowel sounds are about the same as in Spanish or Japanese, more or less like this:

a	ah, as in 'father' or uh, as in 'above'
e	ay, as in 'gay' or eh, as in 'pet'
i	ee, as in 'see'
o	oh, as in 'go'
u	oo, as in 'noon'

Hawaiian has diphthongs, created when two vowels join together to form a single sound. The stress is on the first vowel, though in general if you pronounce each vowel separately, you'll be easily understood.

The consonant *w* is usually pronounced like a soft English *v* when it follows the letters *i* and *e* (the town Haleiwa is pronounced Haleiva) and like the English *w* when it follows *u* or *o*. When *w* follows *a* it can be pronounced either *v* or *w* – thus you will hear both Hawaii and Havaii.

The other consonants – h, k, l, m, n, p – are pronounced about the same as in English.

Glottal Stops & Macrons Written Hawaiian uses both glottal stops and macrons, though in modern print they are often omitted.

The glottal stop (') indicates a break between two vowels producing an effect similar to saying 'oh-oh' in English. A macron, a short straight line over a vowel, stresses the vowel.

Glottal stops and macrons not only affect pronunciation, but can give a word a completely different meaning. There are many words with the same spelling which have different meanings depending on the pronunciation. For example *ai* means either 'sexual intercourse' or 'to eat', depending on the pronunciation.

All this takes on greater significance when you learn to speak Hawaiian in depth. If you're using Hawaiian words in an English-language context (this *poi* is *ono*), there shouldn't be much problem.

Compounds Hawaiian may seem more difficult than it is because many place names are long and look similar. Many begin with *ka*, meaning 'the', which over time simply became attached to the start of the word.

When you break each word down into its composite parts, some of which are repeated, it all becomes much easier. For example:

Kamehameha consist of three compounds Ka-meha-meha.
Humuhumunukunukuapuaa, which is Hawaii's state fish, is broken down into humu-humu-nuku-nuku-a-pu-a-a.

There are some easily recognisable compounds repeatedly found in proper names while some words are doubled to emphasise their meaning. For example:

Wai means 'freshwater' – Waikiki means 'spouting water'.
Kai means 'seawater' – Kailua means 'two seas'.
Hana means 'bay' – Hanalei means 'crescent bay'.
Lani means 'heavenly' – Lanikai means 'heavenly sea'.
Wiki is 'quick' – *wikiwiki* is 'very quick'.

Shaka sign Islanders greet each other with a shaka sign, which is made by folding down the three middle fingers to the palm and extending the thumb and little finger. The hand is then usually held out and shaken in greeting. It's as common as waving.

Common Hawaiian Vocabulary
Learn these words first: *aloha* and *mahalo*, which are everyday pleasantries; *makai* and *mauka*, commonly used in giving directions; and *kane* and *wahine*, often on toilet doors.

aikane
 friend
aina
 land
akamai
 clever

alii
 chief, royalty
aloha
 love, welcome, good-bye
aloha aina
 love of the land
auwe
 Oh my! Alas!
hala
 pandanus
hale
 house
hana
 work; or bay, a compound in place names
haole
 Caucasian
hapa
 half; or person of mixed-blood
hapa haole
 half-white, used for a person, thing or idea
Hauoli Makahiki Hou
 Happy New Year
hau
 lowland tree with flowers resembling hibiscus
haupia
 coconut pudding
heiau
 ancient Hawaiian temple
holoholo
 to walk, drive or ramble around for pleasure
holoku
 a long dress similar to the muumuu, but more fitted and with a yoke
honu
 turtle
hoolaulea
 celebration, party
huhu
 angry
hui
 group, organisation
hula
 traditional Hawaiian dance
ilima
 native groundcover with a delicate yellow-orange flower
imu
 underground earthen oven used in traditional luau cooking

kahuna
  wise person in any field, commonly a priest, healer or sorcerer

kalua
  traditional method of baking in an underground oven

kamaaina
  native-born Hawaiian or a long-time resident; literally 'child of the land'

kane
  man; also the name of one of four top Hawaiian gods

kapu
  taboo, part of strict ancient Hawaiian social system; today often used on signs meaning 'Keep Out'

kaukau
  food

keiki
  child, children

kiawe
  a relative of the mesquite tree introduced to Hawaii in the 1820s, now very common; its branches are covered with sharp thorns

koa
  native hardwood tree often used in woodworking

kohola
  whale

kokua
  help, cooperation; 'Please Kokua' on a trash can is a gentle way of saying 'don't litter'

kona
  leeward, or a leeward wind

konane
  ancient Hawaiian board game similar to checkers

kupuna
  grandparent

lanai
  veranda

lauhala
  leaves of the hala plant used in weaving

lei
  garland, usually of flowers, but also of leaves or shells

lei hulu
  feather lei

lilikoi
  passion fruit

limu
  seaweed

lio
  horse

lolo
  stupid, crazy

lomi salmon
  raw diced salmon marinated with tomatoes and onions

lomilomi
  massage

luau
  traditional Hawaiian feast

mahalo
  thank you

makai
  toward the sea

malihini
  newcomer, visitor

manini
  convict tang (a reef fish); also used to refer to something small or insignificant

mano
  shark

mauka
  toward the mountains, inland

mele
  song, chant

Mele Kalikimaka
  Merry Christmas

muumuu
  long, loose-fitting dress introduced by the missionaries

nene
  Hawaii's state bird, a native goose

ohana
  family, extended family

ono
  delicious; also the name of the wahoo fish

pakalolo
  marijuana; literally 'crazy smoke'

pali
  cliff

paniolo
  Hawaiian cowboy

pau
  finished, no more; *pau hana* means quitting time

pilikia
trouble

puka
any kind of hole or opening

pupu
snack food, hors d'oeuvres; shells

puu
hill, cinder cone

tutu
aunt, older woman

ukulele
stringed musical instrument

wahine
woman

wana
sea urchin

wikiwiki
hurry, quick

Pidgin

Hawaii's early immigrants communicated with each other in pidgin, a simplified, broken form of English. It was a language born of necessity, stripped of all but the most needed words.

Modern pidgin is better defined as local slang. It's extensive, lively and everchanging. Whole conversations can take place in pidgin, or often just a word or two is dropped into a more conventional English sentence.

Even Shakespeare's *Twelfth Night* has been translated (by local comedian James Grant Benton) to *Twelf Nite O Wateva*. Malvolio's line 'My masters, are you mad?' becomes 'You buggahs crazy, o wat?'

Short-term visitors rarely win friends by trying to speak pidgin. It's more like a secret code you're allowed to use only after you've lived in Hawaii long enough to understand the nuances.

Some characteristics of pidgin include: a fast, staccato rhythm, two-word sentences, no 'th' sound, use of loan words from many languages (often Hawaiian) and double meanings which trip up the uninitiated.

Some of the more common words and expressions:

blalah
big Hawaiian fellow

brah
brother, friend; also used for 'hey you'

broke da mouth
delicious

buggah
guy

chicken skin
goose bumps

coconut wireless
word of mouth

cockaroach
steal

da kine
whatchamacallit, thingamajig, doodad etc; used whenever you can't think of the word you want but you know the listener knows what you mean

geev em
go for it, beat them

grinds
food, eat; *ono grinds* is good food.

haolefied
become like a *haole*

howzit?
hi, how's it going?

how you stay?
how are you?

humbug
a real hassle

like beef?
wanna fight?

mo' bettah
much better, the best

stick
surfboard

stink eye
dirty look, evil eye

talk story
any kind of conversation, gossip, tales

tanks
thanks. More commonly *tanks brah*.

tree
three. Dropping the soft 'h' sound from 'th' is common.

Facts for the Visitor

VISAS

The conditions for entering Hawaii are the same as entering any other state in the USA.

Canadians require only proof of Canadian citizenship. Visitors from other countries must have a valid passport and most people require a US visa.

Citizens of the UK, Japan, Switzerland, France, West Germany, Sweden, Italy and the Netherlands may enter the USA without first obtaining a US visa under a new reciprocal visa waiver programme. Under this programme your stay is limited to 90 days and you must have a return ticket that is nonrefundable in the USA. One disadvantage with this visa waiver is that there is no possibility of extending your stay.

Other travellers will need to obtain a visa from a US consulate or embassy. In most countries the process can be done by mail. Your passport should be valid for at least six months longer than your intended stay in the USA and you'll need to submit a recent photo (37 x 37 mm) with the application. Documents of financial stability and/or guarantees from a US resident are sometimes required, particularly for those from Third World countries.

The validity period for US visitor visa depends on what country you're from. The length of time you'll be allowed to stay in the USA is ultimately determined by US Immigration authorities at the port of entry.

ENTRY & EXIT

US Customs allows each person over the age of 21 to bring one litre of liquor and 200 cigarettes duty-free into the USA. Most fresh fruits and plants are restricted from entry into Hawaii and there's a strict quarantine on animals. No immunisations are required to enter Hawaii or any other port in the USA.

Agricultural Inspection All luggage and carry-on bags leaving Hawaii for the US mainland are checked by an agricultural inspector.

You cannot take out gardenia, jade vine, mauna loa flowers or *mokihana* berries, even in *leis*, though most other fresh flowers and foliage are permitted. You can take out pineapples and coconuts but most other fresh fruits and vegetables are banned. Other things not allowed to enter mainland states include plants in soil, fresh coffee berries, cactus and sugar cane (except 'chews'). Seeds and plants which have been certified and labelled for export aren't a problem.

MONEY

US dollars are the only accepted currency in Hawaii.

Foreign travellers will find it easier if their travellers' cheques are already in US dollars, but major currencies can be exchanged at Honolulu International Airport and major banks. Restaurants, hotels and most stores accept US dollar travellers' cheques as if they're cash.

Plastic Money

All major credit cards are widely accepted throughout Hawaii.

Automatic teller machines (ATM) are another plastic alternative. On our last visit to Hawaii we took no travellers' cheques at all, choosing instead to withdraw money from a bank account back home using ATMs. The small service charge worked out cheaper than the 1% service charge for travellers' cheques and we didn't have to carry a bundle of cheques around.

Major banks such as Bank of Hawaii and First Hawaiian Bank have ATMs throughout Hawaii. If you have a money card, your home bank should be able to give you a list of banks in Hawaii which are members of their ATM network.

COSTS

How much money you need for Hawaii

US Dollar & Five Dollar notes

depends on your travelling style. Some people get by quite cheaply while others rack up huge balances on their American Express cards.

The airfare is usually one of the heftier parts of the budget. Fares vary greatly, particularly from the US mainland, so shop around. (Hawaii stopovers are often thrown in free on trips between North America and Asian or Pacific countries.)

Flights between the islands cost about $40 to $50. Hawaii's only ferries do the Lanai-Maui ($25) and Molokai-Maui ($21) runs.

It's a challenge to explore the islands without renting a car, except on Oahu where there's a good public bus system. Hitchhiking is officially illegal and, particularly on Maui and Oahu, not all that common. We met some people biking around the islands, although for the most part they weren't keen on traffic and road conditions.

Fortunately Hawaii has lots of competition in the car rental arena so if you shop around you can often find something for about $80 a week.

Camping is an alternative to paying for a hotel. Every island except Lanai has county park camping grounds, which are inexpensive, and at least one state park with free camping. Maui and the Big Island have national parks with free camping.

Most of the islands have some sort of accommodation, either cheap hotels or B&Bs, in the $25 to $40 range. You'll have to double that price if you want something more middle class and comfortable. If you've got your mind set on a resort-style beachfront hotel, get ready to pay a good $100 a night.

If you're staying awhile, there are ways to cut those costs. Weekly and monthly condo rentals can beat even the cheap hotels. Besides offering more space most condos are turn-key, which means everything you need for comfortable living is provided. This includes cooking facilities so you can save on your food bill.

Another cost-cutter is to travel in the low season, mid-April to mid-December, when accommodation rates are often as much as 30% less.

Hawaii slaps a whopping 9.43% tax on all accommodation rates, though that does include the 4% general excise tax that's already on everything you purchase, including food.

Since much of Hawaii's food is shipped in, grocery prices average 25% higher than on the mainland.

Local restaurants are good value in Hawaii; they're as cheap as you'll find on the mainland.

Lots of things in Hawaii are free. There are no beach or public park entrance fees for instance.

TIPPING

Tipping practices are the same as in the rest of the USA. For hotel and restaurant staff and taxi drivers, 15% is about average.

TOURIST INFORMATION
Hawaii Visitors Bureau

The HVB, which also has offices in various countries around the world, provides free tourist information. Unless you request something special they usually just mail out booklets containing member hotel and restaurant listings and a sightseeing brochure for each island.

The central office, (tel (808) 923-1811), is in the Waikiki Business Plaza, Suite 801, 2270 Kalakaua Ave, Honolulu, HI 96815.

There are branch offices on Maui, Kauai and the Big Island (both Kona and Hilo). The Kauai office has a toll free number – 800-AH-KAUAI. HVB offices outside Hawaii include:

HVB Warrior

On the US mainland
180 N Michigan Ave, Suite 1031, Chicago, IL 60601
3440 Wilshire Blvd, Room 502, Los Angeles, CA 90010
441 Lexington Ave, Room 1407, New York NY 10017
50 California St, Suite 450, San Francisco, CA 94111
1511 K St, NW, Suite 519, Washington, DC 20005

Australia
all c/o Walshe's World
92 Pitt St, 8th Floor, Sydney, NSW 2000; or GPO Box 51, Sydney 2001
307 Queen St, Brisbane, Queensland 4000; or GPO 2211, Brisbane 4001
231 Adelaide Terrace, 4th Floor, Perth, Western Australia 6000

New Zealand
c/o Walshe's World, 87 Queen St, 2nd Floor, Dingwall Building, PO Box 279, Auckland 1

Canada
4915 Cedar Crescent, Delta, BC, V4M 1J9

UK
16 Bedford Square, London WC1B 3JH

Japan
Hibiya Kokusai Building, 11th Floor, 2-2-3 Uchisaiwai-cho, Chiyoda-ku, Tokyo 100

Hong Kong
Suite 3702A, W Tower, Bond Centre, Queensway

For brochures and travel information on Molokai, write to Destination Molokai, Box 960, Kaunakakai, HI 96748.

For a guide to the state parks on all the islands, with a brief description of each including camping information, contact the Division of State Parks (tel 548-7455), Box 621, Honolulu, HI 96809.

Foreign Consulates

In Honolulu there are consulates from Australia, Austria, Belgium, Brazil, Britain, Chile, Cook Islands, Costa Rica, Denmark, Finland, France, Germany, Guatemala, India, Indonesia, Italy, Japan, Korea, Malaysia, Mexico, Nauru, Netherlands, New Zealand, Panama, Peru, Philippines, Portugal, Spain, Sweden, Switzerland and Thailand.

There are also government liaison offices for Tonga, the Samoas and all the Micronesian islands.

Addresses and phone numbers are in the Oahu phone book yellow pages under 'Consulates'.

Information For Disabled Visitors

The Commission on Persons with Disabilities publishes pamphlets for each of the four major islands with travel tips for physically disabled people.

The pamphlets list hotels which have wheelchair access and specially-adapted rooms or facilities. They also list beaches, parks, shopping malls and other attractions with appropriate accessibility and facilities as well as available medical equipment agencies, nursing services and transportation services for the disabled. The Oahu brochure has a map of Waikiki's sidewalk curb cuts.

The brochures are free from the Commission (tel 548-7606), 5 Waterfront Plaza, Suite 210, 500 Ala Moana Blvd, Honolulu, HI 96813.

Hawaiian Weddings

Weddings are big business in Hawaii and the process is fairly simple. Hawaii requires that the prospective bride and groom appear in person together before a marriage licence agent and pay $16 for a licence, which is given out on the spot. There's no residence or citizenship requirements and no waiting period.

The legal age for marriage is 18, or 16 with parental consent. Those under 20 may require proof of age. Women need a health certificate for rubella screening from a doctor. Full information and forms are available from the Department of Health, Marriage License Office, Box 3378, Honolulu, HI 96801.

Pat Kelley (Mother of the Bride, 4633 Aukai Ave, Honolulu, HI 96816; tel 737-1818, 800-367-8047 ext 622 from the USA, 800-423-8733 ext 622 from Canada) organises weddings of all costs and sizes. Her extensive information packet with ideas on wedding locations in gardens and parks, lists of justices of the peace, florists, photographers etc is free on request.

GENERAL INFORMATION

Post

Postage rates for first class mail within the USA are 25 cents for letters up to one ounce (20 cents each additional ounce) and 15 cents for postcards.

International airmail rates are 45 cents for letters per ½ ounce, 39 cents for aerogrammes and 36 cents for postcards. Rates are the same from the USA to all countries, except to Canada (30 cents per ounce for letters, 21 cents for postcards) and Mexico (same as US domestic rates).

Parcels under two pounds airmailed anywhere within the USA cost $2.40. Beyond that, rates differ according to the distance mailed.

First class mail between Hawaii and the mainland usually takes three to four days.

You can have mail sent to you c/o General Delivery at any post office in Hawaii that has its own zip (post) code. Mail is usually held for 10 days before being returned to sender.

Telephones

The area code for all of Hawaii is 808. If

Stamps

you're calling from outside Hawaii, add 808 to all Hawaiian phone numbers in this book.

All numbers listed beginning with 800 are toll free numbers from the US mainland, unless otherwise noted. The same numbers are sometimes toll free from Canada.

To direct dial long distance, dial '1' first.

Local calls within Hawaii cost 25 cents at pay phones. There's no time limit. Any call made from one point on an island to any other point on that island is a local call. Calls from one island to another are long distance.

Most hotels add on a service charge of 50 cents to $1 for each local call. They also have hefty surcharges for long distance calls. Pay phones, found in most lobbies, are always cheaper. You can pump in quarters, use a phone credit card, or make collect calls from pay phones.

In Waikiki there's a private long-distance phone service at the International Market Place. Rates are 45 cents a minute to the US mainland and $6.95 for three minutes to most overseas destinations.

Electricity

Electricity is 110/120 volts, 60 cycles, as it is everywhere else in the USA.

Time

Hawaii does not observe daylight saving time. When it's noon in Hawaii the time in other parts of the world is: 1 pm – Anchorage; 2 pm – Los Angeles; 5 pm – New York; 10 pm – London; 11 pm – Bonn; 7 am next day – Tokyo; 8 am next day – Sydney & Melbourne; 10 am next day – Auckland.

The time difference is one hour greater during those months when other countries observe daylight saving. For example from April to October when it's noon in Hawaii it's 3 pm in LA and 6 pm in New York; and from November to March when it's noon in Hawaii it's 9 am in Melbourne and 11 am in Auckland.

Hawaii has about 11 hours of daylight in mid-winter and almost 13½ in mid-summer. In mid-winter the sun rises at about 7 am and sets about 6 pm. In mid-summer it rises before 6 am and sets after 7 pm.

And then there's Hawaiian Time, a euphemism for being late.

Business Hours

The most common business hours in Hawaii are 8.30 am to 4.30 pm Monday to Friday.

Weights & Measures

Although the USA is supposedly changing to the metric system, it's moving inch by inch. Hawaii is one of the few places in the USA where the metric system is even noticeable. On some islands gasoline is sold by the litre.

The USA basically retains the imperial system of measurement. Distances are in feet, yards and miles, and weights are in ounces, pounds and tons.

For those unaccustomed to the imperial system, there is a metric conversion table in the back of this book.

MEDIA

Newspapers

The two main daily papers are the *Honolulu Advertiser* which comes out in the morning and the *Honolulu Star-Bulletin* which comes out in the afternoon. On Sundays they jointly produce the *Star-Bulletin & Advertiser*.

For copies of either paper, write to the Circulation Department, Box 3350, Honolulu, HI 96801. Single copies sent airmail to the US mainland cost $2.35 for a weekday copy and $5.75 for a Sunday copy. Prices vary to other countries.

The Honolulu papers are sold throughout Hawaii but the neighbouring islands also have their own newspapers.

Several mainland and international newspapers are available, some the same day, including *USA Today, Wall Street Journal* and the *Los Angeles Times*. Look for them in the larger hotels.

Magazines

Honolulu and *Aloha* are Hawaii's two largest general interest magazines. *Honolulu* is geared slightly more toward residents and is published monthly by the Honolulu Publishing Co, 36 Merchant St, Honolulu, HI 96813. *Aloha* (Box 27810, San Diego, CA 92128) is slightly more visitor-oriented and is published six times a year.

There are also numerous tourist magazines distributed free on the main islands. They have maps of varying quality, lots of ads and discount coupons for everything from hamburgers to sunset cruises.

Television & Radio
Hawaii has commercial television stations representing the three major US networks, as well as public broadcasting and cable TV. On cable there's a tourist channel and a Japanese language channel. Almost anything you can watch on the mainland you can watch in Hawaii.

The evening news on Channel 2 has the most local flavour. The newscast ends with some nice slack-key music by Keola and Kapono Beamer and clips of people waving the shaka sign.

Hawaii has about 50 AM and FM stations, with the usual variety of music and programming.

HEALTH
Hawaii is a very healthy place to live and to visit. It's 2500 miles from the nearest industrial centre and there's little air pollution. It ranks first of all the 50 US states in life expectancy, which is currently about 75 years for men and 81 years for women.

There are few serious health concerns. The islands have none of the nasties like malaria, cholera or yellow fever and you can drink water directly out of any tap, though all stream water needs to be boiled or treated.

If you're new to the heat and humidity you may find yourself easily fatigued and more susceptible to minor ailments. Acclimatise yourself by slowing down your pace and setting your body clock to the more kicked-back 'Hawaiian Time'. Drink plenty of liquids.

If you're planning anything strenuous, like cycling across open lava fields or hiking in unshaded areas, take enough water and don't push yourself.

Medical Care
Hawaii has 22 acute care hospitals, 2500 physicians, 1000 dentists and modern facilities. For serious illnesses, most islanders have more confidence in Honolulu hospitals than in neighbouring island facilities.

Travel Insurance
Foreign visitors should be warned that health care in Hawaii is expensive, as the USA has not yet advanced to any form of socialised medical care.

It is, therefore, highly recommended that you take out some kind of travel insurance policy that covers theft, loss and medical expenses. There are a wide variety of policies available but your travel agent should be able to advise on the best choices to cover your trip.

Check the small print because some policies exclude 'dangerous activities' like scuba diving, motorcycling, anything to do with parachutes and even trekking.

Make sure you're covered for ambulance rides and it's wise to get a policy that covers you for an emergency flight home. Some policies even allow for a companion to travel home with you.

Medical Kit
A small first aid kit is a sensible thing to carry on your travels to cope with minor health problems or injuries.

A basic kit should have things like aspirin or panadol for pain or fever; an antihistamine (such as Benadryl) for use as a decongestant, to relieve the itch from insect bites or to help prevent motion sickness; Imodium or Lomotil for stomach upsets; an antiseptic, mercurochrome and antibiotic powder (or dry spray) for cuts and grazes; bandages and bandaids; scissors and tweezers; insect repellent, sunscreen and chap stick.

Don't forget any medication you may already be taking and, if necessary, contraceptive pills or condoms.

Leptospirosis
Visitors to Hawaii should be aware of leptospirosis, a bacterial disease found in

freshwater streams and ponds. The disease is transmitted from animals such as rats, mongoose and wild pigs.

Humans most often pick up the disease by swimming or wading in freshwater contaminated by animal urine. Leptospirosis can exist in any fresh water, including idyllic-looking waterfalls and jungle streams because the water may have washed down the slopes through animal habitats.

Leptospirosis enters the body through the nose, eyes, mouth or cuts in the skin. Wetland taro farmers, hikers and swimmers account for the majority of cases.

Symptoms can occur within two to 20 days after exposure and may include fever, chills, sweating, headaches, muscle pains, vomiting and diarrhoea. More severe symptoms include blood in the urine and jaundice. Symptoms may last from a few days to several weeks.

In 1988 there were 55 confirmed cases statewide. Because symptoms of leptospirosis resemble the flu and hepatitis, other cases have probably gone unconfirmed. Although deaths have been attributed to the disease they are relatively rare, with five fatalities in Hawaii between 1982 and 1989. Leptospirosis is not specific to Hawaii and can be found on the mainland as well.

Some precautions include wearing waterproof *tabis* when hiking and avoiding unnecessary freshwater crossings, especially if you have open cuts.

Leptospirosis can be serious, yet thousands of people swim in Hawaiian streams without contracting it. The state has posted warnings at many trailheads and freshwater swimming areas. Islanders have differing opinions on leptospirosis – some never swim in fresh water because of it, while others consider it such a long shot that they take no precautions at all.

Sunburn

Sunburn is always a concern in the tropics, as the closer you get to the Equator the fewer of the sun's rays are blocked by the atmosphere. Don't be fooled by what appears to be a hazy overcast day as those rays still get through.

Sunscreen with an SPF (sun protection factor) of 10 to 15 is recommended if you're not already tanned. If you're going into the water use one that's water-resistant. Snorkellers may want to wear a T-shirt if they plan to be out in the water a long time. You'll not only be protecting against sunburn but potential skin cancer and premature ageing of the skin.

Fair-skinned people can get both first and second degree burns in the hot Hawaiian sun. The most severe sun is between 10 am and 2 pm.

It's highly recommended that you either take along with you, or buy in Hawaii, a good sun hat and sunglasses.

Fungi & Infections

The same climate that produces lush tropical forests also promotes a prolific growth of skin fungi and bacteria.

Keeping your skin dry and cool and allowing air to circulate is essential. Choose loose cotton clothing rather than synthetics and sandals over shoes.

Cuts are easily infected in Hawaii's hot and humid climate and infections can be persistent. Keep any cut or open wound clean and treat it with an antiseptic solution and mercurochrome. Keep the area protected but, where possible, avoid bandages and band-aids which can keep wounds wet.

Coral cuts are even more susceptible to infection because tiny pieces of coral can get embedded in the skin. These cuts are notoriously slow to heal as the coral releases a weak venom into the wound.

Pesky Creatures

Hawaii has no land snakes but it does have its fair share of annoying mosquitoes as well as centipedes which can give an unpleasant bite.

This being the tropics, cockroaches are plentiful and though they don't pose much of a health problem they do little for the appetite. If you find that the place you're staying at is infested you can always call the manager or the front desk and have them spray poisons – which are no doubt more dangerous than the roaches!

DANGERS & ANNOYANCES
Tsunamis

Tsunamis, or tidal waves, are not common in Hawaii but when they do hit they can be severe.

Tsunamis are generated by earthquakes or other natural disasters. The largest to ever hit Hawaii was in 1946, the result of an earthquake in the Aleutian Islands. Waves reached a height of 55.8 feet, entire villages were washed away and 159 people died.

Since that time, Hawaii has installed a modern tsunami warning system which is aired through yellow speakers mounted on telephone poles around the islands. They're tested on the first working day of each month at 11.45 am for about one minute.

Though tsunamis which travel across the Pacific can take hours to arrive, others can be caused by earthquakes or volcanic eruptions within Hawaii. For these there may be little warning. Any earthquake strong enough to cause you to grab onto something to keep from falling is a natural tsunami warning. If you're in a low-lying coastal area when one occurs, immediately head for higher ground.

Tsunami inundation maps in the front of island telephone books show susceptible areas and safety zones.

Ocean Safety

Drownings are the leading cause of accidental death for visitors.

If you're not familiar with water conditions, ask someone. If there's no lifeguard around, local surfers are generally helpful. They'd rather give you the lowdown on water conditions than pull you out later. It's best not to swim alone in an unfamiliar place.

Shorebreaks Shorebreaks occur where waves break close to or directly on shore. They are formed when ocean swells pass abruptly from deep to shallow waters. If they are only a couple of feet high they're generally fine for novice bodysurfers to try their

hand. Otherwise, they're for experienced bodysurfers only.

Large shorebreaks can hit hard with a slamming downward force. Broken bones, neck injuries, dislocated shoulders and loss of wind are the most common injuries, though anyone wiped out in the water is a potential drowning victim as well.

Rip Currents Rips, rip currents or riptides are fast flowing currents of water within the ocean, moving from shallow shore areas out to sea or caused by the meeting of currents or abrupt changes in depth. They are most common in conditions of high surf, forming when water from incoming waves piles up near the shore. Essentially the waves are coming in faster than they can flow back out.

The water then runs along the shoreline until it finds an escape route out to sea, usually through a channel or out along a point. Swimmers caught up in it can be ripped out to deeper water.

Though rips can be powerful they usually dissipate 50 to 100 yards offshore. Anyone caught in one should either go with the flow until it loses power or swim parallel to shore to slip out of it. Trying to swim against a rip current can exhaust the strongest of swimmers.

Undertows Undertows are common along steeply sloped beaches when large waves backwash directly into incoming surf. The outflowing water picks up speed as it flows down the slopes. When it hits an incoming wave it pulls under it, creating an undertow. Swimmers caught up in an undertow can be pulled beneath the surface. The most important thing is not to panic. Go with the current until you get beyond the wave.

Rogue Waves Never turn your back on the ocean. Waves don't all come in with equal height or strength. An abnormally high 'rogue wave' can sweep over rock ledges such as those circling Hanauma Bay on Oahu or up onto beaches like Lumahai on Kauai. People have been swept into the ocean from both.

If it's stormy, high tide or high surf you need to be particularly cautious.

Some people think rogue waves don't exist because they've never seen one. But that's the point – you don't always see them.

Coral Most coral cuts occur when swimmers are pushed onto the coral by rough waves and surges. Wearing diving gloves is a good idea if you're snorkelling over shallow reefs, and wear shoes if you're walking on coral.

Jellyfish Take a peek into the water before you plunge in to make sure it's not jellyfish territory. Jellyfish are *coelenterates*, or invertebrates with saclike bodies and a single opening, the mouth. The group includes the hydra, sea anemones and corals.

The most common jellyfish, which can measure from less than an inch to up to six feet in diameter, are the disk-shaped animals often found drifting near the shore or washed up on the beach. These consist of 99% water, owing to the composition of the jelly, and most feed on small animals which they catch in their tentacles which are armed with sting cells.

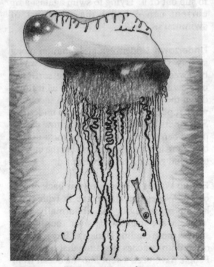

Portugese man-of-war

It's not very pleasant to suddenly find yourself swimming amongst them and though their sting is not dangerous it's not a particularly enjoyable sensation.

Portuguese men-of-war, however, are best avoided. Also known as bluebottles, the men-of-war are not uncommon in Hawaii and are most often found on the windward coasts, particularly after storms. In some waters they have been seen floating in groups of thousands.

The Portuguese man-of-war is actually a *colonial hydrozoan*, or a colony of coelenterates rather than a solitary coelenterate like the true jellyfish. Its body consists of a translucent pink, blue or violet bladder-like float which can be from three to 12 inches long, and may extend up to six inches above the water. Beneath the float are clusters of three types of polyps from which hang tentacles that have been known to measure up to 165 feet long.

The tentacles of one type of polyp contain stinging structures that paralyse small fish and other prey, while the tentacles of another polyp attach to the immobilised victim, spread over it and digest it.

A man-of-war sting is very painful, similar to a bad bee sting except that you're likely to get stung more than once, and can be dangerous. Even touching a bluebottle a few hours after it's washed up on shore can result in a burning sting.

If you do get stung, try applying rubbing alcohol, vinegar, or a meat tenderiser which contains papain (derived from papaya). These all seem to neutralise the toxins. The sting can have serious effects including fever, shock, and interference with heart and lung action. Seek medical attention if you have chest pains or difficulty in breathing.

Cone Shells Cone shells should be left alone unless you're sure they're empty. There's no safe way of picking up a live cone shell as the animal inside has a long harpoon that can dart out and reach anywhere on its shell to deliver a painful sting. The wound should be soaked in hot water and medical attention sought.

The sting of the textile cone, whose shell is decorated with brown diamond or triangular shapes, can even be fatal.

Sea Urchins *Wana*, or spiny sea urchins, have long brittle spines that can puncture the skin and break off, causing burning and possible numbness. They sometimes inflict a toxin as well and can cause an infection. You can try to remove the spines with tweezers or by soaking the area in hot water, though more serious cases may require surgical removal.

Eels *Puhi*, or moray eels, are often spotted by snorkellers around reefs and coral heads. They're constantly opening and closing their mouths to pump water across their gills, which makes them look far more menacing than they are.

Eels don't attack, but they will protect themselves if cornered by fingers jabbing into the reef holes or crevices they occupy. Eels have sharp teeth and strong jaws and may clamp down if someone sticks a hand in their door.

Sharks As Hawaiian waters are abundant with fish, sharks are usually well fed and pose little danger to humans. Sharks are curious and will sometimes investigate divers, though they generally just check things out and then split. If they start to hang around, however, it's probably time for you to go – quietly.

Should you come face to face with a shark the best thing to do is move casually away. Don't panic as sharks are attracted by things that thrash around in water.

A Sea Life Park display suggests thumping an attacking shark on the nose or sticking your fingers into its eyes, which may confuse it long enough to give you time to escape.

Avoid murky waters. After heavy rains sharks sometimes come in around river mouths.

Sharks are attracted by blood. Many attacks on humans come about when the shark is actually going after a spearfishing diver's bloody catch and the diver gets in the way.

According to the University of Hawaii Sea Grant College, only 27 unprovoked shark attacks are known to have occurred in Hawaii since 1900, and only about a third of these were fatal.

Theft & Violence

For the most part, Hawaii is a safe place to be.

However the islands do have notoriety for rip-offs from parked rental cars. The people who break into these cars are good at what they do; they can pop a trunk or pull out a lock assembly in seconds to get to loot inside. What's more, they do it not only when you've left your car in a secluded area to go for a long hike, but also in crowded parking lots where you'd expect safety in numbers.

It's best not to leave anything of value in your car any time you walk away from it. If for some reason you feel you must, at least pack things well out of sight *before* you've pulled up to the place where you're going to leave the car.

The only other real hassles that visitors may experience are from drunks. Be tuned in to the vibes on beaches at night and in places where young guys hang out to drink.

Overall, violent crime is lower in Hawaii than in most of the mainland cities. There are, however, some pockets of resentment against tourists, as well as off-islanders moving in. Oahu tends to be worse than the other islands.

FILM & PHOTOGRAPHY

Film is readily available on all the islands. Kodak and Fuji have labs in Honolulu. Drug stores and department stores, as well as camera shops, often send in to those labs. Longs Drugs is one of the cheapest for both film and developing. All the tourist centres have one-hour print processing shops.

If you're going to be in Hawaii for any length of time consider having your film developed there as the high temperature and humidity of the tropics greatly accelerate the deterioration of film. The sooner the processing the better the results.

Don't leave your camera in direct sun any longer than necessary. A locked car can heat up like an oven in just a few minutes.

Sand and water are intense reflectors and in bright light they'll often leave foreground subjects shadowy. You can try compensating by adjusting your f-stop or attaching a polarising filter or both, but the most effective technique is to take photos in the gentler light of early morning and late afternoon.

ACCOMMODATION

Hawaii has a wide variety of accommodation in all price ranges, including B&Bs, hotels and condominiums. There are also a handful of hostels and state park cabins that are quite inexpensive.

Waikiki has far more hotels than condos, though in Kihei and Kona the opposite is true. In most other major tourist destinations in Hawaii the hotels and condos pretty evenly divided.

Most places to stay in Hawaii have different rates for high season and low season (also called peak season and off season). High season most commonly applies to winter, from 15 December to 15 April, though some places extend the season a few weeks in either direction.

During low season, many places drop their rates by 10% to 35%. The low season is not only cheaper but it's got the best weather. The exception is August which has become busy enough that some hotels now charge high season prices for that month.

During winter many of the best value places to stay, particularly the smaller hotels and condos, are booked out well in advance.

There are more than 69,000 hotel and condo rooms in Hawaii. Oahu, which once boasted all of Hawaii's visitor accommodation and until 20 years ago still had 75%, has now slipped to about 50% as development continues full speed ahead on the neighbouring islands.

The Big Island alone has 44,000 *new* hotel and condo units planned. If it goes unchecked the once sleepy Kona Coast will surpass Waikiki in the next decade.

At most hotels the rooms are basically the same. Rates usually correspond to two variables: the view and the floor. An ocean view often costs 50% to 100% more than a parking lot view, which is usually euphemistically called 'garden view'. Also the higher you go, the higher the tariff as higher floors are generally quieter, especially on busy roads.

The toll free numbers given in this book usually can't be dialled within Hawaii. However, some hotels will accept collect calls from the neighbouring islands – it never hurts to try.

If you have a Hawaii driver's licence, always ask about *kamaaina* rates. Many middle and top-range hotels give residents big discounts.

A combined hotel room and excise tax of 9.43% is added to the price of all accommodation, including B&Bs.

The Hawaii Visitors Bureau (2270 Kalakaua Ave, Honolulu, HI 96815) will mail out on request a free annual accommodation guide listing member hotels with addresses and prices. It includes virtually all of Hawaii's resort hotels and most of those in the moderate range.

Except where noted, the rates given in this book are the same for either singles or doubles.

Condominiums

Condos are individually owned apartments which are usually handled by rental agents, though some complexes have their own front desk. Most condos have more space than hotel rooms, with a living area and a full kitchen. Many also have washer/dryers, sofa beds and a lanai (veranda). What they don't have is daily maid service.

If you're staying awhile or are travelling with several people, condos almost always work out cheaper than all but the bottom-end hotels. However, most condo units booked through rental agents have a three to seven day minimum stay.

Condos usually offer weekly and monthly rates. The general rule is that the weekly rate is six times the daily rate, and the monthly is three times the weekly. In the off season you can usually find someone willing to wheel and deal to beat that.

Bed & Breakfasts

There are hundreds of B&Bs scattered around Hawaii. Some are modest spare bedrooms in family households, others are romantic and private hideaways and a few are full-fledged inns. B&Bs cost as little as $30, though most average $50 or $60 and the most exclusive properties are $100 to $150. Many require a three-day minimum stay. Some give discounts for stays of a week or more. B&Bs vary greatly but for the most part they represent some of the best value accommodation to be found in Hawaii.

Because Hawaii state codes place restrictions on serving home-cooked meals, most B&Bs offer a continental breakfast or provide food for guests to cook their own. Some places do provide full home-cooked breakfasts – they just don't advertise it.

Most home-based B&Bs don't handle their own reservations, but sign up with B&B reservation services. Some of these agencies can also book whole houses, condos and studio cottages as well. All require at least part of the payment in advance and have cancellation penalties. These agencies include:

Pacific-Hawaii Bed & Breakfast, 19 Kai Nani Place, Kailua, HI 96734; Maria Wilson, tel 262-7865 or 800-999-6026. A full directory is sent on request, with a brief description of places. There's no fee.

Bed & Breakfast Honolulu, 3242 Kaohinani Drive, Honolulu, HI 96817; tel 595-7533, 800-288-4666. They provide a sample of listings by mail but don't publish a directory, preferring phone calls. There's a one-time $5 reservation fee for each unit they reserve.

My Island, Gordon & Joann Morse, Box 100, Volcano, HI 96785; tel 967-7216. They book only on the Big Island and don't charge a fee.

Bed & Breakfast Hawaii, Box 449, Kapaa, HI 96746; tel 822-7771 on Kauai, 536-8421 on Oahu. They charge $12.40 for membership and the mailing of their directory, have homes on all the islands and are probably the largest reservation service.

All Islands Bed & Breakfast, 823 Kainui Drive, Kailua, HI 96734; tel 263-2342, 800-542-0344. They book homes throughout Hawaii and there's no fee.

CAMPING

Hawaii has some good public park camping opportunities. In general, the national parks are better than the state parks and the state parks better than the county parks.

Though local people often unofficially camp in places other than the parks, it doesn't necessarily mean that you'll be welcome to join them. They may just be out for a weekend of fishing, or they may be homeless. Either way there could be some turf issues.

Over the years there have been some assaults and numerous thefts targeted at off-island campers. The violence has decreased in most places though a few camping grounds in rough areas, including the entire Waianae Coast of Oahu, are best avoided. The biggest hassles usually come from young local guys who have been drinking. People travelling alone, particularly women, need to be particularly cautious.

As for rip-offs, you'll need to watch your valuables. Generally the less you look like a tourist the less likely you are to have problems.

Pick your park carefully, especially the county parks. Some are well-established with caretakers and attract other campers, while others are pit stops along the road frequented mostly by drinkers.

For the most part the further you are from population centres, the less likely you are to run into hassles. Thieves and drunks aren't big on hiking. Camping in the wilds is generally safe on all the islands – a twisted ankle, a wild boar or a cross-eyed hunter are the biggest safety concerns.

National Parks

The Hawaii Volcanoes National Park is great for camping and hiking; it's the best on the Big Island, if not in all Hawaii. Haleakala National Park on Maui has the best camping on that island. Neither charge camping fees and getting a space is seldom a problem. Both are detailed in their respective sections.

State Parks

The five largest islands have state park

camping grounds. They range from wilderness areas to developed drive-up camping sites, and some also have housekeeping cabins. State parks often have caretakers and better security than county parks.

Camping Camping is allowed in the following places: on Kauai in Kokee, Na Pali Coast and Polihale state parks; on Oahu in Kaiaka, Keaiwa Heiau, Malaekahana, Sand Island and Waimanalo Bay state recreation areas; on Molokai in Palaau State Park; on Maui in Polipoli Spring State Recreation Area and Waianapanapa State Park; and on the Big Island in Kalopa and MacKenzie state recreation areas.

Camping is free by permit and tents are required. Developed camping grounds generally have picnic tables, barbecue grills, drinking water, toilets and showers.

The maximum length of stay in each park is five nights per every 30 days. Camping is allowed on any day, except on Oahu where camping grounds are closed on Wednesday and Thursday nights.

Permits can be obtained on weekdays from any of the following Division of State Parks offices, either in person, by mail or by phone:

Oahu
    1151 Punchbowl St (Box 621), Honolulu, HI 96809; tel 548-7455
Big Island
    75 Aupuni St (Box 936), Hilo, HI 96721; tel 961-7200
Maui
    54 High St (Box 1049), Wailuku, HI 96793; tel 244-4354
Kauai
    3060 Eiwa St (Box 1671), Lihue, HI 96766; tel 245-4444

Applicants must be 18 and include their address and phone number as well as an identification number (driver's licence, passport or social security number) for each camper in the group. Applications must be received at least seven days in advance, but no earlier than one year (30 days on Oahu).

Cabins The state has housekeeping cabins on the Big Island at Kilauea (in the town of Volcano), Kalopa and Mauna Kea state recreation areas and on Maui at Polipoli Spring State Recreation Area and Waianapanapa State Park.

The cabins are generally simple places with kitchens, a common area, bathroom and one to three bedrooms. They have basic furnishings, bedding, hot showers and some cooking and eating utensils. Polipoli has neither electricity nor refrigerators and you'll need a 4WD vehicle or hiking boots to reach it.

The housekeeping cabins are good value: $10 for one person, $14 for two, $19.50 for three, $24 for four, $27.50 for five and $30 for six. The state also has A-frame shelters at Hapuna Beach on the Big Island, which cost $7 per shelter for up to four people.

Reservations can be made at any of the state park offices. These cabins are in demand. Summer is the busiest time, but they're often booked-out all year round. They do, however, get cancellations and if someone with a reservation doesn't pay their deposit in time the computer bounces them and the site opens again.

Cabin cancellations and waiting lists are handled only on the island where the cabins are located. Even at the last moment it's worth calling to see if something is available. If you're a little flexible you might be lucky – as we have been on occasion.

Reservations can be made in person, by phone or by mail; with 50% of the fee due within two weeks of making the reservation. Personal cheques are accepted if you're paying more than 30 days in advance, otherwise you'll need a bank cheque or postal money order. The remainder is due in cash when you check in. Refunds are given with notice 30 days prior to the camping date.

There are concession-run cabins at Malaekahana State Recreation Area on Oahu and Kokee State Park on Kauai (see those sections for reservation information).

County Parks

All the counties have parks with camping areas, though not all are of equal standard.

Maui, which outside Oahu has the lion's share of island hotels and condos, seems more dedicated to getting your dollar than encouraging camping. Camping is allowed at only two county parks, each for only three nights, and neither is recommendable. The fee is $3 per person per night.

The Big Island has 13 county camping grounds and a fee of only $1 which is not always collected.

Kauai has five county camping grounds, including a couple of really nice places on the beach. The fee is $3 per person per night.

Oahu has 14 county camping grounds, a couple of which are safe and recommendable. There are no fees.

Molokai has two county parks with camping areas, one on Hawaii's largest white sand beach, for $3 per person per night. Lanai has no county camping.

Hawaii has many beaches which have been turned into 'beach parks' simply by plopping down restrooms. While some county parks have wonderful white sand beaches and good facilities, others sit beneath oil storage tanks or are merely roadside rest areas. 'County park' may just mean the county owns the shoreline. Just because camping is allowed doesn't mean you'd want to camp there, or even use the beach.

Information on camping at county parks is in the Camping section of each island.

FOOD

Hawaii is a delightful place to eat. Though you can spend a bundle, you don't need to as there are good, cheap neighbourhood restaurants to explore on all the islands.

With Hawaii's ethnic diversity, there are hundreds of different foods to try. There's every kind of Japanese food, an array of regional Chinese cuisines and Korean, Thai, Hawaiian, Filipino and Vietnamese foods. Even McDonald's serves up saimin and Portuguese sausage and Woolworth has sushi at the lunch counter.

On the other end of the spectrum, Hawaii has many restaurants with renowned chefs and gourmet food. Most of them are at the top-end hotels, though a fair number of the more successful chefs have moved on to open their own restaurants.

Fresh fish is readily available throughout the islands. Seafood is generally expensive at places catering fancy meals to tourists, but can be quite reasonable at neighbourhood restaurants.

Note In Hawaii, as in the rest of the USA, 'entrees' refers to the main course or main dish of a meal and 'granola' means cereal.

Fish

Some of the most popular locally caught fish include:

mahimahi	a fish called 'dolphin', (not the mammal)
aku	skipjack tuna
ahi	yellowfin tuna
ono	wahoo
opakapaka	pink snapper
onaga	red snapper
uku	gray snapper
au	swordfish, marlin
akule	mackerel bigeye scad
papio or *ulua*	jack fish
kaku	barracuda
uhu	parrotfish
mano	shark

Fruit

Hawaii has an abundance of fruit including avocado, banana, breadfruit, starfruit, coconut, guava, lychee, mango, papaya, *lilikoi*, or passion fruit, and pineapple. Sweet Kau oranges are grown on the Big Island.

Watermelons grown on Molokai are so famous throughout the islands that the airlines had to create special regulations for passengers carrying them out of Molokai to prevent loose melons from bombing their way down the aisles.

Wild fruits which can be picked along trails include strawberry guava, common

Fruit

guava, thimbleberries, mountain apples, Methley plums and ohelo berries.

Pineapple Hawaii's number one fruit crop is the pineapple. Most Hawaiian pineapple are of the smooth cayenne type and weigh a good five pounds. Pineapples are fairly unique among fruits in that they don't continue to ripen after they're picked. Though they're harvested year round, the long sunny days of summer produce the sweetest pineapples.

Papaya Papayas come in several varieties. One of the best of those found in grocery stores is the Solo, a small variety with pale strawberry-coloured flesh. The flavour of papayas depends largely on where they're grown. Some of the most prized are from the Kapoho area of Puna on the Big Island and the Kahuku area of Oahu. Papayas, which are a good source of calcium and vitamins A and C, are harvested all year round.

Avocado Hawaii has three main types of avocado: the West Indian, a smooth-skinned variety, which matures in summer and autumn; the rough-skinned Guatemalan which matures in winter and spring; and the Mexican variety has a small fruit and smooth skin. Many of the avocados now in Hawaii are a hybrid of the three. Local fruit tends to be larger and more watery than the avocados grown in California.

Mango Big old mango trees are abundant in Hawaii, even in remote valleys. The juicy oblong fruits are about three inches in diameter and four to six inches long. The fruits start out green but take on deeper colours as they ripen, usually reddening to an apricot colour. Mangoes are a good source of vitamins A and C. Two popular varieties, Pirie and Haden, are less stringy than those usually found in the wild. Mangoes are mainly a summer fruit.

Starfruit The carambola, or starfruit, is a translucent yellow-green fruit with five ribs like the points of a star. It has a crisp juicy pulp and doesn't need to be peeled.

Guava The common guava is a yellow, lime-shaped fruit, about two to three inches in diameter. It has a moist, pink, seedy flesh, all of which is edible. Guavas can be a little tart but tend to sweeten as they ripen. They're a good source of vitamin C and niacin and can be found along roadsides and trails.

Lilikoi Passion fruit is a vine with beautiful flowers which grow into small round fruits. The thick skin is generally purple or yellow and wrinkles as it ripens. The fruit inside is juicy, seedy and slightly tart. The slimy texture can be a bit of a put-off the first time, but once you taste it you'll be hooked.

Mountain Apple The mountain apple is a small oval fruit a couple of inches long. The tree is related to the guava, though the fruit is completely different with a crispy white flesh and a pink skin. It fruits in the summer and is common along trails.

Ohelo These berries grow on low shrubs common in lava areas. It's a relative of the cranberry, similar in tartness and size. The fruit is red or yellow and is used in jellies and pies.

Breadfruit The Hawaiian breadfruit is a large, round, green fruit. It's comparable to potatoes in carbohydrates and is prepared much the same way. In old Hawaii, as in much of the Pacific, breadfruit was one of the traditional staples.

Hawaiian Food

The traditional Hawaiian feast marking special events is the *luau*. Local luaus are still commonplace in modern Hawaii for events such as baby christenings. In spirit, these luaus are far more authentic than anything you'll see at a hotel, but they're family affairs and the short-stay visitor would be lucky indeed to get an invitation to one.

The main dish at a luau is *kalua pig*, roasted in an *imu*, which is an underground earthen oven. The shallow imu is prepared by building a fire and heating rocks in the pit. When the rocks are glowing red, layers of moisture-laden banana trunks and green ti leaves are placed over the stones. A pig which has been slit open is filled with some of the hot rocks and laid on top of the bed. Other foods wrapped in ti and banana leaves are placed around it. It's all covered with more ti leaves and a layer of mats and topped off with dirt to seal in the heat which then bakes and steams the food. Anything cooked in this style is called *kalua*.

The process takes about four to eight hours depending on the amount of food. A few of the hotel luaus still bake the pig outdoors in this traditional manner and you can often go in the morning and watch them prepare and bury the pig.

Taro, coconut, bananas, fish, breadfruit, sweet potatoes, chicken and pork are all traditional Hawaiian foods.

Wetland taro is used to make *poi*, a paste pounded from the cooked taro corms. Water is added to make it pudding-like and its consistency is measured in one, two or three-finger poi – which indicates how many fingers are required to bring it from bowl to mouth. Poi is highly nutritious and easily digestible, but an acquired taste. It is sometimes fermented to give it a zingier flavour.

Laulau is fish, pork and taro wrapped in a ti leaf bundle and steamed. *Lomi* salmon (or *lomilomi* salmon) is made by marinating thin slices of raw salmon with diced tomatoes and green onion.

Other Hawaiian foods include baked *ulu* – breadfruit, *limu* – seaweed, *opihi* – the tiny limpet shells which fishermen pick off the reef at low tide, and *pipikaula* – beef jerky. *Haupia* is the standard dessert to a Hawaiian meal. It's a custard made of coconut cream

Poi Pounder

thickened these days with cornstarch, though formerly with arrowroot.

In Hawaiian food preparation, ti leaves are indispensable: food is wrapped in it, cooked in it and served upon it.

Most visitors taste traditional Hawaiian food only at expensive luaus or may sample a dollop of poi at one of the more adventurous hotel buffets. Though Hawaiian food is harder to find than other ethnic foods, there are a few restaurants throughout the islands that serve the real thing and it's some of the cheapest food in Hawaii.

Local Food

The distinct style of food called 'local' usually refers to a fixed plate lunch with 'two scoop rice', a scoop of macaroni salad and a main meal of beef stew, teriyaki chicken or *mahimahi*, generally scoffed down with chopsticks. A breakfast plate might have Spam, eggs, kimchee and, always, two scoop rice.

This is the standard fare in diners and lunch wagons. If it's full of starches, fats and gravies, you're probably eating local.

Snacks

Pupus is the word for all kinds of munchies or hors d'oeuvres. Boiled peanuts, soy-flavoured rice crackers called *kaki mochi* and sashimi are common pupus.

Poke is raw fish marinated in soy sauce, oil, chilli peppers, green onions and seaweed. It's good with beer.

Crack seed Crack seed is a Chinese snack food which can be sweet, sour, salty or a combination. It's often made from dried fruits such as plums and apricots, though more exotic ones include sweet and sour baby cherry seeds, pickled mangoes and *li hing mui*, one of the sour favourites. Crack seed shops often sell dried cuttlefish, roasted green peas, beef jerky and rock candy as well.

Shave Ice Shave ice is similar to mainland snow cones, only better. The ice is shaved as fine as powder snow, packed into a paper cone and drenched with sweet fruit-flavoured syrups. Islanders like the ones with ice cream and/or sweet azuki beans at the bottom. Kids like rainbow shave ice, with colourful stripes of different syrups.

DRINKS

Tap water is safe to drink but water from freshwater streams should be boiled.

Cans of Hawaiian-made fruit juices such as guava-orange or passion fruit are stocked at most stores. They make a good alternative to sodas. They're also good to throw in your daypack for outings as they don't explode when shaken, like soft drinks do, and they taste OK.

Alcohol

The drinking age in Hawaii is 21. It's illegal to have open containers of alcohol in motor vehicles and drinking in public parks or on the beaches is also illegal though it's a common scene.

All grocery stores sell liquor as do most of the smaller food marts. Hawaii has one winery, Tedeschi Vineyards on Maui, which makes a good pineapple wine, grape wine and champagne.

PAKALOLO

Hawaii's *pakalolo* (marijuana) is considered to be some of the most potent anywhere. Occasionally local guys hanging out in beach parking lots will mutter 'buds' as you walk by. It's usually said just loud enough for you to hear if you're listening for it, and miss if you're not.

BOOKS & BOOKSHOPS

Hawaii is said to be the most written-about place in the Pacific. There are books on just about every subject you can think of, from the origin of volcanoes to the history of *hula*. There are even reference books devoted to the books of Hawaii.

The four largest islands all have good bookshops with Hawaiiana sections. Bookshop locations are listed under each island.

Ordering by Mail

The following publishers will send catalogues of their books that can be ordered by mail.

University of Hawaii Press
  2840 Kolowalu St, Honolulu, HI 96822
Bishop Museum Press
  Box 19000-A, Honolulu, HI 96817
Petroglyph Press
  201 Kinoole St, Hilo, HI 96720
Mutual Publishing
  2055 N King St, Suite 201, Honolulu, HI 96819

Reference

The *Atlas of Hawaii* by the Department of Geography, University of Hawaii (University of Hawaii Press, Honolulu, 1983), is loaded with data, maps and tabulations covering everything from land ownership to seasonal ocean wave patterns. This 238-page atlas is the most comprehensive reference book of Hawaii.

Place Names of Hawaii by Mary Kawena Pukui, Samuel H Elbert and Esther T Mookini (University of Hawaii Press, Honolulu, 1974) is a glossary of 4000 Hawaiian place names. The meaning and background of each name is explained.

Hawaiian Dictionary by Mary Kawena Pukui and Samuel H Elbert (University of Hawaii Press, Honolulu, 1986) is the authoritative work on the Hawaiian language. It's in both Hawaiian-English and English-Hawaiian, with 30,000 entries. They also do a $2.95 pocket-size version with 6000 Hawaiian words.

Other Hawaiian language books on the market include grammar texts, conversational self-study guides and books on pidgin.

History & Politics

Hawaiian Antiquities by David Malo (Bishop Museum Press, Honolulu, 1980), written in 1838, was the first account of Hawaiian culture written by a Hawaiian. It gives an in-depth history of Hawaii before the arrival of the missionaries.

Shoal of Time by Gavan Daws (University of Hawaii Press, Honolulu, 1974) is a com-

prehensive and colourful history covering the period from Captain Cook's 'discovery' of the islands to statehood.

Hawaii's Story by Hawaii's Queen by Queen Liliuokalani (Tuttle, 1964) is an autobiographical account of Liliuokalani's childhood and life as a member of royalty as well as the circumstances surrounding her 1893 overthrow.

Fragments of Hawaiian History by John Papa Ii (Bishop Museum Press, Honolulu, 1959) is a first-hand account of old Hawaii under the *kapu* system. Ii lived in Kailua-Kona at the time of Kamehameha I.

Kauai, the Separate Kingdom by Edward Joesting (University of Hawaii Press, Honolulu, 1984) is the authoritative history book on Kauai, the only Hawaiian kingdom never conquered in battle.

The Hawaiian Kingdom by Ralph S Kuykendall (University of Hawaii Press, Honolulu, three-volume set written from 1938 to 1967) covers Hawaiian history from 1778 to 1893. It's considered the definitive work on the period.

Six Months in the Sandwich Islands by Isabella Bird Bishop (University of Hawaii Press, Honolulu, 1964) is the personal account of a Victorian lady's travels around Hawaii in 1873.

The Dark Side of Paradise, Hawaii in a Nuclear World, by Jim Albertini, Nelson Foster, Wally Inglis and Gil Roeder (Catholic Action of Hawaii, Honolulu, 1980) is an enlightening exposé of the military presence in Hawaii.

Fiction

A Hawaiian Reader, edited by A Grove Day and Carl Stroven (Mutual Publishing, Honolulu, 1959), is an excellent anthology with 37 selections, both fiction and non-fiction. It starts with a log entry by Captain James Cook and includes writings from early missionaries as well as Mark Twain, Jack London, Somerset Maugham, David Malo, Isabella Bird, Martha Beckwith and others. If you only have time to read one book about Hawaii this inexpensive paperback is a great choice.

O A Bushnell is one of Hawaii's best-known contemporary authors. The University of Hawaii Press, Honolulu, has published his titles *The Return of Lono* (1971), a historical novel of Captain Cook's final voyage; *Kaaawa* (1972), about Hawaii in the 1850s; *The Stone of Kannon* (1979), about the first group of Japanese contract labourers to arrive in Hawaii, and its sequel *The Water of Kane* (1980).

Stories of Hawaii (Appleton, 1965) is a collection of Jack London's short stories.

Hawaii (paperback: Hodder & Stoughton; Random, 1959), is James Michener's history of the islands, from their volcanic origins to their emergence as a state. This sweeping saga traces the racial origins of modern Hawaiians through several family lines: the Polynesian settlers who became the Hawaiian people; the missionaries and whalers, whose influence on the native culture was both enlightening and disastrous; the White settlers who built empires on sugar cane and cattle; and the Chinese labourers who were brought in to work the plantations.

People

Keneti by Bob Krauss (University of Hawaii Press, Honolulu, 1988) is about the life of Kenneth 'Keneti' Emory, the esteemed Bishop Museum archaeologist. Over the years Emory sailed with writer-adventurer Jack London, and worked with anthropologist Margaret Mead uncovering the ruins of villages and temples throughout the Pacific, recording them before they disappeared forever.

Paddling My Own Canoe by Audrey Sutherland (University of Hawaii Press, Honolulu, 1978) details the author's explorations in an inflatable kayak along the rugged and isolated north shore of Molokai. It inspired a trend toward wilderness kayaking in Hawaii.

Father Damien, the priest who worked in the leprosy colony on Molokai, is the subject of many books including *Holy Man: Father Damien of Molokai* by Gavan Daws (Harper & Row, 1973), *Damien the Leper* by John Farrow (Doubleday & Co, New York 1954) and others.

A Day in the Life of Hawaii by David Cohen and Rick Smolan (Workman, New York, 1984) is a pictorial coffee table book with photographs by some of the world's top photographers, all taken on 2 December 1983.

Aloha Cowboy by Virginia Cowan-Smith and Bonnie Domrose Stone (University of Hawaii Press, Honolulu, 1988) is an illustrated account of 200 years of paniolo life in Hawaii, leading up to today's contemporary cowboys.

Outdoor Activities

Hawaiian Hiking Trails by Craig Chisholm (The Fernglen Press, Lake Oswego, Oregon, 1986) is a good, detailed hiking guide to Hawaii's best-known trails.

Robert Smith (Wilderness Press, Berkeley, California, 1985) has written hiking guides to each of the four major islands: *Hiking Hawaii, Hiking Maui, Hiking Kauai* and *Hiking Oahu*. Smith has combined the main trails on each island into a pocket-size book called *Hawaii's Best Hiking Trails*.

On the Na Pali Coast by Kathy Valier (University of Hawaii Press, Honolulu, 1988) is a guide for hikers and boaters in Hawaii's most spectacular state park. It has maps and narrative covering both ethnobotany and practical details.

Beaches of Oahu (1977), *Beaches of Maui* (1980) and *Beaches of the Big Island* (1985) are by John R K Clark (University of Hawaii Press, Honolulu). These are comprehensive books of each island's coastline and every one of its beaches, covering water conditions, shoreline geology and histories. The Maui edition includes Maui, Molokai, Lanai and Kahoolawe. If you're going to be spending a lot of time exploring beaches, these books are the ones to have.

The Divers' Guide to Hawaii by Chuck Thorne and Lou Zitnik (Hawaii Divers' Guide, Kihei, 1984) is a guide to the best shore dives on the six main Hawaiian islands. It's got comprehensive directions to sites, maps of entry points, what you'll see and

Top: Kodak Hula Show, Kapiolani Park, Oahu
Left: Leis
Right: John Nakai, raku potter, Oahu

Top: Chinese lion dance at Bishop Museum, Oahu
Left: Tattoo Artist, Chinatown, Oahu
Right: Carol Rogers, Kona Arts Center, Holualoa, Big Island

hazards to expect, all written in a light and colourful style. Though it's geared for divers it's of some value to snorkellers as well.

Diving and Snorkeling Guide to the Hawaiian Islands by Doug Wallin (Pisces Books, New York, 1984) is a good guide to both diving and snorkelling on the four main islands. It has colour photos of sites and fish.

Let's Go Shore Dive'n' on the Kona Coast (DPD Associates) is a shore dive guide to the west coast of the Big Island by Dick Dresie, who writes a diving column for *West Hawaii Today*, the local newspaper. Dresie gives first-person accounts of his diving experiences in each spot.

Natural History

Hawaii: The Islands of Life (Signature Publishing, 1988) has strikingly beautiful photos of the flora, fauna and landscapes of areas being protected by the Nature Conservancy of Hawaii. The text is by respected Pacific author Gavan Daws.

The Many-Splendored Fishes of Hawaii by Gar Goodson (Marquest Colorguide Books, California, 1973) is one of the better little fish identification books, with good descriptions and 170 colour drawings.

Hawaii's Birds, edited by Robert J Shallenberger (Hawaii Audubon Society, Honolulu, 1984), is the best pocket-sized guide to the birds of Hawaii. It has colour photos and descriptions of all the native birds and many of the introduced species.

Mammals in Hawaii by P Quentin Tomich (Bishop Museum Press, Honolulu, 1986) is the authoritative book on all the mammals in Hawaii, with interesting stories on their arrival and histories. He includes all species of whales and dolphins found in Hawaiian waters.

Trailside Plants of Hawaii's National Parks by Charles H Lamoureux (Hawaii Natural History Association, 1976) covers common trailside plants and trees in some depth. It's a good book to have if you'll be spending time hiking in the national parks.

Similarly, *Hawaiian Forest Plants* by Mark David Merlin (Oriental Publishing Company, Honolulu, 1976) has descriptions

and colour photos of many of the plants encountered on Hawaii's forest trails.

Plants and Flowers of Hawaii by S H Sohmer and R Gustafson (University of Hawaii Press, Honolulu, 1987) has information on several hundred of the native plants of Hawaii, their habitat and evolution.

Flowers in Hawaii (Hakubundo, Honolulu), with text in both English and Japanese, is a good picture book of common flowers found in Hawaii.

Practical Folk Medicine of Hawaii by L R McBride (Petroglyph Press, Hilo, 1975) has descriptions of many native medicinal plants and their uses.

Maui – How It Came to Be by Will Kyselka and Ray Lanterman (University of Hawaii Press, Honolulu, 1980) is a readable geology book on the evolution of Maui from volcanic formation to present day.

Hawaiian Culture

The Kumulipo by Martha Beckwith (University of Hawaii Press, Honolulu, 1972) is a translation of the Hawaiian chant of creation, with a commentary. The chant of 2077 lines begins in the darkness of the spirit world and traces the genealogy of an *alii* family, said to be the ancestors of humankind.

Hawaiian Mythology by Martha Beckwith (University of Hawaii Press, Honolulu, 1970) has comprehensive translations of Hawaii's old myths and legends.

Nana I Ke Kumu (Look to the Source) by Mary K Pukui, E W Haertig and Catherine A Lee (Hui Hanai, 1972, 2 vols) is a fascinating collection of information on Hawaiian cultural practices, social customs and beliefs.

The Legends and Myths of Hawaii (Charles Tuttle Co, Rutland, Vermont) is a collection of legends as told by King David Kalakaua. It has a short introduction to Hawaiian culture and history as well.

The Hula by Jerry Hopkins (APA Productions, Hong Kong, 1982) is a history of the hula and the musical instruments used in the dance. It includes biographical sketches of some of hula's most important people.

Hawaiian Music and Musicians: An Illustrated History by George S Kanahele

(University of Hawaii Press, Honolulu, 1979) is a history of the islands' music, including singers and composers and some of their song and chants.

Niihau Shell Leis by Linda Paik Moriarty (University of Hawaii Press, Honolulu, 1986) explains the development of the unique Hawaiian craft of shell *lei* making by Niihauans. It also illustrates the styles and varieties.

Hawaiian Petroglyphs by J Halley Cox (Bishop Museum Press, Honolulu 1985) lists petroglyph sites and has extensive photos and illustrations of Hawaiian petroglyphs. The book is artistically striking.

Libraries

Hawaii has a statewide library system. If you present some identification (driver's licence, passport), they'll issue you a free library card on the spot which can be used at any public library in the state.

Books can be checked out for three weeks and can be returned to any library, for example you can check out a book on Kauai and return it on Molokai. Most libraries have a pretty good Hawaiiana section.

MAPS

The drive guides handed out with rental cars have maps of the main roads, as do some of the free tourist magazines. If you really want to explore, a more detailed road map is invaluable.

Rand McNally and Gousha both put out a good Oahu street map, with a well-detailed Honolulu section.

The University of Hawaii makes separate maps for Oahu, Kauai, Maui, the Big Island and Molokai/Lanai. They're the best overall maps for the neighbouring islands as they not only cover roads but also beaches, historical sites and some of the major hiking trails, and have handy indexes. UH maps cost $2.25 to $2.95 and are available in bookstores and general shops frequented by tourists.

Maps & Miscellaneous (tel 538-7429) is a hole-in-the-wall map shop upstairs at 404 Piikoi St, Suite 213, Honolulu, HI 96814, opposite the Ala Moana Center. It carries USGS maps and others. Call first, as business hours are irregular.

On the Big Island, Basically Books (169 Keawe St, Hilo, HI 96720; tel 961-0144) has a comprehensive collection of USGS topographical maps, NOAA nautical charts of Hawaii, UH island maps, street maps and even antique and speciality maps. They also do mail order.

USGS maps can also be ordered from the US Geological Survey, Federal Center, Denver, Colorado 80225. Both full-island and detailed sectional maps are available by mail.

For those who want to dig a little deeper, the basement of Hamilton Library at the University of Hawaii, Manoa campus, has a great map room with thousands of esoteric maps on Hawaii and other Pacific islands. You can't buy them, but you can photocopy them.

ACTIVITIES

Hawaii has an exhaustive variety of sports and recreational activities. Not only are there top conditions for water sports, there's also hiking, biking, jogging, tennis, golf, horseback riding, you name it. There's even snow skiing on the Big Island in winter.

Hawaii is a great place to learn to surf, windsurf or dive – or just rent the equipment if you already know how. Hawaii has 750 miles of coastline and all 283 beaches are public up to the high water mark.

Except for competitions or lengthy excursions, few activities require advance planning before you get to Hawaii.

More detailed information is given in each island section.

Hiking

Hawaii is a first-rate hiking environment. Like the islands themselves, the hiking opportunities are incredibly varied, from desert treks to lush rainforest walks, and from beach strolls to snowline ridge trails.

Trails range from short family-style nature walks to backpacking treks which last several days and require carrying food and gear.

Despite all the development on Hawaii, it's amazing how much of the islands are still in a natural state. There are places where you could walk for days without seeing another soul.

Hawaii's two national parks have hiking opportunities that have no parallels anywhere. Both have barren lunar-like landscapes as well as lush, tropical forests.

The Hawaii Volcanoes National Park on the Big Island has the distinction of containing both the world's most active volcano and largest mountain mass. There are breathtaking hikes down into steaming crater floors and up to the snow-capped summit of Mauna Loa.

At the Haleakala National Park on Maui the volcano is sleepier, but equally awe-inspiring. Hikes into the caldera of the world's largest crater can take half a day and hikes across it can take half a week.

Still, the premier hike in all of Hawaii is on Kauai's Na Pali Coast, where the Kalalau Trail follows an ancient Hawaiian footpath along the edges of some of the most spectacularly fluted coastal cliffs in Hawaii. The trail winds down into lush valleys where camping is allowed and waterfalls and ruins can be explored.

There are also hiking trails into other ancient valleys, such as Waipio on the Big Island and Halawa on Molokai. Some hikes lead to secluded beaches, others to inland waterfalls. There are old 'king's trails' with footpaths worn through lava by the bare feet of travellers over hundreds of years. Every island has ridgeline hikes with panoramic views and there are nature preserves with native plants and birds and lots of solitude.

Safety & Tips A lot of Hawaii's hiking trails take you into steep, narrow valleys with gullies that require stream crossings. The capital rule here is that if the water begins to rise, it's not safe to cross. A flash flood may be imminent so head for higher ground and wait it out.

Flash floods are the biggest dangers on trails, followed by falling rocks. Be wary of swimming under high waterfalls, as rocks can get dislodged from the top, and beware on the edge of steep cliffs as cliffside rock in Hawaii tends to be crumbly.

Darkness sets in soon after sunset in Hawaii and ridgetop trails are not the place to be caught unprepared in the dark. It's a good idea to carry a flashlight when you're hiking, just in case.

Jeans will protect your legs from the overgrown parts of the trail and tennis shoes or sturdy walking shoes are advisable.

Some people prefer *tabi* (reef walkers) for hiking. They have good traction and offer some protection from leptospirosis (see the Health section). They're sold at dive shops and fishing supply shops.

Hawaii has no snakes, no poison ivy, no poison oak and few dangers from wild animals. There's a slim possibility of meeting up with a large boar in the backwoods, but they're unlikely to be a problem unless cornered.

Hiking Information The two most popular hiking books covering trails on all the islands are *Hawaiian Hiking Trails* by Craig Chisholm and *Hawaii's Best Hiking Trails* by Robert Smith. Both are easy to find in Hawaii.

Free recreational maps are available for Maui and Molokai – and should soon be available for Kauai and Oahu – from the Division of Forestry & Wildlife (tel 548-2861), 1151 Punchbowl St, Room 325, Honolulu, HI 96813. The forestry also has some trail descriptions and photocopies of topo maps for some wilderness trails that they'll send out on request. Let them know which islands you'll be hiking on.

The Oahu, Maui, Kauai and Big Island branches of the Sierra Club (Honolulu Merchandise Mart, 1100 Alakea St, Room 330, Honolulu, HI 96813; tel 538-6616) lead guided hikes. For a schedule of hikes, send them a self-addressed envelope with postage for two ounces (45 cents for domestic mail).

Information on the various hiking trails is given in each island section.

Running

There are more than 100 road races, ranging from fun runs to triathlons, held in the islands each year.

Hawaii's best-known races are the Honolulu Marathon held in December and the Ironman Triathlon held in Kona on the Big Island in October. For info on the former contact the Honolulu Marathon Association, 3435 Waialae Ave No 208, Honolulu, HI 96816; and for the latter: 75-5737 Kuakini Hwy, Suite 208, Kailua-Kona, HI 96740 (tel 329-0063).

The Department of Parks & Recreation of the City & County of Honolulu (650 S King St, Honolulu, HI 96813) has an extensive schedule of running events.

Windsurfing

Maui has some of the world's best windsurfing action. Hookipa Beach near Paia hosts some top international windsurfing competitions. Tamer action can be found on other parts of the island.

On Oahu, Kailua Beach draws the biggest crowd with excellent year-round wind. Kauai and the Big Island also have their spots. It's possible to rent gear and take lessons on all four islands.

Although there's good windsurfing conditions in Hawaii year round, winter can have flat periods. The best winds are from June to September.

A useful book for windsurfers is *Windsurfing Guide to the Islands*, published annually by Windward Promotions (Box 52, Paia, HI 96779).

Surfing

Hawaii lies smack in the path of all the major swells that race unimpeded across the Pacific, and the sport of surfing got its start in these islands hundreds of years ago with the early Hawaiians.

Hawaii has good surfing throughout the year although the biggest waves hit from November to February on the north shores. Summer swells break along the southern shores, though they're usually not as frequent and nowhere near as large as winter swells on the northern side.

Oahu's north shore has Hawaii's top surf action. The winter swells at Waimea, Sunset Beach and the Banzai Pipeline can bring in 30-foot waves, creating the conditions that legends are made of. Waikiki has Hawaii's top south shore surfing.

Maui and Kauai also have excellent surfing and, though not as notable, Molokai and the Big Island have surfing spots as well.

In addition to board surfing, bodysurfing and boogie boarding are popular. Boogie boards are small foam boards used to support the upper body when riding a bodysurfing wave.

Diving

Diving is a year-round sport in Hawaii. Under normal conditions, the leeward shores of the islands have the best diving most of the year. The north shores are usually best in the summer.

Hawaiian waters have excellent visibility and water temperatures are 72° to 80°F.

There are almost 700 fish species in Hawaiian waters and about 30% of them are found nowhere else in the world. Reef fish

Diver

are colourful and numerous. There are more than 20 different kinds of butterfly fish, plus rainbow-coloured parrotfish, wrasses, tangs, filefish and pufferfish, just to list a few. There are spinner dolphins, green sea turtles, manta rays and moray eels. Though divers rarely see humpback whales underwater, they do sometimes hear them singing.

Hawaii has underwater caves, canyons, lava tubes, vertical walls and sunken ships. There are all sorts of colourful sponges and corals, including the gem-like black coral.

There are good dive spots off all the islands and numerous dive shops on the four largest islands.

Fishing

The state maintains a few freshwater fishing areas on Kauai, Oahu and the Big Island. Stocked game fish include rainbow trout, largemouth and smallmouth bass, bluegill sunfish, channel catfish, tilapia and carp. Licences are required. It costs non-residents $3.75 for a 30-day licence.

To get a freshwater fishing licence, the booklets *Freshwater Fishing in Hawaii* or *Digest of Fishing Laws and Rules*, contact the Division of Aquatic Resources (tel 548-8766), 1151 Punchbowl St, Room 330, Honolulu, HI 96813.

No licences are required for saltwater fishing. There are, however, seasons, size limits and/or other restrictions on taking *ula* (spiny lobster), crab, octopus (*hee* in Hawaiian, and also called tako or squid), *opihi* (a kind of limpet), Japanese littleneck clams, *limu* (seaweed), and certain kinds of fish.

THINGS TO BUY

Hawaii has a lot of fine craftspeople. Woodworkers generally use the beautifully grained native Hawaiian hardwoods, such as *koa*, to create calabashes and bowls. Traditionally Hawaiian bowls are not decorated or ornate, but rather are shaped to bring out the natural beauty of the wood. The thinner and lighter the bowl, the finer the artistic skill and the greater the value.

There are some excellent island potters, many influenced by Japanese styles and aesthetics. Good raku work in particular can be found throughout the islands at reasonable prices.

Lauhala, the leaves of the pandanus tree which were once woven into the mats that Hawaiians slept on, are now woven into placemats, hats and baskets.

Music shops carry recorded traditional and contemporary Hawaiian music. Hula musical instruments such as nose flutes and gourd rattles are uniquely Hawaiian, as is *kukui* nut jewellery and oils.

Niihau shell *leis*, made from the tiny shells which wash up on the island of Niihau, are one of the most prized Hawaiiana souvenirs. Elaborate pieces can cost thousands of dollars.

Hawaii's island-style clothing is, like Hawaii itself, colourful and light, often with prints of tropical flowers. The classiest *aloha* shirts are of lightweight cotton with subdued colours (like those of reverse fabric prints). Women might want to buy a *muumuu*, a loose, comfortable, full-length Hawaiian-style dress.

Foods are popular purchases. The standard souvenir is macadamia nuts, either canned or covered in chocolate. Kona coffee, macnut butters, *lilikoi* or *poha* berry preserves and mango chutney all make convenient, compact gift items.

Pineapples are not a great choice in the souvenir department. Not only are they heavy and bulky, and you'll probably end up carrying them on the plane, but they're likely to be just as cheap at home.

If you're into Japanese food, Hawaii is a good place to pick up ingredients that might be difficult to find at home. Most grocery stores have a wide selection of things like dried seaweed, mochi and ume plums.

Flowers such as orchids, anthuriums and proteas are good if you're flying straight home. Proteas stay fresh for about 10 days and then can be dried.

WHAT TO BRING

Hawaii has wonderfully balmy weather and a casual attitude toward dress so, for the most part, packing is a breeze.

At the lower elevations it's summer all year. Shorts, sandals and a T-shirt or aloha shirt are the standard day dress. If you don't intend to spend time in the higher country, a light jacket or sweater will be the warmest clothing you'll need.

Pack light. You can pick up something with a floral Hawaiian print when you get there and dress island style.

An aloha shirt and lightweight slacks for men, and a cotton dress for women, is pretty much regarded as 'dressing up' on the islands. Only a few of the most exclusive restaurants require anything dressier and some of those lend their own jackets at the door.

Hawaii does, however, have hilly country and mountains, and most people get at least as far as the former. The hills can be a good 20° cooler than the coast and when the fog blows in and the wind picks up, it gets quite nippy. Plan on another layer of clothes if you'll be spending any time in the hills.

The temperature on the mountain summits on the Big Island and Maui can dip below freezing. If you're going to be hiking there and spending the night, you need to be prepared for cold weather camping. A tent, winter-rated sleeping bag, rain gear and layers of warm clothing, preferably wool, are a must.

Camping on the beach is another matter entirely. A very lightweight cotton bag is the most you'll need. Public camping grounds require tents – and because of mosquitoes they're a good idea anyway. If you don't want to pack camping gear, it can be rented on Kauai, Oahu and the Big Island.

Bring footwear with good traction for hiking. Many people just wear sneakers, though walking on lava can be tough on the ankles. Serious hikers might want to lug along their hiking boots.

You won't regret bringing binoculars for watching whales and birds, and a flashlight is useful to explore caves. We took along a snorkel, mask and fins, but you can also buy or rent them there. Actually, anything you forget or will need you can buy in Hawaii.

Getting There

AIR

Hawaii is a major hub of the Pacific. Most flights to Hawaii land at Honolulu International Airport, though there are a few flights from the US mainland that go on directly to the neighbouring islands.

Most flights between the US west coast and Asia as well as those between the US west coast and Australia, New Zealand and the South Pacific have an intermediate stop in Honolulu, and you can often make a free stopover.

Keeping in mind that all fares are subject to change, the ones listed here should at least give you an idea of relative costs.

The main types of air tickets are:

Advance Purchase Advance Purchase

Excursion tickets must be bought weeks or months prior to departure. These tickets have minimum and maximum stay requirements, strict and heavy amendment and cancellation charges, and often don't allow stopovers.

Economy Class This is a full economy fare ticket. These tickets are valid for 12 months.

MCO Miscellaneous Charges Order is a voucher which can be exchanged with any IATA airline for a flight of your choice. You use it as a flexible alternative to a specific onward ticket.

Standby This can be one of the cheapest ways of flying. You turn up at the airport and if there are spare seats available on a flight

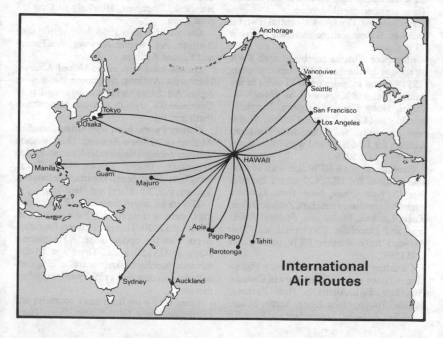

International Air Routes

you can buy a ticket at a considerable discount.

Return With a few exceptions, a return ticket is nearly always cheaper than two one-way tickets. It's generally cheaper to add stops to a long-haul ticket rather than buy a series of short hops.

RTW Round-the-World tickets can be a cheap way of travelling. There are some excellent deals available and you can sometimes get RTW tickets for less than the cost of a return excursion fare.

You must travel around the world in one direction and you cannot backtrack. The number of stopovers you're allowed often depends on the price paid. Tickets are valid for six months to a year although in some cases you can extend this by paying more. RTW tickets offer a combination of airlines, with each airline carrying you on one leg of the journey. Many travel agents will put together RTW tickets using discounted fares on a variety of airlines. These are often excellent value.

Because of Honolulu's central Pacific location, Hawaii can be included on most RTW tickets.

Singapore Airlines combined with TWA offers one of the best RTW fares. It costs US$1899 and includes up to 12 stops in the continental USA, as well as Honolulu, Taipei, Hong Kong, Singapore, Bangkok, Bombay and London, among others. Singapore also has a RTW fare with Canadian Airlines for US$2099 and with Continental Airlines for US$2780.

Continental has a RTW fare with Malaysian Airlines for US$2420 which includes the US West Coast, New York, London, Paris, Amsterdam, Frankfurt, Zurich, Dubai, Kuala Lumpur, Melbourne, Sydney, Auckland and Honolulu. Continental and Thai Airways have another RTW routing for US$2599.

Canadian Airlines combines with Philippine Airlines and includes stops in Canada, Honolulu, Fiji, Australia, New Zealand, Manila, Tokyo, Hong Kong, Rome, Milan, Frankfurt, London, Amsterdam and Paris for US$2499 (C$2999). Canadian Airlines also has RTW fares with Alitalia, Cathay Pacific and Swissair.

Qantas joins with either American Airlines or TWA for a RTW fare of US$2651.

Circle Pacific Tickets For Circle Pacific tickets, two airlines link to allow stopovers along their combined Pacific Rim routes. Rather than simply flying from Point A to Point B, it allows you to swing through much of the Pacific and eastern Asia taking in a variety of destinations - as long as you keep travelling in the same direction.

Continental Airlines links with Garuda allowing stops in places like Honolulu, Auckland, Melbourne, Adelaide, Sydney, Cairns, Brisbane, Bali, Jakarta, Tokyo and the US West Coast.

Continental's link with Singapore Airlines includes the same Australian cities as the Garuda link, as well as Auckland, Christchurch, Tokyo, Taipei, Hong Kong, Bangkok, Singapore, Honolulu and the US west coast.

Continental also links with Philippine Airlines, All Nippon Airways, Air France and Korean Airlines.

Qantas joins with either United Airlines, Northwest Airlines, Singapore Airlines or Japan Air Lines, with routings similar to Continental's, though you can also take in Perth and Fiji.

Cathay Pacific joins with either Canadian Airlines or Air New Zealand. The Canadian Airlines connection includes Vancouver, San Francisco, Tokyo, Taipei, Hong Kong, Bangkok, Singapore, Jakarta, Melbourne, Sydney, Fiji, Auckland and Honolulu.

Tickets for any of these circle Pacific routings, starting from the US West Coast, cost about US$2020. This price covers four stopovers with the option of adding additional stops at US$50 each. There's a 14-day advance purchase requirement, a 25% cancellation penalty and a maximum stay of six months.

Fares vary a bit from other countries and restrictions may be different. From Hong

Kong, Cathay's Circle Pacific fare works out to about US$1830.

Discount Tickets

As well as the good deals provided by RTW or Circle Pacific tickets there are a number of other options for cheaper travel. So rather than just walking into the nearest travel agent or airline office, do a bit of research and shopping around first.

You can start by perusing the travel sections of magazines and weekend papers, like the *New York Times*, the *San Francisco Chronicle-Examiner* and the *Los Angeles Times* in the USA; the Saturday *Age* or the *Sydney Morning Herald* in Australia; and *Time Out* or *TNT* in the UK.

The UK's 'bucket shops' and the various student travel organisations around the world know a lot about cheap tickets and interesting routes, and you don't have to be a student to use their services.

In the USA there's the American Student Council Travel (SCT) and the Student Travel Network; in Canada the equivalent organisation is Travel Cuts; and Australia has STA Travel.

Student Council Travel
Boston
729 Boylston St, Suite 201 (tel (617) 266 1926)
Los Angeles
1093 Broxton Ave (tel (213) 208 3551)
New York
205 East 42nd St (tel (212) 661 1450); and 356 West 34th St (tel (212) 239 4257)
San Diego
5500 Atherton, Long Beach (tel (213) 598 3338)
UCSD Student Center, B-023, La Jolla (tel (619) 452 0630)
4429 Cass St (tel (619) 270 6401)
San Francisco
312 Sutter St, San Francisco (tel (415) 421 3473)
2511 Channing Way, Berkeley (tel (415) 848 8604)
Seattle
1314 North-east 43rd St (tel (206) 632 2448)

Student Travel Network
Dallas
6609 Hillcrest Ave (tel (214) 360 0097)

Honolulu
Suite 202, 1831 South King St (tel (808) 942 7455)
Los Angeles
Suite 507, 2500 Wilshire Blvd (tel (213) 380 2184)
San Diego
6447 El Cajon Blvd (tel (619) 286 1322)
San Francisco
Suite 702, 166 Geary St (tel (415) 391 8407)

Travel Cuts
Travel Cuts is Canada's national student travel agency and has offices in Vancouver, Victoria, Edmonton, Saskatoon, Toronto, Ottawa, Montreal and Halifax.

STA Travel
Adelaide
Level 4, The Arcade, Union House, Adelaide University (tel (08) 223 6620)
Brisbane
Northern Security Building, 40 Creek St (tel (07) 221 9629)
Canberra
Arts Centre, Australian National University, (tel (062) 470 800)
Hobart
Union Building, University of Tasmania, (tel (002) 233 825)
Melbourne
220 Faraday St, Carlton (tel (03) 347 6911)
Perth
Hackett Hall, University of WA, (tel (09) 380 2302)
Sydney
1A Lee St, Railway Square, (tel (02) 212 1255)

Bucket Shops In Europe, two of the best places for buying cheap tickets are London and Amsterdam. There are numerous bucket shops in both places and their services and prices are well advertised.

Bucket shop tickets are generally cheaper than normal Advance Purchase fares and often don't have advance purchase requirements or penalties for cancellation.

Most bucket shops are well established and reliable but it's not unknown for fly-by-night operators to set up office, take the money and disappear before they give you a ticket. Most bucket shops insist on a deposit for a ticket, but you should not hand over the full amount until you have the ticket in your hands.

If you're travelling on a student-discount ticket make sure you have a student card or you may be required to repay the discount at the airport. Tickets, regardless of where they are bought, are non-transferable and airlines usually check that the name on the ticket and the name on your passport match when you check in.

Good, reliable agents for cheap tickets in the UK are: Trailfinders , 46 Earls Court Rd, London W8 (tel 01-938-3366); and STA Travel , Old Brompton Rd, London SW7 and 117 Euston Rd, London NW1 (tel 01-581-1022).

Honolulu International Airport
Honolulu International is a modern and expanding airport but although it is busy it's not particularly difficult to get around.

The airport has all the expected services, including snack bars, restaurants, newsstands, 24-hour sundry shops, lei stands, gift shops, duty-free shops and a mini-hotel for naps and showers. There are car rental counters and hotel/condo courtesy phones in the baggage claim area. The post office is outside the airport but there are mailboxes in front of baggage claim E on the ground level and on the second level opposite the central coffee shop.

The free Wiki Wiki Shuttle (tel 836-2505) connects the more distant parts of the airport. It's available between the waiting area of the main lobby, the outlying gates (6-11 and 26-31) and the inter-island gates (46-62).

Banks Deak International has four currency exchange offices in the airport, including one in the international arrival area (ground level) and another in the central departure lobby.

There's a Bank of Hawaii on the ground level across the street from baggage claim D. It's open from 8.30 am to 3 pm Mondays to Thursdays, and to 6 pm on Fridays.

Baggage Storage There's baggage storage in the baggage claim area near carousel G-5 in the main overseas terminal. It's open 24 hours a day and, depending on the size of the item, it costs $3 to $10 a day.

For small items, there are baggage lockers on the ground level in the parking structure opposite the main overseas terminal. They cost $1 a day.

For information on either call 836-6547.

Airlines serving Honolulu
The following airlines serve Honolulu International Airport on Oahu. A local call, from anywhere in Hawaii, costs 25 cents. To call these airlines, other than those with the toll free 800 number, from outside the state you need to dial the 808 area code.

Air America	tel 834-7172
Air Micronesia	tel 800-231-0856
Air New Zealand	tel 800-521-4059
Air Tungaru	tel 735-3994
Aloha Airlines	tel 836-1111
Aloha IslandAir	tel 833-3219
American Airlines	tel 526-0044
Canadian Airlines	tel 922-0533
China Airlines	tel 836-1052
Continental Airlines	tel 800-231-0856
Delta Air Lines	tel 800-221-1212
Garuda Indonesia	tel 945-3791
Hawaiian Airlines	tel 537-5100
Japan Air Lines	tel 521-1441
Korean Air	tel 923-7302
Northwest Airlines	tel 955-2255
Pan Am	tel 800-221-1111
Philippine Airlines	tel 536-1928
Qantas Airways	tel 800-227-4500
Singapore Airlines	tel 524-6063
TWA	tel 800-221-2000
United Airlines	tel 547-2211
Wardair	tel 955-5981

From the US Mainland
Domestic air fares are constantly in flux. There's usually a lot of competition to Honolulu from the major mainland cities and at any given time any one of the airlines could have the cheapest fare.

The airlines each have their own requirements and restrictions which also seem to be constantly changing. For the latest deals, either find a knowledgeable travel agent or just call the different airlines and compare.

If you call, it's important to ask for the lowest fare, as that's not always the first one they'll quote. Each flight has a limited number of seats available at the cheapest fares. When you make reservations they'll generally tell you the best fare that's still available on the date you give them, which may or may not be the cheapest fare that the airline is currently offering. If you make reservations far enough in advance and are a little flexible with dates, you'll usually do better.

It used to be easy to line up reservations on a couple of flights and if you changed your mind, just not buy the ticket. That's getting more complicated now as some airlines are subscribing to automatic number ID systems. Once you call to make a reservation, not only does your reservation get stored in the computer but so does your phone line. Should you call again from the same phone, your file comes up on their computer screen and they know who you are before they even answer the phone!

Typically the lowest return fares from the US mainland are around $550 to $650 from the east coast, and $300 to $400 from the west coast. These are generally for mid-week flights, with advance purchase requirements and other restrictions. Sometimes tickets are completely non-refundable and non-changeable (though most airlines say they make allowances for medical emergencies if you have a note from a doctor).

When we researched the cost of air tickets most major domestic airlines flying to Honolulu were offering return fares for $378 from the west coast, $558 from the east coast. They required advance purchase, had a 30-day maximum stay and were non-refundable. The departure date couldn't be changed, but the return date could be changed under some very complicated restrictions and with a $75 fee.

Continental had the cheapest 'flexible' ticket. A one-year open ticket from the east coast, that allowed dates to be changed with no penalties and had no advance purchase

requirements, was $702 return. From the west coast the fare was $478. Tickets with a 14-day advance purchase requirement, that allowed maximum stays of 30 days with 50% cancellation penalties, cost $100 less than the flexible fares.

The following airlines, which all have the 800 toll free number, fly to Honolulu from both the US east and west coasts:

American	tel 433-7300
Delta	tel 221-1212
Continental	tel 525-0280
United	tel 241-6522
Pan Am	tel 221-1111
TWA	tel 221-2000
Northwest	tel 225-2525

Hawaiian Airlines (tel 800-367-5320) also flies to Honolulu, from Seattle/Tacoma, San Francisco, Las Vegas, Los Angeles and Anchorage. Its Anchorage to Honolulu fare is $518 with a 14-day advance purchase requirement and a 30-day maximum stay, or $598 with seven-day advance purchase and a 45-day maximum stay. Most of Hawaiian Airlines' west coast fares are about $400 with a 14-day advance purchase. Often a neighbouring island destination can be added on for $20 more. It occasionally offers a Los Angeles to Honolulu special for $238 return.

America West Airlines (tel 800-247-5692) provides non-stop service to Hawaii from Phoenix and Las Vegas. It has a wide range of fares, depending on the day of the week and the time of year. Return fares cost from about $400 to $575.

Air America (tel 800-247-2475) flies between Los Angeles and Honolulu. It sometimes has return fares for as little as $238, though rates usually range from $304 to $448. One-way LA to Honolulu tickets requiring no advance purchase cost $325.

Smaller airlines offering Los Angeles to Honolulu bargains for under $300 return pop up from time to time, though they don't seem to hang on for very long.

Flight time to Honolulu is about 5½ hours from the west coast, 11 hours from the east coast.

From Canada

The return fares (in Canadian dollars) with Canadian Airlines International are: Vancouver to Honolulu $529; Calgary to Honolulu $629; Edmonton to Honolulu $629; and Toronto to Honolulu $799.

Tickets must be purchased seven days in advance and are valid all year round, except 14 to 30 December, and allow a maximum stay of six months. Changes can be made, with seven days advance notice, for $50. There's a $150 fee for cancellations.

Toll free numbers are 800-663-3502 from British Columbia and 800-263-6133 from Toronto's 416 area code.

From Central & South America

Most flights from Central and South America go via Los Angeles, though a few of those from the eastern cities go via New York.

Continental has flights from Mexico and Central America, including Guatemala City, Cancun and Merida. Their lowest Mexico City to Honolulu return fare of $625 allows a maximum stay of 60 days with a seven-day advance purchase requirement.

From Australia

Qantas has Sydney to Honolulu 'value pack' return fares ranging from A$1099 to A$1299, depending on the season. Tickets have a seven-day advance purchase requirement, a minimum stay of seven days and a maximum stay of six months. A free stopover in Fiji is allowed. Date changes can be made on all except the outbound flight at no charge, and there's a cancellation penalty of 50% within 21 days of departure.

Qantas frequently offers special advance purchase fares from Australia or New Zealand to Honolulu and the rest of the USA. It would be worth enquiring whether any of these fare packages are available because they can be up to $200 cheaper than the low season fare.

Air New Zealand also has Sydney to Honolulu return fares from A$1099 to A$1299, depending on the season, with the same basic conditions as the Qantas fare.

Hawaiian Airlines has Sydney to Hono-lulu excursion fares ranging from A$1171 to A$1536 depending on the season. It has one-year tickets with no advance purchase required, though there is a $50 charge for changes and a 25% cancellation penalty.

American Airlines, United Airlines and Continental Airlines also fly from Sydney to Honolulu.

From New Zealand

Air New Zealand's usual Auckland to Honolulu return fare ranges from NZ$1149 (May, June, September, October, November) to NZ$1449 (December). These tickets require purchase 21 days in advance and within seven days of making reservations, and allow stays of up to three months.

Air New Zealand sometimes runs specials as low as NZ$825 return during off periods.

American Airlines has recently begun service between Auckland and Honolulu. They have a ticket valid for stays up to 60 days, with a 21-day advance purchase requirement, ranging from NZ$777 to NZ$998 depending on the season.

Hawaiian Airlines, Continental, United and Qantas also fly between Auckland and Honolulu.

From Fiji

Qantas, Air New Zealand and Canadian Airlines all have Nadi to Honolulu return fares for F$836 (about US$550). The fare is valid all year round, with a one-year maximum stay. There's no advance purchase required and no penalties for changes or cancellations.

Qantas has a one-way fare from Nadi to Honolulu for F$574 with a 14-day advance purchase requirement.

From Other South Pacific Islands

Hawaiian Airlines is the main carrier between Honolulu and Tonga, Tahiti, the Cook Islands and the Samoas.

The lowest Tonga to Honolulu return fare is T$963 (about US$740), with a 30-day maximum stay. It's T$1108 for a one-year return ticket, and half that for one way.

From American Samoa, the lowest Pago Pago to Honolulu return fares are: US$490 with a 30-day maximum stay; and US$590 with a one-year maximum stay. A one-way ticket costs US$295.

From Western Samoa, the lowest Apia to Honolulu return fare is WS$1068 (about US$470) for a 30-day maximum stay. The one-way fare is WS$648.

From Tonga and the Samoas, fares are the same all year round, tickets have a seven-day advance purchase requirement and there's a 25% penalty for changes.

From the Cook Islands, the cheapest fare on Hawaiian Airlines, from Rarotonga to Honolulu, is NZ$970. The ticket is available during the low season months of February, March, October and November, has a 21-day advance purchase requirement and allows a six-month stay. There's a $50 charge for changes and a 25% penalty for cancellations. The one-way fare with 21-day advance purchase, good all year, costs NZ$745.

From Tahiti, Hawaiian Airlines' lowest Papeete to Honolulu return fare is 123,200 CFP (about US$1080). It's available between 25 December and 30 June, has a maximum stay of 45 days, a 14-day advance purchase requirement, and a 25% penalty for changes or cancellations.

From Micronesia
Continental's direct Guam to Honolulu fare is usually around $550 return with a maximum stay of 60 days and a seven-day advance purchase requirement. A one-way ticket is $350.

The more exciting way to go is to take Continental's Micronesia island hopper which stops in Truk, Pohnpei, Kosrae and Majuro before reaching Honolulu. It costs $450 one way. If you're coming from Asia this is a good alternative to a non-stop transpacific flight and a great way to see some of the Pacific's most remote islands without having to spend a lot of money.

Hawaiian Airlines' lowest one-way Guam to Honolulu fare is $295 with a seven-day advance purchase requirement.

From Japan
Northwest Airlines, United Airlines and

Japan Air Lines fly to Honolulu from Osaka and Tokyo. Its cheapest return ticket is about Y165,000 (about US$1148). The regular one-way fare to Honolulu is Y150,000 (about US$1044).

It may be possible to beat these rates, particularly on a one-way fare, by flying first to Guam and then changing to Continental or Hawaiian Airlines to go on to Honolulu.

From South-East Asia
You can fly to Hawaii from either Hong Kong or Bangkok with Cathay Pacific, Japan Air Lines, Korean Airlines, Northwest Airlines or Philippine Airlines. China Airlines also flies out of Hong Kong.

The one-way/return fares to Honolulu on Korean Airlines are: US$491/982 from Bangkok; US$411/822 from Hong Kong; and US$651/990 from Seoul. If you're going one way from Bangkok to Los Angeles on Korean Airlines, it costs US$530 with a free stopover in Honolulu.

Continental's lowest Manila to Honolulu one-year return fare costs from US$750, depending on the season.

Philippine Airlines also flies from Manila to Honolulu. The one-way fare is $432, and its return fare is slightly higher than Continental's.

From Europe
The most common route from Europe is west via Los Angeles or New York. If you're interested in heading east with stops in Asia, it would probably be cheaper to get a RTW ticket than return the same way.

On Continental, the cheapest London to Honolulu return ticket is UK£587 with a six-month maximum stay. Their cheapest Paris to Honolulu return ticket is F7965 with a two-month maximum stay. Both have a 21-day advance purchase requirement and have some change penalties.

On Air New Zealand, the cheapest London to Honolulu return ticket is UK£650, with a three-week advance purchase requirement and a maximum stay of six months. Their cheapest Frankfurt to Honolulu round-trip ticket is DM 2200, valid from October to the end of March.

Customs & Departure Fees

The USA must be one of the few countries in the world that charges to go through Customs. Passengers flying into the USA are charged a $10 Customs fee; it's added on to the price of the airline ticket. Exceptions are passengers arriving from Canada, Mexico or US territories.

There's a $3 departure tax to leave Honolulu International Airport for a foreign destination.

SEA

American Hawaii Cruises (550 Kearny St, San Francisco, California 94108; tel 415-392-9400, 800-227-3666) has two cruise ships, the *Constitution* and the *Independence*, which make seven-day tours around Hawaii. The ships leave Honolulu each Saturday and visit Kauai (Nawiliwili Harbor), Maui (Kahului Harbor) and the Big Island (Kona and Hilo) before returning to Honolulu.

Rates start at $1025 for the 'thrifty inside cabin' and go up to $3695 for the 'deluxe outside two-room suite'. The cheapest outside cabin is $1625. Fares are based on double occupancy.

Alternatives include a three-day cruise with a four-night hotel/car package from $699 and a four-day cruise with a three-night hotel/car package from $849.

Rates don't include airfare to Hawaii, but the cruise line can provide round-trip airline tickets for $559 from the US east coast and for $319 from the west coast.

These are full-fledged cruise ships, 682 feet long, with lavish buffet meals, swimming pools and all that sort of thing. They carry a crew of 330 along with 798 passengers.

Both ships have histories of dumping raw sewage in Hawaii's pristine waters. After dumping human waste in Kailua Bay, angry Kona residents surrounded one of the ships with surfboards, canoes and sailboats in protest. The *Constitution* was fined $25,000

for the incident in 1987. Supposedly, they've since refitted the ships' plumbing and cleaned up their act.

Transpacific Cruises

Travel agents or shops which sell discount cruise tickets are the best sources of information for transpacific cruises, though there are not many to choose from.

In the past Cunard (tel 800-221-4770) has booked the *Queen Elizabeth II* on five-day cruises between Ensenada (Mexico) and Hawaii for about $875 one way. They also book the *Sagafjord* on South Pacific cruises which include Hawaii. These type of cruises are very infrequent, maybe once or twice a year, and some years not at all.

TOURS

Those who want Hawaii in a package all tied up with a bow will find everything they need from travel agents. The full treatment with airfare, lei greeting, hotel and car reservations, sightseeing tours and recreational activities can all be plotted out.

If you want to stay in middle class accommodation and only have time for a quick visit, package tours sometimes work out cheaper than planning the trip yourself.

One-week packages start at around $499 from the US west coast, or $699 from the US east coast, based on double occupancy. If you want to stay somewhere fancy or island hop, they can be much more expensive.

Wilderness Tours

In addition to traditional package tours, there are numerous study and adventure tours to Hawaii.

The University of Research Expeditions Program (University of California, Berkeley, CA 94720; tel 415-642-6586) runs a couple of work/study tours a year assisting scholars in the field with such projects as excavating a heiau or studying the ecology of plants that grow in lava.

Most tours last for about two weeks, and rates range from around $1100 to $1400, including food and simple accommodation but excluding airfare.

Wilderness Hawaii (Box 61692, Honolulu, HI 96822; tel 737-4697) is an outdoor tour company with a philosophy similar to the Outward Bound programmes. Shena Sandler leads four-day wilderness tours on the Big Island, mostly for women who are novice backpackers. They include gear and food for $275.

Island Bicycle Adventures (569 Kapahulu Ave, Honolulu, HI 96815; tel 734-0700, 800-233-2226) organises six-day bike tours of Kauai, Maui or the Big Island. The rate of $785 includes accommodation and meals, but not airfare. Bike rentals are $79 more.

Hawaiian Island Windsurfing (460 Dairy Rd, Kahului, HI 96732; tel 572-5601, 800-367-8047, ext 170) has tour packages for windsurfers which include windsurfing gear, car, accommodation and airfare from the US west coast for $799.

Elderhostel (80 Boylston St, Suite 400, Boston, MA 02116; tel 617-426-7788) is a non-profit organisation offering week-long educational programmes for those aged 60 or older. Elderhostel has its origins in the youth hostels of Europe and the folk schools of Scandinavia. Fees typically include accommodation, all meals and five days of classes, mostly outdoors. One Big Island programme, in conjunction with the Lyman Museum, focuses on Hawaiian culture through archaeology, marine life and museum collections. The fee is $300. Other programmes are held at the Volcano Art Center and at Oahu colleges.

Oceanic Society Expeditions (Fort Mason Center, Building E, San Francisco, CA 941231; tel 415-441-1106, 800-326-749), the environmental travel arm of Friends of the Earth, does eco-tours conducted with a non-invasive approach to viewing wildlife. In Hawaii it has a humpback whale expedition.

The five-day excursions cost $895 including meals and accommodation aboard a 54-foot sailing vessel. The tours sail among the endangered humpbacks, photographing them for identification and recording their underwater songs. There's also snorkelling time off the Kona Coast.

Getting Around

AIR

The major airports which handle jets are at Honolulu (Oahu), Lihue (Kauai), Kahului (Maui), Kona and Hilo (both on the Big Island).

Smaller airports are: Waimea-Kohala, on the Big Island (also called Kamuela); Kapalua-West Maui, on Maui (also called Kapalua/Kaanapali); Hana on Maui; Princeville, on Kauai's north shore; Molokai; Kalaupapa, at Molokai's leper colony; and Lanai.

Aloha Airlines and Hawaiian Airlines are the two major inter-island carriers. Both have frequent flights in modern, full-bodied aircraft between the five major airports.

Overall, Aloha is more professional. On the customer complaint list compiled by the US Department of Transportation, Aloha usually ranks first of all the major US airlines, with the fewest complaints. Hawaiian can generally be found at the other end of the list.

However, when you get right down to it, you're probably just as well off going with whoever has the best price and is leaving when you want to go.

Fares

Flights between any two of the five major airports have the same fare. For both Aloha and Hawaiian airlines, it's currently $50 one way. Round trip tickets are double the one-way fare.

On both airlines, the first and last flights of the day to or from Honolulu and Lihue, Kahului, Kona and Hilo cost $35.

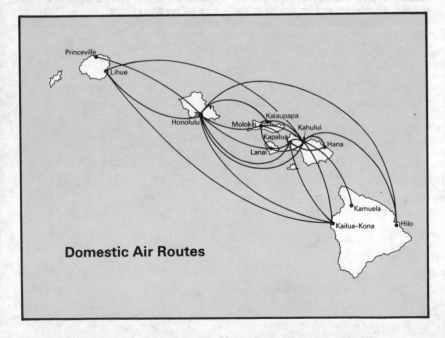

Domestic Air Routes

Both airlines offer coupon booklets, with six tickets good for any sector, for $252. Sometimes you can find the booklets for Hawaiian Airlines discounted to about $185 by local travel agents (check the Honolulu papers).

Both airlines have discount tickets for those aged over 65 ($40) and under 11 ($34).

Periodically there are specials, and Hawaiian generally discounts a little more. Whenever you call, ask for the cheapest fare available.

Hawaiian Airlines Hawaiian has about 250 flights a day between Honolulu, Lihue, Kahului, Kapalua/Kaanapali, Kona, Hilo, Molokai and Lanai. They fly DC-9s between the main destinations and 50-passenger de-Havilland Dash 7 aircraft to the smaller airports.

Their exceptions to the $50 one-way fare are the Honolulu to Molokai and Honolulu to Lanai flights which are $40. Hawaiian Airlines' only round trip ticket is Honolulu-Molokai at $47.

You can book Hawaiian by calling 537-5100 on Oahu; 244-9111 on Maui; 245-3671 on Kauai; 935-0811 on the Big Island; 565-6429 on Lanai; 553-5321 on Molokai; 800-367-5320 from the US mainland; 800-663-2074 from British Colombia; 800-663-6926 from Alberta; 800-663-3389 from Canada's eastern provinces; 02-232-7499 from Sydney; 793-708 from Auckland.

Aloha Airlines Aloha Airlines, which flies 737s between Honolulu, Lihue, Kahului, Kona and Hilo, has about 170 flights a day.

You can book Aloha by calling 836-1111 on Oahu; 245-3691 on Kauai; 244-9071 on Maui; 935-5771 on the Big Island; 800-367-5250 from the US mainland; 800-663-9396 from Alberta and British Colombia; 800-663-9471 from the rest of Canada; 02-261-1866 from Sydney; 008-222-944 from the rest of Australia; 09-797-114 from New Zealand; 03-216-5877 from Tokyo; 06-341-7241 from Osaka and 05-251-365 from Hong Kong.

Aloha IslandAir Aloha IslandAir serves Hawaii's smaller airports. Formerly Princeville Airlines, it was absorbed in 1987 by the Aloha Airgroup which runs Aloha Airlines. It flies 18-passenger deHavilland Dash 6 aircraft.

Aloha IslandAir has flights to Honolulu, Princeville, Molokai, Kalaupapa, Kahului, Hana, Kapalua/Kaanapali, Lanai and Kamuela.

On some of the more remote sectors, flights are only once or twice daily. The more popular routes have eight or nine daily flights.

Fares vary according to the destination. Honolulu to Princeville or Honolulu to Hana is $50 one way. Honolulu to Molokai costs $39 one way. Kahului to Hana is $30. Return fares are double.

You can book Aloha IslandAir by calling 833-3219 on Oahu, 800-652-6541 from the neighbouring islands, 800-323-3345 from the US mainland.

Commuter Airlines Flights on commuter airlines are typically like little sightseeing tours. They provide more personalised service, fly lower and offer better views than the larger airlines. Sometimes you even end up in the co-pilot's seat! Another advantage is that your luggage is loaded and unloaded as you get on and off the plane – so it's rarely misplaced and there's no waiting at the carousel.

If the plane is half empty, you might even be able to talk the pilot into taking an alternative route. We were the only passengers on our last flight out of Molokai to Maui and the pilot took us for a joyride, swinging in and out of Molokai's inaccessible north shore valleys, giving us a bird's-eye view of the world's highest sea cliffs and some incredible waterfalls.

Unfortunately that airline, Air Molokai, folded shortly afterwards, ending 22 years of operation. Small commuter airlines have had a hard time hanging on in Hawaii and the demise of Air Molokai looked like it heralded the end of this alternative island-hopping mode, until a new little commuter airline came along to pick up some of Air Molokai's old routes.

Panorama Air now flies nine-passenger Piper Chieftain aircraft on the Honolulu to Molokai run. The new service also flies from both Honolulu and Molokai to Kahului, and from Honolulu to Kapalua/Kaanapali via Molokai.

The Honolulu to Molokai fare costs $35/$45 one way/return; Honolulu to Kahului is $60/$80; Honolulu to Kapalua is $37/$74; and Honolulu to Kahului is $40/$60.

You can book Panorama Air by calling: 836-2122 on Oahu; 567-6551 on Molokai; 871-5118 on Maui; toll free 800-352-3732 from neighbouring islands to Oahu; or 800-367-2671 from mainland USA.

CAR

As far as the state is concerned, anyone can drive in Hawaii as long as they have a valid driver's licence issued by a country that is party to the United Nations Conference on Road and Motor Transport – which probably covers almost everyone.

As far as major car rental companies are concerned, they'll accept valid foreign driver's licences as long as they're in English. Otherwise most will require an international driver's licence.

Rules of the Road

Hawaii requires the use of seat belts for front-seat passengers. State law also requires the use of car safety seats for children aged three and under. Most of the car agencies rent safety seats, usually from $3 to $5 a day and a little cheaper by the week, but it's best to reserve one in advance.

Hawaiians drive on the right-hand side of the road just like on the US mainland and in Europe.

Drivers in the right-hand lane can turn right at a red light, if there's nothing coming, unless there's a sign at the intersection saying otherwise.

Horn honking is considered very rude in Hawaii unless required for safety.

The police rarely give warnings and if they

stop you for speeding, they'll usually write the ticket. Cruising unmarked police cars come in the most unlikely models and colours.

The word 'highway' on a map doesn't mean a whole lot. Just about every road of any distance gets to be called a highway, including some dinky little secondary roads and even a dirt road or two.

In this book we have tried to use highway numbers because that's what you see on the signs. But islanders generally know roads by names, and often couldn't tell you the route number of the road on which they live.

Note In Hawaii, as in the rest of the USA, a paved road is one that's sealed (tarred) with asphalt (bitumen).

Car Rental

Rental cars are available on all the islands. The market is very competitive and rates are generally cheaper than on the mainland.

With most companies the weekly rate works out far cheaper per day than the straight daily rate. The daily rate for a small car, with unlimited mileage, is around $25 to $30, with weekly rates of $79 to $139. You're usually required to keep the car for a minimum of five or six days to get the weekly rate.

Rates vary greatly from company to company and within each company depending on season, demand and promotions. Call one week and you might find a weekly rate as low as $69. Call a month later and the best deal might be double. Sometimes you have to reserve a week or a month in advance for the best bargains, while other times you can just walk into them.

On our last trip we found our best deals with National and Budget, getting $80 weekly rates with both, though at other times they quoted as high as $120.

You can save money by shopping around. Be sure to ask for the cheapest rate as their first quote is not always the lowest.

It's a good idea to make reservations in advance for each destination. If you don't, the cheapest cars may be sold out. With most reservations, there's no cancellation penalty if you change your mind.

We usually checked out rates after landing at each airport, even when we had an advance booking, and sometimes found a better deal on the spot.

Another advantage of advance reservations is if you have a bottom-line car reserved and there are none in the yard when you show up, the upgrade is free. About half the time we ended up with air-con, though we never paid for it.

Generally the cheapest rates are for small cars, often a Subaru Justy, Nissan Sentra or Toyota Tercel, with standard (manual) transmission and no air-con. You're better off with a standard anyway if you're going to be climbing any hills, and Hawaii does have mountains.

For daily rentals note that most cars are rented on a 24-hour basis so you could get two days use by renting at midday and driving around all afternoon, then heading out to explore somewhere else the next morning before the car is due back. Some companies even have an hour's grace period.

In Hawaii, the rule is generally free unlimited mileage though, on the Big Island at least, a few companies tack on a mileage charge. Also, if you drop off the car at a different location, there's usually a fee added on and sometimes a mileage charge.

Having a major credit card greatly simplifies the rental process. Without one most places require prepayment by cash or travellers' cheques and a deposit, often around $100. Some may even do an employment verification and credit check. Others, like Budget and Dollar, don't do background checks though they reserve the right for the station manager to decide whether to rent to you or not.

Some companies charge $5 a day extra for drivers under 25 and many won't rent to anyone aged under 21.

Insurance

Collision damage waivers (CDW) are the ultimate rip-off and Hawaii used to have the ultimate hard sell. It got such a bad reputation that the state finally put some controls on 'coercive sales tactics'. Still the rental agencies will try to hit you up for $10 to $15 a day for CDW, which can be higher than the rental fee for the car itself. The CDW is not really even insurance (the companies already insure their cars) but rather a guarantee that the rental company won't hold you liable for any damages to their car (though even here there are exclusions!).

If you have collision coverage on your vehicle at home it might cover car rentals in Hawaii. Check with your insurance company before you leave.

A number of credit card companies now offer reimbursement coverage for collision damages if you rent the car with their card. If yours doesn't, it may be worth changing to one that does.

Rental Agencies

All the following car rental agencies have the toll free 800 number:

Budget (tel 527-7000) is at the airports on Oahu, Kauai, Molokai, Maui and the Big Island as well as 15 other locations around Hawaii. People aged between 21 and 25 who want to rent a car must have a credit card in their name. Budget generally only rents to 18 to 20-year-olds if they have some kind of package deal.

National (tel 227-7368) is at the airports on Oahu, Kauai, Maui and the Big Island and at one location in Waikiki.

Avis (tel 831-8000) is at the airports on Oahu, Maui, Kauai, Molokai and the Big Island. Avis also has offices at hotels in Poipu, Waikoloa and Waikiki.

Hertz (tel 654-3131) is at the airports on Oahu, Maui, Kauai and the Big Island and at a number of hotels.

Thrifty (tel 367-2277) is at or near the airports on Oahu, Kauai, and Maui and in Waikiki. If you don't have a credit card you have to deal directly with each location you're renting from, where approval is on a case-by-case basis. They don't have child seats.

Tropical (tel 367-5140; in Hawaii 800-352-3923) is at or near the airports on Oahu, Kauai, Molokai, Maui and the Big Island. Drivers without credit cards must sign a blank personal cheque, imprinted with their name and address (which will be checked for validity). Drivers renting a car must be at least 21 years old.

Sunshine (tel 367-2977 from the US mainland, 800-624-0438 from Canada, 800-522-8440 in Hawaii), a local company, has standard rates for small cars of $24.95 a day or $99 a week, with unlimited mileage. Its collision damage waivers are cheaper than at the larger companies. You must be 21 years or over and have a major credit card. They're near Honolulu International Airport; at Kahului Airport and Lahaina in Maui; and at Lihue, Kona and Hilo airports.

Dollar (tel 367-7006; in Hawaii 800-342-7398) is at the airports on Oahu, Kauai, Molokai, Maui and the Big Island. The company also works in conjunction with Lanai City Service on Lanai. They have fixed prices, with small cars at about $28 a day, $144 a week. They say they don't discount, which makes their prices easy to beat.

There are scores of smaller rental agencies as well, but this is one area where small is not necessarily better. For the most part the big companies have the better deals and the fewer hassles.

BUS
Oahu's excellent all-island public bus system, called TheBus, makes that island the easiest one to get around. You can get almost anywhere on TheBus and the fare is just 60 cents regardless of your destination.

The Big Island has a public bus service between Kailua-Kona and Hilo, and on to Hawaii Volcanoes National Park. The bus runs daily but service is slow and infrequent. It's good for the longer distances, but not for short sightseeing hops back and forth in one day.

Maui has no public buses. There's a new private bus service which runs up and down the length of the Kihei coast and a free bus which covers the distance between Lahaina and Kaanapali. You can get by without a car if you just want to hang out on the west coast beaches and go nowhere else.

Kauai doesn't have a public bus, but there is a little private shuttle service which runs between the airport, Kapaa, Lihue and Poipu.

Molokai has no buses, but there's a mule train.

TAXI
All main islands have taxis, with fares based on mileage regardless of the number of passengers. Rates vary but are about $8 per five miles.

FERRY
There are just two passenger ferries in Hawaii.

Expeditions on Maui (tel 661-3756) runs a 24-passenger boat between Lahaina on Maui and Manele Boat Harbor on Lanai. The boat leaves Lahaina at 6.45 am and 3.45 pm daily and departs Manele at 8 am and 5 pm daily. The crossing takes an hour. One-way fares are $25 for adults, $20 for children.

Sea Link of Hawaii (tel 661-83977 on Maui, 553-5736 on Molokai, 533-6899 on Oahu, 800-833-5800 from the US mainland) has daily service between Kaunakakai on Molokai and Lahaina on Maui on the 118-foot *Maui Princess*. It leaves Kaunakakai at 5.45 am and 4 pm and departs Lahaina at 7.15 am and 5.30 pm. The crossing takes 1¼ hours. One-way fares are $21 for adults, $10.50 for children.

TOURS
There are numerous companies doing tours on different islands. The ones listed here do sightseeing van or bus tours of all the major islands.

Gray Line Hawaii
    Box 30046, Honolulu, HI 96820 (tel 833-8000, 800-367-2420)

Bus Tickets

Robert's Hawaii
    444 Hobron Lane, 5th Flr, Honolulu, HI 96815
    (tel 973-2300)
Trans Hawaiian
    3111 Castle St, Honolulu, HI 96815 (tel 735-
    6467, 800-533-8765)
Akamai Tours
    2270 Kalakaua Ave, Suite 1702, Honolulu, HI
    96815 (tel 922-6485, 800-922-6485)

In addition to tours, Akamai has overnight
packages to the neighbouring islands which
include airfare, car and a hotel. Starting
prices per person, but based on double occupancy, range from $80 on Molokai to $100
on Kauai. If there's two of you and you only
want to go for a day or two it may work out
cheaper than going on your own.

Oahu

Often the images conjured up of Hawaii are those of Oahu – places like Waikiki, Pearl Harbor and Sunset Beach.

Oahu is the most developed of the Hawaiian islands. Quite appropriately, it's long been nicknamed 'The Gathering Place'. The island is home to 830,000 people – more than 75% of the state's population. It's an urban scene, with highways, highrises and crowds. If you're looking for a getaway vacation you'd best continue on to one of the neighbouring islands.

Still, despite all its development, in terms of scenic beauty Oahu holds its own. It has fluted mountains, aqua-blue bays and valleys that look to be almost carpeted with pineapples and sugar cane.

Oahu has excellent beaches. Hanauma Bay is one of the finest easily accessible snorkelling spots in the islands. The north shore has Hawaii's top surfing action and windward Kailua is one of Hawaii's most popular windsurfing beaches.

Honolulu is a modern city with a blend of Eastern and Western influences. Cultural offerings range from Chinese lantern parades and traditional hula performances to ballet and good museums. Honolulu has the only royal palace in the USA, fine city beaches and parks and some great hilltop views. There's a wonderful variety of neighbourhood ethnic restaurants.

Oahu can be the cheapest Hawaiian island to visit. It's the only one you can get around easily without your own transport, thanks to the inexpensive, island-wide bus system. Oahu also has some of Hawaii's cheapest accommodation, including a couple of youth hostels and Ys.

Almost all of Oahu's hotels and tourist facilities are centred in Waikiki. Waikiki resembles a hybrid mix of Miami Beach and Tokyo, with a population density rivalling the latter. There's a lot happening in Waikiki, but to get a better feel for what Hawaii's all about you need to step out of it. There are plenty of places on Oahu worth exploring.

Orientation

Almost all visitors to Oahu land at Honolulu International Airport, the only civilian airport on the island. It's at the western end of the Honolulu district, nine miles west of Waikiki.

If you're going to be doing any exploring at all, it's worth picking up one of the detailed road maps which are readily available at stores around Oahu.

H-1, the main south shore highway, is the key to getting around the island. H-1 connects with Hwy 93, which leads up the leeward Waianae Coast; with Hwy 72, which runs around the south-east coast; with the Pali (61) and Likelike (63) highways, which go to the windward coast; and with H-2, Hwy 99 and Hwy 750, which run through the centre of the island on the way to the north shore.

By the way, H-1 is an *interstate* freeway – an amusing term to use to describe a road on an island state in the middle of the Pacific.

Rush-hour traffic is heavy heading toward Honolulu in the mornings and away from it in the evenings.

Directions on Oahu are often given by using landmarks, in addition to the Hawaii-wide mauka (inland side) and makai (ocean side). If someone tells you to go 'Ewa' (a land area west of Honolulu) or 'Diamond Head' (east of Honolulu) it simply means to head in that direction.

Facts

HISTORY

Oahu was the final island conquered by Kamehameha the Great in his campaign to unite all Hawaii under his sole rule.

Prior to that, however, it was not Kamehameha but Kahekili, the ageing king of Maui, who seemed the most likely candidate to conquer all the islands. In the 1780s Kahekili already ruled neighbouring Molokai and Lanai when he killed his own stepson to take Oahu.

After Kahekili died at Waikiki in 1794 his lands were divided between two quarrelling relatives. His son Kalanikupule got Oahu and his half-brother, King Kaeokulani of Kauai, got Maui, Lanai and Molokai. They immediately went to battle and in the rift Kamehameha moved in.

In 1795 Kamehameha swept through Maui and Molokai before crossing the channel to Oahu. On the quiet beaches of Waikiki he landed his fleet of canoes and marched up toward Nuuanu Valley to meet Kalanikupule, the king of Oahu.

The Battle of Nuuanu

The Oahu warriors were no match for Kamehameha's troops. The first heavy fighting took place around the Punchbowl, where Kamehameha's men quickly circled the fortress-like crater and drove out the Oahuan defenders. Scattered fighting continued up Nuuanu Valley, with the last big battle taking place near the current site of Queen Emma's Summer Palace.

The Oahuans, prepared for the usual spear-and-stone warfare, panicked when they realised Kamehameha had brought in a handful of Western sharpshooters. The foreigners picked off the Oahuan generals and blasted into their ridge-top defences.

What should have been the advantage of high ground turned into a death trap for the Oahuans when they found themselves wedged up into the valley, unable to redeploy. Fleeing up the cliffsides in retreat, they were forced to make their last stand at the narrow precipitous ledge along the current-day Nuuanu Pali Lookout. Hundreds of Oahuans were driven over the pali to their deaths.

Some Oahuan warriors, including King Kalanikupule, escaped into the upland forests. When Kalanikupule surfaced a few months later he was sacrificed by Kamehameha to his war god Ku.

Kamehameha's taking of Oahu marked the last battle ever fought between Hawaiian troops.

GEOGRAPHY

Oahu, which covers 594 square miles, is the third largest Hawaiian island. It has 112 miles of coast and basically has four sides, with distinct windward and leeward coasts and north and south shores. Its highest point is Mt Kaala at 4020 feet. Its extreme length is 44 miles, its width 30 miles.

Two separate volcanoes arose to form Oahu's two mountain ranges, Waianae and Koolau, which slice the island from the north-west to the south-east.

CLIMATE

In Honolulu the average daily maximum temperature is 84°F, and the minimum is 70°F. Temperatures are a bit higher in summer and a few degrees lower in winter. The highest temperature on record is 94°F and the lowest is 53°F.

Waikiki has an average annual rainfall of 25 inches; the Lyon Arboretum in the upper Manoa Valley, north of Honolulu, averages 158 inches. Mid-afternoon humidity averages 56%.

Average afternoon water temperatures in Waikiki are 77°F in March, 82°F in August.

FLORA & FAUNA

Most of the islets off Oahu's windward coast are sanctuaries for sea birds, like terns, noddies, shearwaters, Laysan albatrosses, tropicbirds, boobies and frigate birds. Moku Manu ('bird islands') off Mokapu Peninsula has the greatest variety of species.

Oahu has an endemic genus of tree snail, the achatinella. In former days the forests were loaded with these colourful snails, which clung like gems to the leaves of trees. They were too attractive for their own good and hikers collected them by the handfuls around the turn of the century. Even more devastating has been the deforestation of habitat and the introduction of a cannibal snail and predatory rodents. Of 41

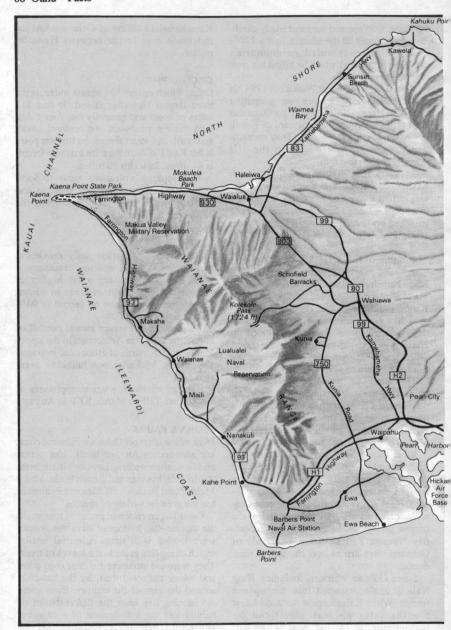

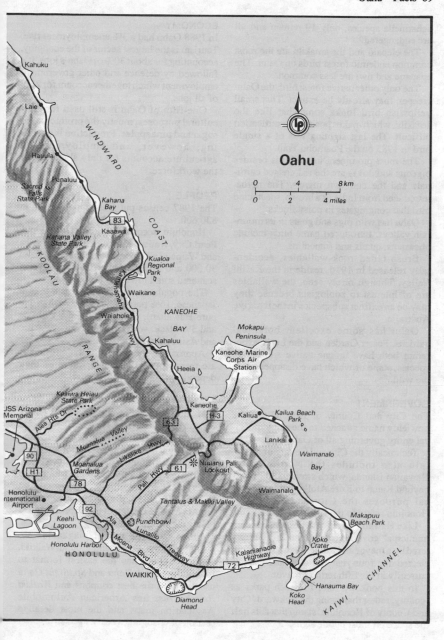

Oahu

0   4   8 km
0   2   4 miles

achatinella species, only 19 remain and all are endangered.

The elepaio and the amakihi are the most common endemic forest birds on Oahu. The apapane and iiwi are less common.

The only other native forest bird, the Oahu creeper, may already be extinct. This small yellowish bird looks somewhat like the amakihi, which makes positive identification difficult. The last sighting was of a single bird in 1985 on the Poamoho Trail.

The most prominent urban birds besides pigeons and doves are the red-crested cardinals and the common mynas. The myna, introduced from India, is a brown, spectacled bird that congregates in noisy flocks.

Oahu has wild pigs and goats in its mountain valleys. Introduced game birds include pheasants, quails and francolins.

Brush-tailed rock-wallabies, accidentally released in 1916, reside in the Kalihi Valley. Though rarely seen, the wallabies are of interest to zoologists because they may be an extinct subspecies in their native Australia.

Oahu has some excellent botanical gardens. Foster Garden and the Lyon Arboretum both have unique native and exotic species, some of which have disappeared in the wild.

GOVERNMENT

The City and County of Honolulu is the unwieldy name attached to the single political entity governing all of Oahu.

Technically the City and County of Honolulu also includes the Northwestern Hawaiian islands, which stretch 1300 miles beyond Kauai to Kure Atoll − but for practical purposes the City and County of Honolulu refers to the island of Oahu.

Like Hawaii's other counties, there are no municipal governments. Oahu is administered by a mayor and a nine-member council, elected for four-year terms. Frank Fasi is currently in his fifth term as mayor.

In this book we refer to beach parks as 'county' rather than using the awkward 'City and County of Honolulu' stamp that fills half the space on most public signs.

ECONOMY

In 1988 Oahu had a 3% unemployment rate. Tourism is the largest sector of the economy, accounting for about 30% of Oahu's jobs. It's followed by defence and other government employment which together account for 22% of all jobs.

One-fifth of Oahu is still used for agricultural purposes, mostly the production of sugar and pineapples. Production is declining, however, and employment in agriculture accounts for only about 2% of the workforce.

PEOPLE

The 1987 census put Oahu's population at 830,600.

Honolulu accounts for 381,100 people. Pearl City, Kailua, Kaneohe, Wahiawa, Aiea and Waipahu all have populations of between 30,000 and 50,000. Other Oahuans live in scattered small towns and rural areas.

The population is 27% Caucasian, 24% Japanese, 16% part-Hawaiian (less than 1% pure Hawaiian), 10% Filipino, 6% Chinese and 3% black, with numerous other Pacific and Asian minorities.

Approximately 15% of Oahu's residents are members of the armed forces or their dependants.

TOURIST INFORMATION

The main office of the Hawaii Visitors Bureau (tel 923-1811) is at 2270 Kalakaua Ave, Suite 801, Honolulu, HI 96815. It's loaded with free brochures and magazines, including those for the neighbouring islands. Hours are from 8 am to 4.30 pm Monday to Friday.

The HVB also has an information desk at the Ala Moana Center, at the street level just below the central escalator.

Numerous free tourist magazines are available at the airport and around Waikiki. *Guide to Oahu* has the easiest format to follow, *This Week Oahu* and *Spotlight Oahu* usually have the best coupons and *Waikiki Beach Press* has American Automobile Association maps and the most detailed section of changing weekly events.

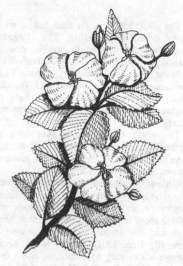

Ilima Flower

GENERAL INFORMATION
Official Oahu
Oahu is nicknamed 'The Gathering Place'. Its flower is the delicate native ilima, which is yellow-orange, the island's official colour.

Money
There are hundreds of banks on Oahu. In Waikiki, there's a Bank of Hawaii office at 2220 Kalakaua Ave. Automatic teller machines can be found at the Ala Moana Center, the airport, some Foodland supermarkets and many other places.

Banks are generally open from 8.30 am to at least 3 pm Mondays to Thursdays and from 8.30 am to 6 pm Fridays.

Post
The Ala Moana Center post office (tel 946-2020) is open from 8.30 am to 5 pm Monday to Friday and from 8.30 am to 4.30 pm on Saturdays. It's at street level on the mountain side of the centre at the Sears end.

The main Oahu post office is at 3600 Aolele St (tel 423-3990) in Honolulu. The Waikiki post office (tel 941-1062) is at 330 Saratoga Rd.

Media
The two English dailies are the morning *Honolulu Advertiser* and the afternoon *Honolulu Star-Bulletin*. They put out a joint Sunday paper, the *Star-Bulletin & Advertiser*. There's also one daily newspaper each in Korean, Chinese and Japanese/English.

Honolulu has 27 radio stations and seven TV stations. Channels 6 and 8 have Visitor-Cable Network with programmes about Hawaii, mostly geared for tourists.

Bookshops
Honolulu Book Shops has a good selection of general, Hawaiiana and travel books. They're at the corner of Bishop and Hotel streets in downtown Honolulu and in the Ala Moana, Hawaii Kai, Pearlridge and Kailua shopping centres.

The Waldenbooks chain has shops in the Royal Hawaiian Shopping Center in Waikiki, Ward Warehouse, Kahala Mall, Koko Marina Shopping Center, Windward Mall and Pearlridge Center.

Used Books Froggies (tel 942-8686), at the corner of Kalakaua and King streets in Honolulu, has an excellent selection of used books, including good-sized Hawaiiana and travel sections. You might want to give them a call before you visit, as they were planning to move. They are open from 9 am to 10 pm daily.

Jelly's Comics and Books (404 Piikoi St, tel 538-7771), opposite the Ala Moana Center, also has a pretty good collection of used books. It's open from 9 am to 10 pm Monday to Saturday and until 7 pm on Sundays.

Other used book stores in Honolulu include Interlude (opposite Froggies on the corner of Kalakaua and King streets, tel 944-2665), Rainbow Books and Records (University and King streets, tel 955-7994) and Gecko Books (Waialae and Koko Head avenues, tel 732-1292).

Libraries
Hawaii's statewide library system has its main library (tel 548-4775) in downtown

Honolulu, next to Iolani Palace. There are 21 other public libraries around Oahu.

Photocopying
Dittos (2570 S Beretania St, tel 943-0005) is open 24 hours a day and has quality photocopiers at six cents a copy. It's up by the university, opposite the Down to Earth health food store. There's another Dittos at 833 Kapiolani Blvd.

Weather
The National Weather Service provides recorded weather forecasts for Honolulu (tel 833-2849) and all Oahu (tel 836-0121) as well as surf conditions (tel 836-1952) and a marine forecast (tel 836-3921).

KPOI, an FM rock music radio station, also provides surf reports (tel 538-7131).

Night Sky
The Hawaiian Skyguide (tel 948-0759) is a recording with information on the current stars and planets visible in the Hawaiian sky.

Emergency
Dial 911 for all police, fire and ambulance emergencies. A crisis line (tel 521-4555) operates 24 hours a day.

Hospitals with 24-hour emergency services include the Queen's Medical Center (1301 Punchbowl St, Honolulu; tel 538-9011), Straub Clinic & Hospital (888 S King St at Ward, Honolulu; tel 522-4000), Castle Medical Center (640 Ulukahiki, Kailua; tel 263-5500), Kahuku Hospital (Kahuku; tel 293-9221) and Wahiawa General Hospital (128 Lehua St, Wahiawa; tel 621-8411).

Divers with the bends are sent to the UH Hyperbaric Facility (42 Ahui St, Honolulu; tel 523-9155).

ACCOMMODATION
All but 10% of Oahu's nearly 40,000 visitor rooms are in Waikiki. Unlike on the neighbouring islands, where there are multiple destinations, outside Honolulu there are only two resort hotels: the Sheraton Makaha on the Waianae Coast and the Turtle Bay Hilton, on the northern tip of the island.

The Waikiki/Honolulu area has a wide range of accommodation. The cheapest places are the two youth hostels, one in Waikiki and one by the university, with dorm beds for about $10. After that, there are Ys in the range of $25 per person and Waikiki hotels that start around $35 a single or double. Waikiki has lots of middle-range and luxury hotels as well as some condos.

The north shore gets its fair share of surfers hanging out on a budget and though there are no hotels there is some cheaper accommodation to be found there.

Unless otherwise noted, rates given throughout this book are the same for either singles or doubles and don't include the 9.43% room tax. Establishments often have high and low seasons. The high season is generally from 15 December to 15 April, though it can vary by establishment a few weeks in either direction. The rest of the year is the low season.

If you're calling from outside Hawaii, add the 808 area code to all numbers. Numbers beginning with 800 are toll free from the US mainland and sometimes from Canada as well.

Camping
Camping is allowed at 13 county beach parks, one county botanic garden and five state recreation areas.

All county and state camping grounds on Oahu are closed on Wednesday and Thursday nights, ostensibly for maintenance, but also to prevent permanent encampments.

Although thousands of visitors use these camping sites each year without incident, Oahu has more of a reputation for trouble than other islands. Rip-offs at roadside and beachfront camping grounds are not uncommon.

State Parks Camping is free by permit at Sand Island and Keaiwa Heiau, both in the greater Honolulu area; Malaekahana, in Laie; Kaiaka, near Haleiwa; and in Waimanalo state recreation areas.

Keaiwa Heiau is a good choice for an inland park, Malaekahana for a coastal. Malaekahana is the only public park on Oahu with housekeeping cabins (see the Windward Oahu section).

Permit applications must be submitted at least seven days and no more than 30 days before the first camping date. Applications may be made by mail, by phone or in person between 8 am and 4 pm on weekdays from the Division of State Parks (tel 548-7455), 1151 Punchbowl St (Box 621), Honolulu, HI 96809.

County Beach Parks Camping is free at county parks but permits are required. Pick up permits between 8 am and 4 pm weekdays at the Department of Parks & Recreation (tel 523-4525) on the ground floor of the Municipal Office building (650 S King St, Honolulu, HI 96813), the tall grey building on the corner of King and Alapai streets. Permits are also available from any satellite city hall, such as at Ala Moana Center (tel 945-2677) or in Kailua (tel 261-8575).

Camping is allowed from 8 am Friday to 8 am Wednesday at Kahe Point, Nanakuli, Lualualei and Keaau beach parks on the Waianae Coast; Mokuleia and Haleiwa beach parks on the north shore; and Hauula, Kahana Bay, Swanzy, Kualoa, Bellows Field, Waimanalo and Makapuu beach parks on the windward shore.

Kualoa, in one of the nicest beach settings, is the only county beach park with a caretaker and gates that are locked at night. Camping along the Waianae Coast is not recommended.

County Botanic Garden Hoomaluhia is an inland park in Kaneohe at the base of the Koolau Range. It has Oahu's safest camping and is unique among the county camping grounds in that it's operated by the botanic gardens division. Reservations can be made by mail. For an application, send a business-sized, self-addressed envelope to Hoomaluhia, Box 1116, Kaneohe, HI 96744.

Back-Country Camping The state forestry allows back-country camping along several valley and ridge trails, including three in Hauula on the windward coast and along the Waimano Trail north of Pearl City. There's also a cabin at the end of the 3½-mile Poamoho Ridge Trail, which begins near the Dole Pineapple Pavilion in Wahiawa and leads to the Koolau Range summit.

All back-country camping requires a permit from the Division of Forestry & Wildlife (tel 548-8850), 1151 Punchbowl St, Honolulu, HI 96813. The forestry will send maps for these trails on request.

Fellow hikers on back-country trails are likely to be pig hunters.

Camping Supplies Omar The Tent Man (650A Kakoi St, Honolulu, HI 96819; tel 836-8785) rents two-person tents for $32 a week, stoves for $14 a week, frame backpacks or sleeping bags for $20 a week, plus lanterns, pads and coolers.

ENTERTAINMENT

For up-to-date entertainment information, check the Friday listings in the *Honolulu Advertiser*, or the free tourist magazines – especially the *Waikiki Beach Press*.

The free *Island Entertainment* paper comes out bimonthly and has club listings, but it's harder to find. The Island Entertainment Hotline (tel 847-INFO) has a recorded listing of nightclub news, coming concerts and other shows.

The gay scene is centred around the Kuhio District in Waikiki and is described in the Waikiki Entertainment section.

Oahu has more than 40 movie theatres, including three drive-ins. Check the papers for details.

Call 527-5666 for a recorded listing of free performances and activities presented by the City and County of Honolulu.

For festivals, fairs and competitions, see the Holidays & Festivals section in the Facts about the Islands chapter. For details of specific venues, see the relevant town or city.

Luaus

Oahu's two main luaus, *Paradise Cove* and *Germaine's Luau*, are both huge impersonal commercial affairs held nightly out in the Barbers Point area. They each cost about

$40, which includes a 35 minute bus ride from Waikiki hotels, buffet dinner and show. This area of Oahu is dry and dusty and the whole scene is a long way from most people's visions of paradise.

For something on a more reasonable scale, walk down to the beach in front of the Outrigger Waikiki Hotel and take a free peek at *Chuck Machado's Luau* (tel 836-0249) at 7 pm on Tuesdays, Fridays and Sundays. Or join in for $24.50.

The *Royal Hawaiian Hotel* (tel 923-7311) has a luau on Sundays on the lawn by the beach.

Hawaiiana

Some of the best Hawaiian entertainment can be found at community events, such as competitions between the hula schools. These generally take place outside Waikiki; check the papers for more information.

Some of the better contemporary Hawaiian musicians to look for are Olomana, Cecilio and Kapono, Kapono and Keola Beamer, the Peter Moon Band, Brother Noland (with a reggae sound) and the rock band Kalapana.

For a more traditional Hawaiian sound there are Makaha Sons of Niihau, Genoa Keawe, Mahi Beamer and Haunani Apoliona, among others.

ACTIVITIES
Swimming

Oahu boasts 60 beach parks, most of which have restrooms and showers, and 19 are patrolled by lifeguards. The island's four distinct coastal areas have their own peculiar seasonal water conditions. When it's rough on one side, it's generally calm on another, so you can find places to swim and surf year round.

Oahu's south shore extends from Barbers Point to Makapuu Point and includes the most popular beaches on the island, including the white sand beaches of Waikiki and Ala Moana.

The windward coast extends from Makapuu Point to Kahuku Point. It catches the trade winds which provide great year-round sailing conditions. Kailua Beach Park, Oahu's busiest windsurfing spot, is one of the best all-around beaches on this side. Other nice beaches are at Waimanalo, Kualoa and Malaekahana.

The north shore extends from Kahuku Point to Kaena Point. It has spectacular waves in winter, but can be as calm as a lake in summer.

The leeward Waianae Coast extends from Kaena Point to Barbers Point. It's the driest, sunniest side of the island, with long stretches of white sands. The most popular beach on this side is Makaha.

The county maintains 17 community swimming pools. Pools in the greater Honolulu area are at Palolo Valley Field (2007 Palolo Ave), Manoa Valley Field (2721 Kaaipu Ave) and Booth Playground (2331 Kanealii Ave).

Surfing

In winter, the north shore gets some of Hawaii's most spectacular surf, with swells reaching 20 to 30 feet. This is the home of the Banzai Pipeline, Sunset Beach and some of the world's top surfing competitions.

Makaha is the top winter surf spot on the leeward Waianae Coast. The south shore gets its best surfing waves in summer, with Waikiki and Diamond Head having some of the best breaks.

Surf News Network (tel 531-SURF) has a recorded surfline reporting winds, wave heights and results of surfing contests, updated three times a day. The National Weather Service (tel 836-1952) has a recorded surf forecast.

The county's Haleiwa Surf Center (tel 637-5051), at Haleiwa Alii Beach Park, holds free surfing lessons from 9.30 am to noon Saturdays and Sundays. Call them for details even if you just want to know if the surf's up.

Local Surfer Magazine is a free newspaper with local surfing news, contest info and a tide chart. It's available at 7-11 stores and shops catering to surfers around the island.

Surf-N-Sea (tel 637-9887), just beyond the Anahulu Bridge in Haleiwa, rents surfboards for $5 for the first hour, $3.50 for each additional hour, and up to $18 per day. Two-hour surfing lessons cost $35; they also sell new and used surfboards.

Local Motion rents surfboards at five Oahu locations, including 1714 Kapiolani Blvd (tel 955-7873), the Windward Mall in Kaneohe (tel 263-7873) and Koko Marina in Hawaii Kai (tel 396-7873).

You can also rent boards at concession stands on the beach in Waikiki.

Bodysurfing, Snorkelling & Boogie Boarding

The most popular boogie boarding place for beginners in Waikiki is at Kapahulu Groin.

Waimanalo Beach Park and nearby Bellows Beach Park have gentle shorebreaks good for beginning bodysurfers.

The two hottest (and most dangerous) spots for experts are Sandy Beach Park and Makapuu Beach Park in south-east Oahu. Other top shorebreaks are at Makaha on the Waianae Coast, Waimea Bay on the North Shore, and Kalama Beach in Kailua and Pounders in Laie on the windward coast.

The University of Hawaii Sea Grant College (Marine Advisory Program, 2540 Maile Way, Spalding 252B, Honolulu, HI 96822) has a free pamphlet on bodysurfing. It details 17 bodysurfing spots on Oahu as well as techniques, Hawaiian etiquette (hog someone's wave and you ask for a fight) and safety tips.

The snorkelling mecca of Hanauma Bay is on the south shore. North shore beaches such as Shark's Cove draw snorkellers in summer, as do some Waianae Coast locations like the Makaha Caverns at Makaha Beach.

If you're going to be doing much snorkelling or boogie boarding, you're better off buying your own equipment. Otherwise, there are stands along Waikiki Beach renting both. Prices vary slightly and you may save a few dollars by checking out different stands. Boogie boards cost about $3.50 to $5 an hour and $12 to $15 a day. Snorkel sets are usually a bit cheaper.

Elsewhere on the island, Surf-N-Sea (tel 637-9887) in Haleiwa rents boogie boards for $3 for the first hour and $2 for each additional hour, and snorkel sets for $6.50 half a day. It's open from 9 am to 6 pm daily.

The Leeward Dive Center (tel 696-3414) in Maili, on the Waianae Coast, rents snorkel sets for $9 a day. Naish Hawaii (tel 261-6067) in Kailua, on the windward coast, rents boogie boards and snorkel sets.

Windsurfing

Kailua Bay is Oahu's number one windsurfing spot. It has flat water, waves and good trade winds. Windsurfing shops set up there daily, renting boards and giving lessons. It's a great place for beginners.

Windsurfers can be found along much of the windward coast, which catches the trade winds. Other good spots include Diamond Head for speed and jumps and Backyards for north shore challenges.

Naish Hawaii (as in windsurfing champion Robbie Naish) sells and rents equipment, gives lessons and arranges windsurfing vacations. They're at 130 Kailua Rd, Kailua, HI 96734 (tel 261-6067), near Kailua Beach Park. Introductory group lessons are $35 for three hours. Private

Windsurfer

lessons are $30 an hour. Rental rates vary with board and rig, starting at $20 per half day.

Next door, the Kailua Sailboard Company (130 Kailua Rd, Kailua, HI 96734; tel 262-2555) rents boards for $20 per four hours, $27 a day and $95 a week. One-hour private lessons cost $25; three-hour beginner's lessons are $35. Call them for a wind report.

Aloha Windsurfing (tel 926-1185) does excursions to Kailua Beach Park from Waikiki, including hotel pick-up, for $47 with about 4½ hours of sailing time. They also rent equipment on the beach at $10 an hour, $20 for three hours and $50 for a coupon book good for 10 hours. A three-hour lesson costs $35 and, like the others, includes equipment.

Waikiki Windsurfing (tel 949-8952) at Fort DeRussy Beach rents windsurfing equipment for $18 for the first hour and $12 for each additional hour. It's $30 for a 1¼-hour lesson.

In Haleiwa, Surf-N-Sea (tel 637-9887) rents windsurfing equipment for $10 for the first hour and $5 for each additional hour. Two-hour windsurfing lessons cost $30.

Windsurfing Hawaii (156C Hamakua Drive, Kailua, HI 96734; tel 261-3539) also has rentals, lessons and tours.

Diving

The Waianae Coast and prime locals on the north shore like Shark's Cove at Pupukea Beach Park attract divers in summer. At Waianae's Makaha Beach they go out to the Makaha Caverns beyond the reef. In case of the bends or other diving accidents, 24-hour emergency treatment is available at the UH Hyperbaric Facility (tel 523-9155), 42 Ahui St, Honolulu.

Aloha Dive Shop (Koko Marina Shopping Center, Honolulu, HI 96825; tel 395-5922) in Hawaii Kai has two-tank boat dives off Koko Head for $62. Half-day introductory dives at Hanauma Bay are $52. Divers can be certified in four half-day sessions for $295. They offer free transport to and from Waikiki hotels. The shop sells and rents

scuba and snorkelling gear. It's open from 8 am to 5.30 pm daily.

Leeward Dive Center (87-066 Farrington Highway, Maili, HI 96792; tel 696-3414, 800-255-1574) has dives to Makaha Caverns, the WW II minesweeper *Mahi* and an aeroplane wreck. Two-tank boat dives cost $65 during the day and $70 at night. Introductory dives for beginners cost $65, snorkelling trips are $30. Certification courses in both PADI and NAUI, camera rentals and video services are available.

Surf-N-Sea (tel 637-9887), in Haleiwa, has boat dives for $45 for one-tank dives, $75 for two-tank dives. Daily rental rates for diving gear are $6 for tanks, $2.50 for weight belts and $7.50 for regulators or wet suits. Air fills cost $3. They can certify in PADI and offer intro dives.

Snuba looks like it could be fun. It's a sort of scuba diving for snorkellers, using long air hoses attached to a tank on an inflatable raft. The diver simply wears a mask and weight belt and can dive down as far as the air hose allows and stay down as long as the tank has air. For more information call Snuba (tel 922-7762).

For snorkelling tours, see the Hanauma Bay section.

Hiking

The trail that leads three-quarters of a mile from inside the crater of Diamond Head up to its summit is the most popular hike on Oahu. It's easy to get to from Waikiki and ends with a panoramic view of greater Honolulu.

The Manoa Falls Trail, just a few miles above Waikiki, is another short hike – a quiet walk through an abandoned arboretum of huge trees to a nice waterfall.

The Tantalus and Makiki Valley area has the most extensive trail network around Honolulu, with fine views of the city and surrounding valleys. Amazingly, though it's just two miles above the city hustle and bustle, the quiet solitude of this lush forest reserve is unspoiled.

On the western edge of Honolulu, the Moanalua Trail goes deep into the Moanalua

Top: View of Honolulu & Diamond Head from Round Top, Oahu
Left: Divers at Koko Crater, Oahu
Right: Waikiki, Oahu

Top: Waikiki Beach, Oahu
Left: Surfer, Waikiki
Right: Weighing in octopus & parrotfish, Molokai

Valley. You can hike it on your own or join a guided walk.

At Keaiwa Heiau State Park, just northwest of Honolulu, the Aiea Loop Trail leads 4½ miles along a ridge with views of Pearl Harbor and Diamond Head to the south and the Koolau Range to the north and east.

The Kaena Point Trail is a coastal hike through a natural area reserve on the westernmost point of Oahu.

On the windward side, a trail in the Sacred Falls State Park goes up a narrow valley in the Koolau Range to a waterfall. There's another hike in nearby Kahana Valley State Park.

There are short walks from the Nuuanu Pali Lookout, along Nuuanu Pali Drive, around Hanauma Bay and along countless beaches.

All hikes are described in their respective sections.

Guided Hikes Notices of hiking club outings are run in the Friday edition of the *Honolulu Star-Bulletin* in the 'Pulse of Paradise' column. By joining one of these clubs you get to hike with ecology-minded islanders; it may also be a good way to get to the backwoods if you don't have a car, as they often share rides.

The *Sierra Club* (1100 Alakea St, Room 330, Honolulu, HI 96813; tel 538-6616) leads hikes nearly every Sunday. For most outings, hikers meet at 8 am at the corner of Hotel and Alakea streets, near the Bear and Cubs statue in front of the Honolulu District Court building. City parking is not a hassle on Sundays and you can usually find space along Alakea or Richards streets. The hike fee is $2 for non-members. Bring lunch and water.

The *Hawaiian Trail and Mountain Club* (Box 2238, Honolulu, HI 96804; tel 734-5515) meets for hiking at 8 am most Sundays on the mountain side of Iolani Palace. The hike fee is $1 for non-members. Bring lunch and water. Send a stamped, self-addressed envelope for a copy of their hiking schedule.

The two hiking groups join forces on weekends to clear Oahu trails. If you want to

join them, bring a machete or sickle and head for Iolani Palace. They generally go out on Saturday one week, Sunday the next.

Friends of Foster Garden (50 N Vineyard Blvd, Honolulu, HI 96817; tel 537-1708) leads hikes to places like Sacred Falls, Manoa Falls and Koko Crater for $5.

The *Hawaii Audubon Society* (212 Merchant St, No 320, Honolulu, HI 96813; tel 528-1432) leads bird-watching hikes, usually on the third Sunday of each month. Binoculars and a copy of *Hawaii's Birds* are recommended. Call them for more information.

Note Anyone who has hiked on Oahu should scrub their shoes and wash their socks and long pants before hiking on other islands to avoid transferring clinging *Clidemia hirta* seeds, which are practically invisible. This weed has infested much of Oahu, overrunning trails and choking out native plants, but it's not yet widely established on the neighbouring islands. It's presumed that the patches of this invasive plant found along trails on Molokai and Maui hitchhiked there on an Oahuan hiker's boot.

Horse Riding
Sheraton Makaha Lio Stables (tel 695-9511) in Makaha has one-hour rides in groups of up to five people for $18.50 each. The stables are closed on Mondays.

Kualoa Ranch (49-560 Kamehameha Highway, Kualoa; tel 237-8515) has trail rides at 2 pm Monday to Friday and at 9 or 11.30 am and 1.30 pm on Saturdays. It costs $15 for a one-hour ride and $25 for a two-hour ride. Reservations are required.

Tennis
Oahu has 172 county tennis courts. There are 10 courts at Ala Moana Beach Park (tel 521-7664) and nine at the Diamond Head Tennis Center (tel 971-7150) at the Diamond Head end of Kapiolani Park. Court time is free on a first-come first-served basis.

With ground space at a premium, few Waikiki hotels have tennis courts. The Ilikai (tel 949-3811, ext 6428) leads with five courts, rentals, a pro shop and even stadium seating for the occasional championship match. Rates are $8 per hour per person and $2 extra for night games.

The Pacific Beach Hotel has two courts and the Hawaiian Regent has one, both costing $8 per person per hour.

The Honolulu Tennis Club (2220 S King St, tel 944-9696) has four tennis and three racquetball courts and offers transport to and from Waikiki. It's $8 to $10 per hour per person for tennis and $6 for racquetball.

The Sheraton Makaha Resort in Makaha (tel 695-9511) has four courts for $10 per hour per court, and the Turtle Bay Hilton in Kahuku (tel 293-8811) has 10 courts at $8 per person.

Golf

Oahu has four municipal golf courses. The 18-hole courses are: the Ala Wai Golf Course (tel 296-4653) on Kapahulu Ave, mauka of the Ala Wai Canal near Waikiki; the Pali Golf Course (tel 261-9784), 45-050 Kamehameha Highway, Kaneohe; and the Ted Makalena Golf Course (tel 296-7888), Waipio Point Access Rd, Waipahu. Rates are $8 on weekdays and $12 on weekends and holidays. The nine-hole Kahuku Golf Course (tel 293-5842) in Kahuku costs $4 on weekdays and $6 on weekends. Most require reservations a week in advance.

The Sheraton Makaha (tel 695-9511) claims to have the number one USGA-rated golf course on Oahu. There's a driving range, putting green and shoe and club rentals. The cost is $47.50 for nine holes and $95 for 18 holes for non-guests (about half that price for guests) including a cart. It's open from 7.30 am to 6 pm daily.

The Turtle Bay Hilton has an 18-hole golf course around the same price.

Running

Oahu is big on jogging. It's estimated that Honolulu has more joggers per capita than any other city in the world. Kapiolani Park and Ala Moana Park are two favourite spots. There's also a 4.8 mile run around Diamond Head crater that's a pretty beaten track.

There are more than 100 road races each year, from one mile fun runs and five mile jogs to competitive marathons, biathlons and triathlons.

For an annual schedule of running events with times, dates and contact addresses, write to the Department of Parks & Recreation, City and County of Honolulu, 650 S King St, Honolulu, HI 96813.

Oahu's best-known race is the Honolulu Marathon held in December. For information send a stamped, self-addressed envelope to Honolulu Marathon Association, 3435 Waialae Ave, No 208, Honolulu, HI 96816.

The Department of Parks & Recreation holds a Honolulu Marathon Clinic at 7.30 am every Sunday (except for three-day holidays) at the Kapiolani Park Bandstand. It's free and open to everyone from beginners to seasoned marathoners. Runners join groups of their own speed.

Cricket

The Honolulu Cricket Club plays at 2 pm on Sundays at Kapiolani Park. Visiting players are welcome, but call first (tel 261-4042) to confirm.

Skydiving

Skydive Hawaii (tel 521-4404) says for $150 they'll attach you to the hips and shoulders of a skydiver so you can jump together from a plane at 10,500 feet, freefall for 50 seconds and finish off with a couple of minutes of canopy ride. The more daring can take a quick lesson and then jump independently with a static line for the same price. Experienced skydivers are charged $35 for jumps. They take off from Dillingham Airfield in Mokuleia.

Hang Gliding

Tradewinds Hang Gliding (380-H Haleloa Place, Honolulu, HI 96821; tel 396-8557) and Airsport (41-014 Ehukai, Waimanalo, HI 96795; tel 259-8192) both offer hang gliding lessons for beginners, taking off from Makapuu Point.

THINGS TO BUY

Honolulu is a large, cosmopolitan city with plenty of sophisticated shops. If you're looking for crafts, the best deals will be at one of the craft shows that are held from time to time around the city (check the papers).

If you just want to buy a carton of macadamia nuts, Longs Drugs has better prices than almost anything you'll find in Waikiki. There's a Longs as well as 180 other stores at Ala Moana Center, which boasts being the 'largest open-air shopping center in the world'.

For kitsch souvenirs there are scores of shops selling fake Polynesian stuff, from Filipino shell hangings and carved coconuts to cheap seashell jewellery and wooden statues of ET.

For more local flavour, the Aloha Flea Market (tel 239-9101), at Aloha Stadium out near Pearl Harbor, has more than 1000 sellers from 7.30 am to 3 pm Wednesdays, Saturdays and Sundays.

At the county-run People's Open Market Program, farmers sell local produce for one hour a week at each of 21 locations around Oahu. For a schedule call 523-4730.

GETTING THERE & AWAY

Most flights into Hawaii land at Honolulu International Airport, the only commercial airport on Oahu. All inter-island airlines that serve the neighbouring islands also land at Honolulu.

See the Getting There and Getting Around chapters in the front of the book for information.

GETTING AROUND
Airport Transport

From the airport you can easily get to Waikiki by local bus (if your baggage is limited), by a number of airport shuttle services, by taxi or by renting a car. Most of the many car rental agencies have booths in or nearby the airport. A taxi to Waikiki from the airport will cost about $15, with baggage charges extra. Taxis are readily available.

The easiest way to drive to Waikiki from the airport is to take Hwy 92, which starts out as Nimitz Highway and turns into Ala Moana Blvd, leading directly into Waikiki. Though this route hits more local traffic, it's hard to get lost on it.

If you're into life in the fast lane, connect instead with the H-1 freeway heading east.

On the return to the airport from Waikiki, take note not to miss the poorly marked interchange where H-1 curves down toward the airport. It takes 20 to 30 minutes to get from Waikiki to the airport via H-1 if you don't hit traffic.

Airport Bus Travel time is about an hour between the airport and the far end of Waikiki on No 19 and No 20 buses. TheBus (see the Bus section) stops at the 'Passenger Drop' areas in front of the airline counters. Luggage is limited to what you can hold on your lap or store under your seat, the latter space comparable to the space under an airline seat.

Airport Shuttle The ride between Waikiki and the airport takes about 45 minutes by shuttle bus.

The *Waikiki Express* (tel 942-2177) runs between the airport and Waikiki every half hour from 4.45 am to midnight. It costs $5. From Waikiki to the airport, call in advance for a reservation, as there are no scheduled pick-up stops. From the airport, use the courtesy phone.

The *Airport Motor Coach* (tel 926-4747) leaves Waikiki for the airport by reservation (and only in that direction) between 6.30 am and 10 pm. The cost is $5 for adults, $2.50 for children.

Both allow two suitcases and one carry-on bag.

Bus

Oahu has a very good public bus system – the only extensive one in Hawaii. It's called simply TheBus and it's easy to use.

TheBus has 59 routes covering most of Oahu. You can take the bus to watch windsurfers at Kailua or surfers at Sunset Beach or Makaha, visit Chinatown or the Bishop Museum, snorkel at Hanauma Bay or hike Diamond Head. Some of the island's prime viewpoints are beyond reach, however. TheBus doesn't stop at the Nuuanu Pali Lookout, go up to Tantalus or out to Kaena Point.

Each bus route can have a few different destinations. The destination is written on the front of the bus next to the number.

Buses generally keep the same number when inbound and outbound. For instance, the No 8 bus can take you either into the heart of Waikiki or out away from it toward Ala Moana – so note both the number and the written destination before you jump on.

When in doubt ask the bus driver. They're used to disoriented visitors and most drivers are remarkably patient and helpful.

Though TheBus is convenient enough, this isn't Tokyo – if you set your watch by the bus here you'll come up with Hawaiian Time.

In addition to not getting hung up on schedules, buses can bottleneck, with one packed bus after another cruising right by crowded stops. Saturday nights between Ala Moana and Waikiki can be a particularly memorable experience.

Overall the buses are in excellent condition – if anything they're too modern. Newer buses are air-conditioned, with sealed windows and climate-control. They're so out of 'control' that drivers wear jackets to keep from freezing!

Still, TheBus usually gets you where you want to go and as long as you don't try to cut anything close or schedule too much in one day it's good value.

Fares The fare to anywhere is 60 cents – *exact change only*.

Monthly bus passes valid for unlimited rides in a calendar month cost $15. Passes are available at all Foodland supermarkets, satellite city halls and 7-11 stores.

Transfers are given free when more than one bus is required to get to a destination. Ask when you board.

Children under the age of six ride free.

Common Routes Bus Nos 8, 19 and 20 run between Waikiki and Ala Moana Center,

Honolulu's central transfer point. There's usually a bus every 10 minutes or less. From Ala Moana you can connect with a broad network of buses to points mauka and Ewa.

Bus Nos 2, 19 and 20 will take you between Waikiki and downtown Honolulu.

Bus No 4 runs between Waikiki and the University of Hawaii.

Circle Island Route It's possible to circle the island, beginning at Ala Moana Center. The No 52 Wahiawa-Circle Island bus goes clockwise up Hwy 99 to Haleiwa and along the north shore. At the Turtle Bay Hilton, on the northern tip of Oahu, it switches signs to No 55 and comes down the windward coast to Kaneohe and down the Pali Highway back to Ala Moana. The No 55 Kaneohe-Circle Island bus does the same route in reverse. If you do it nonstop it takes about four hours.

For the south-east Oahu loop, from Waikiki it's bus No 58 to Sea Life Park and then No 57 up to Kailua and back into Honolulu.

Because you'll need to change buses, ask for a transfer when you first board. Transfers have time limits and aren't meant to be used as stopovers but you can grab a quick break at Ala Moana. Anytime you get off to explore along the route you'll need to pay a new 60-cent fare when you reboard.

Bus Schedules TheBus has a great telephone service. As long as you know where you are and where you want to go, you can call 531-1611 anytime between 5.30 am and 10 pm daily and they'll tell you not only which bus to catch but what time the next one will be there.

You can get printed timetables at TheBus office at the corner of Kapiolani and Cooke streets in Honolulu (7.30 am to 4 pm weekdays) or by sending a self-addressed stamped envelope to MTL, 1133 Alapai St, Honolulu, HI 96813.

There are useful bus route maps in the front of the Oahu yellow pages phone book.

If you're going to be using TheBus extensively, pick up a bus guide. There are a few of them on the market. We found *TheBus*

Guide (Maui Pacific Traders) to be well worth the $2. Be sure to get the most up-to-date version.

Shuttle Bus

Private shuttle buses run from Waikiki to the Arizona Memorial (tel 923-2999 or 926-4747, $4 return), to Hanauma Bay (tel 677-9600, $3 return) and to the flea market at Aloha Stadium (tel 955-4050, $6 return including admission).

The *Waikiki Trolley* is a tourist trolley bus that runs between Waikiki and Honolulu, stopping at Ala Moana Center, Honolulu Academy of Arts, Iolani Palace, Aloha Tower, Chinatown and a few other sights and shopping centres. Passengers can get off at any stop and then get on the next trolley; they stop once an hour. A day pass is $7 for adults and $4 for children. In Waikiki they leave on the hour from 8 am to 3 pm from the Royal Hawaiian Shopping Center.

Taxi

Metered taxis usually start with a flagfall fee of $1.40 and then notch up $1.20 per mile.

Taxis are readily available at the airport, but otherwise hard to find and you generally need to phone. They're not allowed to cruise, but if you do see one passing by you can try flagging it down. If they're not going for a pick-up they'll usually stop.

Car

Budget (tel 922-3600), National (tel 922-3331), Hertz (tel 836-2691), Avis (tel 834-5536), Thrifty (tel 836-2388), Sunshine (800-522-8440), Dollar (tel 926-4250) and Tropical (tel 836-1041) all have desks at Honolulu International. Toll free numbers are in the Getting Around chapter in the front of the book.

All things being equal, try to rent from a company with its lot inside the airport. The major companies, like Budget, National, Hertz and Avis, are all inside. Getting to their lots is quicker but, more importantly, on the way back all the highway signs lead to these in-airport car returns.

During our last visit to Honolulu we rented from Alamo, which is outside the airport, and found returning the car to be a long process. After dropping our bags at the airport, we had to go back outside and find the Alamo depot on a side street. Alamo didn't make things any easier. On top of the usual delay at the counter, there was a good 20-minute wait for their shuttle van to arrive. All in all, it killed close to an hour.

You can also rent cars in Waikiki at dozens of locations, most commonly in the lobbies of large hotels, but you usually get the best deals at the airport or with advance reservations.

Budget gives renters a coupon booklet with one free admission to Sea Life Park, the Bishop Museum, Queen Emma Summer Palace, Waimea Falls Park, the Polynesian Cultural Center and a few other sights and eateries. You don't have to buy one to get one, so for a single person it's all free. This is a particularly good deal if you're only renting a car for a day or two and want to catch some of the sights.

United Car Rental (234 Beach Walk, tel 922-4605) rents old, rusting compacts for $10.50 a day based on availability. Other local companies advertising low rates include Waikiki Rent-A-Car (corner of McCully and Kalakaua Ave, tel 946-2181), Honolulu Rent-A-Car (1856 Kalakaua Ave, tel 941-9099) and Discount Rent-A-Car (tel 949-4767).

At the other end of the price range, you can rent a Porsche, Corvette, Rolls Royce, Mercedes or other luxury car from Odyssey Rentals (tel 947-8036), Silver Cloud Exotic Car Rentals (tel 599-3999) or Ferrari Rentals (tel 942-8725).

Moped

The Easy Rider (tel 922-7924) moped rental desk at the Waikiki Grand Hotel (134 Kapahulu Ave) has mopeds for $7.77 per half day. They also have a branch at the Seagull Restaurant (2463 Kuhio Ave, tel 922-8868) parking lot.

Budget (tel 922-3600) is the only major rental company that rents mopeds, but they're not as good a deal: $10 for four hours or $21 for 24 hours, plus $5 a day mandatory $100-deductible loss damage waiver.

Actually, moped rental desks are almost as common as hamburger joints in Waikiki and can be found on many street corners.

Bicycle

There's a lot more traffic on Oahu than on the other islands and bicycle rentals seem to be a foreign concept there.

The Hawaii Bicycling League (Box 4403, Honolulu, HI 96812; tel 988-7175) holds bike rides every Saturday and Sunday, ranging from 10 mile jaunts to 112 mile treks around Oahu. Rides are free and open to the public.

For details on coming bicycle races, send a stamped, self-addressed envelope to the US Cycling Federation, 14-1 Kaalalo Place, Wahiawa, HI 96786.

Tours

For sightseeing tours by van or bus, try Trans Hawaiian (tel 735-6467), E Noa Tours (tel 599-2561), Akamai Tours (tel 922-6485), Sun Tan Tours (tel 839-0944) or Robert's Hawaii (tel 947-3939).

Full-day circle-island tours cost about $35 to $40. Other tours go up the Waianae Coast and to places such as downtown Honolulu, Diamond Head, the Nuuanu Pali Lookout and Pearl Harbor.

Gliding Glider Rides (tel 677-3404) offer 20-minute trips from Dillingham Airfield in Mokuleia. While the views are pretty, they're not spectacular. In winter the salt spray can hang in the air like a haze. However it is an experience, soaring silently, and the only other glider rides in Hawaii are given on Kauai and cost far more. Rides cost $40 for one person and $60 for two. Flights go daily between 10.30 am and 5.30 pm.

Helicopter Not every seat in all copters is a window seat. The most common configuration is two passengers up front with the pilot and four sitting across the back. The two back middle seats don't give the photo opportunities proclaimed in the brochures. It's like being a mid-seat rear passenger on a scenic drive – only there's no getting out at viewing points up there. People are usually seated according to weight, so if you're dishing out a lot of money make sure it's clear where you're going to be sitting.

Royal Helicopters (tel 941-4683) and Hawaii Pacific Helicopters (tel 836-1566) both take off from a little helipad on the beach by the Hilton Hawaiian Village and do five-minute twirls over the greater Waikiki area for $28, a 22-minute Hanauma Bay loop for $78 and a 55-minute Oahu flight for $187.

Cruises Sunset sails, moonlight sails, dinner cruises and party boats leave daily from Kewalo Basin, just Ewa of Ala Moana Park. Rates are anywhere from $15 to $80, with dinner cruises averaging about $35. Many provide transport to and from Waikiki and advertise all sorts of come-ons and specials.

Some of the cruising vessels are catamarans in name only; they're more like cattle boats in reality. If it matters, go down to the harbour and check them out for yourself before signing up.

The Hyatt Regency Waikiki's Manu Kai catamaran (tel 923-1234) leaves from the beach at Waikiki. They have hour-long cruises during the day for $12 including sandwiches and a drink, and 1½-hour sunset cruises for $18 including pupus and mai tais.

Hawaiian Cruises (tel 947-9971) has one-hour glass-bottom boat rides leaving from Kewalo Basin at 10 and 11 am, 1.30 and 2.30 pm daily. It costs $10.40 for adults, $5.75 for children, and free transport from Waikiki can be arranged.

Atlantis Submarines (tel 522-1710) has a 65-foot, 46-passenger sightseeing submarine that goes down a mile off Diamond Head. The tour lasts about one hour and 45 minutes, starting with a catamaran ride out to the sub. About 45 minutes are spent cruising beneath the surface surrounded by tropical fish. Tours leave Hilton Hawaiian Village on the hour from 8 am to 4 pm and cost $70 for adults, $35 for children.

Captain Bob's (tel 926-5077) has daily snorkel cruises from Kaneohe Bay. Free transport is available.

Waikiki

Waikiki has an amazing density of highrise hotels along an attractive stretch of white sand beach. It was once Hawaii's only tourist destination and still accounts for nearly half of the visitor accommodation in Hawaii. It's crowded with package tourists from both Japan and mainland USA.

Waikiki has 24,000 permanent residents and some 65,000 visitors on any given day, all in an area roughly 1½ miles long and half a mile wide. It has 450 restaurants, 350 bars and clubs, and more shops than you'd want to count. Its 34,000 hotel and condo rooms have a year-round occupancy rate of 87%.

While the beaches are packed during the day, at night most of the action is along the streets, where window shoppers, cruising pedicabs, time-share touts and prostitutes all go about their business. There's all sorts of music and dancing in the clubs and hotel lounges, including disco and Hawaiian guitar.

Visitors who are into city lights or singles scenes often find what they're looking for here, while many seasoned travellers and a fair number of Oahu residents avoid Waikiki like the plague.

In an effort to upgrade Waikiki's image, the beachfront Kalakaua Ave has just undergone an $11 million beautification project, and Waikiki hotels are in the midst of their own half billion dollar face-lift. With all the construction and jackhammers, it can be very noisy.

Waikiki Beach has wonderful orange sunsets, with the sun dropping down between cruising sailing boats. It's the one time of day that the area approaches the romantic image that the travel brochures like to portray.

Just beyond Waikiki is Diamond Head, a landmark so dominant that it's used as a directional marker – people say 'go Diamond Head' instead of 'head east'.

History

At the turn of the century, Waikiki was almost entirely wetlands. It had more than 50 acres of fishponds as well as extensive taro patches and rice paddies. Fed by mountain streams from the upland Manoa and Makiki

Rice Paddies 1930's

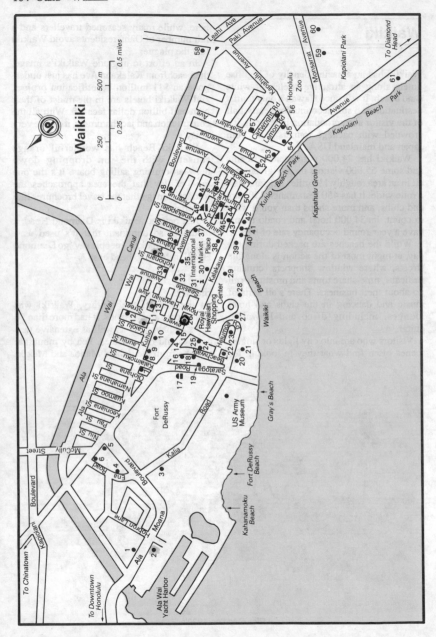

1	Ala Wai Terrace	32	Waikiki Trade Center
2	Ilikai Hotel	33	Outrigger Waikiki Surf
3	Hilton Hawaiian Village	34	Ilima Hotel
4	Five Spices	35	Pizza Hut
5	Sizzler	36	Food Pantry
6	Pink Cadillac	37	Outrigger East
7	Kuhio Twins Theatre	38	Sheraton Princess Kaiulani
8	Hula's Bar & Lei Stand	39	Moana Surfrider
9	Hamburger Mary's	40	Board Rentals
10	Hotel Honolulu	41	Police
11	Waikiki Surf West	42	Wizard Stones
12	Zuke Bistro	43	Hyatt Regency Waikiki
13	Waikiki Surf West	44	Waikiki Prince Hotel
14	Kyotaru	45	Hale Aloha Hostel
15	Moose McGillycuddy's	46	Inter Club Hostel Waikiki
16	New Tokyo Restaurant	47	Continental Surf
17	Waikiki Post Office	48	Waikiki Sand Villa Hotel
18	The Breakers	49	Royal Grove Hotel
19	Urasenke Tea Ceremony	50	Waikiki Circle Hotel
20	Outrigger Reef Hotel	51	Pacific Beach Hotel
21	Halekulani	52	St Augustine's Church
22	Outrigger Waikiki Tower	53	Hawaiian Regent
23	Waikiki Parc Hotel	54	Holiday Inn Waikiki Beach
24	Niihau Apartment Hotel	55	Waikiki Grand
25	Outrigger Coral Seas	56	Queen Kapiolani Hotel
26	Malia's Cantina	57	Quality Inn
27	Sheraton Waikiki	58	Waikiki Library
28	Royal Hawaiian Hotel	59	Kodak Hula Show
29	Outrigger Waikiki	60	Waikiki Shell
30	Waikiki Beachcomber	61	Waikiki Aquarium
31	Hawaii Visitors Bureau		

valleys, Waikiki was one of Oahu's most fertile and productive areas.

By the late 1800s Waikiki's narrow beachfront was lined with private gingerbread-trimmed cottages, built by Honolulu's more well-to-do.

Robert Louis Stevenson, who frequented Waikiki in those days, wrote:

If anyone desires such old fashioned things as lovely scenery, quiet, pure air, clear sea water, heavenly sunsets hung out before his eyes over the Pacific and the distant hills of Waianae, I recommend him to Waikiki Beach.

Tourism took root in 1901 when the Moana opened its doors as Waikiki's first hotel. A tram line was constructed to connect Waikiki to downtown Honolulu and city folk crowded aboard for the beach. Tiring quickly

of the pesky mosquitoes that thrived in the wetlands, these early beach-goers pressured to have Waikiki's 'swamps' brought under control.

In 1922 the Ala Wai Canal was dug to divert the streams that flowed into Waikiki. Old Hawaii lost out, as farmers had the water drained out from under them. Coral rubble was used to fill the ponds, creating what was to become Hawaii's most valuable piece of real estate. Water buffaloes were replaced by tourists.

Waikiki's second hotel, the Royal Hawaiian, was built in 1927 and became the crown jewel of the Matson Navigation Company.

The Royal was the land component for cruises on the *Malolo*, one of the premier luxury ships of the day. The $7.5 million ship, built while the $2 million hotel was under construction, carried 650 passengers from San Francisco to Honolulu each fortnight. The Pink Palace, as the hotel was nicknamed, opened with an extravagant $10-a-plate dinner.

Hotel guests ranged from the Rockefellers to Charlie Chaplin, Babe Ruth to royalty. Some of the guests brought dozens of trunks, their servants and even their Rolls Royces.

The Depression put a damper on things and WW II saw the Royal Hawaiian turned into an R&R centre for servicemen.

Waikiki had 1400 hotel rooms in 1950. In those days surfers could drive their cars to the beach and park on the sand. In the 1960s tourism took over in earnest and by 1968 Waikiki had 13,000 hotel rooms. By 1988 that number had more than doubled.

The boom goes on. St Augustine's Catholic Church, standing on what may have been the last speck of property along busy Kalakaua Ave left uncommercialised, was recently sold to a Tokyo developer for $45 million.

Orientation

Waikiki is bounded on two sides by the Ala Wai Canal and on one by the ocean. The eastern boundary varies according to who's drawing the line, but it's usually considered to be Kapahulu Ave.

There are two main roads: the coastal strip is Kalakaua Ave, named after King David Kalakaua; Kuhio Ave, the main drag for Waikiki's buses, is named after Prince Jonah Kuhio Kalanianaole, a respected Hawaiian statesman.

City buses are no longer allowed on Kalakaua Ave, now a one-way street, and trucks are prohibited at midday. The avenue is no longer as congested as it was in years past, but taxis and cars now tend to zoom by all the faster.

Walking along the beach is an alternative to using the crowded sidewalks. It's possible to walk the full length of Waikiki along the sand and the seawalls. Though it's hot and crowded at midday, it's pleasant at other times. At night it's dark enough for you to see the stars. Cops patrol the beach on dune buggies after sunset.

Information

Tourist Information
The Hawaii Visitors Bureau (tel 923-1811) is at 2270 Kalakaua Ave, Suite 801, in the Waikiki Business Plaza.

Freebie tourist magazines can be found on street corners and in hotel lobbies throughout Waikiki.

The Waikiki Public Library (400 Kapahulu Ave, tel 732-2777) is open from 10 am to 5 pm Monday to Saturday and until 8 pm on Mondays and Wednesdays. This is a relatively small library, but it holds newspapers from the neighbouring islands and a few from the mainland.

The Waikiki post office is at 330 Saratoga Rd. For details on banks refer to the Oahu general information section.

Telephone Phone Line Hawaii (tel 923-1214), on the second level of International Market Place, is a long distance phone service. Three-minute calls to Canada cost $4, while those to most Pacific and European destinations are $7. Calls to anywhere in the USA cost 45 cents a minute. Phone Line Hawaii is open from 8.30 am to 11 pm daily.

Shopping Waikiki is as commercial as they come. There's no lack of souvenir shops, swimsuit and T-shirt shops, quick-stop convenience marts, boutiques or other stores. You won't have any problem finding beach mats or macadamia nuts. Everything's geared towards tourists, most of it bordering on either the tacky or the slick.

The Royal Hawaiian Shopping Center is Waikiki's biggest shopping centre, spanning three blocks along Kalakaua Ave in the centre of Waikiki. It has about 100 shops, restaurants and offices, including a post office, Aloha Airlines, Budget Rent A Car, American Express, Waldenbooks and about 25 eateries, from Baskin Robbins and McDonald's to Chinese and Greek. Most other shops are pricey speciality and jewellery stores. The centre is open from 9 am to 9 pm daily.

International Market Place was Waikiki's original shopping centre. It has lots of ticky-tacky shops and stalls tucked in around a large banyan tree. Many people consider the Market Place one of Waikiki's biggest eyesores and for years it's been targeted for demolition. The latest idea is to build a convention centre in its place. There's a pretty good gallery upstairs that has island photography, paintings and raku pottery.

Liberty House, a somewhat up-market department store with good quality clothing, is next door at the Waikiki Beachcomber.

For better deals, try the Ala Moana Center, Aloha Flea Market or the craft shows that pop up around the city.

Grocery Stores The best place to get groceries in Waikiki is at the Food Pantry, 2370 Kuhio Ave, which is open 24 hours a day. Their prices are higher than those of the supermarkets but lower than those of the smaller convenience stores.

Otherwise the easiest supermarket to get to without a car is Foodland at the Ala Moana Center. There's a Times Supermarket at 3221 Waialae Ave, between 5th and 6th avenues, and a Foodland a few blocks away near the eastern intersection of King and Kapiolani. There are grocery stores along Beretania as well.

Film & Photography Longs Drugs is one of the best places to pick up film and to have prints and slides processed. All their stores send out to Kodak, and most also do Fuji. Slides generally take two to three days and it's a buck or two cheaper than the camera shops.

There's a Longs on the top floor of the Ala Moana Center and another next to Times Supermarket at 3221 Waialae Ave.

Parking Parking in Waikiki is a hassle. Many of the hotels charge an additional $6 to $10 a day at their parking garages.

There's a small underground parking lot next to the Tradewinds Plaza on Lemon Rd,

a couple of buildings down from Queen Kapiolani Hotel. It costs $1 for overnight parking and $2 to park all day.

The parking lot at the zoo on Kapahulu Ave has meters and costs 25 cents an hour with a four-hour parking limit.

Emergency Dial 911 for all police, fire and ambulance emergency services.

Doctors On Call has four private clinics in Waikiki. They have doctors available 24 hours a day at the Hyatt Regency (Diamond Head Tower, 4th Floor, tel 926-4777) and during more standard hours at the Reef Towers Hotel (tel 926-0664), the Hawaiian Regent Hotel (tel 923-3666) and Hilton Hawaiian Village. Appointments aren't necessary. They have X-ray and lab facilities and even make housecalls. A standard office visit costs $45.

Time-Share Hassles There's been a clampdown on the hustlers who used to push time shares and other con deals from every other street corner in Waikiki. They're not totally gone – there are just fewer of them. If you see a sign touting car rentals for $5 a day, you've probably found one.

Time-share salespeople will offer you all sorts of deals, from luaus to sunset cruises, if you'll just come to hear their 'no obligation' pitch. *Caveat emptor*.

Waikiki Beaches

The two mile stretch of white sand that runs from the Hilton Hawaiian Village to Kapiolani Park is commonly called Waikiki Beach, though sections along the way have their own names and characteristics.

In the early morning the beach belongs to walkers and joggers – and it's surprisingly quiet. Strolling down the beach toward Diamond Head at sunrise can actually be a meditative experience.

By midmorning it looks like a normal resort beach, with boogie board and surfboard concessionaries setting up shop and catamarans pulling up on the beach offering $20 sails. By noon it is packed and the challenge is to walk down the beach without stepping on anyone.

Most of Waikiki's beautiful white sands are not its own. Tons of sand have been barged in over the years, much of it from Papohaku Beach on Molokai.

As the beachfront developed, landowners haphazardly constructed seawalls and off-shore barriers to protect their property. In the process they blocked the natural forces of sand accretion, and erosion has long been a serious problem at Waikiki.

Sections of the beach are still being replenished with imported sand. Much of it ends up washing into the ocean, filling channels and depressions and altering the surf breaks.

Waikiki is good for swimming and other beach activities most of the year. Between May and September, summer swells can make the water a little rough. At such times it's better for surfing than swimming.

Overall, Waikiki beaches aren't that good for snorkelling. The best of them is Sans Souci. There are lifeguards and showers at most of the beaches.

Kahanamoku Beach Kahanamoku Beach, fronting the Hilton Hawaiian Village, is the westernmost section of Waikiki. It was named for Duke Kahanamoku, a surfer and swimmer who won Olympic gold in the 100-metre freestyle in 1912 and became a Hawaiian celebrity.

Kahanamoku Beach is protected by a breakwater at one end and a pier at the other, with a coral reef running between the two. It's a calm swimming area with a sandy bottom that slopes gradually.

Kahanamoku is not as crowded as the central Waikiki beaches, though you do have to deal with the Hilton crowd and all the toys, from huge floating aqua-cycles and glass-bottom paddleboats to a helicopter pad.

There's a large saltwater lagoon just inland of the beach, which has pumps to drain and circulate the water. It reaches a depth of 15 feet in the middle and is like a giant swimming pool.

Fort DeRussy Beach Fort DeRussy Beach,

one of the least crowded Waikiki beaches, borders 1800 feet of the Fort DeRussy Military Reservation. Like all beaches in Hawaii, it's public. The federal government provides lifeguards.

The water is usually calm and good for swimming. It's marked by buoys and has a floating raft you can swim to. You can snorkel there, though it's nothing to rush down for. There's also boogie boarding and surfing. The stretch from the lifeguard tower down to the Hilton pier is open to windsurfers.

A grassy lawn under shade palms provides an alternative to frying on the sand.

There are two beach huts where you can rent water sports equipment. Prime Time rents boogie boards for $3.50 for the first hour and $2.50 for each additional hour, and snorkel sets for $3 for one hour and $6 for three hours.

Waikiki Windsurfing (tel 949-8952) rents windsurfing equipment for $18 for the first hour and $12 for each additional hour. It's $30 for a 1¼-hour lesson.

Gray's Beach Gray's Beach is on the Ewa side of the Halekulani Hotel. The sandy channel that runs out from the beach and crosses the reef is a popular spot for local distance swimmers.

The seawall in front of the Halekulani was built so close to the waterline that the beach is often totally submerged.

Between the Halekulani and the Royal Hawaiian Hotel the beach varies in width from season to season. The waters are shallow and calm.

Central Waikiki Beach The area between the Royal Hawaiian Hotel and the Waikiki Beach Center is the busiest section of the whole beach.

Most of the beach has a shallow bottom with a gradual slope. There's pretty good swimming, though there's a lot of activity, with catamarans, surfers and plenty of other swimmers in the water. Keep your eyes open.

Offshore are Queen's Surf and Canoe's Surf, Waikiki's best-known surf breaks.

Waikiki Beach Center The area opposite the Hyatt Regency Waikiki is the Waikiki Beach Center. There are restrooms, showers, a police station and rental concessions.

The Wizard Stones of Kapaemahu – four boulders on the Diamond Head side of the police station – are said to contain the secrets and healing powers of four sorcerers – Kapaemahu, Kinohi, Kapuni and Kahaloa – who arrived from Tahiti in ancient times. Before returning to Tahiti they transferred their powers to these stones.

Star Beach Boys rents out surfboards and boogie boards for $5 for the first hour and $3 for each additional hour. They also give outrigger canoe rides for $5. Down by the Surfrider another concession stand rents boogie boards for $3 an hour and $5 for two hours.

Kuhio Beach Park Kuhio Beach Park is marked on one end by Kapahulu Groin, a walled storm drain with a walkway on top that juts out into the ocean from the end of Kapahulu Ave.

A low breakwater seawall runs about 1300 feet out from Kapahulu Groin, paralleling the beach. It was built to control sand erosion and in the process two enclosed swimming pools were formed. The breakwater is called The Wall. Local kids walk out on The Wall, but it's very slippery and to the uninitiated can be dangerous.

The pool closest to the groin is best for swimming, with the water near the breakwater likely to be over your head. However, because water circulation is limited it can get murky and sometimes collects a noticeable film of suntan oil.

The 'Watch Out Deep Holes' sign refers to holes in the sandy bottom that can be created by swirling currents. They can take waders by surprise.

The park is named after Prince Kuhio, who maintained his residence on this beach. His house was torn down in 1936, 14 years after his death, in order to expand the beach. Old timers gather each afternoon to play chess and cribbage at the sidewalk pavilions.

Kapahulu Groin Kapahulu Groin is one of Waikiki's hottest boogie boarding spots. If the surf's right you can find a few dozen boogie boarders, mostly teenage boys, riding the waves.

The kids ride straight for the wall and then veer away at the last moment, drawing 'oohs' and 'ahs' from the tourists who gather to watch them. Boogie boards can be rented from a stand for $5 an hour and $15 a day.

This is also a great place to catch sunsets.

Kapiolani Beach Park Kapiolani Beach Park starts at Kapahulu Groin and runs down to the Natatorium, past Waikiki Aquarium.

Queen's Surf is the wide midsection of Kapiolani Beach. The area around the pavilion is a popular beach with the gay community. It's a pretty good area for swimming, with a sandy bottom. The section between here and Kapahulu Groin is shallow and has a lot of broken coral.

Kapiolani Beach is a relaxed place with little of the frenzy of activity found in front of the central strip of Waikiki hotels. It's a popular weekend picnicking spot for local families who unload the kids to splash in the water as they line up the barbecue grills.

There's a big grassy field to lay out on, good for spreading out a beach towel and unpacking a picnic basket. There's free parking near the beach off Kalakaua Ave.

The surfing area offshore is called Public's.

Natatorium The Natatorium, at the Diamond Head end of Kapiolani Beach, is a 100-metre-long saltwater swimming pool built after WW I as a memorial for soldiers who died in that war. There were once hopes of hosting an Olympics, with this pool as the focal point.

Waves bouncing off the Natatorium, which is now closed and in disrepair, create erosion problems but because of its status as a memorial, sentiment has been against tearing it down.

Sans Souci Beach Down by the New Otani Kaimana Beach Hotel, Sans Souci Beach is a nice little sandy beach away from the main tourist scene.

A shallow coral reef close to shore makes for calm, protected waters and provides reasonably good snorkelling. Better coral can be found by following the Kapua Channel, which cuts through the reef.

Among those who come down for their daily swim is Arthur Murray, the ageing dance school master.

There are outdoor showers and a lifeguard at Sans Souci, and restrooms next door at the Natatorium.

Royal Hawaiian Hotel

The Royal Hawaiian was Hawaii's first luxury hotel. With its pink turrets and Moorish/Spanish architecture, it's a throwback to the era when Rudolph Valentino was *the* romantic idol and travel to Hawaii was by luxury liner.

The hotel was originally on 20 acres of coconut grove but over the years the grounds have been chipped away by a huge shopping centre on one side and a highrise mega-hotel on the other. The Royal Hawaiian is a survivor.

Inside, the hotel is lovely and airy with high ceilings and chandeliers and everything in rose colours. The gardens are filled with bird song, a rare sound in most of Waikiki. It's a neat place to walk through.

Fort DeRussy

Fort DeRussy Military Reservation is a US Army post used mainly as a recreation centre for the armed forces. This large chunk of Waikiki real estate was acquired by the US Army a few years after Hawaii was annexed to the USA. Before that it was swampy marshland where Hawaiian chiefs hunted ducks.

The Hale Koa Hotel on the property is open only to military personnel and their families and guests. The army is considering plans to develop a much larger resort. There's a public beach and a military museum on the grounds.

US Army Museum of Hawaii Battery Randolph, a reinforced concrete building built in 1911 as a coast artillery battery, houses the army museum at Fort DeRussy. It once held two 14-inch disappearing rifles with a 14-mile range designed to recoil below the concrete walls for reloading after each firing. A 55-ton lead counter weight would then return the carriage to position.

The museum is full of weapons, war stories and military history as it relates to Hawaii. It's open from 10 am to 4.30 pm daily except Mondays. Admission is free.

Oceanarium

The Pacific Beach Hotel (2490 Kalakaua Ave) houses an impressive three-storey 280,000-gallon aquarium that forms the backdrop for three of their restaurants. They claim it's the world's largest. Divers enter the Oceanarium to feed the tropical fish at 9 am, noon and 1, 5.30, 7 and 8 pm daily. Show up then for the show or anytime to take a look.

Dolphins

The Kahala Hilton, in the Kahala area beyond Diamond Head, has three Atlantic bottlenose dolphins in a lagoon as well as penguins, green sea turtles and tropical reef fish on display. Coached by trainers from Sea Life Park, the dolphins put on a short show for smelt and herring at 11 am and 2 and 4 pm. They jump and dive, stand on their tails, vocalise, hula dance, play volleyball and the like. The show is free but you may have to pay to park.

Damien Museum

St Augustine's Church, off Kalakaua Ave and Ohua St, has been a quiet little sanctuary in the midst of the hotel district. Dwarfed by the block-long Hawaiian Regent Hotel on one side and the Pacific Beach on the other, it's scheduled to be demolished to make way for yet another hotel.

If it's still there you might want to check out the Damien Museum, honouring Father Damien, who lived and worked in the leper colony on Molokai.

Murals

Waikiki has two particularly noteworthy murals. The outside wall of Wave Waikiki, a nightclub at 1877 Kalakaua Ave, has an interesting ukiyoe-influenced mural; and the First Hawaiian Bank, 2181 Kalakaua Ave, has murals with scenes of Hawaiian life by the late Jean Charlot.

Ala Wai Canal

Late in the afternoon, outrigger canoe teams can be seen paddling up and down Ala Wai Canal.

Kapiolani Park

The nearly 200-acre Kapiolani Park, at the Diamond Head end of Waikiki, was a gift from King Kalakaua to Honolulu in 1877. It was Hawaii's first public park and he dedicated it to his wife, Queen Kapiolani.

In its early days, horse racing and band concerts were its biggest attractions. Although the race track has gone, the concerts continue and Kapiolani Park is still the site of all sorts of community activities.

The park contains the Waikiki Aquarium, built in 1904, as well as the Honolulu Zoo, Kapiolani Beach Park, the Waikiki Shell, Kodak Hula Show grounds, Kapiolani Bandstand and tennis courts. Parades marching through Waikiki usually end up at the park. It has sports fields, huge lawns and tall banyan trees.

The Royal Hawaiian Band presents free concerts from 2 to 3.30 pm every Sunday at the Kapiolani Bandstand. Dance competitions, Hawaiian music concerts and other activities occur throughout the year. Check the Honolulu papers for schedules.

The Waikiki Shell is an outdoor amphitheatre with symphony, jazz and rock concerts. For information on performances, check the papers or call the Blaisdell Center (tel 521-2911).

Kapiolani is one of the top-rated kite-flying parks in the USA. Kite Fantasy (tel 922-KITE), a kite shop at the nearby New Otani Kaimana Beach Hotel, puts on kite shows from 11 am to 2 pm on Tuesdays, Wednesdays and Thursdays on the grassy lawns beyond the tennis courts.

It's a pleasant park and despite all the activities that go on, it's large enough to have a lot of quiet space.

Waikiki Aquarium This aquarium (2777 Kalakaua Ave; tel 923-9741) has sharks, moray eels, flash-back cuttlefish wavering with pulses of light, and rare Hawaiian fish with names like the bearded armorhead and the sling-jawed wrasse.

One tank displays the mudskippers of a mangrove swamp, another the swaying tentacles of corals which help build Micronesian reefs.

In 1985 the aquarium was the first to breed the Palauan chambered nautilus in captivity. One of these sea creatures, with its unique spiral, chambered shell, is on display.

There are also some giant clams from Palau that were less than an inch long when acquired in 1982 and now measure several feet, the largest in the USA.

An outdoor tank re-creates a rocky Hawaiian shore and has some of the more common tropical fish found in inshore waters. There's also a touch tank for children, a green sea turtle and a Hawaiian monk seal.

The aquarium is not large, but it's well worth the $2.50 admission fee (free for children under 16). It's open from 9 am to 5 pm daily. Reef walks, lectures and travel programmes are occasionally offered.

Honolulu Zoo The zoo is somewhat stark and artificial, with lots of small concrete cages. It has elephants, tigers, bears, white rhinos, storks, flamingos, giraffes, monkeys and Galapágos tortoises.

The reptile building has the tiny bright-green and black poison arrow frog from Panama, introduced into Manoa Valley in 1932 for mosquito control, and the green iguana, also found on Oahu.

A sign that reads: 'This is the best zoo to be found for 2300 miles in any direction', is a slight exaggeration as Hilo's rainforest zoo, though smaller, is more natural and better.

The zoo is open from 8.30 am to 4 pm

Artist Earl Shimokawa, at the Art fence in
Kapiolani Park

daily. Admission is $1 but children under 12
accompanied by an adult are admitted free.

In front of the zoo there is a large banyan
tree which is home to hundreds of white
pigeons – escapees from a small group
brought to the zoo in the 1940s.

Art in the Park Local artists have been
hanging their paintings on the fence around
the zoo on weekends for more than 25 years.
If you'd like a painting, it's a good place to
buy directly from the artist. The artwork is
on display from 10 am to 4 pm on weekends.

Kodak Hula Show The Kodak Hula Show,
off Monsarrat Ave near the Waikiki Shell, is
a staged photo opportunity of hula dancers,
ti-leaf skirts and ukuleles. The musicians are
a group of older ladies who performed at the
Royal Hawaiian Hotel in days gone by.

This is the scene in postcards where
dancers hold up letters forming the words
'Hawaii' and 'Aloha'. The whole thing is
quite touristy, though entertaining if you're
in the mood, and it's free.

Kodak has been putting on this show since
1939. The benches are set up stadium-style

around a grassy stage area with the sun at
your back. The idea is for everyone to shoot
a lot of film. It works. Even though Kodak
doesn't monopolise the film market
anymore, the tradition continues.

Shows are held from 10 to 11.15 am on
Tuesdays, Wednesdays and Thursdays.
Make sure you're on time because once it
starts they only admit people between acts.
The gates open at 8.30 am.

Places to Stay
Waikiki's main beachfront strip, Kalakaua
Ave, is largely lined with highrise hotels and
$100-plus rooms.

The best value are the smaller and less
pretentious hostelries on the side streets. A
few hotels in the Ala Wai Canal area are just
as nice as hotels on the beach but half the
price. The fact that they are less crowded and
less impersonal can well make up for the
walk to the beach, which is never more than
10 or 15 minutes away anyway.

In many hotels the rooms themselves are
the same, only the views vary; generally the
higher the floor, the higher the price. On the
main drags the lower floors can get a lot of
traffic noise. Some of the cheaper side streets
are less hectic. Our own preference is for the
quieter east end of Waikiki, down near
Kapahulu Ave and the zoo.

There are no laws governing what kind of
rooms can be said to have ocean views or to
front the ocean. Some 'ocean views' are mere
glimpses of the water seen through a series
of highrises. If you're paying a lot for the
view, check out the room first.

Many of Waikiki's hotels are undergoing
major renovations and as they're completed,
room rates climb.

Waikiki has many more hotel rooms
than condos. Most Waikiki condos are
filled with long-term residents and there
isn't the proliferation of vacation rental
agents that there is in Kihei and Kona. The
best way to find a condo is to look in the
Vacation Rentals section of the daily paper.
If you're staying a long time, condos are
usually the best deals.

Places to Stay – bottom end

Hale Aloha Hostel (2417 Prince Edward St, Honolulu, HI 96815; tel 926-8313), a member of AYH and IYHF, is a 50-bed hostel on a back street a few short blocks from Waikiki Beach. Dorm beds are $11.50. There are a few studios for couples at $26, each with small refrigerators, TVs and their own bathrooms. For studios, paid reservations are required; you can book a maximum of three nights. Office hours are from 8 to 10 am and from 5 to 9 pm. Dorms are locked during the day. Reservations and hostel membership are required. If you can't get a bed, try the hostel up by the university – you can buy hostel membership there as well. Both hostels are run by Thelma Akau and her family.

InterClub Hostel Waikiki (2413 Kuhio Ave, Honolulu, HI 96815; tel 924-2636) is one of a small Australian/American chain of hostels. There are 63 bunk beds, usually arranged five to a room, with shared bathrooms. To get in you need a passport and can't be working in Hawaii (they ask people who get work passing out flyers to leave!). Reservations aren't taken, so if they're full (which they often are), show up in the morning and hang around until someone leaves. If you call from the airport and a bed is available, they say they'll hold it long enough for you to get there by bus. Office hours are from 8 am to midnight.

The staff include international travellers working for room and board and lots of languages float in the air. Guests are mostly backpackers and younger travellers. Unlike the AYH hostel, you can come and go as you please all day and there aren't lots of rules. There's a weekly beer and wine party, a communal kitchen and a washer/dryer. The rooms closest to the heavy traffic on Kuhio can be very noisy. It costs $18 a night per person.

Waikiki Prince Hotel (2431 Prince Edward St, Honolulu, HI 96815; tel 922-1544) has 30 units next door to Hale Aloha Hostel. Rooms are basic and not all that cheery, but the people working there make up for it with aloha spirit. They get an inter-national crowd, with a lot of backpackers in the summer. Standard rooms cost $34 a day and $230 a week, while rooms with kitchenettes cost from $38 a day and $255 a week, but note that these rates include the 9% tax. All rooms have cable TV and air-con. Parking costs $3 a day.

Waikiki Circle Hotel (2464 Kalakaua Ave, Honolulu, HI 96815; tel 923-1571) has 100 rooms with lanais and TVs. They're nothing special but there's nothing wrong with them either – and you can't beat this price and still be right opposite Waikiki Beach. Singles/doubles cost $39/42, while rooms with an unobstructed view of the ocean cost $5 more.

A fair number of retirees return each winter to *Royal Grove Hotel* (151 Uluniu Ave, Honolulu, HI 96815; tel 923-7691). Kitchenette units cost $35 in the old wing (with no air-con) and from $44 in the new wing (with air-con). Rooms without kitchenettes cost $30/34 in the old/new wing. There's a small pool.

Tradewinds Plaza, 2572 Lemon Rd, is a condo complex near Queen Kapiolani Hotel. Sheila Bangert (1015 Wilder Ave, No 603, Honolulu, HI 96822; tel 538-0679) handles eight of the units, which cost from $40 to $59 a day. There are weekly and monthly rates, and rates are about 10% less in the low season. The best is the 10th floor studio, which has a queen-size bed, a TV, a phone on which you can make free local calls, air-con, a refrigerator, a microwave, free parking and a bit of an ocean view. It can also be rented by the month for $1100. It's a nice unit, but if you're not an early riser the incredibly noisy garbage trucks that service the nearby hotels in the morning may annoy you.

The Queen Kapiolani Hotel (tel 922-1941) manages the *Coral Surf* apartments, next door to Tradewinds. They are rented by the month, for $800.

Niihau Apartment Hotel (247 Beachwalk, Honolulu, HI 96815; tel 922-1607) is one of Waikiki's better condo bargains. However, only 20 of the 43 units are in the rental pool and winter residency is booked up far in advance. The units have kitchens, lanais and TVs. One-bedroom units cost $45, while two-bedroom units for up to four people cost $66. There's a three-night minimum stay period, no pool and no parking.

Places to Stay – middle

Ilima Hotel (445 Nohonani St, Honolulu, HI 96815; tel 923-5200; 800-367-5172 from the USA, 800-663-1118 from Canada, 008-335-046 from Australia) is a great deal. You could easily spend twice as much in many of the big Waikiki hotels and not match what you get here. All room are studios – very large and light with lanais, kitchens and tasteful rattan furnishings. Local phone calls and parking are free, which is rare in Waikiki. The lobby is decorated with koa wood and colourful Hawaiiana paintings, including a large mural of the god Ku and the goddess Hina in an ocean of eternal bliss. It's in a less hurried section of Waikiki, a 15 minute walk from the beach. There's a pool and sauna. Low season rates start at $56/63 for single/double studios on the 4th floor, and rise to $78/89 for those on the top floor. There are 99 rooms, including some one and two-bedroom suites. Everything's $12 more from 15 December to 31 March.

Waikiki Sand Villa Hotel (2375 Ala Wai Blvd, Honolulu, HI 96815; tel 922-4744; 800-247-1903 from the mainland, 800-342-1557 from the neighbouring islands) is a 223-room hotel on Ala Wai Canal, a 10 minute walk from Waikiki Beach. Rooms have cable TV, refrigerators and nice wall prints. Each has a lanai, some with views across the golf course toward Manoa Valley. Standard rooms cost $49/59 in the low/high season. It's good value for this price range.

Continental Surf (2426 Kuhio Ave, Honolulu, HI 96815; tel 922-2755, 800-245-7873) is a 140-room 21-storey hotel a few blocks from the ocean. Rates are $47 for standard rooms and $62 for rooms with kitchenettes. In the high season it's $14 more. All rooms are the same size (small), so the ones with kitchenettes are a bit squeezed. The decor is uninspiring but it's a modern hotel and good

value. Many units have views of the ocean or the mountains. The higher you go, the better the view, and the rates are the same on all floors.

Outrigger (Box 88559, Honolulu, HI 96830; tel 926-0679; toll free 800-367-5170 from the USA and Canada, 0014-800-125-642 from Australia) is buying up Waikiki's middle-range hotels left and right and has just put $125 million into renovating a number of them.

At last count Outrigger had 21 hotels. Generally they're pretty good deals, though there's a wide range in price and quality. If they're still running their 'Free Ride' promotion you'll get a free rental car for the length of your stay if you request it at the time you make reservations.

Outrigger Waikiki Surf (2200 Kuhio Ave, tel 923-7671) is Outrigger's best deal. The 288 recently refurbished rooms are small but nice, each with a tiny refrigerator. Rooms cost from $50, kitchenette units from $65, and one-bedroom units for up to four people from $75. Rates are $5 less in the low season. The pool is minuscule and practically on the sidewalk. The staff are friendly, they'll store your luggage, and there's a hospitality shower if you have a late flight out.

If the Waikiki Surf is full, Outrigger's *Waikiki Surf East* (422 Royal Hawaiian Ave) and *Waikiki Surf West* (412 Lewers St) are right around the corner. Rates at both begin at $45/50 in the low/high season, and all rooms have kitchenettes.

Outrigger also has two hotels, the Coral Seas and the Waikiki Towers, on Lewers St, closer to the beach. Both can be recommended.

The 109-room *Outrigger Coral Seas* (250 Lewers St, tel 923-3882) has standard rooms for $50/60 in the low/high season. Kitchenette units cost from $65/70 in the low/high season. Though the hotel is not much to look at from the outside, the rooms are pretty nice.

The 440-room *Outrigger Waikiki Tower* (200 Lewers St, tel 922-6424) is a modern highrise. Rooms have lanais and are comfortable and nicely decorated in pastels. Rooms from the 6th floor down cost $70/80 in the low/high season. Kitchenettes begin at $85. It's a five minute walk to the beach.

Ala Wai Terrace (1547 Ala Wai Blvd, tel 926-0679), at the edge of the Ala Wai Canal, between Waikiki and the Ala Moana Center, is the cheapest Outrigger property. Studios costs from $40/45 in the low/high season.

Outrigger has two hotels right on the beach: the *Outrigger Reef*, with rooms from $100 to $185, and the *Outrigger Waikiki*, with rooms from $120 to $195. Despite the price, these are not luxury hotels by any means.

Hotel Honolulu (376 Kaiolu St, Honolulu, HI 96815; tel 926-2766; 800-426-2766 from the USA) is Waikiki's only gay hotel. It's a quiet oasis on a side street a block from busy Kuhio Ave and the heart of the gay district. The three-storey hotel has the character of an unhurried inn, with helpful management, lots of hanging ferns and potted orchids and a peach-coloured cockatoo at the front desk. There's a bulletin board, a roof deck for sunning and Dutch coffee and doughnuts available all day. The 19 units are decorated with flair, each with its own theme, such as 'Safari', 'Rangoon' or 'Norma Jean'. They are large and very comfortable, with lanais, kitchens, ceiling fans and air-con. Studios cost from $49 to $64 and one-bedroom units from $79 to $96. Parking is free. This is a hotel for tourists and travellers, not a local hang-out, and straights are also welcome.

Waikiki Grand (134 Kapahulu Ave, Honolulu, HI 96815; tel 923-1511) is a 172-room hotel opposite the zoo. It may be a bit noisy as it's undergoing renovations, but in the meantime rates start at $55 for a standard room and $75 for a room with a kitchenette.

Quality Inn (175 Paoakalani Ave, Honolulu, HI 96815; tel 922-3861; 800-367-2317) has 451 rooms. It doesn't have a whole lot of character, and orange vinyl predominates. However this is the cheapest of the nationwide chain hotels, and it has a couple of non-smoking floors. Rooms cost from $65 to $99 in the old tower and from $83 to $121 in the spiffier Pali Tower. They're all $9 cheaper in low season.

The Breakers (250 Beachwalk, Honolulu, HI 96815; tel 923-3181, 800-426-0494) is a lowrise hotel with 66 kitchenette units surrounding a well-used courtyard pool. This is one of the more pleasant places at the western end of town and the staff are upbeat and friendly. Rooms cost from $79/82 a single/double. Avoid the rooms close to Saratoga Rd, which carries lots of traffic.

Queen Kapiolani (150 Kapahulu Ave, Honolulu, HI 96815; tel 922-1941, 800-367-5004) is a 315-room hotel at the quieter end of Waikiki. Standard-looking rooms cost from $92 to $125. This is an older hotel with an ageing regal theme – chandeliers, high ceilings and fading paintings of Hawaiian royalty. The small pool has an unobstructed view of Diamond Head.

Places to Stay – top end

These hotels all have standard 1st class amenities and in-house restaurants. All are on the beach or across the street from it and all except the New Otani have swimming pools.

The new 298-room *Waikiki Parc Hotel* (2233 Helumoa Rd, Honolulu, HI 96815; tel 921-7272; 800-422-0450) is across the street from its more up-market sister, the Halekulani. The comfy rooms have lots of nice touches, like ceramic tile floors, white shuttered lanai doors, remote-control TV and two phones. It has a pleasant, understated elegance and is more relaxed and appealing than the Halekulani. Standard rooms cost from $105, while those with an ocean view cost from $165.

The pink Moorish/Spanish-style *Royal Hawaiian Hotel* (2259 Kalakaua Ave, Honolulu, HI 96815; tel 923-7311; 800-325-3535) was Waikiki's first luxury hotel. In terms of atmosphere it's still its finest. It's a beautiful hotel – cool and airy and loaded with charm. The older section maintains the original character, some of the rooms having quiet garden views. It's easier to book too, since most guests prefer the modern highrise wing with its ocean views. Rates are from $160/195 in the low/high season. It's owned by the Sheraton.

The *Hyatt Regency Waikiki* (2424 Kalakaua Ave, Honolulu, HI 96815; tel 923-1234; 800-228-9000) has twin 40-storey towers with 1230 newly renovated rooms. There is a maximum of 18 rooms per floor, so it's quieter and feels more exclusive than other hotels its size. Rooms are nicely decorated in pastels with rattan furnishings and cost from $150 to $235, depending on the view. Between the towers there's a large atrium with cascading waterfalls and orchids, red torch ginger and other tropical vegetation.

The *New Otani Kaimana Beach Hotel* (2863 Kalakaua Ave, Honolulu, HI 96815; tel 923-1555; 800-421-8795) is on Sans Souci Beach on the quieter Diamond Head side of Waikiki. It has 125 units with rooms from $95 to $160 and studios with kitchenettes from $100. The hotel's Hau Tree Lanai restaurant is right on the beach.

The *Hawaiian Regent* (2552 Kalakaua Ave, Honolulu, HI 96815; tel 922-6611; 800-367-5370 from the USA or Canada, 0014-800-125-666 from Australia) has 1346 rooms and is maze-like. The challenge is to find the lobby. Rooms are quite ordinary for the money. Rates range from $130 to $210.

The 716-room *Holiday Inn Waikiki Beach* (2570 Kalakaua Ave, Honolulu, HI 96815; tel 922-2511; 800-877-7666) looks almost like a reflection of the bigger Hawaiian Regent across the street, and the rooms are just as nice, though cheaper. Rates start at $90/105 in the low/high season.

The 1150-room *Sheraton Princess Kaiulani* (120 Kaiulani Ave, Honolulu, HI 96815; tel 922-5811) is the Sheraton's cheapest Waikiki property. It was built in the 1950s by Matson Navigation to help develop Waikiki into a middle-class destination. From the outside it looks like an inner city housing project. From the inside it's nice enough, but pricey at around $95 to $160. It's in the busy heart of Waikiki, across the street from the beach.

The *Sheraton* pretty much owns a little stretch of the beach, boasting 4138 rooms in its Waikiki hotels. The toll-free numbers for all Sheraton's hotels are 800-325-3535 from the USA and Canada and 008-222-229 from Australia.

The Moana was Hawaii's first beachfront hotel, built in 1901. It's now the *Sheraton Moana* and has recently undergone a $50 million historic restoration, authentic right down to the elegant carved columns on the porte-cochere. Unfortunately, the highrise *Sheraton Surfrider* has been joined to the Moana, crowding in on her original charm. The 224 rooms in the original Moana are called the Banyan Wing after the 100-year-old tree in the rear courtyard. Rates start at $175/210 in the low/high season. Rooms in the highrise Tower Wing start at $120/180 in the low/high. It's being renamed the *Moana Surfrider* (tel 922-3111), and is at 2365 Kalakaua Ave, Honolulu, HI 96815.

Sheraton Waikiki (2255 Kalakaua Ave, Honolulu, HI 96815; tel 922-4422) is a 1900-room mega-hotel that looms over the Royal Hawaiian Hotel. The bustling lobby resembles an exclusive Tokyo shopping centre, lined with lots of expensive jewellery stores and boutiques with French names and designer labels. The hotel has central elevators and some of the longest corridors in Hawaii, though it tries to compensate for long walks through winding hallways with trippy tropical jungle wallpaper. Rates start at $150.

Hilton Hawaiian Village (2005 Kalia Rd, Honolulu, HI 96815; tel 949-4321; 800-445-8667) is Hawaii's largest hotel, with 2522 rooms. The ultimate in mass tourism, the 'Home of Don Ho' is practically a package-tour city unto itself. It's self-contained for people who never want to leave the hotel grounds. Everything's busy and impersonal, right down to the roped-off lines at the front desk, which resembles an airline check-in counter. The Hilton is on a nice beach, though it's anything but low-key and buzzes with activities ranging from aqua-cycles to helicopters. Rates start at $160.

Places to Stay – deluxe

Halekulani (2199 Kalia Rd, Honolulu, HI 96815; tel 923-2311; 800-223-6800) is considered to be Waikiki's premier hotel. The

412 rooms are very modern and boast all amenities right down to three phones per room just in case you didn't want to get away from it all. Rooms come with deep soaking tubs, silent refrigerators, fresh flowers and homemade chocolates. It's all very sophisticated and elegant, if a little pompous. Rooms with garden views are $195 and those fronting the ocean are $320. Suites cost from $475.

Kahala Hilton (5000 Kahala Ave, Honolulu, HI 96816; tel 734-2211; 800-367-2525) is in the exclusive Kahala residential area on its own quiet stretch of beach. This is where the rich and famous go when they want to avoid the Waikiki scene 10 minutes away. Rather than formal opulence, the Kahala Hilton has a more appealing casualness. It's subdued and private. Staff who have been working there for decades and guests who return year after year know each other by name. The guest list is Hawaii's most regal: Charles and Di, King Juan Carlos and Queen Sofia, and the last five US presidents. The two-storey older wing has some rooms on the hotel's enclosed lagoon, with dolphins swimming just beyond the lanais. Rooms are large and plush, but not extravagant. Prices range from $195 for a mountain view to $1875 for the presidential suite. (See the South-East & Windward Oahu map.)

Places to Eat

Waikiki has no shortage of places to eat, though the vast majority of the cheaper ones are easy to pass up. Generally the best inexpensive food is found outside Waikiki, where most Honolulu residents live and eat. Waikiki's top-end restaurants, on the other hand, are some of the island's best, though they'll quickly burn a hole in your wallet.

About a mile up Kapahulu Ave from Waikiki Beach there's a row of ethnic restaurants with Hawaiian, Japanese, Thai, Korean, Vietnamese, Chinese and Mexican food. Keo's, the crown jewel of the neighbourhood, is the only one that's neither cheap nor a hole in the wall. Keo's is included

with the middle-range restaurants; all the others come into the bottom-end category.

If you don't have a car, you're better off walking from Waikiki than taking a bus, as bus stops along Kapahulu Ave aren't conveniently located and most of the routes loop off before you get to the restaurants anyway.

Breakfast Ideas Waikiki has a wide range of breakfast options. Signs draped from buildings advertising breakfast specials for a few dollars are commonplace. *McDonald's*, *Jack in the Box* and *Burger King* offer quick and inexpensive breakfasts from just about every other corner. If you're really hungry, the $4 breakfast buffet at *Perry's Smorgy* is a great deal.

From around $8 to $12, you can try one of the breakfast buffets offered by many of the hotels but few are worth the money.

For a real treat, there's breakfast at *Michel's* right on Sans Souci beach. You can get croissants and coffee for as little as $5, or a full breakfast served on fine china for the same money as the hotel buffets – and it's a much classier experience. The following sections have more details on these restaurants.

Sunday Brunches Waikiki's most renowned Sunday brunch buffet is at Orchid's at the Halekulani hotel. Its top competition is across town at the Kahala Hilton. Orchid's has the better view, while the Kahala is more relaxed.

Orchid's (tel 923-2311) has an ocean view and a soothing flute and harp duo. You'd best have reservations or be ready for a two-hour wait. They have sashimi, rack of lamb, roast beef and turkey, wonderful-looking sauces and a rich dessert bar. It's open from 10 am to 2.30 pm and costs $25.

The *Kahala Hilton* (tel 734-2211) has Sunday brunch in two places. The Hala Terrace (11.30 am to 1.30 pm), the more casual of the two, is open-air with an ocean view and you have the option of ordering from the menu. The Maile Terrace (10 am to 12.30 pm) is enclosed and overlooks the dolphin lagoon; it has a buffet only, including made-to-order omelettes and Belgian waffle bars. Both have salads, hot meals and desserts prepared by the same chef for around $20. The restaurants will validate your ticket for free parking.

The *Parc Cafe* (tel 921-7272) in the Waikiki Parc Hotel has a Sunday brunch from 11 am to 2 pm with a buffet of eggs benedict, grilled ono in lemon sauce, ginger chicken, sesame beef, fruits and pastries for $13. The setting is casually elegant and though it doesn't have as much variety as the other buffets it's perhaps the best value.

Michel's at the Colony Surf (tel 923-6552) has champagne Sunday brunch, not a buffet. Meals range from $15 for a fresh spinach omelette to $25 for opakapaka and include fruit, muffins, sweet rolls, champagne cocktail and Kona coffee. If you get a seat by the window you can't beat it.

More details about these restaurants are provided in the following sections.

Places to Eat – bottom end

The *New Tokyo Restaurant* (286 Beach Walk) is a popular local lunch spot with good, cheap Japanese food served in a pleasant setting. Oyako-ju, which is chicken, steamed egg and onions with a sweetened sauce over rice, costs $3.50. The yakizakana plate with grilled fish (we were served salmon!) and rice is $4. Both are served with miso, pickles and rice. Other lunch specials cost from $3 to $7. Dinner prices are about double the lunch prices. It's closed on Sundays.

Five Spices (432 Ena Rd) has inexpensive Cantonese and Sichuan dishes. The lunch special (until 5 pm) for $5.55 comes with soup (the hot and sour is good), brown rice and a choice of dishes. The eggplant with sweetened hot Sichuan sauce can be recommended, though beware if you're not used to spicy food. They'll cool it down on request. Most meat and duck standards cost $6 to $7, and vegetarian dishes are about $1 cheaper. This is a casual sort of place, the kind where the owner sits at a dining room table shelling peas. It's open from 11 am to 10.30 pm.

The *Shore Bird Broiler* at the Outrigger Reef Hotel (2169 Kalia Rd) has a big grill at the end of the dining room where everyone cooks their own meal. Fish costs $7, garlic or teriyaki chicken $10 and steak $12. Meals come with chilli, rice and a simple salad bar with slices of papaya and pineapple. The salad bar alone costs $6. There's usually a coupon in *This Week* magazine that knocks $1 off the price of all meals. The Shore Bird fronts the ocean and has tables inside and out. It's a bustling place that becomes a disco in the evening.

Perry's Smorgy at the Outrigger Waikiki Hotel (2335 Kalakaua Ave) has one of the best breakfast deals around and a great beach view if you get one of the dozen lanai tables. It's a buffet, with fresh pineapple, papaya, bananas and watermelon on ice surrounded by a zillion orchids. They also have breakfast standards like pancakes, eggs, sausage, danish and slices from a round of ham. It's a touristy crowd and the food isn't top quality, but the fruit's as fresh as that available anywhere, and you can't beat the $4 price. Breakfast is served from 7 to 10.30 am, there's a buffet lunch from 11 am to 2.30 pm for $5.45, and dinner is served from 5 to 9 pm for $8. On Tuesdays, Fridays and Sundays when the Outrigger does its beachfront Polynesian show below, Perry's lanai tables become free balcony seats.

Malia's Cantina (311 Lewers St) has authentically spicy, inexpensive Mexican food. Two vegetarian tacos cost $2.50, two beef or chicken $4; and rice and beans are $1 extra. The corn tortillas are handmade and portions are generous. They have good homemade salsa and chips. There's a bar and music videos. The margarita grande is $2.25 from 2 to 8 pm. The restaurant is open from 11 am to 2 am daily.

Hamburger Mary's (2109 Kuhio Ave) is a restaurant and bar in the middle of the gay district. Burgers range from $4.25 for a standard to $6.25 for an avocado burger. A variety of salads served with multigrain bread are about the same price. They have creative homemade soups, such as gazpacho and cinnamon fruit, for $3 a bowl. For appetisers the sautéed mushrooms with cheddar cheese is good, though it costs

$6.75. Servings aren't as large as they used to be.

The *Noodle Shop* in the Waikiki Sand Villa Hotel (2375 Ala Wai Blvd, tel 922-4744) serves a breakfast of sliced pineapple, egg, pancakes and coffee for $3 from 7 to 10.30 am. At dinner they have Italian pastas, oriental noodles like saimin and udon, fish and meat dishes and a salad bar. Prices are moderate. They sometimes have an all-you-can-eat spaghetti dinner with salad for $5. Dinner is served from 5 to 8 pm.

It's Greek To Me in building A of the Royal Hawaiian Shopping Center has gyros, souvlaki, spanakopita and other Greek dishes. You can get a complete lunch for $7 and dinner for $3 to $4 more. Big slices of baklava cost $2. It's open from 9 am to 10 pm. Belly dancers perform nightly.

Moose McGillycuddy's (310 Lewers St) has 17 types of breakfast omelette for $4.50 each, including such all-time favourites as the pina colada with pineapple, coconut and cheese and the Euell Gibbons' Memorial topped with Grape Nuts. Until 9.30 am, two eggs, bacon, toast and orange juice cost $2.30. Moose's is popular with the college crowd and has an extensive menu of burgers, sandwiches, pizza, salad, pupus and drinks at moderate prices. It's open from 6.30 am to 10.30 pm daily. All drinks are half-price from 4 to 8 pm.

The *Bar-B-Q Center* (797 Kapahulu Ave) is a family-run neighbourhood restaurant with authentic Korean food. The mixed plate of barbecue chicken and man doo is $5.50 and is recommended. Without the man doo it's $4.25. Huge portions of barbecued meats come with rice, kimchee and half a dozen little dishes of pickled and marinated vegetables. Don't be put off by the filmy windows and vinyl decor, as the food is good. It's open from 10 am to 10 pm daily. The takeaway special available from 10 am to 4 pm comprises three main dishes, vegetables and rice for $3.85.

Ono Hawaiian Food (726 Kapahulu Ave) is *the* place to get Hawaiian food served Hawaiian-style. It's none too fancy looking, but people line up outside waiting to get in.

A kalua pig plate costs $4.45 and a laulau plate $4.70. Both come with pipikaula, lomi salmon and haupia with rice or poi. The photographs lining the walls are of professional wrestlers and people of local fame. It's open from 11 am to 7.30 pm Monday to Saturday.

New Kapahulu Chop Suey (730 Kapahulu Ave) serves big plates of Chinese food. Lunch specials are $3.20, dinner specials $4. It's a lot of food for the money and the restaurant is usually pretty crowded.

Irifune's (563 Kapahulu Ave) is a funky little joint complete with Japanese country kitsch and a waiting room that resembles the anteroom of a bordello. They don't use MSG in the kitchen and you can bring in beer. (There's a liquor store a few minutes' walk up the road.) The gyoza is good at $2.50 as is the garlic tofu with vegetables at $5.50. Kushiyaki and combo dinners are around $7.

KC Drive Inn (1029 Kapahulu Ave), way up the road almost as far as the freeway, features peanut butter shakes for $2, waffle dogs (a hot dog wrapped in a waffle) for about $1.50 and plate lunches. It's been a local favourite since 1929. Just recently they dropped their car-hop service.

Fast food is well represented: there are three *Burger King*, four *McDonald's* and six *Jack in the Box* restaurants. In addition to the standards, they add some island touches, such as passion fruit juice, Portuguese sausage and saimin. Lots of people have breakfast or lunch there, saving up for a splurge at dinner. All three chains usually have discount coupons in the freebie tourist magazines.

Places to Eat – middle

The *Parc Cafe* (tel 921-7272) in the Waikiki Parc Hotel has continental-style dining. It's pleasant and a bit up-market. The daily breakfast buffet from 7 to 10 am includes breakfast meats, eggs, French toast and hot cakes with guava syrup, fresh fruits, pastries and coffee for $8. At lunch, sandwiches and salads average about $5, with hot main dishes from $7 to $12. At dinner they have fish, chicken and red meat dishes. Seafood pasta or broiled fresh ahi with sage butter cost $13.

For a silver service breakfast with an open-air view of the ocean, there's the *Hala Terrace* (tel 734-2211) at the Kahala Hilton. 'Just for the Health of It' is a fruit smoothie, muffins, coffee and half a papaya with bananas, granola, yoghurt and honey for $11. Other dishes range from thin pancakes with maple butter for $6.75 to opakapaka fillet with hash browns and toast for $14.25. Breakfast is served from 6.30 to 11 am daily. Lunch, served from 11.30 am to 2.30 pm, is in the same price range.

The *Surf Room* at the Royal Hawaiian Hotel has a nice beach setting. Breakfasts are pricey, costing from $9 (apple crepes with macadamia nuts and coffee) to $15.75. Lunch is a better deal, with sandwiches and salads priced from $6.50 to $9.50.

Zuke Bistro (tel 922-0102) was until recently The Stuffed Potato, an intimate place tucked into a courtyard behind Hamburger Mary's. They had fine seafood, with dinners like jumbo shrimp pernod or opakapaka with dill cream sauce for about $15. Now they're changing their name, expanding the menu and moving to the Coconut Plaza Hotel on the corner of Ala Wai and Lewers. It's worth checking out, though the new menu will be à la carte and therefore more expensive.

Kyotaru (2160 Kalakaua St, next to the Pizza Hut) is part of a small Kyoto-based chain with reasonably good Japanese food. The tempura and sashimi plate is $6.75 at lunch and $10 at dinner. Una-jyu (eel dinner) is $11.25. They also sell inexpensive takeaway sushi rolls and soba. It's open from 11 am to 2 pm and 5 to 9.30 pm daily.

The *Hard Rock Cafe* (1837 Kapiolani Ave) is decorated with old surfboards and enlivened with loud rock music. A 1959 Cadillac 'woody' wagon hangs precariously over the bar. They serve burgers from about $6 and other all-American food including barbecue ribs and milkshakes, but it's the atmosphere, not the food, that draws most people. It's open from 11.30 am to at least midnight daily.

The *Oceanarium Restaurant* in the Pacific Beach Hotel (2490 Kalakaua Ave) has standard fare with anything but standard views. The dining room wraps around an enormous three-storey aquarium filled with colourful tropical fish. At breakfast, hot cakes or oatmeal with papaya cost $4 and a full buffet is $9.75. They serve lunch and dinner as well. The more expensive Neptune (seafood) and Shogun (teppanyaki, sushi bar) restaurants in the same hotel also have views of the aquarium.

Keo's (625 Kapahulu Ave, tel 737-8240) is widely regarded as Hawaii's top Thai restaurant. It's decorated with sprays of orchids, original Thai paintings and dozens of photos of owner Keo Sananikone posing with celebrity diners, including the likes of Jimmy Carter, Stevie Wonder and Shirley MacLaine. Prices are surprisingly moderate considering the valet parking and the popularity. House specialities are the Evil Jungle Prince dish ($7.95), spring roll appetisers ($5.95 for pork or tofu) and green papaya salad ($4.95). Main meals and curries cost $12 at the most. It won't break the bank to dine with the stars there. It's open from 5.30 to 11 pm nightly.

Places to Eat – top end

The *Maile Restaurant* (tel 734-2211), at the exclusive Kahala Hilton, is considered by many to be the best restaurant in Honolulu for traditional dishes, such as rack of lamb. Roast duckling served with Grand Marnier sauce, lychees and burgundy peaches is a speciality. Main dishes are priced from $24 to $30. There's a complete dinner with appetiser, salad, main course, dessert and coffee for $48. Jackets are required, though if you arrive without one they'll lend you one. It's open from 6.30 pm nightly. Dignitaries, movie stars and Imelda Marcos' shoes are frequently seen there.

Bagwells 2424 (tel 922-9292) is in the Hyatt Regency Waikiki. One of the nice things about the place is that you can sit in the lounge and munch on small 'grazing portions' chosen from the menu, thereby sampling some of Waikiki's finest food without picking up a $50 tab. Opakapaka-filled filo on mango puree costs $3.50 grazing and $9 as an appetiser in the dining room. Broiled lamb chops with a red bell pepper and garlic sauce costs $7.25 grazing and $28 as a main dish. A grazing dessert and a cup of tea will cost about $6.

Michel's at the Colony Surf Hotel (2895 Kalakaua Ave, tel 923-6552) is often hailed as Oahu's most romantic restaurant. It's formal, fine dining with crystal, china and chandeliers, fronting Sans Souci Beach. When you make reservations be sure to ask for a window table – it's a whole different experience without it. Dinner will cost around $50 and lunch about half that. One of their specialities is opakapaka, which costs $36 at dinner and $20 at lunch, à la carte. At breakfast you can get a cup of coffee and two croissants for $5 or Belgian waffles, fresh strawberries and coffee for $9.50. Breakfast is served from 7 to 10 am and dinner from 6 to 11 pm daily. Lunch is available from 11.30 am to 2.30 pm on weekdays.

La Mer (tel 923-2311) in the Halekulani Hotel has a top reputation for both its very creative French menu with Hawaiian influences, and its fine ocean view. It's expensive, quite formal and perhaps a bit too fastidious for some diners to feel relaxed. It's open nightly and jackets are required.

The Third Floor (tel 922-6611) in the Hawaiian Regent Hotel is another restaurant with expensive formal dining. They reputedly serve good country European food with traditional dishes and heavy sauces. They have nice touches like complimentary Indian naan bread and high-back wicker chairs. Dinner is served from 6.30 pm nightly; jackets are suggested.

Entertainment

Classics & Concerts *The Waikiki Shell*, in Kapiolani Park, draws big national and international names and large audiences for both classical and contemporary concerts. Call the Blaisdell box office at 521-2911 for information.

Hawaiiana Many major Waikiki hotels have Hawaiian-style entertainment, from Polynesian shows with beating drums and grass skirts to mellow duos playing ukulele or slack-key guitar.

Of the splashy musical revues with hula troupes, the Brothers Cazimero is the best. They perform from Tuesday to Saturday at the *Royal Hawaiian Hotel* (tel 923-7311), at 7 pm for the dinner seating ($49.50) and 9 pm for the cocktail seating ($19.50). There's an extra cocktail show at 10.30 pm on Fridays and Saturdays for $14. You can also have a drink in the bar and hear them across the lawn.

Dancing & Disco Many of the major Waikiki hotels have a disco or nightclub with dancing.

Wave Waikiki (1877 Kalakaua Ave, tel 941-0424) has a disco between bands playing progressive rock, new wave and oldies. The Wave has been one of Waikiki's hottest clubs since opening in 1980. It's open from 9 pm to 4 am and costs $4 on weekdays and $5 on weekends.

The nearby *Pink Cadillac* (478 Ena Rd, tel 942-5282) pulls in the early-20s crowd with rock videos, a beach night, a college night and contests. It's open from 9 pm to 2 am nightly, and usually charges $4 for those aged 21 or older and $10 for those under 21.

The *Shore Bird Beach Broiler* at the Outrigger Reef Hotel (2169 Kalia Rd, tel 922-2887) has beachfront dancing with a laser light show and 10-foot video screen from 9 pm to 2 am nightly.

For people with finer threads, more sophisticated dance scenes with live music can be found at *Nick's Fishmarket* at the Waikiki Gateway Hotel (2070 Kalakaua Ave, tel 955-6333) and at the disco at *Spats* in the Hyatt Regency Waikiki (tel 923-1234).

Gay Scene The gay scene is centred around the Kuhio District, along Kuhio Ave from Kalaimoku to Kaiolu streets.

Hula's Bar & Lei Stand (2103 Kuhio Ave, tel 923-0669) is an open-air video dance club under a big banyan tree. It's open from 2 pm to 2 am daily.

Katz (870 Kapahulu Ave, tel 737-4661) is a new disco. Shuttle vans run from Hotel Honolulu every half hour from 6 pm. It's open to 2 am.

Other gay hangouts include *CC's* (2155 Lauula St, tel 923-1640) and the bar at *Hamburger Mary's* (2109 Kuhio Ave, tel 922-6722).

Partner's (802 Kapiolani Blvd, tel 545-7810) is a women's bar with a pool table, videos, DJ and dancing. It's open from 3.30 pm to 2 am daily.

Pacific Ocean Holidays (Box 88245, Honolulu, HI 96830; tel 923-2400; 800-735-6600) produces a small booklet called *Pocket Guide to Hawaii*, geared to the gay community. You can get a copy by sending them $3. They also arrange vacation tours for gay men and women.

Comedy Frank DeLima, one of Honolulu's most popular comedians, pokes fun at Hawaii's multi-ethnic community, doing a fair amount of local inside material. He performs at 9.30 and 11 pm Wednesday to Sunday at the Noodle Shop (tel 922-4744) in the Waikiki Sand Villa Hotel. There's a $5 cover charge and a two-drink minimum. Reservations may be necessary.

Movie Theatres Movie theatres in Waikiki include the Waikiki Twins (tel 923-2394) on Seaside Ave near Kalakaua Ave; Waikiki 3 (tel 923-5353) on Kalakaua near Seaside; and Kuhio Twins (tel 941-4422) at 2095 Kuhio Ave.

Tea Ceremony *The Urasenke Foundation of Hawaii* (245 Saratoga Rd, tel 923-3059) has tea ceremony demonstrations on Wednesdays and Fridays, bringing a rare bit of serenity to busy Saratoga Rd. Students dressed in kimonos perform the ceremony on tatami mats in a formal tea room.

It costs $1 to be served green tea, but you can watch the ceremony for nothing. Each demonstration lasts about 45 minutes. The first sitting is at 10 am, the last at 11.45 am. The building is across the street from and makai of Waikiki's post office.

Free Things The Royal Hawaiian Band performs at 2 pm at the Kapiolani Park Bandstand. There are also occasionally other free concerts at the bandstand – call 527-5666 for details.

McDonald's in the Royal Hawaiian Shopping Center, building C, has a surprisingly high quality collection of native Hawaiian artwork. It includes feather leis and war spears; a work by Hawaii's most renowned oil painter, Herb Kane; and wooden sculptures and pencil drawings by native Hawaiian artist Rocky Jensen. The works are displayed on both floors of the restaurant. You can pick up a free brochure there detailing the exhibit.

Hyatt's Hawaii, on the 2nd floor of the Hyatt Regency Waikiki (near the waterfall), is a tiny folk-style museum of Hawaiian crafts. Tapa, quilts, weavings and feather work are on display. Aunty Malia Solomon, who runs the gallery, sometimes demonstrates crafts or Hawaiian games.

The *Royal Hawaiian Shopping Center* has free lessons in such things as quilting, ukulele playing and the Hawaiian language from 9.30 to 11.30 am Monday to Friday on the 3rd floor bridgeways between the buildings. Some, like the hula lessons, are popular with retirees.

The *Polynesian Cultural Center* puts on a free mini-show from 9.30 to 11.30 am on Tuesdays, Thursdays and Saturdays on the ground floor between buildings B and C of the Royal Hawaiian Shopping Center. For details of other free events, pick up a schedule at the shopping centre.

Hilton Hawaiian Village lets off fireworks at 7.30 pm on Fridays, following a torch-lighting ceremony and preceding a hula show and Hawaiian music.

Teenage hula students perform in a free Polynesian show at 7 and 8 pm nightly near the top of the escalator on the 2nd floor of *Kuhio Mall*.

Honolulu

The first foreign ship to sail into what is now called Honolulu Harbor was the English frigate *Butterworth* in 1793. Its captain, William Brown, named the harbour Fair Haven. Ships that followed called it Brown's Harbor. In time the name Honolulu (sheltered bay) came to be used for both the harbour and the seaside district that the Hawaiians had called Kou.

As more and more foreign ships found their way to Honolulu a harbourside village of thatched houses sprouted up and the town became Hawaii's centre of trade.

In 1809 Kamehameha I moved his royal court to Honolulu from Waikiki. On what today is the southern end of Bethel St, Kamehameha set up residence to keep an eye on all the trade that moved in and out. From there, sandalwood was shipped to Canton in exchange for weapons and luxury goods, which Kamehameha loaded into his harbourside warehouses.

In the 1820s whaling ships began pulling into Honolulu for supplies, liquor and women at the same time as Christian missionaries were coming ashore to save souls. The Protestant mission and Episcopal and Catholic churches all established their Hawaiian headquarters in downtown Honolulu.

A century later luxury liners docked alongside Honolulu's Aloha Tower, bringing the first tourists to the islands.

All have left their mark. Downtown are the offices of the 'Big Five' corporations that were in control of most of Hawaii's commerce by the turn of the century. It's no coincidence that their lists of corporate board members – Baldwin, Alexander, Cooke and Dole – read like a roster from the mission ships.

The whalers left a different legacy. Hotel St, a line of bars and strip joints a few blocks from the harbour, remains the city's red light district.

By the early 1900s Honolulu had expanded into a sprawling cosmopolitan city, but the downtown area up from the harbour remains the heart of Honolulu.

Honolulu Today

Honolulu is the only major city in Hawaii. It has a population of 365,000 and is the state's centre of business, culture and politics. It's been the capital of Hawaii since 1845. Honolulu International Airport and Honolulu Harbor are Hawaii's busiest ports.

Honolulu is home to people from throughout the Pacific: it's a city of minorities, with no ethnic majority.

Honolulu's ethnic diversity can be seen on almost every corner – the sushi shop next door to the Vietnamese bakery, the Catholic church around the block from the Chinese temple, and the rainbow of schoolchildren waiting for the bus.

The main federal, state and county offices and the state's highest concentration of historic buildings are found in downtown Honolulu.

DOWNTOWN HONOLULU

Downtown Honolulu is a city that's grown up since the mid-1800s, and its older, most handsome buildings are all within walking distance.

The area is a hodgepodge of past and present. There's a royal palace, a modernistic state capitol, a coral-block New England missionary church and a Spanish-style city hall all within sight of one another. Downtown has both modern highrises and stately Victorian-era buildings.

You can take in a Friday noon band concert on the palace lawn, lounge in the open-air courtyard of Hawaii's central library or catch a view of it all from the top of the Aloha Tower.

Information

Downtown Honolulu is a hassle to drive around, not only because of traffic congestion but also because of the one-way streets and confusing intersections. During the week, it's not a bad idea to take the bus. Bus Nos 2, 19 and 20 run between downtown and

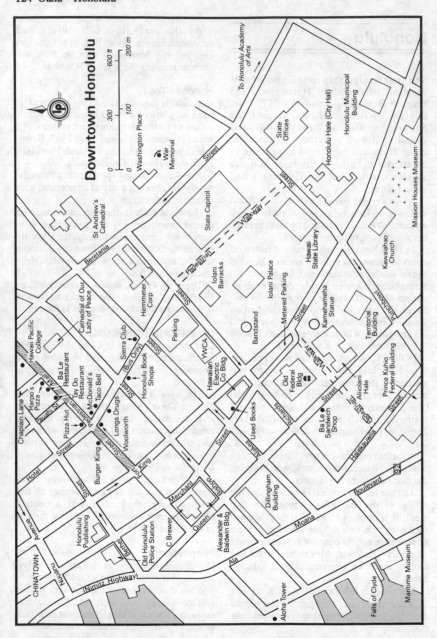

Downtown Honolulu

0 300 600 ft
0 100 200 m

To Honolulu Academy of Arts

Washington Place
War Memorial

St Andrew's Cathedral

State Offices
Honolulu Hale (City Hall)
Honolulu Municipal Building

State Capitol

Beretania

Cathedral of Our Lady of Peace

Hemmeter Corp

Pedestrian Walkway

Iolani Barracks
Iolani Palace

Hawaii State Library

Mission Houses Museum
Kawaiahao Church

Sierra Club (Bus Only)
Parking
YWCA
Bandstand
Metered Parking
Kamehameha Statue

Puowaina

Punchbowl

Territorial Building

Hawaii Pacific College

Ba Le Restaurant
Harpo's Pizza
Tay Do Restaurant
McDonald's
Taco Bell
Pizza Hut
Longs Drugs
Woolworth
Burger King

Honolulu Book Shops

Hawaiian Electric Co Bldg

Used Books

Old Federal Bldg
Ba Le Sandwich Shop
Aliiolani Hale

Prince Kuhio Federal Building

Richards

Alakea

King

Merchant

Bishop

Queen

Dillingham Building

Alexander & Baldwin Bldg

Moana

Ala

Honolulu Publishing
Old Honolulu Police Station
C Brewer

Boulevard

CHINATOWN

Nuuanu
Hotel Street
Bethel
Chaplain Lane
Nuuanu Avenue

Fort Street
King Street
Pauahi St
Maunakea St

Nimitz Highway

Aloha Tower
Falls of Clyde
Maritime Museum

Waikiki. On weekends the traffic is light and parking isn't difficult.

Lots of city bus routes converge downtown – so many that Hotel St, which begins downtown and crosses Chinatown, is for bus traffic only.

Post Dowtown Honolulu's main post office is at 3600 Aolele St. There's also one in the Ala Moana Center.

Walking Tours Kapiolani Community College leads walking tours with varied historical themes – from ghosts of old Honolulu to the crime beat of the 1920s. Schedules are available from the Office of Community Services (tel 734-9211), Kapiolani Community College, 4303 Diamond Head Rd, Honolulu, HI 96816. Advance registration is required. Tours cost $5 for adults and $2 for children.

For Chinatown walks, see the Chinatown section. For other walking tours, check the 'Honolulu Calendar' in the *Honolulu Advertiser*.

Shopping Honolulu's major shopping centre is the Ala Moana Center (see the Ala Moana section).

Ward Warehouse at the corner of Ala Moana Blvd and Ward Ave has Waldenbooks, Birkenstock Footprints, The Artist Guild with fine local crafts and about 50 other shops and eateries including the Old Spaghetti Factory, Dave's Ice Cream, the Coffee Works and Stuart Anderson. There's free garage parking. Bus Nos 8, 19 and 20 stop there.

Goodwill (780 S Beretania St) is open from 9 am to 6 pm daily. It has racks of used aloha shirts for $5, jeans for $4 and muumuus for $6. There's another thrift shop at St Andrew's Cathedral.

Parking At the corner of Alakea and Hotel streets, weekday parking is 25 cents per half-hour for the first two hours and 50 cents per half-hour thereafter. On Saturdays, Sundays and holidays it's a maximum of $1 all day.

Iolani Palace ticket

Iolani Palace

Iolani Palace is the only royal palace in the USA. It was the official residence of King Kalakaua and Queen Kapiolani from 1882 to 1891 and to Queen Liliuokalani, Kalakaua's sister and successor, for two years after that.

Following the overthrow of the Hawaiian kingdom in 1893, the palace became the capitol – first for the republic, then for the territory and later for the state of Hawaii.

It wasn't until 1969 that the current state capitol was built and the legislators moved out of their cramped quarters. The Senate had been meeting in the palace dining room and the House of Representatives in the throne room. By the time they left the palace was in shambles, the grand koa staircase termite-ridden and the Douglas fir floors pitted and gouged.

After extensive $7 million renovations, the palace was largely restored to its former glory and opened as a museum in 1978. Visitors must wear booties over their shoes to protect the highly polished wooden floors.

Iolani Palace was modern for its day. Every bedroom had its own full bath with hot and cold water running into copper-lined tubs, a flushing toilet and a bidet. According to the guides, electric lights superseded the gas lamps here four years before the White House in Washington got electricity.

The throne room, decorated in red and gold, features the original thrones of the king and queen, and a kapu stick made of the long spiral ivory tusk of a narwhal. In addition to celebrations full of pomp and pageantry, it was there that King Kalakaua danced his favourite Western dances – the polka, the waltz and the Virginia reel – into the wee hours of the morning.

Not all the events that took place there were joyous. Two years after she was dethroned, Queen Liliuokalani was brought back to the palace and tried for treason in the throne room. In a move calculated to humiliate the Hawaiian people she spent nine months as a prisoner in Iolani Palace, her former home.

Guided tours leave every 15 minutes from 9 am to 2.15 pm Wednesday to Saturday and are worth the $4 admission. Sometimes you can join up on the spot, but it's advisable to make reservations by phoning 522-0832.

Palace Grounds Before Iolani Palace was built, there was a simpler house on these grounds that King Kamehameha III used when he moved the capital from Lahaina to Honolulu in 1845. In ancient times it was the site of a heiau.

The ticket window and gift shop are in the former barracks of the Royal Household Guards. The barracks look oddly like the uppermost layer of a fort from the Middle Ages sliced off and plopped on the ground.

The domed pavilion on the grounds was originally built for the coronation of King Kalakaua in 1883 and is still used for inauguration of governors and concerts by the Royal Hawaiian Band.

The grassy mound surrounded by a wrought iron fence was the site of a royal tomb until 1865 when the remains of King Kamehameha II and Queen Kamamalu (who both died of measles in England in 1824) were moved to the Royal Mausoleum in Nuuanu.

The huge banyan tree between the palace and the state capitol is thought to have been planted by Queen Kapiolani.

Hawaii State Library

The central branch of the state-wide library system (tel 548-4775) is at the corner of King and Punchbowl streets. Its collection of half a million titles is the state's best and includes a good Hawaii & the Pacific section. The library's open-air garden courtyard is a nice place to sit and read.

Hours are from 9 am to 5 pm Mondays, Wednesdays, Fridays and Saturdays and from 9 am to 8 pm Tuesdays and Thursdays.

The Hawaii State Archives (tel 548-2355) next door holds official government documents and an extensive photo collection. It's open to the public for research.

Queen Liliuokalani Statue

The statue of Hawaii's last queen stands between the capitol and Iolani Palace. It faces Washington Place, Liliuokalani's home, and place of exile for more than 20 years. The statue is holding *Aloha Oe*, the hymn she composed; *Kumulipo*, the Hawaiian chant of creation; and the Hawaii constitution which Liliuokalani wrote in 1893, in fear of which American businessmen overthrew her.

The statue is often draped with leis of hibiscus or maile.

State Capitol

Hawaii's state capitol is not your standard gold dome. Constructed in the late 1960s, it was a grandiose attempt at a 'theme' design.

Its two central legislative chambers are cone-shaped to represent volcanoes; the rotunda is open-air to let gentle trade winds blow through; the supporting columns represent palm trees; and the whole structure is encircled by a large pool symbolising the ocean surrounding Hawaii.

The building not only symbolises the elements but has been quite effective in drawing them in. The pool draws brackish water; rain pouring in the rotunda has necessitated the sealing of many of the skylights; and Tadashi

Sato's 'Aquarius' floor mosaic, meant to show the changing colours and patterns of Hawaii's seas, has been so weathered it's undergoing a $60,000 reconstruction.

If you're downtown you might want to take a look at the modernistic chambers used by the Senate and House of Representatives, with their huge wall tapestries. From the capitol's top floor there's a view of the downtown area, though it's largely of rooftops.

In front of the building is a statue of Father Damien, the Belgian priest who volunteered to work amongst the lepers of Molokai and died of the disease 16 years later, aged 49. The stylised sculpture was created by Venezuelan artist Marisol Escubar.

War Memorial
The war memorial is a sculptured eternal torch dedicated to soldiers who died in WW II. It sits between two underground garage entrances on Beretania St, directly opposite the state capitol.

Washington Place
Washington Place, the governor's official residence, is a large colonial-style building, with stately trees, built in 1846 by US sea captain John Dominis. The captain's son John married the Hawaiian princess who later became Queen Liliuokalani. After the queen was dethroned she lived at Washington Place in exile until her death in 1917.

The large tree to the right of the walkway is a pili nut tree, recognisable by the buttress-like roots extending from the base of its trunk. In South-East Asia the nuts of these trees are used to produce oil.

St Andrew's Cathedral
King Kamehameha IV was attracted by the royal trappings of the Church of England and decided to build his own cathedral. He and his consort Queen Emma founded the Anglican Church of Hawaii in 1858.

The cornerstone was finally laid in 1867 by King Kamehameha V. Kamehameha IV had died four years earlier on St Andrew's Day – hence the church's name.

The church is of French Gothic architecture, shipped in pieces from England. Its most striking feature is the impressive window of hand-blown stained glass that forms the western facade and reaches from the floor to the eaves. In the right section of the glass you can see the Reverend Thomas Staley, the first bishop sent to Hawaii by Queen Victoria, alongside Kamehameha IV and Queen Emma.

St Andrew's is on the corner of Alakea and Beretania streets.

A thrift shop in the church grounds is open from 9.30 am to 4 pm on Mondays, Wednesdays and Fridays and from 9 am to 1 pm on Saturdays. If you're lucky you might find an aloha shirt for $4 or a 10-speed bicycle for $10. Used paperbacks are 25 cents. It appears Episcopalians have fairly good taste in literature and you might find something worth reading.

Hemmeter Corporation
The elegant five-storey building on Richards St opposite the state capitol looks like it could be the governor's mansion but is actually the headquarters of the Hemmeter Corporation. Chris Hemmeter is the developer behind Hawaii's fantasy hotels, including the Hyatt Regency Waikoloa and the Westin Kauai.

The building has something of the appearance of a Spanish mission, including courtyards and ceramic tile walls and floors. Built in 1928, it served as the YMCA Armed Services building until Hemmeter's recent purchase. It's just undergone a multimillion dollar face-lift.

Fort Street Mall
Fort St is a pedestrian shopping mall lined with benches and trees. It's not very interesting in itself, but if you're downtown it's a good place to eat – not as good as Chinatown, but a few blocks closer. Sometimes classical music flautists, folk guitarists or other street musicians play for coins.

Cathedral of Our Lady of Peace
The oldest Catholic cathedral in the USA is

the Cathedral of Our Lady of Peace, at the Beretania St end of Fort St Mall. Built of coral blocks in 1843, it's older and more ornate than St Andrew's Cathedral.

Father Damien, who later served Molokai's leper colony, was ordained there in 1864.

Aliiolani Hale

Aliiolani Hale (House of Heavenly Kings) was the first major government building built by the Hawaiian monarchy. Since its construction in 1874 it has housed the Supreme Court. In earlier times it was also home to the legislature. The building has a distinctive clock tower and was originally designed by Australian architect Thomas Rowe to be a royal palace, although it never was used as such.

It was on these steps in January 1893 that Sanford Dole proclaimed the establishment of a provisional government and the overthrow of the monarchy.

Kamehameha Statue

The statue of Kamehameha the Great stands

Kamehameha Statue

in front of Aliiolani Hale, opposite Iolani Palace. It was cast by Thomas Gould in 1880. This one is actually a recast, as the first statue was lost at sea near the Falkland Islands. The original statue, recovered after this second version was dedicated, now stands in Kohala, the Big Island birthplace of Kamehameha.

On 11 June, a state holiday honouring Kamehameha, both statues are ceremoniously draped with layer upon layer of 12-foot leis.

Honolulu Hale

City Hall, also known as Honolulu Hale, is largely of Spanish mission design with a tile roof, decorative balconies, arches and pillars. Built in 1927, it bears the initials of C W Dickey, Honolulu's most famous architect of the day. The open-air courtyard in the centre of the building is often used for concerts and art exhibits.

Kawaiahao Church

Oahu's oldest church, on the corner of Punchbowl and King streets, was built on the site where the first missionaries constructed a grass thatch church shortly after their arrival in 1820. The original was an impressive structure, measuring 54 feet by 22 feet, which could seat 300 on lauhala mats.

Still, thatch wasn't quite what the missionaries had in mind so they designed a more typically New England-style Congregational church with simple Gothic influences.

Built between 1838 and 1842, the church is made of 14,000 giant coral slabs, many weighing more than 1000 pounds. Hawaiian divers chiselled the huge blocks of coral out of Honolulu's underwater reef.

The clock tower was donated by Kamehameha III and the clock, built in Boston and installed in 1850, still keeps accurate time.

Inside the church is breezy and cool. The rear seats, marked by feather *kahili* staffs and velvet padding, were for royalty and are still reserved for descendants of royalty today.

The church is open to visitors from 8 am to 4 pm daily.

Top: Hanauma Bay, Oahu
Left: Manoa Falls, Oahu
Right: Toilet Bowl, Hanauma Bay, Oahu

Top: Kite Festival, Kapiolani Park, Oahu
Bottom: Outrigger canoe race, Molokai

The tomb of King Lunalilo, the successor to Kamehameha V, is in the church grounds at the main entrance. Lunalilo ruled for only one year before his death in 1874 at the age of 39.

Around the back is a cemetery where many of the early missionaries were buried.

Mission Houses Museum

Three of the original buildings of the Sandwich Islands Mission headquarters still stand: the Frame House (built in 1821), the Chamberlain House (1831) and the Printing House (1841).

Together they're open to the public as the Mission Houses Museum (553 S King St, tel 531-0481). The houses are authentically furnished with handmade quilts on the beds, settees in the parlour and iron pots in the big stone fireplaces.

Tickets to the museum are sold in the coral-block Chamberlain House. Levi Chamberlain was the man appointed by the mission to buy, store and dole out supplies to the missionary families who each had an allowance. Account books show that in the late 1800s 25 cents would buy either one gallon of oil, one pen knife or two slates.

The Chamberlain House was the early mission storeroom, a necessity as Honolulu had few shops in those days. Upstairs are hoop barrels and wooden crates packed with dishes and a big desk with pigeon-hole dividers and the quill pen Levi used to work on accounts.

The first missionaries packed more than their bags when they left Boston – they actually brought a pre-fabricated wooden house around the Horn with them! Designed to withstand cold New England winter winds, the small windows instead block out Honolulu's cooling trade winds, keeping the two-storey house hot and stuffy. The Frame House is the oldest wooden structure in Hawaii.

Inside the Printing House, an interpreter in period dress uses lead type to print pages in Hawaiian.

The Mission Houses are open from 9 am to 4 pm daily except major holidays. Admission of $3.50 for adults and $1 for children includes a 45-minute guided tour of the three buildings.

The best day to visit is Saturday, the day of the living history programme. Costumed actors portray the missionary residents of 1831, as well as sea captains and native Hawaiians of the time.

Visitors can engage in lively debate with Hiram Bingham, Honolulu's first Christian minister, an opinionated and prejudiced evangelist. The actors don't step out of character or the period when they answer questions and show complete puzzlement about the existence of such things as cameras or the state of California.

On Saturdays tours are given every hour on the hour. There's no extra fee for the living history programme. Tours on other days begin whenever a small group gathers, starting from 9.30 am.

If you're not into all that, a walk around the grounds and a peek inside open doors and windows is free.

Other Historic Buildings

The Hawaiian Electric Company's four-storey administrative building, on the corner of Richards and King streets, is of Spanish colonial architecture. It has an arched entrance, some fine wrought-iron grilles and neat old chandeliers with gas-type bulbs hanging from hand-painted ceilings. Walking through the front door is like stepping back into the 1920s. It's the entrance to the customer service department and it's OK to walk in and take a look.

Diagonally opposite, on Merchant St, is the Old Federal Building, another interesting edifice with Spanish colonial features. Completed in 1922, it holds a post office and customs house.

Also noteworthy is the three-storey YWCA at 1040 Richards St. It was built in 1927 and designed by architect Julia Morgan, who also designed William Randolph Hearst's San Simeon estate in California.

The old Honolulu Police Station (1931 to 1961), at the corner of Bethel and Merchant streets, has beautiful interior ceramic tile work in earthen tones on its counters and walls. It now houses the state departments of Housing and Finance.

The four-storey Alexander & Baldwin building at the corner of Bishop and Queen streets was built in 1929. The columns at the front entrance are carved with tropical fruit and the Chinese characters for prosperity and long life. Inside the portico there's an interesting ceramic tile mural of Hawaiian fish.

Samuel Alexander and Henry Baldwin, both sons of missionaries, vaulted to prominence in the sugar industry and created one of Hawaii's 'Big Five' controlling corporations. The other four – Theo Davies, Castle & Cooke, Amfac and C Brewer – all have their headquarters within a few blocks of here.

The four-storey 60-year-old Dillingham building at the corner of Bishop and Queen streets is of Italian Renaissance-style architecture with arches, marble walls, elaborate elevator doors and an arty brick floor. It's a study in contrasts, mirrored in the reflective glass exterior of the nearby 30-storey Grosvenor Center.

Honolulu Academy of Arts

The Honolulu Academy of Arts (900 S Beretania St, tel 538-1006) is an exceptional museum, with permanent Asian, European, American and Pacific art collections from ancient times to the present.

Just inside the door and to the right is a room with works by Matisse, Monet, Cezanne, Gauguin, Van Gogh and Picasso and a welcoming place to sit in the middle of the room to take it all in.

The building is open and airy and has numerous small galleries around six garden courtyards. The Spanish Court has benches and a small fountain surrounded by Greek and Roman sculpture and Egyptian reliefs dating back to 2500 BC.

There are sculptures and miniatures from India, jades and bronzes from ancient China, Madonna and child oils from 14th century Italy and James Michener's collection of Japanese prints, to name just a few.

The Hawaiian section is small but choice, with feather leis, tapa beaters, poi pounders and koa calabashes. The collection from Papua New Guinea, Micronesia and the South Pacific includes ancestor figures, war clubs and masks.

The museum is off the tourist track and seldom crowded. To top it all off, admission is free, though donations are appreciated.

It's open from 10 am to 4.30 pm Tuesday to Saturday and from 1 to 5 pm on Sundays. Gallery tours are given at 2 pm on Thursdays, 1 pm on Sundays and 11 am on Tuesdays, Wednesdays, Fridays and Saturdays. Tours change with the interests of each group and last about an hour.

The on-site Academy Theatre presents more than 400 programmes each year, including foreign and independent films, classical music concerts and art lectures. An events calendar is available at the museum. There's also a gift shop, library and lunch cafe (by reservation).

Hawaii Theatre

The neo-classical Hawaii Theatre (1130 Bethel St), with its art deco neon signs, first opened in 1922 with silent films to the tune of a pipe organ. It ran continuous shows during the war but the development of mall cinemas in the 1970s was its undoing.

After closing in 1984, its future looked dim, even though it was on the Register of Historic Buildings. The volunteer Hawaii Theatre Center group has raised a couple of million dollars and is now renovating the theatre, which it recently purchased from the Bishop Estate.

Aloha Tower

The top-floor observation deck of the Aloha Tower offers a sweeping view of Honolulu's big commercial harbour and downtown area.

Built in 1926, the 10-storey Aloha Tower is a Honolulu landmark. For years it was the city's tallest building.

Back in the days when all tourists arrived by ship, the four-sided clock tower greeted incoming passengers with the word 'Aloha'. Cruise ships still pull in beneath the tower, which is part of the US Customs building.

Aloha Tower is at Pier 9, off Ala Moana Blvd at the harbour end of Fort St. The observation deck is open from 8 am to 9 pm daily. Admission is free. Drive or walk up to the 2nd storey and from there take an elevator to the 10th floor. There's metered parking below the tower.

Hawaii Maritime Center

The Hawaii Maritime Center is at Honolulu Harbor on the Diamond Head side of the Aloha Tower. The centre contains a museum; the *Falls of Clyde*, said to be the world's last four-masted four-rigged ship; and the double-hulled sailing canoe *Hokulea*.

The 60-foot *Hokulea* has made three voyages from Hawaii to the South Pacific, retracing the routes of the early Polynesian seafarers using traditional means of navigation, including wave patterns and the stars. Its final voyage took place between July 1985 and May 1987, when it sailed from Hawaii to Tahiti, the Cook Islands, New Zealand, Tonga and Samoa and from the Tuamotus back to Hawaii.

The 266-foot iron-hulled *Falls of Clyde* was built in Glasgow, Scotland, in 1878. In 1899 Matson Navigation bought the ship and added a deck house, and the *Falls* began carrying sugar and passengers between Hilo and San Francisco. It was later converted into an oil tanker and eventually stripped down to a barge.

After being abandoned in Ketchikan, Alaska, where it had been relegated to the function of a floating oil storage tank, the *Falls* was towed to Seattle. A group of Hawaiians raised funds to rescue the ship in 1963, just before it was scheduled to be sunk to create a breakwater off Vancouver. With the aid of the Bishop Museum, the *Falls* was eventually brought to Honolulu and restored to its former Matson-era grace.

The new museum has a mishmash of maritime artefacts, model replicas of ships, a reproduction of a stateroom and interesting old photos of Waikiki in the days when just the Royal Hawaiian and the Moana hotels shared the horizon with Diamond Head. Both hotels belonged to Matson, who spearheaded tourism in Hawaii and ironically sold out to the Sheraton in 1959 just before the jet age and statehood launched sleepy tourism into a booming industry.

To get there by bus, take a No 8, 19 or 20 from Waikiki. By car, it's off Ala Moana Blvd, about a mile west of Ward Warehouse. There's metered parking between the museum and Aloha Tower. The museum is open from 9 am to 5 pm daily. Admission of $6 for adults and $3 for children includes boarding the *Falls*.

Sand Island State Recreation Area

Sand Island is a 500-acre island on the western side of Honolulu Harbor. About a third of it is a state park.

Sand Island is heavily used by local people, who camp and picnic there on weekends. It has little appeal to the casual visitor and you won't find many tourists.

The park is not reached from the downtown area, but by an access road a few miles west, off the Nimitz Highway. Sand Island Access Rd leads 2½ miles down to the park through an industrial area with a waste-water treatment plant, oil tanks, scrap metal yards and the like. The airport is directly across the lagoon and Sand Island is on the flight path.

The park has showers, restrooms and a white sand beach that is not particularly clean.

Chinatown

Chinatown proper is the area immediately west of central Honolulu, bounded by Honolulu Harbor, Nuuanu Ave, River St and North Beretania St.

A walk through Chinatown is like a journey to Asia. Though it's predominantly Chinese, it has Vietnamese, Thai and Filipino influences as well.

Chinatown is busy and colourful. It has a lively market that could be right off a back street in Hong Kong and good cheap ethnic restaurants. You can get tattooed, consult with a herbalist, munch on moon cakes or slurp a steaming bowl of Vietnamese soup. There are temples and shrines, noodle factories, antique shops and art galleries.

History Chinese immigrants who had worked off their sugar cane plantation contracts began settling in Chinatown and opening up small businesses there around 1860.

In December 1899 the bubonic plague broke out in the area. The 7000 Chinese, Hawaiians and Japanese who made the crowded neighbourhood their home were cordoned off and forbidden to leave.

As more plague cases arose, the Board of Health decided to conduct controlled burns of infected homes. On 20 January 1900 the fire brigade set fire to a building on the corner of Beretania St and Nuuanu Ave. The wind suddenly picked up and the fire spread out of control, racing toward the waterfront. To make matters worse, police guards stationed inside the plague area attempted to stop quarantined residents from fleeing. Nearly 40 acres of Chinatown burned to the ground.

Not everyone thought the fire was accidental. Just the year before, Chinese immigration into Hawaii had been halted after the USA annexed the islands, and Chinatown itself was prime real estate on the edge of the burgeoning downtown district.

1	Cathedral of Our Lady of Peace	16	Antique Shops
2	Hawaii Pacific College	17	Chinatown Marketplace
3	Hawaii Theater	18	Oahu Market
4	Pegge Hopper Gallery	19	Ba Le Sandwich Shop
5	Former Pantheon Bar	20	Armstrong Building
6	Lai Fong Department Store	21	To Chau Restaurant
7	Sharps & Flats	22	His Island Tattoo Shop
8	Police Station	23	Cebu Pool Hall
9	Krung Thai	24	Chinatown Cultural Plaza
10	Chinese Chamber of Commerce	25	Sun Yat-Sen Statue
11	Nature Conservancy	26	Doong Kong Lau Restaurant
12	Shung Chong Yuein	27	Izumo Taisha Shrine
13	Wo Fat	28	Taoist Temple
14	Cindy's Lei Shop	29	Kuan Yin Temple
15	Bank of Hawaii		

Despite the adverse climate the Chinese held their own and a new Chinatown arose.

In the 1940s, thousands of American GIs walked the streets of Chinatown before being shipped off to Iwo Jima and Guadalcanal. Many spent their last days of freedom in Chinatown's 'body houses', pool halls and tattoo parlours.

Chinatown Today Today Chinatown is where East meets East, as new Asian immigrants stake out their claim.

The stone block Armstrong building on the corner of River and King streets houses Vietnamese and Thai businesses. Nearby, posters advertise Vietnamese movies like *The Moon Chasing Beauty* and *Gone With the Time*.

The section of Hotel St by the river is the Filipino area, with Cebu Pool Hall and My Sista's Place bar.

North Hotel St is Chinatown's seamier side. Darkened doorways advertise 'video peeps' for 25 cents and the lounges have names like Risque Theatre and Club Hubba Hubba.

Chinatown is undergoing some urban renewal, particularly on its downtown edge. Though many of Chinatown's historic buildings have recently been renovated, others deemed less worthy have been razed, some for open space and others for affordable highrise housing.

Information To get to Chinatown by car from Waikiki, take Ala Moana Blvd and turn at Smith St or Bethel St. Or take Beretania St and head makai down Nuuanu Ave or Maunakea St. Hotel St is open only to bus traffic.

Chinatown is full of one-way streets and it's often difficult to find a parking space. Cars line up at parking lots waiting for spaces to become available.

You can avoid parking hassles by taking the bus. Nos 2 and 20 run to Chinatown from Waikiki; get off at Maunakea St or Hotel St.

Tours The Chinese Chamber of Commerce (42 N King St, tel 533-3181) leads tours at 9.30 am on Tuesdays for $4, with the option of lunch at Wo Fat for $5 extra. Reservations are required.

The Hawaii Heritage Center (1128 Smith St, 2nd Floor; tel 521-2749) leads tours from 9.30 am to 12.30 pm on Mondays and Fridays for $4.

While the guides do give some historical insights, it feels pretty touristy being led around in a group. It's more fun to poke around on your own.

Oahu Market The heart of Chinatown is Oahu Market, at the corner of Kekaulike and King streets. It's been an institution since 1904.

Everything the Chinese cook needs is on display: pig heads, ginger root, fresh octopus, quail eggs, salted jellyfish, slabs of tuna, jasmine rice and long beans, just to name a few items.

In 1984 the tenants of Oahu Market organised and purchased the market to save it from falling into the hands of developers.

Ba Le Sandwich Shop, across the street, makes the best French bread in Honolulu.

Don't leave Chinatown without having at least one meal and picking up some Chinese pastries (see the Places to Eat section).

Maunakea Street Wo Fat, the distinctive pink restaurant at the corner of Hotel and Maunakea streets, is a Chinatown landmark with a facade that resembles a Chinese temple. It's the oldest restaurant in Honolulu and has been on this site since just after the Chinatown fire of 1900. Interesting photos lining the stairwell depict the lives of the Chinese immigrant families of that period.

Shung Chong Yuein (1027 Maunakea St) sells delicious moon cakes and almond cookies for a mere quarter. This is the place for dried and sugared foods – everything from candied ginger and pineapple to candied squash and lotus root. They also carry boiled peanuts, which are actually quite good if you can resist comparing them to roasted peanuts.

Across the street is Cindy's Lei Shop, a friendly place with leis made of maile, ilima and Micronesian ginger in addition to the more common orchids and plumeria. The colours and fragrances are heady.

Nuuanu Avenue The new Chinatown Police Station is on the corner of Hotel St and Nuuanu Ave in the circa 1888 Perry Block building. Newly renovated, the inside has dome lights, walls of koa panels and enough 1920s touches to resemble a set from 'The Untouchables'.

Next door to the police station, at 1109 Nuuanu Ave, is Sharps & Flats, a music store stuffed with second-hand instruments. More colourful than the store itself is owner Jack C Young, who sits out the front bedecked in as many rings as fingers, each made from an American gold coin. He's been in business for almost 50 years and claims to play all instruments and be master of none.

Just down the street is the Pantheon Bar, now abandoned, the oldest watering hole in Honolulu and a favourite of sailors in days past.

Across the street, Lai Fong Department Store sells antiques, knick-knacks and old postcards of Hawaii. They also make Chinese silk dresses to order.

The granite blocks used for sidewalks on Nuuanu Ave were the ballast used in the ships that brought tea from China in the 1800s.

Antiques & Arts Chinatown is becoming trendy for antique shops and art galleries.

Pegge Hopper, whose prints of Hawaiian women adorn many a wall in the islands, has her gallery at 1164 Nuuanu Ave. Well-known island photographer William Waterfall's gallery is at 1160A Nuuanu Ave.

There's a line-up of antique shops at the waterfront end of Maunakea St, including Bushido Antiques (936 Maunakea St), which sells Japanese swords, Korean ceramics and Paul Jacoulet prints.

Chinatown Cultural Plaza This plaza covers the better part of a block along North Beretania St from Maunakea St to River St.

The modern complex doesn't have the character of Chinatown's older shops, but inside it's still Chinatown, with tailors, acupuncturists and calligraphers alongside travel agents, restaurants and a Chinese newspaper press. One of the kiosks inside the Asia Mall section sells nuts, dried fruit and local honey at good prices. There's a post office and restrooms.

There's a small statue of Kuan Yin, where elderly Chinese light incense and leave mangoes. The lychee tree at the centre of the plaza blooms in July.

River St Pedestrian Mall The River St pedestrian mall has covered tables beside Nuuanu Stream, where old men play mahjong and checkers. A statue of Chinese revolutionary leader Sun Yat-Sen stands at the end of the pedestrian mall near North Beretania St.

There are eat-in and take-out restaurants along the strip, including Mongolian barbecue, Japanese and good Hakka Chinese food.

Other Shops Chinatown herbalists are both physicians and pharmacists, with a wall full of small wooden drawers each filled with a different herb. They'll size you up, feel your pulse and listen to you describe your ailments before deciding which drawers to open, mixing herbs and flowers and wrapping them for you to take home and boil up together. The object is to balance Yin and Yang forces. A-1 Pacific Herb Shop (182 N King St) is one such shop. You can buy ginseng root there too.

There are half a dozen noodle factories in Chinatown. If you look inside you'll see clouds of white flour hanging in the air and thin sheets of dough running around rollers and coming out as noodles. Yat Tung Chow Noodle Factory (150 N King St), next to Ba Le, makes nine sizes of noodles, from skinny golden thread to fat udon. None cost more than $1 a pound.

Tino Camanga, a former Big Island cowboy, has been tattooing Honolulu's sailors since 1946. He's one of the last survivors from the days when there was a tattoo shop on every block in town. His Island Tattoo Shop is a hole in the wall on River St near N Hotel St.

Hakubundo (100 N Beretania St) sells Japanese swords and dolls, kung fu uniforms, origami and calligraphy supplies.

Other cubbyhole shops sell teapots, bamboo steamers, dried lotus leaves, salted duck eggs and strands of freshwater rice pearls.

Taoist Temple The Lum Sai Ho Tong Society was organised in 1889, one of the more than 100 societies started by Chinese immigrants in Hawaii to help preserve their cultural identity. This one was for the Lum clan, who hail from west of the Yellow River. At one time the society had more than 4000 members, and even now there are nearly 900 Lums in the Honolulu phone book.

The society's Taoist temple at the corner of River and Kukui streets honours the goddess Tin Hau, a Lum child who rescued her father from drowning and was later deified as a saint. Many Chinese claim to see her apparition when they travel by boat. The elaborate altar inside the temple is open for viewing when the street-level door is unlocked. The caretaker is friendly, though he doesn't speak English.

Izumo Taisha Shrine The Izumo Taisha shrine, across the river on Kukui St, is a small wooden Shinto shrine built in 1923. Hundred-pound sacks of rice sit near the altar.

Foster Botanic Garden
This garden covers 20 acres at the northern end of Chinatown. The entrance is on Vineyard Blvd, near its intersection with River St. The garden was established in 1850 by German botanist William Hillebrand on five acres of land purchased from Queen Kalama. The towering trees in the centre of the garden were planted by Hillebrand.

Captain Foster bought the property in 1867 and continued the planting. In the 1930s the tropical garden was bequeathed to the city of Honolulu, and it's now a city park.

The garden is laid out in sections, with areas for palms, orchids, plumerias and poisonous plants, among other plants.

If you've ever wondered how nutmeg, allspice or cinnamon grow, stroll through the Economic Garden. There's also a black pepper vine that climbs 40 feet up a gold tree, a vanilla vine and other herbs and spices.

The herb garden was the site of the first Japanese language school in Oahu. Many Japanese immigrants sent their children there to learn to read Japanese, hoping to maintain their cultural identity and the option of someday returning to Japan. During the bombing of Pearl Harbor a stray artillery shell exploded into a room full of students. A memorial marks the site.

At the other end of the park, the wild orchid garden is a beauty and a good place for close-up photography. Unfortunately this side of the garden is skirted by the H-1 freeway, which detracts from what would otherwise be a peaceful stroll.

The garden's East African *Gigasiphon macrosiphon*, a tree with white flowers which open in the evening, is thought to be extinct in the wild. The tree is so rare that it doesn't have a common name.

The native Hawaiian loulu palm, taken long ago from the upper Nuuanu Valley, may also be extinct in the wild. The garden's chicle tree, New Zealand kauri tree and Egyptian doum palm are all reputed to be the largest of their kind in the USA. Oddities include the cannonball tree, the sausage tree and the double coconut palm with a single 50-pound nut.

In the true spirit of a community garden, there's a plot near the entrance (labelled 'The Garden') where neighbourhood folks tend little patches of taro, tomatoes, chard and other backyard crops for their own use.

Foster Garden is open from 9 am to 4pm and admission costs $1 for those aged 13 and over. Trees are marked and a corresponding self-guided tour booklet is available at the entrance.

The Friends of Foster Garden (tel 533-3406) provides volunteer guides who lead 45-minute walking tours at 1 pm on Mondays, Tuesdays and Wednesdays. It's best to call ahead.

Kuan Yin Temple

The Kuan Yin Temple (170 N Vineyard Blvd) is next to the entrance of Foster Garden. It's a bright red Buddhist temple with a green ceramic tile roof. Inside it's ornate and richly carved and is filled with the sweet pervasive smell of burning incense.

The temple is dedicated to Kuan Yin Bodhisattva, goddess of mercy, whose statue is the largest in the prayer hall. Devotees burn paper money for prosperity and good luck. Offerings of oranges, fresh flowers and vegetarian food are placed at the altar. The large citrus fruit that is sometimes stacked pyramid-style is the pomelo, considered a symbol of fertility because of its many seeds.

Hawaii's multi-ethnic Buddhist community worships there and respectful visitors are welcome.

Ala Moana

Ala Moana means 'path to the sea'. Ala Moana Blvd (Hwy 92) connects the Nimitz Highway (leaving the airport) with downtown Honolulu and continues into Waikiki. Ala Moana is also the name of Honolulu's largest beach park and a land area, but the words are most often spoken (and sung in commercials) in reference to the Ala Moana Center.

Ala Moana Center Ala Moana is Hawaii's biggest shopping centre, with over 180 shops. When neighbouring islanders fly to Honolulu to shop, they go to Ala Moana. Tourists wanting to spend the day at a mall usually head there too. The centre is Honolulu's major bus transfer point and tens of thousands of passengers transit through Ala Moana daily, so it's pretty easy to get there.

Ala Moana has the Sears, Liberty House, J C Penney, Longs Drugs, Foodland supermarket, Waldenbooks, Sharper Image and Banana Republic chain stores. It also has a great food court with 21 ethnic fast-food stalls, a post office, a satellite city hall and a visitor information centre with bus schedules and tourist brochures. There's a kite shop selling Molokai kites and a shop selling old Hawaiian stamps and coins.

Shirokiya is an authentic Japanese department store, from the saleswomen in blue uniforms chirping 'arigatos' to the top-floor Japanese food market where sushi in little plastic containers sells for $3.

At the Crack Seed Center people scoop from jars full of pickled mangoes, li hing pears, rock candy, salty red ginger, cuttlefish legs, roasted green peas and something called tourist plum.

Ala Moana Beach Ala Moana Beach Park is a fine city park with much less hustle and bustle than Waikiki. The park is fronted by a broad white sand beach nearly a mile long which is buffered from the traffic noise of Ala Moana Blvd by a spacious grassy area with shade trees.

This is where Honolulu residents go to jog after work, play volleyball on the beach and enjoy weekend picnics. There are several softball fields and tennis courts. It's a very popular park yet big enough to feel uncrowded.

Ala Moana is generally a safe place to swim and popular with distance swimmers. However the deep channel that runs the length of the beach can pose a danger at low tide, particularly to poor swimmers who don't realise it's there. A former boat channel, it drops off suddenly to depths of about 30 feet.

The 43-acre artificial peninsula jutting from the Diamond Head side of the park is Aina Moana State Recreation Area, otherwise known as Magic Island. There's a nice walk around the perimeter of Magic Island and sunsets can be picturesque with sailboats pulling in and out of the adjoining Ala Wai Boat Harbor. This is also a hot summer surf spot.

Ala Moana Park is directly opposite the Ala Moana Center. The park has full facilities, free parking and even its own Burger King.

AROUND DOWNTOWN HONOLULU
Bishop Museum

The Bishop Museum (1525 Bernice St, tel 847-3511) is considered by many to be the best Polynesian anthropological museum in the world. It also has Hawaii's only planetarium.

One side of the main gallery, the Hawaiian Hall, has three floors covering the cultural history of Hawaii. The first floor is dedicated to pre-Western contact Hawaii and has a full-size pili-grass thatched house.

The most impressive display on this floor is a large yellow feather cloak made for Kamehameha I and passed down to subsequent kings. It was created entirely of the yellow feathers of the now-extinct mamo, a predominately black bird with a yellow

Bishop Museum ticket

upper tail. Around 80,000 birds were caught, plucked and released to create this cloak.

The 2nd floor is dedicated to 19th century Hawaii and the top floor to the various ethnic groups that comprise present-day Hawaii. Like Hawaii itself, the museum has a bit of everything, including samurai armour, Portuguese festival costumes, Taoist fortune-telling sticks and Queen Liliuokalani's royal coach.

The Polynesian Hall contains masks from Melanesia, stick charts from Micronesia and weapons and musical instruments from Polynesia. The Cooke Rotunda features an exhibit detailing how ancient Pacific navigators journeyed vast distances, tuning into the seas and the skies for direction.

The Hall of Discovery is a hands-on centre aimed at getting kids interested in museums. There are Hawaiian toys to play with, pre-contact tools to try, large turtle shells to crawl under and peek out of and collections of butterflies and seashells, with magnifying glasses to inspect them with.

In the Atherton Halau, hula shows are presented at 1 pm daily. From 9 am to 3 pm craftspeople demonstrate Hawaiian quilting, lauhala weaving, lei making or other traditional crafts.

Bishop Museum is well-respected, not only for its collections but for the ethnological research it has spearheaded. Beginning in the 1920s, supported by mainland philanthropy and Ivy League scholars, it organised teams of archaeologists and anthropologists and sent them to record the cultures of the Pacific islands before they were forever lost.

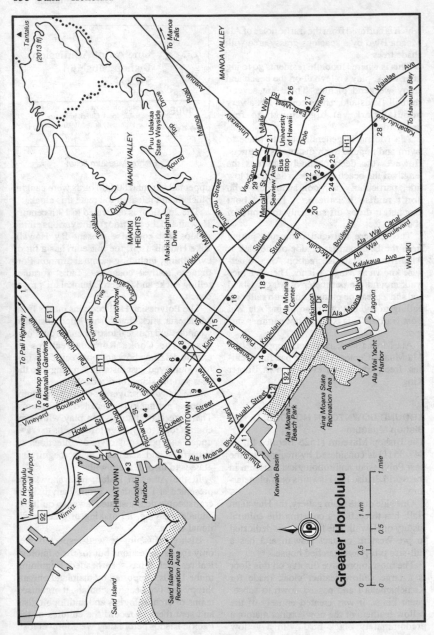

Greater Honolulu

1	Royal Mausoleum State Monument	16	Mekong
2	Foster Botanic Garden	17	Fernhurst YWCA
3	Aloha Tower	18	Froggies
4	Iolani Palace	19	Central Branch YMCA
5	Restaurant Row	20	Chiang Mai
6	Goodwill	21	Honolulu International Youth Hostel
7	Thomas Square	22	Anna Bannanas
8	Honolulu Academy of Arts	23	Yakiniku Camellia
9	Yanagi Sushi	24	Down to Earth Natural Foods
10	Blaisdell Center	25	Chan's Chinese Restaurant
11	Ward Warehouse	26	East-West Center
12	Ward Center	27	Burns Hall
13	Jelly's Maps & Misc	28	Foodland
14	El Burrito	29	Manoa Valley Inn
15	Auntie Pasto's		

The most renowned of the researchers was Kenneth Emory, a local boy who spoke Hawaiian and thus had the linguistic underpinnings to understand all Polynesian dialects. For five decades he sailed schooners and mailboats to the far corners of the Pacific, cranking out film footage of native dancers, recording their songs, measuring their temples (both buildings and skulls!) and transcribing their folklore. Emory's treatises are the most important (and sometimes the only) anthropological recordings of many Pacific island cultures, from Lanai to Tuamotu. Now in his 90s, he's still affiliated with the museum.

Admission The Bishop Museum is open from 9 am to 5 pm Monday to Saturday and on the first Sunday of each month. Admission of $5 for adults and $2.50 for children aged 6 to 17 includes all exhibits, demonstrations and the planetarium.

Planetarium shows are held at 11 am and 2 pm. On Fridays and Saturdays there's an extra show at 7 pm followed on clear nights by viewing from the observatory telescope. Admission to the planetarium alone costs $2.50 for adults and $1.25 for children.

Resources The museum library has nearly 100,000 books on the Pacific. It's open to the public from 10 am to 3 pm Tuesday to Friday and from 9 am to noon on Saturdays. The visual history collection (movies and old photographs) is open from 1 to 4 pm Tuesday to Thursday and from 9 am to noon on Saturdays.

The museum shop has many books on the Pacific not easily found elsewhere and a gift shop. There's also a small cafeteria.

Getting There & Away From Waikiki, take the No 2 School/Middle St bus to Kapalama St, walk toward the ocean and turn right on Bernice St. By car, take Exit 20A off H-1 and drive a couple of blocks mauka of the freeway.

Moanalua
In olden times Moanalua was a stopover for people travelling between Honolulu and Ewa as well as a vacation spot for Hawaiian royalty. In 1884 Princess Pauahi Bishop willed the valley to Samuel M Damon. It's now privately owned by his estate.

Moanalua Gardens Moanalua Gardens is a large grassy park with grand shade trees. It's maintained by the Damon Estate as a public park and is a popular weekend picnic spot.

On the grounds, Kamehameha V's gingerbread-trimmed summer cottage overlooks a taro pond. Above it a Chinese-style hall is fronted by carp ponds and a stand of golden-stemmed bamboo. The centre of the park has a grassy stage where the Prince Lot Hula Festival is held on the third Saturday in July.

To get there, take the Puuloa Rd/Tripler Hospital exit off Hwy 78 and then make an immediate right-hand turn into the gardens.

Moanalua Trail The trail up Moanalua Valley is along a gravel and dirt road, once a cobblestoned valley road. This is a dry area and there is only partial shade along the trail. There are both native and introduced plants, and lots of bird calls can be heard. Seven stone bridges remain along the path in various stages of disrepair.

The non-profit Moanalua Gardens Foundation works to preserve Moanalua Valley in its natural state. Their efforts to raise public awareness of the valley's history and environmental uniqueness helped defeat plans which would have routed the new H-3 freeway through Moanalua Valley.

The foundation gives interpretive walks into Moanalua (Kamananui) Valley on the second Saturday and fourth Sunday of each month. The easy five-mile walks begin at 9 am and finish around noon. Reservations are requested a week in advance (tel 839-5334) though if it's not crowded they may let you join in on the spot.

You can also hike the trail on your own. Numbered posts along the first half of the trail correspond to a self-guide brochure available from the Moanalua Gardens Foundation office (1352 Pineapple Place, Honolulu, HI 96819) for $2 or by mail for $2.50.

If you follow the road all the way in, it's about four miles. It's also possible to branch off before the end of the road and take a trail up to the ridge.

To get to the trailhead, take the Moanalua Valley/Red Hill exit off Hwy 78 (one exit past Moanalua Gardens). Stay to the right and follow the Moanalua Valley sign uphill 1½ miles past the golf course to where the road ends at a parking lot. There are restrooms and drinking water.

Royal Mausoleum State Monument
The Royal Mausoleum contains the remains of Kings Kamehameha II, III, IV and V as well as King David Kalakaua and Queen Liliuokalani, the last reigning monarchs.

The only one missing is Kamehameha I, the last king to be buried in secret in accordance with Hawaii's old religion.

The original mausoleum building is now a chapel and the caskets are in nearby crypts. Other markers honour John Young and Charles Reed Bishop, husband of Bernice Pauahi Bishop.

The mausoleum, at 2261 Nuuanu Ave (just before the avenue meets the Pali Highway), is open from 8 am to 4 pm Monday to Friday.

Hsu Yin Temple
Part of the Chinese-Buddhist Association of Hawaii, the Hsu Yin Temple is on Kawananakoa Place, just across Nuuanu Ave from the Royal Mausoleum.

This is a nice Buddhist temple, with the standard offerings of Sunkist oranges and burning incense. Prints on the walls tell Buddha's life story.

Punchbowl
Punchbowl is the bowl-shaped remains of a long-extinct volcanic crater. At an elevation of 500 feet it sits a mile above the downtown district and offers a fine view of the city out to Diamond Head and the Pacific beyond.

Early Hawaiians called the crater Puowaina, 'Hill of Human Sacrifices'. It's believed there was a heiau there and that kapu breakers were brought to Punchbowl to be slain and burned on an altar.

Today it's site of the 115-acre National Memorial Cemetery of the Pacific. The remains of Hawaiians sacrificed to appease the gods now share the crater floor with the bodies of more than 25,000 soldiers, more than half of whom were killed in the Pacific during WW II.

The remains of Ernie Pyle, the distinguished war correspondent who covered both world wars and was hit by machine gun fire in Okinawa during the final days of WW II lies in section D, grave 109. His place is marked with the same style of flat granite stone that marks each of the graves.

A huge memorial at the head of the cemetery has eight marble courts representing different Pacific regions and is inscribed with the names of the 26,280 Americans missing in action from WW II and the Korean War.

The cemetery is open from 8 am to 5.30 pm in winter and until 6.30 pm from March to September. The entrance into Punchbowl is off Puowaina Drive. There's a marked exit as you start up the Pali Highway from H-1; it comes up quickly!

University of Hawaii

The University of Hawaii at Manoa, the central campus of the statewide college system, is east of downtown Honolulu and two miles north of Waikiki.

The university has strong programmes in astronomy (thanks to Mauna Kea), geophysics, marine sciences and Hawaiian and Pacific studies. The campus attracts students from islands throughout the Pacific.

The outside walls of the Campus Center have a great Hawaiiana mural, with scenes based on photos from a classic August 1981 *National Geographic* article on Molokai.

Manoa Garden restaurant in Hemenway Hall is a student hangout that sometimes has live music. Hemenway Hall and the Campus Center are behind Sinclair Library, which fronts University Ave opposite Burger King and the bus stop. Parking at UH is a hassle; you're better off arriving by bus or on foot.

The Hamilton Library has an excellent map room, though the downtown public library has a better collection of general interest books and periodicals than the university libraries.

Information The Information Center (tel 948-7235) in the Campus Center has campus maps and arranges tours.

Attending University You can get information on undergraduate studies from the Admissions & Records Office (tel 948-8975), Sakamaki Hall, 2530 Dole St, Honolulu, HI 96822, and on graduate studies from the Graduate Division (tel 948-8544), Spalding Hall, 2540 Maile Way, Honolulu, HI 96822.

The summer session consists of two six-week terms. Tuition is $100 per credit for non-residents and $50 per credit for residents. For the summer catalogue contact the Summer Session (tel 948-7221), Box 11450, Dept PA, Honolulu, HI 96828.

Activities & News *Campus Calendar* is a free weekly newsletter detailing campus exhibitions, seminars and performances, many of them open to the public. *Ka Leo O Hawaii* is the student newspaper. Both are free and can be found at the campus libraries.

Hemenway Theater (tel 948-6468) in Hemenway Hall shows foreign flicks, select Hollywood movies and local surf films. Admission is $3. Printed schedules are available at the theatre and posted on the bulletin boards.

Bulletin Boards Boards around campus have notices of rooms for rent, cars and surfboards for sale and campus activities. The best boards are in front of Sinclair Library.

There's another board strictly for information about rooms for rent but it's tricky to find. Ask at the Campus Center for directions. The majority of rentals are for rooms in shared student households and most advertisers are looking for long-term roommates.

East-West Center

The East-West Center (1777 East-West Rd, Honolulu, HI 96848; tel 944-7111) is a federally funded educational institution whose stated goal is to promote mutual understanding among the people of Asia, the Pacific and the USA.

Some 2000 researchers and graduate students work and study there. They examine development policy, the environment, communication and other Pacific issues.

The centre has multicultural programmes open to the public. Almost every week there's a music performance such as Chinese lute music or a Dixieland jazz band. Admission is usually $5 to $10. For information call 944-7666.

On most weekdays the centre presents documentary or travel videos on Pacific locales or scholastic seminars on such topics as living in another culture, conflict resolution in Thailand or the homeless in Hawaii. Pick up a *Centerweek* newsletter at Burns Hall (at the corner of Dole St and East-West Rd) or call 944-7283 for the weekly schedule.

Free one-hour tours of the East-West Center's facilities and Japanese garden are held at 1.30 pm Tuesday to Thursday. Meet at the Friends Desk on the garden level of Jefferson Hall.

UPPER MANOA VALLEY

The Upper Manoa Valley, mauka of the university, ends at forest reserve land. There's a hike to Manoa Falls, trails through Lyon Arboretum and the touristy Paradise Park.

The drive up the valley is through a well-to-do residential neighbourhood. Not as exclusive as nearby Makiki Heights, the yards reflect the individual character of the residents rather than professional gardeners. Some yards are nicely planted with orange trees and flowering shrubs, others have tasteful Japanese touches such as stone lanterns, rock gardens and tile roofs.

Paradise Park

Paradise Park is disappointing, with birds in stark cages and a tour bus crowd. It's open from 10 am to 5 pm daily. Admission is $7.50.

Manoa Falls Trail

The trail to Manoa Falls is a beautiful hike, especially for one so close to the city. The trail runs for three-quarters of a mile above a rocky streambed that leads up to the falls. It takes about 30 minutes one way.

You get the feeling you're walking through a thick rainforest a long way from anywhere, surrounded by lush damp vegetation and moss-covered stones and tree trunks; where the only sounds the birds have

to compete with are the rush of the stream and waterfall.

There are all sorts of trees along the path, including tall *Eucalyptus robusta* trees with their soft spongy reddish bark, flowering orange African tulip trees, and lofty varieties which creak like wooden doors in old houses. Many of them were planted by the Lyon Arboretum, which at one time held a lease on the property.

Wild purple orchids and red ginger grow up near the falls. The ginger can be seen inside the fenced watershed area to the left of the falls. The falls are steep and drop about 100 feet vertically into a small shallow pool. It's not deep enough for swimming, and occasional falling rocks don't make it advisable anyway, but there are pools in the stream that you can at least get wet in. The area is quiet and peaceful.

The trail is usually a bit muddy but not too bad if it's not been raining lately. Be careful not to catch your foot in the exposed tree roots – they're potential ankle breakers, particularly if you're moving with any speed. The packed clay can be slippery in some steep places, so take your time and enjoy the trail.

Aihualama Trail About 75 feet before Manoa Falls an inconspicuous trail starts to the left of the chain-link fence. This is the Aihualama Trail, well worth a little 15-minute side trip. Just a short way up you get a broad view of Manoa Valley.

After about five minutes you'll enter a bamboo forest with some massive old banyan trees. When the wind blows the forest releases eerie crackling sounds. It's a trippy forest, enchanted or spooky depending on your mood.

You can return to the Manoa Falls Trail or go on another mile to Pauoa Flats where the trail connects with the Puu Ohia Trail in the Tantalus area.

Lyon Arboretum

The Lyon Arboretum (3860 Manoa Rd, tel 988-7378) is a great place to go after hiking to Manoa Falls if you want to identify trees and plants you've seen along the trail.

LYON ARBORETUM
University of Hawaii

Lyon Arboretum Button

Dr Harold Lyon, after whom the arboretum is named, is credited with introducing 10,000 exotic trees and plants to Hawaii. Approximately half of these are represented in this 124-acre arboretum, which is part of the University of Hawaii.

This is not a landscaped tropical flower garden, but a mature and largely wooded arboretum, where related species are clustered in a semi-natural state with trails meandering through.

The Hawaiian ethnobotanical garden has mountain apple, breadfruit and taro; ko, the sugar cane brought by early Polynesian settlers; kukui, which produced lantern oil; and ti, used medicinally since ancient times and for moonshine after Westerners arrived.

The arboretum also has herbs and spices and cashew, cacao, papaya, betel nut, macadamia nut, jackfruit and calabash trees, as well as greenhouses and classrooms.

The 20-minute walk up to Inspiration Point is a good choice. There are wonderful scents, stone benches along the way and lots of bird calls. The path loops through ferns, bromeliads and magnolias and passes by tall trees, including a bo tree, a descendant of the tree Gautama Buddha sat under when he received enlightenment.

Inspiration Point has a view of the hills that enclose the valley. It'd be a pleasant place to have a picnic lunch.

The arboretum is open from 9 am to 3 pm Monday to Friday and from 9 am to noon on Saturdays. They ask for a $1 donation. Free guided tours are given at 1 pm on the first Friday and third Wednesday of each month

and at 10 am on the third Saturday of each month.

The reception centre (tel 988-3177) has a book and gift shop and helpful staff members. They can give you maps and brochures of the garden and information on outings and community workshops in horticulture, Hawaiiana and arts and crafts.

They also offer two-hour workshops where children can make their own tapa, Hawaiian toys or artwork from natural objects found in the garden, for just 50 cents.

Getting There & Away

From Ala Moana Center take the No 5 Manoa bus to the end of the line, which is the parking lot below Paradise Park. From there it's a five-minute walk to the road's end, where the Manoa Falls Trail begins. Lyon Arboretum is off to the left just before the trailhead.

To get there by car, simply drive to the end of Manoa Rd. There's room to park at the trailhead, but don't leave anything valuable in the car. Parking is more secure at Lyon Arboretum.

TANTALUS & MAKIKI HEIGHTS

Just two miles from downtown Honolulu a narrow switchback road cuts its way up the lush green forest reserve land of Tantalus and the Makiki Valley. The road climbs up almost to the top of 2013 foot Mt Tantalus, with swank mountainside homes tucked in along the way.

Though it's one continuous road, the western side is called Tantalus Drive and the eastern side Round Top Drive. The 8½-mile loop is Honolulu's finest scenic drive, with great views of the city below.

The road is winding and steep, but it's a good paved road. Amongst the profusion of dense tropical growth, eucalyptus, bamboo, ginger and elephant-ear taro are easily identified. Vines climb to the top of telephone poles and twist their way across the wires.

A network of hiking trails runs between Tantalus and Round Top drives and throughout the forest reserve. The amazing thing about hiking there is that the trails are seldom

Tantalus, Makiki Valley & Manoa Falls

crowded. Perhaps because the drive itself is so nice, the only walking most people do is between their car and the lookouts.

The Makiki Heights area below the forest reserve is one of the most exclusive residential areas in Honolulu and the site of a museum of contemporary art. There's bus service as far as Makiki Heights, but none around the Tantalus-Round Top loop drive.

Puu Ualakaa State Wayside Park

From Puu Ualakaa State Wayside Park you can see an incredible panorama of all Hono-

lulu. The park entrance is 2½ miles up Round Top Drive from Makiki St.

The sweeping view from the lookout extends from Kahala and Diamond Head on the far left, across Waikiki and downtown Honolulu, to the Waianae Range on the far right. The tan buildings inland on the left are the University of Hawaii at Manoa; below, and to the right, you can see clearly into the green mound of Punchbowl Crater; the airport is out on the edge of the coast; and Pearl Harbor is beyond that.

Although the best time for photos is usually during the day, this is also a fine place to watch evening settle over the city. Arrive at least 30 minutes before sunset to see the hills before they're in shadow.

The park gates are locked from 6.45 pm (7.45 pm in summer) to 7 am. For night (and anytime) views, there are a couple of scenic pull-offs before the park.

In olden times, the slopes of Puu Ualakaa (Rolling Sweet Potato Hill) were planted with sweet potatoes, which were said to have been dug up and rolled down the hill for easy gathering at harvest time. The hill's other name, 'Round Top', is more recent.

The Contemporary Museum

The new Contemporary Museum (2411 Makiki Heights Drive, tel 526-1322) is housed in a classy 1925 tropical-design estate with 3½ acres of Japanese gardens.

The estate was built for Mrs Charles Montague Cooke, whose other former home is the present site of the Honolulu Academy of Arts.

You enter the museum through a covered courtyard with copper and bronze gates and an arrangement of parabolic mirrors reflecting the view hundreds of times over.

Inside are several galleries of paintings, sculpture and other contemporary artwork by both local and international artists. A newer building holds the museum's most prized piece, a vivid environmental installation by David Hockney based on his sets and costumes for *L'Enfant et les Sortileges*, Ravel's 1925 opera. There's also a bookshop with a tea room.

The museum is near the intersection of Mott-Smith Drive and Makiki Heights Drive. The No 15 bus from downtown Honolulu gets you there.

It's open daily except Tuesdays, from noon to 4 pm on Sundays and from 10 am to 4 pm on other days. Admission is free on Thursdays and $3 other days.

Meditation Center

The Honolulu Siddha Meditation Center (1925 Makiki St, Honolulu, HI 96822), for followers of Gurumayi Chidvilasananda, has programmes open to interested visitors.

These sessions, which generally include chanting and a video of Gurumayi, are held from 7.30 to 9 pm on Wednesdays and Saturdays. Special programmes with festive dinners or potluck meals take place on holy days.

For registration and information call 942-8887. The ashram is in a big house behind the main road.

Hiking Tantalus

A network of hiking trails crosses forest reserve land in the Makiki/Tantalus area, with numerous trailheads off Tantalus Drive and Round Top Drive.

Three of the hiking trails can be combined to make a 2½-mile loop through Makiki Valley.

The Puu Ohia Trail leads to the Nuuanu Valley Lookout and also connects with another trail that leads across to Manoa Valley.

Makiki Valley Loop Trail

Maunalaha and Kanealole, two of the three trails that form the Makiki Valley Loop Trail, start at the baseyard of the Makiki Forest Recreation Area. The Makiki Valley Trail crosses the upper Makiki Valley, connecting the Maunalaha and Kanealole trails.

The loop is through a lush and varied tropical forest that starts out in Hawaii's first state nursery and arboretum. In this nursery, hundreds of thousands of trees were grown to replace the sandalwood forests that had been levelled in Makiki Valley and throughout Hawaii in the 1800s. The new saplings were planted to stem the erosion and loss of watershed caused by the deforestation.

The Maunalaha Trail (three-quarters of a mile) begins behind the second building below the baseyard parking lot. It first crosses a bridge, passes taro patches and proceeds to climb the east ridge of Makiki Valley, passing Norfolk pine, bamboo and fragrant allspice and eucalyptus trees. There are some good views along the way.

Before reaching the Makiki Valley Trail junction you see avocado trees on the right. In early fall they're ripe for the picking.

The mile-long Makiki Valley Trail is the left fork of the four-way trail intersection. It passes up and down through small ravines and across gentle streams with patches of ginger. Near the Moleka Stream crossing are mountain apple trees (related to allspice and guava), which flower in the spring and fruit in the summer. Edible yellow and strawberry guavas also grow along the trail. There are some fine views of the city below.

The Kanealole Trail begins as you cross Kanealole Stream and then follows the stream down to the baseyard, three-quarters of a mile away. The trail leads down through a field of Job's-tears. The bead-like bracts of the female flowers of this tall grass are often picked to be strung in leis. Kanealole Trail is usually muddy, so wear shoes with good traction and pick up a walking stick. Halfway down there's a grove of introduced mahogany.

Getting There & Away To get to the baseyard, turn left off Makiki St and go about half a mile up Makiki Heights Drive. Where the road makes a sharp bend, proceed straight ahead through a green gate into the Makiki Forest Recreation Area. Keep going until you come to the Forestry & Wildlife baseyard. There's a parking lot on the right.

You can also take the No 15 bus, which runs between downtown and Pacific Heights. Get off near the intersection of Mott-Smith Drive and Makiki Heights Drive and walk down Makiki Heights Drive to the baseyard. It's about a mile to the trailhead.

An alternative is to hike just the Makiki Valley Trail, which you can reach by driving up Tantalus Drive two miles from its intersection with Makiki Heights Drive. As you come around a sharp curve, look for the wooden post marking the trailhead on the right. You can take this route in as far as you want and backtrack out or link up with other trails along the way.

Puu Ohia Trail
The Puu Ohia Trail leads up to a lookout with a great view of Nuuanu reservoir and valley. It's two miles one way and makes a hardy hike.

The trailhead is at the very top of Tantalus Drive, 3.6 miles up on the left from its intersection with Makiki Heights Drive. There's a large turn-off opposite the trailhead where you can park.

The Puu Ohia Trail leads through bamboo groves and guava, and lots of eucalyptus which is a fast growing tree planted to protect the watershed. About half a mile up, the trail reaches the top of 2013 foot Mt Tantalus (Puu Ohia).

From Mt Tantalus, the trail leads into a service road. Continue on the road to its end, where there's a Hawaiian Telephone building. The trail picks up again behind the left side of the building.

Continue down the trail until it leads into the Manoa Cliff Trail. Go left on the Manoa Cliff Trail a short distance until you come to another intersection where you turn right. This is the continuation of the Puu Ohia Trail which now leads down into Pauoa Flats and on to the lookout. The flats area can be muddy. Be careful not to trip on exposed tree roots.

You'll pass two trailheads before reaching the lookout. The first is Nuuanu Trail, on the left, which runs three-quarters of a mile along the western side of Upper Pauoa Valley and offers broad views of Honolulu and the Waianae Mountains.

The second is Aihualama Trail, a bit farther along on the right, which takes you the 1¼ miles to Manoa Falls through bamboo groves and huge old banyan trees. If you were to follow this route you could then hike less than a mile down the Manoa Falls Trail to Paradise Park and from there catch a bus back to town (see the Manoa Valley section).

PLACES TO STAY
Places to Stay – bottom end
Honolulu International AYH-Hostel (2323A Seaview Ave, Honolulu, HI 96822; tel 946-0591) is in a residential neighbourhood near the University of Hawaii. The main house is

a dormitory for Pacific Island students attending the university. Out the back, seven dorms with bunk beds can accommodate 40 travellers, with men and women in separate dorms. There are no rooms for couples. Rates are $8 per night for IYHF or AYH hostel members and $11 per night for non-members. AYH membership is sold there for $20. Telephone reservations are accepted. Office hours are from 7.30 to 9.30 am and from 5 to 9 pm. Guests must be out during the day.

The bulletin board has useful information for new arrivals and beach mats are lent free. There's a laundry room, a TV room and the manager sometimes puts a movie on the VCR. From Ala Moana, catch a No 6 or No 18 (University or Woodlawn) bus and get off at the corner of University Ave and Metcalf. Seaview Ave is one block up.

Fernhurst YWCA (1566 Wilder Ave, Honolulu, HI 96822; tel 941-2231) has rooms for women only in a three-storey building about a mile from the university. There are 60 rooms, each intended for two guests, with two single beds, two locked closets, a desk and dresser. Two rooms share a bathroom.

It costs $20 per person for YWCA members and $23 for non-members. If you get a room to yourself (easier during the low season), it costs $5 more. Rates include buffet-style breakfasts and dinners daily except Sundays and holidays.

Guests staying more than three days must become Y members ($20 a year). Payment is required weekly in advance. There's a linen-use fee of $4.50. Reservations can be made by mail by sending one night's deposit by cashier's check or postal money order.

Fernhurst is near the intersection of Wilder and Punahou, on the No 4 bus line. It's a quiet community setting and there's a laundry room, security guard and a garden courtyard with a small pool. Office hours are 8.30 am to 10.30 pm.

The *Central Branch YMCA* (401 Atkinson Drive, Honolulu, HI 96814; tel 941-3344), on the Diamond Head side of the Ala Moana Center, has rooms for men only. Rates are

$25 with shared bath, $30.50 with private bath. For doubles they charge $10 more and add a rollaway bed. The hard part is getting in as it's always full and they don't take reservations. Your best bet is to call at around 8 am when they set up a waiting list and again at around 11 am to check on your status. The 115 rooms are simple but clean, each with a bed, desk and closet. Guests receive YMCA privileges which includes free use of the sauna, lap pool, gym and handball courts. There's a coin-operated laundry and a TV lounge for residents.

During the school year, the *Atherton YMCA* (1810 University Ave, Honolulu, HI 96822; tel 946-0253) operates as a dorm for full-time University of Hawaii students only. During summer holidays (mid-May to mid-August) it's open on a space-available basis to non-students. Rates are $18/25 a single/double. Reservations are made by application (available by mail) with a $115 security deposit. The Y is next door to Burger King, directly opposite the university.

Sailors, both male and female, between ships can try their luck getting one of the 23 rooms at the *Seaman's Home*, next to the Marine Firemen's Union, 707 Alakea St, just up from Honolulu Harbor. The rooms are spartan and the toilets are down the hall, but at $12 a night, no-one's complaining.

Places to Stay – middle

The *Pagoda Hotel* (1525 Rycroft, Honolulu, HI 96814; tel 941-6611, 800-367-6060) has two sections. The cheapest rooms, which are $65 studios in the apartment complex section, are run down and a bit on the seedy side. The $70 hotel rooms are nicer and have kitchenettes and a central lobby. It's nothing special, but it's one way to avoid Waikiki. It has a nice restaurant with a carp pond.

Places to Stay – top end

Manoa Valley Inn (2001 Vancouver Drive, Honolulu, HI 96822; tel 947-6019, 800-634-5115), formerly the John Guild Inn, is on a quiet side street near the University of Hawaii. The back porch and garden have views of the sunset and the highrises of

Waikiki, which is a 10-minute drive and a whole world away.

Crazy Shirts owner Rick Ralston spent $750,000 authentically restoring the house's Victorian decor, right down to the floral wallpaper stretched over cheesecloth. The inn is on the National Register of Historic Places. All eight rooms are beautiful and filled with period antiques, one with a four-poster bed, another with furnishings that belonged to the silent film star Frances Beaumont. Other nice touches include complimentary sherry and mineral water, fruit and cheese in the afternoon, lounging robes and fresh flower bouquets. There's lots of common space, a parlour and a pool table. It would be a delightful place to stay.

Rates are $80 for rooms with a shared bathroom and from $95 to $145 for rooms with a private bathroom, and include a continental breakfast buffet. No children under 14 are allowed.

Places to Stay – near the airport

If you've got some dire need to be near Honolulu International, there are three hotels outside the airport along a busy highway and beneath flight paths.

For long layovers or midnight flights, there are two cheaper places where you can catnap or just take a shower. Both shower services provide towels, shampoo, razors and hair dryers and are open 24 hours a day.

The *Honolulu Airport Mini Hotel* (Terminal Box 42, Honolulu, HI 96819; tel 836-3044) is in the airport's main terminal, between lobbies five and six. It has 17 private rooms, each with a single bed and its own bathroom and shower. Overnight (eight-hour) stays are $22.75. Showers only are $7.50. Between 7 am and 7 pm you can catch a few winks for $4 an hour. Reservations are not taken for the per-hour sleeps or showers, but are for overnight stays.

Nimitz Shower Tree (tel 833-1411) is at 3085 N Nimitz Highway in an industrial area not far from the airport hotels. The private 'roomettes' are just a line of three-walled cubicles with curtains that can be drawn

across the front. It's $18 per person for an eight-hour sleep and shower or $7.50 for a shower only. They can store luggage, provide transport to and from the airport and have a courtesy phone in the baggage claim areas.

Holiday Inn-Honolulu Airport (3401 N Nimitz Highway, Honolulu, HI 96819; tel 836-0661, 800-465-4329), at the corner of Rodgers Blvd and Nimitz Highway, has 310 rooms at $92/99 for singles/doubles. It's about 10% cheaper in the low season.

Best Western Plaza Hotel-Honolulu Airport (3253 N Nimitz Highway, Honolulu, HI 96819; tel 836-3636, 800-528-1234) has 268 rooms starting at $76/87 for singles/doubles.

The *Pacific Marina Inn* (2628 Waiwai Loop, Honolulu, HI 96819; tel 836-1131), slightly further along in an industrial area, is an unappealing three-decker motel with rooms for $64/68 for singles/doubles.

All three hotels have swimming pools and provide 24-hour free transport to and from the airport, about 10 minutes away. The Holiday Inn and Best Western have restaurants. The Sizzler Steak House is nearby.

PLACES TO EAT

Honolulu has an incredible variety of good ethnic food. If you know where to look it can also be quite cheap. The trick is to get out of the tourist areas and eat where the locals do.

Around the University

The area just below the University of Hawaii at Manoa has some great restaurants. All these listings are within a five-minute walk of the three-way intersection of King St, Beretania St and University Ave – except Chiang Mai, which is about 10 minutes away.

Yakiniku Camellia (2494 S Beretania St) has an all-you-can-cook buffet Korean lunch for $7. It's a great deal and the food is delicious. The mainstay is pieces of chicken, pork and beef, which you select from a refrigerated cabinet and grill at your table. Accompanying this are 18 marinated and pickled side dishes, miso and seaweed soups, fresh vegetable salads and fruit. The mung bean and watercress dishes tossed with sesame seeds are sweet and mild. As for the kimchee and other marinated dishes, generally the redder they are, the hotter they are. At dinner the same buffet costs $10, but they throw in sashimi and oysters. This place is the real thing; there's even a newspaper vending machine selling a Korean-language daily.

Chan's Chinese Restaurant (2600 S King St) is the place to go for inexpensive dim sum. The chicken-filled half moons and the shrimp gau at 45 cents each are recommended. The chicken pies and curry turnovers cost 60 cents each, have a wonderful flaky crust and are potentially addictive. Chan's has noodles, chow mein and other Chinese dishes as well. Lunch specials are in the $4 range. It's open from 9 am to midnight daily.

India House (2632 S King St, tel 955-7552) serves aromatic Indian dishes in an almost hole-in-the-wall setting. Tandoori chicken is $7.50 à la carte or $11.75 with pullao rice and naan bread. Chef Ram Arora is credited with introducing naan to the prestigious Third Floor restaurant before opening his own place. It's open from 5 to 9.30 pm most nights and occasionally for lunch.

Anna Bannanas (2440 S Beretania St, tel 946-5190), a combined bar and restaurant, has reasonably priced Mexican food and sandwiches. It's best known as a rockin' nightspot and is a little dark at lunch time.

Chiang Mai (2239 S King St, tel 941-1151) serves northern Thai cuisine such as spring rolls, crispy noodles and chicken with eggplant. The food is good, the decor interesting and it's not too difficult to get in on a weekend night. It's open from 11 am to 2 pm Monday to Friday and from 5.30 to 10 pm nightly.

Down to Earth Natural Foods (2525 S King St) is a fantastic natural foods supermarket. If it's healthy and you can eat it, you'll probably find it there. They have everything from Indian chapattis and dahl to pure maple syrup and sesame oil on tap, as well as local organic produce and a dozen varieties of granola sold in bulk. It's a great place to shop and prices are surprisingly low. The good yoghurts and whole-grain breads that some of Honolulu's more with-it supermarkets sell are substantially cheaper at Down to Earth. It's open from 8 am to 10 pm daily.

Natural Deli, inside Down to Earth, is a snack bar serving vegetarian food only. It has a salad bar from which you can select salad for $3 per pound, sandwiches for $2 and barbecued soyburgers for $3.25. It's open from 10 am to 9 pm daily.

The University of Hawaii has two unexciting campus cafeterias operated by Marriott: the *Hamilton Snack Bar* (next to Hamilton Library), where you can fill up for $3 or $4, and the *Manoa Garden*, where the food is slightly better and prices slightly higher. *Burger King* and *Pizza Hut* are just across University Ave.

Ala Moana

Ala Moana Center's central food court is a circus, with neon signs, 800 tiny tables crowded together and 21 fast food stands circling it all. There's something for everyone, from salads to daiquiris, ice cream to pizza, and Chinese, Japanese, Korean, Hawaiian, Thai, Filipino and Mexican specialities.

This is a good place to stop when you're between buses if you've got the munchies. It's like window shopping. If you come in here hungry you'll go crazy. It's open from 9.30 am to 9 pm Monday to Friday, from 9.30 am to 7 pm on Saturdays and from 10 am to 5 pm on Sundays.

Kitchen Garden specialises in salads such as curried chicken, Thai peanut pasta, Waldorf, fruit, marinated vegetable and just plain green. They're good and healthy and range in price from $2.95 to $4.50.

Panda Express has Mandarin and Sichuan food. It's our favourite choice here, with dishes like spicy chicken with peanuts, broccoli beef and shrimp with garlic sauce. Combination plates with fried rice or chow mein and two dishes are $3.55, three dishes $4.35. The food is fresh and you can walk through and pick what looks best from the steamer trays.

Patti's Chinese Kitchen is the other big-volume Chinese restaurant, with 20 to 30 dishes to choose from. It costs $3.20 for two selections, $4 for three selections. If you really want to indulge you can get a whole roast duck for $8. It has a limited selection of dim sum and desserts, including almond cookies for a dime. Patti's is the busiest place in the food court.

Two tasty skewers of chicken satay at *Little Cafe Siam* are $1.55.

Big slices of acceptable pizza at *Sbarro* cost between $1.50 and $2.

Ward Warehouse
The *Old Spaghetti Factory* is hands down the best deal at Ward Warehouse, which is on the corner of Ala Moana Blvd and Ward Ave. The restaurant is filled with old antiques, heavy woods, Tiffany stained glass – even an old street car. At lunch you can get spaghetti with tomato sauce for $3.10, with clam sauce for $3.85, or with meatballs for $5. All meals come with warm sourdough bread and a green salad. At dinner time they add coffee and spumoni ice cream and raise the prices by $1. To top it off, window tables have a view of the boat harbour across the street.

For dessert, *Dave's Ice Cream* sells chunks of chocolate-covered frozen bananas rolled in nuts for 25 cents, as well as ice cream and sherbet in macadamia nut, lychee, passion fruit and other Hawaiian flavours.

Coffee Works has coffees, desserts such as carrot cake and apple pie, and sandwiches on healthy breads at reasonable prices.

Stuart Anderson's is heavy on the steak and ribs, in the $5 to $10 range for lunch and about double that for dinner.

Fisherman's Wharf, across the street at Kewalo Basin, is disappointing – at least for lunch.

Restaurant Row
The new and rather sterile complex of Restaurant Row on the corner of Ala Moana Blvd and Punchbowl St caters to the downtown business crowd. It seems to have more offices than eating places and, despite the name, isn't worth going out of your way to get to.

The top draws are the *Black Orchid*, a fine-dining restaurant co-owned by actor Tom Selleck; *Trattoria Manzo*, an Italian restaurant frequented by Mayor Fasi; and *Studebaker's*, which is a nightclub. There's also a *Burger King*, *Marie Callender's* and a sandwich shop.

The pop-art revolving clock in the central fountain is from the 1986 Expo in Vancouver, or so we've been told.

Fort St Mall
The Fort St Mall, on the edge of the downtown district, has cheap restaurants within walking distance of Iolani Palace. It's convenient for downtown workers and sightseers, but not a draw if you're elsewhere around town.

Taco Bell, *McDonald's*, *Burger King* and *Pizza Hut* are all near the intersection of Hotel St and the pedestrian-only Fort St Mall.

The following three restaurants are lined up a block away, on Fort St Mall between Pauahi St and Chaplain Lane.

At *Harpo's Pizza* you can get a slice of pepperoni pizza, tossed green salad and soft drink for $3.55.

Tay Do, a new Vietnamese restaurant, has lunch plates such as spicy lemon grass chicken or barbecued pork that come with consomme, rice and salad for $4.25. Noodle dishes and the Vietnamese soup pho are the same price. It's open from 8.30 am to 7 pm daily except Sundays.

Ba Le, a branch of the Ba Le Vietnamese restaurant in Chinatown, has great French bread, sandwiches, manapua, good shrimp rolls and French coffee. It's open from 7 am to 6 pm Monday to Friday, and from 9 am to 2 pm on Saturdays.

There's another Ba Le on Queen St near the Old Federal Building.

Chinatown

Wo Fat (on the corner of Hotel & Maunakea streets) is large and lively, with bright colourful decor that includes fire-breathing dragons climbing the central pillars. A lunch plate of egg rolls, beef broccoli, won ton, chicken chow mein and rice costs $4. Add spare ribs and 55 cents for dinner. They have a buffet lunch on weekdays for $7.50 with dishes from Peking duck to almond pudding, but the regular plates are big enough to fill you up at half the price. It's open from 10 am to 9 pm daily. Waikiki bus Nos 2 and 20 stop out the front.

Krung Thai (1028 Nuuanu Ave, tel 599-4803), on the edge of Chinatown between the business and red light districts, is a real find. It's run by a friendly Thai family with a knack for cooking. There's a garden courtyard out the back. The chicken Panang has a great spicy peanut sauce and costs $4.25. They have papaya salad, spring rolls and vegetarian, seafood and meat dishes. Nothing on the menu is over $6. Liquor's not served but you can bring your own. Dinner is from 5.30 to 8 pm on Mondays, Wednesdays and Fridays. Lunch is geared to the business community's 30-minute lunch breaks, with dishes ready in steamer trays. One item costs $2.65, two items $3.55 and all are served with rice or noodles. It's open from 10.30 am to 2.30 pm Monday to Saturday.

Ba Le Sandwich Shop (150 N King St) bakes terrific French bread, with a delicate and crisp crust that can't be beaten. Baguettes cost 35 cents, or filled as sandwiches they cost $1 for vegetarian and $2.25 with meat. Sweet, strong French coffee with milk costs $1.25 hot or cold. They make good croissants, Vietnamese manapua and soursop candies. It's a great place for a simple breakfast if you're in Chinatown.

The speciality at the Vietnamese restaurant *To Chau* (1007 River St), is pho, a delicious soup of beef broth with rice noodles and thin slices of beef garnished with cilantro and green onion. It comes with a second plate of fresh basil, mung bean sprouts and slices of very hot red chilli to add

at will. It's $3.50 for a regular bowl and $4 for an extra-large one. The shrimp rolls with peanut sauce ($2.50) are good, and they also have noodle and rice dishes, but just about everybody comes for the soup. It's so popular for lunch that even at 10.30 am you may have to wait for one of the 16 tables. It's well worth it.

Doong Kong Lau (River St pedestrian mall) has an extensive menu that includes the expected Chinese standards as well as more exotic dishes from the mountainous Hakka region of China. Most dishes, from fresh island prawns to preserved eggs with tofu, cost from $4.50 to $8. Salt-roasted chicken roasted in a paper bag is a speciality. Lunch specials are large, delicious and cheap. The shrimp and scallops in garlic sauce is full of flavour and costs $3.65. If you order a noodle dish, splurge and pay the extra 75 cents for the cake noodles, pressed and cooked to a crisp on the edges. Meals include soup. It's open from 8 am to 9.30 pm daily.

Other Places to Eat

El Burrito (550 Piikoi St, up from Ala Moana Center) could be a neighbourhood restaurant on a back street in Mexico City. It's a real hole-in-the-wall with about a dozen tables squeezed in. The food's good and authentic. Chicken enchiladas with rice and beans are $5.25 and recommended. Other plates are priced from $3.75. At dinner time it's a busy little place with people waiting outside for tables. Inside it's noisy, crowded and alive with people laughing and chattering – often in Spanish. It's open from 11 am to 8 pm Monday to Thursday and to 9 pm on Fridays and Saturdays.

Mekong (1295 S Beretania St, tel 521-2025) is the original Keo's (now in Waikiki), and still has the original Thai cook. It doesn't look like much from the outside, but inside it's got a touch of class, with live orchids and white linen. The menu is similar to that of Keo's, but in the Mekong, Thai posters replace the original artwork, you bring your own booze and prices are all about a third less. The famous Evil Jungle Prince and most other beef or chicken dishes are $5.25. The $8 fresh fish saute is the most expensive item. The restaurant is open from 11 am to 2 pm on weekdays and from 5 to 9.30 pm nightly. Reservations are taken from Monday to Thursday only.

The *Garden Cafe* (tel 531-8865) is an open-air lunch restaurant in the Honolulu Academy of Arts (900 S Beretania). It's run by volunteers with proceeds going to the museum. They cook up something different every day, and it costs $6 including a beverage. It's usually a sandwich or a salad such as chicken curry with chutney, along with homemade soup. Dessert or wine costs $1.50 extra. Seatings are at 11.30 am and 1 pm Tuesday to Friday. Call in the morning to see what's on the menu and to make reservations. On Thursdays there's a 6.30 pm supper.

Auntie Pasto's (1099 S Beretania, tel 523-8855) has excellent Italian food at moderate prices. The $7.50 eggplant parmigiana is recommended. Pasta costs $4.50 with tomato sauce, $6.95 with creamy pesto or $5.95 heaped with fresh vegetables in a butter and garlic sauce. The parmesan cheese is freshly grated and the Italian bread is served warm. Dishes and prices are the same at lunch and dinner. It's a bustling, popular, high-energy place that's off the tourist track. Even at lunch you may have to wait for a table, and dinner on weekends can be nuts. It's open from 11 am to 10.30 pm Monday to Friday and 4 to 10.30 pm on Saturdays and Sundays.

The *Pagoda Floating Restaurant* at the Pagoda Hotel (1525 Rycroft, tel 941-6611) is surrounded by gardens, waterfalls and a carp pond. The breakfast menu (7 to 11 am) is extensive, with many choices from $3 to $5.75. It has menu lunches from about $5 and a lunch buffet for $8.50 from Monday to Friday. The dinner buffet for $14 ($12 from 4.30 to 5.30 pm) features prime rib, Alaskan snow crab and teppanyaki. It's open daily.

Willows (901 Hausten St, tel 946-4808) has been a Honolulu attraction for 45 years, as much for the atmosphere as the food. You can even dine in thatched huts. Their Hawaiian Poi Supper is a good alternative to being soaked at an impersonal luau and there's more Hawaiiana at Willows anyway. Dishes range from Sri Lankan curry to wok specialities and fresh fish. It's open for lunch and dinner, there's a Sunday brunch and prices are moderate.

Yanagi Sushi (762 Kapiolani Blvd, tel 537-1525) and *Sada's* (1432 Makaloa, tel 949-0646) are two good places for sushi. Yanagi Sushi is open from 11 am to 2 pm daily and from 5.30 pm to 3 am daily except Sundays. Sada's is open from 11 am to 2 pm Monday to Saturday and from 5 pm daily until at least 11 pm.

Compadres is a hopping place at the Ward Center, 1200 Ala Moana Blvd. Lots of margaritas and nachos are downed there on late Friday afternoons, with the noise level rising as the daylight fades. A single enchilada, burrito or taco with beans, rice and salad costs $8. Larger combinations start at $10.

The new *Coasters* restaurant, behind the Hawaii Maritime Center at Pier 7, is open for snacks, lunch and dinner from 10.30 am to 10 pm. Chef Bones Yuen is well known around town for his former gourmet restaurant, Serendipity.

John Dominis (43 Ahui St, tel 523-0955), on the Ewa side of Kewalo Basin, is rather expensive but it has good fresh seafood and a great ocean view.

ENTERTAINMENT
Classics & Concerts

Honolulu has a symphony orchestra, opera company, ballet troupes, community theatre groups and chamber orchestras.

The *Blaisdell Center* at 777 Ward Ave in Honolulu draws big national and international names. Call the Blaisdell box office (tel 521-2911) for information.

The *Academy Theater* of the Honolulu Academy of Arts and the *East-West Center* both present quality multi-cultural shows, such as performances by members of the Beijing Opera and recitals of Japanese lute music.

Dancing & Disco

At the Ala Moana Hotel (410 Atkinson Drive), near the Ala Moana Center, you can find top-40 bands at *Nicholas Nickolas* (tel 955-4466) and a video disco at the newly renovated *Rumours* (tel 955-4811).

The *Black Orchid* restaurant (tel 521-3111) in Restaurant Row (500 Ala Moana Blvd) has jazz from 7 to 9 pm, top-40 or Hawaiian groups from 9 pm to 1 am, and a genteel crowd.

Studebaker's (tel 531-8444), also in Restaurant Row, is into a '50s trip with a real red Studebaker, checked linoleum, vinyl bar stools and glitzy neon tube lights. It's a popular spot.

Or try *Anna Bannanas* (2440 S Beretania St, tel 946-5190) on Fridays and Saturdays when the house band, the Pagan Babies, plays roots dance music (African, reggae and soca) from 9 pm to 1 am. On salsa night Hawaii's Latinos come out to dance. Anna's is also a restaurant and bar, specialising in Mexican food. It's refreshingly unpretentious.

Comedy

The *Honolulu Comedy Club* (tel WACKY-98), atop the Ilikai Hotel, has stand-up comedians from Wednesday to Saturday.

Movie Theatres

For something progressive, there's the *Academy Theatre* (tel 538-1006) at the Honolulu Academy of Arts and the *Hemenway Theater* (tel 948-6468) at the university.

Free Things

Centerstage at the Ala Moana Center features local performers in free shows. There's some sort of performance going on at noon and 7 pm most days.

The Young People's Hula Show with little keiki dancers at 9 am Sundays draws the biggest crowd.

The Royal Hawaiian Band usually performs at noon on Wednesdays or Thursdays. Sometimes they get into big band jazz, and other times they play numbers from old musicals. Other performers include church choirs, high school groups and rock bands.

The Royal Hawaiian Band also performs from noon to 1 pm on Fridays in the grounds of the Iolani Palace.

Call 527-5666 for recorded details of free performances and activities presented by the City and County of Honolulu, including occasional concerts at *Honolulu Hale* (City Hall).

The *Ward Centre* (1200 Ala Moana Blvd, tel 531-6411) has jazz concerts from 5 to 7 pm on the first Friday of each month. They sometimes feature top musicians such as saxophonist Gabe Baltazar.

For a different sort of entertainment the following are also free: the Honolulu Academy of Arts, daily except Monday; the Contemporary Art Museum on Thursdays; and the Punchbowl memorial.

Pearl Harbor Area

On 7 December 1941 a wave of more than 350 Japanese planes attacked Pearl Harbor, home of the US Pacific Fleet.

Some 2335 US soldiers were killed during the two-hour attack. Of those, 1177 died in the battleship USS *Arizona* as it took a direct hit and sank in less than nine minutes. Twenty other ships were sunk or seriously damaged and 188 aeroplanes were destroyed.

USS Arizona Memorial

Over 1.5 million people 'Remember Pearl Harbor' each year by visiting the USS Arizona Memorial run by the National Park Service. It is Hawaii's most visited attraction.

The visitor centre includes a museum and theatre as well as the off-shore memorial at the sunken USS *Arizona*. The park service provides a 75 minute programme that includes a 21 minute documentary film followed by a boat ride out to the memorial and back. Everything is free.

The film gives the history of the *Arizona* from the day it was launched to the day it

USS Arizona Memorial

went under, with a spiel emphasising military preparedness.

The 184 foot memorial, built in 1962, sits directly over the *Arizona* without touching it. It contains the *Arizona*'s bell and a wall inscribed with the names of those who went down with the ship. The average age of the enlisted men on the *Arizona* was 19.

From the memorial the battleship can be viewed eight feet below the surface. The ship rests in about 40 feet of water and even now oozes a gallon or two of oil each day. In the rush to recoup from the attack and prepare for war, the navy exercised its option to leave the men in the sunken ship buried at sea. They remain entombed in its hull.

The visitor centre (tel 422-2771; recorded information: tel 422-0561) is open from 7.30 am to 5 pm daily except Thanksgiving, Christmas and New Year's Day. There's a snack bar and a souvenir shop.

Programmes run every 15 or 20 minutes from 8 am to 3 pm. As soon as you arrive, pick up a ticket at the information booth; the number on the ticket corresponds to the time the tour begins. Summer months are busiest, with an average of 4500 people taking the tour daily, and the allotment of tickets is sometimes gone by 11 am. Generally the shortest waits are in the morning. Children shorter than 45 inches are not allowed on the boat.

There's a little open-air museum to keep you occupied while you're waiting. It has interesting photos from both Japanese and US military archives showing Pearl Harbor before, during and after the attack. There's a photo of Harvard-educated Admiral Yamamoto, the brilliant military strategist who planned the attack on Pearl Harbor even though he personally opposed going to war with the USA. Rather than relish the victory, he stated after the attack that he feared Japan had 'awakened a sleeping giant and filled him with a terrible resolve'.

Another photo shows the Micronesian atoll of Bikini going up in a nuclear explosion in 1946. A number of US battleships that the Japanese had missed at Pearl Harbor five years earlier – including the *Nevada* and the *Pennsylvania* – were nuked along with Bikini during the atomic bomb test.

Getting There & Away The visitor centre is off Kamehameha Highway (Hwy 90) on the Pearl Harbor Naval Base just south of Aloha

The Bowfin Submarine

Stadium. Follow highway signs for the Arizona Memorial, not Pearl Harbor.

If you're travelling by public transport, take the No 20 Airport bus from Waikiki. It takes about 1¼ hours.

The private Arizona Memorial Shuttle Bus (tel 926-4747) runs direct from Waikiki every half hour between 6.50 am and 1 pm. The last return trip leaves the memorial at 4 pm. The ride takes about 45 minutes and costs $4 return.

There are private boat cruises to Pearl Harbor leaving from Kewalo Basin. They should be avoided as passengers are not even allowed to board the memorial.

Bowfin Park

Adjacent to the Arizona Memorial visitor centre is Bowfin Park (tel 423-1341), which contains the Pacific Submarine Museum and a moored WW II submarine, the USS *Bowfin*.

The museum traces the development of submarines from the turn of the century to the nuclear age.

The *Bowfin*, commissioned in May 1943, sank 44 ships in the Pacific before the end of the war. The sub tour is self-guided, with a hand-held radio receiver that picks up recorded messages as you walk through. Admission of $4 for adults and $1 for children includes both the sub and the museum.

There's no charge to enter the park and inspect the conning tower and periscopes, which can be moved around to scan Pearl Harbor or the Japanese *kaiten*, or suicide torpedo, that sits in the grounds.

The kaiten is just what it looks like: a torpedo with a single seat. As the war was closing in on the Japanese homeland, the kaiten was developed in a last-ditch effort to ward off an invasion. It was the marine equivalent of the kamikaze pilot and his plane. A volunteer was placed in the torpedo before it was fired. He then piloted it to its target. At least one US ship, the USS *Mississinewa*, was sunk by a kaiten. It went down off Ulithi Atoll in November 1944.

If you have to wait an hour or two for your Arizona Memorial tour to begin, you might want to stroll over to this park, which is open from 8 am to 4.30 pm daily.

PEARL CITY

Pearl City is the largest city outside Honolulu. It's home to 43,000, including a lot of military people and civilians who work on the bases. There's not much of interest there.

If you're not going into Pearl City, stay on H-1 and avoid the parallel Kamehameha Highway (Hwy 90), as it's all stop-and-go traffic, fast food and malls.

Pearlridge Shopping Center is a massive mall that runs between H-1 and Kamehameha Highway. A swap meet is held a block west of the shopping centre on Saturdays, Sundays, Wednesdays and holidays at the drive-in theatre.

KEAIWA HEIAU STATE PARK

This park in Aiea, north of Pearl Harbor, covers 334 acres and contains an ancient medicinal temple, camping grounds, picnic facilities and a scenic loop trail. The park is open from 7 am to sunset for day visitors. As with all state parks, there are no fees.

At the park entrance is Keaiwa Heiau, a religious site used by Hawaiian *kahuna lapaau* (herbalist healers). The kahunas used hundreds of medicinal plants and grew many on the grounds surrounding the heiau. Among those still found here are noni, whose pungent yellow fruits were used to treat heart disease; kukui, whose nuts were an effective laxative; and ulu, whose sap soothed chapped skin. Ti leaves were wrapped around a person to break a fever. Many of the medicinal plants around the heiau are marked.

The heiau is 100 by 160 feet, a single terraced stone structure. Not only did the herbs have medicinal value but the heiau itself was considered to possess life-giving energy. The kahuna was able to draw forth the powers from both.

People wishing to be healed still place offerings within the heiau. The offerings reflect the multiplicity of Hawaii's cultures: rosary beads, New Age crystal pendants and cans of Campbell's tomato soup sit beside flower leis and rocks wrapped in ti leaves.

Aiea Loop Trail

The 4½ mile Aiea Loop Trail begins at the top of the park's paved loop road next to the restrooms and comes back out at the camping ground, about a third of a mile below the start of the trail.

The trail starts off in a forest of eucalyptus and ironwood trees and runs along the ridge. Other trees along the way are Norfolk Island pines, edible guava and native ohia lehua, with its fluffy red flowers.

There are vistas of Pearl Harbor, Diamond Head and the Koolau Range. About two-thirds of the way along, the wreckage of a C-47 cargo plane that crashed in 1943 can be spotted through the foliage on the eastern ridge. The hike takes 2½ to three hours. It's a fairly easy, well-maintained trail.

Camping

The camping area can accommodate 100 campers. Each site has its own picnic table, barbecue grill and trash can. Sites are not crowded together, but because they're largely open there's not a lot of privacy either. There's a distant view of Honolulu's airport a couple of miles to the south.

If you're camping in winter make sure your gear is waterproof, as it rains a lot at this 880-foot elevation. The temperature is usually pleasant. There are restrooms, showers, a phone and drinking water.

For Oahu, it's a good choice for a camping ground. There's a caretaker by the front gate, and the gate is locked at night for security.

Permits are issued for up to five nights and must be reserved a week in advance. Like all Oahu public camping grounds, it's closed on Wednesdays and Thursdays.

Getting There & Away

From Honolulu, head west on Hwy 78 and take the Aiea Stadium turn-off onto Moanalua Rd. Turn right onto Aiea Heights Drive at the first traffic light. The road passes the Aiea sugar refinery and winds up, through a residential area, 2½ miles to the park. The ride up the hill has good views of the city and Pearl Harbor.

South-East Oahu

Some of Oahu's finest scenery is along the south-east coast, which curves around the tip of the Koolau Mountains. Diamond Head, Hanauma Bay and the island's most famous bodysurfing beaches are all just a 20-minute ride from Waikiki.

East of Diamond Head, H-1 turns into the Kalanianaole Highway (Hwy 72), following the south-east coast up to Kailua. It passes the exclusive Kahala residential area, a run of shopping centres, and housing developments that creep up into the mountain valleys.

The highway rises and falls as it winds its way around the Koko Head area and Makapuu Point, with coastal views along the way. The area is geologically interesting, with boldly stratified rock formations, volcanic craters and lava sea cliffs.

DIAMOND HEAD

Diamond Head is a tuff cone and crater that was formed by a violent steam explosion deep beneath the surface long after most of Oahu's volcanic activity had stopped.

As the backdrop to Waikiki, it's one of the best-known landmarks in the Pacific. The summit is 760 feet high.

The Hawaiians called it Leahi and built a luakini heiau on the top where human sacrifices took place. But ever since 1825, when British sailors found calcite crystals sparkling in the sun and mistakenly thought they'd struck it rich, it's been called Diamond Head.

In 1909 the US Army began building Fort Ruger at the edge of the crater. They built a network of tunnels and topped the rim with cannon emplacements, bunkers and observation posts. Reinforced during WW II, it's been a silent sentinel whose guns have never fired.

Today there's a Hawaii National Guard base inside the crater as well as Federal Aviation Administration and civil defence facilities. The best reason to visit Diamond Head is to hike the trail to the crater rim for the panoramic view.

Diamond Head is a state monument, with restrooms, drinking water, picnic tables and interpretive plaques. The gates are open from 6 am to 6 pm.

Hiking Diamond Head

The trail to the summit was built in 1910 to service the military observation stations along the crater rim.

It's a fairly steep hike, with a gain in elevation of 560 feet, but it's only three-quarters of a mile to the top and plenty of people of all ages hike up. It takes about 30 minutes one way. The trail is open and hot and you might want to take along something to drink.

As you start up the trail, you can see the summit ahead at about 11 o'clock.

The crater is dry and scrubby with kiawe, koa haole, grasses and wildflowers. The little yellow-orange flowers along the way are native ilima, Oahu's official flower.

About 20 minutes up the trail you enter a long, dark tunnel. Because the tunnel curves you don't see light until you get close to the end. It's a little spooky, but the roof is high enough for you to walk through without bumping your head, and there is a hand rail. Your eyes should adjust enough to make out shadows but if you don't like walking in the dark, bring a flashlight.

The tunnel itself seems like it should be the climax of the long climb, but on coming out into the light you're immediately faced with a steep 99-step staircase.

Persevere! After this there's a shorter tunnel, a narrow spiral staircase inside an unlit bunker and the last of the trail's 271 steps.

From the top there's a fantastic 360° view taking in the south-east coast to Koko Head and Koko Crater and the leeward coast to Barbers Point and the Waianae Mountains. Below is Kapiolani Park and the orange seats of the Waikiki Shell. You can also see the lighthouse, coral reefs, sailboats and even surfers waiting for waves at Diamond Head Beach.

Watch your footing at the top. There are some steep drops.

Getting There & Away Bus Nos 3 and 58 stop at Diamond Head. It's about 15 minutes walk from the bus stop to the trailhead above the parking lot. Once you walk through the tunnel you're in the crater.

By car, take Monsarrat Ave (which goes by the zoo) to Diamond Head Rd and then take the right after Kapiolani Community College into the crater.

Diamond Head Beach

Diamond Head Beach is popular with both surfers and windsurfers.

To get there from Waikiki, follow Kalakaua Ave to Diamond Head Rd. There's a parking lot just beyond the lighthouse. At the end of the lot is a paved trail down to the beach. The beach has showers but no other facilities.

Conditions at Diamond Head are suitable for intermediate to advanced windsurfers,

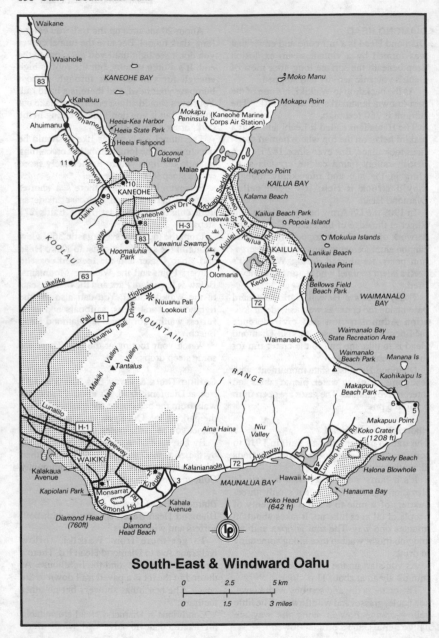

South-East & Windward Oahu

| 0 | | 2.5 | | 5 km |
| 0 | 1.5 | | 3 miles | |

and when the swells are up they really ride the waves – surfing more than sailing.

HANAUMA BAY BEACH PARK

Hanauma is a wide, sheltered bay of sapphire and turquoise waters set in a rugged volcanic ring. No visitor to Oahu should miss it, even if you only go there to look.

Hanauma (curved bay) was once a popular fishing spot. It had nearly been fished out when it was designated a marine life conservation district in 1967. Now that the fish are fed instead of eaten, they swarm in by the thousands.

From the overlook you can peer into crystal waters and see the entire coral reef that stretches across the width of the bay. You can see glittery schools of silver fish, the bright blue flash of parrotfish and perhaps a lone sea turtle. To see an even more colourful scene, put on a mask, jump in and view it from beneath the surface.

The large sandy opening in the middle of the coral, called the Keyhole, is where most beginning snorkellers start. Divers and veteran snorkellers go beyond the reef to deeper parts of the bay.

Hanauma seems to get as many people as fish. With some three million visitors a year, it's always busy and often crowded. But go anyway! It's for good reason that everyone's there.

If you ask an islander about snorkelling conditions elsewhere on Oahu, the answer you'll get most often is 'It's not Hanauma'.

Hanauma is both a county beach park and a state underwater park. It has a grassy picnic area, lifeguards, showers, restrooms, changing rooms and access for the disabled.

The snack bar has hamburgers, hot dogs, popcorn, soda and long queues. Snorkel sets are rented at a concession stand for $5 between 8 am and 4 pm.

Paths lead along low ledges on both sides of the bay. Be cautious when the sea is rough or the tide is high, as waves can wash over the ledges.

More people drown at Hanauma than at any other beach on Hawaii. Although the figure is high largely because there are so many visitors to the beach, people drowning in the Toilet Bowl or being swept off the ledges have accounted for a fair number of deaths.

Toilet Bowl

A 15-minute walk out to the point on the left side of the bay brings you to the Toilet Bowl, a small natural pool in the lava rock. The Toilet Bowl is connected to the sea by an underwater channel, which enables water to surge into the bowl and then flush out from beneath.

People going into the pool for the thrill of it can get quite a ride as it flushes down four to five feet almost instantly. However the rock around the bowl is slippery and hard to grip, and getting in is far easier than getting out. It definitely shouldn't be tried alone.

You can also walk to the Toilet Bowl from above the parking lot. Go up and around the fence and walk south-east.

Witches Brew

A 10-minute walk along the right side of the bay will take you to the rocky point that juts out about two-thirds of the way down. Witches Brew is the name for the turbulent waters that swirl and churn in the cove on the southern side of this point.

There's a nice view of Koko Crater from there. Green sand made of olivine can be found along the way.

Snorkelling & Diving

Snorkelling is good at Hanauma Bay year

round. Mornings are better than afternoons, as swimmers haven't stirred up the sand.

The inner reef is an excellent place for novice snorkellers. The deepest water is 10 feet, though it's very shallow over the coral. It's well-protected and usually swimming-pool calm.

Hanauma's got big rainbow parrotfish crunching off chunks of coral, moray eels, bright yellow butterflyfish, goatfish, Moorish idols and numerous other tropicals. Drop in some bread if you want to start a feeding frenzy.

For confident snorkellers, it's better on the other side of the reef where there are larger coral heads, bigger fish and fewer people. Swim out to the red flag marking the channel on the right side of the beach and go out just beyond the boulders. Then snorkel down to the left parallel with the beach. There's a bit of a current in the channel, especially at low tide when you can feel it pull out as you come back in.

Don't swim outside the reef when the water is rough or choppy. Not only will the channel current be strong, but the sand will be stirred up and visibility poor anyway.

Divers have the whole bay to play in, with clear water and coral gardens, sea turtles and lots of fish. Beware of currents when the surf is up; surges in the Witches Brew, on the right hand side; and the Molokai Express, a treacherous current that runs just outside the mouth of the bay.

An interpretive board in front of the snack bar clearly illustrates water conditions in different parts of the bay and is worth looking at. It also names the fish that can be seen.

Getting There & Away
Hanauma is about 10 miles from Waikiki along Hwy 72.

TheBus runs a 'Beach Bus' to Hanauma (and on to Sea Life Park) about every 40 minutes, but only on weekends, holidays and school vacations (including all summer). The last bus back is at 4.55 pm.

Alternatively, you could take bus No 58 to the Koko Marina Shopping Center, but it's a mile-long uphill walk from there.

From the highway bus stop it's 10 minutes walk down to the beach. Look for the dirt path short cut leading to the parking lot.

A private bus (tel 677-9600) runs to Hanauma daily. It makes eight trips from Waikiki between 9 am and 1 pm, with return trips between noon and 4.30 pm. It collects passengers at 16 bus stops in Waikiki and costs $1.50 one way.

There are a number of snorkel tours to Hanauma for $5 to $10, including snorkel gear and transport to and from Waikiki hotels. You might try Hanauma Bay Snorkeling (tel 523-1023), Steve's Diving Adventures (tel 947-8900), Hawaii Snorkeling (tel 944-2846) or Ocean Snorkel Rentals (tel 955-5680) or check the free tourist magazines.

KOKO HEAD REGIONAL PARK
The entire Koko Head area is a county regional park. It includes Hanauma Bay, Koko Head, Halona Blowhole, Sandy Beach and Koko Crater.

Koko Head is backed by Hawaii Kai, an expansive development of condos, houses, a marina and a golf course – all overplanned and quite sterile.

Koko Crater and Koko Head are both tuff cones created about 10,000 years ago in Oahu's last gasp of volcanic activity.

Koko Head
Koko Head, not to be confused with Koko Crater, overlooks and forms the south-western side of Hanauma Bay.

The one mile walk up the road to the summit has fine coastal views that light up nicely at sunset. The road starts near the highway at the Hanauma Bay entrance.

There are two craters atop Koko Head, as well as telecommunications facilities on the 642-foot summit. The Nature Conservancy maintains a preserve in the shallow Ihiihilauakea Crater, the larger of the two. The crater has a unique vernal pool and a rare fern, the *Marsilea villosa*. For information on work parties or weekend excursions call 537-4508.

Top: Petroglyphs, Puako, Big Island
Left: Puuhonua O Honaunau National Historical Park, Big Island
Right: Fishing God

Top: Crossing Hanakapiai Stream, Kalalau Trail, Kauai
Left: Waimea Canyon, Kauai
Right: Trail through ironwood trees, Palaau State Park, Molokai

Lookouts & Halona Blowhole

Less than a mile past Hanauma is a lookout with a view of striking coastal rock formations and crashing surf.

Less than a mile further is the pull-off for Halona Blowhole. Here water surges through a submerged tunnel in the rock and spouts up through a hole in the ledge. It's usually preceded by a gushing sound, as air is forced out immediately before the water.

Down to the right of the parking lot is Halona Cove, the beach where the risque love scene with Burt Lancaster and Deborah Kerr in *From Here to Eternity* was filmed in the 1950s.

Atop Halona Point Japanese fishermen have placed a little stone monument to those lost at sea.

Sandy Beach

Sandy Beach is one of the most dangerous beaches on the island if measured in terms of lifeguard rescues and broken necks. It has a punishing shorebreak, a powerful backwash and riptides.

Nevertheless, the shorebreak is extremely popular with bodysurfers who know their stuff. People go to Sandy Beach to watch them being tossed around in the transparent waves.

Sandy Beach is beneath Koko Crater. The beach is wide and very long and, yes, sandy. It's popular with sunbathers, young surfers and their admirers, and high school students cruising the parking lot. When the swells are big, board surfers hit the left side of the beach.

There's a zone for everyone; like the grassy strip where model aircraft can be operated between 7 am and noon and kites can be flown from noon to 6 pm!

For the more sedate, sifting through the sand will produce lots of white augers and other small shells.

The park has restrooms, showers and lifeguards. Lunch wagons usually park across the street.

In the past few years one of Oahu's biggest environmental struggles has been centred around Sandy Beach. In a major anti-development coup, islanders have united in a grassroots movement to 'Save Sandy Beach' from a planned golf course development. To block the plan, the movement sponsored a 1988 county ballot initiative to rezone 31 acres of coastal land around Sandy Beach from residential status to preservation status. It was passed with overwhelming support.

Koko Crater

According to Hawaiian legend, Koko Crater is the imprint left by the vagina of Pele's sister Kapo, sent there from the Big Island to lure the pig-god Kamapuaa away from Pele.

Inside the crater there's a neglected botanic garden with ageing plumeria trees that the county has plans eventually to revive. To get there, take Kealahou St off Hwy 72 opposite Sandy Beach. Just over half a mile in, turn left at the road to Koko Crater Stables (no trail rides) and drive in.

On the outside of the crater on the Hanauma side there's an unmaintained hiking trail. It follows an abandoned railroad track that once served a former army missile base on the 1208-foot summit.

Places to Eat

Koko Marina Shopping Center, at the corner of Lunalilo Home Rd and Hwy 72, has a *Sizzler Steak House*, a *Korean Bar-B-Q*, *Domino's Pizza*, a *Kentucky Fried Chicken*, *McDonald's* and other restaurants as well as ice cream, shave ice and yoghurt shops.

The centre also has the Aloha Dive Shop, a Foodland supermarket, Waldenbooks, banks, drugstores, twin theatres and gas stations. The bulletin board around the side of Foodland is a good place to check for information about rooms to rent.

Yen King (tel 732-5505), in the Kahala Mall Shopping Center off H-1 in Kahala, has good northern Chinese food. Their kung pao shrimp is recommended and they also do a good shredded pork and string bean saute. Prices are more moderate at lunch time.

Roy's (tel 396-7697) at Hawaii Kai Corporate Plaza on Hwy 72 is the new locale of renowned chef Roy Yamaguchi. The restaurant serves lunch, dinner and Sunday brunch and has wrap-around windows and a view of Maunalua Bay. Roy's combines European and Oriental influences in dishes such as grilled shrimp with Thai curry sauce and chutney. Dinner for two costs about $50.

MAKAPUU

Makapuu Point (647 feet) is the easternmost point of Oahu. A lighthouse marks its tip.

About 1½ miles north of Sandy Beach there's a lookout with a view down onto Makapuu Beach, with aqua-blue waters outlined by white sand and black lava. You can sometimes watch hang gliders taking off from the cliffs.

The largest of the two offshore islands is Manana, otherwise known as Rabbit Island. This ageing volcanic crater has a feral rabbit population that coexists with burrowing wedge-tailed shearwaters. Birds and rabbits sometimes even share the same burrows.

The island also looks vaguely like the head of a rabbit, and if you try hard you may see it, ears folded back. If that doesn't work, try to see it as a whale.

In front of it is the smaller Kaohikaipu Island. All it looks is flat.

There's a coral reef between the two islands that divers sometimes explore, but to do so usually requires a boat.

Makapuu Beach Park

Makapuu Beach is one of Oahu's top winter bodysurfing spots, with waves reaching 12 feet and higher. It has the island's best shorebreak, but there are also dangerous currents to contend with. As with Koko Head's Sandy Beach, Makapuu is for bodysurfers who can handle rough water conditions. Surfboards are prohibited.

The Makapuu Body Surfing Championships are held at this beach around the first weekend in March. In summer, the waters can be calm and good for swimming in.

The beach is opposite Sea Life Park in a pretty setting, with cliffs in the background and a glimpse of the lighthouse. There are restrooms, showers, a daily lifeguard and drinking water. Two native Hawaiian plants are plentiful – naupaka by the beach and the yellow-orange ilima by the parking lot.

Sea Life Park

Sea Life Park (tel 259-7933) is Hawaii's only marine park. Its 300,000-gallon aquarium is Oahu's best, with turtles, eels, eagle rays, hammerhead sharks and thousands of reef fish. A spiral ramp circles the aquarium, which is 18 feet deep, and allows you to see it from different depths.

In one of two outdoor amphitheatres, jumping dolphins and waddling penguins perform the standard marine life park tricks.

In the other, the Whaler's Cove, a 1500-pound false killer whale and a group of dolphins give a choreographed performance. The dolphins tail walk, do the hula and give rides to a 'beautiful island maiden'. It borders on the kitsch.

There's a large pool of California sea lions and a smaller pool with harbour seals and a rare Hawaiian monk seal. The turtle lagoon holds hawksbill, loggerhead and green sea turtles. Another section of the park has nesting red-footed boobies, albatrosses and great frigate birds, which are all sea birds indigenous to Hawaii.

Hanging from the ceiling of the park's little Pacific Whaling Museum is the skeleton of a 38-foot sperm whale that was washed up off Barbers Point in 1980. After the Coast Guard damaged a ship propeller unsuccessfully trying to tow the 20-ton mammal out to sea, they turned the carcass over to Sea Life Park. The park removed almost 38,000 pounds of flesh from the skeleton using many of the antique whaling tools that were on display in the museum. The whole process took the better part of two years.

The museum also has a fine collection of whaling-era scrimshaw, from toys and bird cages to suggestive 'porno' pieces. Implausibly, the gift shop at the side continues the trade in whale-bone scrimshaw. The museum closes one hour before the rest of the park.

On Mondays, Tuesdays, Wednesdays and Saturdays the park is open from 9.30 am to 5 pm, with the last series of shows beginning at 3.15 pm. On Thursdays, Fridays and Sundays the park closes at 10 pm, with the last series of shows from 7 pm, plus a Hawaiian music and dance performance at 8.30 pm. The Friday show sometimes features top island musicians.

Admission is $10 for adults, $7.75 for children aged seven to 12 and $3.75 for those aged four to six. Bus No 58 stops at Sea Life Park.

You can visit the whaling museum and the park restaurant (hamburgers and buffet-style food) without paying admission. There you also get a free glimpse into the seal and sea lion pools from the side of the museum.

WAIMANALO

Waimanalo Bay has the longest continuous stretch of beach in Oahu: 5½ miles of white sand stretching north from Makapuu Point to Wailea Point. A long coral reef about a mile out breaks up the biggest waves, protecting much of the shore.

Waimanalo has three beach parks with camping. The setting is pleasant, though the area isn't highly regarded for safety.

Waimanalo Beach Park

Waimanalo Beach Park has an attractive beach of soft white sand and the water is excellent for swimming.

It's an in-town county park with a grassy picnic area, restrooms, changing rooms, showers, roadside camping, baseball fields, basketball and volleyball courts and a playground.

The park has ironwood trees, but overall is more open than the state park and Bellows Field park up the road. The scalloped hills of the lower Koolau Range rise behind and Manana Island and Makapuu Point are visible to the south.

Waimanalo Bay State Recreation Area

Waimanalo Bay State Recreation Area is about a mile north of the county beach park.

For board surfers and bodysurfers this area has Waimanalo Bay's biggest waves.

The locals call the park Sherwood Forest because hoods and car thieves used to hang out there in the 1960s, and it hasn't totally shaken its reputation. Just as a park ranger in Honolulu was telling us that the incidence of crime on the windward coast is exaggerated, his co-worker reminded him of a friend, who recently, while setting up camp at Waimanalo, had watched helplessly as someone drove off with his car!

The state has spruced up the place with brand new facilities and camping sites on the beach under ironwood trees.

Bus No 57 stops in front and it's a third of a mile further to the beach and camping ground. The gate is open from 7 am to sunset.

Bellows Field Beach Park

The beach fronting much of Bellows Air Force Base is open to civilians for day use and camping on weekends only. It's a long beach with fine, hard-packed sand in a natural setting of ironwood trees. The small shorebreak waves are good for beginner bodysurfers and board surfers.

There's a lifeguard, showers, restrooms and water. The 50 camping sites are under the trees. Permits are available from the county Department of Parks & Recreation.

The marked entrance is a quarter of a mile north of the state recreation area. Bus No 57 stops in front of the entrance road and from there it's 1½ miles to the beach.

Places to Eat

Bueno Nalo (tel 259-7186) is between the state and county beaches, just north of Waimanalo's post office. It serves good homestyle Mexican food with most combo plates in the $7 to $8 range. You can bring in beer and wine, which you can pick up next door at Bobby's grocery store. It's open for dinner from 5 to 9 pm nightly except Mondays.

There's a *McDonald's* just south of the state recreation area.

Pali Highway

The Pali Highway (Hwy 61) runs between Honolulu and Kailua, cutting through the spectacular Koolau Range. It's a scenic little highway with one of Oahu's best views. Many Kailua residents commute to work this way; which wouldn't be a bad way to start the day!

Honolulu-bound traffic can be heavy in the morning, and outbound traffic heavy in the evening, though most day trippers will be travelling against the traffic. City buses travel the Pali Highway but none stop at the lookout.

Up past the four-mile marker, look for two notches cut about 15 feet deep into the crest of the pali (cliff). The notches are thought to have been dug as cannon emplacements by Kamehameha I.

If it's been raining heavily, look up at the mountains to the left – every fold and crevice will have a lacy waterfall streaming down it.

The original route between Honolulu and windward Oahu was via an ancient footpath that wound its way perilously over these cliffs. In 1845 the path was widened into a horse trail and later into a cobblestone carriage road.

In 1898 the Old Pali Highway (as it's now called) was built following the same route. It was abandoned in the 1950s after tunnels were blasted through the Koolau Range and the present multi-lane Pali Highway opened.

You can still drive a loop of the Old Pali Highway (called Nuuanu Pali Drive) and hike another mile of it from the Nuuanu Pali Lookout.

Queen Emma Summer Palace
At the Pali Highway two-mile marker is the Queen Emma Summer Palace, which belonged to Queen Emma, the consort of Kamehameha IV.

Emma was three-quarters royal Hawaiian and a quarter English, a granddaughter of the captured sailor John Young who became a friend and adviser of Kamehameha I. The house is also known as Hanaiakamalama, the name of John Young's home in Kawaihae on the Big Island, where he served as governor.

The Youngs left the home to Queen Emma, who often slipped away from her formal downtown home to this cooler retreat. It's a bit like an old Southern plantation house, with a columned porch, high ceilings and windows to catch the breeze.

The home was forgotten after Emma's death and was scheduled to be razed in 1915, as the estate was being turned into a public park. The Daughters of Hawaii rescued it and now run it as a museum.

The house has period furniture collected from five of Emma's homes. Some of the more interesting pieces are a cathedral-shaped koa cabinet made in Berlin and filled with a set of china from Queen Victoria; feather cloaks and capes; and Emma's necklace of tiger claws, a gift from the Maharaja of India.

It is open from 9 am to 4 pm daily except holidays. Admission is $4.

Nuuanu Pali Drive
For a scenic side trip through a shady green forest, turn off the Pali Highway onto Nuuanu Pali Drive, half a mile past the Queen Emma Summer Palace. The 2½-mile road runs parallel to the Pali Highway and then comes back out to it before the Nuuanu Pali Lookout, so you don't miss anything by taking this side loop – in fact, quite the opposite.

The drive is through mature trees that form a canopy overhead, all draped with hanging vines and wound around with philodendrons. The lush vegetation includes banyan trees with hanging aerial roots, tropical almond trees, overgrown banana trees, bamboo groves, orange trumpet vines and lots of impatiens.

Judd Trail If you want to get off the road and into the woods, you might try Judd Trail. The full trail is a 1½-mile loop, but it's not all that well maintained and most people just take it as far as Jackass Ginger, a little freshwater pool about 10 minutes in.

About a mile up Nuuanu Pali Drive, there's a dirt parking lot on the right. It's soon after Poli Hiwa Place and just before a small bridge.

The trail starts below the parking lot at a stream crossing. The trail runs parallel to the stream but goes uphill a bit, so you'll need to keep an eye out for the pool. Sometimes it's a good place for a dip, other times it's muddy; and the mosquitoes there are hungry!

Trees along the way include large banyans, ironwood, *Eucalyptus robusta* and Norfolk pine.

Nuuanu Pali Lookout

Whatever you do, don't miss the Nuuanu Pali Lookout (Nuuanu Pali State Wayside) with its broad view of the windward coast from a height of 1200 feet. You can see Kaneohe and Kailua ahead, and Chinaman's Hat (Mokolii

Island) and the coastal fishpond at Kualoa Park to the far left.

This is already *windward* Oahu – and winds that funnel through the pali are so strong that you can sometimes lean against them. It gets cool enough to make taking a jacket worthwhile.

In 1795 Kamehameha routed Oahu's warriors up the Nuuanu Trail in his invasion of the island. On these steep cliffs Oahu's warriors made their last stand. Hundreds were thrown to their death over the pali as they were overcome by Kamehameha's troops. During the construction of the Old Pali Highway in the 1890s, more than 500 skulls were found at the base of the cliffs.

The abandoned Old Pali Highway winds down from the right of the lookout, ending abruptly at a barrier along the current highway about a mile away. Few people realise the road is there, let alone venture down it. It makes a nice walk and takes about 20 minutes one way. There are good views looking back up at the jagged Koolau Mountains and out across the valley.

As you get back on the highway, it's easy to miss the sign leading you out of the parking lot. Go to the left if you're heading toward Kailua, to the right if heading towards Honolulu.

Windward Oahu

Windward Oahu is the island's eastern side, following the Koolau Range along its entire length. The mountains looming inland are lovely, with scalloped folds and deep valleys. In places they come so near to the shore that they seem almost to crowd the highway into the ocean.

The windward coast runs from Kahuku Point in the north to Makapuu Point in the south. (For the Waimanalo to Makapuu area, see the South-East Oahu section.)

The two main towns are Kaneohe and Kailua, both largely nondescript dormitory suburbs of Honolulu, about 10 miles away.

North of Kaneohe, the windward coast

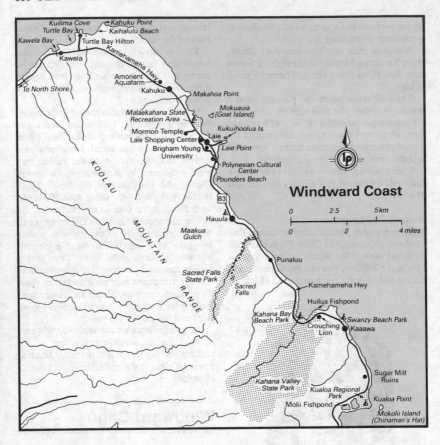

is rural Hawaii, where many Hawaiians struggle along, close to the earth, making a living with small papaya, banana and vegetable farms. It's generally wetter on the windward side, and the vegetation is lush and green.

The windward coast is exposed to the north-east trade winds. This is a popular area for anything that requires a sail – from windsurfing to yachting. Swimmers should keep an eye out for stinging Portuguese man-of-war, which are often washed in during storms.

Though there are a few nice beaches on the windward coast, many more are silted and others are right in town in less than ideal settings. Most of the offshore islands along this coast are bird sanctuaries.

Camping

The two best beach camping grounds on the windward coast are at Malaekahana State Recreation Area and Kualoa Regional Park. Other beach camping grounds along this coast aren't highly recommended.

The best camping on the windward coast, if you don't mind being away from the beach, is at the Hoomaluhia Park in Kaneohe.

Getting There & Away

Two highways cut through the Koolau Range to the windward coast. The Pali Highway (Hwy 61) goes straight into Kailua.

The Likelike Highway (Hwy 63) runs directly into Kaneohe and, though it doesn't have the scenic stops the Pali Highway has, it is in some ways more dramatic. Driving away from Kaneohe it feels like you're heading straight into the mountains – tall, fairy-tale mountains, often shrouded in clouds and laced with waterfalls. Then you suddenly shoot through a tunnel and when you emerge on the Honolulu side, the drama is gone.

If you're heading both to and from windward Oahu through the Koolau Range, take the Pali Highway up from Honolulu and the Likelike Hwy back for the best of both. (See the Pali Highway section for details on that drive.)

KAILUA

Kailua Bay and neighbouring Lanikai are fronted by fine white sand beaches.

In ancient times Kailua was loaded with legends. It was home to a giant turned into a mountain ridge, the island's first menehunes and numerous Oahuan chiefs.

But that's all history. Kailua today is an ordinary middle-class community and other than its beach has little of interest. It's the third largest city in Hawaii, beating Hilo by a few heads.

Ulupo Heiau

Ulupo Heiau is a large open platform temple, made of stones piled 30 feet high for 140 feet. Its construction is attributed to menehunes, the little people legends say created much of Hawaii's stonework, finishing each project in one night. Ulupo means 'night inspiration'.

If you walk out across the top of the heiau you get a view of Kawainui Swamp, one of the largest water-bird habitats in Hawaii. Legends say the swamp's ancient fishpond had edible mud at the bottom and was home to a *moo*, or lizard spirit.

This is the best preserved heiau in these parts, but if you're not too interested in heiaus, you could easily pass it up.

Ulupo Heiau is one mile south of central Kailua. Coming up the Pali Highway from Honolulu, take Uluoa St, the first left after passing the Hwy 72 junction. Then turn right on Manu Aloha St and right again. The heiau is behind the YMCA.

Kailua Beach

Kailua Beach Park is at the south-eastern end of Kailua Bay. The white sand beach is long and broad and the water a beautiful aqua.

Kailua Bay is the top windsurfing spot in Oahu. Onshore trade winds are predominant and windsurfers can sail there every month of the year. Around the bay there are a variety of water conditions, some good for jumps and wave surfing, others for flatwater sails. Several windsurfer companies rent boards and give lessons at the beach park daily.

Kailua Beach Park has a gently sloping sandy bottom with waters that are generally flat and calm. Swimming is good year round.

Kaelepulu Canal divides the park into two sections, though the canal waters are usually prevented from emptying into the bay by a sand bar.

The park has restrooms, showers, lifeguards, a snack shop, a volleyball court and large grassy expanses for picnicking or sunbathing. Most facilities are on the Lanikai side of the park; there's a small boat ramp at the far end.

The island offshore is Popoia (or Flat) Island, a bird sanctuary where landing is allowed.

While surfers do use the beach park, the surf is bigger at the northern end of Kailua Bay. Kalama Beach, an unimproved beach just north of the park, has gentle waves good for beginner bodysurfers. Board surfers often go further north to Kapoho Point or to a break called Zombies.

To get to Kailua Beach Park, take bus Nos 56 or 57 from Ala Moana Center and transfer to a No 70 in Kailua.

Lanikai Beach

Along the coastal road south-east of Kailua Beach Park there's a makai pull-off with a great view of Kailua Bay.

Just beyond is Lanikai, a rather exclusive residential neighbourhood. Lanikai Beach has gorgeous clear aqua waters and powdery white sand – at least what's left of it. Much of the sand has washed away as a result of the retaining walls built to protect the homes plopped right on the shore.

The sandy bottom slopes gently and the waters are calm, offering safe swimming conditions similar to those at Kailua. The twin Mokulua islets sit directly offshore.

From Kailua Beach Park, the road turns into the one-way Aalapapa Drive, which comes back around as Mokulua Drive to make a 2½ mile loop. There are 11 narrow beach access walkways off Mokulua Drive. For the best stretches of beach, try the one opposite Kualima Drive or any of the next three.

Places to Stay

Kailua has no hotels, but there are furnished beachfront cottages and vacation houses for rent, and quite a few people rent out rooms in their homes. Many are either advertised in the newspaper or handled by B&B reservation services. You can also check with the windsurfing shops. Most places have a three to seven-day minimum stay.

Pacific-Hawaii Bed & Breakfast (Maria Wilson, 19 Kai Nani Place, Kailua, HI 96734; tel 262-7865; 800-999-6026 from the USA and Canada) lists more than 50 B&Bs in Kailua, with rates as low as $35.

Pat's Kailua Beach Properties (204 S Kalaheo Ave, Kailua, HI 96734; tel 261-1653) handles about 45 vacation rentals. Studio cottages cost from about $50 a day or $1000 a month. Two-bedroom places cost from $55 to $100 a day or from $1100 to $2100 a month. They also have larger luxury homes, some accommodating up to 10 people, and will send descriptions on request.

Abacus Vacation Rentals (48 Kailua Rd, Kailua, HI 96734; tel 263-8828; 800-752-5528) rents studios from $50, cottages from $65 and homes from $100.

Places to Eat

Kailua has a full selection of fast food and diner-style restaurants. Near the intersection

Kailua Beach Park

of Kailua and Kuulei roads are *Pizza Hut*, *McDonald's* and *Gee A Deli*, a halfway decent sandwich shop.

If you want to fuel your body with something a bit more positive, try the food bar at *Good N' Natural*, a small health food store at 124 Oneawa St. They have falafel sandwiches, salads, smoothies, vegetarian chilli and hardy homemade soups. Everything's under $5. The food bar is open from 9 am to 3 pm Monday to Saturday. The store stays open until 5 pm and has Maya yoghurt, juices and vitamins.

If you want Mexican food, we've been told *Cisco's Cantina* (123 Hekili) is good.

Buzz's (413 Kawailoa Rd; tel 261-4661) near Kailua Beach Park is open from 5 to 10 pm daily. Prices range from $8 for the kebab to $25 for steak and lobster. They also have fresh fish, a salad bar and appetisers such as artichokes and escargot.

For something a little up-market, you could try *L'Auberge Swiss Restaurant* (117 Hekili St, tel 263-4663). They have continental food at moderately expensive prices.

KANEOHE

Kaneohe is Oahu's fourth largest town, with a population of about 35,000.

Kaneohe Bay stretches from Mokapu Peninsula all the way up to Kualoa Point, seven miles north. It's the state's largest bay and reef-sheltered lagoon, though inshore it's largely silted. The near-constant trade winds that sweep across the bay are some of the best on the islands for sailing.

Two highways run north to south through Kaneohe. Kamehameha Highway is closer to the coast and goes by Heeia State Park. Kahekili Highway runs inland from the outskirts of Kaneohe, where it intersects the Likelike Highway, and goes north by Byodo-In. They merge into a single route, Kamehameha Highway (Hwy 83), just north of Ahuimanu.

Kaneohe Marine Corps Air Station occupies the whole of Mokapu Peninsula. H-3, the new cross-island highway under construction, terminates at its gate. When completed, the highway should connect with Pearl Harbor.

H-3 Freeway

Construction of final sections of the controversial H-3 freeway, opposed by environmentalists for years, is now underway after courts allowed the highway to be made exempt from a law prohibiting the use of federal moneys on highway projects using public parkland. Islanders opposed H-3 not only because it will cut across Hoomaluhia Park but also because it will open the windward coast to further development.

Controversy also surrounds the Omega station, which emits electromagnetic signals that can be picked up by ships and planes. Vessels aligning themselves with two such stations can pinpoint their exact location anywhere on the globe.

No-one knows what effect the signals have on humans, but the new highway may help them find out: H-3 passes right through the Haiku Naval Reservation from which the electromagnetic signals are sent. One plan actually calls for the highway to be strung with a mile-long tunnel of grounding wires to keep pacemakers from short-circuiting!

Hoomaluhia Park

The county's newest and largest botanic garden is Hoomaluhia, a 400-acre park in the uplands of Kaneohe. The park is planted with groups of trees and shrubs from tropical regions of the world.

It's a peaceful, lush green setting, with a stunning pali as a backdrop. This is not a landscaped flower garden but more of a natural preserve. Trails lead up to the park's 32-acre lake (no swimming allowed).

The little visitor centre has displays on the history of the park which was originally built by the US Army Corps of Engineers as flood protection for the valley below. There are also displays on flora, fauna and Hawaiian ethnobotany.

These are the same folks who run Foster Garden in Honolulu. They give a fine ecological perspective. Ask for the interesting free booklet detailing 30 of the labelled trees and shrubs in Pa Launa, the garden just beyond the visitor centre.

The park is at the end of Luluku Rd, which starts 2¼ miles down Kamehameha Highway from the Pali Highway. Bus Nos 55 and 56 go to Windward City Shopping Center opposite the start of Luluku Rd. It's

1½ miles up Luluku Rd from the highway to the visitor centre and another 1½ miles from the visitor centre to the far end of the park so, if you use the bus, expect to do some walking.

The park is open from 9 am to 3 pm daily and admission is free.

Two-hour nature hikes are held at 10 am Saturdays and 12.30 pm Sundays. There are also bird walks, moonwalks, ethnobotany walks and lei-making workshops. Call the centre (tel 235-6636) for registration.

Restrooms are at the visitor centre and at each of the camping areas. There's a pay phone and drinking water.

Camping Hoomaluhia has the best non-beach camping in Oahu. There are five camping areas. The one farthest in is on an open grassy expanse with great views.

Camping is allowed from 9 am Thursday to 9 am Tuesday. There's no fee but reservations must be made two weeks (and not more than six months) in advance at the centre or with the county Department of Parks & Recreation. It's possible to do it all by mail. For an application send a business-size, self-addressed stamped envelope to Hoomaluhia, Box 1116, Kaneohe, HI 96744.

With a resident caretaker and gates that are locked to non-campers at 3 pm, they haven't had any safety problems since the park was opened to camping in 1982.

Valley of the Temples & Byodo-In

The Valley of the Temples is an interdenominational cemetery in a beautiful setting just off the Kahekili Highway (No 47-200) north of Kaneohe. The main attraction of the valley is Byodo-In, the 'Temple of Equality', which is a replica of the 900 year old temple of the same name in Uji, Japan. This one was dedicated in 1968 to commemorate the 100th anniversary of Japanese immigration to Hawaii.

Byodo-In sits against the Koolau Range. The rich red of the temple against the verdant fluted cliffs is a pretty scene, especially when mist settles in on the pali.

The temple is meant to symbolise the mythical phoenix. Inside the main hall is a nine-foot gold-lacquered buddha sitting on a lotus. Wild peacocks roam the grounds and hang their tail feathers over the upper temple railings.

A carp pond fronts the temple, with cruising bullfrogs and cooing doves. A three-ton brass bell beside the pond brings tranquillity and good fortune to those who ring it.

It's all very Japanese, right down to the gift shop selling sake cups, daruma dolls and happy buddhas. This scene is as close as you'll get to Japan without having to land at Narita.

A traditional Japanese tea ceremony is held outdoors a couple of times each year. For information call 239-5570.

Admission to the temple is $2. It's open from 8.30 am to 4.30 pm daily. On the way out, you might want to head up to the hilltop mausoleum with the cross on top and check out the view.

Heeia State Park

Heeia State Park is on Kealohi Point, just off Kamehameha Highway. It has a good view of Heeia Fishpond on the right and Heeia-Kea Harbor on the left.

Heeia Fishpond is owned by the Bishop Estate, as was Coconut Island, visible beyond the pond. The mangrove that grows above the fishpond is an introduced invasive plant that takes root between the rocks and has done more damage than hundreds of years of waves and storms.

Coconut Island was a royal playground in times past and was named for the coconut trees planted there by Princess Bernice Pauahi Bishop. In the 1930s it was the estate of Christian Holmes, heir to the Fleischmann Yeast fortune, who dredged the island, doubling its size to 25 acres. During the war the estate served as an R&R facility and even had a brief stint as a hotel. The Hawaii Institute of Marine Biology of the University of Hawaii occupies a niche on the island, which is otherwise privately owned.

You can walk around the grounds of Heeia State Park and take in the view but otherwise there's not much to do here.

Places to Eat

Haiku Gardens (tel 247-6671) is a restaurant with simple open-air dining and a picturesque view of a lily pond tucked beneath the Koolau Mountains. It's open for lunch and dinner daily except Mondays, but you can also come just for the view and to stroll around the lily pond.

Lunch is from 11.30 am to 2.30 pm. There's a buffet for $10 and a Hawaiian lunch that includes kalua pork or steamed laulau, chicken luau, tripe stew, lomi salmon, poi, pipikaula, yams and haupia for $9.50. There are also sandwiches with fries from $5.25 and seafood and steak dishes. Dinner costs a few dollars more.

From Kamehameha Highway turn left on Haiku Rd just past Windward Mall. After Haiku Rd crosses Kahekili Highway, Haiku Gardens is a quarter of a mile farther up, on the left.

The Windward Mall on Kamehameha Highway is a large two-level mall with a Liberty House, Sears, JC Penny, Waldenbooks, a bank, a pharmacy and a lot of other shops. Eateries include *Arby's*, *Baskin-Robbins*, *Orange Julius*, *Marie Callender's*, *Yami Yogurt* and *McDonald's*.

Best of all is the Windward Mall's Food Court – sort of a mini Ala Moana with a line of food stalls selling hot cinnamon rolls, deli items and Japanese, Mexican and Korean foods and pizza by the slice. *Patti's Chinese Kitchen* has good inexpensive buffet-style plate lunches. Prices range from $1.10 for a pint of chow mein to $8.25 for one of the hanging ducks. There are good Chinese pastries there too, such as almond cookies and coconut-filled gin doi.

The strip of Kamehameha Highway south of Windward Mall has a *Pizza Hut*, *Kentucky Fried Chicken*, *Taco Bell*, *Jack in the Box*, *Edokko* (fast Japanese food), *Burger King* and *McDonald's*.

WAIAHOLE & WAIKANE

Waiahole and Waikane mark the beginning of rural Oahu. There are lots of nurseries and small farms, with coconut groves, banana fields and papaya and lemon orchards.

Waikane has a couple of fruit stands and a little store on the side of the road.

Large tracts of Waikane Valley were leased by the military during WW II and used as training areas. The military continued to use it for shelling up until the 1960s and now claims the land has so many live ordnances that it can't be returned to the families it was leased from.

KUALOA

Kualoa Regional Park, a 153-acre county park on Kualoa Point, is bounded on its southern side by Molii Fishpond. From the road south of the park the fishpond is visible through the trees as a distinct green line in the bay.

Kualoa is a nice beach park in a scenic setting. The mountains looming precipitously across the road are, appropriately enough, called Pali-ku, meaning 'vertical cliff'. When the mist settles it looks like a scene from a Chinese watercolour.

The main island offshore is Mokolii, which in more recent times has come to be known as Chinaman's Hat. In Hawaiian legend, Mokolii is said to be the tail of a nasty lizard or a dog – depending on whose story you read – which was slain by a god and thrown into the ocean.

Apua Pond, a three-acre brackish salt marsh on the point, is a nesting area for the endangered aeo (Hawaiian stilt). If you walk down the beach beyond the park you'll see a bit of Molii Fishpond, but it's hard to get much of a perspective on it. The rock walls are covered with mangrove, milo and pickleweed.

The park is largely open lawn with a few palm trees. It has a long thin strip of beach with shallow waters and safe swimming. There are picnic tables, restrooms, showers, a phone, camping space, and a lifeguard on winter weekends. The park is open for day use between 7 am and 8 pm, after which the gate is locked for security.

Lots of islanders camp there on weekends – so many, in fact, that they open a second camping ground on the bay side of the point, which is more shaded than the camping ground at the head of the beach. Camping is free from Friday to Tuesday nights with a permit from the county.

Kualoa used to be one of the most sacred places on Oahu. When a chief stood on the point, passing canoes lowered their sails in respect. The children of chiefs were brought there to be raised and it may also have been a place of refuge. It was at Kualoa that the double-hulled canoe *Hokulea* landed in 1987, following a two-year rediscovery voyage through Polynesia that retraced the ancient migration routes.

Kualoa Ranch

The horses grazing on the green slopes across the road from Kualoa Park belong to Kualoa Ranch. The ranch offers all sorts of activities from kayaking to target shooting but, except for horseback riding which is open to the public with reservations, everything's packaged for Japanese honeymooners, who are shuttled in from Waikiki by helicopter.

Back in 1850 Kamehameha III leased about 625 acres for $1300 to Dr Judd, a missionary doctor who became one of the king's advisers. Judd planted the land with cane, built flumes and imported Chinese labourers to work the fields. His sugar mill trudged along for a few decades but went under just before the reciprocity agreement with the USA opened up mainland sugar markets.

You can still see the remains of the mill's stone stack and a bit of the crumbling walls a third of a mile north of Kualoa Park, just after the 31-mile marker.

KAAAWA

In the Kaaawa area, the road hugs the coast and the pali moves right on in. There's only enough space to squeeze a few houses in between the base of the cliffs and the road.

Swanzy, a neighbourhood beach park used mainly by fishermen, is fronted by a shore wall. Across the road is a 7-11 store, a gas station and Kaaawa Country Kitchen, a takeaway restaurant with a couple of tables out the front. Plate lunches cost around $4, fishburgers $1.65.

Crouching Lion

The crouching lion is a rock formation at the back of the restaurant of the same name.

The stone is said to be a demigod from Tahiti who was cemented to the mountain during a fight between the jealous sisters Pele, the volcano goddess, and Hiiaka. When he tried to free himself by pulling into a crouching position, he was turned to stone.

To find him, glance at the inn's logo at the entrance to the parking lot. Then stand with your back to the Crouching Lion Inn sign and look straight up to the left of the coconut tree. The lion is on a cliff in the background.

The inn itself has a tour bus ambience. Burgers, fries and coleslaw are about $6 at lunch.

Continuing north, just past the inn you get a glimpse of Huila Fishpond on the right.

Places to Stay

Plantation Spa (51-550 Kamehameha Highway, Kaaawa, HI 96730; tel 237-8685) is modelled on a European health spa. This new retreat serves gourmet vegetarian meals and has an exercise schedule including aerobics, yoga and canoeing. Rates are about $1500 a week all inclusive.

KAHANA

In old Hawaii the islands were divided into *ahupuaa* – pie-shaped land divisions reaching from the mountains to the sea which provided everything the early Hawaiians needed for subsistence. Kahana Valley, four miles long and two miles wide, is the only publicly owned ahupuaa in Hawaii.

Kahana is a wet valley. Rainfall ranges from about 75 inches along the coast to 300 in the mountains. In pre-contact times Kahana Valley was planted with wetland taro. The overgrown remnants of more than 130 terraces and irrigation canals have been uncovered in the valley.

In the early 1900s the area was planted with sugar cane. The sugar cane was hauled north to the Kahuku Mill via a little railroad. The upper part of the valley was used as a military training jungle during WW II.

Kahana Valley was purchased by the state in 1965 from one of the Robinsons of Kauai (owners of Niihau) to preserve it from development. Kahana's inland state park and county beach park are opposite each other one mile north of Crouching Lion Inn.

Kahana Valley State Park

The state park hasn't really been developed and Kahana Valley still has 140 residents. An orientation centre and restrooms built a decade ago were never opened and sit at the park entrance wasting away.

There are plans eventually to incorporate the families living in the valley into a 'living park' concept, with the residents acting as interpretive guides. In the meantime there's not much to the park other than a muddy 4½-mile trail along a jeep road to a swimming hole at a gauging station.

Kahana Bay Beach Park

Kahana Bay is set deep and narrow. The protected beach provides safe swimming, with a gently sloping sandy bottom. The tree-lined beach park is used primarily by island families.

Camping is allowed from Friday to Tuesday with a permit from the county. There are restrooms and a phone at the northern end of the park.

PUNALUU

Punaluu is more of a scattered little beach community than a town. It has a condo, a couple of restaurants and a beach park.

Punaluu Gallery has a nice collection of quality arts and crafts, all locally made. They have stained glass, watercolours, sculptured candles, wood carvings, prints and photographs. The gallery is just north of Punaluu Beach at 53-352 Kamehameha Highway. It's open daily.

Punaluu Beach Park

Punaluu's narrow beach provides good swimming, with its offshore reef protecting the shallow inshore waters in all but stormy weather. Be cautious in the area by the mouth of the Waiono Stream and in the channel leading out from it, as currents are strong when the stream is flowing quickly or the surf is high.

Places to Stay

Pat's at Punaluu (53-567 Kamehameha Highway, Box 359, Hauula, HI 96717; tel 293-8111) is a 136-room condo half a mile north of the 24-mile marker. Standard units are none too spiffy, but they're fairly large, with kitchens, TVs and a spare bed in the living room. They cost $58.

Countryside Cabins (53-224 Kamehameha Highway, Punaluu, HI 96717; tel 237-8169) is just past the 25-mile marker. Rates are $20 with shared bath and no kitchen, and $30 a day or $175 a week for a studio with kitchen and private bath. It's an older place. Don't expect anything fancy. The owner keeps the gate locked to keep her dog in, so call before you get there.

Places to Eat

Paniolo Cafe, just before the 25-mile marker, has pretty good sandwiches and burgers with fries for $5.25 to $6.50.

Pat's at Punaluu, at the condo of the same name, has a 'Plate Lunch & Sandwich Buffet', with cafeteria-quality dishes, cold cuts and white bread. At $8.75, you can do better almost anywhere else. Dinners are in the $10 to $18 range.

SACRED FALLS STATE PARK

Sacred Falls is a 1374-acre state park with a two-mile trail leading up the narrow Kaliuwaa Valley which folds deeply into magical-looking mountains. The park is north of the 23-mile marker.

The trail begins across an old cane field and follows Kaluanui Stream through a narrow canyon. The upper end of the trail leads to an 80-foot waterfall beneath high, rocky cliffs. The falls are nice but not spectacular and there are lots of mosquitoes.

The hike is not terribly strenuous and takes about 1½ hours return. There are a couple of stream crossings on the way that have slippery rocks and, more importantly, are subject to flash flooding. Even when it's sunny on the valley floor, a quick rain storm in the mountains can wash down suddenly.

The trail may be closed if the weather is sufficiently bad. Decisions are made daily and posted at the park; you can call 548-7455 to find out the status.

The falls may be sacred, but the hike isn't blessed. Though it's generally safe to hike, and thousands do, caution is definitely warranted.

In the past decade a number of hikers have been swept to their deaths in flash floods, at least one other killed by falling rocks and another by a slip over a ledge. Other hikers have been stranded during flash flooding, at least once requiring rescue by helicopter.

Flash floods give little warning. Hikers caught in them here have reported hearing a sudden loud crack and then seeing a wall of water pour down the stream bed; they've had just five seconds to reach higher ground. If the water starts to rise or you hear a rumbling, get up on a bank and wait it out. Don't try to cross the stream if the water reaches above your crotch. Use a walking stick.

An infamous incident occurred in 1984 when 25 hikers were ambushed at the falls and robbed at gunpoint in the worst of a rash of trail robberies. These days robberies don't seem to be a problem but thefts from parked cars are notorious. We pulled up to the roadside parking lot one Sunday afternoon as several hikers were returning to find their car locks had been popped and their cars ransacked. This was in broad daylight, with a full parking lot and plenty of traffic passing by. One hiker had $2000 worth of cameras and money taken from the trunk of his car. Obviously, you shouldn't leave anything valuable in your vehicle here (or anywhere else, for that matter).

HAUULA

Hauula is a rather tired-looking town with a fine backdrop of hills and Norfolk pines. There's a 7-11 store and a few small eateries.

The in-town beach looks none too appealing for swimming but it occasionally gets waves big enough for local kids to ride. The beach is actually a county park that allows

camping, though it's mostly local families that camp there.

The stone ruins of Lanakila church (circa 1853) sit perched on a hill opposite Hauula Beach, next to the newer Hauula Congregational church.

Trails

The Division of Forestry & Wildlife maintains three trails in the forest reserve behind Hauula: Hauula Loop (2½ miles), Maakua Gulch (three miles) and Maakua Ridge (2½ miles).

The trailhead to all three is at a bend in Hauula Homestead Rd, about a quarter of a mile up from Kamehameha Highway. Apparently it's possible to camp along the trails. For information, a trail map and camping permit call 548-8850.

LAIE

In ancient times Laie was thought to have been the sight of a *puuhonua* – a place where kapu breakers and fallen warriors could seek refuge. Today Laie is a Mormon town.

The first Mormon missionaries to Hawaii arrived in 1850. After an attempt to establish a Hawaiian 'City of Joseph' on Lanai failed amidst a land scandal, the Mormons moved shop to Laie, where in 1865 they purchased 6000 acres of land.

In Laie, the Mormons cultivated the land and slowly expanded their influence. In 1919 they constructed a temple, a smaller version of the one in Salt Lake City. It sits at the end of a promenade above their residential community at the foot of the Koolau Range. The temple is very stately and like nothing else on the windward coast. Though there's a visitor centre where eager guides will tell you all about Mormonism, tourists are not allowed to enter the temple itself.

Nearby is the Hawaii branch of Brigham Young University, with scholarship programmes bringing in students from islands throughout the Pacific.

In the long run the university may be more effective than missionary proselytising in spreading Mormon influence, as more and more students with Brigham Young degrees return to their home islands seeking positions of authority.

Information

Laie Shopping Center, about half a mile north of the Polynesian Cultural Center, has restaurants, a laundromat, a movie theatre and a Bank of Hawaii.

T T Surf Shop (55-730 Kamehameha Highway, tel 293-5363), next to Cackle Fresh Egg Farm, rents surfboards for $14 a day, boogie boards for $10 a day and snorkel sets for $8 a day. They also sell new and used boards.

There are a handful of vacation rental signs in front of private houses around this area.

Polynesian Cultural Center

The Polynesian Cultural Center (tel 293-3333), called the PCC by locals, is a 'non-profit' organisation belonging to the Mormon Church. The centre draws more tourists than any other attraction in Hawaii with the exception of the USS Arizona Memorial.

The park has seven theme villages representing Samoa, New Zealand, Fiji, Tahiti, Tonga, the Marquesas and Hawaii. They have authentic-looking huts and ceremonial houses, many elaborately built with twisted sennit ropes and hand-carved posts. The huts hold weavings, tapa cloth, feather work and other handicrafts.

People of Polynesian descent in native garb demonstrate poi pounding, coconut frond weaving, dances, games and the like.

Many of the people working here are Pacific Island students at the nearby Brigham Young University. They don't all end up at the 'village' of their home islands. Apparently there are more Samoans than Hawaiians, for instance, so you may well find a Samoan student demonstrating Hawaiian weavings. People are pretty friendly and you could easily spend a few hours wandering around chatting or trying to become familiar with a craft or two.

The admission price includes boat rides along the waterway that winds through the park, and the Pageant of the Long Canoes, a sort of trumped-up floating talent show at 1, 2, 3 and 4 pm.

The theme park is open from 12.30 to 6 pm daily except Sundays. The last half hour of the day ends with a grand finale canoe pageant that's worth catching if you've dished out the cost of admission.

Although PCC is interesting and is, to a surprising degree, sensitively presented, it is also very touristy and hard to recommend when the admission price is $25 for adults and $10 for children.

The 'Voyager' ticket costing $37 for adults and $15 for children includes a buffet dinner and evening show as well. The buffet is a mass production with uninspiring cafeteria food. There's also a luau for an extra $5, with much the same food and the addition of an imu-baked pig.

'This is Polynesia', the evening song and dance show, runs from 7.30 to 9 pm. It's partly authentic, partly Hollywood-style and much like an enthusiastic college production with elaborate sets and costumes. The fire show at the end is a highlight.

Laie Beaches

The 1½ miles of beach fronting the town of Laie between Malaekahana State Recreation Area and Laie Point is used by surfers, body-surfers and windsurfers.

Pounders is an excellent bodysurfing beach, but the shorebreak, as the name of the beach implies, can be brutal. There's a strong winter current. The area around the old landing is usually the calmest. Summer swimming is generally good and the beach is sandy.

Pounders is half a mile south of the main entrance to PCC. Pit toilets are the only facilities provided.

From Laie Point there's a good view of the mountains to the south and of tiny offshore islands. The island to the left with the hole in it is Kukuihoolua, otherwise known as Puka Rock.

To get to the point, head makai on Anemoku St, opposite the Laie Shopping Center, then turn right on Naupaka St and go straight to the end.

Malaekahana State Recreation Area

Malaekahana Beach stretches between Makahoa Point to the north and Kalanai Point to the south. The long narrow sandy beach is backed by ironwoods. Swimming is good year round, though there are occasionally strong currents in winter. It's a popular family beach and good for most water activities, including swimming, bodysurfing, surfing and windsurfing.

Kalanai Point, the main section of the state park, is less than a mile north of Laie and has picnic tables, barbecue grills, camping, restrooms and showers. Papaya trees heavy with fruit grow inland of the picnic and camping areas. It may be hard to find a ripe one though as they're harvested regularly.

Mokuauia (Goat Island), a state bird sanctuary just offshore, has a nice sandy cove with good swimming and snorkelling. It's possible to wade over to the island – best when the tide is low and the water's calm. Be careful of the shallow coral and sea urchins.

You can also snorkel across to Goat Island and off its beaches. There's sometimes a rip current off the windward end of the island, though that's where the deeper water is.

Camping You can camp in the park's main Kalanai Point section, or you can rent a cabin or camp for a fee in the Kahuku section, three-quarters of a mile to the north.

A booth near the northern entrance handles the rentals (call 293-1736 for reservations). The five cabins have either three or six bedrooms and cost from $20 to $40 a night, depending on the number of people. They don't look terribly well maintained. Tent camping in this section costs $3 per person. Dome tents can be rented for $5 to $7 a night, tarps for $2.50. Boogie boards and surfboards cost $6 for six hours.

In the Kalanai Point section tent camping is free if you have a state park permit. This is the best camping ground at this end of the

windward coast. It has lots of marked tent sites and is seldom crowded, though weekends are busier.

Places to Stay

Laniloa Lodge (55-109 Laniloa St, Laie, HI 96762; tel 293-9282, 800-367-8047 ext 359) is a two-storey motel with a pool. It's comfortable enough, though ordinary. Each room has a lanai, TV, tub, air-con and mini-refrigerator. Rates are $55/60 a single/double. It offers package deals, one of which combines a room and rental car for $70 a double. Another adds in a visit to the Polynesian Cultural Center, which is right next door.

Hale Kekela (55-113 Kamehameha Highway, Laie, HI 96962; tel 293-9700) is a quarter of a mile past Pounders Beach. There's a beachfront duplex, with each side sleeping up to six people for $120 a day or $720 a week. Next to the duplex is a three-bedroom, three-bath house that can sleep up to 12 people at double the price. The place includes TVs, phones, kitchens, lanais, washer/dryers and gates that are locked at night. It has a beach house feel.

Places to Eat

Country Health Foods in the Laie Shopping Center makes simple salads, burritos and sandwiches (tuna, vegie and protein burgers). Everything on the menu is under $4. Fruit smoothies are $2. The store has no fresh produce and a limited dairy section, but it has most of the packaged standards. They also have Haagen-Dazs ice cream, trail mix and dried fruits. It's open from 9 am to 7 pm Monday to Saturday.

Laie Chop Suey in the Laie Shopping Center has plate lunches with two dishes and rice for $3.50 as well as many of the standard Chinese dishes. Most dishes are $4 to $6. It's open from 10 am to 8.45 pm Monday to Saturday.

Laie's *McDonald's* has a little more character than the usual McDonald's. The building resembles a Polynesian long-house with a peaked roof. Inside there's even a waterfall. The restaurant was built for Laniloa Lodge next door, but when their restaurant folded, McDonald's moved in.

KAHUKU

Kahuku is a former sugar town with little wooden cane houses lining the road. The mill in the centre of town belonged to the Kahuku Plantation which produced sugar here from 1890 until 1971 when it closed. It was a relatively small concern, unable to keep up with the increasingly mechanised competition of the bigger mills.

Kahuku Sugar Mill

A fledgeling shopping centre has been set up inside the old sugar mill, with small shops ringing the old machinery. The mill's enormous gears, flywheels and pipes have been painted in bright colours to attract visitors who might be interested in seeing how a sugar mill works. The steam systems are red, the cane juice systems light green, hydraulic systems dark blue and so forth. It looks like something out of *Modern Times* – you can almost imagine Charlie Chaplin caught up in the giant gears.

You can walk around the machines and read the plaques which explain the process. Shops include a florist, camera shop and restaurant, among others.

Amorient Aquafarm

Less than a mile north of the old mill is the Amorient Aquafarm. Founded in 1978, the farm has 143 one-acre ponds producing both saltwater and freshwater shrimp. The ponds are drained to harvest the shrimp. Catfish, tilapia and silver carp are also raised on the farm.

You can get a fresh shrimp cocktail at the farm food stand for $3.25, shrimp tempura for $6, or you can take home live prawns for $10 a pound. Zoning rules restrict them to selling only what they raise, so you might want to pick up something to drink in town or at Tanaka's store just north of the farm.

Water birds are drawn to the ponds like kids to a candy store. They include night heron, coots, stilts, black swans, ducks and cattle egrets. If you're taking the circle-island bus and want a break, it stops right in front.

As you continue along to the north shore there are papaya farms, banana trees, a university livestock station, and some high-tech windmills on the hill.

Turtle Bay Hilton

The Turtle Bay Hilton, the sole hotel in Kahuku, is not exactly welcoming, with its guard booth and its parking fees. But the hotel is near shallow Kuilima Cove which is one of the area's best swimming spots.

Parking costs $1 for the first half-hour and 50 cents for each additional half-hour. For a hotel out in the middle of nowhere, charging parking fees is inexcusable.

Kaihalulu Beach

Kaihalulu is one of the few hidden beaches on the north shore of Oahu. It's a beautiful curved white sand beach fronted by ironwoods and still in a natural state. Though a shoreline lava shelf and rocky bottom make the beach poor for swimming, it's good for beachcombing and you can walk east about a mile to Kahuku Point. Local fishermen cast thrownets from the shore and pole fish from the point. The dirt road just in from the beach is also used as a horse trail.

To get there turn into the Turtle Bay Hilton and just before the guard booth turn right into an unmarked parking lot, where there are free spaces for beachgoers. Walk straight out along the dirt road toward the ironwoods. It's less than five minutes to the beach. There are no facilities.

Places to Stay

The *Turtle Bay Hilton & Country Club* (Kahuku, HI 96731; tel 293-8811; 800-445-8667) is a self-contained resort and the only 1st class hotel on the windward and north shores. It's on Kuilima Point, between Turtle Bay and Kuilima Cove. All 486 rooms are said to have ocean views and Kuilima Cove is good for swimming. Rates are from $135 to $300. There's an 18-hole golf course, two pools, stables and 10 tennis courts.

Places to Eat

Country Kitchen in the Kahuku Sugar Mill is a family-style restaurant with breakfast served all day. It's $3 for two eggs, hash browns and toast and $4.25 with bacon. Sandwiches and fries are $4 to $5. Dinner is but a few dollars more and there's a kid's menu. The setting is interesting.

Huevos has home-style cooking with standard breakfast fare (yes they have eggs) and hearty sandwiches at lunch time. Fresh fish and meat dishes are served at dinner, weekends only. Prices are reasonable. It's in a residential area among plantation houses just beyond the highway. Turn right at Kahuku High School onto the dirt road. It's a few houses down.

The Turtle Bay Hilton has two restaurants with lunch buffets. Both look fairly good though neither are knock-outs. *Bay View Lounge* has a lovely view of Kuilima Cove. It has a deli luncheon from 11.30 am to 2 pm for $9, with soup, salad bar, luncheon meats and desserts. It has a limited selection but pretty good-looking salads. At night, Bay View turns into a disco.

The *Palm Terrace* lunch buffet costs $11.50. It has hot dishes such as chicken and ribs in place of luncheon meats, and a few more salad and dessert selections than Bay View. Palm Terrace is also open for breakfast and dinner.

Central Oahu

Central Oahu is the saddle between the Waianae Mountains on the west and the Koolau Mountains on the east.

Three routes lead north from Honolulu to Wahiawa, the town smack in the middle of Oahu. The freeway, H-2, is the fastest route and Highway 750, the farthest west, is the most scenic. Highway 99 catches local traffic as it runs through Miilani, a modern, sterile dormitory suburb.

Most people just zoom up through central Oahu on their way to the north shore. If your time is limited this isn't a bad idea. There are

a few sights along the way and some nice scenery, but Wahiawa doesn't really warrant much more than a zip through anyway.

From Wahiawa two routes then head north to Haleiwa on the north shore. They are both fine scenic roads and if you're not circling the island you might as well go up one and down the other.

Highway 750

Highway 750 (Kunia Rd) adds a few miles to the drive through central Oahu but if you have the time it's worth it. Follow H-1 to the Kunia Rd/Hwy 750 exit, three miles west of where H-1 and H-2 diverge.

After you turn up Hwy 750 (also marked Hwy 75) you enter plantation lands, with sugar cane spreading out as the road leads up hill. This route runs along the foothills of the Waianae Range. The countryside is all agricultural between here and Schofield Barracks.

Up the road 2½ miles, a narrow strip of corn fields acts as a boundary between cane to the south and pineapple to the north. In these fields the Garst Seed Co grows three generations of corn each year, which makes it possible to develop hybrids of corn seed at triple the rate it would take on the mainland. Little bags are placed over each ear of corn to prevent them from being cross pollinated.

Further north is one of the most scenically situated pineapple fields in Hawaii. There are no buildings and no development – just red earth carpeted with long green strips of pineapples stretching to the edge of the mountains.

From the Hawaii Country Club up the road, there's a distant view of Honolulu all the way to Diamond Head.

Kunia

Kunia is the little Del Monte town in the midst of the pineapple fields. If you want to see what a plantation town looks like turn west off Hwy 750 on Kunia Drive, which makes a 1¼-mile loop through the town.

Rows of green-grey wooden houses stand on low stilts. The simple buildings have corrugated tin roofs, and chickens in the yards.

People take pride in their gardens, with bougainvillaea and orange trumpet vines adding a splash of brightness to an already lush green area.

Kunia Drive intersects the highway at about 5½ miles north of the intersection of Hwy 750 and H-1 (there's a store and post office near the turn-off) and again at the six-mile marker.

Kolekole Pass

Kolekole is the gap in the Waianae Mountains that Japanese fighter planes flew through on their way to bomb Pearl Harbor. The scene was recreated there 30 years later for the shooting of the film *Tora, Tora, Tora*.

The pass, at an elevation of 1724 feet, sits above Schofield Barracks on military property. It can be visited as long as the base isn't on some sort of military alert.

Access is through Foote Gate, on Hwy 750. About a third of a mile south of its intersection with Hwy 99. After being logged in at the gate, take the first left onto Road A, then the first right onto Lyman Rd. The drive is 5¼ miles up past the barracks, golf course and bayonet assault course. The parking lot is opposite the hilltop with the big white cross, which is visible from miles away.

It's a five-minute walk to the top of the pass. From there you can see straight down to the Waianae Coast.

A large ribbed stone sits atop the ridge. A woman named Kolekole is said to have taken the form of this stone so as to become the perpetual guardian of the pass.

Along the side of the stone are a series of ridges, one of them draining down from a bowl-like depression on the top. Shaped perfectly for a guillotine, the depression has given rise to a more recent 'legend' that Kolekole served as a sacrificial stone for the beheading of defeated chiefs and warriors. The fact that military bases flank both sides of the pass has no doubt had a little influence on this one.

Just west of the pass the road continues through a Navy base down to the Waianae Coast, but you can't take it. The Navy base

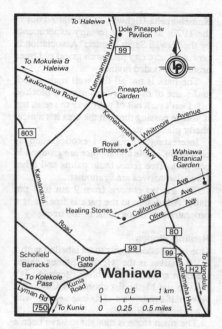

is a stockyard for nuclear weapons and there's no public access through their side.

WAHIAWA

Wahiawa is a GI town. Just about every fast-food chain you can think of is there – and as if that weren't enough, one local sit-down restaurant in the middle of town has even named itself 'Fast Food'. Tattoo parlours and pawn shops are the town's only refinements; if you're looking for a little excitement there are some rough and tumble bars.

To go through town and visit the botanic garden, healing stones and royal birthstones, take Kamehameha Highway (which is Hwy 80 as it goes through town, though it's Hwy 99 before and after Wahiawa). To circle around Wahiawa, stick with Hwy 99.

Wahiawa Botanical Garden

The Wahiawa Botanical Garden, 1396 California Ave, is less than a mile east of the

Kamehameha Highway. What started out in the 1920s as a site for forestry experiments by the Hawaii Sugar Planters' Association is now a 27 acre city park with grand old trees around a wooded ravine.

The park is not all that well maintained, and some of the walkways may be blocked off. Don't rush out of your way to see it, but if you're passing through the area it's a nice, shady place to stroll.

Interesting 60-year-old exotics such as cinnamon, chicle and allspice are grouped in one area. Tree ferns, loulu palms and other Hawaiian natives are in another.

The garden is open from 9 am to 4 pm daily. Admission to the park is free, as is a brochure describing some of the trees.

Healing Stones

One of the odder sights to be labelled with a HVB marker is the 'Healing Stones' caged inside a small concrete block 'temple'. It's next to the Methodist church on California Ave, half a mile west of its intersection with Kamehameha Highway.

The main stone is thought to have been a gravestone of a powerful Hawaiian chief, moved long ago from the original burial place in a field a mile away to a graveyard at this site. In the 1920s people thought the stone had healing powers and thousands made pilgrimages to it before interest waned. The streets, housing development and church came later, crowding in on the graveyard and leaving the stones sitting out on the sidewalk.

There are many stories about people who built around the graveyard being beset with bad luck, divorces and other misfortunes.

A local group with roots in India who sees a spiritual connection between Hawaiian and Indian beliefs now visit the temple, so you might see coconuts, flowers or little elephant statues placed around the stones. The story is actually more interesting than the sight, however.

Royal Birthstones

Kukaniloko, a group of royal birthstones where queens gave birth, is just north of

Wahiawa. The stones are thought to date back to the 12th century. It was said that if a woman lay properly against the stones while giving birth, her child would be blessed by the gods. Many of Oahu's great chiefs were born at this site.

These stones are one of only two documented birthstone sites in Hawaii (the other's in Kauai). Many of the petroglyphs on the stones are of recent origin, but the eroded circular patterns are original. The stones are being studied at solstices for possible astrological alignments.

To get to them from town, go three-quarters of a mile north on Kamehameha Highway from its intersection with California Ave. Turn left onto the red dirt road directly opposite Whitmore Ave. The stones are a quarter of a mile down through a pineapple field, amongst a stand of eucalyptus and coconut trees. If it's been raining, be aware that the red clay can cake onto your car tires, and once back on the paved road the car may slide as if it's driving on ice.

WAHIAWA TO THE NORTH SHORE

Highways 803 and 99 both lead from Wahiawa through pineapple country and down through cane fields on the way to the north shore.

Highway 803 (Kaukonahua Rd) is a slightly shorter way to Mokuleia than Hwy 99 and about the same distance to Haleiwa, though it by- passes some of the attractions. As it approaches Thompson Corner the road is lined with ironwood trees and has fine mountain and coastal views.

Highway 99 (Kamehameha Hwy) passes the pineapple garden, from where it's 6½ miles to Weed Circle. At Weed Circle, you can go left to Mokuleia or right (Hwy 83) to Haleiwa.

About two miles north-west of Wahiawa on either road, you can see Kolekole Pass on your left.

Pineapple Garden

There's a pineapple demonstration garden in a triangle at the intersection of Hwy 99 and Hwy 80.

'Smooth cayenne', the commercial variety of pineapple grown in Hawaii, is shown in various growth stages. Each plant produces just two pineapples. The first takes nearly two years to reach maturity, the second about one year more. Other commercial varieties grown in Australia, the Philippines and Brazil are on display, as well as many varieties of decorative bromeliads. You can pull off to the side of the road and walk through on your own at any time.

Dole Pineapple Pavilion

The Dole Pineapple Pavilion is a gift shop on Hwy 99 a bit north of the pineapple garden.

You can get a cup of pineapple juice for 65 cents or a pineapple freeze for $1.25. They also sell pineapples ready to take home – three for $8. It's open from 9 am to 5.30 pm daily.

Dole's processing plant is across the street and pineapple fields surround the area. A few miles north the country changes from pineapple to cane fields, and broad views of the ocean can be seen.

North Shore

Oahu's north shore is synonymous with surfing and prime winter waves. Sunset Beach, the Banzai Pipeline and Waimea Bay are among the world's top surf spots and draw some of the best international surfers.

Other north shore surf breaks may be less well known but with names like Himalayas and Avalanche, they're not exactly for neophytes.

On winter weekends convoys of cars drive up from Honolulu to watch the action from the beach. People set up stands beside the road to sell fruit and shell mobiles. You can beat much of the traffic simply by coming up on a weekday.

It's believed that the earliest Polynesians to arrive on Oahu were drawn to the north shore by the region's rich fishing grounds, cooling trade winds and moderate rain. The areas around Mokuleia, Haleiwa and Waimea all once had sizeable Hawaiian settlements. Abandoned taro patches still remain in their upland valleys.

By the turn of the present century the Oahu Railroad & Land Company had extended the railroad around Kaena Point and along the entire north shore, linking the area with Honolulu and bringing in the first beachgoers from the city. Hotels and private beach houses sprang up, but when the railroad stopped running in the 1940s the hotels shut down for good. Sections of track are still found along many of the beaches.

Waikiki surfers started taking on north shore waves in the late 1950s and big-time surf competitions followed a few years later. Each December there are three major surf competitions, known as the Triple Crown, with prize purses reaching six figures.

Surf mania prevails even in the restaurants, which serve up omelettes with names like 'Pumping Surf' and 'Wipe Out'. Half the north shore population can be found on the beach when the surf's up.

Swimming

With the exception of Haleiwa Beach Park, north shore beaches are notorious for treacherous winter swimming conditions. There are powerful currents along the entire shore. If it doesn't look calm as a lake, it's probably not safe for swimming or snorkelling.

During summer, waves along the whole north shore can mellow right out. Shark's Cove is then a prime snorkelling and diving spot and Waimea Bay is a popular swimming and snorkelling beach.

WAIALUA

Waialua is a quiet little sugar town about a mile west of Haleiwa. Waialua Sugar Mill, the smaller of Oahu's two working sugar mills, is owned by Castle & Cooke.

Down by the mill the Sugar Bar, in an old Bank of Hawaii building, sells beer and Bavarian food.

The most scenic route between Haleiwa and Waialua is along Haleiwa Rd.

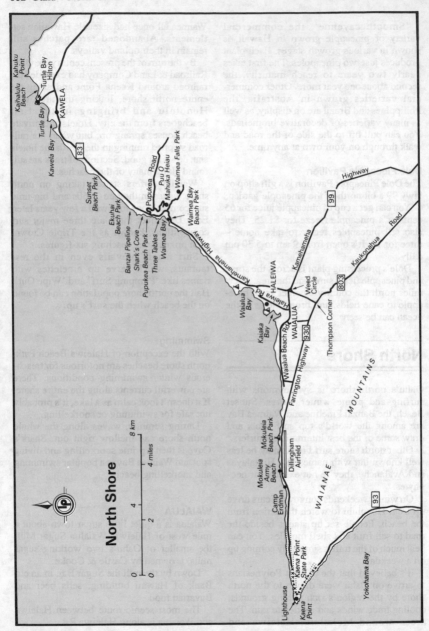

North Shore

Map labels:

Kahuku Point
Kahalulu Beach
Turtle Bay Hilton
Turtle Bay
KAWELA
Kawela Bay
Sunset Beach Park
Ekuhai Beach Park
Banzai Pipeline
Shark's Cove
Three Tables
Pupukea Beach Park
Waimea Bay
Puu O Mahuka Heiau
Waimea Falls Park
Waimea Bay Beach Park
Pupukea Road
83
Kamehameha Highway
Highway
99
Kamehameha Highway
Kaukonahua Road
Weed Circle
803
HALEIWA
Haleiwa Rd
Waialua Bay
Kaiaka Bay
WAIALUA
Waialua Beach Rd
930
Thompson Corner
Farrington Highway
Mokuleia Beach Park
Mokuleia Army Beach
Dillingham Airfield
Camp Erdman
MOUNTAINS
WAIANAE
93
Kaena Point State Park
Lighthouse
Kaena Point
Yokohama Bay

N
0   2   4   miles
0   4   8 km

Kukui Nut Factory

The Kukui Nut Factory (66-935 Kaukonahua Rd) in Waialua sells jewellery and skin oil products made from native kukui nuts. The rock-hard nuts are polished to make necklaces and the kernels are squeezed for their oil. Visitors are given a mini-tour of the small factory to show how the nuts are processed. It's open from 9 am to 5 pm daily. There's a general store and a bakery nearby.

Places to Stay

The *B&B Plantation House* (Kyla & Michael DuBois, Box 857, Waialua, HI 96791; tel 637-4988) in Waialua has two bedrooms, one with a private bath for $65 single or double. The other has a shared bath and twin beds for $45/55 a single/double. There's a two-night minimum stay and small children are not allowed. There's a swimming pool. Rates include a continental breakfast.

MOKULEIA

The Farrington Highway (Hwy 930) runs west from Thompson Corner to Dillingham Airfield and Mokuleia Beach. (Both this road and the road along the Waianae Coast are called Farrington Highway, but both stop about 2½ miles short of Kaena Point.)

Mokuleia Beach is a six-mile stretch of white sand running from Kaiaka Bay toward Kaena Point. Though there are some GIs there, the beaches don't draw much of a crowd and the area has sort of a boonies feel to it. The nearest store is in Waialua.

Dillingham Airfield is the take-off site for glider rides and sky diving. There are two developed public access beaches opposite the airfield.

Mokuleia Beach Park

Mokuleia Beach Park, the first west along the road, has a large open grassy area with picnic tables, restrooms, showers and a phone. The county allows tent and trailer camping.

Mokuleia is popular with windsurfers in spring and autumn and is known for its consistent winds. In winter there are dangerous currents.

Mokuleia Army Beach

Mokuleia Army Beach, opposite the western end of Dillingham Airfield, has the widest stretch of sand on the Mokuleia shore. The beach is open to the public and there's a lifeguard, though only military personnel and their guests are allowed to camp.

The beach is unprotected and has very strong riptides, especially during winter high surf. Surfing is sometimes good.

Army Beach to Kaena Point

From Army Beach, you can drive another 1½ miles down the road, passing still more white sand beaches with aqua waters. You'll usually find someone shorecasting and occasionally some campers.

The paved road goes past Camp Erdman, the YMCA Boy Scout Camp, and ends at old railroad tracks from where the terrain is pretty much scrubland reaching up to the base of the Waianae Range. Near the end of the road the coastline is littered with rubbish; there are even a few torched cars on the beach below. It's not too inviting.

It's possible to walk the 2½ miles to Kaena Point along state park lands, but it's more attractive from the other side (See Kaena Point State Park in the Waianae Coast section).

HALEIWA

Haleiwa is the gateway to the north shore and the main town catering to the multitude of day-trippers who make the circle-island ride.

The 3000 townspeople are a multi-ethnic mix of families who have lived there for generations and the more recently arrived surfers, artists and New Age folks.

Most of Haleiwa's shops are lined up along Kamehameha Ave (Hwy 83), the main drag through town. Haleiwa has a picturesque boat harbour, bounded on both sides by beach parks. One is known for its winter surfing, the other for the north shore's safest year-round swimming.

The Anahulu River, flowing out along the boat harbour, is spanned by a bridge with distinctive white arches. Take a glimpse up the river from the bridge. It's still a bucolic

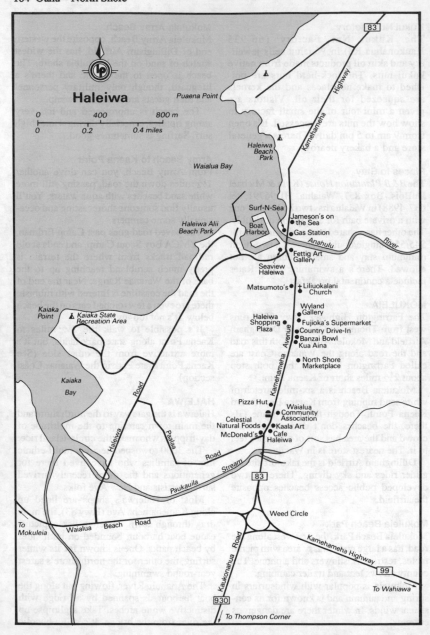

Haleiwa

0 — 400 — 800 m
0 — 0.2 — 0.4 miles

Puaena Point

Waialua Bay

Haleiwa Beach Park

Kamehameha Highway

Anahulu River

Surf-N-Sea

Boat Harbor

Jameson's on the Sea

Gas Station

Fettig Art Gallery

Haleiwa Alii Beach Park

Seaview Haleiwa

Matsumoto's

+ Liliuokalani Church

Kaiaka Point

Kaiaka State Recreation Area

Wyland Gallery

Haleiwa Shopping Plaza

Fujioka's Supermarket

Country Drive-In

Banzai Bowl

Kua Aina

North Shore Marketplace

Kaiaka Bay

Haleiwa Road

Paalaa Road

Paukauila Stream

Kamehameha Avenue

Pizza Hut

Waialua Community Association

Celestial Natural Foods

Kaala Art

McDonald's

Cafe Haleiwa

Weed Circle

To Mokuleia

Waialua Beach Road

Kaukonahua Road

Kamehameha Highway

To Wahiawa

99

930

To Thompson Corner

scene and it's easy to imagine how it must have looked in ancient Hawaii when the riverbanks were lined with taro patches.

In the summer of 1832, John and Ursula Emerson, the first missionaries to the north shore, built a grass house and missionary school beside the Anahulu River. They called the school Haleiwa. Over time the name, which means house (hale) of the great frigate bird (iwa), came to refer to both the beach and village.

Matsumoto's

For many people the circle-island drive isn't complete without lining up at Matsumoto's ancient general store for shave ice.

Hawaiian shave ice is a bit like a snow cone, though better because the ice is finer. The cloyingly sweet syrups are no different, however. Shave ice here costs from 70 cents for the small plain version to $1.40 for a large with ice cream and azuki beans.

Liliuokalani Protestant Church

The church opposite Matsumoto's takes its name from Queen Liliuokalani, who summered on the shores of Anahulu River and attended services here. Though the church dates from 1832, the current building was built in 1961. As late as the 1940s services were held entirely in Hawaiian.

Of most interest is the unusual seven-dial clock which shows the hour, day, month and year as well as the phases of the moon. Queen Liliuokalani presented the clock, on the face of which her 12-letter name replaces the numerals, to the church in 1892. Nearly 100 years later it still keeps time. The church is open whenever the minister is in, which is usually in the mornings.

Shops & Galleries

Kaala Art has some nice tapa hand made by a Tongan woman who lives on Oahu. The shop also sells tie-dyed and printed Bali and local pareos, hand-screened T-shirts, wood block prints and Hawaiian and Pacific handicrafts at good prices. It's next to Cafe Haleiwa and a neat place to explore if you have to wait for a table.

Wyland Gallery (66-150 Kamehameha Ave) features whales, painted and sculptured in many mediums. Marine artist Wyland is best known for his 'Whaling Wall' mural on Waikiki's Ilikai hotel. The gallery is open from 9 am to 7 pm daily.

Fettig Art Gallery has paintings of local and rural scenes, such as seascapes and plantation shacks. It's on the main drag by the boat harbour.

Haleiwa Shopping Plaza has a Bank of Hawaii, IGA supermarket and restaurants. Across the street is the more colourful Fujioka's supermarket.

The bulletin boards in front of IGA and Celestial Natural Foods are good places to check for rooms for rent, surfboards for sale and the like.

Kaiaka State Recreation Area

The 53-acre Kaiaka State Recreation Area is on Kaiaka Bay, about a mile west of town. This would be a good place for a picnic as there are shady ironwood trees, but the beaches in town are better choices for swimming. Two streams empty out into the bay, muddying up the beach after rainstorms. There's a view of the Waialua sugar mill. Kaiaka has the state's newest camping ground.

Haleiwa Alii Beach Park

Surfing is king at Haleiwa Alii Beach Park. This is the site of several tournaments in the winter, when north swells can bring waves as high as 20 feet.

When waves are five feet and under lots of younger kids bring their boards out. Any time they're six feet or better there are also strong currents and it's more suited to experienced surfers.

The 20-acre park has restrooms, showers, picnic facilities and a lifeguard tower. The shallow areas on the southern side of the beach are generally the calmest for swimming.

Haleiwa Beach Park

Haleiwa Beach Park is across the bridge over the Anahulu River, on the eastern shore of Waialua Bay. The beachfront is protected by a shallow shoal and a 160-foot breakwater that follows the shore. The waters are usually very calm and see little wave action, though north swells occasionally ripple into the bay.

In addition to full beach facilities the 13-acre county park has camping for both tents and trailers, basketball and volleyball courts, an exercise cluster and baseball and softball fields. It also has a good view of Kaena Point.

The Anahulu River enters the bay just south of the beach, and if it's been raining hard the water may be full of sediment. It's not an overly attractive beach.

Places to Stay

Jim's at the Beach (61-545 B Pohaku Loa Way, Haleiwa, HI 96712; tel 637-5100) has 32 beds in dorm-style rooms in a two-storey house right on the beach. Four to eight people share each small but clean room, with just enough space to squeeze in the bunk beds. The house has two bathrooms and showers. A third shower is outdoors. Beds are $15 a night and $84 a week. It's geared for international travellers and passports are supposedly required, but apparently if the house is not full, the staff may be flexible. There's a shared kitchen and a small common room with a fine sunset view. Transport from Honolulu Airport can be arranged. Jim's is north of Haleiwa, half a mile past the three-mile marker on Kamehameha Highway.

Places to Eat

The *China Inn* in the North Shore Marketplace has filling meals at low prices. One dish is $2, two are $3 and three are $3.75, each including noodles or fried rice. If you select carefully the food is good for the price. Cashew chicken and dishes with lots of vegetables are good, but batter-dipped dishes are heavy on the batter. It's open from 9 am to 10 pm daily but Mondays.

The *Coffee Gallery* in the North Shore Marketplace has steamed coffees, scones, Belgian waffles, lox & bagels and the like at quite reasonable prices.

Cafe Haleiwa, on the right as you come into town, is the best inexpensive eatery on the north shore. Portions are huge and the food is excellent. It's a simple place with cement floors, surfing photos on the wall and the kitchen at the end of the room. Sautéed vegie and cheese burritos with rice and beans cost $3.50. The home fries are terrific. You can get two huge whole-wheat pancakes loaded with blueberries for $1.55 in a half order, which is a meal in itself. Daily specials include fresh fish. It's open from 6 am to 2 pm weekdays and from 7 am to 2 pm weekends. The only catch is getting in, particularly on weekends when the queue forms outside. It's well worth the wait.

If you're looking for fast food, there's a *McDonald's* across the road in an Old West-style building.

Celestial Natural Foods, opposite Cafe Haleiwa, is a fine health food store with fresh produce, Alta Dena kefir and yoghurt and just about everything else you'd expect to find. Prices are reasonable. In the back of the store is *Galaxy Juice Works*. You can get a bowl of vegetable chilli over brown rice for $1.75, sandwiches for $3 to $4, salads for $2 to $3, Tex-Mex food and smoothies.

Pizza Bob's in the Haleiwa Shopping Plaza has passable pizza at reasonable prices. It costs about $7 for a regular pizza with one topping. From 11 am to 4 pm daily you can get two slices of pizza or a sandwich with salad and soft drink for $3.85. It's open from 11 am to 10 pm daily. This is one of those restaurants where all the window seats are reserved for smokers and non-smokers are relegated to the darker corners.

Steamer's in the Haleiwa Shopping Plaza is one of the nicer places to eat in town. They put on a good $12.50 Sunday brunch from 10 am to 3 pm. In addition to an all-you-can-eat buffet of meats, salads and good-looking desserts, the brunch has made-to-order omelettes and pancakes. At lunchtime salads, burgers and sandwiches cost about $5 to $7, and dinners range from $15 to $20.

Country Drive-In, opposite the Haleiwa Shopping Plaza, serves breakfast until 11.30 am. Two eggs, coffee and toast costs $2.

There are 21 different plate lunches, including some Korean dishes, for $3.25 to $4.50. *Banzai Bowl* next door is a sit-down place with the same food at the same prices.

Nearby *Kua Aina* is a popular sandwich and burger shop. Prices range from $3 for a cheese sandwich to $4.40 for a mahimahi sandwich.

Seaview Haleiwa, a family restaurant on the boat harbour, has an extensive menu of sandwiches, burgers, saimin, and meat and potato dishes at moderate prices.

Jameson's on the Sea, north of the bridge, is Haleiwa's up-market seaside eatery. Seafood is a speciality and people drive all the way up from Honolulu to eat there. Dinner is served upstairs in an attractive setting with white tablecloths, cool ceiling fans and views across the boat harbour down to Kaena Point. Dishes like shrimp curry with mango chutney, or clams diablo, cost from $15. Dinner is served from 5 to 10 pm nightly except Mondays. Lunch is served downstairs from 11 am to 5 pm daily. Salads and hot sandwiches cost from $6 to $9.

WAIMEA
Waimea Valley was once heavily settled. The lowlands were terraced in taro, the valley walls dotted with house sites and the ridges topped with heiaus. Just about every crop grown in Hawaii thrived in the valley, including a rare pink taro fancied by the alii .

Waimea Stream, now blocked at the beach, used to open into the bay and canoes could be paddled upstream to the villages. The sport of surfing was immensely popular here centuries ago, when the early Hawaiians rode the world's top waves on their long boards.

When Captain Cook's ships sailed into Waimea to collect water in 1779, shortly after Cook's death on the Big Island, an entry in the ship's log noted how uncommonly beautiful and picturesque the valley was.

In 1792 Captain Vancouver, who had been an officer on one of Cook's vessels, anchored in Waimea. While three of his men were collecting water on shore they were attacked and killed. It's thought that their bodies were taken up to Puu O Mahuka Heiau on the ridge above the beach and sacrificed. When Vancouver returned a year later demanding justice, the high chief turned over three islanders. Though Vancouver doubted they had anything to do with the murders, he had come to set an example so he ordered their execution.

Deforestation above the valley contributed to a devastating flood in Waimea in 1894. In addition to water damage an enormous volume of mud washed through the valley, so much so that it permanently altered the shape of Waimea's shore. After the flood, most residents resettled elsewhere.

Waimea Beach Park
Waimea Bay's mood changes with the seasons: it can be tranquil and as flat as a lake in summer and savage with incredible surf and the islands' meanest riptides in winter.

Waimea has Hawaii's biggest surfable waves and holds the record for the highest waves ever ridden in international competition. As at Sunset Beach, the huge north swells bring out crowds of spectators who throng to watch Waimea surfers perform their near-suicidal feats on waves of up to 35 feet.

On winter's calmer days the boogie boarders are out in force, but even then sets come in hard and people get pounded. Winter water activities here are not for novices.

From June to September is usually the only time the water is calm enough for swimming and snorkelling.

Waimea Bay is a very beautiful, deeply inset bay with turquoise blue waters and a wide white sand beach almost 1500 feet long. Ancient Hawaiians believed the waters here were sacred.

Waimea Beach Park is the most popular north shore beach. There are showers, restrooms, picnic tables, a phone and a lifeguard on duty daily. Parking is tight.

Waimea Falls Park
Waimea Falls Park (tel 638-8511), across the highway from Waimea Bay Beach Park, is a

botanical garden, cultural preserve and tourist park in one.

The main park trail leads three-quarters of a mile up the Waimea Valley past extensive naturalised gardens including sections of ginger, hibiscus, heleconia and medicinal plants. At Waimea Falls, cliff divers plunge 60 feet into the waterfall pool five times a day to thrill spectators.

Along the hike to the falls there are ancient stone platforms and terraces and some replicas of thatched buildings the early Hawaiians might have used. Hula dances, mini-tours, Hawaiian games and other demonstrations are scheduled a few times a day.

The park can be pleasant to wander through and the valley is naturally pretty but the cost of admission is a bit high. It's $9.95 for adults, $6 for children aged seven to 12 and $2 those for under seven. The park is open from 10 am to 5.30 pm daily and there's an in-park restaurant called the *Proud Peacock.*

Free one-hour moonlight walks are held twice monthly at 8.30 pm on or near the full-moon night. The No 52 bus stops at the highway, a third of a mile from the gate.

St Peter & Paul Church

The church of St Peter & Paul stands beneath the tall unassuming tower on the northern side of Waimea Bay. The structure was originally a rock-crushing plant built to supply gravel for the construction of the highway in the 1930s. After it was abandoned, the Catholic church converted it into Oahu's most unlikely chapel.

Puu O Mahuka Heiau State Monument

Puu O Mahuka is a long low-walled platform heiau perched above Waimea. Its construction is attributed to the legendary menehunes and it's the largest heiau on Oahu.

The terraced stone walls are a couple of feet high but most of the heiau is now overgrown. This was an incredible site for a temple and it's definitely worth a ride up for the view. Sunsets can really be nice here.

Walk to the far side of the heiau from the parking lot for a view of Waimea Valley and Waimea Bay. The plateaus above the southern side of the valley are covered with sugar cane. You can see all the way out along the coast to Kaena Point. There are guava trees down the slope from the end of the parking lot.

To get there, turn up Pupukea Rd at the Foodland supermarket. The marked turn-off to the heiau is about half a mile up the road and from there it's about three-quarters of a mile in. On the drive up there's a good view of Pupukea Beach Park.

Pupukea Beach Park

Pupukea Beach Park is a long beach along the highway that includes Three Tables on the left and Shark's Cove on the right.

In the middle is Old Quarry, full of jagged rock formations and tidepools. This is a very scenic beach, with deep blue waters, a varied coast and a mix of lava and white sand beach. The rocks and tidepools are tempting to explore but be careful because they're razor sharp and if you slip it's easy to get a deep cut.

The waters off Pupukea Beach are a marine-life conservation district. There are showers and restrooms in front of the Old Quarry. The beach entrance is opposite the Shell gas station.

Three Tables Three Tables, at the western end of the beach, gets its name from the ledges rising above the water. It's possible to see some action by snorkelling around the tables, but the best coral and fish as well as some small caves, lava tubes and arches are in deeper water farther out. It makes a good shore dive. This is a summer-only spot. In winter there can be dangerous riptides. Beware of sharp rocks and coral.

Shark's Cove Shark's Cove is beautiful both above and below the water's surface. The naming of the cove was done in jest – sharks aren't a particular problem. In the summer,

Banzai Pipeline

this is Oahu's most popular cavern dive and one of the north shore's best snorkelling spots. A fair number of beginner divers take lessons here, though the underwater caves will thrill advanced divers.

To get to the caves, swim out of the cove and around to the right. Some of the caves are very deep and labyrinthine, so caution should be used exploring them. There have been a number of drownings there.

The large boulders out on the end of the point to the far right of the cove are said to be followers of Pele. She gave them immortality by turning them to stone.

Ekuhai Beach Park

The main reason people come to Ekuhai Beach Park is to watch the pros surf the world-famous Banzai Pipeline, a few hundred feet to the left of the park.

The Pipeline breaks over a shallow coral reef and can be a death-defying wave to ride.

At Ekuhai Beach itself, many board riders and bodysurfers brave a hazardous current and ride the waves. Water conditions mellow out in summer, when it's good for swimming.

Ekuhai Beach Park is opposite the Sunset Beach Elementary School but roadside

parking isn't permitted and they do tow cars away. To get to the beach, continue past the school and turn in opposite the huge roadside totem which marks a souvenir shop. Then turn left on the beach road and go down to the parking lot. There's a lifeguard, restrooms, showers, picnic tables and a phone.

Sunset Beach Park

Sunset Beach Park is near the nine-mile marker. This roadside beach is Oahu's classic winter surf spot with incredible waves and challenging breaks. It's such a big name you expect a big beach but it's just a little roadside attraction without even a sign. All the action here is in the water.

Winter swells create powerful riptides. Even when the waves have mellowed in the summer, there's still an along-shore current for swimmers to deal with.

Two portable toilets and a lifeguard tower are the only facilities. Across the street is a little market and food stand. That white dish on the hill behind the beach is a COMSAT station for commercial satellite communications.

Backyards, the surf break off Sunset Point at the northern end of the beach, draws a lot of top windsurfers. There are sometimes mammoth waves in winter. There's also a shallow reef and strong currents to contend with, but Backyards has the island's biggest waves for sailing.

Places to Stay

Vacation Inns (59-788 Kamehameha Highway, Haleiwa, HI 96712; tel 638-7838) has a couple of different set-ups opposite Three Tables at Pupukea Beach. It's pretty much a surfers' hangout, and beach-house casual. One house has four bunk beds to a room, for $12 a bed. Another has double rooms for $35. Both houses have shared bathrooms and kitchens. Expect clutter and three-legged furniture, but if you're just looking for a place to crash you can't beat the price. They have beach parties and barbies and there's no curfew. Snorkels and boogie boards are lent free. Across the road on the beach are eight studios with TVs and kitchens from $55 a night, $300 a week, for up to four people.

Ke Iki Hale (59-579 Ke Iki Rd, Haleiwa, HI 96712; tel 638-8229) has 12 units, some fronting a white sand beach and others, the cheaper ones, by the road. Studios cost from $65, beachfront one-bedroom units $85 and two-bedroom units $125. All have the atmosphere of a beach cottage. To get there turn at Ke Iki Rd, the first makai road north of Pupukea Beach Park.

The Pupukea Foodland has a bulletin board that may have notices of roommates wanted and apartments for rent.

Waianae Coast

The Waianae Coast is the arid leeward side of Oahu.

In 1793 Captain Vancouver, the first Westerner to drop anchor there, found a barren wasteland with a few scattered fishing huts. Two years later, however, Kamehameha invaded Oahu and many Oahuans who had

been living in more desirable areas were forced to flee to the dry and isolated Waianae Coast.

Today it is still separate from the rest of the island. There are no gift shops or sightseeing buses on the Waianae Coast. When you get right down to it, watching surfers at Makaha is probably the biggest drawcard as there aren't a whole lot of sights to see.

Although developers are beginning to grab farmland for golf courses, for the time being leeward Oahu is the island's least touristed side. The area has a history of resisting development and a reputation for not being receptive to outsiders. In the past, visitors have been the targets of assaults and muggings. There's still a major problem with thefts from cars and camping sites, and though things aren't as hostile as they used to be, many locals aren't keen on sharing their space with tourists.

With overseas developers now buying up Waianae land and evicting tenant farmers, the conflict could become more intense.

Overall, you need to be attuned to the mood of the people. This is the only place in Hawaii where the park brochures say camping opportunities are for *local* residents.

Farrington Hwy (Hwy 93) runs the length of the leeward coast. There are long stretches of white sand beaches, some quite attractive, others littered with rubbish. In winter most have treacherous swimming conditions but at that time they also have some of the island's more challenging surfing. Though the towns themselves are ordinary, the cliffs and valleys cutting into the Waianae Range form a lovely backdrop.

At road's end, there's an undeveloped mile-long beach and a fine nature hike out to scenic Kaena Point.

KAHE POINT
Kahe Point Beach Park
There's no beach at this park, just the rocky cliffs of Kahe Point. There are standard

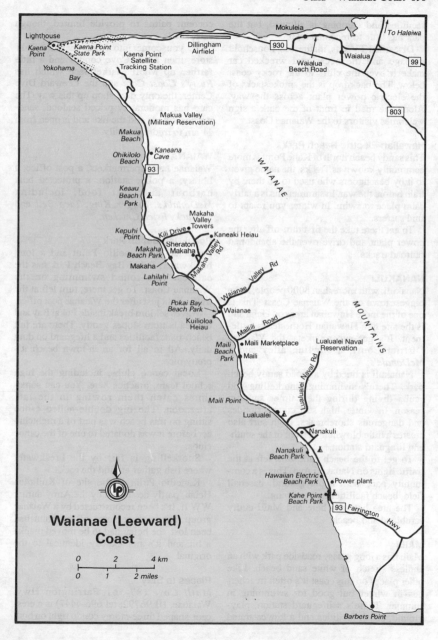

Waianae (Leeward) Coast

0   2   4 km
0   1   2 miles

facilities and camping is allowed, but the park has little to recommend it.

Discarded TV sets, mattresses, household garbage and the occasional wrecked car make it over the cliffs to the rocky coast below. The backdrop is the smokestacks of the electric power plant across the way. Along the road in front of the park a sign welcomes visitors to the Waianae Coast.

Hawaiian Electric Beach Park

This sandy beach north of Kahe Point is more commonly known as Tracks, the name given to it by beachgoers who used to go there by train before the war. In summer this is a fairly calm place to swim. In winter you're apt to find surfers.

To get there take the first turn-off after the power plant and drive over the abandoned railroad tracks.

NANAKULI

Nanakuli, with more than 8000 people, is the biggest town on the Waianae Coast. This is one of the more Hawaiian areas on Oahu and is the site of a Hawaiian Homesteads settlement. It's got supermarkets, the Waianae District Court, a bowling alley and a *McDonald's*.

Nanakuli is lined by a broad sandy beach park. There's swimming, snorkelling and scuba diving during the calmer summer season. In winter, high surf creates riptides and dangerous shorebreaks. High surf also creates a little blowhole in front of the south-end lifeguard station.

To get to the beach park, turn left at the traffic lights on Nanakuli Ave. This is a community park with a playground, baseball field, beach facilities and camping.

The area between here and Maili is dry scrubland and beach.

MAILI

Maili has a long grassy roadside park with an endless stretch of white sand beach. Like other places on this coast it's often treacherous in winter but good for swimming in summer. There's a lifeguard station, playground, beach facilities and a few castrated

coconut palms to provide limited, though safe, shade.

As you come into Maili there's a 7-11 store, then Maili Cove condos and a little farther up Maili Marketplace which has *Rusty's Coast Cafe* and the Leeward Dive Center, the only dive shop up this way. The cafe has moderately priced seafood, sandwiches, salads and the like and is open from 11 am to midnight daily.

WAIANAE

Waianae has supermarkets, a post office, a library, a police station, a protected boat harbour and fast food, including *McDonald's*, *Burger King*, *Taco Bell* and *Kentucky Fried Chicken*.

Pokai Bay Beach Park

Protected by Kaneilio Point and a long breakwater, Pokai Bay Beach Park has the calmest year-round swimming on the Waianae Coast. To get there, turn left at the traffic light just after the Waianae post office.

Waves seldom break inside Pokai Bay and the sea bottom slopes gently. There are full beach-park facilities and a lifeguard on duty daily. All in all for an in-town beach it's pretty nice.

Local canoe clubs, including the high school team, practice here. You can sometimes catch them rowing in the late afternoon. The big double-hulled canoe sitting on this beach was part of a nightclub act before it was donated to one of the canoe clubs.

Snorkelling is fair by the breakwater where fish gather around the rocks.

Kaneilio Point is the site of Kuilioloa Heiau, partly destroyed by the Army during WW II. It's been reconstructed by a Waianae group, but because some of the point had been lost, the heiau had to be moved mauka a bit and it's not exactly identical to the original.

Places to Stay

Maili Cove (87-561 Farrington Hwy, Waianae, HI 96792; tel 696-4447) is a crescent-shaped three-storey condo right on both

Top: Pahoehoe & Aa lavas
Left: Haleakala Crater, Maui
Right: Devastation Trail, Hawaii Volcanoes National Park, Big Island

Top: Kailua Pier, Kona, Big Island
Bottom: Guided Mule Tours, Molokai

the highway and the beach, between Waianae and Makaha. The large one-bedroom units cost $530 a week or $1340 a month. All have lanais with ocean views and most have cable TV and phones. There's a pool.

MAKAHA

Makaha means 'ferocious', and in days past the valley was notorious for the bandits who used to hang out along the cliffs waiting for travellers to pass.

Makaha has world-class surfing, Oahu's best-restored heiau, a few condos and a Sheraton up in the valley.

Makaha Beach Park

Makaha Beach is broad, sandy and crescent-shaped, with some of the most daunting surf in the islands. Experienced surfers and body-surfers both hit the waves there.

The beach is home to some major surf competitions. The most colourful is the Buffalo Big Board Surfing Classic held in March using old-style surfboards called 'tankers' which are sometimes 12 feet long and weigh 80 pounds. As surfers today go for small, light boards, most competitors are of an older generation of surfers.

When the surf's not up, Makaha is a popular swimming beach. When it is up the swimming conditions are hazardous; there is a strong shorebreak, dangerous riptides and stray surfboards.

In summer the slope of the beach is relatively flat. In winter it's fairly steep. The beach sand is slightly coarse and of calcareous origin with lots of mollusc shell fragments. As much as half of it temporarily washes away during winter erosion. Even then, Makaha is still an impressive beach.

Snorkelling is good offshore during calm summer weather. Makaha Caves, out where the waves break furthest offshore, feature underwater caverns, arches and tunnels at depths of 30 to 50 feet. It's a popular leeward diving spot.

Makaha Beach has a lifeguard on duty daily and full beach facilities.

Kepuhi Point, at the northern end of Makaha Beach, has some blowholes. To look

for them, turn down Makau St, north of Makaha Shores condos. Kepuhi means 'to blow'.

Makaha Valley

Up in Makaha Valley you'll find Kaneaki Heiau, a couple of condos and the Sheraton hotel and golf course.

If you turn mauka onto Kili Drive, just north of Makaha Beach Park, the drive up the valley is beside scalloped green cliffs.

An estimated 3000 wild peacocks live in the valley, including about 25 white ones. They come out in the early evening, sometimes gathering at the intersection by the Makaha Valley Towers condos, a mile up from the Farrington Hwy.

At the Towers turn right onto Huipu Drive. Just a third of a mile down on the left is Mauna Olu St, which leads a mile into Mauna Olu Estates and Kaneaki Heiau.

The Sheraton is at the intersection of Huipu Drive and Makaha Valley Rd. Most of the hotel activity is centred around the golf course.

Makaha Valley Rd comes back down to Farrington Hwy through a residential neighbourhood.

Kaneaki Heiau Kaneaki Heiau, in the centre of Makaha Valley, was originally a Lono temple, dedicated to the god of agriculture. In its final days it was rededicated by Kamehameha I as a luakini war temple. It remained in use until the time of Kamehameha's death, in 1819.

Restoration, which was done by the Bishop Museum and completed in 1970, added two prayer towers, a taboo house, drum house, altar and god images. It was reconstructed in the traditional manner using ohia logs and pili grass shipped over from the Big Island.

Supposedly the guard at the Mauna Olu Estates gatehouse lets visitors drive through to the heiau between 10 am and 2 pm daily, though when we were there they were only allowing visitors on weekends. You might want to call the Sheraton (tel 695-9511) first to inquire. Admission is free.

Places to Stay

The Waianae Coast doesn't have a lot of accommodation for short-term visitors. Apart from the Sheraton, all are condos and most require you to stay for at least one week.

Makaha Surfside is a four-storey cinder-block apartment complex a mile south of Makaha Beach. Though it's mostly residential, some of the 450 units are rented out through the Makaha Surfside Homeowner's Association (85-175 Farrington Hwy, No A222, Makaha, HI 96792; tel 696-2105). One-bedroom units cost $343 a week in the low season or $413 in the high season. They also have a studio for $273 a week. It's a very ordinary-looking complex, though there are pools, barbecue grills and a sauna.

Makaha Shores (Hawaii Hatfield Realty, 85-833 Farrington Hwy, Suite 201, Waianae, HI 96792; tel 696-8415) is a condo right on the northern end of Makaha Beach. In winter, studios cost $400 for one week, $575 for two weeks or $825 a month. In the low season they're $325 a week or $700 a month. They tack on a $35 cleaning fee. There are one and two-bedroom units as well. It's tough to book in the high season, as a lot of retired people winter there.

There are two other seaside condo complexes in Makaha, and they're next to each other. The *Hawaiian Princess*, which looks the nicer of the two, has one-bedroom units for $75 a night or $500 a week. The other complex is the *Makaha Beach Cabanas*, but under no circumstance should you think 'cabana' for this plain concrete highrise. One-bedroom units cost $70 a night or $375 a week.

Both places can be booked through Peggy Hill (84-965 Farrington Hwy, No 107, Waianae, HI 96792; tel 696-2756). There's a $35 cleaning fee and you must stay a minimum of three days. Monthly rates are substantially cheaper.

At the *Sheraton Makaha Resort & Country Club* (84-626 Makaha Valley Rd, Makaha, HI 96792; tel 695-9511; 800-325-3535) the theme is country club right down to the brochure that shows a young couple practising their putts in the bedroom. The 200 rooms have lanais and refrigerators. The hotel has an 18-hole golf course, an Olympic-size pool, lighted tennis courts, horseback riding and restaurants. Rates are from $95 to $165.

Up in Makaha Valley, there are two other large complexes: *Makaha Valley Plantation* and *Makaha Valley Towers*. Both give the impression they're under siege, with guards and gates to keep outsiders at bay. Of the two, Makaha Valley Towers seems the better value. Inga's Realty (84-1170 Farrington Hwy, Makaha, HI 96792; tel 695-9055) handles 100 of the 586 units. Studios cost $400 a week, one-bedroom units $475, plus there's a $45 'check-out' cleaning fee. You also have to pay large deposits, though it's all a bit cheaper in the low season. The peacocks that hang around can be noisy in the mornings.

Places to Eat

The Sheraton has a lobby lounge, a poolside cafe open from 7 am to 5 pm daily, and a more elegant dining room for dinners and Sunday brunch.

Cornet Village, at the corner of Farrington Hwy and Makaha Valley Rd, has a store and deli (and also a laundromat). There's a 7-11 store on the opposite corner.

NORTH OF MAKAHA
Keaau Beach Park

Keaau Beach Park is another long open grassy strip, this time bordering a rocky shore, with camping, showers, drinking water, picnic tables and restrooms. A sandy beach begins at the very northern end of the park, though a rough reef, sharp drop and high seasonal surf make swimming uninviting.

Driving north along the coast you'll see low lava sea cliffs, white sand beaches and patches of kiawe. On the mauka side there are glimpses of a run of little valleys.

Kaneana Cave

Kaneana Cave, a massive cave on the

right-hand side of the road about two miles north of Keaau Beach Park, was once underwater. Its size is the result of wave action wearing away loose rock around an earthquake crack and expanding the cavern over the millennia, as the ocean slowly receded.

It's a somewhat uncanny place – often a strong wind gusts near the cave while it's windless just down the road.

Hawaiian legend tells of a child named Nanaue who was born with a open space between his shoulders. Unknown to his mother, the child's father was the king of sharks who had taken on the guise of a man. Nanaue was born half man, half shark. He was human on land, but when he entered the ocean the opening on his back became a shark's mouth. After a nasty spell in which many villagers were ripped to shreds by a mysterious shark, Nanaue was discovered and forced to swim from island to island as he was hunted down. For a while he lived near Makua and took his victims into Kaneana Cave via an underwater tunnel.

Hawaiian kahunas once performed rituals inside the inner chamber. Older Hawaiians consider it a sacred place and won't enter for fear it's haunted by the spirits of deceased chiefs. From the collection of broken beer bottles and graffiti inside it's obvious not everyone shares their sentiments.

From Ohikilolo Beach, below the cave, you can see Haena Point ahead. The beach is sometimes called Barking Sands, as the sand is said to make a 'woofing' sound if it's walked on when very dry.

It's rugged country around here with grasses, high cliffs and, for some reason, lots of dead trees.

Makua

Scenic Makua Valley is wide and grassy. It serves as the ammunition field of the Makua Military Reservation.

The makai road opposite the south end of the reservation leads to a little graveyard shaded by yellow-flowered be-still trees. This is all that remains of the Makua Valley community, forced to evacuate during WW II so the US military could use the entire valley for bombing practice. The valley is now fenced off with barbed wire and signs that warn of stray explosives.

Makua Beach, the white sand beach opposite the reservation, was a canoe landing in days past. A movie set, of Lahaina as it was during the 1800s, was built on Makua Beach for the 1966 movie *Hawaii* which starred Julie Andrews and Max von Sydow. No trace of it remains.

Satellite Tracking Station

Just before the start of Kaena Point State Park a road leads up to Kaena Point Satellite Tracking Station, operated by the US Air Force. The tracking station's domes and antennas sit atop the mountains above the point.

There are a couple of trails above the tracking station that can be hiked – one of them a two-mile ridge trail. You need to obtain a permit in advance from the Division of Forestry & Wildlife (tel 548-8850).

KAENA POINT STATE PARK

Kaena Point is the sharp, westernmost point of Oahu. Kaena Point State Park is an undeveloped 853-acre coastal strip that runs along both sides of the point.

Until the mid-1940s the Oahu Railroad ran up from Honolulu and around the point, carrying passengers on to Haleiwa.

The attractive mile-long sandy beach on this side of the point is Yokohama Bay, so named for the large numbers of Japanese fishermen who came here during the railroad days.

Winter brings huge pounding waves and Yokohama is a popular surfing and bodysurfing spot. It is, however, best left to the experts because of the submerged rocks, strong riptides and dangerous shorebreak.

Swimming is pretty much limited to the summer, and then only during calm conditions. When the water's flat, the rocky areas should provide half-decent snorkelling. There are restrooms and showers but no drinking water.

In addition to being a state park, Kaena Point has been designated a natural area reserve because of its unique ecosystem. The extensive dry, windswept coastal dunes that rise above the point are the habitat of many rare native plants. The endangered Kaena akoko that grows on the talus slopes is found nowhere else.

More common plants are the beach naupaka, the white flowers of which look like they've been torn in half; pau-o-Hiiaka, a vine with blue flowers; and beach morning glory, sometimes found wrapped in the parasite plant kaunaoa, which looks like orange plastic fishing line.

Sea birds common to the point include shearwaters, boobies and the common noddy, a dark-brown bird with a greyish crown.

Dirt bikes and 4WD vehicles have, until recently, created a great deal of disturbance in the dunes. It was only after Kaena Point became a natural area reserve in 1983, that vehicles were prohibited.

It's hoped that the reserve will again become a nesting site for the Laysan albatross and green sea turtles, and for the Hawaiian monk seals that on rare occasions bask in the sun there. Controversial on-again, off-again proposals to connect Farrington Hwy around the point, however, threaten it all.

Legends

Early Hawaiians believed that when people went into a deep sleep or lost consciousness their souls would wander. Souls that wandered too far were drawn west to Kaena Point. If they were lucky they were met here by their *aumakua* (ancestral spirit helper) who led their soul back to their body. If unattended, their soul would be forced to leap from Kaena Point into the endless night, never to return.

On clear days Kauai can be seen from the point. According to legend, it was at Kaena Point that the demigod Maui attempted to cast a huge hook into Kauai and pull it next to Oahu to join the two islands. But the line broke and Kauai slipped away, with just a small piece of it remaining near Oahu. This is Pohaku O Kauai, a rock off the end of Kaena Point.

Hiking

A 2½-mile (one way) coastal hike runs from Yokohama Bay to Kaena Point, following the old railroad bed. Along the trail are tide pools, sea arches, great coastal views and the lofty sea cliffs of the Waianae mountain range. There's a graffiti-covered light beacon on the point, but otherwise it's a totally undeveloped area. The hike is unshaded. Take plenty of water and don't leave anything valuable in your car.

Hawaii – The Big Island

The island of Hawaii, commonly called the Big Island, is twice the size of all the other Hawaiian islands combined. Geographically, it is so incredibly varied that it resembles a mini-continent. Climates range from tropical to arid. Landscapes include one of just about everything: desolate lava flows, lush coastal valleys, high sea cliffs, rolling pastures, deserts and rainforests.

Geologically, it's the youngest Hawaiian island and the only one still growing. Kilauea, the most active volcano on earth, has added 100 acres of coastal land and new black sand beaches to the island since its latest series of eruptions began in 1983.

The Big Island has Hawaii's highest mountains, which rise almost 14,000 feet above sea level. Some people liken them to icebergs, not only for their seasonal snow-caps but because their summits are merely the tips of mountain masses which rise 32,000 feet from the ocean floor.

The mountains create a huge windscreen that blocks the moist north-easterly trade winds and makes the leeward western side of the Big Island the driest region in Hawaii. This sunny western side's Kona and Kohala coasts have the island's best beaches and water conditions.

The windward east coast catches the rain. Parts of it are planted in expansive fields of green sugar cane. The rest is a rugged coastline with pounding surf, lush tropical rainforests, deep ravines and impressive waterfalls.

The Hawaii Volcanoes National Park encompasses incredible volcanic sites. It also has excellent hiking and camping, ranging from black sand beaches to the 13,679-foot summit of Mauna Loa. You can drive or cycle around the rim of Kilauea's huge caldera or walk across still-steaming crater floors.

The Big Island also has the largest privately owned cattle ranch in the USA and the world's top collection of astronomical observatories. The latter dot the summit of Mauna Kea, Hawaii's highest point at 13,796 feet. The Big Island has important historical sites including Hawaii's best petroglyphs and some of its most important heiaus.

Orientation

There are two distinct centres on the Big Island. Hilo, on the lush rainy east coast, is the island's only real city. It's the oldest city in Hawaii and it shows its age with character. But it's Kona, on the dry, sunny west coast that draws the visitors. It's got most of the island's accommodation, with the majority of rooms in condos, and is the centre of most recreational activities, including excellent diving and deep-sea fishing.

The Big Island has some neat small towns that remain unchanged by tourism. A couple of them have old-fashioned hotels with $20 rooms and small downstairs restaurants. Things move slower in these rural spaces and there's a nice sense of community.

The Big Island is big on space and few places feel crowded. It attracts a lot of adventurous people. It's got cowboy country, traditional fishing villages, valleys with taro farmers and wild horses, and a fair number of alternative folks living off the land.

The Big Island's main airports are in Hilo and Kona. The Hilo Airport is in town.

Most visitors land in Kona at Keahole Airport. This can be a shock if you're expecting tropical greenery and waving palm trees because it looks more like a black lava wasteland, as if the island had been paved over in asphalt. Don't panic! It's but one face of the island and even here if you look closer you can catch a glimpse of some fine secluded white sand beaches squeezed between the lava and the turquoise waters.

Hwy 19 runs along the Kona Coast. From the airport to Kailua- Kona, seven miles south, you'll see black lava accented with white coral graffiti and blazing bougainvillea. Waikoloa is 12 miles to the north through similar scenery.

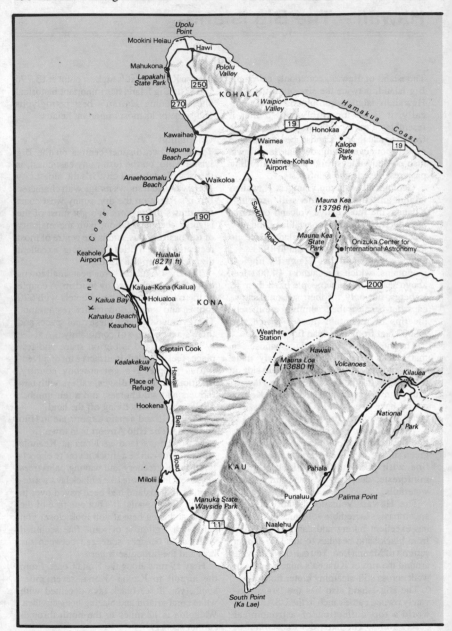

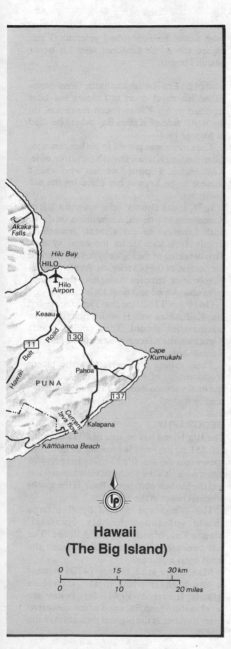

**Hawaii
(The Big Island)**

```
0        15       30 km
0     10      20 miles
```

The Hawaii Belt Rd circles the island, taking in the main towns and many of the sights. Different segments of the road have different highway numbers and names, but it's easy to follow.

From Kona to Hilo, the northern half of the belt road is 93 miles and the journey takes about two hours non-stop. The southern Kona-Hilo route is 125 miles and takes approximately three hours.

Facts

HISTORY

By and large the history of the Big Island is the history of Hawaii. It's widely believed that the first Polynesian settlers landed on this island. It was on the Big Island that the first luakini heiau (temple of human sacrifice) was introduced and the kapu system of strict taboos which regulated all aspects of daily life came into being. It was also here, six centuries later, that the old gods were overthrown and replaced by those of the Christians.

English explorer Captain Cook died on the Big Island in 1779, a year after 'discovering' Hawaii, and this was where Kamehameha the Great rose to power.

The Kamehameha Era

Kamehameha I Kamehameha was born on the Big Island. As a young boy he was brought to Kealakekua Bay to live at the royal court of his uncle, Kalaniopuu, high chief the island.

Kamehameha went on to become Kalaniopuu's fiercest general. To help him amass even more strength, Kalaniopuu appointed Kamehameha guardian of the war god Kukailimoku, the 'snatcher of land'.

The god was embodied in a coarsely carved wooden image with a bloody red mouth and a helmet of yellow feathers. Kamehameha carried it into battle with him and it was said that during the fiercest fighting the image would screech out terrifying battle cries.

Immediately after Kalaniopuu's death in 1782, Kamehameha led his warriors against Kalaniopuu's son, Kiwalao, who had taken the throne. Kiwalao was killed and Kamehameha emerged as ruler of the Kohala region and one of the three ruling chiefs of the Big Island. The other two were Kahekili of Maui and Kamehameha's cousin, Keoua.

But Kamehameha's ambitions went beyond sharing the control of the islands. In 1790, with the aid of a captured foreign schooner and two shipwrecked sailors, Isaac Davis and John Young, whom he used as gunners, Kamehameha attacked and conquered Maui.

Shortly after, Kamehameha was in Molokai preparing for the invasion of Oahu when word reached him that Keoua, chief of the Kau region, was attacking the Hamakua Coast. Keoua had pillaged sacred Waipio Valley where Kamehameha had received his war god a decade earlier.

As an angry Kamehameha set sail for home, Keoua's soldiers retreated to Kau, passing beneath the slopes of the volcano, Kilauea. The volcano erupted and many of the warriors were instantly killed by toxic fumes and ashes that swept over them. It is the only known volcanic explosion in Hawaiian history to have resulted in such fatalities. Casts of their footprints remain on the trail today.

Around this time Kamehameha was told by a prophet from Kauai that if he built a new heiau to honour his war god, Kukailimoku, he would become ruler of all the islands.

Kamehameha did so, completing Puukohola Heiau in Kawaihae in 1791. He then sent word to Keoua that his appearance was requested at the heiau for reconciliation. Keoua, well aware that this was a luakini temple, probably knew his fate was sealed.

Upon landing, Keoua and his party became the heiau's first sacrifices. With Keoua's death, Kamehameha became sole ruler of the Big Island.

Over the next few years Kamehameha conquered all the islands (except for Kauai over which he established suzerainty) and named the entire kingdom after his home island, Hawaii.

End of an Era Kamehameha the Great established his royal court in Lahaina but later returned to his Kamakahonu residence, on the north side of Kailua Bay where he died in May 1819.

The crown was passed to his hesitant son, Liholiho, and Kamehameha's favourite wife, Kaahumanu, a spirited woman who wasn't content to be kept in her place by the old traditions.

In Kamakahonu, six months after Kamehameha's death, Kaahumanu sat down with Liholiho to eat a meal, something strictly forbidden under the kapu system. This breaking of the kapus by royalty marked the demise of the old religion. Almost immediately after, temples throughout the islands were abandoned and their idols burned.

On 19 April 1820 the ship *Thaddeus* sailed into Kailua Bay with Hawaii's first Christian missionaries aboard. They landed beside Kamehameha's recently desecrated heiau at Kamakahonu.

Their timing was perfect as the recent abandonment of the old religion had left a spiritual vacuum into which the missionaries readily moved.

GEOGRAPHY

The Big Island has an area of 4035 sq miles (10,451 sq km) and is growing as new lava spews into the sea. It's 93 miles long and 76 miles wide. It's the youngest Hawaiian island and the farthest east. South Point is the southernmost point in the USA.

The island was formed by five large shield volcanoes: Kohala, Hualalai, Mauna Kea, Mauna Loa and Kilauea. The last two are still active with Kilauea the most active on earth.

Mauna Kea at 13,796 feet (4205 metres) is the highest point in the Hawaiian islands. It extends 19,680 feet below sea level to the ocean floor and when measured from its base, is the highest mountain in the world.

Mauna Loa, at 13,679 feet (4169 metres) above sea level, is the largest mountain mass in the world when measured from the ocean floor.

CLIMATE

Rainfall and temperatures vary more with location than with the seasons. The leeward north-west coast between Lapakahi and Waikoloa is the driest region in the state. Kawaihae, in the centre of this strip, averages less than 10 inches of rain a year.

On the windward side of Mauna Kea, near the 2500 foot elevation, 300 inches of rain falls each year. So much rain is squeezed out of the clouds as they rise up Mauna Kea and Mauna Loa that only about 15 inches of precipitation reaches the summits, much of it as snow. Heavy subtropical winter rainstorms in Hilo occasionally bring blizzards to the mountains, as low as the 9000-foot level.

Elevation makes enough of a difference that even within the city of Hilo, annual rainfall ranges from 130 inches on the shore to 200 inches on the higher slopes. Trivia buffs may be interested to know that Hilo has the world's largest measured raindrops, 4 to 8 mm in diameter!

Annual rainfall in Volcano is 101 inches. At Kailua-Kona it's 25 inches. Though winter is wetter than summer, location again is the key. In Kona seasonal rainfall variations are marginal. At Volcano it's about twofold.

Average January temperatures are 65°F at Hawaii Volcanoes National Park, 79°F in Hilo and 81°F in Kailua-Kona. In August, they are 71°F, 83°F and 85°F respectively. Night-time lows are about 15° less.

'Vog' is a word coined on the Big Island to define the volcanic haze that has been hanging over the island since Kilauea's latest eruptive phase began in 1983.

It usually blows toward Kona and though at times it's not noticeable, conditions can resemble a mild city smog when the trade winds falter. Vog consists of water vapour, carbon dioxide and significant amounts of sulphur dioxide.

Nene

FLORA & FAUNA

The nene, the endangered goose that is Hawaii's state bird, lives on the upland slopes of Mauna Kea, Mauna Loa and Hualalai. As recently as 100 years ago there were an estimated 25,000 nene on the Big Island. They now number just a few hundred. Still, they're a friendly species and you might come across them, particularly if you camp in the national park.

Two varieties of silversword grow on the Big Island, one on Mauna Kea and the other on Mauna Loa. They're related to their better- known Maui cousin. They grow in remote areas and few people see them.

In the first 30 years of the 1800s, Hawaii's once extensive sandalwood forests were stripped from every accessible niche of the islands, the fragrant wood shipped off to China. Only a few inaccessible areas escaped the devastation.

One of the last virgin sandalwood forests in Hawaii is on the Kona Coast on the slopes above Kealakekua where the ancient trees, three foot in diameter, are being logged by a land developer from South Africa and pulled out of the rugged back country by helicopter. As in the olden days, they're then placed on ships for the Orient where each of the big trees brings in about $20,000.

Many native birds that once lived in Hawaii's sandalwood forests have already become extinct and the logging represents a major habitat loss for those remaining. It's also a significant loss of watershed. Amazingly, it's all legal and the sandalwood forests remain unprotected.

There are wild horses in Waipio Valley and feral cattle on the slopes of Mauna Kea. More recently introduced on Mauna Kea are mouflon sheep which eat the seed pods of mamane trees, the same food source of the endangered palila, a small yellow bird which survives solely on Mauna Kea's slopes. The Big Island also has wild pigs and goats.

GOVERNMENT

The Big Island is one county unto itself with a mayor and a nine-member council. Hilo is the county seat and political centre.

There's ongoing rivalry between old established Hilo and boomtown Kona.

The biggest political issue on the island, as elsewhere in Hawaii, is rampant development. Mayor Bernard Akana, a Republican on a heavily Democratic island, was a relative unknown before being swept into office in 1988 by a rogue wave of anti-growth sentiment.

ECONOMY

The Big Island's unemployment rate is about 5%. Employment is fairly diversified with the retail trade, government, hotels and construction industries employing about half of the workforce.

Agriculture accounts for almost 15% of the workforce. The Big Island produces most of Hawaii's macadamia nuts, coffee and tropical flowers. It also exports papayas, bananas and ginger root. Cocoa has recently been introduced.

There's also an illicit and far more profitable underground agriculture in pakalolo. Some 90% of all marijuana confiscated in Hawaii is from the Big Island. In 1987, 1,737,685 pot plants were destroyed.

Sugar production, though still important, is in decline. Sugar companies are diversifying into fields ranging from macadamia nuts to slaughterhouses.

The Big Island has several sizeable cattle ranches. Spurred by Hawaii's population growth, the cattle business is booming.

Kona Coffee Missionaries introduced the first coffee trees to Hawaii in 1827. By the early 1900s coffee was an important cash crop, planted throughout the islands.

The erratic rise and fall of coffee prices eventually drove most coffee farmers out of business. Only the coffee thriving in the upland areas of south Kona was of high enough quality to find a market during gluts in world markets.

By 1980 coffee production had dropped dramatically but a rising interest in gourmet coffee sparked sales of the highly aromatic Kona coffee. Today coffee farming is thriving among small growers. Kona coffee is the only commercially grown coffee in the USA and commands top prices.

High Technology Some of the world's most expensive and intricate astronomical observatories sit on the summit of Mauna Kea.

The Big Island is also leading in the research and development of alternative energy projects in hydroenergy and geothermal energy. It's widely believed that the Big Island has enough natural energy potential to supply all of Hawaii's energy needs.

The state has spent about half a million dollars to study the feasibility of a commercial space launching pad in the Kau area. The Big Island would have the advantage of being the only US launch site with the capability of sending spacecraft into either equatorial or pole-crossing orbits. Plans originally focused on South Point, but are now centred on Palima Point, 23 miles up the coast to the north-east. Many of the islanders including native Hawaiians and local fishermen in the South Point area are against these plans and do not want to see the proposed project built anywhere in Kau.

Development Growth is a big issue on the Big Island which has more new hotel and condo developments planned than all the other islands combined. There are currently 20,904 new hotel units and 22,910 condo units on the drawing board, almost all of them in the Kona and Kohala areas. Some are planned for beaches which are now totally undeveloped and secluded, such as Makalawena and Kukio Bay, while others will be attached to existing Waikoloa resorts including Mauna Kea and Mauna Lani. To get an idea of the scale, in 1988 there were 69,000 visitor accommodation units in the entire state of Hawaii.

The ultimate real estate deal was the 1989 sale by Castle & Cooke to a Japanese developer of almost the entire North Kohala coast from Mahukona to Pololu Valley.

The scale of this rampant development has not only Big Island residents but neighbour islanders concerned. Besides losing the finest stretch of secluded beaches anywhere in Hawaii, the developments raise major infrastructure problems, from water and energy supplies to a serious lack of affordable housing.

PEOPLE

The population of the Big Island was 114,400 in 1987. The Hilo district has about 40% of the island's population, but the Big Island's demographics are changing rapidly.

Between 1970 and 1980, North Kona (which includes Kailua-Kona) was the fastest growing district in the state with a growth rate of 185%. In the '80s it settled down to a relatively modest 50% making it the fourth fastest growing district in the state. Since then Puna and South Kohala have edged it out. (In case you're wondering, the number one is Kauai's North Shore.)

The Big Island's ethnic breakdown is 30% part-Hawaiian, 24% Caucasian, 20% Japanese, followed by mixed non-Hawaiian, Filipino and Chinese. There are 666 full-blooded Hawaiians.

Ohia Lehua

TOURIST INFORMATION

There are two Hawaii Visitors Bureau offices: 180 Kinoole St, Hilo, HI 96720 (tel 961-5797) and 75-5719 W Alii Drive, Kailua-Kona, HI 96740 (tel 329-7787).

GENERAL INFORMATION
Official Hawaii

The Big Island's official flower is the ohia lehua. Ceremonial leis are made from its fluffy red pompom blossoms. The official colour is red.

Media

West Hawaii Today (tel 329-9311) is the Kona Coast newspaper, published daily except Saturdays. Hilo's *Hawaii Tribune-Herald* (tel 935-6621) is published daily.

Free tourist magazines such as *This Week Hawaii* and *Guide to Hawaii* are easily available at the airport, in hotel lobbies and around town. The monthly *Harry Lyons' Kona Coast Magazine*, geared for both residents and visitors, is also free. They're all good sources of information and include discount coupons for a range of activities throughout the island.

Maps

The best map of the Big Island is the one put out by the University of Hawaii and is available in shops around Kona and Hilo.

Libraries There are public libraries in Kailua-Kona, Kealakekua, Holualoa, Hilo, Waimea, Pahoa, Pahala, Naalehu, Mountain View, Laupahoehoe, Kapaau, Honokaa and Keeau.

Weather

The National Weather Service has recorded forecasts for the Big Island in general (tel 961-5582), for Hilo and vicinity (tel 935-8555) and water conditions (tel 935-9883).

Hawaii Volcanoes National Park (tel 967-7977) has recorded information on current volcano eruptions and viewing points.

Temporary/Part-time Employment

Job openings are listed at the state employment service (tel 322-9344 in Kealakekua, 961-7481 in Hilo). The Kona and Waikoloa resort areas have a steady demand for service jobs.

Coffee farms need pickers during the harvest season which peaks during autumn. Going rates are about $20 to $30 per bag. Three or four bags a day is average. A really good picker might get six.

Check the Honokohau Harbor bulletin board for possible crew jobs.

Emergency

For ambulance or fire emergencies, dial 961-6022. Each town has different telephone numbers for police: Kailua-Kona is 323-2645; Hilo is 935-3311. The island-wide crisis line is 329-9111.

The main hospitals are in Hilo (tel 969-4111) and Kealakekua (tel 322-9311).

ACCOMMODATION

Most of the island's accommodation is centred around Kailua-Kona, with the majority of the rooms in condos – though some of these are run like hotels with a front desk and daily rates. If you're staying a week or more, condos are often a better deal than hotels.

Because the island is so big, it's worth considering moving around and exploring from a couple of different bases.

The cheapest places to stay in the Kona area (and on the whole island) are mauka of Kailua, in small local hotels in the towns of Holualoa, Honalo, Kealakekua and Captain Cook.

Waimea has some delightful B&Bs as well as a couple of small motels.

Rainy Hilo doesn't see a great many visitors and choices aren't as varied as you might expect for a city. There are a couple of good moderately priced places to stay and a handful of ordinary tourist hotels.

Waikoloa, north of Kona, has expensive resorts. The Mauna Lani and Mauna Kea attract the rich who want elegant hideaways and not much excitement. Kona Village plays out the getaway fantasy in comfortable Polynesian thatched huts. The Hyatt Regency Waikoloa is loaded with splashy high-tech toys for those who want constant titillation.

My Island (Gordon & Joann Morse, Box 100, Volcano, HI 96785; tel 967-7216) is a no-fee reservation service for 19 Big Island B&Bs. Their own B&B in the village of Volcano (near Hawaii Volcanoes National Park) is the cheapest, from $25. Others start at $40, with most around $55. Other B&B services are listed in the front of the book.

Places to stay are listed in these sections: Kona, South Kona, North of Kona, North Kohala, Waimea, Hamakua Coast, Hilo, Puna, Hawaii Volcanoes National Park and Kau.

Unless otherwise noted, the rate given is the same for either singles or doubles. If calling from outside Hawaii, add the 808 area code.

Camping

At first glance, the list of Big Island camping grounds seems to read like some sort of 'Campers Guide to Hell': Laupahoehoe Beach where a village was washed away in a tidal wave; Halape Beach where an earthquake sank the shoreline 30 feet; and Kamoamoa Beach where a lava flow recently wiped out the nearby ranger station!

Actually there's little to worry about. Hawaii's lava isn't the rushing type which sweeps through camping grounds overnight and tsunami speakers have been set up to warn of approaching tidal waves.

Some of the best and safest camping is found in Hawaii Volcanoes National Park. Other good campsites are found on beaches, in upland forests and on the floor of lush Waipio Valley. There are also a few semi-secluded beaches where campers have been known to unofficially set up for a night or two.

State Parks Tent camping is allowed at Kalopa, MacKenzie and Manuka state parks. There are no fees but permits are required.

The state maintains A-frame shelters at Hapuna, self-contained housekeeping cabins at Mauna Kea and Kilauea and cabins for up to eight people at Kalopa.

The whole system is computerised and reservations can be made at state park offices on any island. The Big Island office (tel 961-7200) is at 75 Aupuni St (Box 936), Hilo, HI 96721.

The A-frame shelters at Hapuna are single rooms with screened windows, a picnic table and wooden sleeping platforms for up to four people. Shared facilities include restrooms, cold showers and a pavilion with refrigerator, electric range, sink and tables. The cost is $7 per shelter per night.

Cabin prices depend on the number of people and range from $10/14 for singles/doubles to $30 for six people.

The cabins and shelters are popular and most require booking months in advance. Cancellations do occur. If you're flexible and lucky, you might be able to get a day or two without advance reservations. As soon as you arrive, call to see if anything is open. The main drawback is that even if you're on the western side of the island you'll have to drive over to Hilo to register if there's no time to do it by mail.

County Beach Parks The county allows camping at 13 of its beach parks: Kealoha, Kolekole, Laupahoehoe and Onekahakaha, all near Hilo; Harry Brown and Isaac Hale in Puna; Spencer, Keokea, Kapaa, Mahukona and Milolii, all on the western side; and Whittington and Punaluu in Kau.

Permits are required and they may be obtained by mail or in person from the Department of Parks & Recreation (25 Aupuni St, Hilo, HI 96720; tel 961-8311). Office hours are 7.45 am to 4.30 pm Monday to Friday.

Permits may also be picked up at the Yano Center in Captain Cook (tel 323-3046), opposite the Manago Hotel. It's open from 8 am to noon and 1.30 to 4.30 pm (to 4 pm on Fridays).

In Waiohinu, permits are issued by the public works office at the Kau Base Yard (tel 929-7189) from 7 am to 3.30 pm on weekdays. Turn at the sign for Discovery Harbor, next to Kauahaao Church.

The caretaker at Spencer Beach Park sells permits on weekdays. At Keokea Beach Park, the caretaker comes by in the morning to collect fees from campers who have arrived without permits.

Fees are $1 per person per day. Camping is allowed up to two weeks in each park (one week in the summer). Permits are issued for specific parks, or you can get a two-week open permit and move around as you like. The Big Island tends to be more relaxed than the other islands about permits.

Beach parks in the Puna and Kau areas are sometimes closed during winter storms.

Hawaii Volcanoes National Park The Hawaii Volcanoes National Park section has details on the park's three drive-up camping grounds and on trail shelters for backcountry hikers. They're all free and rarely filled.

Camping Supplies Pacific Rent-All (1080 Kilauea Ave, Hilo, HI 96720; tel 935-2974) rents pup tents for $7/28/56 a day/week/month, larger tents for $20/40/120, cotton summer-weight sleeping bags for $6/18/36, plus stoves, lanterns, water jugs and other supplies.

ENTERTAINMENT

Some of the larger Kona and Waikoloa hotels have Hawaiian music, usually duos or trios strumming in the early evening. The hotels often have dance bands, piano music and jazz groups as well.

Kona's singles scene centres around the discos: Mitchell's in the Keauhou Shopping Center and Eclipse on Kuakini Hwy in Kailua. Both are restaurants during the day, with dancing nightly. Mitchell's sometimes has live music. Eclipse tends to have a younger crowd. Poo Ping II at Kamehameha Square in Kailua is the newest disco; it's open from 10 pm to 2 am nightly.

Keauhou Beach Hotel's Makai Bar, an open-air thatched building right on the shoreline, has good sunset views and live Hawaiian music from 5 pm nightly. They sometimes feature a $2 tropical drink. Uncle George Naope & Friends present an authentic hula show several nights a week in the hotel lounge.

Kona has no shortage of sunset views or happy hour come-ons at restaurants and bars all along Alii Drive.

Kona Lagoon Longhouse at Kona Lagoon Hotel was the biggest concert hall before the Hyatt came along. I can hold up to 1000 people uncomfortably and has attracted the likes of Kenny Loggins and Bonnie Raitt.

The Hyatt Waikoloa sometimes brings in big-name entertainers appropriate for their clientele, such as Liza Minnelli or Rich Little.

In Hilo, Harrington's on Reed's Bay has a guitarist or jazz piano in its lounge from Tuesday to Saturday. The Reflections Restaurant at 101 Aupuni St has live top-40 bands and dancing from Tuesday to Saturday. Uncle Billy presents a hula show during dinner time at 6 pm nightly at the Hilo Bay Hotel restaurant.

Fiasco's on Hwy 11 near Banyan Drive has dancing to '50s and '60s music from 8.30 pm to 1 am Thursdays, Fridays and Saturdays.

Waimea's Kahilu Theater at the Parker Ranch Shopping Center presents occasional plays, classical music concerts, dance troupes and other productions.

Luaus Kona Village Resort (tel 325-5555) has the most authentic luau in Hawaii. It's Friday nights only, costs $46 and sometimes books out weeks in advance.

Hotel King Kamehameha in Kailua has a luau on Tuesdays, Thursdays and Sundays on its beach in front of Ahuena Heiau for $36. Kona Hilton in Kailua and the Hyatt and Royal Waikoloan in Waikoloa also have luaus and Polynesian shows.

Movies Theatres at Prince Kuhio Plaza and Waiakea Shopping Plaza in Hilo and at Hualalai Theatres on Kuakini Hwy in Kailua serve up a standard Hoywood diet.

World Square Theater in Kailua's Kona Marketplace has a mix of Hollywood movies and a few alternative films. They sell baked goodies from Aloha Cafe in Kainailu.

Free Polynesian Show The Kona Surf Resort in Keauhou has a free Polynesian show from 5.30 to 6.30 pm Tuesdays and Fridays. It's at the Nalu Terrace lounge.

ACTIVITIES

The vast majority of the Big Island's recreational activities take place in West Hawaii. In addition to those listed here, most of the Waikoloa resorts have a wide variety of activities, including water sports, cruises and dive trips. They advertise mainly to their guests, but are usually open to the public as well and generally charge higher-than-average rates.

Beaches

The Big Island has 313 miles of shoreline. What it doesn't have are the expansive stretches of sandy beaches that you'll find on Maui or Oahu. Most of the Big Island's beachfront borders its bays and coves.

The best spots are on the west coast. Kailua-Kona has a few good beaches, though the better ones are up the Kona Coast to Waikoloa and Kohala. Anaehoomalu and Hapuna are both beautiful public beaches. There are also a number of isolated gems dotting the coast that are well worth the effort to get to.

Hilo is not as well endowed with beaches, though there are a few places to swim and snorkel on the east side of Hilo Bay.

The Puna and Kau districts have black sand beaches though generally unfavourable swimming conditions.

Kamoamoa Beach in Hawaii Volcanoes National Park is a gorgeous new black sand beach pounded by rugged surf. The waters are too treacherous for swimming, but it's fun to walk on.

Swimming

The county has public pools at Honokaa High School in Honokaa, Kamehameha Park in Kapaau, Konawaena High School in Kealakekua, Kau High School in Pahala, Laupahoehoe High School in Laupahoehoe and at the old Hilo airport and the Hoolulu Complex in Hilo. All county pools are free to the public for lap swims and open pool use, scheduled at different hours.

There's a coastal saltwater pool with public access behind Kona by the Sea condos in Kailua.

Surfing

Though the Big Island has its surfing spots, it's not the best choice in Hawaii. Many of the island's surf spots are rocky and it is advisable to check out conditions before hitting the waves.

Honolii Beach Park, north of Hilo, is popular on the eastern side. In Kona, Kahaluu Beach in Keauhou and near the banyan tree before Magic Sands Beach in Kailua are popular spots.

Magic Sands Beach is also one of the best places on the Kona Coast for boogie boarding and bodysurfing.

Windsurfing

Most windsurfers head to Anaehoomalu Bay up in Waikoloa, where there are good wind and water conditions. You can rent boards from the beach hut in front of the Royal Waikoloan for $16 an hour. Two-hour lessons cost $35.

Kawaihae Harbor and Hilo Bay are other spots that see some activity.

Diving

The Big Island has excellent diving on the leeward Kona and Kohala coasts. Overall the best conditions are in spring and summer, though there are good, calm dive spots all year round.

The Kona Coast has many good shore dives, including steep near- shore drop-offs with lava tubes, caves and diverse marine life. Diving is far more limited on the Hilo side where the season is basically from April to September.

A good reference is the book *Let's Go Shore Dive'n' on the Kona Coast* by Dick Dresie, who has a dive column in *West Hawaii Today*.

Kona has lots of dive operations and the cost of one-tank dives averages about $55, two-tank dives about $75, including gear and often lunch. Several places offer introductory dives, night dives and certification courses.

One favoured dive is Red Hill, about 10 miles south of Kona. It's a cinder cone with beautiful lava formations, including ledges and lots of honeycombed lava tubes nicely lit by streaks of sunlight. There are coral pinnacles and many brightly coloured nudibranchs.

Another good spot is Suck-em-up Caves off Kaiwi Point, south of Honokohau Harbor. It's a series of little lava tubes. If the surge is right you can enter one and it'll pull you through. There are small white-tipped reef sharks, manta rays and sometimes a sea turtle or two.

Kealakekua Bay has good coral and marine life in a very protected cove that's calm all year round. There are about 40 other boat dives along the Kona Coast, including an aeroplane wreck off Keahole Point.

Jack's Diving Locker (Box 5306, Kailua-Kona, HI 96740; tel 329-7585; 800-345-4807), in the Coconut Grove Marketplace opposite the Hilton is a friendly little operation. It organises trips to Suck-em-up Caves and

Red Hill but will take divers almost anywhere they want to go. It also sponsors the local dive club.

Dive Makai (74-5590 Alapa, Kailua-Kona, HI 96740; tel 329-2025) gets a lot of return business as it has a good reputation. It's in the industrial area.

Sea Dreams Hawaii (Box 4886, Kailua-Kona, HI 96745; tel 329-8744) takes up to eight people out in a 28-foot power catamaran, and organises trips usually to caves, archways and lava tubes north of Kailua.

Kona Coast Divers (75-5614 Palani Rd, Kailua-Kona, HI 96740; tel 329-8802) is a larger operation. It's professional but not as personal as the smaller services.

Sea Paradise Scuba (Box 5655, Kailua-Kona, HI 96745; tel 322-2500, 800-322-5662) is at Keauhou Bay. It organises trips mostly to Red Hill or Kealakekua Bay in the south.

Kohala Divers (Box 4935, Kawaihae, HI 96743; tel 882-7774), at the shopping centre in Kawaihae, organises trips up the Kohala Coast in the north.

Mauna Loa Diving Service (97 Haili St, Hilo, HI 96721; tel 935- 3299) doesn't have a boat but does shore dives for $35 (one tank), $45 (two tanks) and a snorkelling tour to Richardson's for $15. Though they won't take recreational divers out with them, they do support dives for Cousteau and other film crews photographing lava flows entering the ocean.

Live-Aboard Boat The Kona Aggressor (Live-Dive Hawaii, Box 2097, Kailua-Kona, HI 96745; tel 329-8182; 800- 344-5662) is a 110-foot live-aboard dive boat that accommodates up to 18 people. All-inclusive one-week trips cost $1600, starting and ending each Saturday.

Dive Club Kona's Humuhumu Dive Club is a good place to find dive buddies and directions to local dive spots. When the group is active they go out twice a month, usually on weekends. Most of their dives are shore dives. They're into reef ecology and don't allow spear fishing. Dives are announced on the radio or in West Hawaii Today. For information call 329-7585.

Snorkelling

For snorkelling, there are some good spots south of Kailua-Kona. Kahaluu Beach is teeming with fish and is one of the best easy-access snorkelling spots in Hawaii. There's terrific snorkelling in the calm, clear 30-foot waters near Captain Cook's monument at the north end of Kealakekua Bay. The north side of the Place of Refuge is another fine snorkelling spot.

Snorkelling Cruises The most common snorkelling cruise is to Kealakekua Bay. (If you want to enjoy it without taking a boat, you can also hike down.) The cruise prices given here all include snorkelling gear. Some have free beverages and pupus and lower rates for kids.

Fairwind (tel 322-2788) has snorkelling trips to Kealakekua Bay aboard a 50-foot trimaran. They start from Keauhou Bay which allows more snorkelling time than on boats leaving from Kailua. The morning trip leaves at 8.30 am, has 2½ hours of snorkelling and includes lunch for $49. The afternoon trip leaves at 1 pm and has 1½ hours of snorkelling time for $30. They also have an $80 introductory dive for beginners on the morning trip. It includes instruction before the cruise and an hour of diving in the bay at 30 to 50 feet. They have free transportation to the boat.

Captain Zodiac (tel 329-3199) does four hour tours aboard bouncy Zodiac rubber rafts. They leave Honokohau Harbor at 8.30 am and 1.30 pm and cost $52. After 45 minutes of snorkelling at Kealakekua Bay they go south to sea caves around the Place of Refuge.

Kamanu Charters (tel 329-2021) takes a 36-foot catamaran out of Honokohau Harbor to a cove 45 minutes south. They usually use the sail on the way back. The three hour trips start at 9.30 am and 1.45 pm and cost $30. They also have a sunset sail.

Sea Breeze Cruises (tel 326-1311) takes a 42-foot catamaran out of Kailua Pier for two-hour cruises at 9 and 11.30 am and 2 pm. Their snorkelling spot at the north end of Kailua Bay is a 15 minute run. It costs $23.

Capt Beans' Cruises (tel 329-2955) has the high-profile boat with the tacky yellow lights and orange sails. Though it's a huge boat, it usually doesn't draw a big crowd on its snorkelling tours to Kealakekua Bay. It leaves at 8.30 am and the trip costs $25.

Capt Beans' also has a glass-bottom boat cruise from 1.30 pm for $10 and a touristy dinner cruise in the evening. All leave from Kailua Pier.

Capt Cook (tel 329-6411) is another large-boat operation going to Kealakekua from Kailua, which costs the same as Capt Beans. Both have about 45 minutes of snorkel time and entertain non-swimmers with divers who go under the glass bottom and feed the fish.

Snorkellers can sometimes tag along with divers on dive tours if space is available. Kohala Divers charges snorkellers just $10. Most charge about $25.

Snorkelling Equipment Kona Water Sports (tel 329-1593) at Banyan Court in Kailua rents boogie boards or snorkel sets for $5 a day. Weekly prices are competitive with Snorkel Bob's. They also have a few masks with corrective lenses at $8 a set and under-water cameras for $10 to $20. Rates are for 24 hours.

Snorkel Bob's (tel 329-0770), off Alii Drive by the Hilton, has snorkel sets for $15 a week. They also rent boogie boards and corrective-lens masks.

Fairwind at Keauhou Bay and Hawaiian Pedals in the Kona Inn Shopping Village rent snorkel sets for $5 a day.

Hotel King Kamehameha's beach hut rents snorkel sets for $5 a day and kayaks from $7.50 an hour. Sailboats are $15 to $20 the first hour and a bit cheaper after that. Sailing instructions are $10 per hour plus the rental.

If you want to buy snorkel gear, Windsong, behind Pottery Steakhouse in Kailua, sells masks and snorkels for quite a bit less than the dive shops. B & L Bike &

Sports in Kailua also sells reasonably priced snorkelling equipment in addition to daypacks and cycling accessories.

Fishing

Kona is a world-renowned deep-sea fishing spot for Pacific blue marlin, spectacular fighting fish with long swords. Kona holds most of the world records, with marlin topping 1000 pounds reeled in each year. Kona's also known for its record catches of ahi (yellowfin tuna).

Kona has plenty of charter boats. It costs about $90 to go out for half a day, sharing a boat with five others; and about $200 to $350 to charter a boat for half a day, depending on the size of the boat. Generally all tackle and gear is supplied.

These centres each book several dozen boats:

Kona Activities Center (Box 70, Kailua-Kona, HI 96745; tel 329-3171; 800-367-5288);

Kona Charter Skippers Association (75-5663 Palani Rd, Kailua- Kona, HI 96740; tel 329-3600; 800-367-8047);

Kona Coast Activities (Box 5397, Kailua-Kona, HI 96745; tel 329-2971; 800-367-5105).

The Hawaiian International Billfish Tournament held each August is the Super Bowl of fishing tournaments and includes a week-long festival with a parade.

Whale Watching

The best whale watching is off Maui, but the Big Island's not a bad second. Pilot, sperm, false killer whales and four dolphin species can be found in Kona waters all year round. The humpback season starts in December and runs through March or April.

The Pacific Whale Foundation (tel 329-3522) in Kona Inn Shopping Village does whale-watch tours at least once daily during the season from Kailua Pier, as long as they have a minimum of six people. The three-hour cruises cost $30 for adults, $15 for children. They guarantee humpback whale sightings or you'll get a 'just a fluke' coupon for a free trip within the year.

Dan McSweeney of the West Coast Whale Research Foundation also sometimes leads tours, though he doesn't have his own boat.

Hiking

Some of the Big Island's best and most varied hikes are in Hawaii Volcanoes National Park. Park trails lead across lava flows and steaming crater floors, through dense native forests and up to the peak of Mauna Loa.

North of Kona, you can hike in from the highway to secluded beaches. You can also explore portions of ancient footpaths and petroglyph fields. Mauna Lani Resort and Lapakahi State Park have easy trails around ancient fishponds and through abandoned villages, marked with interpretive plaques.

There are steep cliffs and deep valleys on the northern tip of the island which can be approached from either end. It's a 30-minute hike to the beach of Pololu Valley on the north-west side. On the south-east side, you can take a 30-minute walk down into verdant Waipio Valley or backpack on into remote Waimanu Valley.

South of Kona, a trail leads to the spot where Captain Cook died on the edge of Kealakekua Bay. A strenuous hike leads to the summit of Mauna Kea with its observatory domes. On the slopes below, Kalopa State Park has easy forest trails.

The Sierra Club's Moku Loa Group in Hilo holds hikes two to four times a month, usually on weekends. They vary between overnight backpacking campouts, day hikes and service projects. Hikes are announced about a week in advance in the two daily newspapers.

Cycling

B & L Bike & Sports (tel 329-3309), on Pawai Place in Kailua's industrial area, has 10-speeds for $12/60 a day/week and mountain bikes for $15/75.

Dave's Triathlon Shop (tel 329-4522), also on Pawai Place in Kailua, has mountain bikes for $18/70 a day/week.

Hawaiian Pedals (tel 329-2294) in the Kona Inn Shopping Village in Kailua has mountain bikes for $15 a day, tandem bikes for $25 a day and car bike racks for $5 a day.

Ciao (tel 969-1717) on Banyan Drive, in front of Hilo Hawaiian Hotel in Hilo, has mountain bicycles of all speeds. Five-speeds cost $15 for eight hours though sometimes you can wheel and deal for a better price.

Horse Riding All stables provide basic riding instruction for beginners. Some require reservations at least a day in advance.

Waiono Meadows (tel 329-0888) in Holualoa does trail rides through the pastures of Waiono Ranch and up the slopes of Hualalai. One-hour rides are $17 and two-hour rides cost $34. A common weather pattern on Hualalai is clear in the morning, clouding up around noon and rainy in the afternoon. You get great views of Kailua's turquoise waters sparkling below.

Waikoloa Stables (tel 883-9335) in the village of Waikoloa has 1½ hour cross-country ranch rides for $30 by appointment. The rides start in high desert and go up to the Parker Ranch meadows. They use rodeo, polo and show horses and generally follow stock trails, walking the horses in rocky areas, trotting and cantering in others.

Ironwood Outfitters (tel 885-4941) has rides through high mountain forest and grassland in the Kohala Mountains above Waimea, starting at the 4000-foot level. Rides cost $40 for 1½ hours and $65 for three hours.

Mauna Kea Stables (tel 882-7222) leaves from behind the Parker Ranch Shopping Center in Waimea. It's $25 an hour for open range riding.

Giddy-Up Go Trail Rides (tel 964-5713) in Pepeekeo, north of Hilo, has one-hour rides for $15 and three-hour rides for $35. There's a minimum charge of $40 per group and discounts for groups of four.

Waipio on Horseback, booked through Hawaii Resorts Transportation (tel 885-7484), has 2½ hour horseback rides in Waipio Valley for $65.

Tennis

The county has free public tennis courts at

Kailua Playground and the Old Kona Airport Park in Kailua, Honokaa Gym in Honokaa, Hoolulu Complex in Hilo and Waimea Park in Waimea.

At the old Kona airport, if you show up with racket in hand there's a good chance you'll find a partner. There are four well- lit outdoor courts there. Hilo's Hoolulu Complex has lighted indoor courts.

The King Kamehameha, Kona Hilton and Kona Surf hotels in Kona have tennis courts open to the public at reasonable fees.

Golf

The Waikoloa area resorts have world-class golf courses laid out on top of lava flows. The brilliant greens contrasting with the black lava are stunning.

The Westin Mauna Kea Golf Course (tel 882-7222), Francis Ii Brown Golf Course at Mauna Lani Resort (tel 885-6655) and the Waikoloa Beach Resort Golf Club (tel 885-6060), all 18 holes, are the big-time, big-buck courses. Mauna Kea charges non-guests $100. The other two cost a little less.

For more reasonable turf, the Hilo Municipal Golf Course (tel 959-7711) on Haihai St in Hilo has 18 holes for $6 on weekdays.

Other courses include Naniloa Country Club in Hilo, nine holes; SeaMountain Golf Course at Punaluu, 18 holes; Kona Country Club in Keauhou, 27 holes; Waikoloa Village Golf Club in Waikoloa, 18 holes; and Volcano Golf and Country Club in Hawaii Volcanoes National Park, 18 holes. Fees are $25 to $50.

Skiing

Skiing in Hawaii is primarily a curiosity. Snow does fall each winter on the upper slopes of Mauna Kea, though the timing is unpredictable. There are good years and bad years, though the last few haven't been too good.

The ski season starts anywhere from early January to late February and on a lucky year lasts until June. The altitude can be tough and the slopes can have exposed rocks. It's not your standard skiing, but it's an experience.

Perhaps the most unusual ski service in the USA is Ski Shop Hawaii (Box 8232, Honolulu, HI 96830; tel 737-4394). They run you back up the slopes in their 4WD vehicle which doubles as the warming hut. Tours including all ski equipment, though not clothing (which can be rented separately), cost $126 a day with a minimum of eight skiers.

Another service is Ski Guides Hawaii in Waimea (Box 2020, Kamuela, HI 96743; tel 885-4188).

Sporting Competitions

The Ironman triathlon combines a 2.4 mile ocean swim, 112 mile bike race and 26.2 mile marathon into one exhaustive endurance event. It's held each October, beginning and ending near Kailua Pier.

More than 1000 men and women from about 50 countries compete in the Ironman each year, with worldwide media coverage. The course record is around 8½ hours. For information: Ironman (75-5737 Kuakini Hwy, Suite 208, Kailua-Kona, HI 96740; tel 329-0063)

Each January, the Kilauea Volcano Wilderness Marathon and Rim Runs are held at Hawaii Volcanoes National Park. There's a 10- mile run around the rim of Kilauea's caldera, a 5½ mile race that goes down into Kilauea Iki Crater and a 26.2 mile marathon through the Kau Desert. Runs are limited to 200 to 500 people, depending on the race. An international crowd competes. Contact the Kilauea Visitor Center (tel 967-7311) for information.

West Hawaii Road Runners (Box 5519, Kailua-Kona, HI 96745) prints up an annual calendar of Big Island sporting events a year in advance. It's available at B & L Bike & Sports in Kailua and is also mailed out on request. It lists dozens of fun runs, marathons, triathlons, hiking outings, canoe races, regattas and swimming events.

THINGS TO BUY

Kona coffee and macadamia nuts are the Big Island's most common souvenirs. If you're buying coffee, note that 'Kona blend' is only 10% Kona coffee. If you want the real thing make sure it says 100%. Prices change with the market, but it is one of the more expensive gourmet coffees, usually around $10 a pound.

Supermarkets and discount stores (Longs, Pay'N Save) usually have the best deals on coffee. Rooster Farms produces an organically grown coffee which is sold at Kona Healthways at Kona Coast Shopping Center in Kailua and a few other places.

Shops selling local arts and crafts are plentiful. Good places to start are at the Volcano Art Center, galleries in Holualoa and at Potter's Gallery in Hilo.

GETTING THERE & AWAY
Air
The Big Island has two main airports, in Kona and Hilo. Hawaiian Airlines and Aloha Airlines connect both airports with the other main islands. Kona is by far the busiest of the two and has a few direct flights from the mainland with United Airlines.

There's also a small airport in Waimea, officially called the Waimea-Kohala Airport, but referred to as Kamuela (the old name for Waimea) by Aloha IslandAir, the only airline which serves it. Aloha IslandAir flies between Kamuela and Honolulu, Molokai, Princeville in Kauai, and Kahului and Kapalua/Kaanapali in Maui.

Fares on all three airlines are $49.95 from any destination, except for the first and last flights from Honolulu on Hawaiian and Aloha airlines, which are $34.95.

Hilo Airport General Lyman Airport in Hilo is just off Hwy 11, just under a mile south of its intersection with Hwy 19. It has a visitor information booth, restaurant, gift shop, lei stand, taxi stand and car rental booths. There's no bank or foreign money exchange counter at any of the Big Island airports.

Kona Airport Keahole Airport is on Hwy 19, about seven miles north of Kailua-Kona. It has a snack bar, car rental booths, visitor

information booth, mailbox, newspaper stands and a gift shop which sells the University of Hawaii map of the Big Island. For a relatively busy airport, it's surprisingly casual and all open-air (there's not enough rain to justify sealing it up!).

GETTING AROUND
Bus
Hele-On is the county public bus. Service between Kona and Hilo is along the northern route of the Hawaii Belt Rd once in each direction Monday to Saturday. The bus leaves the South Kona town of Kealia at 5.45 am and makes many stops along the way, including Kona Surf in Keauhou at 6.25 am, Mokuaikaua Church in Kailua at 6.43 am, Waimea at 7.45 am and Honokaa at 8.25 am, arriving in Hilo at the Mooheau terminal at 9.45 am and Prince Kuhio Plaza at 10.05 am.

The return trip leaves Prince Kuhio at 1.10 pm and arrives in Kailua at 4.32 pm. Fares are based on distance. The one-way fare between Kailua and Hilo is $5.25.

Drivers accept only the exact fare unless you have a ticket. Bus tickets sold around the island have a 10% discount. Luggage and backpacks are each $1 extra.

There are three other routes: Pahoa to Hilo, Laupahoehoe to Hilo, and Waiohinu to Hilo via Volcano. Each has service once a day in each direction Monday to Friday.

There's limited service around the city of Hilo for 75 cents per ride.

You can get a schedule and information from Mass Transportation Agency (tel 935-8241), 25 Aupuni St, Hilo, HI 96720.

Taxi
The taxi flag-down fee costs $2. It costs $1.60 a mile after that. The approximate fare from Kona's Keahole Airport is $15 to Kailua, $45 to Waikoloa.

Car
The companies mentioned here have car rental booths at Kona's Keahole Airport: Budget (tel 329-8511), Avis (tel 329-1745), National (tel 329-1674), Sunshine (tel 329-2926), Hertz (tel 329-3566), Dollar (tel

329-2744), Tropical (tel 329-2437) and Alamo (tel 329-8896).

Budget also has an office at Kona Inn Shopping Village (tel 329- 0721) and Dollar has offices at Hotel King Kamehameha (tel 326- 1123), the Kona Hilton (tel 326-2082) and Kona Surf Resort (tel 322-2261). Tropical has an office at Keauhou Beach Hotel (tel 322-9104).

At Hilo Airport you'll find Budget (tel 935-6878), Tropical (tel 935-3385), Alamo (tel 961-3343), Sunshine (tel 935-1108), Avis (tel 935-1290), National (tel 935-0891), Hertz (tel 935-2896) and Dollar (tel 961-6059).

Toll free numbers are in the front of the book.

Local companies often do better on daily rates, though seldom on weekly. Honolulu Rent-A-Car (tel 329-7328) on Pawai Place in the industrial area in Kailua has four-year-old Chevettes for about $14 a day with free mileage and free hotel pick-up. If you don't have a credit card they'll take a $200 cash deposit and prepayment in advance.

Otherwise, probably the best daily deal you'll find will be about $20 a day. Try World Rent-A-Car (tel 329-1006) next to Sizzler in Kailua, or National.

Harper Car & Truck Rentals (1690 Kamehameha Avenue, Hilo; tel 969-1478) has 4WD vehicles adjusted for use at Mauna Kea's high altitude and there're no restrictions on going to the summit. Isuzu Troopers cost $60 a day, $360 a week. They also have cars and vans plus free pick-up around Hilo.

Some of the other rental companies have 4WD vehicles, but they prohibit their use not only on the Summit Rd but also on the Saddle Rd. Also, they're likely to be 4WD more in name than in actuality.

Hilo is a good place to gas up, as gas is much cheaper there than in Kona.

Motor Scooter

Rent-Scootah (tel 329-3250), in Kailua's industrial park, has Honda 50cc scooters for $12.95 from 8 am to 5 pm or $21.95 for 24 hours. A credit card is required. There's free shuttle service from anywhere between Kona Surf and the airport.

Budget (tel 329-8511) in Kailua rents Yamaha scooters from $9.95 per four hours to $89 weekly. The price is a bit of a joke, however, as there's a mandatory '$100 deductible Loss Damage Waiver' at $5 a day. They open at 9 am at Kona Inn Shopping Village and at 7 am in their office in Kailua's industrial park.

You can also rent motor scooters in Kailua from $12.95 from a concessionaire who sets up in the parking lot on Alii Drive in front of Huggo's.

Ciao (tel 326-4177), which is in a kiosk opposite the Hotel King Kamehameha in Kailua rents mopeds for $25 a day and 150cc scooters for $45 a day. Ciao in Hilo (tel 969-1717) on Banyan Drive, in front of Hilo Hawaiian Hotel, also has mopeds and motorcycles.

Tours

Helicopter The most popular Big Island helicopter tour is to Kilauea, especially when it's acting up.

The cost largely depends on where you leave from. From Kona, it costs $245 with Kona Helicopters (tel 329-0551); from Hilo, it's $145 with Hilo Bay Air (tel 969-1545); from the 18th hole of the Volcano Golf Course, it's $105 with Volcano Heli-Tours (tel 967- 7578).

There are several other companies including Papillon (tel 885- 5995) from Waikoloa; Io Aviation (tel 935-3031) and Orchid Isle (tel 969-6664) from Hilo; and Kenai Helicopters (tel 329-7424) from Kona. It's worth checking the free tourist magazines for discount coupons and calling around to compare prices.

The cheapest way to fly over the volcano is with Hawaii Pacific Aviation (tel 961-5591), but they use a small plane instead of a helicopter. Their volcano tours leave from Hilo and cost $55.

If it's raining it's not worth going up. If

you're coming from Kona, call first to see what the weather's like.

Bus Trans Hawaiian – Jacks Tours (tel 329-2555), Akamai Tours (tel 329-7324; 800-922-6485) and Polynesian Adventure Tours (tel 329-8008) have day-long circle-island minibus tours for about $40.

The first two also have shorter, cheaper tours to smaller sections of the island.

Submarine Atlantis Submarines (tel 329-6626), based at Hotel King Kamehameha in Kailua, has one-hour rides in a submarine which dives down 100 to 150 feet in a coral crevice in front of Kona Hilton.

The sub has 26 side portholes and carries 46 passengers. It goes out six times daily and costs $58 ($29 for children).

Kona

Kona literally means 'leeward'. The Kona Coast refers to the dry, sunny west coast of the Big Island. However, to make matters a little more confusing, Kona also refers to Kailua, the largest town on the Kona Coast. The town's name is compounded Kailua-Kona by the post office and other officialdom to avoid confusion with Kailua on Oahu.

The weather is so consistent on this side of the island that the local paper usually just alternates two forecasts: 'Sunny morning. Afternoon clouds with upslope showers' or 'Sunny morning. Cloudy afternoon with showers over the slopes.'

The showers that hit the higher slopes rarely touch the coastline a couple of miles

1	Kaahumanu Plaza	31	Ocean View Inn
2	Kailua Candy Co	32	Banyan Court
3	Budget	33	Poki's Pasta
4	Rent-Scootah	34	Suzanne's Bakeshop
5	B & L Bike & Sports	35	Hulihee Palace
6	Salvation Army Thrift Shop	36	Mokuaikaua Church
7	Pawai Center	37	Laundromat
8	Lanai Siamese Kitchen	38	Kona Plaza
9	Laundromat	39	Eclipse
10	Kamehameha Square	40	Kona Center
11	North Kona Shopping Center	41	Kona Marketplace
12	Gas Station	42	McDonald's
13	Kona Coast Shopping Center	43	Kona Bay Hotel
14	Sizzler	44	Kona Inn Shopping Village
15	First Hawaiian Interstate Bank	45	7-11 Store
16	Burger King	46	Bank of Hawaii
17	Hilo Hattie	47	Gas Station
18	Longs Drugs	48	Library
19	Lanihau Center	49	St Michael's Church
20	Bowling Alley	50	Kealaokamalamalama Church
21	Waldenbooks	51	Waterfront Row
22	Kona Coast Divers	52	Jolly Roger
23	Pizza Hut & Taco Bell	53	Islander Inn
24	Gas Station	54	Kona Alii
25	Kona Seaside Hotel	55	Hualalai Theatres
26	Quinn's	56	Kailua Playground
27	Hotel King Kamehameha	57	Huggo's
28	Ahuena Heiau	58	Kona Hilton
29	Kona Ranchhouse	59	Hale Kona Kai
30	Old Kailua Cantina		

Hawaii – The Big Island – Kona 215

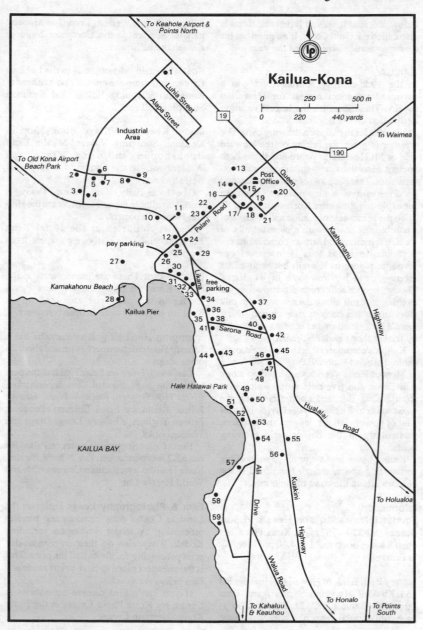

Kailua-Kona

To Keahole Airport &
Points North

To Waimea

Industrial
Area

To Old Kona Airport
Beach Park

Post
Office

pay parking

Kamakahonu Beach

Kailua Pier

free
parking

Palani Road

Likana

Sarona Road

Hale Halawai Park

KAILUA BAY

Alii
Drive

Kuakini
Highway

Hualalai
Road

Kaahumanu
Highway

To Holualoa

To Kahaluu
& Keauhou

Walua Road

To Honalo

To Points
South

0   250   500 m

0   220   440 yards

below. Because it sees so little rain, Kona is also called the Gold Coast. It's a good bet for a sunny vacation any time of the year.

KAILUA

In the 19th century Kailua-Kona was a favoured vacation retreat for Hawaiian royalty. These days it's the largest vacation destination on the Big Island.

It's got a lot to make it a drawing card. The weather is great, the setting on the leeward side of Mt Hualalai is pretty and it has both ancient Hawaiian and missionary-era historic sites. There are lots of places to stay and good restaurants. Kailua makes a good base for exploring the entire Kona west coast.

To the south-east of Kailua are a couple of small hillside towns with a pleasant mix of local, alternative and artisan communities.

Kailua-Kona has long been one of our favourite places in Hawaii, but with all its recent growth it's lost some of its charm. Though people still come downtown in the evening to stroll along the sea wall and talk story under the banyan trees, much of the town's historic character is being smothered by trinket shops and mini-malls.

Kailua's commercial activities are mostly centred around Kailua Bay.

Most of Kona's condos are lined up along Alii Drive, the five-mile strip, which runs from Kailua Bay and continues along the coast south to Keauhou. Alii Drive also sees a lot of power walkers, joggers and strollers, particularly in the cooler early morning hours.

Kailua has a few swimming, snorkelling and surfing spots, though the island's best beaches are up the coast to the north.

Information

Tourist Information The Hawaii Visitors Bureau (tel 329-7787) is in Kona Plaza. It's open 8 am to noon and 1 to 4.30 pm Monday to Friday.

Money Both Bank of Hawaii (at Hualalai Rd and Kuakini Hwy intersection) and First Interstate Bank (75-7522 Kuakini Hwy) have full-service branches with automatic

teller machines. Western Union has a money transfer service at the Computer Store in Kamehameha Square.

Post The main post office is in the Lanihau Center; and there are contract post offices at Kona Inn Shopping Village and Keauhou Shopping Village.

Media Keauhou Village Book Shop in Keauhou Shopping Village, Middle Earth Bookshoppe in Kona Plaza and Waldenbooks in the Lanihau Center are all well stocked.

The local daily, *West Hawaii Today*, is readily available around town, as are the Hilo and Honolulu papers.

Resort Sundries at the Hotel King Kamehameha sells daily newspapers from the mainland.

Laundromat There are laundromats in the North Kona Shopping Center, near Pawai Center in the industrial area, and up on Kuakini Highway near Eclipse restaurant.

Shopping Hotel King Kamehameha has a Liberty House department store and about 20 other shops.

Lanihau Center on Palani Rd has the post office, the huge Food 4 Less supermarket, Royal Jade Garden, Rocky's Pizza, Orange Julius, Kentucky Fried Chicken, Penguins Frozen Yoghurt, a bakery, Longs Drugs and Waldenbooks.

Kona Coast Shopping Center on Palani Rd has a KTA supermarket, Pay'N Save, Sizzler, Kona Healthways, Paniolo Country Cafe and World Rent-a-Car.

Film & Photography Longs Drugs in the Lanihau Center sells cameras and handles processing by major developers including Kodak. They also do their own same-day print processing for about half the price. This is the cheapest place to have prints made and film prices are good.

If you can't find camera accessories at Longs, try Kona Photo Center in the North Kona Shopping Center.

Parking Kailua's little central area can get quite congested and finding a parking space in town can be a challenge. There's free public parking in the lot behind Kona Seaside Hotel between Likana Lane and Kuakini Hwy, at Hale Halawai Park, and for library users at the library off Hualalai Rd.

Parking is at such a premium that Kailua has built its first underground parking lot, at Waterfront Row.

Hotel King Kamehameha, at the north end of Alii Drive, has a big pay-parking lot behind the hotel. The first 30 minutes is free and it's not terribly expensive after that. If you spend a few dollars in one of the shops or restaurants, you can get a voucher for free parking.

Hotel King Kamehameha

Be sure to take a stroll through the sprawling lobby of the Hotel King Kamehameha which is full of museum-quality Hawaiiana displays. It includes items such as feather capes and leis, temple drums, quilts, war clubs, *pahoa* daggers, calabashes and gourd containers.

The musical instrument display has a nose flute, coconut shell knee drum, shell trumpet, bamboo rattles and hula sticks. Other displays are on traditional foods and fishing.

There's an interesting painting of King Kamehameha at Kailua Bay by native Hawaiian artist Herb Kane near the front desk.

There are interpretive plaques and you can also get a free brochure at the activity desk which explains the displays in more depth.

The hotel has guided historical and ethnobotanical tours free to the public. Some of the tours visit the indoor displays and others take in the grounds. Hula teacher Ulalia Berman does the best tours. She also puts on a fine hula show with her students in the hotel lobby. Check the hotel activity desk (tel 329-2911 ext 102) for the current schedule.

Kailua Pier

Kona has Hawaii's best deep-sea fishing and several world-class tournaments. Though most charter fishing boats now use the larger Honokohau Harbor north of Kailua, several still pull in each afternoon at Kailua Pier to hoist their catch on the scales. The Kona Coast is the world's number one fishing spot for Pacific blue marlin and some catches top 1000 pounds.

Cattle Drive at Kailua Pier

Kailua Bay was once a major cattle shipping area. Cattle driven down from hill ranches were stampeded into the water and forced to swim out to waiting steamers where they were hoisted aboard by sling and shipped to Honolulu. Kailua Pier was built in 1915 and until the 1960s cattle pens were still in place.

Pa O Umi Point

In the 16th century the great King Umi moved his royal court from Waipio to Kona. He is thought to have landed at a lava outcropping on the north-east side of Kailua Bay. This rocky point is called Pa O Umi, 'Umi's enclosure'.

A sea wall has been built over it but you can see just the tip of the lava point by looking over the wall in the area directly across the street from the Ocean View Inn.

The tiny sandy beach between Pa O Umi and Kailua Pier is Kaiakeakua, 'sea of the gods'. It was once Kamehameha's canoe landing.

Hulihee Palace

Hulihee Palace, a modest two storey house, was built in 1838 by Governor 'John Adams' Kuakini as his private residence.

Kuakini was also the Mokuaikaua Church contractor and both buildings were of the same lava construction. The palace got its current look in 1885 when it was plastered over inside and out by King Kalakaua who had taken to a more polished style after his travels abroad.

The palace belonged to a succession of royal owners until the early 1900s when it was abandoned and fell into disrepair. The Daughters of Hawaii, a group founded in 1903 by daughters of missionaries, took it over and now operate the property as a museum.

Hawaiian royalty were huge people and everything inside the palace takes on those proportions, including a bed which is seven feet long.

Princess Ruth Keelikolani, who owned the palace in the mid-1800s, was indeed a lady of some presence, said to have weighed more than 400 pounds. She was an earthy woman,

preferring to live in a big grass hut on the palace grounds rather than being confined within the palace.

After her death the wooden posts from her grass house were carved with designs of taro, leis and pineapples and used as posts in one of the beds upstairs.

The palace is furnished with antiques, many picked up on royal jaunts to Europe. Of the more Hawaiian pieces, there's an armoire made in China of Hawaiian sandalwood and inlaid with ivory. One table is inlaid with 25 kinds of native Hawaiian woods, some of which are now extinct. Kamehameha the Great's personal war spears are also on display.

The palace is open from 9 am to 4 pm daily. Admission costs $4 and includes a 30-minute tour. Although it's interesting enough, there's a bit of a haughty air about the place.

There's no charge to visit the gift shop or walk around the grounds. The stocked fishpond behind the palace once served as a queen's bath and before that was a canoe landing.

Sea Wall Walkway

A walkway along the sea wall begins behind the Hulihee Palace and continues south to the Kona Inn Shopping Center.

The wall is a nice place to sit and watch the surf break, people fishing and boats pulling in and out of the harbour. It's typical Kona lava coastline with lots of sea urchins and scurrying black crabs camouflaged among the black rocks. This is a quieter side of Kailua-Kona and it's possible to be totally unaware of all the traffic, shops and tourist attractions behind you.

Mokuaikaua Church

On 4 April 1820 Hawaii's first Christian missionaries landed at Kailua Bay, stepping out on a rock that is now said to be one of the footings for the pier. They had no way of knowing that the old religion had been abolished on this spot just six months before. They established Hawaii's first Christian church a few minutes walk from

Kamehameha's ancient heiau at Kamakahonu.

The Mokuaikaua Church was built in 1836 and is a handsome building with walls of lava rock held together with a mortar of sand and coral lime.

The posts and beams are of ohia wood, a strong termite-resistant wood which was hewn with stone adzes and smoothed down with chunks of coral. The pews and the pulpit are made of koa. At 112 feet, the church steeple remains the highest structure in Kailua.

There's usually an interpreter around to talk about the church's history from 9 am to noon and from 1 to 4 pm Monday to Saturday. A model of the brig *Thaddeus*, which brought those first Congregational missionaries, is on display.

St Michael's Church

The pink church opposite Waterfront Row is St Michael's. In the cemetery next to the church, a tiny grass hut marks the spot of an earlier thatched chapel, the first Catholic church on the Big Island.

Kealaokamalamalama Church

The green and white Kealaokamalamalama, 'path of the light', Church, is south and mauka of St Michael's Church. It is an independent Hawaiian Congregational church. A look inside is a pleasant surprise to those who might be expecting it to be dark and gothic as you'll find tropical flowers and a big rainbow painted on the wall.

Hale Halawai Park

Hale Halawai is a quiet beachfront park with a few benches under shade trees. The coast is rocky and the sand full of coral chunks. It's not a sunbathing spot, but it's a fine place to read the morning paper.

A prison and courthouse once stood there. Now there's a pavilion used by community

Ahuena Heiau

groups for flea markets and pancake breakfasts. This is your best bet for public parking on the south side of downtown.

Kamakahonu Beach

Kamakahonu which means 'eye of the turtle' is a beach at the north end of Kailua Bay. It was the site of an ancient heiau and the home of Kamehameha the Great.

Shortly after his death here in 1819, Kamehameha's successors came to Kamakahonu and ended the traditional kapu system, sounding a death knell for the old religion.

The ancient sites are now part of the grounds of the Hotel King Kamehameha, where a few thatched structures along with carved wooden kii gods have been reconstructed. Ahuena Heiau, once a place of human sacrifice, juts out into the cove and offers protection to swimmers. The waters here are the calmest in Kailua Bay.

The hotel has a beach hut that rents snorkels, sailboats, kayaks, floats with windows and giant aqua-cycles. It's the only downtown swimming spot and it's popular with kids.

Old Kona Airport Beach Park

The old Kona Airport, which was superseded by the current Keahole Airport in 1970, has been turned into a state recreation area and beach park. It's about a mile north of downtown Kailua, at the end of Kuakini Hwy.

The runway skirts a long sandy beach, but lava rocks run the length of the beach between the sand and the ocean. This makes for poor swimming conditions, but good tidepooling and fishing.

Some of the rocks have intriguing little aquarium-like pockets holding tiny sea urchins, crabs and bits of coral.

There are a couple of breaks in the lava that allow entry into the water. There's one in front of the first picnic area.

A little cove which can be reached by a short walk from the north end of the beach is a good area for confident snorkellers and scuba divers. The reef fish are large and plentiful and in deeper waters there's good coral and a steep coral wall harbouring big

moray eels and a wide variety of other sea creatures such as lionfish and cowries.

When the surf's up there's an offshore break that's popular with local surfers. In high surf it's too rough for other water activities.

This local park is popular with families, picnickers, people drying reef fish and the like, however, the park is much too big to ever feel crowded. There are restrooms, showers and covered picnic tables there.

The Kailua end contains soccer and softball fields, four outdoor lighted tennis courts and horseshoe pits.

Directly behind the tennis courts there's a break in the wall marked 'Shoreline Public Access'. This leads to an exclusive subdivision but the beach is public. Walk along the beach a few minutes toward Kailua-Kona and you'll come to a sandy area with a big wading pool a few feet deep. It's a great place for kids.

The old runway makes a perfect drag strip and the park has had a rowdy night time reputation. These days the gates close at 8 pm and a police substation has been set up there.

Saltwater Pool

One of Kona's best-kept secrets is a saltwater swimming pool in a little lava outcropping so close to the ocean that waves lap in over the side. It is as large as most condo pools and it's open to the public.

The pool was once part of a retired admiral's private estate. By the time it was sold to developers (Kona by the Sea condos are here now) all coastline had become public domain.

Kona by the Sea has put in four public beach access spaces in its parking lot. There's a narrow path on the northern side which leads down to the pool.

The admiral had good taste. You float above the ocean and can glance over the edge and watch surfers riding into shore. Watch it when you're getting into the pool as the steps are slippery.

Magic Sands Beach Park

It's called Magic Sands, White Sands and

Disappearing Sands, but it's all the same beach, midway between Kailua and Keauhou. The sand can disappear in the winter literally overnight, leaving only rocks on the shore. And then just as magically it returns and again becomes a fine white sand beach.

This is a very popular bodysurfing beach when the rocks aren't exposed. There's also a volleyball court and usually plenty of action. One area of the beach has restrooms and picnic tables.

Places to Stay

In Kona, condos outnumber hotels many times over. Most are fairly new, have complete kitchens and are fully furnished with everything from linens to cooking utensils. The general rule is that the weekly rate is six times the daily rate and the monthly rate is three times the weekly.

Condos tend to be cheaper than hotels if you're staying awhile. Generally, except for those condos run like hotels, you'd have to pay a security deposit, often around $150, which is not refunded until a week or two after you move out. For advance reservations there are usually deposits and cancellation penalties to deal with.

Most condos have a three-day minimum though some, including those handled by Triad Management, have a seven-day high season minimum.

If you take your chances and wait until you arrive in Kona to look for a place, you can sometimes find the best condo deals in the classified ads of *West Hawaii Today*. During the high season, however, it's risky as most places are booked up months in advance.

All Kona hotels and condos listed here have swimming pools unless otherwise noted.

Places to Stay – middle

Kona Seaside Hotel (75-5646 Palani Rd, Kailua-Kona, HI 96740; tel 329-2455) has two sections. One's a modern six-storey building with comfortable $58 rooms with the standard amenities. The older refurbished Hukilau wing has rooms for $52, though you can get a cheaper local rate if you call within

Hawaii. Their special of $39 for one night and $68 for two nights seems to be perpetually advertised in the Sunday Honolulu paper. Packages including a car cost about $15 more a night.

For those who want to be right in the centre of town, there's Uncle Billy's *Kona Bay Hotel* (75-5739 Alii Drive, Kailua-Kona, HI 96740; tel 329-1393; 800-367-5102). The older cinder block buildings lack charm but at $49 it's one of the cheaper hotels.

Kona Tiki Hotel (Box 1567, Kailua-Kona, HI 96745; tel 329-1425), on Alii Drive at the one-mile marker, is an older three-storey complex, which has 15 rooms all with refrigerators and breezy beachfront lanais. It's unpretentious, with a friendly management and some nice touches including complimentary breakfasts of Kona coffee, rolls and fruit. Though it's right on the road the surf drowns out the traffic. Rates are $35 for standard rooms, $40 with kitchenettes and for a third person it is $5 more.

For cheaper local accommodation in nearby towns, see South Kona – Places to Stay.

Places to Stay – top end

The 460-room *Hotel King Kamehameha* (75-5660 Palani Rd, Kailua-Kona, HI 96740; tel 329-2911; 800-367-5170) is on Kailua Bay and the only beach in town. The sprawling koa wood lobby is full of Hawaiiana displays and this is the site of King Kamehameha's former residence. Rates range from $85 to $145.

Kona Hilton (Box 1179, Kailua-Kona, HI 96740; tel 329-3111; 800-445-8667) has a beachfront location on the edge of town. There's no actual beach but there is a shallow saltwater pool built out of a tidepool that's deep enough to swim and snorkel. There are 452 rooms, with rates from $95.

Places to Stay – condos

The *Kona Islander Inn* (75-5776 Kuakini Hwy, Kailua- Kona, HI 96740; tel 329-3181; 800-922-7866) is an older development in the town centre. Some of the units are musty,

- Kona Islander Inn
- Kona Alii
- Kona Billfisher

Kona Hilton •
Hale Kona Kai •
Kona Reef •

Walua Road

- Malia Kai Apts
- Kona Pacific
- Kona Mansions

Kona Tiki Hotel •

Sea Village •
Alii Villas •
Royal Sea Cliff Resort •

Kona Shores
Kona Makai

Casa de Emdeko •
Kona by the Sea •

Kona Isle

Kona Riviera Villa

Ala Kala Condo •
Hal Kai O Kona •

Hale Pohaku
Kona Nalu

Kona Bali Kai •
Banyan Tree •

- Holualoa Bay Villas

- Banyan Surf Apts
- Royal Kahili

- Kona Palms

Kona Magic Sands •
White Sands Village •

Kona White Sands
• Apartment Hotel

Alii

MAGIC SANDS BEACH

St Peter's Church •

Drive

KAHALUU BAY

Keauhou Beach Hotel

Kona Lagoon •
Keauhou-Kona Surf
& Racquet Club •

Keauhou
Shopping
Village

King Kamehameha III Road

Kona Coast Resort •

Keauhou Palena •
Kanaloa at Kona •

KEAUHOU BAY

• Country Club Villas
Keauhou Resort Condo
Kona Country Club

Kona Surf Resort •

Keauhou Akahi

Keauhou Punahele •

Kailua–Keauhou Condos

particularly those on the bottom floor. Aston handles 67 of the 150 units and maintains a front desk, running them like a hotel. They charge $80 for rooms with refrigerators, plus $10 more if you want a kitchenette.

The handful of units rented by Hawaii Resort Management (next door on Alii Drive) are a better deal. They charge $40/55 for low/high season, with a three-day minimum, and their units include hot plates and microwaves. Parking can be a problem there in the high season.

Kona Billfisher is mauka of the Hilton. The units are large and quite well furnished with kitchens, lanais, sofa beds and both ceiling fans and air-con. One-bedroom units cost $50/65 for the low/high season, two-bedroom units are $70/85, through Hawaii Resort Management. There's a three-day minimum. It's good value for this price range.

Malia Kai Apartments, inland from the Hilton on Walua Rd, has 21 units, each with three levels. The bottom level has a carport and washer/dryer. The second floor has a lanai, living room with sofa bed and kitchen. The third floor has one main bedroom with sliding shoji doors separating it from another room with a sofa bed.

The complex has a nice garden courtyard with a small pool. The units aren't all that spiffy but if you're with a few people it could be economical. Rates are $70/420 a day/week in the high season, $55/330 in the low season, through Triad Management.

Hale Kona Kai (75-5870 Kahakai Rd, Kailua-Kona, HI 96740; tel 329-2155) is a real find, right on the ocean in a quiet corner just beyond the Hilton. The 39 one-bedroom units aren't brand new, but they're comfortable with all the standards like cable TV and sofa beds. All have lanais with great ocean views and the sound of the surf. Rates are $65. It's $10 more for a corner unit with wrap-around lanai and $5 more for the third and fourth person. There's a three-day minimum, no Sunday or holiday check-in and a 20% discount for monthly stays.

Kona Reef (75-5888 Alii Drive, Kailua-Kona, HI 96740; tel 329-4780), south of the Hilton, is a condo complex run like a hotel by Hawaiiana Resorts. It's modern, with all amenities including washer/dryers. Rates are $80 to $100 for up to four people in a one-bedroom unit. In low season it's $10 less and the seventh night is free.

Kona Pacific up on Walua Rd is a big place with big units. It's comfortable and has everything you need, but it's a bit impersonal with underground parking, elevators and the like. Rates for one-bedroom units with two bathrooms, a lanai and a sofa bed are $65/390 per day/week through Kona Vacation Resorts.

Kona Mansions is a quiet place on Walua Rd which has about 90 units. There's a minimum stay of five days. Its good value one-bedroom units may be as low as $40 a day, or $840 a month through Triad Management.

Sea Village (75-6002 Alii Drive, Kailua-Kona, HI 96740; tel 329-1000) is a notch up from next-door Kona Shores, but it's run like a hotel. One-bedroom units are $60/81 in the low/high season and two-bedroom units are about $20 more. The minimum stay is three nights. They have tennis courts.

Kona Shores (75-6008 Alii Drive, Kailua-Kona, HI 96740; tel 329-3663) is largely local housing with a fairly young crowd. There are only a handful of vacation rentals, and the walls between the units are far from soundproof, but it's a relatively cheap place to try for longer stays. Studio units are $250/750 for a week/month. During the off-season you might be able to work out a better deal, although they try to lease long-term from March to November.

Alii Villas (75-6016 Alii Drive, Kailua-Kona, HI 96740; tel 329-1288) has 126 units. It's a comfortable and quiet place with good ocean breezes. The units are large and they each have a private lanai, cable TV and washer/dryer. Most have a phone and sofabed. One-bedroom units are about $275 to $425 a week, depending on the season.

Kona Makai, on the ocean side of Alii Drive next to Alii Villas, has one-bedroom units with everything including washer/dryer from $80 through Kona Vacation Resorts. There's an exercise room and tennis courts.

Casa de Emdeko (75-6082 Alii Drive, Kailua-Kona, HI 96740; tel 329-2160) is a newer complex. The one-bedroom units are pleasant and have all the standard amenities though there's little beachfront and the lanais line up facing other lanais. There are fresh and saltwater pools. Rates for one-bedroom units are $50/65 in low/high season through Hawaii Resort Management and from $75 through Kona Vacation Resorts.

Royal Sea-Cliff Resort (75-6040 Alii Drive, Kailua-Kona, HI 96740; tel 329-8021; 800-922-7866) is modern and architecturally striking, with angular lines. The units are some of the nicest in Kona, with large balconies, stylish furnishings and very full kitchens. There are tennis courts, pools and a sauna. Aston runs it like a hotel, with a front desk and there's no minimum stay. Studios are $115/95 in high/low season. The units are ritzier than Aston's more expensive Kona by the Sea complex.

The *Kona White Sands Apartment Hotel* is a two-storey building with 10 units, all with kitchenettes and lanais. Studios cost $45, one-bedroom units cost $50 if booked through Hawaii Resort Management. It's opposite the White Sands Beach. There's no pool.

Vacation Rental Agencies Many condo complexes each have a few rental agencies handling different units. For condos with an address listed here you can write directly to the condo. Either they handle their own bookings or they'll pass correspondence on to the agent that does.

For the rest, units are handled by at least one of the three following agencies. They'll send their latest listings and rates upon request. It's worth comparing lists.

Hawaii Resort Management (tel 329-9393; 800-553-5035), 75-5782 Kuakini Hwy, Suite C-1, Kailua-Kona, HI 96740

Kona Vacation Resorts (tel 329-6488; 800-367-5168), 77- 6435 Kuakini Hwy, Kailua-Kona, HI 96740

Triad Management (tel 329-6402), North Kona Shopping Center, 75-5629-P Kuakini Hwy, Kailua-Kona, HI 96740

Places to Eat

Kona has lots of restaurants including fast food, good ethnic food and fine beachfront spots. It also has quite a number of mediocre tourist traps.

Our favourite places, both for taste treats and value, are Cafe Sibu, Poki's Pasta, Royal Jade Garden, Poo Ping II and the French Bakery.

Places to Eat – bottom end

For a good cheap meal on the run try the *French Bakery* at Kaahumanu Plaza in the industrial area. This is Kona's best bakery, with good French bread, tempting strudels and hearty three-seed muffins. The cheese bread which costs $1.50 is the equivalent of a mozzarella cheese sub and is big enough for two. They also have croissant sandwiches for $2.25 and quiche slices, microwaved on request. It's open from 6 am to 5 pm Monday to Saturday.

Lanai Siamese Kitchen (tel 326-1222), near Pawai Center in the industrial park, has just six tables on a small porch surrounded by hanging plants. The food is good and authentically Thai, though everything is á la carte and portions are rather small. Vegie yum, a noodle dish with tofu and macadamia nuts, is good value at $5.25. Sates, curries and seafood dishes are mostly in the $6 to $12 range. Dinner is served from 5 to 9 pm daily except Sundays.

Poo Ping II in Kamehameha Square has a good $5.50 buffet lunch with eight Thai main dishes plus jasmine, brown and fried rice. There's usually chicken curry, one other curry, a noodle dish and a vegetable tempura with sweet and sour sauce.

Other buffet courses change daily, but include dishes like Pad Khing Moo Kai, which is fried pork or chicken with thick

slices of fresh ginger, oyster mushrooms and onions ($5.75 on the menu). Poo Ping is run by the Kanchanawat family who grow their own mint leaves, lemongrass, chillies and dozens of different varieties of other herbs up in Captain Cook. A few samples are planted around the courtyard. Both the buffet and menu have vegetarian selections. The buffet is available from 11 am to 3 pm, with menu service until 9 pm, daily except Sundays. The restaurant turns into a disco from 10 pm to 2 am nightly.

For a healthy fast-food alternative, *Kona Healthways* in the Kona Coast Shopping Center has fresh green salads made with organically grown island produce for $2.50. It also has a few prepared sandwiches, snacks, juices and yoghurt. Some of the locally made items include spirulina flakes, dried shittake mushrooms, Rooster Farms' organic coffee, guava leather and macadamia nuts. It's open daily.

Paniolo Country Cafe, in the Kona Coast Shopping Center, is a family restaurant, with everything from pizza to barbecued ribs. The food's ordinary, but Wednesday taco nights are a good value, featuring 99-cent tacos and $1.50 magaritas.

The *Sizzler* in the Kona Coast Shopping Center has the best salad bar in town, with a good selection of vegies and fresh fruit plus a tortilla bar for $5.49. This is also a family-style steak and seafood restaurant. The air-con provides an Arctic blast – bring a sweater.

The *Royal Jade Garden* in the Lanihau Center has excellent Chinese food at bargain prices. Prepared food is served cafeteria-style and you can eat there or takeaway. You can have a hearty meal for $3 to $4, selecting combos from beef and broccoli, sweet and sour pork, egg foo yung and the like.

The Royal Jade does such a volume, particularly at lunch and dinner hours, that the food in the buffet trays is constantly replenished and is always very fresh. For a few dollars more you can order from the menu. It's open from 10.30 am to 10.30 pm daily.

Rocky's Pizza, at Lanihau Center, is Kona's most popular pizza restaurant. In

Top: Halemaumau Crater, Hawaii Volcanoes National Park, Big Island
Left: Akaka Falls, Big Island
Right: Puuhonua O Honaunau National Historical Park, Big Island

Top: Mauna Kea with snow, Big Island
Bottom: Waipio Valley, Big Island

addition to whole pizzas, they sell slices for $1.25 to $1.75.

Quinn's, on Palani Rd opposite the Hotel King Kamehameha, serves dinner until 1 am. The crowd is mostly long-time residents who come for both the bar and the consistently good fish and steak dinners. For the setting, prices aren't cheap, but fish portions are huge.

The unassuming *Ocean View Inn* on Alii Drive has been a central Kona landmark for generations. This is where local folks come to eat local food. Complete breakfasts with coffee cost $2.50 to $4.25. Sandwiches cost around $1 to $2. You can get good inexpensive Chinese, American and Hawaiian foods and it's a good place to try lomi salmon marinated with tomatoes and green onion for $1.50 or a side of poi. There's a view of Kailua Bay through the louvred windows.

Subway, at Kona Center, is a fast-food submarine sandwich shop. It's cheapest to buy a foot-long sub, which costs from $3 to $7 and split it, but they also come in the six-inch size.

Waterfront Row has *Flying Fruit Fantasy* which is a fruit shake and yoghurt bar, and *Coffee Pub of Kona* which has quiche, cheesecake, tortes and espresso.

Kona's other fast food outlets include *McDonald's*, *Pizza Hut*, *Taco Bell*, *Kentucky Fried Chicken* and *Orange Julius*, all close to the Palani Rd and Kuakini Hwy intersection.

Poo Ping I is in the Kona Inn Shopping Village. It's open from 5 to 9.30 pm nightly, with menu service only.

Cafe Sibu at Banyan Court serves delicious Indonesian food in a casual cafe setting. The combination plates for $7.75 to $8.50 offer three dishes (with choices like ginger beef, spicy Indian curry and chicken sate) over brown rice. The huge gado gado, served over rice and covered with peanut sauce costs $6.50. The shrimp sate marinated in spicy coconut milk is good. They also have a daily Italian dish, vegetarian dishes and good karma. It's open from 11.30 am to 9 pm daily.

Poki's Pasta (tel 329-7888) is a hole-in-the-wall Italian bistro in the Kailua Bay Inn Shopping Plaza. Owner Poki Goold makes her own fresh pasta and gourmet sauces. Most of the dishes cost $7 to $10 and include things like lasagne, eggplant parmigiana and chicken cannelloni. It also has seafood and clam dishes. Try the toasted French bread with jumbo cloves of baked elephant garlic – it spreads like butter and is surprisingly mild. You can bring in a bottle of wine (the nearest liquor store is next to Ocean View Inn) and they'll put it on ice, bring chilled glasses and not even charge a corkage fee. Poki's is open from 4 to 9 pm daily.

Suzanne's Bakeshop, on Likana Lane below the public parking lot, sells pastries, desserts and coffee from 4.45 am to 9.30 pm daily. Sometimes in the evenings they clear out doughnuts and apple fritters at three for $1, instead of the regular 80 cents each. There are a few cafe tables set out on the sidewalk.

Kona Ranchhouse (tel 329-7061), off Kuakini Hwy, south of Palani Rd serves good breakfasts between 6.30 am and noon, from about $3. At lunch time, a half sandwich with soup and salad costs $3.95. The triple-decker Kona clubhouse makes a decent light lunch. Dinner costs $8 to $20, with an emphasis on barbecued meats. Weekend evenings are busy. If you make reservations, you get the classier front room. For a glimpse of paniolo Hawaii check out the photos of island ranches hanging from the dining room walls.

Kona Chuckwagon, in front of Casa de Emdeko on Alii Drive, is the bargain of buffets. The all-you-can-eat breakfast (7 to 10 am) costs $4.50, lunch (11 am to 5 pm) $5.50 and dinner (5 to 9 pm) costs $7.95. It has the ambience of a diner, though the food is a notch or two better than at most diners. Lunch and dinner always have a fresh salad bar, fruit, soup, chilli, beverages and a few main meat dishes such as fried chicken and ribs. At dinner they throw in a ham and roast beef.

Old Kailua Cantina is a second floor open-air Mexican restaurant opposite the

Kailua Pier. Between 4 and 6 pm they have early bird specials on food and drink and if you get a window seat you can watch fishermen bring their boats into harbour and hoist up their catch of marlin and tuna. Prices are moderate. The food's OK, though a bit bland.

Jolly Roger at the southern end of Kailua near Waterfront Row, serves ordinary and slightly overpriced American fare, but you can't get any closer to the water than their beachfront tables. They're open for breakfast, lunch and dinner.

Huggo's is on the beachfront beside the Hilton. The most popular meal is the $6.95 lunch time ribs special every Tuesday and Thursday from 11.30 am when there can be a line of people waiting for tables. Dinner is largely seafood and steak with prices ranging from $12 to $20.

Attila's Bar & Grill (tel 326-BEER), at Honokohau Harbor, boasts Kona's longest bar and largest wall-mounted Pacific blue marlin. Open-air tables overlook the harbour and fishermen and yachties hang out there, downing large schooners of draft beer ($1.75). The food's not as interesting as the setting, but it's adequate. Sandwiches cost about $4 and a plate of fish & chips costs $7. It's open from 10.30 am to 8.30 pm daily except Sundays.

Places to Eat – top end

The *Chart House*, upstairs at Waterfront Row, has a good salad bar, with fruit, pastas and fresh-baked breads. It's $9.95 alone, with main dishes ranging from $12.65 for teriyaki steak kabobs to about $28 for lobster and steak. It's fine dining with good ocean views and food that's better than most places in the area, including the overrated and disappointing Fisherman's Landing.

The *Beach Club* (75-6106 Alii Drive, Kailua-Kona; tel 329-0290) is at the Kona by the Sea condo complex. They have beachside dining under the stars, which is inexplicably rare in Hawaii. Chef Mark Tuhy is creative and changes the menu at whim. His specialities are seafood and pasta dishes with Thai, Cajun and Mexican influences. Main courses range from $12 to $20. For an appetiser, the Aztec shrimp with papaya relish is a treat at $6.75.

The Beach Club is low profile and tucked out of the way, but it gets a lot of rave reviews. The food takes precedence over service and even with reservations you can have a long wait. They have an indoor dining area as well, so when you make reservations be sure to ask for outdoor seating.

Jameson's by the Sea (tel 329-3195) on Magic Sands Beach is a spin-off of the popular Oahu north shore restaurant. Fresh seafood is a speciality, with dinners from $13.95 up. They have a good reputation. It's open for lunch from Monday to Friday and dinner from Monday to Saturday.

Kona Inn, in the centre of town, opened in 1929 and was the Big Island's first hotel. It's now a shopping centre with a large and popular restaurant of the same name. Steak and seafood dinners are in the $12 to $18 range. Their light meals are available from 11.30 am to midnight and include croissant sandwiches for $5 and steak sandwiches for $10. Kona Inn and Quinn's are two of the few late night places to eat in town.

Pottery Steakhouse is at the end of Walua Rd up on Kuakini Hwy. The steak, which costs $12 to $17, is good but in this price range you'd hope for a view or some Hawaiiana and it's got neither.

Buffets

The best of Kona's buffets is the Sunday champagne brunch at the *Kona Hilton* (tel 329-3111). If you can swallow the $17.95 price tag, you can feast for hours on jumbo shrimp, crab claws, tempura, sushi, a few dozen main dishes and all sorts of salads, cheeses and fruits. To finish off the decadence, there's an array of desserts that includes a Haagen-Dazs sundae bar. It's open from 9 am to 1 pm.

The Hilton's international buffet on Sunday nights, which costs about $15, also looks good, with treats ranging from oysters on the half shell to chocolate-dipped strawberries.

The *Keauhou Beach Hotel* (tel 322-3441) in Keauhou has a fine-looking seafood buffet from 5 to 9 pm Friday to Sunday for about $17. Fried oysters, steamed clams, sashimi, crab legs, marlin and prime rib are featured. They also have a Chinese buffet Monday to Thursday for about $10 and a Sunday champagne brunch buffet for $16.

Moby Dick at the Hotel King Kamehameha puts on a Sunday champagne brunch for $17. It's a quite respectable buffet, yet it's not on par with the one at the Hilton or Keauhou Beach. Also, it's indoors with air-con whereas the other two have nice open-air dining next to the ocean.

Entertainment

Kona has no shortage of sunset views or happy hour come-ons at restaurants and bars all along Alii Drive.

The *Eclipse* restaurant on Kuakini Hwy has dancing nightly. It tends to have a younger crowd.

Poo Ping II at Kamehameha Square is the newest disco; it's open from 10 pm to 2 am nightly.

Luaus The *Kona Hilton* has luaus and Polynesian shows.

Hotel King Kamehameha has a luau on Tuesdays, Thursdays and Sundays on its beach in front of Ahuena Heiau for $36.

Movies The *Hualalai Theatre* on Kuakini Hwy has the standard Holywood films. The *World Square Theatre* in the Kona Marketplace has a mix of Hollywood movies and a few alternative films.

KEAUHOU

Keauhou is the coastal area immediately south of Kailua-Kona. It starts at Kahaluu Bay and runs down beyond Keauhou Bay and the Kona Surf Resort.

Keauhou contains a planned community of three hotels, nine condo complexes, a shopping centre and a 27-hole golf course. It's neatly spaced out with a country club atmosphere. Bishop Estate, Hawaii's largest private landholder, owns the land.

There was once a major Hawaiian settlement there, supported by an abundance of fresh spring water. Several historical sites can still be explored, although they now share their grounds with the hotels and condos.

Information

Tourist Information Keauhou Visitors Association (78-6831 Alii Drive, Suite 234, Kailua-Kona, HI 96740; tel 322-3866), upstairs in the Keauhou Shopping Village, has information on Keauhou, brochures and helpful staff. It's open from 8 am to 4.30 pm Monday to Friday.

Keauhou has a free on-call shuttle service (tel 322-3500) which runs around the resort between 8 am and 4 pm.

Hula Children from Ulalia School of Hawaiian Dance practice traditional hula dances at 8 am on Saturdays in the outdoor plaza at Keauhou Shopping Village.

Shopping Keauhou Shopping Village, the shopping centre at the corner of Alii Drive and King Kamehameha III Rd, has a large KTA supermarket, newspaper stands, a contract post office and 37 shops and restaurants. Keauhou Village Book Shop has a good collection of travel guides and books on Hawaii. Alapaki's has museum-quality Hawaiian crafts and Showcase Gallery has contemporary fine arts and crafts; both are worth seeing, though neither is inexpensive.

Liberty House has a clearance store at Keauhou Beach Hotel. They have good-quality clothing at discounted prices and you can sometimes find a good selection of aloha shirts.

Produce Sellers On Friday and Saturday mornings local produce and flowers are sold along the roadside opposite the Keauhou Beach Hotel.

Papayas, mangoes, starfruit and anything else that's in season are fresher and cheaper there than you'll find in the grocery stores.

St Peter's Church

The little blue church on the north side of

Kahaluu Bay is St Peter's Catholic Church. This church dates back to 1880 and it was moved from White Sands Beach to this site in 1912. Tidal waves have since attempted to relocate it on a couple of occasions.

This is Hawaii's most photographed 'quaint church' which is still used for Sunday services and weddings.

Beside the church is what remains of the foundation of Kuemanu Heiau, a surfing temple. Hawaiian royalty surfed the waters at the north end of Kahaluu Bay and paid their respects at this temple before hitting the waves.

There's also a square spring-fed pond where the alii used to bath after surfing and in later years local families washed clothes.

Locals keep up the surfing tradition, though high surf usually generates dangerous northward rip currents.

Kahaluu Beach

Kahaluu, 'the diving place', is the island's best drive-up snorkelling spot. The bay is like a big natural aquarium and it's a good place to learn to snorkel. It's not even necessary to go out over your head to enjoy it.

Large rainbow parrotfish, schools of silver needlefish, brilliant yellow tangs and colourful wrasses are among the numerous tropicals easily seen here. Spotted moray eels are not that hard to find either.

The fish are tame enough to come and eat out of your hand. If you hold out some bread or peas the frenzied swarms can give quite a rush!

There are lots of fish in the shallows but generally the deeper the water the better the coral and the larger the fish.

An ancient breakwater, said to have been menehune-built, is on the reef and protects the bay. Still, when the surf is high Kahaluu can have strong currents that pull in the direction of the rocks near St Peter's Church and it's easy to drift away without realising it. Check your bearings occasionally to make sure you're not being pulled by the current.

A plaque by the picnic pavilion explains water conditions and gives a little info on marine life in the bay. Check it out before you go in.

A lifeguard is on duty daily except Wednesdays and Thursdays. There's usually a snack van here. Another van rents snorkel sets at $3 for the first hour and $1 an hour after that as well as 35mm underwater cameras for $12.50 an hour.

The park has a sandy beach, showers, restrooms, changing rooms and a basketball hoop. It's a popular place and often draws a crowd.

Keauhou Beach Hotel

The grounds of Keauhou Beach Hotel, immediately south of Kahaluu Beach, contain some easily explored historical sites. The hotel brochure has a map of the sites and a one-page historical hand-out is available at the front desk.

The remains of Kapuanoni, a fishing temple which contains an old koa canoe, is on the north side of the hotel.

The reconstructed summer beach house of King Kalakaua is inland, beside a spring-fed pond once used as a royal bath. You can peek into the simple two-room cottage and see a portrait of the king in his European-style royal dress, a Hawaiian quilt on the bed and lauhala mats on the floor.

Other heiau sites are on the south side of the hotel. The remains of Keeku Heiau, just beyond the footbridge which leads to Kona Lagoon Hotel, is thought to have been a luakini heiau.

There are some great tidepools there, in a low shelf of smooth *pahoehoe* lava, which are best explored when the tide is low. The pools contain numerous sea urchins, including spiny and slate pencil types, and small tropical fish. Petroglyphs are supposedly visible in this area at low tide but we had no luck spotting them.

The Keauhou Beach Hotel grounds also have a fertility pit, carved wooden god images, historic *kuula* stones sacred to fishermen and a house site or two.

Kona Lagoon Hotel is being converted from 454 rooms into 250 suites. Both Keauhou Beach Hotel and Kona Lagoon

Hotel are owned by Azabu USA, which has a master plan calling for the development of a swimming lagoon and white sand beach.

Keauhou Bay

Keauhou Bay, which has a launch ramp and space for two dozen small boats, is one of the most protected bays on the west coast.

Snorkelling is pretty good in the bay, but you have to watch out for the boat traffic. There are restrooms and showers there.

A stone marking the site where Kamehameha III was born in 1814 is in a small garden just south of the dive shacks. The young prince was said to have been stillborn and brought back to life on this rock by a visiting kahuna.

There are two ways to get to the bay: you either turn makai off Alii Drive onto King Kamehameha III Rd; or drive down Kaleopapa Rd toward Kona Surf Resort but instead of turning into the resort continue to the end of the road.

Manta Rays

If you're looking for something to do in the evening, you could go down to Kona Surf Resort and watch the manta rays which sometimes gather in the late evening at the rocky outcropping below the resort's saltwater pool. They're attracted by the spotlights which shine down onto the ocean which means they are less likely to make a showing during full moon.

The wingtips of these impressive creatures often measure up to 12 feet across and their white underbellies flash against the dark waters as they cruise around in the surf. They're hypnotic to watch.

Places to Stay

The 318-room *Keauhou Beach Hotel* (78-6740 Alii Drive, Kailua-Kona, HI 96740; tel 322-3441; 800-367-6025) adjoins Kahaluu Beach Park. The grounds have interesting historical sites and tidepools to explore. Rates range from $70 to $110.

Kona Surf Resort (78-128 Ehukai St, Kailua-Kona, HI 96740; tel 322-3411; 800-367-8011) is a modern, sprawling,

553-room, Japanese-oriented hotel. It has some interesting Polynesian carvings and decor, a little wedding chapel, tennis courts and both salt and freshwater pools. It's rather isolated on a rugged and rocky lava point on the south side of Keauhou Bay. Rates range from $95 to $145. There's a daytime shuttle service between there and town.

Keauhou Resort Condominiums (78-7039 Kamehameha III Rd, Kailua-Kona, HI 96740; tel 322-9122; 800-367-5286) has 48 units with dishwashers and washer/dryers. Though the units are about 20 years old they are well maintained and are the cheapest in Keauhou. One-bedroom units are $60/67 in the low/high season with a garden view, $70/75 with an ocean view. The minimum stay is five days. It's near the golf course and there's a pool.

At the other end of the spectrum is *Kanaloa at Kona* (78-261 Manukai St, Kailua-Kona, HI 96740; tel 322-2272; 800-367-6046), operated by Colony Hotels & Resorts. It has 114 condo units ranging from $125/145 in the low/high season for up to four people in a one-bedroom apartment with a golf course view to $205/240 low/high season for up to eight people in a three-bedroom unit which fronts the ocean. The units have lanais with wet bars and kitchens with microwave ovens. The oceanfront suites have jacuzzis. There are three pools and two lighted tennis courts.

Other Keauhou condos are priced between the two and are largely booked through vacation rental agents. Kona Vacation Resorts (77-6435 Kuakini Hwy, Kailua-Kona, HI 96740; tel 329-6488; 800-367-5168) handles units in most of them.

Places to Eat

The Terrace Restaurant is outdoors at the Kanaloa at Kona condos. It's got a poolside condo atmosphere but it's on the beach and the food's OK. Lunch is available from 11.30 am to 2.30 pm. The chef's salad is good at $5.95. Sandwiches and other dishes cost from $5 to $7. To get there, turn makai off Alii Drive onto King Kamehameha III Rd and then right onto Manukai St. Ask the gatekeeper where to park.

Mitchell's, the night time disco in the Keauhou Shopping Center, has breakfast from 7 to 11 am daily. The menu is large and prices moderate, with omelette plates which include half a papaya for $5. Lunch is served until 2 pm, with burger plates from $6.

Drysdale's Two in the Keauhou Shopping Center is popular for sandwiches and burgers in the $5 range and is a hot spot for watching ball games on TV. It's open from 11 am to midnight.

Rocky's Pizza at Keauhou Shopping Center sells pizza by the slice or the pie. Keauhou Shopping Center also has Baskins Robbins ice cream and a shave ice stand.

Keauhou Beach Hotel and *Kona Surf Resort* both have a few restaurants. Keauhou Beach Hotel is the better choice and has good buffets.

Entertainment
Some of the larger hotels have Hawaiian music, usually duos or trios strumming in the early evening. The hotels often have dance bands, piano music and jazz groups as well.

Keauhou Beach Hotel's *Makai Bar*, an open-air thatched building right on the shoreline, has good sunset views and live Hawaiian music from 5 pm nightly. It sometimes features a $2 tropical drink. Uncle George Naope & Friends present an authentic hula show several nights a week in the hotel lounge.

The Kona Surf Resort has a free Polynesian show from 5.30 to 6.30 pm Tuesdays and Fridays. It's at the Nalu Terrace lounge and no doubt they appreciate you buying a drink.

Mitchell's in the Keauhou Shopping Center is a restaurant during the day with dancing nightly. It sometimes has live music too.

The *Kona Lagoon Longhouse* at Kona Lagoon Hotel was the biggest concert hall before Hyatt Waikoloa came along. It can hold up to 1000 people uncomfortably and

has attracted the likes of Kenny Loggins and Bonnie Raitt.

For the latest entertainment listings, check *West Hawaii Today*, especially on Fridays.

HOLUALOA
Holualoa is perched in the hills, 1400 feet above Kailua-Kona. The slopes catch afternoon showers so it's lusher and cooler there than on the coast below.

Holualoa is an artist's community with craft shops, galleries and a community art centre. It's a friendly place with lots of aloha.

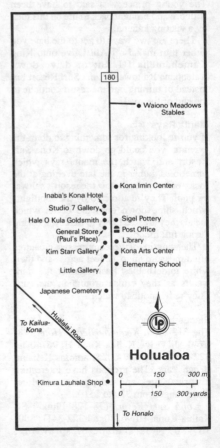

Holualoa

This is pretty much a one-road village, with everything lined up along Hwy 180. There's a general store, a Japanese cemetery, an elementary school, a couple of churches and a stable. The library is open from 1 to 5 pm on Tuesdays and 9 am to 1 pm on Saturdays.

There are two places to stay. Inaba's Kona Hotel retains the small town character (and room rates!) of a bygone era. Holualoa Inn is a lovely modern B&B off the main road.

From Kailua-Kona, it's a scenic four miles up Hualalai Rd to Holualoa. The landscape is bright with flowers, coffee bushes, and fruit trees of all kinds.

Kona's relentless development is creeping up this way. Older homes half-hidden by jungly gardens are being joined by a jumble of new houses and a spate of 'For Sale' signs. It's an enviable location, with a fine view of Kona's sparkling turquoise waters below.

Kimura Lauhala Shop

The Kimura Lauhala Shop (tel 324-0053), at the intersection of Hualalai Rd and Hwy 180, sells items woven from lauhala, the leaf (lau) of the hala tree.

This was once an old plantation store which sold salt and codfish. During the Depression of the 1920s, Mrs Kimura started weaving lauhala hats and coffee baskets and taking them down to the plantations to sell.

Three generations of Kimuras still weave lauhala, the work is supplemented by the wives of local coffee farmers who do piecemeal work at home when it's not coffee season. It's a fading art. The shop also stocks baskets from China and the Philippines.

The hardest part, the Kimuras say, is preparing the lauhala which is messy work, complicated by the sharp spines along the leaf edges. The easy part is the weaving. Once the lauhala is ready to weave, it takes a couple of hours to make a placemat which sells for around $8.

The most common items are placemats and open baskets, as well as hats of a finer weave. The shop is open from 9 am to 5 pm Monday to Saturday.

Kona Arts Center

The Kona Arts Center (Box 272, Holualoa, HI 96725) is in a ramshackle ex-coffee mill, with a tin roof and hot-pink doors.

Bob and Carol Rogers are the directors of this nonprofit organisation. She teaches crafts and he teaches visual arts. They've been there since 1965, nurturing the spirit as much as the art. Beginners are especially encouraged.

This is a community scene and everyone's welcome. It costs $20 a month to use the centre, which includes workshops up to five times a week. Classes include pottery, batik, tie dye, basketry, weaving and painting.

Visitors who drop in to look around are offered postcards and Kona coffee. Both the centre and the gallery are open from 10 am to 4 pm Tuesday to Saturday.

Little Gallery

The Kona Arts Center's Little Gallery, across the road, is in a restored church originally built by Japanese Christians around 1900. The gallery is light and airy, with benches and recorded flute music.

Items for sale include handblown glass, batiks, weavings and baskets of natural fibres like sea grass, coconut palm leaves and banana poka vine. Some, but not all, are made at the arts centre. The gallery show changes each month.

Studio 7 Gallery

Studio 7 Gallery (tel 324-1335) opened in 1980 to showcase the artwork of owner Hiroki Morinoue who works in watercolours, oils, wood block and 3D sculpture. His wife, Setsuko, is a potter and the gallery's director.

Studio 7 now exhibits some 30 top-notch artisans, about half of whom come from the Kona area. Works include ceramics, natural-dyed fabrics, sculpture, basketry, blown glass and pit-fired raku.

The gallery is like a little museum and the zen-like setting blends both Hawaiian and Japanese influences, with wooden walkways over lava stones. It's open from 10 am to 4 pm Tuesday to Saturday.

Kona Imin Center

Holualoa's most famous son, astronaut Ellison Onizuka, died in the 1986 Challenger space shuttle disaster. His portrait hangs in the Kona Imin Center.

This senior centre was a Japanese language school until WW II at which time immigrants were banned from studying Japanese.

Places to Stay

If you want to be on the cool slopes above Kailua-Kona, Holualoa has two unique alternatives.

Holualoa Inn (Desmond & Karen Twigg-Smith, Box 222, Holualoa, HI 96725; tel 324-1121) is a beautiful contemporary B&B atop 40 acres of sloping meadows with great views of the Kona Coast.

The house was built as a getaway by Desmond's uncle, president of the *Honolulu Advertiser*, who at the time of construction owned a sawmill. The exterior is all western red cedar and the interior floors are red eucalyptus from Maui. Although there are only four bedrooms, the house is 5000 square feet. There's a large swimming pool, billiard room, rooftop gazebo and lounge with TV and video. Wine, cheese and their own home-grown Kona coffee are complimentary and they serve a continental breakfast which includes fruit from the garden. There are plans to add bungalows and a restaurant. As it stands now, it's one of Hawaii's best finds. Rates are $75 to $120.

Inaba's Kona Hotel (Hwy 180, Holualoa, HI 96725; tel 324-1155) is in Holualoa's town centre. This old local hostelry has high ceilings and some nice views. Rooms are very basic with just a bed and dresser but the price is right at $12/20 for singles/doubles. Bathrooms are shared and down the hall. Rumour has it that the mattresses in the street-side rooms are the most comfortable as the burly construction workers who sometimes stay there during the work-week favour the ocean side. With only 11 rooms, getting a room here is pretty hit and miss.

South Kona

Hwy 11 heads south out of Kailua-Kona through a number of small communities: Honalo, Kainaliu, Kealakekua, Captain Cook and Honaunau. These are upland towns with coffee farms and macadamia nut groves.

Spur roads off Hwy 11 lead to Kealakekua Bay, Puuhonua O Honaunau National Historical Park (better known as the Place of Refuge) and the old fishing villages of Hookena and Miloli'i. South Kona is short on

1	Daifukuji Mission
2	Teshima's Restaurant/Inn
3	Laundromat
4	Kona Lodge & Hostel
5	Aloha Cafe
6	Kona Coffee Roasters
7	Flea Market
8	Mrs Fields
9	Kahanahou
10	Hospital
11	Post Office
12	McDonald's
13	Canaan Deli
14	Bank of Hawaii
15	Library
16	Natural Foods Coop
17	Kona Historical Society Museum
18	Tropical Temptations
19	Captain Cook Monument
20	Manago Hotel
21	State & County Offices
22	Post Office
23	Kealakekua Ranch Center
24	Captain Cook Coffee Company
25	Royal Kona Coffee Mill
26	Coffee Trees
27	Kona Country Fair
28	Kona Coast Macadamia Nut & Candy Factory
29	Bong Brothers
30	St Benedict's Painted Church
31	Morihara Store

South of Kona

beaches but there are a couple of excellent spots for snorkelling and diving.

Kona coffee is the only coffee grown on a commercial scale in the USA. Almost all of it is planted in these hillslope towns, from Holualoa in the north to Honaunau in the south. The coffee trees thrive in the rich volcanic soil and the cloud cover that moves in nearly every afternoon.

During coffee season buyers hang out signs announcing how much they'll pay for the 'cherries' which are the red coffee berries. In a good year they may offer 90 cents a pound.

Coffee trees must be handpicked several times a year as not all the berries ripen at once. The harvesting season begins in August. Coffee farmers at the lowest elevations may finish harvesting by December, while those at the 2000-foot level might harvest into March.

HONALO

Honalo is a small village at the intersection of Hwy 11 and Hwy 180.

Daifukuji Soto Mission, on the mauka side of Hwy 11, is a big Buddhist temple with two altars, gold brocade, huge drums

Kona Coffee Bags

and incense burners. Visitors are welcome to view the main altar but as with all Buddhist temples, you must leave your shoes at the door.

Places to Stay

The *Kona Lodge & Hostel* (Box 645, Kealakekua, HI 96750; tel 322-9056) on Hwy 11 in Honalo is a good place to meet other travellers. Bunk and dormitory rates start at $8 per person for those with American Youth Hostel cards, $12 otherwise. Dormitory guests have bunk duties. Very simple private rooms start at $20/25 for singles/doubles. It's a steep $14 to pitch a tent in the grounds. Bathrooms are shared and there's a communal kitchen. Smoking is not allowed. The location is out of the way for anyone without transportation.

Teshima's Inn (tel 322-9140) on Hwy 11 in Honalo has 10 rooms in a building behind Teshima's restaurant. However, most of the rooms are usually rented out on a monthly basis. Rooms are adequate with private bathrooms, but don't expect any frills. Rates are $12/24 for singles/doubles. Ask for Mrs Teshima at the restaurant.

Places to Eat

Teshima's is an unpretentious cafe that serves authentic Japanese food. The best deal is the lunch teishoku of miso soup, sashimi, sukiyaki, tsukemono (pickled cabbage), sunomono (vinegared cucumber, daikon, carrot) and rice for $4.75. At dinner the same meal with the addition of shrimp tempura costs $9.50. It also has inexpensive sandwiches. There's a bar at the side of the restaurant.

KAINALIU

Kainaliu is a little town with positive energy. Aloha Cafe and the adjoining theatre and natural food store are the focal point.

Aloha Theatre, which is the home of the Kona Community Players, presents performances with progressive themes and you can get a good feel for the community by attending one.

There are a couple of interesting shops in town. Kimura's Fabrics started out in 1926 as a country store and the Kimuras have been operating there ever since. A more recent newcomer is Crystal Star Gallery, a New Age shop specialising in crystals, metaphysical books and the like.

Kona Coffee Roasters has a little lanai out the back where you can sip a cup of fresh-brewed coffee.

Places to Eat

The *Aloha Cafe* is the place to eat in these parts and well worth the drive up from Kailua-Kona. The food is fresh, with lots of vegetarian dishes and good salads, as well as chicken and wonderful fresh fish specials. Full dinners cost from $6 to $11. It has good sandwiches, fresh fruit smoothies, carrot juice and pastries from carrot cake to chocolate chip cookies. The burrito especiale is good and very big, topped with sour cream and guacamole, with a generous side salad for $5.25. A bowl of homemade soup with bread costs $3.25. The outside terrace has a distant ocean view. It's open from 8 am to 8 pm Monday to Saturday. If you come up for dinner in the winter bring a sweater as it gets cool in the evenings.

Next door is the *Aloha Village Store*, a fully stocked natural foods store.

KEALAKEKUA

Kealakekua means 'path of the gods'. A series of heiaus once ran from Kealakekua Bay, a few miles south of town, north to Kailua-Kona.

These days Kealakekua is the banking centre for Kona's hill towns. The Kona Coast's new hospital is on the north side of town, a quarter of a mile mauka of Hwy 11. The state employment services office is on Halekii Rd, next to the post office.

Kealakekua has the best library on this side of the island. It's open from 10 am to 8 pm Mondays, to 5 pm on Tuesdays to Fridays, and to 1 pm on Saturdays.

Next door to the library is the coral mortar and lava Kona Union Church, which dates back to 1854. The sign out the front proclaims 'Keepers of the Light, Lamp to Laser'.

Kahanahou

Kahanahou (tel 322-3901) is a non-profit native Hawaiian handicraft workshop, which sells hula instruments and native crafts such as nose flutes, split bamboo dancing sticks and gourd masks at reasonable prices. They even grow their own gourds – look on the roof.

Mrs Fields Factory

Mrs Fields, on Halekii Rd just off Hwy 11, sells nuts and all the standard Mrs Fields cookies. It's open from 8.30 am to 5.30 pm daily and informal free tours of its small macadamia nut factory are conducted every half an hour or so. The cracked nuts come down a chute where they are hand sorted, dried, graded, salted and vacuum packed. It's not all that dynamic, but if you're curious it only takes a few minutes to walk through and see the process. The shop isn't pushy about sales and free samples are given .

Flea Market

A little farther down Halekii Rd on the right, a small flea market is held every Thursday and Saturday from 8 am to 3 pm. You can buy local produce and an assortment of other typical flea market merchandise. Check out the clothing carefully. Ned bought a fine-looking $20 cotton shirt that fell apart on the first washing!

Kona Historical Society Museum

Kona Historical Society (tel 323-3222) is just south of Kona Meat Company and north of the Kealakekua Grass Shack gift shop. The stone and mortar building, built in the mid-1800s, was once a general merchandise store-cum-post office.

These days it's the society's office and archives with a little museum. There are some interesting displays of the area's local history, including old photos and bottles and other memorabilia. It's open from 9 am to 3 pm Monday to Friday and though there's no admission fee per se, donations are appreciated. They sell some interesting historical post cards.

Tropical Temptations

Tropical Temptations, at the south end of town, sells fruit dried without preservatives. The sign out front tells local growers which fruit they're buying each day. It takes seven pounds of bananas, 11 pounds of pineapples or 15 pounds of papayas to make one pound of dried fruit.

They also sell macadamia nuts and roasted coffee beans dipped in date-sweetened carob and sometimes have samples to try.

Places to Eat

Ohana O Ka Aina Cooperative is a natural foods cooperative on Hwy 11. It has a wide selection of organic produce, nuts, grains, fruit juices and dairy products, as well as some of the standard packaged health foods. There's a community bulletin board out the front.

Canaan Deli on Hwy 11 is a New York style deli. It has a variety of sandwiches for about $3.75 to $5.50 plus spaghetti, pizza and some rather lacklustre deli standards. It's open from 7 am to 8 pm daily except Sundays.

There's also a *McDonald's* nearby on Hwy 11.

Napoopoo Road

Napoopoo Rd leads makai from the north end of the town of Captain Cook, down to a coffee mill and Kealakekua Bay. The rural road passes coffee farms and a few banana and papaya orchards on the way down to the coast.

At the fork, which is 2¾ miles from Hwy 11, bear to the left to go to St Benedict's Painted Church, or to the right to get to the coffee mill. All of these roads make nice short country drives.

Royal Kona Coffee Mill

Once a week Royal Kona Coffee Mill fires up its old roaster and cooks 500 pounds of coffee. After 20 minutes it's roasted down to 425 pounds.

On any day you can stop and get a free cup of fresh-brewed Kona coffee and learn a little about the coffee biz. They have a showroom with historical artefacts, a three-minute video about coffee picking and photos from the early 1900s.

In the early days donkeys (called Kona nightingales, because of their braying) trans-

ported the coffee down Kona's stony hills but in the 1950s they were replaced by jeeps. Photos from 1953 show coffee growers parading through town on lei-draped donkeys lamenting the mechanisation with such banners as 'Kona's reached a doleful pass, when our bray gives way to gas'.

A separate lanai area has displays of macadamia nuts in various stages. There's even a 1950s vintage macadamia nut husker with a Goodyear car tyre serving as the grinding wheel.

Both macadamia nuts and coffee are processed out the back. They sell coffee, seedlings and souvenirs here, but it's low-key. It's open from 8 am to 4.30 pm daily and admission is free.

KEALAKEKUA BAY

Kealakekua Bay is a large bay, a mile wide at its mouth. Napoopoo Beach Park and Hikiau Heiau are at the south end of the bay. The north end has a protected cove with some of the best snorkelling spots on the Big Island.

Steep sea cliffs separate the two ends of the bay and there's no land passage between them. The northern end can be approached only by sea or by a hike from the town of Captain Cook.

Kealakekua Bay is a state underwater park and marine life conservation district. Fishing is restricted and the removal of coral and rocks prohibited.

Captain James Cook, the first Westerner to visit Hawaii, sailed into Kealakekua Bay at dawn on 17 January 1779. The beaches were lined with 10,000 onlookers and 1000 canoes sailed out to greet him.

Cook's tall ships with high sails appeared to fulfil a prophecy of the return of the god Lono who was to arrive on a floating island covered with tall trees.

On his first evening ashore, Cook was brought to Hikiau Heiau where the high priest performed a series of ceremonies recognising Cook as the incarnation of the god Lono.

Eleven days later at the heiau, Cook performed a burial service for sailor William

Whatman who had died of a stroke. The inauspicious death of his mate raised a few questions about Cook's own mortality.

On 14 February, Cook was tragically killed in a scuffle at the north end of the bay. Ironically, the world's greatest navigator was such a poor swimmer that he apparently stumbled into the direction of an angry crowd rather than trying to swim a few metres out to a waiting boat.

An obelisk monument on the north side of the bay marks the spot where Cook died at the water's edge.

Napoopoo Beach Park

Napoopoo Beach Park is on Middle Keei Rd (see the South of Kona map).

Hikiau Heiau is the large platform heiau above the beach. The busy park has a boat landing, restrooms and showers.

Two elderly Hawaiian women run a tiny snack shop near the heiau, selling mangoes, papayas and limes at bargain prices. They also string plumeria leis which they sell for $1.50.

The beach is rather rocky, with grey sand and because it's small it often feels crowded. This end of the bay is moody and the surf can sometimes get rough, though occasionally there are good surfable waves.

The real prize is the cove at the north end of the bay. Some people snorkel over from Napoopoo Beach when it's calm, but it's a long haul and only strong swimmers should consider it.

From the park you can continue four miles south along a narrow road through scrub brush and lava flows to Puuhonua O Honaunau, the Place of Refuge. The road is bumpy, but paved and passable. Be careful if you pull over as there are roadside trenches. Most of the stone walls which parallel parts of the road were built in the early 1900s to keep cattle from straying.

Captain Cook Monument Trail

If you're up to a hike, the trail to Captain Cook Monument and the cove at the north end of Kealakekua Bay makes a good day outing. To get to the trailhead, turn off Hwy 11 onto Napoopoo Rd and go down about 200 yards to the dirt road on the right after the second telephone pole.

Less than a minute's walk down the dirt road, just before reaching a metal gate marked 'Private Property', there's a parting through tall grasses on the left. This is the start of the trail. Don't expect a well-beaten path. Also, it's not a good hike to do in sandals.

The first half of the trail is like a jungle walk through shoulder-high elephant grass. Still, the path is fairly simple and in most places runs between two rock fences on an overgrown jeep road. When in doubt, stay to the left.

Eventually the coast becomes visible, the vegetation sparser and the trail easier to walk. The trail veers to the left along a broad ledge, leads through an old wooden gate and goes down to the beach. Once you're at the water, it's less than five minutes to the left to the monument marking Cook's deathplace.

The hike takes about 1¼ hours down, 1¾ hours up. It's not a particularly strenuous hike, but it is hot and largely unshaded, and it's uphill all the way back. On the return, about five minutes up from the beach, there's a small fork in the trail where there are lots of air plants; bear to the right and you'll be on your way back.

There are no facilities at the bottom. Be sure to take drinking water and snorkelling gear.

Snorkelling There's fairly easy entry from the rocks on the left side of the cement dock in front of the Captain Cook Monument. The water starts out about five feet deep and slopes gradually to about 30 feet. The cove is protected and usually very calm. Both coral and fish are plentiful, there's great visibility and it's a terrific place to snorkel.

Snorkelling tour boats (see the Activities section) pull into the bay in the morning, but they don't come ashore and they generally leave before lunch time. Anyway, the cove is big enough so it doesn't feel crowded.

Exploring This area was once the Hawaiian village of Kaawaloa. Old lava stone walls still go all the way out to Cook's Point at the north end of the bay. There's a small light beacon on the point.

Queen's Bath, which is a small lava pool with brackish spring-fed water, is on the edge of the cove, a few minutes walk from the monument. The water is cool and refreshing. This age-old equivalent of a beach shower is a great way to wash off the salt before hiking back. However, the mosquitoes can get a bit testy here.

A few minutes beyond the Queen's Bath, the path ends at the cliffs called Pali-kapu-o-Keoua, the 'cliff sacred to the chief Keoua'. The cliffs contain numerous caves which were the burial places of Hawaiian royalty. It's speculated that some of Captain Cook's bones were placed there. As late as 1887 villagers from Kaawaloa were in the employ of King Kalakaua to maintain the burial grounds.

A few lower caves are accessible but they don't contain anything other than beer cans. The ones higher up are fortunately not as easy to get to and probably still contain bones. All are sacred and should be left undisturbed.

This is an interesting area. Although it's not officially permitted, it seems like a tempting place to camp for a day or two and explore.

CAPTAIN COOK

The town named for the Pacific navigator is on Hwy 11 above the bay where he met his end. Captain Cook has some county and state offices, a shopping centre, a hotel and a couple of restaurants.

Kealakekua Ranch Center has a Sure Save supermarket, Ben Franklin store, Harvest Moon Books, a hardware store and Mexican and Chinese restaurants.

The Chevron gas station north of Manago Hotel is open 24 hours. Mauna Loa Gallery shows paintings, sculpture and photography by Hawaiian artists.

Kona Coffee

Captain Cook Coffee Company runs a little stand at the side of Hwy 11 at the south end of town. There's an area to sit out the back with a pretty view of Kealakekua Bay. They sell doughnuts and give out free coffee samples. A few cofffee trees grow by the parking area.

If you just want to examine coffee trees, there's a pull-off for that purpose about a mile south, marked with an HVB sign. Coffee trees are planted in the front and macadamia trees beyond.

Coffee, a relative of the gardenia, has fragrant white blossoms in the spring. In the summer the trees have green berries, which turn red in the autumn as they ripen.

Kona Country Fair

Kona Country Fair is a large new flea market on a rather remote stretch between Captain Cook and Honaunau. It's not exactly homespun but with its broad vista of the south Kona Coast it's hard to beat the setting. Their 90-foot lava tube and tall totem pole are worth looking at.

This is an ambitious project with plans to eventually add a restaurant, shops and tour bus parking. It's controversial among islanders who feel it might end up a tacky tourist trap like Waikiki's International Market Place. It's open from 8 am to 3 pm Wednesdays, Fridays and Saturdays.

Places to Stay

Manago Hotel (Hwy 11, Box 145, Captain Cook, HI 96704; tel 323-2642) is a family-run hotel started in 1917 as a restaurant serving bowls of udon to salespeople on the then-long journey between Hilo and Kona. Those wanting to stay overnight were charged $1 for a futon on tatami mats. These days the basic rooms in the original roadside building show their age without much grace but rates are only $16/19 for singles/doubles. The furniture is rickety and there are shared baths down the hall.

If you want comfort over character, go for one of Manago's 42 rooms in the newer wing at the rear. The motel-style rooms are ordinary but sufficient, with private baths and radios. The highlight is the lovely unobstructed lanai view of Kealakekua Bay a mile below. Rates are $26 to $29 for singles, $29 to $32 for doubles; the higher rates are for better views. There's a communal TV room near the restaurant. Although it's pure local flavour, Manago draws many international travellers.

Adrienne's B&B (RR1, Box 8E, Captain Cook, HI 96704; tel 328-9726) is a three-room accommodation in the home of Reginald & Adrienne Ritz-Baty, enthusiastic hosts who enjoy talking about the island. Adrienne is a former national archery champion. All the rooms have private baths and cable TV. There's a hot tub on the lanai with a view of the distant coast, access to the kitchen and the washer/dryer and they have a collection of 800 videos. Rates are $40/45 for singles/doubles and include breakfast of homemade bread or muffins and fruit from the yard. They're on Hwy 11 about a mile south of the Place of Refuge.

RBR Farms B&B (Box 930, Captain Cook, HI 96704; tel 328- 9212) is in Captain Cook on a coffee and macadamia nut farm. It's a comfortable, secluded place at the end of a three-quarter mile dirt road. Rooms with shared bathroom cost $50. A cottage with private bath, kitchen, living room and lanai costs $100 for up to four people. There's a pool.

Places to Eat
Manago Restaurant, which is in the Manago Hotel, is a Japanese version of a meat and potatoes eatery, and is known for its pork chops. It's not health food, but the portions are large. Two big chops, rice, potato salad and side dishes such as tofu curd cost $6. Sandwiches and burgers are around $2. Breakfast is available from 7 to 9 am, lunch 11 am to 2 pm and dinner from 5 to 7 pm.

HONAUNAU
Honaunau's main attraction is Puuhonua O Honaunau National Historical Park, commonly called the Place of Refuge, but there are other things to see there as well.

On Hwy 11, just south of Middle Keei Rd, Bong Brothers has a little shop where they

sell their own coffee as well as organic and locally grown produce.

At Morihara Store, Hwy 160 connects with Hwy 11 and leads down to the Place of Refuge, passing Painted Church Rd, Wakefield Botanical Gardens and rural scenery with grazing horses, stone walls and brilliant bougainvilleas.

Macadamia Nut Factory
The Kona Coast Macadamia Nut & Candy Factory, on Middle Keei Rd near Hwy 11, has a little display with a hand-cranked husking machine and nut cracker. You can try it out, one nut at a time, and eat the final product.

The showroom overlooks the real operation out the back, where bags of nuts are husked and sorted. The shop sells both raw and roasted macadamia nuts as well as macadamia nut honey. They also sell edible rejects (mostly a bit over-roasted) for about $2 a pound.

Middle Keei Rd continues down to Kealakekua Bay, passing the Royal Kona Coffee Mill on the way.

St Benedict's Painted Church

This church is noted for its painted interior done by John Berchmans Velghe, a Catholic priest who came from Belgium in 1899.

He painted the walls with a series of Biblical scenes as an aid in teaching the Bible to natives who couldn't read. He designed the wall behind the altar to resemble the gothic cathedral in Burgos, Spain. The ceiling is a Hawaiian sky with clouds and birds.

When Father John arrived, the church was on the coast near the Place of Refuge. One of his first moves was to bring the church two miles up the slopes to its present location. It's not clear whether he did this as protection from tsunamis or just to be on the rise – both actually and symbolically – from the old gods of 'pagan Hawaii'.

The tin-roofed church still holds Sunday services, with hymns sung in Hawaiian. There's a big breadfruit tree out the front.

The church is on Painted Church Rd. Turn north at the one-mile marker on Hwy 160. It's a quarter of a mile down the road.

Wakefield Botanical Gardens

Wakefield Botanical Gardens on Hwy 160 has free self-guided walks and there are lots of interesting plants here with names like snow on the mountain, Moses in the basket, cup of gold, ponytail palm and cardboard plant, as well as cactus, bonsai and more typical tropical flowers. The only price you pay is feeding the mosquitoes. The gardens are owned by island artist Arlene Wakefield.

There is a restaurant there which sells sandwiches, fruit salads and cold drinks. Meals are in the $5 to $6 range. The macadamia nut pie for $1.95 should satisfy the strongest of sugar urges. Lunch is served from 11 am to 3 pm.

PLACE OF REFUGE

Puuhonua O Honaunau National Historical Park (tel 328-2288) preserves ancient temples, royal grounds and a puuhonua, a place of refuge or sanctuary. The park fronts Honaunau Bay.

Puuhonua O Honaunau is a tongue-twister

Puuhonua O Honaunau National Historical Park

of a name which simply means 'place of refuge at Honaunau'.

In old Hawaii, breaking any of the many kapus which strictly regulated all daily interactions was thought to anger the gods who just might retaliate with a natural disaster or two. To appease the gods the offender was hunted down and killed.

Commoners who broke a kapu, as well as defeated warriors and ordinary criminals, could all have their lives spared by reaching the sacred ground of the puuhonua.

This was more of a challenge than it might appear. Since royalty and their warriors lived on the grounds immediately surrounding the refuge, kapu breakers were forced to swim through open ocean, braving currents and sharks to get to the puuhonua.

Once inside the sanctuary, priests performed ceremonies of absolution which apparently placated the gods. Kapu breakers could then return home with a clean slate.

Hale O Keawe Heiau, the temple on the point of the cove, was built around 1650. The bones of 23 chiefs were buried there. It's thought that the mana of the chiefs remained in their bones and added a spiritual power to those who came into the grounds. The heiau has been authentically reconstructed. The carved wooden statues which stand erect beside it are called kii and are said to embody the ancient gods.

The heiau is at the end of a large stone wall built around 1550. It's called the Great Wall and is more than 1000 feet (304 m) long and 10 feet (three m) high. The west side of the wall was the puuhonua and the east side was the royal grounds.

A self-guided walk corresponding to the park brochure passes by Hale O Keawe Heiau, two older heiaus, a petroglyph, legendary stones, a fishpond, lava tree moulds and a few thatched huts and shelters. The canoe on display is hand carved from koa wood.

There's also a stone board for konane, a game similar to checkers. The game pieces are small stones of black lava and white coral. Get a copy of the game rules at the park entrance and try your hand.

Medicinal plants around the grounds include the noni tree with its pear-sized warty-looking fruit. The fruit, which was eaten in times of famine, tastes as bad as it smells. More often it was used to make dyes or as a treatment for diabetes and high blood pressure.

Check out the tidepools in the pahoehoe lava at the south end of the park. The tiny black speckles dotting the shallow pools behind the heiau are pipipi, a kind of periwinkle. The tidepools near the picnic area further south are even better. They have coral, black-shelled crabs, small fish and eels, sea hares, and sea urchins with rose-coloured spines.

Twenty-minute orientation talks are given at 10, 10.30 and 11 am and at 2.30, 3 and 3.30 pm daily. They're largely geared to people on tour buses who don't have time to see the whole park. There's good background information in the park brochure and the audio displays at the entrance.

Some of the rangers are native Hawaiians. You'll occasionally find one dressed in a malo or tapa demonstrating traditional pili grass thatching, feather cape weaving, canoe carving or kii statue making.

A programme in Hawaiian studies is held at 7.30 pm on the first Wednesday of each month in the park's amphitheatre. A festival with traditional displays and food, hukilau (net fishing) and a 'royal court' is held on the weekend closest to 1 July. Local students compete in Hawaiian sports on the first Friday of February and November.

Admission is $1; good for repeated visits over six days.

Honaunau Beaches

Place of Refuge Swimming is allowed at Keoneele Cove inside the Place of Refuge. The cove was once the royal canoe landing and it's shallow with a gradual decline. Snorkelling is best when the tide is rising; not only is the water a bit deeper, but it brings in fish. Sunbathing is discouraged here.

South end of the Park Near the Place of Refuge visitor centre there's a road leading a quarter of a mile south to a beach park with picnic tables and some quiet sandy patches.

Winter surf is rough here and it's probably best to stick to the Keoneele Cove area for swimming and snorkelling.

North end of the Park There's a terrific place to snorkel and dive just north of the Place of Refuge. From the park's parking lot, take the narrow road to the left with the 15 mph sign.

Go down about 500 feet and park just past the boat ramp. There's a little park mauka of the road. St Benedict's Painted Church was originally on this site.

Snorkellers step off a lava ledge immediately north of the boat ramp into about 10 feet of water. It then drops off fairly quickly to about 25 feet. There are some naturally formed lava steps which make it fairly easy to get in and out.

Visibility is excellent, with good-sized reef fish and corals close to shore. The predatory crown of thorns starfish can be seen here feasting on live coral polyps.

For divers, there's a ledge a little way out which drops off about 100 feet.

In winter the water can get rough when the surf is high.

South on Highway 11

For about 15 miles south on Hwy 11 after the Place of Refuge turn-off, the road is narrow and winding with some fairly steep drops. Be careful when driving as there are sections that have no shoulder at all.

At night, sudden oncoming headlights and fog can make it particularly tricky, especially if you're tired from a long haul between Hilo and Kona.

HOOKENA BEACH

Hookena was once a bustling village with two churches, a school, court house and post office. King Kalakaua sent his friend Robert Louis Stevenson here in 1889 to show him a typical Hawaiian village. Stevenson stayed a week with the town's judge and wrote about Hookena in *Travels in Hawaii*.

In the 1890s Chinese immigrants began to move into the village setting up shops and restaurants. A tavern and a hotel opened and the town got rougher and rowdier.

In those days Big Island cattle were shipped from Hookena's landing to market in Honolulu. When the circle-island road was built, the steamers stopped coming and the townspeople moved away. By the 1920s the town was almost deserted.

These days Hookena is a tiny fishing community with a small county beach park. The storm-beaten remains of the landing are in front of the park restrooms.

Hookena is 2¼ miles down a narrow road from Hwy 11. The marked turn-off is between the 101 and 102-mile markers, opposite the water tank that supplies the village with drinking water.

The beach has very soft black sand. The bay is backed by lava sea cliffs and there are trees for shade. When winter surf is up, kids boogie board there.

When it's calm, you can snorkel straight out from the landing. It drops off pretty quickly, from 10 feet to about 30 feet, and there's lots of coral. Pygmy dolphins occasionally come into the bay, sometimes as

many as 100. If you take a loaf of bread out, they'll greet you but do not go too far out as there're strong currents.

There are showers here but the water is brackish and not suitable for drinking. A shack on the beach sells reasonably priced drinking coconuts, shave ice and soft drinks.

Hookena is a popular weekend picnic spot. Officially there's no camping, but there are often a few islanders with tents up.

MILOLII

Milolii is the most traditional fishing village remaining in Hawaii. Families who have been fishing these waters for generations still set out in outrigger canoes each morning before dawn.

Milolii means 'fine twist'. Historically the village was known for it's skilled sennit twisters who used bark from the olona shrub to make fine cord and highly valued fishing nets.

Milolii sits on the edge of an expansive 1926 lava flow that covered the nearby fishing village of Hoopuloa.

Milolii has about 125 residents and many of the homes there are simple, shanty-like wooden structures. There's no running water or village-wide electricity, though a solar-powered desalinisation plant is being planned. The state is also providing funds to tear down some of the old shacks and replace them with new houses.

The fishermen there use an age-old method resembling aqua farming. They sail out to feed papaya and taro to opelu, a type of mackerel. After months of the fattening and taming process they return to net the fish.

Folks in Milolii have long-standing complaints with some commercial fishing boats that ply their fishing grounds and scoop up the opelu they've fattened. Things seem destined to get worse if the massive new Riviera resort complex planned for Kahuku, south of Milolii, builds its proposed 400-boat marina.

Milolii Beach Park, which is past the town's little boat ramp, has grills and a thatched picnic pavilion, but no drinking water. The village has just one ageing little store and it's only occasionally open.

Tidepools of both red and black lava provide a splashy backdrop to white coral and colourful fish. When the waters are calm the snorkelling is good. The coconut trees along the coast have nuts so huge that they're the topic of legends.

Camping is officially allowed in the beach park but it's right in the village and there's not a lot of space or privacy. This place is also the village's playground and volleyball court. If you're thinking of camping, check it out first. Sentiments towards outsiders may be affected by the controversial Riviera development which many see as a threat to their privacy and lifestyle.

The turn-off to Milolii is just north of the 88-mile marker. It's five miles down a paved but steep and winding single-lane road that cuts across the lava flow. Use low gear or your brakes will smoke on this one.

MacFarms of Hawaii

Just before entering the Kau district, Hwy 11 passes through the 3800 acres of MacFarms of Hawaii, the largest macadamia nut orchard in Hawaii. The orchards were started by a partnership which included Jimmy Stewart, Julie Andrews and other Hollywood stars.

MacFarms has introduced biological insect controls, composting and the use of grazing sheep for weed control in an effort to go organic.

The orchards annually produce about 10 million pounds of nuts which are husked, processed and packaged on site.

North of Kona

Hwy 19 (Queen Kaahumanu Hwy) runs north 33 miles from Kailua-Kona up the Kona Coast to Kawaihae in the South Kohala district.

This is hot arid country. Clumps of bougainvillea planted along the road look striking in their pink brilliance against the jet black lava but otherwise, the vegetation is mainly sparse tufts of grass that survive the dry winds.

Honokohau Harbor and a new historical park are just a couple miles north of Kailua-Kona. Tiny fishing villages once dotted this sparsely populated coast but were wiped out by the tsunami of 1946.

There are beautiful secluded beaches and coves on the north Kona Coast which are hidden from the road and are accessible only on foot (or by boat). Once you hike in, you'll find white sand beaches tucked between a sea plain of lava and a turquoise ocean. A few of these beaches are nesting sites of the threatened Pacific green sea turtle.

There are wonderful drive-up beaches at the Waikoloa hotels and the nearby beach parks of Anaehoomalu and Hapuna.

From along much of the coast you can look inland and see Mauna Kea, and to the south of it Mauna Loa both of which often have snowcaps in winter.

The Big Island's fanciest resorts are in the Waikoloa area on the South Kohala Coast. They have artwork collections, some excellent restaurants and world-class golf courses. This was an important area in Hawaiian history. Temples, fishponds, petroglyphs and ancient stone-paved trails can all be explored.

Hwy 19 is flat and straight and it's easy to zoom along but it's also a hot spot for radar speed traps, particularly on the stretch between the airport and Kailua. Most police cruise in their own unmarked cars, anything from Trans Ams to Broncos, and they're tough to spot.

From Kawaihae you can continue 27 miles up the coast along Hwy 270 to Pololu Valley or head 10 miles inland along Hwy 19 to Waimea.

Hwy 19 is part of the Ironman triathlon route. Wide, smooth bike lanes border both sides of the road but cyclists should be aware that when the air temperature is about 80°F, reflected heat from asphalt and lava can edge the actual temperature above 100°F. There's no drinking water or services between OTEC Beach and the Waikoloan hotels.

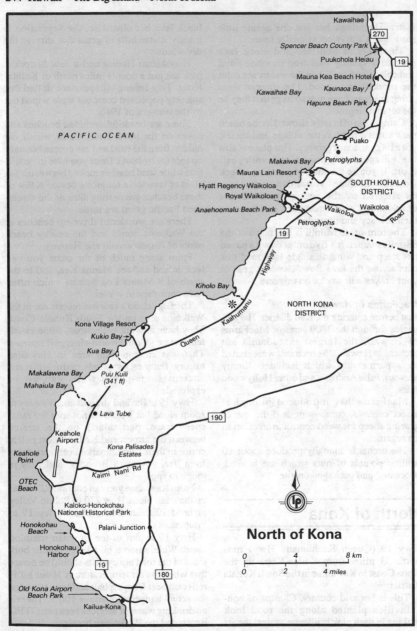

North of Kona

PACIFIC OCEAN

Kawaihae

Spencer Beach County Park
Puukohola Heiau
Mauna Kea Beach Hotel
Kawaihae Bay
Kaunaoa Bay
Hapuna Beach Park

Puako
Petroglyphs
Makaiwa Bay
Mauna Lani Resort
Hyatt Regency Waikoloa
Royal Waikoloan
Anaehoomalu Beach Park
Petroglyphs

SOUTH KOHALA
DISTRICT

Waikoloa
Waikoloa Road

Kiholo Bay

NORTH KONA
DISTRICT

Kona Village Resort
Kukio Bay
Kua Bay
Makalawena Bay
Mahaiula Bay

Puu Kuili
(341 ft)

Lava Tube

Keahole
Airport

Keahole
Point

OTEC
Beach

Kona Palisades
Estates

Kaimi Nani Rd

Kaloko-Honokohau
National Historical Park

Honokohau
Beach
Honokohau
Harbor

Palani Junction

Old Kona Airport
Beach Park

Kailua-Kona

0   4   8 km

0   2   4 miles

HONOKOHAU HARBOR
Honokohau Harbor was built in 1970 to take some of the burden off Kailua Pier. The majority of the 155 buoys are occupied by charter fishing boats and these days most of Kona's catch comes in here, not to Kailua.

The harbour is about two miles north of Kailua on Hwy 19. In case you're wondering about the plaques in front of the coconut trees that line the road down to the harbour – they show who donated each of the 243 trees for this beautification project.

The marina complex has Attila's Bar & Grill, shops dealing with marine activities and a bulletin board with notices of boats and cars for sale plus crew jobs.

Honokohau Beach
Honokohau Beach, just north of the harbour has long been Kona's nude beach, though its days are probably numbered as the beach is being added to the new Kaloko-Honokohau National Historical Park.

The beach is composed of large-grained sand, a mix of black lava, white coral and rounded shell fragments. Walking along the sand gives a good foot massage. It's not a bad beach for swimming and snorkelling, though the bottom is a bit rocky.

To get there, turn onto the harbour road from Hwy 19, then turn right in front of the marina complex and follow the road a quarter of a mile. Pull off to the right after the dry dock boat yard. The trail begins at a break in the lava wall on the right. It's about a five-minute walk along a well-beaten path to the beach. (As development proceeds on the new park, a new trail is likely to follow.)

There are no facilities at the beach, but there are showers and toilets back at the marina. You might want to take along some insect repellent in case the gnats are feasting.

Aimakapa Fishpond, just inland from the beach, is the largest pond on the Kona Coast and an important bird habitat. It's a pretty view looking across the grass-fringed pond to the hills beyond. You're likely to see black-necked stilts (aeo) and Hawaiian coots (alae-keokeo), both endangered native waterbirds.

KALOKO-HONOKOHAU NATIONAL HISTORICAL PARK
Kaloko-Honokohau is a new national historical park which is still under development. When completed it'll encompass about 1200 acres and will include Aimakapa and Kaloko fishponds, ancient heiau and house sites, burial caves, petroglyphs, a queen's bath and the beachfront from Kaloko to Honokohau Harbor.

There's speculation that the bones of Kamehameha the Great were secretly buried near Kaloko. This, combined with the fact that Aimakapa Fishpond is a habitat for endangered waterbirds, was enough to help Congress win the slim majority that it needed to go ahead with the national park designation in 1978.

The park is being slowly pieced together by acquiring land from a few private owners and the state. The park entrance leads to Kaloko Fishpond, acquired in 1986 from Huehue Ranch in exchange for 300 acres of federal land on the mainland.

Over the past two decades, mangrove has invaded and spread rapidly throughout Kaloko Fishpond and native birds have abandoned the habitat. The park service is eradicating the mangrove in the hope that the birds will return. They've tried cutting and torching, but the pervasive mangrove keeps sending up new shoots. Now they're tearing them up one by one and burning the roots. Unfortunately mangrove is now invading Aimakapa Fishpond as well.

Plans call for the Kaloko Fishpond area to eventually have a centre for native Hawaiian crafts and cultural interpretation. A visitor centre is being built near the highway.

The park (tel 329-6881) entrance is off Hwy 19, about half a mile north of the 97-mile marker. It's open from 7.30 to 4 pm daily.

Queen's Bath
The queen's bath is a spring-fed pool with brackish water in the middle of a lava flow. Even though it's inland, the water level changes with the tide. At high tide more saltwater seeps in and the water rises.

You can get there by walking south for

about 15 minutes from Kaloko Fishpond or inland from the north end of Honokokau Beach. The queen's bath is marked by stone cairns as well as Christmas berries, always a dead giveaway that freshwater is nearby.

KEAHOLE POINT/OTEC BEACH

The turn-off to OTEC Beach and the National Energy Laboratory of Hawaii (NELH), a state hydroenergy research facility, is one mile south of the Keahole Airport.

At Keahole Point the seafloor drops steeply just offshore providing a continuous supply of both cold water from 600-metre depths as well as warm surface waters. These are ideal conditions for ocean thermal energy conversion (OTEC).

The OTEC system operates like a steam turbine, with the difference in temperature between the cold and warm waters providing the energy source. They've successfully produced electricity there and are now building a larger experimental 165 kilowatt-per-hour power plant.

The nutrient-rich cold waters which are pumped up there are also used in spin-off aquaculture projects to cultivate salmon, Maine lobster and abalone. Other ponds produce beta-carotene and spirulina.

From the highway it's about a mile in to OTEC (Wawaloli) Beach. There are toilets and showers and drinking water is available. This is a windswept lava coastline and it's rocky and not very good for swimming but when it's calm it's possible to snorkel and dive nearby.

If you follow the dirt road leading south from the beach there are a couple of small blowholes about a third of a mile down. There's an inlet through the lava nearby that allows snorkellers and divers to get out to a steep wall drop which has interesting formations and marine life.

Though it's posted 'no camping' it's not uncommon to see a few tents at the south end of the beach.

Lava Tube

There's a big open lava tube mauka of Hwy 19, two miles north of the turn-off to Keahole Airport, just before a speed limit sign. It might seem rather ordinary if you've been to Hawaii Volcanoes National Park, but interesting if you haven't.

The tube and the expansive lava flow which surrounds the airport are all from the last eruption of Mt Hualalai, in 1801.

KUA BAY

Kua Bay, also known as Maniniowali, has a beautiful secluded beach with turquoise waters and gleaming white sands. It's picture postcard material.

It has a gentle slope and inviting waters for swimmers most of the year round and for boogie boarders and bodysurfers in the winter. Though it's generally calm, winter storms can kick up currents in the bay.

The turn-off to the beach is just north of both the 88-mile marker and the grassy 341-foot Puu Kuili, the highest cinder cone on the makai side of the highway. Look for the stop sign and red gate at the head of the road.

The road down is rough and over loose lava stones. Some people do drive in about half a mile and park near the roadside, but if you park near the highway it only takes about 20 minutes to walk in.

At the end of the road there's a public access sign and a beaten path over the rocks to the south end of the beach.

Kua Bay is one of the nicest of the isolated Kona Coast beaches and you might not feel the need to go any farther. However, if you do want to explore, there's a trail leading along the coast to Makalawena, about two miles to the south. Makalawena is another beautiful stretch of beach. It's backed by sand dunes and contains some fine coves with good swimming and snorkelling.

You could also walk north along the coast about a mile to Kukio Bay, which has a long stretch of white sand beach and an absolutely lovely cove with good swimming. There's a huge condo-hotel under construction there.

In the evenings donkeys come down from the hills to drink at the spring-fed watering holes and to eat the seed pods from the kiawe trees along the coast near the Kona Village Resort. The donkeys, called Kona nightingales, are descendants of the pack animals which were used on coffee farms until the 1950s. They were largely forgotten until Hwy 19 went through in 1974.

The donkeys now need to cross the road so it's worth keeping an eye out for them at night as they don't always pay attention to the donkey crossing markers on the highway there!

Kona Village Resort

Kona Village Resort is the most unique of Hawaii's getaway hotels. The accommodation is in thatched Polynesian 'hales' on stilts spaced around a spring-fed lagoon and along the beach. The grounds have flowering tropical plants and trees, petroglyphs and lots of birds.

The resort is on the secluded Kahuwai Bay, surrounded by huge expanses of barren lava. There was a fishing village there years ago but it got washed away in the 1946 tidal wave. When the resort opened in 1965 it was so isolated it had its own airstrip to shuttle in guests. The highway wasn't built for another decade.

Guided tours are given at 11 am from Monday to Friday and the staff are very friendly.

The resort recently opened its dining to non-guests, with outdoor buffet lunches from 12.30 to 2 pm and fine dining nightly except Wednesdays and Fridays from 6 to 9 pm.

The dining room has the roof of a traditional New Hebrides building and is lined with lauhala matting. The 75-foot tapa cloth draped from the ceiling was a gift from the king of Tonga after his stay there.

The turn-off is just before the 87-mile marker. There's public parking and beach access to the south side of Kahuwai Bay. Unlike the sandy beach in front of the resort, this end is rocky and not that great and is mostly used by divers going spear fishing.

Kiholo Bay

Halfway up the coast, near the 82-mile marker, there's a lookout which commands great views of Kiholo Bay. It appears like a little oasis in the midst of the lava, with intense blue waters and coconut trees. An inconspicuous trail down to the bay starts about 200 yards south of the 81-mile marker. It follows a 4WD road, the beginning of which has been blocked off by boulders to keep vehicles out. The hike down takes about half an hour.

Kiholo Bay is almost two miles wide and the south end of the bay has a lovely, large spring-fed pond called Luahinewai. It's refreshingly cold and fronted by a black sand beach. There's also good ocean swimming there when it's calm.

In ancient times Kiholo provided a respite along the king's trail which ran along the coast. It was a fishing village famed for a large fishpond built by Kamehameha. The fishpond was filled in by a 1859 lava flow.

Cattle were shipped from here in the 1890s and there was once a small hotel. Now there are just a few private homes on the bay, including one owned by country-western singer Loretta Lynn.

Places to Stay

Kona Village Resort (Box 1299, Kaupulehu, HI 96745; tel 325-5555; 800-367-5290) is on a secluded beach with 125 Polynesian-style free-standing 'hales'. They look like rustic thatched huts on the outside but are modern and very comfortable inside with high ceilings, rattan furnishings, ceiling fans and louvred windows.

The village is intended to be a getaway and the units do not have phones or TVs (the front office has both). It's all low-key and relaxed though there are activities available including tennis, sailboats, glass-bottom boats and outrigger canoes. The meals are reputedly excellent and include seven-course dinners. Daily rates range from $265 to $485 for singles, $345 to $565 for doubles, and include all meals and recreational activities. Despite the obvious irony of paying this kind of money to 'go native' there seem to be few unhappy campers here.

Entertainment

The *Kona Village Resort* (tel 325-5555) has the most authentic luau in Hawaii. It's Friday nights only, costs $46 and sometimes books out weeks in advance.

WAIKOLOA BEACH RESORT

Just after crossing into the South Kohala district, a single turn-off leads to the Royal Waikoloan and Hyatt Regency Waikoloa hotels and to Anaehoomalu Beach Park.

When you get to the stop sign, there are a field of petroglyphs to the right, the beach to the left and the hotels straight ahead.

Petroglyphs

The two-acre lava field beside the resort's golf course is etched with an impressive number of petroglyphs, many dating back to the 1500s. Some are graphic (humans, birds, canoes), others cryptic (dots and lines). Western influences show up in the form of horses and English initials.

Although the footpath which leads through the petroglyphs is called the 'king's trail', this section was actually a horse and cattle trail built in the late 1800s. The trail once connected Kailua with Kawaihae. It's possible to continue on the trail to a historical preserve at the Mauna Lani Resort, about two miles away. It's a unshaded walk over lava.

Anaehoomalu Beach

Anaehoomalu Beach is a long, sandy beach which curves along an attractive bay. The waters are popular for swimming and windsurfing and have a gently sloping sandy bottom. Winter weather can produce rip currents but most of the time the water is quite calm.

The south end of the beach has public facilities, with showers, toilets, changing areas and parking. The north end of the beach fronts the Royal Waikoloan hotel.

Both ends of the bay are composed of prehistoric lava flows from Mauna Kea, with rough *aa* lava to the north and smooth pahoehoe to the south.

The beach hut in front of the hotel has a good aerial photo showing the coral and rock formations in the bay and can give you the latest on water conditions. It rents out snorkel sets at $4.50 an hour. You can rent windsurfing equipment for $16 an hour and take two-hour lessons for $35. They have a beginners scuba pool lesson for $20 and one-tank beach dives for $55.

Anaehoomalu was once the site of royal fishponds. Archaeologists from the Bishop Museum have found evidence of habitation dating back more than 1000 years.

There are two large fishponds just beyond the line of coconut trees on the beach. A short trail starts near the showers and winds by the fishponds, caves, ancient house platforms and a shrine. Interpretive plaques along the way explain the area's history. It's a nice little walk and this is a fine beach to drive up to if you're staying in Kona.

Hyatt Regency Waikoloa

The 62-acre Hyatt Regency Waikoloa is the most extravagant resort development on the Big Island. It has the air of a sophisticated theme park and islanders have nicknamed it 'Disneyland'.

The Hyatt had no beach, so it built its own. There's a four-acre saltwater lagoon stocked with tropical fish, a 'river' with a current for rafting and a dolphin pool.

Canopied boats cart guests between buildings along artificial canals and there's a modernistic tram that looks like it was intended for downtown Tokyo.

There's free parking at the hotel or you can walk over from the Royal Waikoloan, a quiet 15-minute stroll up the lava coast.

As you climb up the back steps of the Hyatt there are no clues as to what's on the other side of the fortress-like wall. Then suddenly you're in the midst of it all, crossing a rope walkway over sprawling swimming pools with cascading waterfalls and shrieking kids flying down a waterslide.

When it opened in 1988 the Hyatt billed it as the world's most expensive resort at a cost of $360 million. But for all the extravagance it's surprisingly casual and anyone can cruise around in the free boats and tram.

The Hyatt has a multi-million dollar art collection along a mile- long walkway which runs in both directions from the front lobby. The museum-quality pieces include extensive collections from Melanesia, Polynesia and Asia.

They're particularly big on Papua New Guinea, with war clubs and spears, spirit boards, carved fighting shields and a partial replica of a ceremonial house. There's a collection of Han pottery which dates back to 2,000 years, antique dolls and Noh masks from Japan, jumbo marble urns and Bali puppets. They've even managed to slip in a little Hawaiiana section next to the Palace Tower.

Quite amazingly, much of the artwork is touchable even though some of the pieces look rather vulnerable to this hands-on concept.

The Hyatt holds star-gazing with a Celestron-8 telescope at 7 and 8.15 pm Wednesday to Sunday. It's free to the public but space is limited. Call 885-1234 for reservations.

WAIKOLOA
Waikoloa village is a modern residential development and bedroom community for workers in the nearby resorts. There's not much there of interest to visitors, though there's a golf course, horse stables and a little village store.

The 12-mile Waikoloa Rd runs through the village connecting Hwy 190 and Hwy 19.

Places to Stay
The 523-room *Royal Waikoloan* (Box 5000, Waikoloa, HI 96743; tel 885-6789; 800-537-9800 from the USA and Canada, 0014-800-125-642 from Australia) is a former Sheraton. This is the 'budget' hotel in Waikoloa, with rooms beginning at $155 in high season, $100 in the low season.

Hyatt Regency Waikoloa (1 Waikoloa Beach Resort, Waikoloa, HI 96743; tel 885-1234; 800-228-9000) is a mega-hotel with 1241 rooms. It was developed by Chris Hemmeter and is the most indulgent of his Hawaii fantasy resorts. By and large the hotel seems to draw a similar crowd to Disneyland, with lots of families with video cameras and kids running around. Rates start at $215 for garden views and $285 for partial ocean views and go up to $2700 for the presidential suite.

Waikoloa Villas, a modern lowrise condo development in Waikoloa village, is the cheapest accommodation up this way. One- bedroom units cost $75/$90 in low/high season; the weekly rate is $450. Two-bedroom units cost $90/105 for low/high season and the weekly rate is $540. Three-bedroom units cost $110/125 low/high; $660 weekly. They have full kitchens, lanai, swimming pools and all that sort of thing. It's on the Waikoloa golf course, not the beach, and is part of Hawaiian Islands Resorts (Box 212, Honolulu, HI 96810; tel 531-7595; 800-367-7042).

Places to Eat
The Garden Cafe, in the Royal Waikoloan, has a relaxing setting with pleasant carp pools. Sandwiches or quiche with salad are in the $6 to $7 range.

Cascades, in the Hyatt Regency Waikoloa, which is quite casual, is open for breakfast, lunch and dinner. It's a very pleasant setting overlooking a pond with exotic waterbirds. It has good sandwiches made with nine-grain breads and hot dishes in the $6 to $9 range. The $13.95 brunch buffet is pretty good with champagne, crepes, a few Hawaiian dishes and lots of fruits and salads. Ask for a swan-view table.

This is the best value of the Hyatt's moderate-range restaurants. The Hyatt also has expensive Japanese, Italian and continental restaurants.

Entertainment
The hotels in Waikoloa have Hawaiian music, usually duos or trios strumming in the evenings and quite often dance bands, piano music and jazz groups as well.

The *Hyatt Regency Waikoloa* sometimes brings in big-name entertainers appropriate for their clientele, such as Liza Minnelli or Rich Little.

Luaus Both the *Hyatt Regency Waikoloa* and

the *Royal Waikoloan* have luaus and Polynesian shows.

MAUNA LANI RESORT

After starting off with coconut palms and bright bougainvilleas at the highway entrance, Mauna Lani Drive heads through a long stretch of lava with virtually no vegetation. Halfway, there's a strikingly green golf course sculptured into the black lava. Mauna Lani Bay Hotel is at the end of the road.

The hotel is ritzy, but still low-key, a modern open-air structure centred around a breezy atrium which holds waterways, bamboo stands and full-grown coconut trees. A saltwater stream which runs through the hotel and outdoors into the sun holds black-tipped sharks and a variety of colourful reef fish.

Mauna Lani has good beaches and historical sights and there's public access to both. A free self-guided trail map is available at the concierge desk. One-hour historical tours, which are free to the public, leave from the pool desk at 3.30 pm on Tuesdays and Fridays.

Beaches

The beach in front of the hotel is protected but the water is rather shallow. There's a coral reef beyond the inlet that snorkellers might want to explore. Check at the beach hut for water conditions.

There's also a spring-fed pool and a less-frequented cove down by the beach club restaurant, a 15-minute walk to the south.

An old coastal foot trail leads about a mile further south to Honokaope Bay. It passes by a few historical sites, including a fishermen's house site and other village remains. The southern end of Honokaope Bay is protected and good for swimming and snorkelling when the seas are calm.

The same coastal trail leads about a mile north from the hotel to Pauoa Bay. This stretch is good for surfing in the winter. A Ritz-Carlton Hotel is going up there.

Fishponds

The ancient Kalahuipuaa fishponds are along the beach just south of the hotel in a shady grove of coconut palms and milo trees.

The ponds are stocked with awa, or milkfish. Water circulates from the ocean through traditional *makaha* sluice gates which allow small fish to enter but keep the older fattened ones from leaving. The fish sporadically jump into the air and slap down on the water, an exercise which knocks off parasites.

These are among the few continuously working fishponds in Hawaii and awa from here have been used to provide stock for commercial fisheries.

Historical Trail

The Kalahuipuaa Trail begins opposite the resort's little grocery store, at a turn-off mauka of the hotel entrance.

The trail meanders through a Hawaiian settlement which dates from the 1500s. There are cave shelters, a few petroglyphs and other archaeological and geological sites marked by interpretive plaques.

It's a neat little walk which ends at the fishponds and the beach. If you loop around the largest fishpond and head back it's about 1½ miles round trip.

Places to Stay

The open-air interior of the *Mauna Lani Bay Hotel* (Box 4000, Kohala, HI 96743; tel 885-6622, 800-367-2323) is luxuriant with gardens and waterways and Hawaii's most spectacular atrium. Rates for the 340 rooms start at $250 for a garden view, $325 for an ocean view.

The *Mauna Lani Point* condos at Mauna Lani Resort are booked through Classic Resorts (50 Nohea Kai Drive, Lahaina, HI 96761; tel 667-1400; 800-642-6284). One-bedroom units start at $180/225 in the low/high season.

Places to Eat

If you want to splurge, try Mauna Lani Bay Hotel's (tel 885-6622) Sunday brunch buffet at the *Bay Terrace*. It starts out with a sushi and sashimi table, has waffles and omelettes to order, meats and fishes, lots of salads and a great-looking dessert table. It's open from 11.30 am to 2 pm Sundays for $17.50.

The *Third Floor* has formal dining with high-backed chairs in an elegant setting. They specialise in seafood and both the food and service have a good reputation. Main dishes range from about $25 for roast duckling to $40 for Maine lobster with fettucine. A nice touch is the Indian naan bread served with meals.

The *Canoehouse Restaurant* features Pacific Rim cuisine with dishes like kiawe-grilled Pacific spiny lobster and wok-fried Kohala Coast snapper. It's informal dining on the water with an ocean view and there's both indoor and outdoor seating.

There's a casual restaurant at the end of Kaniku Drive on the south side of the hotel, fronting a small swimming cove. Sandwiches cost $4 to $6.25. Parking is marked for members and resort guests, but if the gate is open it doesn't seem to be a problem for non-guests.

HAPUNA BEACH PARK

The long beautiful stretch of white sand along Hapuna Bay is the Big Island's most popular beach.

When it's calm Hapuna Beach Park has good swimming, snorkelling and diving. In the winter it's a hot bodysurfing and boogie boarding beach. The high winter surf can produce strong rip currents and a pounding shorebreak, and so waves over three feet should be left for experts only. Hapuna has had a number of drownings.

There's a tiny secluded cove with a small sandy beach about five minutes walk to the north. Just follow the shoreline trail and you'll come across steps leading down to it. The water is calmer there and in winter there's less sand kicked up by the waves.

The 61-acre Hapuna Beach State Recreation Area includes the beach, A-frame cabins for overnight stays and a landscaped park with picnic facilities, showers, drinking water and telephone. There are plans to open a snack bar and to staff the beach with lifeguards.

Mauna Kea Properties has plans to build a 350-room hotel adjacent to the northern end of the beach. The community remains divided after an initiative to stop the development failed in the 1988 election. 'Save Hapuna Beach' stickers are still prominent on car bumpers around the island.

Hapuna to Mauna Kea An easy trail runs along the craggy coast from the north end of Hapuna Beach to the south end of Kaunaoa (Mauna Kea) Beach. As part of the trail goes through stands of kiawe, watch out for the sharp thorns which can puncture flip-flops. The walk takes about 20 minutes.

MAUNA KEA HOTEL & BEACH

In the early 1960s, Laurance Rockefeller obtained a 99-year lease on the land around Kaunaoa Bay from his friend Richard Smart, owner of Parker Ranch. Five years later he opened Mauna Kea Beach Hotel, the first luxury hotel on the outer islands.

Kaunaoa Bay is a gorgeous crescent bay with a white sand beach. It has a gradual slope and fine swimming conditions most of the year. There's good snorkelling on the north side when it's calm.

Inside the hotel, a large collection of Asian and Pacific artwork is on display. Bronze temple toys on wheels from India are lined up opposite the elevators on the 5th floor. Thai guardian dogs, Hawaiian quilts and hanging batiks decorate other corners.

Their most prized possession is the 7th century pink granite meditating Buddha which sits in the north garden. It was taken from a temple in South India.

To use Mauna Kea Beach, ask at the gatehouse for one of the 30 beach access parking spaces allotted for non-hotel guests.

Other visitors are allowed a complimentary hour at the hotel. If you stay longer than that and you don't eat at one of the restaurants, there's supposedly a $10 charge but they don't always enforce it.

Places to Stay

Mauna Kea Beach Hotel (Box 218, Kohala, HI 96743; tel 882-7222; 800-228-3000 from the mainland, 800-952-7235 in Hawaii) is a

Westin property. The 310 rooms start at $230. Throw in another $100 for a beach view. From 10 December to 25 March, rooms are only available with breakfast and dinner included at an additional rate of $62.50 per person.

Places to Eat

We found the *Mauna Kea Beach Hotel's* daily lunch buffet to be overrated and disappointing. The food's not as fresh as it should be, nor is it inspired enough to warrant the $18.25 price tag.

The *Batik Room* (tel 882-7222) has a Sri Lankan theme with dishes ranging from Indian curry and fresh fish to chateaubriand. It's open for dinner only. There's dance music and it's quite expensive.

PUAKO

Puako is a quiet one-road coastal village where everyone either lives on the beach or across the street from it. It'd be a tempting place to take a long vacation.

Puako is lined with giant tidepools. The sea washes in and stays in the swirls and dips of the pahoehoe lava which forms the coastline. Some of the pools are deep enough to shelter live coral and diverse marine life.

You can take any of the many beach access points off Puako Rd and explore the area. Snorkelling is said to be excellent, though the surf can be rough in winter. There's a narrow beach of pulverised coral and lava lining much of the shoreline.

Hoku Loa Church, which dates back to 1859, is about half a mile beyond the Puako Bay boat ramp. It's a plain plastered building with a few simple wooden pews and doors that don't lock. Though it looks quite forgotten, services are still held there.

The turn-off to Puako is marked on Hwy 19 but you can also reach Puako from Hapuna Beach Park along a passable route that's more patchwork than road.

Puako Petroglyphs

Puako has the largest concentration of petroglyphs in Hawaii. The human figures drawn in simple linear forms are some of Hawaii's oldest. Those with triangular shapes and curved forms are from more recent times.

The start of the trail to the petroglyphs is on the mauka side of Puako Rd just beyond house number 153.

It's about 15 minutes walk and the arrows painted on the lava lead to a path through kiawe woods. There are petroglyphs in a couple of places along the trail, but they are mostly right at the end, where you'll find hundreds.

The ageing petroglyphs are fragile as they're carved into an ancient lava flow which is brittle and cracking. Stepping on the petroglyphs can damage them, so don't.

After returning from the trail you can walk directly across the street to the beach to find a few more petroglyphs, a konane game board chinked into the lava and tidepools deep enough to cool off in.

Places to Stay

In Puako, there are often 'For Rent' signs staked out in front of a few of the beach houses. You could either drive by and check them out or try calling Ednie Realty (tel 885-4445) or Royal Coast Realty (tel 882-1038).

Puako Beach Condominiums (tel 882-7711) has one three-bedroom, two-bath unit for rent for $600 a week.

SPENCER BEACH COUNTY PARK

The Spencer Beach County Park, beneath Puukohola Heiau, is a family beach good for keikis. The shallow sandy beach is protected by a reef and by the jetty to the north. If anything, it's a bit too protected and the water tends to get silty.

The rocky south end of the beach past the pavilion is better for snorkelling, though entry is not as easy.

Spencer has full facilities, a lifeguard and camping. During the week, Hilo people working on this side of the island sometimes camp here instead of commuting daily and on weekends quite a few families show up.

Though it's a well-used beach park, the grounds are larger here than at most county parks. Campers might want to avoid setting up near the picnic pavilion area, which can

Puukohola Heiau

get noisy. If you don't have a county park permit, you can just camp the first night and register the next day with the park attendant.

PUUKOHOLA HEIAU

The Puukohola Heiau National Historic Site, which is at the side of the road leading down to Spencer Beach, contains the last major temple built in Hawaii.

In 1790, after his attempts to take over the neighbouring islands in battle were thwarted, King Kamehameha sought the advice of Kapoukahi, a famous soothsayer from Kauai.

Kamehameha was told that if he built a temple to his war god here above Kawaihae Bay the other islands would fall to him in battle. Kamehameha immediately began construction of Puukohola Heiau, completing it in 1791.

Kamehameha then held a dedication ceremony and invited his last rival on the Big Island, Keoua, the chief of Kau. When Keoua's canoe came ashore, he was killed and brought up to the temple as the first offering to the gods. With Keoua's death, Kamehameha had sole control of the Big Island, and he went on

to fulfil the prophecy by conquering the other islands.

Puukohola Heiau, terraced in three steps, was covered with wooden idols and thatched structures, including an oracle tower, altar, drum house and the home of the high priest.

After Kamehameha's death in 1819, his son Liholiho and powerful widow Kaahumanu destroyed the heiau's wooden images and the temple was abandoned. These days only the basic rock foundation remains but it's still an impressive site.

Puukohola means 'hill of the whales'. Migrating humpbacks can be seen offshore during winter.

The visitor centre (tel 882-7218), which is open from 7.30 am to 4 pm daily, has a few simple displays and a detailed brochure. The park covers 77 acres and includes other historic sites, though they are of minor interest. There are no entrance fees.

A trail which takes about an hour to walk starts at the visitor centre, which is on Hwy 19 just south of the road leading to Spencer Beach Park. However, if you want to cut time off the hike, just drive down the beach road to the heiau.

Opposite Puukohola Heiau are the ruins of Mailekini Heiau which predates Puukohola and was later turned into a fort by Kamehameha. A heiau dedicated to shark gods is submerged just offshore and you can still see the stone leaning post where the high chief watched sharks bolt down the offerings he made.

The path continues down by the creek to Kamehameha's former house site. Warbling silverbills, doves and mosquitoes frequent the kiawe woods, but there's not much to see.

The trail continues across the highway to the site of John Young's homestead. Young, a shipwrecked British sailor, served Kamehameha as a military advisor and governor of the island. There's not much to see here either.

KAWAIHAE

Kawaihae has the Big Island's second largest deep-water commercial harbour. There are plans to expand the adjacent small boat harbour to accommodate as many as 300 boats and allow the development of a large charter fishing industry.

The harbour has fuel tanks and cattle pens and a little local beach park. Appropriately enough, most visitors stop in Kawaihae just long enough to eat and fuel up on their way to somewhere else.

All the restaurants are along Hwy 270 which passes through the town. Kawaihae Shopping Center has two restaurants, an ice cream shop, a 7-11 store and Kohala Divers.

Places to Eat

Cafe Pesto (tel 882-1071), formerly We're Talk'n Pizza, serves up gourmet pizza – the best we found in Hawaii. It's a class act with lemon in the water glasses, nasturiums in the tossed salad and fresh basil leaves on the side. Pizza toppings are an inch deep and a small pizza will feed two people. The Greek Pizza is topped with feta cheese, fresh spinach, olives and peppers for $6.95. There are many combos, both standard and exotic.

The lunch special is a slice of pizza, dinner salad and soft drink for $3.65. It's on the lower level of the Kawaihae Shopping Center and is open from 11 am to 9 pm on weekdays, to 10 pm weekends.

Harrington's (tel 882-7997), upstairs from Cafe Pesto, specialises in seafood and steak. Main dishes cost $12 to $19. It's open from 5.30 pm nightly.

Harbor Hut has breakfast from 7.30 to 11 am, with two eggs & bacon, coffee and all-you-can-eat pancakes for $3.99.

Jinho's Fast Food Service has shave ice, plate lunches and sandwiches.

North Kohala

The north-west tip of the Big Island is dominated by a central range, the Kohala Mountains.

The leeward side of the mountains is dry and desert-like. The windward side is wet and lush with steep coastal cliffs and spectacularly cut hanging valleys.

North Kohala is often bypassed by travellers as it's off the main track, but it has a couple of impressive historical sites, a few sleepy towns to poke around in and a lovely valley lookout at the end of the road.

There are two ways to get to North Kohala, an inland road and a coastal road. You could go up one and down the other.

Highway 250 (Waimea to Hawi)

Hwy 250 (Kohala Mountain Rd) runs north for 20 miles from Waimea to Hawi. This is a very scenic drive along the upland slopes of the Kohala Mountains. The road is lined in places with ironwood trees and goes through rolling green hills dotted with grazing cattle. At its northern end there's even a little llama farm.

As you head north, Maui rises out of the mist, with the crater of Haleakala showing up red. Mauna Kea is behind you. There are views of the coast and Kawaihae Harbor below and a scenic pull- off to take it all in.

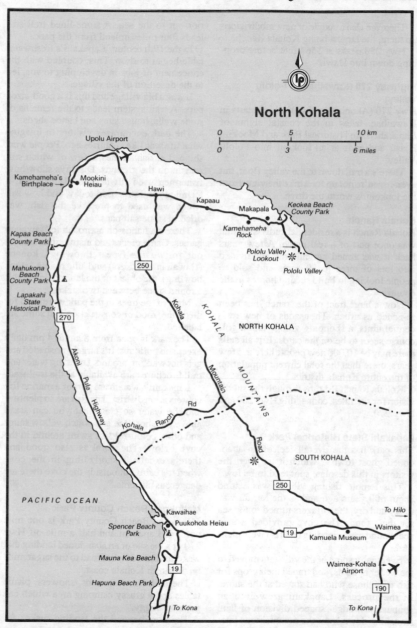

There are also a couple of new subdivisions up there, the largest being Kohala Ranch.

Hwy 250 peaks at 3564 feet before dropping down into Hawi.

Highway 270 (Kawaihae to Pololu Valley)

Hwy 270 (Akoni Pule Hwy), which starts in Kawaihae, takes in the coastal sights of Lapakahi State Historical Park and Mookini Heiau and ends at an lookout into Pololu Valley.

There's a trail down to the valley floor, but even if you're not up for a hike the view from the lookout is worth the drive.

Kohala Ranch

Kohala Ranch is a residential sudivision that was once part of a real ranch. A few years back it was zoned agricultural, subdivided into lots of three to 10 acres and sold to people looking to build second homes in the country.

Now a large tract of the 'ranch' has been re-zoned as urban. Thousands of new residential units, a shopping village and a golf course seem to be on the cards. If it all sells there may be 10,000 new people here in a few years, more than the total current population of the entire Kohala district.

Kohala Ranch Rd runs through the subdivision for six miles, connecting Hwy 250 and Hwy 270.

Lapakahi State Historical Park

This park has the overall feel of an abandoned ghost town – which it is. Even the visitors in this desolate spot tend to be few.

This remote fishing village was settled about 600 years ago and as the terrain was rocky and dry, the villagers turned to the sea for their food. The cove provided a safe year-round canoe landing and fish were plentiful.

Eventually some of the villagers moved to the wetter uplands, and traded their crops for fish with those who had stayed at the shore. In the process, Lapakahi grew into an ahupuaa, a wedge- shaped division of land stretching down from the mountainous interior out to the sea. A stone-lined trail still leads four miles upland from the park.

In the 19th century Lapakahi's freshwater table began to drop. This, coupled with the enticement of jobs in developing towns, led to the desertion of the village.

It was a big village and this is a good-sized park. A trail system leads to the remains of stone walls, house sites and canoe sheds.

The park encourages visitors to imagine what life was like centuries ago. People worshipped at fish shrines, a few of which still remain on the grounds. Displays show how fishermen used lift nets to catch opelu, a technique still practised today, and how salt which was used to preserve the fish, was dried in stone salt pans.

There's a hands-on approach to Hawaiian games. Game pieces and instructions are laid out for *oo ihe* (spear throwing), konane (Hawaiian checkers) and ulu maika (stone bowling), the object of the latter being to roll a round stone between two stakes.

Most of the trees in the park were used for medicine, food or construction and some are labelled.

The park is open from 8 am to 4 pm daily except on holidays. It's largely unshaded and gets hot walking around. Drinking water and trail brochures are available at the trailhead.

Lapakahi's waters are part of a marine life conservation district. The fish are so plentiful and the water so clear that you can stand above the shoreline and watch yellow tangs and other colourful fish swim around in the cove below. The coral is also good and there's excellent snorkelling in the cove when it's calm but outside the cove there are dangerous currents.

Mahukona Beach County Park

Mahukona Beach County Park is one mile north of Lapakahi and half a mile off Hwy 270. It's the site of an abandoned landing that was once linked by railroad to the sugar mills on the north Kohala coast.

The park has restrooms, showers, picnic tables and a grassy camping area which can get a bit buggy.

The area beyond the landing makes for

Top: Waimea, Big Island
Bottom: Halemaumau Trail, Hawaii Volcanoes National Park, Big Island

Top: Kona Coast, Big Island
Left: Rainbow at Haena Beach, Kauai
Right: Waipio Valley, Big Island

interesting snorkelling and diving, though it's too rough in winter. Entry is in about five feet of water. Heading north, it's possible to follow an anchor chain out to a submerged boiler and the remains of a ship in about 25 feet of water. There's coral on the bottom and visibility is good.

Kapaa Beach County Park
Kapaa Beach County Park is 1¼ miles north of Mahukona and nearly a mile off Hwy 270. Its biggest selling point is its view of Maui.

Camping is allowed and there are full facilities, but there's no sand beach and it's rather dumpy.

MOOKINI HEIAU
Mookini is a massive heiau set atop a grassy knoll on the desolate northern tip of the Big Island. It has a clear view out across the ocean to Maui. There's a sense of timelessness and a certain eerie aura.

Chants date Mookini Heiau back to 480 AD. This is a luakini heaiu, where the alii offered human sacrifices to the war god Ku.

According to legend, it was built in one night with basalt stones from Pololu Valley which were passed along a human chain stretching 13 miles.

A kapu which once prevented commoners from entering the heiau grounds was lifted only a decade ago. It will probably just be you, the wind and the spirits there.

The heiau is 250 feet long, with rock walls reaching a good 25 feet high. The entrance through the wall into the heiau itself is on the west side. The large scallop-shaped altar on the north end is thought to have been added by Paao, a Tahitian priest who arrived around the 12th century.

The current kahuna nui priestess is Leimomi Mookini Lum, the most recent in a long line of Mookinis tracing their lineage back to the temple's first high priest. On Children's Day every November, school children are bused in from all over the Big Island for a heritage programme.

To get there turn left off Hwy 270 at the 20-mile marker and go two miles down to Upolu Airport. At the airport, turn left onto the road which parallels the coast. After 1½ miles you'll come to a fork. The left road leads up to the heiau, a quarter of a mile more. This red dirt road can get very muddy after heavy rains.

Kamehameha's Birthplace
Kamehameha the Great was said to have been born on a stormy winter night in 1758 on this rugged windswept coast. If you continue straight ahead at the fork below the heiau, the road leads a short way to his birthsite. There's supposed to be an HVB marker there but it keeps disappearing.

According to one story, Kamehameha's mother was told by a kahuna that her son would become a destroyer of chiefs and a powerful ruler. The high chief of the island didn't take well to the prophecy and in a King-Herod-like scenario, he ordered the newborn killed.

Immediately after birth, the baby was taken to Mookini Heiau for his birth rituals and then into hiding in the Kohala Mountains.

HAWI
Hawi (pronounced Hah-vee), with a population of less than 1000, is the largest town in North Kohala. It has a small grocery store, a post office, a couple of gas stations, a little hotel, laundromat, video arcade and a few restaurants.

North Kohala used to be sugar country and Hawi was the biggest of a half dozen sugar towns. Kohala Sugar Company, which had incorporated all of the mills, closed down its operations in 1975. Hawi now has more storefronts than stores and there's really not much happening there.

The park on Hwy 250 in front of the post office is cool and shady with giant banyan trees. It would be a fine place for a picnic. Behind the park is the old sugar mill tower, a remnant of the town's former mainstay. You can still see the occasional strip of feral cane amongst the pastures outside town.

Places to Eat
Ohana Pizza on Hwy 270 has pretty good

pizza and a variety of sandwiches. Lasagne with salad and garlic bread costs $5. There's a bar and the place has a country and western feel.

Kohala Inn Bar & Restaurant on Hwy 250 near Hwy 270 is a local diner serving breakfast, lunch and dinner.

KAPAAU

The statue of Kamehameha the Great on the front lawn of the North Kohala Civic Center may look familiar. Its lei-draped and much-photographed twin stands opposite the Iolani Palace in Honolulu.

The statue was made in 1880 in Florence, Italy, by American sculptor Thomas Gould. The ship delivering it sank off the Falkland Islands and a duplicate made from the original mould arrived in 1883 and took its place in downtown Honolulu.

Later the sunken statue was recovered from the ocean floor and it completed its trip to Hawaii. The original statue was then sent here, to Kamehameha's childhood home where it stands watching the traffic trickle along in quiet Kapaau.

Kapaau has a new courthouse and police station and Kamehameha Park which includes a large, modern gymnasium and everything from a ball park to a swimming pool. The town has a little library, a Bank of Hawaii and a couple of interesting shops.

Still, it's an ageing town. The only crowd is at the senior centre, which is part of the civic centre. The senior citizens sometimes staff a table on the porch with visitor information.

Kalahikiola Church

Protestant missionaries Elias and Ellen Bond, who arrived in Kohala in 1841, built Kalahikiola Church in 1855. An earthquake damaged it in 1973 but it's since been restored and the church is still in use today.

If you want to take a look, turn mauka off Hwy 270 onto an unmarked driveway about half a mile east of Kamehameha's statue, near the 24-mile marker. The church is about half a mile up from the highway.

The land and buildings on the drive in to the church are part of the Bond estate, proof enough that the missionary life wasn't total deprivation.

If the doors of the church seem to be locked it's because they don't push or pull, but rather slide open.

Places to Eat

Don's Family Deli on Hwy 270 is the place to eat in Kapaau. Mahimahi sandwiches, quiche with salad or tofu burgers cost $4. They also have meat and cheese sandwiches, Portuguese bean soup, espresso and cappuccino. New Age music plays in the background.

For dessert you could walk down the street to *Tropical Dreams* for a scoop of gourmet ice cream or sorbet or one of their macadamia butter cookies. Tropical Dreams makes delicious macadamia nut butters in flavours such as Kona coffee, mocha java, or ambrosia with chunks of pineapple, currants and almonds. They're sold here and in speciality shops around the island and make a great gift. They give out little samples of the nut butters, coffees and cookies they sell.

Mit's Drive-In is just east of Kapaau Post Office, next to H Naito general store. Mit's has inexpensive breakfasts, plate lunches and burgers.

KAPAAU TO POLOLU VALLEY
Kamehameha Rock

Kamehameha Rock is on the right-hand side of the road, about two miles east of Kapaau, just over a small bridge. It's said that Kamehameha carried this rock up from the beach below to demonstrate his strength.

A road crew once attempted to move the rock to a different location, but though they managed to get it up onto a wagon the rock fell off – an obvious sign it wanted to stay where it was. Not wanting to mess with Kamehameha's mana, the workers obliged.

Right around the corner is the Kohala Tong Wo Society, founded in 1886. Hawaii once had many Chinese societies which provided immigrants with a place to preserve their cultural identity, speak their native language and socialise. This is the last one remaining on the Big Island.

Pololu Valley

Makapala

The little village of Makapala has a few hundred residents. The last place to get anything to drink before Pololu Valley is just past the school on the left where there's a soda machine.

Keokea Beach County Park

Keokea Beach County Park is on a somewhat scenic rocky coast. There's no sandy beach and it's not great for water activities.

The park is most active on weekends and camping is allowed on the grassy section below the pavilion. If you arrive without a permit you can get one from the caretaker who comes by in the morning. There are covered picnic areas, restrooms, showers, drinking water, barbecue grills and electricity.

The marked turn-off is about 1½ miles before Pololu Valley Lookout. The park is rather secluded and it's about a mile in from the highway.

There's an old Japanese cemetery on the way to the park. Most of the gravestones are in kanji and a few have filled sake cups in front of them.

Pololu Valley Lookout

Hwy 270 ends at a lookout looking down into the scenic Pololu Valley and out along the steep scalloped coastal cliffs to the east.

Pololu was once thickly planted with wetland taro, and the Pololu Stream fed the valley, carrying heavy rainfall from the interior to the valley floor. When the Kohala Ditch was built, however, it siphoned off much of the water and put an end to the taro production. The valley slopes are now forest reserve land.

Pololu Valley Trail The trail from the lookout down to Pololu Valley only takes about 20 minutes to walk. It's steep and can be hot walking, but it's not overly strenuous. Much of the trail is packed clay which can be slippery when wet.

Look for passion fruit to the right near the start of the trail. The round juicy yellow fruit makes a nice treat.

Cattle and horses roam in the valley. There's a gate at the bottom of the trail which keeps them in.

The black sand beach stretches for about half a mile. Driftwood collects in great quantities and on rare occasions glass fishing floats get washed up as well.

Surf is usually high in winter and though it's a bit tamer in summer, there can be rip currents year round.

Kohala Ditch

Kohala Ditch is an intricate series of ditches, tunnels and flumes that lead from Waikaloa Stream in the rugged wet interior of the Kohala Forest Reserve out to the Hawi area. Waikaloa Stream is midway between Pololu and Waipio valleys.

The ditch was built in 1906 to irrigate Kohala sugar cane fields. The last Kohala cane was cut in the 1970s, but the ditch continues to be a source of water for Kohala ranches and farms.

It was engineered by a sugar man, John Hind, with the financial backing of Samuel Parker of Parker Ranch. Kohala Ditch runs 22½ miles and was built by Japanese immigrant labourers who were paid about $1 a day for the hazardous work. More than a dozen of them died during the construction.

There were once miles of mule and footpaths along the ditch which were used for maintenance but the trails are now overgrown.

Much of the ditch runs through 19,000 acres of Kohala land which Castle & Cooke recently sold to a Japanese developer.

Places to Stay

Kohala Lodge (Box 200, Hawi, HI 96719; tel 889-5577), at the intersection of Hwy 270 and Hwy 250 in downtown Hawi, has been through a succession of names and management. When we were last there it appeared to be largely low-income housing and the managers weren't particularly friendly or interested in dealing with overnight guests. However, a new and friendlier manager has since taken over and there are 23 motel-style units. Rates are $35/39.50 for singles/doubles and longer stays cost as little as $110/360 a week/month.

Kohala Club Hotel (tel 889-6793) is midway between Hawi and Kapaau makai of Hwy 270. Even though there's a sign,

you get the impression they don't see many tourists there. The 'hotel' is a little duplex cottage with two very basic rooms that are connected with a shared bathroom and each room costs $30.

Waimea

Waimea has a pretty setting in the foothills of the Kohala Mountains at an elevation of 2670 feet. It's cooler than the coast, with more clouds and fog. There are gentle rolling hills and frequent afternoon rainbows.

This is the headquarters of Parker Ranch, Hawaii's largest cattle ranch, which spreads across nearly one-ninth of the Big Island. Almost everything in Waimea is owned by, run by or leased by Parker Ranch.

Waimea has its cowboy influences, but it's rapidly growing and becoming more sophisticated. It's the main town serving the new subdivisions being developed on former ranches in the Kohala Mountains. Many of the newcomers are wealthy mainlanders. Waimea is also home to some of the international astronomers who work on Mauna Kea.

Waimea has a handful of restaurants started by renegade chefs from the island's best hotels, with food so good that people regularly drive up from Kona and even fly in from Maui. There are several places to stay, including some delightful B&Bs.

This is not a big tourist town with a lot of action or sightseeing attractions. There are a couple of museums and the green pastures are scenic, but for most visitors Waimea is just a stopover on the drive between Kona and Hilo.

Information

Waimea is also referred to as Kamuela. Waimea's post office is named Kamuela, the Hawaiian spelling of Samuel. Though some say the post office was named after former postmaster Samuel Spencer, most claim it's for Samuel Parker of Parker Ranch fame.

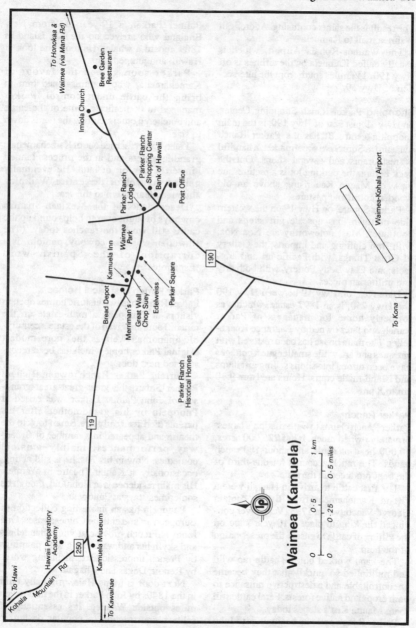

To Honokaa &
Waimea (via Mana Rd)

Bree Garden
Restaurant

Imiola Church

Parker Ranch
Shopping Center

Parker Ranch
Lodge

Bank of Hawaii

Post Office

190

Waimea Park

Kamuela Inn

Bread Depot

Merriman's

Great Wall
Chop Suey

Edelweiss

Parker Square

Waimea-Kohala Airport

To Kona

19

Kohala Mountain Rd

250

Hawaii Preparatory
Academy

Kamuela Museum

Parker Ranch
Historical Homes

To Hawi

To Kawaihae

Waimea (Kamuela)

1 km

0 · 5 miles

0 · 5

0 · 25

0 · 5

The result is the same: confusing. Address all Waimea mail to Kamuela.

The Waimea-Kohala Airport, which is usually called Kamuela by the airlines is off Hwy 190, 1¾ miles south from the intersection of Hwy 19.

Shopping Parker Ranch Shopping Center, on Hwy 19 just east of Hwy 190, is the main shopping centre. It has the Parker Ranch museum, a Sure Save supermarket, a handful of restaurants and several shops. Out the back behind the parking lot is a picturesque view of Mauna Kea rising above an old wooden corral and pastures.

Parker Square, on Hwy 19 on the western side of town, has upscale gift shops and boutiques. Most noteworthy are Noa Noa, with Bali clothing and imports; the Gallery of Great Things, with Pacific art and artefacts; and Clay Body Pottery, with both arty and utilitarian pieces.

Hale Kea, on Hwy 19 between Hwy 190 and Hwy 250, is an 1897 estate, which was formerly home for managers of Parker Ranch and later owned by Laurance Rockefeller. The main house has been restored with antiques and art, while smaller guest cottages have been turned into shops selling gift items and island-made crafts. Hours are from 9.30 am to 8 pm.

Parker Ranch
Parker Ranch claims to be the nation's largest privately owned ranch. It has 225,000 acres, 50,000 head of cattle and about 100 ranch hands. The ranch accounts for one-third of the beef produced in the state.

The first cattle to arrive in Hawaii were a gift to Kamehameha from British captain George Vancouver in 1793. Vancouver convinced the king to place a 10-year kapu on the killing of cattle to ensure the preservation of the herd.

The kapu worked but the cattle ran wild and multiplied so quickly that they became uncontrollable and a destructive nuisance to both crops and native forests. Feral cattle still roam Mauna Kea's slopes today.

Parker Ranch owes its beginnings to John Palmer Parker, a 19-year-old from New England who arrived on the Big Island in 1809 aboard a whaler. He took one look at Hawaii and jumped ship.

Parker soon gained the favour of Kamehameha, who commissioned him to bring the cattle under control. Parker managed to domesticate some of the cattle and butchered others, cutting the herds down to size.

Later, Parker married one of Kamehameha's granddaughters and in the process landed himself a tidy bit of land. He eventually gained control of the entire Waikoloa ahupuaa clear down to the sea.

Descendants of the Mexican-Spanish cowboys brought over to help round up the cattle still work the ranches today. (The Hawaiian word for cowboy, paniolo, is a corruption of the Spanish word 'Espanoles'.)

Parker Ranch Historical Homes
Parker Ranch has two historic homes open to visitors at Puuopelu, a mini-estate on the ranch. Tours are given of the estate's century-old manor as well as the more modest original Parker home which has been reconstructed next door.

Current Parker Ranch owner Richard Palmer Smart, the great-great-great grandson of John Palmer Parker, was raised at Puuopelu by his grandmother after his parents died at an early age. Smart took to the theatre and appeared in a number of Broadway performances, mainly musical comedies. Now in his 70s, he is still acting, occasionally at Kahilu Theatre in Waimea. His main residence is in Honolulu, though he sometimes stays at Puuopelu.

Puuopelu has an interesting collection of European art and antique Chinese vases. One room is French provincial with chandeliers and skylights and walls hung with paintings by French impressionists, including works by Renoir, Degas and Chagall.

Next door is Mana Hale, originally built in the 1840s by John Parker in the hills seven miles outside Waimea. It's essentially of saltbox construction, a popular design in

Parker's native Massachusetts where the sloping roof deflects winter's cold north-east winds. The house is simple and aesthetically striking with walls, ceilings and floors made entirely of koa. The interior of Mana Hale was recently dismantled board by board and rebuilt here at Puuopelu but the exterior is a replica.

Mana Hale is decorated with period furnishings and interesting old photos of the hardy-looking Parker clan.

The turn-off to the homes is on Hwy 190, about three-quarters of a mile south of its intersection with Hwy 19, on the west side of the road. Hours are 9.30 am to 4.30 pm daily and admission costs $5.

Parker Ranch Visitor Center

Parker Ranch Visitor Center in the Parker Ranch Shopping Center is a little museum of the ranch's history showcasing Parker family memorabilia such as portraits, lineage charts, quilts and dishes. There's a little cowboy hut with saddles and branding irons.

There are also stone adzes, lava bowls, tapa bedcovers and other Hawaiian artefacts, though for Hawaiiana alone other Big Island museums have more extensive collections. Actually the museum is not terribly dynamic. Perhaps most interesting are the old photos and the 15-minute movie on Parker Ranch, including footage of cowboys rushing cattle into the sea and lifting them by slings onto the decks of waiting steamers.

A separate room is dedicated to Duke Kahanamoku. Duke, who was of royal Hawaiian lineage, won Olympic gold in the 100-metre freestyle swim in 1912 and 1920 and he is credited with introducing surfing to Australia in 1912. Duke went on to play small roles in Hollywood movies, was sheriff of Honolulu for 25 years and was the city's 'ambassador' until his death in 1968 at age 77. The museum holds his trophies and mementoes, including a photo of Britain's Queen Elizabeth dancing the hula with Duke in a Honolulu restaurant.

Hours are from 9 am to 4.30 pm daily and admission costs $4.

Parker Ranch Tours

Parker Ranch (tel 885-7655) runs a shuttle bus every 10 to 15 minutes from 9 am to 3.30 pm daily from the visitor centre to the ranch stables, then to the historic homes at Puuopelu and back to the visitor centre. The fee of $15 includes admissions.

A second tour takes you to these areas plus includes lunch and visits to the original Mana Hale homestead, the Parker family cemetery and working field areas for $38. There are two tours daily, from 9 am to 1 pm and from noon to 4 pm.

There's also a 25-minute helicopter tour of the ranch and the nearby Kohala mountain range for $70.

Children are charged half the price on all Parker Ranch tours and attractions except for the helicopter.

Church Row

Waimea's churches are lined up side by side in an area called Church Row. Imiola Congregational Church is the oldest and the green steepled church next to it is Ke Ola Mau Loa Church, an all-Hawaiian church. Buddhists, Baptists and Mormons also have churches in the row.

Imiola Congregational Church Waimea's first Christian church was a grass hut built in 1830. It was replaced in 1838 by a wood and coral structure, built with coral stones carved out of the reef and carried inland on the backs of Hawaiian Christians. They named it Imiola, 'seeking salvation'.

The current building was constructed in 1857 and restored in 1976. The interior is simple and beautiful and it's built entirely of koa, most of it dating back to the original construction.

In the churchyard is the grave of missionary Lorenzo Lyons who arrived in 1832 and spent 54 years in Waimea. He wrote many of the hymns, including the popular 'Hawaii Aloha', that are still sung in Hawaiian here each Sunday. Also in the garden is the church bell, too heavy for the church roof to support.

Kamuela Museum

There's a lot of history crammed into the homespun Kamuela Museum (tel 885-4724) at the junction of Hwy 19 and Hwy 250. There's all sorts of Hawaiiana including tapa beaters, 18th century feather leis braided with human hair, fish hooks made of human bones, a stone knuckle duster and a dog-toothed death cup. Some items are very rare and many once belonged to royalty. The museum has Kamehameha the Great's sacred chair and tables of teak and marble from Iolani Palace.

This museum is like one of those Chinese grocery stores that has one of everything – you just have to find it. The non- Hawaiian part of the collection ranges from a Tibetan prayer horn and stuffed moose heads from Canada to a piece of rope used on the Apollo II mission.

Equally interesting is the owner, Albert Solomon – a spry octogenarian, colourful storyteller and former boxer. His wife Harriet is a descendant of John Palmer Parker.

There's a great view of Mauna Kea and Mauna Loa framed by a picture window inside the museum as well as from out beyond the parking area. Hours are 8 am to 5 pm daily. Admission costs $2.50 for adults, $1 for children under 12.

Places to Stay

Waimea is upcountry and if you equate Hawaii with beach life and constant sun you may be disappointed making a base here. If country settings and open spaces are what you're looking for, there are some fine choices.

The best of them is *Puu Manu Cottage* (Doug & Dodie MacArthur, Box 1958, Kamuela, HI 96743; tel 885-6247). This B&B has horses in the back pasture and a straight-on view of Mauna Kea out through French glass doors. The setting is a knock-out. The cottage has skylights, raised beam ceilings, two bedrooms, a modern kitchen, a fireplace, phone and even a stereo. It's $85 for two, but big enough to hold two couples comfortably. It's in a secluded spot with plenty of privacy. There are bicycles you can

use as well. It's two miles from Waimea on the Hilo side.

Hawaii Country Cottage (Box 1717, Kamuela, HI 96743; tel 885-7441) is good value at $65. This B&B has double and single beds, a large living room with fireplace, Douglas fir floors and raised beam ceilings. The owner, Gale, has the 'tutu nene' cottage industry making the stuffed cotton nene found in gift shops around the island. There's a distant sunset view of the ocean and a stream running alongside the property. It's just a little way up Hwy 250.

Waimea Gardens Cottage (Box 563, Kamuela, HI 96743; tel 885-4550) looks like an old shack from the outside, but it's nice inside with a full kitchen and rustic charm. You can walk right outside the cottage amidst the clucking hens and collect your breakfast eggs. Owner Charlie Campbell is a veterinarian. He provides blankets but there's no fireplace and it might get a bit chilly on a winter's night. It's near the intersection of Hwy 19 and Hwy 250. The rate is $75.

Puu Manu, Hawaii Country and Waimea Gardens cottages all have privacy, cooking facilities and TVs. Smoking is limited to the 'great outdoors'. All include breakfast or fixings to make your own, have three-day minimums and charge $10 each for a third or fourth person.

Kamuela Inn (Box 1994, Kamuela, HI 96743; tel 885-4243) is somewhat in between an inn and a small hotel in both layout and atmosphere. The cheaper of its 20 rooms are rather small but all have some nice touches like ceramic Chinese lamps or framed prints. Standard rooms are $44 to $55 and suites with kitchenettes are $72 for up to four people. All include continental breakfast.

Parker Ranch Lodge (Box 458, Kamuela, HI 96743; tel 885- 4100) is a one-story motel. The rooms in the new wing are a bit spiffier, while those in the older wing are larger, less boxy and have kitchenettes. All have good views of the mountains out the back. All 20 rooms are $52/58 for singles/doubles.

The Log House B&B (Bruce & Robin Hall, Box 1495, Honokaa, HI 96727; tel

775-9990) is in Ahualoa on the Old Mamalahoa Hwy east of Waimea. It's a neat place, quiet and friendly. The exterior is of white pine logs and the inside looks like a New England inn. A fire is lit most nights in the stone fireplace in the downstairs common room. There's a room downstairs with a king-size bed and private bathroom for $65. Upstairs is a three- room suite with queen and double beds, bathroom and living room for $80. A hearty breakfast is included.

Places to Eat

In a town where Volvos are taking over, it's important to have restaurants with name chefs. There are now four chefs who have left the Waikoloa resort scene to start their own restaurants in the hills of Waimea: Merriman's, Edelweiss, Bree Garden and Hale Kea.

Merriman's (tel 885-6822) in Opelo Plaza has American regional cuisine, with a focus on fresh products from Big Island farmers. It uses local fern shoots, herbs from Kealakekua and nori and freshwater shrimp from a local aquaculturist. A speciality is the wok-charred ahi, blackened-style on the outside and like sashimi on the inside. Other dishes include pineapple lamb curry served Thai-style with rice and papaya-grilled flank steak. Vegetarian meals are available on request. Two people can have an excellent dinner here with wine for $50. Chef Pete Merriman made his reputation at the Gallery Restaurant in Mauna Lani before starting up here. It's open from 11.30 am to 1.30 pm weekdays, 5.30 to 9 pm nightly and for Sunday brunch from 10.30 am to 1.30 pm. Reservations are recommended.

Edelweiss (tel 885-6800) on Hwy 19 also has a reputation for good food, though heavy on the meats. German chef Hans-Peter Hager has built his following around such German-Austrian dishes as roast pork with sauerkraut and wiener schnitzel. Full dinners cost $11.50 to $18. Lunches are lighter with burgers, sandwiches and salads starting at about $5. Lunch is from 11.30 am to 1.30 pm, dinner is from 5 pm and they really pack 'em in.

In 1989 Chef Bernd Bree left the Mauna Kea Beach Hotel and opened up *Bree Garden Restaurant* (tel 885-5888). The menu is continental with a different ethnic dish each night. It features locally grown food and has vegetarian dishes. It's behind the Ironwood Center and open 4.30 to 9.30 pm daily.

The newest arrival is the restaurant at *Hale Kea* estate, with chef Steve Hupp, formerly of the Mauna Lani Resort. The menu features fresh fish, island lamb, steaks and seafood. Lunch is 11 am to 3.30 pm, dinner is from 5 pm (reservations are recommended; tel 885-6095) and Sunday brunch is from 10 am to 3 pm.

The *Bread Depot* in Opelo Plaza bakes its own breads and pastries. At lunch time, 11.30 to 3 pm, they make good sandwiches for $3.75. Homemade soup or chowder is $2.50. This is a busy place and the five small tables are often full.

Auntie Alice's in the Parker Ranch Shopping Center has doughnuts, pies and coffee-shop-style meals. You can get two eggs, home fries and toast there for $2.50 and sandwiches and burgers in the $3 to $4 range. It's open 6 am to 5 pm daily except Sundays.

Waimea Corral at the Parker Ranch Shopping Center has a lunch time soup and salad bar for $6.95 or with a few lacklustre buffet dishes for $9. It's open from 11 am to 2.30 pm and 4.30 to 8.30 pm.

Paniolo Country Inn, next to Parker Lodge, has the same food as Paniolo Pizza in Kailua-Kona. Pizza, burgers and other family-style meals are fairly inexpensive, particularly at lunch time, but they're not exciting.

If you're just looking for something light, you could pick up a power bar, yoghurt and juice at *Big Island Natural Foods* in the Parker Ranch Shopping Center. They have a good selection for a shopping centre health food store.

Entertainment

Waimea's entertainment scene is limited, perhaps because cowboys rise at dawn and astronomers work all night!

Kahilu Theatre at the Parker Ranch

Shopping Center presents occasional plays, classical music concerts, dance troupes and other productions.

Getting There & Away

Waimea is 40 miles from Kona along Hwy 190. From Kona the road climbs out of residential areas into a mix of lava flows and dry grassy rangeland studded with prickly pear cactus. There's a little one-room church, broad distant coastal views, wide-open spaces and tall roadside grasses that have an incredible golden hue in the morning light.

If you come back on this road at night the highway reflectors light up like an airport runway to guide you along.

Waimea to Honokaa Hwy 19 heads east from Waimea to Honokaa through rolling hills and cattle pastures, with views of Mauna Kea to the south.

For a peaceful, scented backroad turn right off Hwy 19 onto the Old Mamalahoa Hwy near the 52-mile marker. (If you're coming from Hilo, turn left at the 43-mile marker opposite Tex Drive Inn and then take the next immediate right.)

The 10-mile detour winds through hill country, with small roadside ranches, old wooden fences and grazing horses. This is an untouristed Hawaii. Nobody's in a hurry on this road, if they're on it at all and it's also a great alternative route for cyclists.

AROUND WAIMEA
Mana-Keanakolu Road

To get closer to Mauna Kea for photography or views you could drive part way down Mana Rd, the start of a road which curves around the eastern flank of Mauna Kea. It begins off Hwy 19 at the 55-mile marker on the eastern side of Waimea. After 15 miles the road becomes Keanakolu Rd and continues about 25 miles before reaching Summit Rd (the road leading up Mauna Kea) near the Humuula Sheep Station.

Only the first part of the Waimea section is paved. The entire road is passable on horseback or by 4WD vehicle but you have to open and close a couple of dozen cattle

gates as you proceed. It's mostly ranchers and hunters that come this way.

David Douglas Memorial A memorial to David Douglas, the Scottish botanist for whom the Douglas fir tree is named, is on Mana-Keanakolu Rd about halfway between Waimea and the Saddle Rd. Douglas died in 1834 at this spot.

The circumstances of Douglas' death are somewhat mysterious as his gored body was found trapped with an angry bull at the bottom of a pit. Hunters commonly dug such pits and camouflaged them with underbrush as a means of trapping feral cattle, but the probability of both Douglas and a bull falling into the same hole seemed highly suspicious. Fingers were pointed at Ned Gurney, an escaped convict from Botany Bay who had been hiding out in the area and who had been the last person to see Douglas alive.

Hamakua Coast

The Hamakua Coast is the north-eastern coast of the Big Island, stretching 50 miles from Waipio Valley down to the city of Hilo.

From Waimea, it's 15 miles east on Hwy 19 to the town of Honokaa. If you detour there and drive nine miles north-west on Hwy 240 you'll reach Waipio Valley Lookout, one of the most spectacular valley views in Hawaii.

Much of the north end of the Hamakua Coast is owned by Hamakua Sugar and is planted in vast fields of green sugar cane. The rest of the Hamakua Coast is rugged with steep cliffs and luxuriant rainforests laced with streams and waterfalls. The Hawaii Belt Rd (Hwy 19) is an impressive engineering feat where it runs along the wet windward slopes of Mauna Kea, spanning deep green ravines with a series of sweeping cantilevered bridges. Hamakua's character comes out in its road signs: 'Slow Moving Cane Trucks' and 'Road Subject To Washout'.

Hwy 19 also passes small towns that are

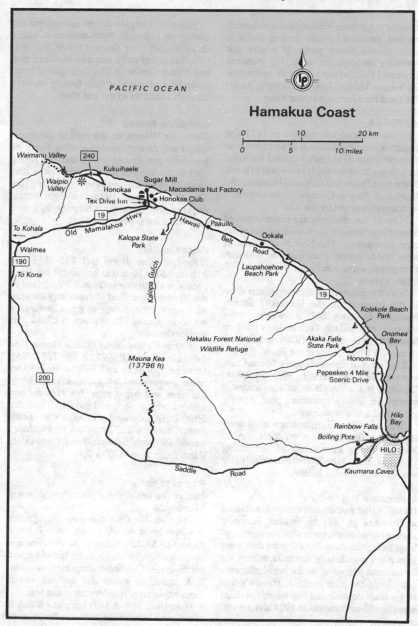

Hamakua Coast

PACIFIC OCEAN

0   10   20 km

0   5   10 miles

Waimanu Valley

Waipio Valley

Kukuihaele

240

Honokaa

Sugar Mill

Macadamia Nut Factory

Tex Drive Inn

Honokaa Club

19

Hawaii

Paauilo

Old Mamalahoa Hwy

To Kohala

Waimea

190

To Kona

Kalopa State Park

Belt

Kalopa Gulch

Ookala

Road

Laupahoehoe Beach Park

19

200

Mauna Kea (13796 ft)

Hakalau Forest National Wildlife Refuge

Kolekole Beach Park

Akaka Falls State Park

Onomea Bay

Honomu

Pepeekeo 4 Mile Scenic Drive

Hilo Bay

Rainbow Falls

Boiling Pots

HILO

Kaumana Caves

Saddle   Road

home to sugar cane workers and homesteaders and unmarked roads leading down to unfrequented beach parks. If you're just whizzing through on your way between Kona and Hilo, at the very least make time for Waipio Valley Lookout, majestic Akaka Falls and the four-mile scenic drive.

HONOKAA

Honokaa's sugar mill opened in 1873 and sugar has been the mainstay of this town ever since. In those days flumes carried the sugar cane down from the fields to the mill in town. Sugar cane fields still surround Honokaa and Hamakua Sugar Company maintains a working mill down by the bay.

Most of the residents are descendants of immigrants brought in to work on the sugar cane plantations. The Scotch and English were first to arrive. Then came the Chinese, Portuguese, Japanese, Puerto Ricans and Filipinos in turn.

With a population of 2000, this quiet town is the biggest on the Hamakua Coast. Mamame St (Hwy 240) is the main street through town and most of the shops lined up here date to around the 1920s and haven't changed a whole lot over the years.

The centre of activity is the Honokaa Club, a hotel and restaurant, built in 1908. Honokaa has a couple of antique shops, a post office, library, swimming pool, grocery stores and a few restaurants.

In ancient Hawaii, Honokaa was an overnight stop for travellers on their way to Waipio. Today there's talk of developing Honokaa into a bedroom community for workers at Waikoloa hotels.

Macadamia Nut Factory

Hawaii's first macadamia trees were planted in Honokaa in 1881 by William Purvis, a sugar plantation manager who brought seedlings from Australia. For 40 years they were grown in Hawaii, as in Australia, mainly for ornamental purposes, as the nut shells were considered too hard to crack. Hawaii's first large-scale commercial macadamia orchard was planted in Honokaa in 1924 and it's still producing.

Hawaiian Holiday has its macadamia nut factory on Lehua St, three-quarters of a mile down the hill from the post office. For visitors, this is basically just a store where nuts and cookies are sold. The 'self-guided tour' essentially means watching factory workers through windows in the gift shop.

Kamaaina Woods

Kamaaina Woods, on the road to the macadamia nut factory, makes quality bowls of koa, milo and mango woods and everything sold in the shop is made there. Prices start around $18 with many bowls well over $100. The thinnest and lightest-weight bowls require the greatest craftmanship and command the highest prices.

Places to Stay

Honokaa Club Hotel (tel 775-0678) on Mamane St in Honokaa has simple but clean rooms, with private baths and TVs. Many of the 20 rooms are filled with monthly lodgers, so it's not always easy to get a room on a walk-in basis. Rates are $29/32 for singles/doubles.

Waipio Wayside B&B (Jackie Horne, Box 840, Honokaa, HI 96727; tel 775-0275), between Honokaa and Waipio, is an older home surrounded by gardens, macadamia nut trees and sugar cane. It's pleasant and relaxed with a deck and gazebo. There are four nicely decorated bedrooms with shared bath. There's a full breakfast that includes smoothies with bananas from the garden. Rates range from $40 to $60.

Places to Eat

Except for Tex's, these places are all along Mamane St.

The *Honokaa Club*'s massive dining room is where most people eat in town. It has a variety of $3.75 lunches of sandwiches and burgers which include a limited salad bar and coffee or tea. The dinner menu is fairly extensive, including steaks and seafood, and is more expensive. It serves breakfast too.

Honokaa Pizza & Subs has pizza which is bready and unexciting, calzones for $5, subs for about $4 and 60 cent hot dogs. This is the local video game hangout.

Dairy Queen has the usual fast food, with hamburgers for $1.50, plate lunches from $3.75 and soft ice cream.

At *Richard's Fruit Stand* the ongoing special is six papayas for $1. It has a good variety of other seasonal local fruits as well.

Tex Drive Inn is up on Hwy 19 and if you're driving by in the morning, say on your way from Waimea to Hilo, you could stop over for a couple of malasadas (45 cents each) and a cup of coffee. Malasadas are Portuguese pastries of sweet fried dough, rolled in sugar and served warm – like a doughnut without the hole. There's a convenience store next door and a laundromat across the road.

KUKUIHAELE
About seven miles beyond Honokaa heading toward Waipio Valley, on the right, there's a loop road off Mamane St which goes down to the tiny village of Kukuihaele.

The village's Last Chance Store is just that, as there's no food or supplies in Waipio Valley. At Last Chance you can get Alta-Dena yoghurt, crackers and canned food. Hard-boiled eggs cost a quarter, though most items are marked up a bit more than at shops in the town centre. Waipio Wagon Tours and the post office are also here.

Farther down the road is Waipio Woodworks which sells quality island-made crafts and where arrangements are made for the Waipio Valley Shuttle.

Kukuihaele means 'travelling light' and refers to the ghostly night marchers who pass through on their way to Waipio.

Places to Stay
Hamakua Hideaway (Box 5104, Kukuihaele, HI 96727; tel 775-7425) in Kukuihaele is a cottage with a fine view down the coast to Waipio Valley. There's a fireplace, sunken tub, kitchen and the sounds of a 50-foot waterfall which you can hear but not see. Rates are $50 a night, $300 a week and $1000 a month.

WAIPIO VALLEY
Hwy 240 ends abruptly at the edge of cliffs overlooking Waipio Valley. The view is glorious. Waipio is the largest and southernmost of the seven spectacular amphitheatre valleys on the windward side of the Kohala Mountains. Waipio is a mile wide at the coast and nearly six miles deep. Some of the near-vertical pali wrapping around the valley reach heights of 2000 feet.

Everything is lushly green, a mix of tangled jungle, flowering plants, taro patches and waterfalls. The mouth of the valley is fronted by a black sand beach and the Waipio Stream divides the beach in two.

On the opposite cliff face you can see the switchback trail which leads to Waimanu Valley and glimpses of the rugged coastal cliffs which stretch out to the north-west.

The narrow, paved, mile-long road which leads down into Waipio Valley is so steep (25% grade) that it's restricted to all but hikers and 4WD vehicles. A couple of tour companies make the run daily, and the walk down is easier than it looks. There are restrooms and drinking water at the lookout.

History
Waipio means 'curving water' and is often referred to as the 'Valley of the Kings'. In ancient times it was the political and religious centre of Hawaii and home to the highest chiefs. Waipio was a very sacred place and there were a number of important heiaus there. The most sacred, Pakaalana, was also the site of one of the island's two major puuhonua or places of refuge.

Umi, the Big Island's ruling chief in the early 1500s, is credited with laying out Waipio's taro fields, many of which are still in production today. Waipio is also where Kamehameha the Great received his fearsome war god.

According to oral histories at least 10,000 people – or possibly many times more – lived in Waipio during pre-contact times. It was the most fertile and productive valley on the Big Island.

In 1823 William Ellis, the first missionary to visit the valley, guessed the population to

Air Plants

be about 1300. Later in that century immigrants, mainly Chinese, began to settle in Waipio. At one time the valley had schools, restaurants and churches as well as a hotel, post office and jailhouse.

In 1946 the most devastating tsunami in Hawaii's history swept great waves far back into Waipio Valley. Afterwards most people evacuated and resettled elsewhere on the Big Island and Waipio has been sparsely populated ever since.

Waipio Valley Today

Taro remains important in Waipio. Most of the valley's 30 to 40 residents have taro patches and you may see farmers knee- deep in the muddy ponds.

Other Waipio crops include lotus (for its roots), avocados, breadfruit, oranges and limes. There are kukui and mahogany trees, huge elephant ears, Turk's cap hibiscus, air plants, ferns and vines, and pink and white impatiens which climb the cliff walls along the road.

Most of Waipio Valley is owned by the Bishop Museum which has been negotiating selling the land to the state's Department of Land & Natural Resources.

Exploring Waipio

The walk from the lookout to the valley floor and back is not terribly difficult, though if you are not in good shape you may notice some forgotten muscles the next day. It takes about 30 minutes to get down and about 45 minutes to go up. The road is carved into the cliffs at an angle that provides hikers with shade much of the way.

From the bottom of the hill, if you walk to the left for about five minutes there's a fair chance you'll see wild horses grazing along the stream. It's a picturesque scene set against the steep valley cliffs.

You'll also get a distant view of Hiilawe Falls, which with a sheer drop of more than 1000 feet, is Hawaii's highest free-fall waterfall. Hiking to Hiilawe Falls is difficult as there's no real footpath and it's mainly bushwhacking. There are a lot of 'Private Property' signs and generally the further back in the valley you go, the less friendly the dogs become.

According to legend the god Lono looked down from the heavens and discovered Kaikilani, the beautiful woman who was to become his wife, sitting beside Hiilawe Falls. Lono slid down to the falls on a rainbow – which is definitely the preferred way to get there.

In the 1970s an elaborate mirrored restaurant surrounded by a carp pond was built back in the valley. It looks straight on to Hiilawe Falls in one direction and out to the valley mouth in the other. The location is lovely but the restaurant wasn't allowed to open due to objections from residents and it was later given to the Bishop Museum.

Waipio Beach

It takes about 10 minutes to walk to the beach from the bottom of the hill. After heavy rains, the road can be like a slippery mud pie.

Waipio Beach is lined with ironwood trees that act as an effective windbreak against the strong wind that sometimes picks up here. It was an ancient surfing beach that occasionally still sees some action but there are usually rip currents and when the surf is high the waters can be outright treacherous.

Walk along the beach toward the stream mouth for a good view of Kaluahine Falls which cascade down the coastal cliffs to the east. It's easier to look at than to get to however, as the coast between Waipio Beach and Kaluahine Falls is loose lava rock and rather rough walking and dangerous as the surf sometimes breaks up over the uppermost rocks. Local lore has it that ghost marchers periodically come down from the upper valley and march down the beach where there's a hidden entrance into the netherworld, called Lua O Milu.

Precautions

As you walk around the valley, you might come across wild horses or stray dogs along the road though both tend to veer off if you come too close.

Because of all the feral animals roaming this Eden-like valley, precautions against leptospirosis are advisable (see the Health section). Taro farmers in Waipio have one of the highest incidence rates on the islands.

Don't drink from the Waipio Stream without first boiling or treating the water. There's a freshwater spring up from the beach that most people use for drinking water.

Waipio Tours

Waipio Valley Shuttle first introduced tours into the valley some 20 years ago. The tour lasts 1½ hours and though Land Rovers are used, it's not all that adventurous. It's more of a taxi ride for those who don't care to walk down. The driver points out waterfalls, identifies plants and throws in a bit of history. Sit as close to the driver as you can as it's nearly impossible to hear the spiel if you're bouncing around in the back.

Reservations (tel 775-7121) are made at Waipio Woodworks in Kukuihaele. It costs $20 for adults, $10 for children under 12. The tours run on the hour from 8 am to 4 pm daily. Despite the name, it's not really a shuttle. However if you've already walked into the valley and don't want to hike back up you can try flagging them down at the bottom of the jeep road. They sometimes take passengers back up to the lookout for $5.

Hawaii Resorts Transportation Company (tel 885-7484) has a 1½-hour mini-van tour into Waipio Valley for $20, starting at the macadamia nut factory in Honokaa.

Akamai Tours (tel 329-7324) has a half-day mini-van tour to Waipio Valley for $35. It leaves from Kona and includes Waimea.

Waipio Valley Wagon Tours (Box 1340, Honokaa, HI 96727; tel 775-9518) has two-hour valley tours in a 10-passenger open-air wagon pulled by two mules, Lehua and Nui. Tours leave from Waipio Valley Lookout at 10, 11.30 am, 1.30 and 3 pm. Passengers are taken to the valley floor by 4WD where they meet the wagon. It's $25 and arrangements are made at Last Chance Store in Kukuihaele.

Switchback Trail to Waimanu Valley

The switchback trail leading up the northwest cliff face of Waipio Valley is an ancient Hawaiian footpath. Though it looks arduous, it really isn't all that bad if you're not carrying a heavy backpack. It's a well-beaten path, a few feet deep in places, almost like walking in a little trough.

Doing part of the trail makes a nice day hike if you're camping in Waipio. It takes about 1½ hours from the floor of Waipio Valley to the third ravine where there are little pools and a small waterfall. The trail is used by hunters as well as hikers and you might come across old timers on donkeys heading for the backwoods to hunt wild boar.

The trail continues up and down a series of ravines to Waimanu Valley. From Waipio to Waimanu it's about nine miles. About two-thirds of the way along there's a trail shelter.

Waimanu is a smaller valley than Waipio though it's similar in appearance. Now abandoned, it once had a sizeable Hawaiian settlement.

Most of Waimanu Valley is estuarine sanctuary and belongs to the state. It's OK to camp and you don't need a permit but as with all streams in Hawaii, boil or treat the water before drinking.

Places to Stay

Tom Araki's hotel (c/o Sueno Araki, 25 Malama Place, Hilo, HI 96720; tel 775-0368) is back to basics on the floor of Waipio Valley. The hotel is about a 15-minute walk inland from the bottom of the hill, just on the other side of the stream. It once served Peace Corps instructors who trained new recruits in the valley before they went off on assignment in other Pacific and Asian jungles.

The hotel has five rooms in a straight line looking out on a taro patch and it's all quite in keeping with its surroundings. The rooms are rustic and simple, but comfortable enough, and blankets and linens are provided. You'll have to bring in all your own food. There's no refrigerator or electricity, but there is a communal kitchen with a double gas burner, sink and a jug of drinking water. Kerosene lanterns provide lighting and it's a custom to bring along a bottle of sake to pass the evening.

Tom is often booked out and suggests making reservations at least three weeks in advance, though we found rooms available without a reservation when we were there. Rates are $10 per person.

Camping Hamakua Sugar Company (tel 776-1211) issues permits for camping on the section of Waipio Beach they control. Permits are free but must be picked up in person at their office, which is next to the post office in Paauilo, just off Hwy 19 about six miles south of Honokaa. The crux of the application seems to be a release and a promise to carry in a shovel to bury waste and to carry out your trash. The office is open from 7.30 am to 4 pm Monday to Friday.

Not all campers here know about permits. We met people who had been camping for more than a week without them and some locals said it's OK to just camp along the beach for a day or two as long as you respect the area.

KALOPA STATE PARK

Kalopa State Park is a few miles south-east of Honokaa and about three miles inland from the marked turn-off on Hwy 19.

The park contains 100 acres of native rainforest as well as picnic sites, camping sites in a fragrant eucalyptus grove and cabins that hold up to eight people. It's at an elevation of 2000 feet and cooler than the coast. Kalopa averages about 90 inches of rain a year.

A new four-acre arboretum to the right of the park entrance contains both native and Polynesian introduced plants. Though the tropical plants brought to Hawaii by the early Polynesian settlers have problems with the temperatures up there, native koa is thriving. The first year the seedlings were planted they shot up eight feet!

A nature trail just beyond the arboretum loops for three-quarters of a mile through an ancient ohia forest where some of the trees are more than three feet in diameter.

There are also hikes to Kalopa Gulch in the adjoining forest reserve. The hike along Robusta Lane starts on the left after the caretaker's house. It's about three-quarters of a mile round-trip to this gulch (ravine). A trail continues along the rim of the gulch for another mile. The deep gulch was formed by melting glaciers that originated at Mauna Kea.

An easily spotted native forest bird here is the elepaio. It's brown with a white rump and about the size of a sparrow and it makes a loud whistle that mimics its name.

LAUPAHOEHOE POINT

Laupahoehoe means 'leaf of pahoehoe lava'. It's a flat peninsula-like point jutting out from the coastal cliffs, formed by a late eruption of Mauna Kea which poured lava down a ravine and out into the sea.

Laupahoehoe Point is midway between Honokaa and Hilo. A highway sign marks the steep winding road down to the point. There are views of the north coast cliffs on the way down and after heavy rains waterfalls come to life in all directions.

Tragedy hit Laupahoehoe on 1 April 1946

when tsunami waves up to 30 feet high wiped out the schoolhouse on the point, killing 20 children and four adults. After the tsunami the whole town moved uphill, though a few families have since settled back in. A monument down by the water lists those who died.

Laupahoehoe is a rugged coastal area and is not suitable for swimming. The surf is usually rough and pounding and can sometimes crash up over the rocks and onto the lower parking lot near the monument.

Inter-island boats once landed here. Many of the immigrants who came to work the sugar cane fields along the Hamakua Coast first set foot on the Big Island at Laupahoehoe.

There is a county beach park on the point. It has restrooms, campsites, showers, drinking water, picnic pavilions and electricity, and as it's off the highway it's relatively secluded. All this makes it convenient for camping, but makes it ideal for late-night partying too. Locals who use the park as a drinking hangout sometimes get fairly wasted and rowdy.

AKAKA FALLS
To get to Akaka Falls, turn mauka off Hwy 19 onto Akaka Falls Rd (Hwy 220), midway between the 13 and 14-mile markers. The road passes through the town of Honomu and ends at the falls 3½ miles away.

Honomu
Honomu is an old sugar town that if not for being on the route to Akaka Falls might have been forgotten.

As it is, things are pretty slow here. There's a place to get shave ice, Ishigo's store and bakery (which sometimes rents a few rooms above the store for $25) and the Crystal Grotto shop which sells crystals, crafts and New Age books.

Akaka Falls State Park
Akaka Falls State Park has the Big Island's most impressive easy-to-view waterfall. A half-mile rainforest loop trail passes through dense and varied vegetation including massive philodendron vines, fragrant yellow

and red gingers, hanging heliconia and cool bamboo groves. Look up and you'll even find orchids growing wild in the trees.

If you start the loop trail by going to the right you'll first come to the 100-foot Kahuna Falls. It's a nice waterfall but the real treat is still to come. Up ahead is Akaka Falls dropping a sheer 442 feet down a fern-draped cliff. Its mood depends on the weather – sometimes it rushes with a mighty roar and other times it cascades gently. Either way it's always beautiful. Sometimes there's even a rainbow in the spray.

One legend says that whenever a branch of the lehua tree lands on a particular stone at the top of the falls, it will begin to rain. If so, there are apparently a lot of loose lehua branches upstream! You might want to bring an umbrella.

Hakalau Forest National Wildlife Refuge
Inland from Akaka Falls is the Hakalau Forest National Wildlife Refuge which protects a portion of the state's largest koa-ohia forest, habitat for native forest birds and the hoary bat. The refuge is comprised of 15,000 acres acquired by the Nature Conservancy and turned over to the US Fish & Wildlife Service. Another 16,000-acre parcel is expected to be added in the near future.

There's currently no public access to the refuge, though the Sierra Club occasionally has volunteer workdays to help eliminate invasive weeds.

PEPEEKEO FOUR-MILE SCENIC DRIVE
Between Honomu and Hilo there's a delightful four-mile side loop off Hwy 19. It's a drive through lush tropical jungle. The road crosses a string of one-lane bridges over little streams. In places it's almost canopied with African tulip trees, which drop their orange flowers on the road, and with passion fruit, guava and tall mango trees. The fruit can be picked up along the roadside in season.

The road is well-marked on the highway at both ends, with the south end about seven miles north of Hilo.

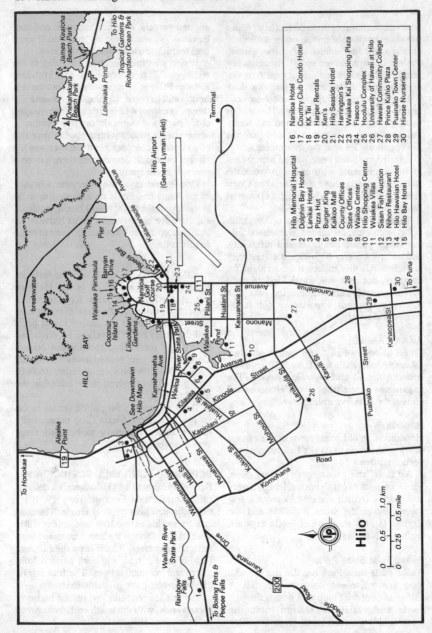

1	Hilo Memorial Hospital
2	Dolphin Bay Hotel
3	Lanikai Hotel
4	Pizza Hut
5	Burger King
6	Kaikoo Mall
7	County Offices
8	State Offices
9	Wailoa Center
10	Hoolulu Complex
11	Waiakea Villas
12	Sisan Fish Auction
13	Nihon Restaurant
14	Hilo Hawaiian Hotel
15	Hilo Bay Hotel
16	Naniloa Hotel
17	Country Club Condo Hotel
18	KK Tei
19	Harper Rentals
20	Ken's
21	Hilo Seaside Hotel
22	Harrington's
23	Waiakea Kai Shopping Plaza
24	Fiascos
25	Hooulu Complex
26	University of Hawaii at Hilo
27	Hawaii Community College
28	Prince Kuhio Plaza
29	Puainako Town Center
30	Hirose Nurseries

Hawaii Tropical Botanical Garden

If somehow the four-mile scenic drive isn't enough, there's also the Hawaii Tropical Botanical Garden along the way. The garden is a rainforest nature preserve with a lily pond, 1000 species of tropical plants and several streams and waterfalls.

Visitors buy tickets at the old yellow church mauka of the road and are shuttled by van down to the valley garden at nearby Onomea Bay.

This non-profit foundation charges an $8 admission fee. You're given a self-guided trail map and are free to wander as long as you like. It's open daily 8.30 am to 5.30 pm.

Hilo

Hilo is the county capital and commercial centre of the Big Island. It's on a large crescent-shaped bay and has Hawaii's second largest port. The population is 42,000, which is one-third the island's total.

In terms of lush, natural beauty, Hilo beats Kona hands down any day – the only catch is in finding a sunny one. During an average year in Hilo, measurable rain falls on 278 days.

Though the rain dampens some spirits, it feeds the waterfalls, gardens and jungle-like valleys. Flowers are big business in Hilo and orchids and anthuriums thrive there.

Many of Hilo's buildings are old and weathered and some of the small businesses within them look as if they've been there a hundred years. The parking meters out the front still take pennies.

Hilo is ethnically diverse, with a lot of people of Japanese and Filipino descent. There's also an alternative community that's been filtering in since the '70s, attracted by Hilo's affordability and the windward coast's scenic appeal.

Hilo is a survivor. Natural forces threaten it from both sides, tidal waves from one and lava from the other. Two devastating tsunamis have hit in this century and as recently

as 1984 a lava flow from Mauna Loa stopped short eight miles above town.

Hilo's reputation for wet weather has protected it from the invasive development that has spread elsewhere on the island. In many ways Hilo is the last remaining Hawaiian city unaffected by tourism.

Not that attempts haven't been made. In the 1970s Hilo built a new airport and a few deluxe hotels and resorts and started a media blitz. The airlines began direct flights from the mainland, but the tourists never showed.

'America's rainiest city' just couldn't compete with the sunny Kona Coast. The flights have all been dropped and some of the hotels have been turned into condos or cheap local housing.

Information

Tourist Information The Hawaii Visitors Bureau (tel 961-5797), 180 Kinoole St, near Hilo Hotel, is open from 8 am to noon and from 1 to 4.30 pm Monday to Friday.

For camping permits, the County Department of Parks & Recreation (tel 961-8311) is at 25 Aupuni St and the Division of State Parks (tel 961-7200) is at 75 Aupuni St. Both are near Wailoa River State Park.

The Hilo (General Lyman) Airport is just off Hwy 11, three-quarters of a mile south of its intersection with Hwy 19.

Aloha Airlines (tel 935-9385) is in Hilo Shopping Center and Hawaiian Airlines (tel 935-0858) is at 120 Kamehameha Ave.

Money The Bank of Hawaii has offices at 117 Keawe St, 120 Pauahi and 427 Kawili. There are numerous other banks around town.

Post Hilo has two post offices. The main one (tel 935-2821) is on the road into airport and the other is downtown in the federal building (tel 935-6685).

Bookshops Basically Books (169 Keawe St, tel 961-0144) is a great little book and map store. It specialises in Hawaiiana, including travel guides, diving guides, out-of-print books and Hawaiian dictionaries and literature. They also have a good general travel section and all sorts of maps, including USGS topo maps of Hawaii and the Pacific.

Other bookstores include Serendipity Bookshop in Puainako Town Center, Waldenbooks in Prince Kuhio Plaza and Book Gallery in Kaikoo Mall.

Laundromat Hilo Quality Coin Laundry, 210 Hoku St, which is a side street off Kilauea Ave opposite the Kaikoo Mall, is open from 5 am to 9 pm.

Shopping Puainako Shopping Center on Hwy 11 and Puainako St has a KTA supermarket, Pay'N Save, Ting-Hao Mandarin Restaurant, Pizza Hut and Jack in the Box.

Prince Kuhio Plaza on Hwy 11, opposite Puainako Shopping Center, has Liberty House, Sears, Longs Drugs, Woolworth, Safeway supermarket, Arby's Roast Beef, Prince Kuhio Theatres and a one- hour photo place.

Waiakea Kai Shopping Plaza, 88 Kanoelehua Ave (Hwy 11), has a McDonald's, Magoo's Pizza and three movie theatres.

Hilo Shopping Center on Kekuanaoa St and Kilauea Ave has Dick's Coffee House, Lanky's Pastries & Deli and Aloha Airlines.

Emergency Hilo Memorial Hospital is at 1190 Waianuenue Ave, near Rainbow Falls. Dial 969-4100 for emergencies.

DOWNTOWN HILO

Downtown Hilo is a mishmash of classic old buildings from the early 1900s, many on the National Register of Historic Places, and ageing wooden storefronts, some newly renovated, others falling apart.

One short walk that takes in historical sites and some interesting shops starts at the intersection of Kalakaua and Keawe streets, goes down Keawe, up Wailuku Drive, along Kinoole St past Kalakaua Park and back down Kalakaua St.

If you wander a little further astray you can explore the back streets. There are little Japanese restaurants with faded kanji signs,

barber shops with hand-pumped chairs and old pool halls.

The Lyman Museum puts out the brochure *Discover Downtown Hilo: A Walking Tour of Historic Sites*, which is available free at the museum, the HVB, hotels and downtown stores. The American Association of University Women puts out a similar brochure, a two-mile walking tour of *Old Hilo Town*, sold for $1 at Basically Books.

Keawe Street

The north end of Keawe St has been spruced up. The old welfare office has been turned into a Cajun restaurant and the old shops along the street have trendy new businesses.

Bears' Coffee is the place to hang out. It has great espresso and cinnamon rolls.

The nearby Chocolate Bar makes homemade chocolates, specialising in dipped fruits, truffles and candy made to look like sushi.

The Potter's Gallery, on the corner, has a nice collection of island pottery at reasonable prices as well as quality glasswork, weavings, woodwork and other crafts from about 40 Big Island artists.

Maui's Canoe

If you continue walking along Keawe St just beyond Wailuku Drive, you'll be on the Puueo St Bridge which crosses over the Wailuku River. The large rock in the river upstream on the left is called Maui's Canoe.

Legend has it the demigod Maui paddled his canoe with such speed across the ocean that he crash landed here and the canoe turned to stone. Ever the devoted son, Maui was rushing to save his mother, Hina, from a water monster who was trying to drown her by damming the river and flooding her cave beneath Rainbow Falls.

Kalakaua Park

In the late 1800s King David Kalakaua established Hilo as the county seat. Kalakaua Park is a quiet downtown park with a statue of the king sitting under the shade of a huge banyan tree, a sundial erected by the king in 1877, a

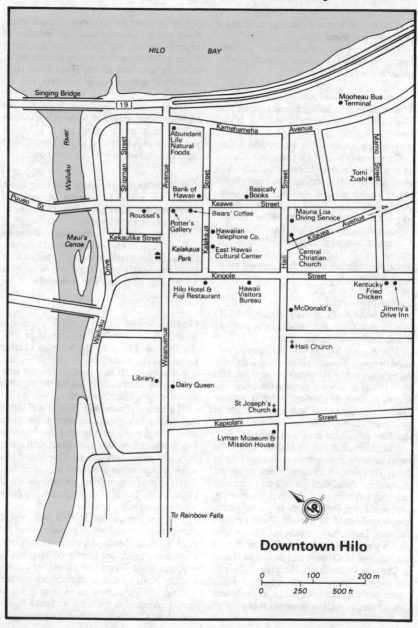

HILO BAY

Singing Bridge

19

Mooheau Bus
● Terminal

Wailuku River

Shipman Street

Kamehameha   Avenue

● Abundant
Life
Natural
Foods

Mamo Street

Avenue

Street

Tomi
● Zushi

Bank of
● Hawaii

Puueo St

● Basically
Books

Keawe   Street

● Roussel's

● Potter's
Gallery

Bears' Coffee

Mauna Loa
Diving Service

Avenue

Kekaulike Street

Kalakaua
Park

Hawaiian
Telephone Co.

East Hawaii
Cultural Center

Kilauea

Central
Christian
Church

Kalakaua Street

Haili Street

Maui's
Canoe

Wailuku Drive

Kinoole   Street

Hilo Hotel &
Fuji Restaurant

Hawaii
Visitors
Bureau

Kentucky ●●
Fried Chicken

● McDonald's

Jimmy's
Drive Inn

Waianuenue

† Haili Church

● Library

● Dairy Queen

St Joseph's †
● Church

Street

Kapiolani   Street

Lyman Museum &
Mission House

To Rainbow Falls

Downtown Hilo

0   100   200 m

0   250   500 ft

war memorial and a reflecting pool filled with carp and water lilies.

The site of the king's former summer home, Niolopa, is opposite the park at what today is the Hilo Hotel.

Around Kalakaua Park

The old federal building opposite the park on Waianuenue Ave was built in 1919. It's of neo-classical design with high columns and a Spanish tile roof. It houses the post office.

On the other side of the park, on Kalakaua St, the East Hawaii Cultural Center has taken over the old police station. The centre hosts changing art exhibits and has a gift shop. Admission is free. There are plans to eventually put in a performing arts centre upstairs.

Next door is the Hawaiian Telephone Company building, designed by Honolulu architect C W Dickey in the 1920s. It's an attractive building of Spanish mission influence with nice tile work.

Lyman Museum

Lyman Museum (276 Haili St, tel 935-5021) is a first-class museum and a great place to spend a rainy afternoon.

The ground floor covers the island's cultural heritage. Displays show things like how adzes were made of volcanic clinkstone, and how kukui nuts were skewered on coconut leaves to burn as candles. Exhibits include feather leis, tapa cloth and a house made of pili grass. Mana, kahunas and *awa* (kava) drinking are all succinctly explained.

The different lifestyles of those who came as indentured immigrants and stayed on to form Hawaii's multi-ethnic society are all given their due. Displays include costumes, cultural artefacts and detailed interpretive plaques. From Portugal there's a braginha, the forerunner of the ukelele. There's even a full-size Taoist shrine made in China, which was disassembled and carried aboard ship in the luggage of Chinese emigrating to Hilo.

Upstairs in the Earth Heritage Gallery is the largest mineral collection in the Pacific. There are thousands of rocks, crystals and gemstones, as well as minerals that glow in the dark.

The lava section explains volcanic eruptions and lava formations with samples of spatter, olivine and Pele's hair and tears. Other exhibits include native insects, birds, seashells and land shells. Hawaii has 1000 land shell species found nowhere else on earth.

The museum is open from 9 am to 5 pm Monday to Saturday, with Mission House tours at 9.30, 10.30 and 11.30 am and 1, 2, 3 and 4 pm. Admission to both is $3.50. The gift shop has a good selection of Hawaiiana books.

Sampan Tours Museum director Leon Bruno has a special interest in sampans, which are modified autos with two rows of seats running along their length.

These minibuses were the forerunner of today's vans. In his restored 1948 Plymouth, Dr Bruno (or a staff member) chauffeurs an enjoyable one-hour narrated tour of Hilo for $6.50 per person. The schedule is by reservation.

Mission House

Next door to the museum is the large missionary house built by the Reverend David Lyman and his wife Sarah in 1839. They had eight children of their own and in the attic boarded a number of island boys who attended their church school.

The mission house tour is brief and informal, led by an enthusiastic docent. You get a good feel for the people who lived in this house. Things are faded and used, such as the very old patchwork quilts. The house has many of the original furnishings including Sarah Lyman's melodeon, rocking chair and china dishes. Some of the original wavy glass windows are still in place.

The mattresses are stuffed with wood shavings, a material which provided a bed for bugs as well (hence the expression 'Good night, sleep tight, don't let the bedbugs bite').

Pages from Mrs Lyman's diaries are on display. Notice the erratic handwriting of the section written during more than a dozen earthquakes and eruptions from both Kilauea and Mauna Loa which hit on a single day in

1868. Some of her diaries have been published in the book *The Lymans of Hilo*.

Churches

Haili St was once called Church Row for the churches which lined up along it. The three that remain, one Catholic and two Congregational, are worth visiting.

St Joseph's Church, at the corner of Haili and Kapiolani streets, is a beautiful pink church in Spanish mission style that looks as if it came right out of Southern California. It was built in 1919 and has an old cracked bell, stained glass windows and an arched entrance topped with angels.

Haili Church, at 211 Haili St, was built in 1859. It has straight lines and a boxy square tower, somewhat resembling a New England barn. Services are conducted in both Hawaiian and English.

The Central Christian Church, on the corner of Kilauea and Haili streets, was built in the Victorian style in the early 1900s by Portuguese immigrants.

Hilo Library

Hilo has a good public library. It's on Waianuenue Ave, and is open from 9 am to 5 pm daily except Sundays, and until 8 pm Mondays and Wednesdays.

The two large stones on the library's front lawn are the Naha and Pinao stones. The Pinao Stone was an entrance pillar to an old Hawaiian heiau.

The Naha Stone, from the same temple grounds, is said to weigh 2½ tons. According to legend any person who had the strength to budge the stone would have the strength to conquer and unite all the islands. Kamehameha I reputedly met the challenge and overturned the stone in his youth.

Wailoa River State Park

On 1 April 1946 Hilo Bay was inundated by a tsunami which had raced its way across the Pacific from an earthquake in the Aleutian Islands. It struck at 6.54 am without warning.

Fifty-foot waves jumped the sea wall and swept into the city. They tore the first line of buildings off their foundations, carrying them inland and smashing them into the rows behind. As the waves pulled back, they sucked much of the splintered debris and a number of people out to sea.

By 7 am the town was littered with shattered buildings as far as the eye could see. The ground was not visible through the pile of rubble. Throughout Hawaii the tsunami killed 159 people and racked up $25 million in property damages. The hardest hit was Hilo, with 96 fatalities.

Hilo's bayfront 'Little Tokyo' bore the brunt of the storm and Shinmachi, which means 'New Town' in Japanese, was rebuilt on the same spot.

Fourteen years later, on 23 May 1960, an earthquake off the coast of Chile triggered a tsunami which made a beeline for Hilo at a speed of 440 miles per hour. A series of three tidal waves washed up in succession, each one sweeping farther up into the city.

Though the tsunami warning speakers roared this time, many people didn't take them seriously. The tiny tsunamis of the 1950s had been relatively harmless and a few people actually went down to the beach to watch the waves.

Those along the shore were swept inland, while others farther up were dragged out into the bay. A few lucky ones who managed to grab hold of floating debris were rescued at sea. In the end there were 61 deaths and property damage of over $20 million.

Again Shinmachi was levelled but this time, instead of rebuilding, the low-lying bayfront property was turned into parks and the survivors moved to higher ground.

All along Kamehameha Ave you can still see the curbstone cuts which once led to streets or to the driveways of businesses that made up Shinmachi.

Park Attractions Wailoa River State Park is mostly open grassy expanses where Shinmachi once stood. The park has two memorials, one for the tsunami victims, the other a Vietnam memorial with an eternal flame.

Wailoa River flows through the park and most of Waiakea Pond is within the park boundaries. This spring-fed estuarine pond has both saltwater and brackish water fish species, mostly mullet. There's a boat launch ramp near the mouth of the river; only non-motor boats are allowed and fishing licenses are required.

The park's Wailoa Center is a state-run art gallery with quality multi-media exhibits which change monthly. Photos of the tsunami damage are on display downstairs. It's open from 8 am to 4.30 pm on Mondays, Tuesdays, Thursdays and Fridays; from noon to 8.30 pm Wednesdays and from 9 am to 3 pm Saturdays. Admission is free.

Banyan Drive

Banyan Drive goes around the edge of Waiakea Peninsula which juts into Hilo Bay. The road skirts the Liliuokalani Gardens, the nine-hole Naniloa Golf Course and Hilo's bayfront hotels.

Banyan Drive is lined with big banyan trees planted in the 1930s by royalty and celebrities, including the likes of Babe Ruth and Amelia Earhart. Plaques beneath the trees identify the planters.

Suisan Fish Auction

Local fishermen sell their catch every morning except Sundays at Suisan Fish Auction, near the intersection of Lihiwai and Banyan Drive, on the western side of the peninsula.

The auction is a lively and colourful scene where bids are shouted out in Hilo's unique blend of pidgin. Open to the public, it's best to get there by 8 am, as the whole thing's usually wrapped up by 9 am.

Next door there's a fish market with the freshest fish on the island.

Liliuokalani Gardens

Hilo's 30-acre Japanese garden is named for Queen Liliuokalani, Hawaii's last queen. This waterfront park is filled with ponds and waterways complete with mullet that jump clear out of the water, little Japanese pagodas and covered sitting areas, stone lanterns, arched bridges and patches of bamboo.

The gardens are a monument of sorts to the Japanese presence in Hawaii. Natural

forces have had a hand in shaping and reshaping the park. The last big tsunami, in 1960, wiped out the dry gardens. Many of the lanterns and pagodas that dot the park were donated by Japanese regional governments and sister cities in honour of the 100th anniversary of Japanese immigration to Hawaii.

It's a pleasant place to walk around, though after heavy rain you'll need to stick to high ground.

Coconut Island

Coconut Island, which is connected to land by a footbridge, sticks out into the bay opposite the Liliuokalani Gardens. The island is a county park with opportunities for picnicking, swimming and fishing. Hilo's Fourth of July fireworks display is shot off from here.

In ancient times Coconut Island was called Moku Ola, 'island of life'. It was known as a place of healing, and had a special healing stone as well as medical kahunas whose invocations could cure the sick by ridding them of demonic spirits. Moku Ola also had pure spring water, which was said to bring good health, and a birthing stone which instilled mana to the children born there.

Beaches

Hilo is not a city for beach bums. Still, there are some decent beaches along Kalanianaole Ave, a four-mile stretch on the eastern side of Hilo. The road is basically a continuation of Kamehameha Ave, starting in front of the Hilo Seaside Hotel.

Onekahakaha County Beach Park This park is a quarter of a mile off Kalanianaole Ave. The turn-off is just before the Hilo Tropical Gardens.

The park has a big sandy-bottomed pool formed by a large boulder enclosure. The water's just a foot or two deep in most places and it's popular with families with young children.

On the Hilo side of the park there's an unprotected cove that is sometimes used by snorkellers on calm days but be careful as it has a seaward current. The park department cautions swimmers and snorkellers not to venture beyond the breakwater at any time.

There are camping sites, restrooms, showers and a picnic area. Campers usually set up their tents around the edge of the lawn near the tree line at the Hilo end of the beach. But at any rate, avoid low ground because when it rains in Hilo, it pours.

James Kealoha Beach Park Kealoha is an unmarked county park known locally as Four-Mile Beach because of the distance between the park and the downtown post office. It's just before the Mauna Loa Shores apartments and has camping, showers and restrooms.

For swimming and snorkelling most people go to the eastern side which is sheltered by an island and a naturally occurring rocky breakwater. It's generally calm there with clean, clear water and pockets of white sand.

The Hilo side of the island is open ocean and much rougher. You can sometimes find people net fishing here. It's also a popular winter surfing spot, though there are strong rip currents which run out to sea.

Across Kalanianaole Ave is Lokowaka Pond, a fishpond where trout and mullet are harvested. You're welcome to go over and take a look around. There's a little restaurant there which serves trout dinner by reservation.

Richardson Ocean Park This park, just before the end of the road, has a small black sand beach fronting Hilo's most favoured snorkelling site. The left side of the bay tends to be colder due to springs in the water. These are less common on the right side where the snorkelling is better.

The old house at the water's edge holds a centre for marine education run by the county. There are a couple of nature displays there and you can pick up a plant identification guide to the park's short shoreline trail. The trail passes over a fishpond fed by freshwater springs and through a little fern grotto. Periodically public workshops are offered on kayaking, shoreline fishing, limu pressing etc. The park has restrooms and showers.

Rainbow Falls
Rainbow Falls is on the western side of Hilo, off Waianuenue Ave, just below the hospital.

Waianuenue, 'rainbow seen in water', is the Hawaiian name for this pretty 80-foot waterfall. The huge cave beneath the falls is said to have been the home of Hina, mother of Maui. The falls are usually seen as a double drop which flows together before hitting the large pool at the bottom.

The best time to see rainbows is in the mornings, though they're by no means guaranteed. Most people just look at the falls straight on from the viewpoint in front of the parking lot, but there's another lookout which gives a far better angle for catching rainbows in the mist. It's up on the left near the beginning of a short loop trail. The trail then continues past a giant banyan tree and through a shady wooded area.

Lots of tour buses pull in and out at Rainbow Falls. There are restrooms and drinking water.

Boiling Pots
Peepee Falls and Boiling Pots are up Waianuenue Ave, about 1½ miles past Rainbow Falls.

These impressive falls drop from a sheer rock face and as the water runs downstream over a series of basalt depressions in the river, it swirls and churns into bubbling pools which have earned it the name Boiling Pots.

Boiling Pots is as interesting as Rainbow Falls, though few tour buses come this way.

Kaumana Caves
The Kaumana Caves were formed by an 1881 lava flow from Mauna Loa. As the flow subsided, the outer edges of the deep lava stream cooled and crusted over in a tunnel-like effect. The hot molten lava inside drained out, creating these caves.

The caves are wet and mossy, thickly covered with ferns and impatiens. If you have a flashlight you might want to explore them, though they tend to be drippy.

The caves are marked and are on the right, a couple of miles up Kaumana Drive (Hwy 200).

Orchids

Nurseries & Gardens

Most of the state's orchids are grown on the Big Island, earning it one of its nicknames 'The Orchid Island'. Hilo is the centre of activity and from here orchids, anthuriums and other tropical flowers are flown to florists around the world.

Many of Hilo's working nurseries open their greenhouses and gardens to visitors free of charge, but because of a serious anthurium blight that can be spread by people moving among the plants, fewer are now open to the public.

Hilo Tropical Gardens This is Hilo's nicest free garden. An old moss- covered sign hanging in the garden quotes Kipling, 'Gardens Are Not Made By Sitting In The Shade' and this two-acre garden is obviously the result of years of labour. Paths wind around lotus ponds, orchids, azaleas, hibiscus, ginger and all sorts of tropical flowers. There's a nursery and gift shop out the front.

Inside the garden is a little homegrown cafe featuring the unlikely combination of pizza and chocolate truffles. The truffles are great (try the kahlua and cream) and you can

also get a pretty good cup of Kona coffee there.

The garden is at 1477 Kalanianaole Ave, just past Onekahakaha Beach, on the left. It's open from 8.30 am to 5 pm daily.

Hirose Nurseries Hirose Nurseries has a small greenhouse with some of the prettiest orchids in Hawaii. Orchids and anthuriums are for sale in the shop out the front. It's a friendly place and female visitors are likely to get a free orchid pinned in their hair. Hirose is on Kahaopea St, across Hwy 11 from Puainako Town Center.

Rainbow Tropicals Rainbow Tropicals is on Mamaki St near Hwy 11, on the way to the zoo. There's a small shop and a large screenhouse loaded with anthuriums and other tropical flowers.

Nani Mau Gardens Nani Mau Gardens is a commercial garden on the tour bus route. There are several acres of flowering plants, including a large orchid section, and almost everything is labelled. It's a newly planted garden, however, with wide concrete paths and tram rides and so it's not very natural. Nani Mau is about three miles south of Hilo. The turn- off from Hwy 11 onto Makalika St is marked with an HVB warrior. Admission is $5 plus $3 more for the tram. It's open from 8 am to 5 pm daily.

Panaewa Rainforest Zoo

Panaewa Rainforest Zoo, the only tropical rainforest zoo in the USA, is in a forest reserve which gets 125 inches of rain every year.

It's a respectable little zoo and good for an hour of strolling. Four impressive and healthy looking tigers, two of them born there, roam a large natural pit-style cage. There are giant anteaters, pygmy hippos, monkeys, alligators and hoofed animals. Peacocks and guinea fowl have the run of the place. You can also see some of Hawaii's endangered birds here, such as the nene and the Hawaiian duck, hawk and owl.

To get there, turn off Hwy 11 onto Mamaki

St (also called Kulani and Stainback Hwy), a few miles south of town. The zoo is one mile west of Hwy 11. It's open from 9 am to 4 pm daily and admission is free.

Mauna Loa Macadamia Nut Visitor Center

Mauna Loa Macadamia Nut Visitor Center is on Macadamia Rd off Hwy 11, about five miles south of Hilo. The 2¾-mile road to the centre cuts across row after row of papaya trees and macadamia trees, as far as the eye can see.

C Brewer Co, which owns Mauna Loa, produces most of the world's macadamia nuts. This large, impersonal centre packs the tourists in but it's essentially just a gift shop and snack bar.

To the side is a working factory with an outside walkway with windows that allows visitors to view the large, fast-paced assembly line inside.

The little planted area out behind the visitor centre with its labelled fruit trees and flowering bushes is worth walking through if you've come this far. The centre is open from 9 am to 5 pm daily.

Places to Stay

Partially due to the weather, Hilo has no self-contained resorts. People don't come to Hilo to hang around a pool, but to visit the sights and then head on.

Though rents are relatively cheap in Hilo, hotels aren't the bargain you might expect. This is in part because former hotel space has been turned into residential units, lowering competition. The 'vacation rental' condo market that's so common on the Kona Coast is virtually non-existent here.

Places to Stay – bottom end

Dolphin Bay Hotel (333 Iliahi St, Hilo, HI 96720; tel 935-1466) is a gem. It's a very friendly place and, unlike many other small inns, they welcome travellers with children. It's on a hill just above downtown. All 18 units have kitchens, fans and sliding glass doors. All except the standard rooms have sunken bathtubs. Fresh-picked fruit from the backyard is available in the lobby.

This is one of the few hotels in Hilo with a continuously high occupancy rate and reservations are suggested. There's a two-night minimum stay and standard rooms cost $29/39 for singles/doubles; $8 for each additional person and $10 more for superior rooms. They also have one-bedroom/two-bedroom units for $59/$69. Weekly rates are available. Dolphin Bay has no swimming pool or restaurant, but it has plenty of sightseeing tips to share.

Hilo Hotel (142 Kinoole St, Box 726, Hilo, HI 96720; tel 961-3733) is an old-fashioned downtown hotel built in the 1950s on the former site of King Kalakaua's summer home. Rooms are good-sized though simple and a little faded. There's a community lounge with a TV. Complimentary sweet rolls are available in the mornings. Rates with/without TV cost $39/$32. A two-bedroom suite with kitchen is $68 for up to four people.

The *Country Club Condo Hotel* (121 Banyan Drive, Hilo, HI 96720; tel 935-7171), fancy name aside, is a former Travelodge that's dingy and weathered. Rooms start around $35, but they're not worth it. Weekly rates start around $150, monthly around $300, but applications must first be filed and approved. Units with kitchens are about $50 more a month.

Lanikai Hotel (100 Puueo St, Hilo, HI 96720; tel 935-5556) conjures up images from poverty-in-America documentaries. The 30 rooms in this rundown triple decker cost $18 to $25 a night, $205 to $300 a month.

Lihi Kai (Amy Gamble Lannan, 30 Kahoa Rd, Hilo, HI 96720; tel 935-7865) is a B&B in Amy's home on a cliff directly above Hilo Bay, two miles from town. There's a small swimming pool. Rooms are $40 single or double. There's a two-night minimum or an extra $5 charge.

Places to Stay – middle

Waiakea Villas (400 Hualani St, Hilo, HI 96720; tel 961-2841; 800-367-7042) has 147 units spread over 14 acres of gardens and ponds. Rooms are quite nice with a touch of tropical decor. They're only mildly faded, which in Hilo is relatively spiffy. Standard rooms cost $40/$240 a day/week and rooms with kitchens start at $50/300 a day/week. The complex has a couple of restaurants, shops and offices.

Hilo Seaside Hotel (126 Banyan Drive, Hilo, HI 96720; tel 935-0821; 800-367-7000) is a 145-unit two-floor motel-style complex with a nice carp pond out the front. Rooms are on the small side and rather standard, though each has a small refrigerator. The rooms around the pool can get a bit noisy. Past visitors might remember this as the Hukilau, part of a small Hawaiian hotel chain of reliable budget stand-bys. The hotels have all been renovated and prices now start at a more moderate $48. However, if you book within Hawaii and ask for the special it's often at least $10 cheaper.

Uncle Billy's *Hilo Bay Hotel* (87 Banyan Drive, Hilo, HI 96720; tel 961-5818; 800-367-5102 from the US mainland, 800-442-5841 in Hawaii) is a 130-room lacklustre hotel. Things change slowly in Hilo – standard rooms here still have B&W TVs. Rates range from $59 standard to $74 beachfront; and cost $10 less in low season.

Places to Stay – top end

Hilo Hawaiian Hotel (71 Banyan Drive, Hilo, HI 96720; tel 935-9361; 800-367-5004 from the US mainland, 800-272- 5275 in Hawaii) is a 285-unit highrise hotel overlooking Coconut Island. Rooms are comfortable and modern though overpriced at $73/76 for singles/doubles. If you want your lanai overlooking the ocean instead of the parking lot it's $21 more.

Naniloa Hotel (93 Banyan Drive, Hilo, HI 96720; tel 969- 3333; 800-367-5360 from the US mainland, 800-442-5845 in Hawaii) is a 400-room highrise, Hilo's largest. The rooms have recently been renovated and are nice enough, but cost $80 to $130 depending on the view. It's popular with Japanese tour groups.

Places to Eat

Hilo has lots of hole-in-the-wall restaurants and cheap places to eat. Many places have salad-to-dessert lunch specials for around $5. Even some of the best restaurants have 'business lunches' for just a bit more than that.

Places to Eat – bottom end

Bears' Coffee, 106 Keawe St, is a nice place for a light lunch or breakfast. They have a wide selection of good pastries, from croissants and muffins to cheesecake and raspberry linzertorte. There are also quiches, deli sandwiches, burritos and build-your-own bagels with more than a dozen fillings. Everything costs less than $5. It's open from 7 am to 5 pm Monday to Friday, 8 am to 4 pm Saturdays.

The unpretentious *Tomi Zushi*, 68 Mamo St, could easily be on a back street arcade under a Tokyo train station. It has seven vinyl-backed booths and not a fork in sight. The best deal is the special bento for $2.50, available from about 9 am as a takeaway picnic lunch. They also have sushi, tempura, udon and other Japanese standards.

KK Tei, 1550 Kamehameha Ave, is a family restaurant with all the Japanese standards as well as Western dishes such as steaks and hamburgers. At lunch time, oyako donburi (egg and chicken over rice) with miso soup and tea costs $4.25 and teishokus are $6.25. Dinners average a few dollars more. It's open from 11 am to 2 pm Monday to Saturday and 5 to 9 pm daily.

Jimmy's Drive Inn at 362 Kinoole St, next to Kentucky Fried Chicken, is a busy local eatery. They serve generous portions of inexpensive Korean, Japanese, Hawaiian and American food, although they all tend to blend in flavour. The Korean combo plate of kalbi, mundoo, barbecued chicken and kimchee costs $4.25. Seafood dishes start around $5. They also have cheap and hearty breakfasts.

Dick's Coffee House in the Hilo Shopping Center on Kilauea Ave is another cheap diner. Complete meals cost from $3.40 for spaghetti to $6.70 for steak and come with salad and soup. At breakfast, omelettes with hash browns and toast start at $2.50. It's not exciting but it's cheap.

Abundant Life Natural Foods, 90 Kamehameha Ave, is a nice large natural food store with a wide variety of health foods including cheeses, yoghurt, kefir and deli items.

Hilo has an abundance of fast food restaurants, including *McDonald's, Pizza Hut, Jack in the Box* and the like. *Ken's House of Pancakes*, 1730 Kamehameha Ave, is open 24 hours daily.

Places to Eat – moderate

Fiascos, 200 Kanoelehua Ave (Hwy 11), is a bustling place serving burgers, omelettes and quiche in addition to dishes ranging from fajitas for $4.25 to fillet and artichoke bearnaise for $16.95. Salad bar with soup cost $6.50. It's open from 11.30 am to 11 pm daily, and until midnight on Fridays and Saturdays.

Ting-Hao Mandarin Restaurant in Puainako Town Center on Hwy 11 is a popular Chinese restaurant. They have vegetarian dishes such as broccoli with garlic and mapo tofu in the $5 range as well as other standard Sichuan and Mandarin dishes for $4 to $9. They do not use MSG. It's open 10.30 am to 2.30 pm Monday to Saturday, and 4 to 9 pm nightly.

Nihon Restaurant at 121 Lihiwai St, next to Liliuokalani Gardens, is on the second floor of Nihon Cultural Center with a fine view of Hilo Bay. At lunch time there's a special for $6.25 which includes two main dishes such as sashimi, tonkatsu or tempura along with nigiri rice, kappamaki, miso soup and tossed salad. Dinner teishokus are a few dollars more. They also have a good, inexpensive sushi bar and one-bowl dishes like donburi, soba and udon. Lunch is from 11 am to 2 pm and dinner is 5 to 9 pm. The lobby has a small display of Japanese textiles and crafts.

Fuji Restaurant in the Hilo Hotel, 142 Kinoole St, has a serene atmosphere with shoji screens and windows looking out onto a garden and the food's good. Tempura costs $7.90 at lunch, $9.70 at dinner, and yakitori donburi is $5.90 at lunch, $6.50 at dinner. It's open from 11 am to 2 pm and 5 to 9 pm daily except Mondays.

Places to Eat – top end

For something different you might try *Seaside* (tel 935-8825), opposite the Four-Mile Beach on Kalanianaole Ave, just before Mauna Loa Shores apartments. This is an aquafarm raising trout and mullet with a small dining area serving the same. Meals from salad to dessert cost about $12. Reservations are required, with a minimum of four people. If a party of four has already booked, they'll accept smaller groups.

Harrington's (tel 961-4966), right on Reeds Bay, is a small bayfront restaurant with wooden beam ceilings. Seafood, steak and other dishes range from about $12 to $18. It's open from 5.30 pm daily. There's another Harrington's in Kawaihae.

Roussel's (tel 935-5111), 60 Keawe St, is Hilo's French Creole restaurant. Most main dishes at lunch time are around $9 and include dishes like shrimp creole, oysters rockefeller and blackened mahimahi. Dinner time dishes range from $10 for trout to $16 for duck. It's open weekdays for lunch and from 5 to 10 pm Monday to Saturday for dinner.

Entertainment

Harrington's on Reeds Bay has a guitarist or jazz piano in its lounge from Tuesday to Saturday.

The *Reflections Restaurant* at 101 Aupuni St has live top- 40 bands and dancing Tuesday to Saturday.

Uncle Billy presents a hula show during dinner time at 6 pm nightly at the Hilo Bay Hotel restaurant.

Fiascos on Hwy 11 near Banyan Drive has dancing to '50s and '60s music from 8.30 pm to 1 am Thursdays, Fridays and Saturdays.

Movies The theatres at *Prince Kuhio Plaza* and *Waiakea Shopping Plaza* have the standard Hollywood films.

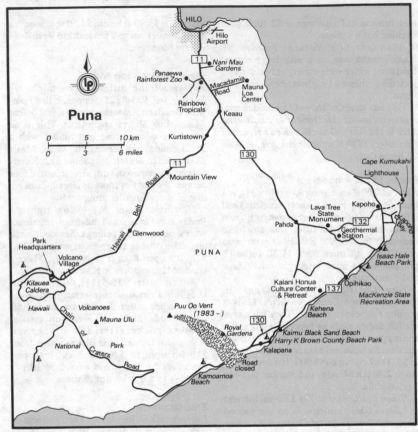

Puna

Puna is the diamond-shaped easternmost point of the Big Island. Its main attractions are in lava: vast fields of it covering former villages, an ancient forest of lava tree moulds, lava tidepools and black sand beaches. These days the highway into Puna ends abruptly at a steaming lava flow that glows red after dark.

Kilauea Volcano's active east rift zone slices clear across Puna. The most recent series of eruptions has been spewing lava since 1983, burying nearly 100 homes and creating about 100 acres of new coastal land.

Puna has Hawaii's cheapest land. The closer to the rift, the greater the volcanic activity and the cheaper it gets.

A growing number of people are drawn here by the idea of homesteading but many have found it tough making a living off a lava flow. Pakalolo is one alternative and Puna grows a lot of it. More than a few marijuana connoisseurs rank 'Puna butter' at the top of the list.

The Big Island accounts for 90% of all pot confiscated by Hawaii police, with the vast majority taken in Puna. Each spring Operation Green Harvest strikes with para-military raids, landing in helicopters, tearing up plants and rounding up entire families at gunpoint. They also conduct aerial assaults, spraying herbicides over huge tracts of state land. After two weeks of spraying in 1989 the state boasted it had wiped out about half of the area's estimated one million marijuana plants. In addition to killing the pakalolo, the drifting herbicides also enter local farms and gardens and contaminate drinking water, which in Puna is mostly from local catchment.

Deserved or not, Puna has the reputation of being less than friendly. If you're travelling the main roads you probably won't pick up on those vibes at all but if you're cruising around off the beaten path you may raise a suspicious eye.

Puna is also a major producer of anthuriums, grows the best papayas in Hawaii, and grows many of the orchids that get credited to Hilo.

Puna is not known for its beaches, other than the curiosity of its black sands, and for the most part waters along the coast are subject to strong currents and riptides.

Puna & Pele
In the Hawaiian language there are several proverbial expressions that link Puna with the volcano goddess Pele. As an example, to express anger, someone might say Ke lauahi maila o Pele ia Puna, 'Pele is pouring lava out on Puna'.

Equally common are both historic and modern stories of a mysterious woman travelling alone through Puna. Sometimes she's young and attractive, other times she's old and wizened and often she's seen just before a volcanic eruption. Those who stop and pick her up hitchhiking or show some other kindness are often protected from the lava flow.

After the 1960 lava flow in Kapoho, stories circulated on how the lightkeeper in the spared lighthouse had offered a meal to an elderly homeless woman who had showed up at his door on the eve of the eruption.

Orientation
Keaau is the entrance to Puna, where Hwy 11 and Hwy 130 intersect. From there, Hwy 130 goes south 11 miles to Pahoa and then continues on to the coast.

Maps which show Hwy 130 winding down through Puna and up the Chain of Craters Road to Hawaii Volcanoes National Park were made obsolete in 1988 when a lava flow buried a large section of the road. The national park can now be entered only via the Hawaii Belt Rd (Hwy 11), which makes Puna more time consuming to visit, as you need to backtrack out the same way you go in. If you don't have a lot of time, Puna could easily be bypassed.

Hwy 11, on the way to the national park, passes through the towns of Kurtistown, Mountain View and Glenwood, as well as side roads leading into some of Puna's largest subdivisions.

KEAAU
Keaau is the town at the northern end of Puna. Keaau Town Center, Puna's only shopping centre, is at the intersection of Hwy 11 Hwy 130. It has a grocery store, post office, Dairy Queen, pizza place and Mexican restaurant. Keaau Natural Foods is opposite the centre on an old road which parallels the highway. They have baked goods, produce and a full line of health foods. It's open daily.

Though there's not much to Keaau's old town centre, opposite the kite shop there's an interesting old building with a juice bar in front and a homebrew supply store at the back. It's worth stopping there to check out the fading turn-of-the-century photos of plantation workers and Japanese mail-order brides that are nailed to the wall along the wooden plank hallway there.

PAHOA
Pahoa is the heart of Puna. It's a funky little town with raised wooden sidewalks and cowboy architecture. The town has an untamed edge. There are influences from the '60s and '70s but there are other more time-less ones as well like the rough and tumble bar just a few doors down from the health food store.

If you'd like to take a look at life on a lava flow as you're driving around, stop by Pahoa Realty (tel 965-9500) and pick up their sub-division map.

Prices start as low as $3500 an acre (no electricity, water by catchment) for land in Royal Gardens, a subdivision partly covered by a 1988 lava flow. The lower-risk Hawaiian Beaches area (with water, electricity and paved roads) has quarter-acre lots for around $11,000.

Wild orchids grow like weeds along the roadsides around Pahoa and throughout Puna. There are fields of cultivated orchids and lots of anthurium nurseries as well, including one right in Pahoa, which is open to visitors.

Places to Stay

Kalani Honua Culture Center & Retreat (RR2, Box 4500, Pahoa, HI 96778; tel 965-7828; 800-367-8047 ext 669) is a New Age retreat between the villages of Opihikao and Kehena. Workshops for things like Iyengar Yoga, Crystal Transformation, Kahuna Arts, massage and dance are offered. You can also spend the night without participating in the programmes.

There are 31 rooms in two-storey cedar lodges which have beamed ceilings, lots of wood and a screened common area with shared kitchen. Rates are $50/60 for singles/doubles with private bath, $40/48 with shared bath. They also have cottages with one bedroom, bath and living room for $72. Tents can be pitched on the grounds for $13. There's a sauna, pool and tennis courts, which are free to guests and open to the public for a small fee.

The *Merry Whales Hotel* (Box 1130, Pahoa, HI 96778; tel 965-8334) rents out rooms behind the Paradise West bar in Pahoa. The building which dates back to the 1920s has seven rooms; all have cable TV and shared baths. Rates are $15 to $25 nightly, and from $75 weekly. On Fridays and Saturdays there's a band at the bar that can be heard throughout Pahoa. On weekends people from subdivisions without electricity sometimes come into town and spend the night here.

Places to Eat

Not Jest Juice has felafels, smoothies, soups, salads and sandwiches and, of course, vegetable and fruit juices. They make a good avocado and cheese sandwich for $3. Ask for the miso-honey dressing.

Luquin's is an inexpensive Mexican restaurant. A taco or enchilada will cost you $1.50 and combination plate lunches range from about $3 to $6. The salad bar is small but fresh and costs $3.50.

Pahoa Natural Groceries is a good well-stocked natural foods store with a full dairy section and healthy homemade bakery items like 'chocolate-honey pahoehoe pie'.

Pahoa also has a ribhouse restaurant, Chinese restaurant, Dairy Queen, sandwich stand, coffee shop with burgers, produce stands and a grocery store where you'll find the local bulletin board.

Onward from Pahoa

The usual route after Pahoa is to make the triangle down Hwy 132 past Lava Tree State Monument, then Hwy 137 along the shore to Kalapana and back to Pahoa via Hwy 130.

From Pahoa, Hwy 132 passes through tropical forest reserve. The area is very lush and jungle-like, with ferns growing on the bark of trees and a thick ground cover of impatiens.

Lava Tree State Monument

The lava moulds at Lava Tree State Monument were created in 1790 when this former ohia rainforest was engulfed in pahoehoe from Kilauea's east rift zone. The lava was free-flowing and moved quickly, like a river flooding its banks.

As the molten lava ran through the forest, some of it began to congeal around the moisture-laden ohia trunks while the rest of the flow moved on through and quickly receded.

Though the trees burned away, the moulds of lava which had formed around them remained. Now, 200 years later, there's a ghost forest of lava shells.

A 20-minute loop walk winds around most of the 'lava trees'. Some are a good 10 feet high and others are short enough to look down into and shelter ferns within their hollows.

Be careful if you walk off the path as in places the ground is crossed by deep cracks, some hidden by new vegetation. It's thought one deep fracture caused by an earthquake at the same time as the flow may have drained much of the lava back into the earth.

The park is on Hwy 132, 2½ miles east from its intersection with Hwy 130. The mosquitoes can be wicked there.

Geothermal Plant

An experimental geothermal plant a few miles south-east of Pahoa produces electricity from hot 675°F subterranean water rising from a deep well.

There are plans to develop a large 25-megawatt plant on the site and schemes to eventually cable 'volcanic electricity' directly to Oahu.

Greenpeace, the Hawaii Rainforest Action Group and the Pele Defense Fund are opposing development of expanded geothermal energy projects in Puna, as plans call for many of the wells to be placed within a rare lowland tropical rainforest. There is also concern about the unknown environmental hazards of extensive drilling into an active volcano. In addition, many Hawaiians feel the proposed plant is sacrilegious and inviting Pele's wrath. Others oppose it on baser grounds, as the release of hydrogen sulphide makes the area smell like rotten eggs.

A number of small homegrown businesses have set up around the plant. One uses a geothermal kiln to dry koa for woodworking, another uses a geothermal dehydration cabinet to dry papaya and pineapple from surplus local crops.

The plant's visitor centre is open from 7.30 am to 5.30 pm. To get there, take the first right just beyond Lava Tree State Monument onto Pahoa-Pohoiki Rd. It's about a mile down on the left.

KAPOHO

Hwy 132 heads east through papaya orchards and long rows of vanda orchids to what was once Kapoho, a farming town of about 300 people.

On 13 January 1960 a fountain of fire half a mile long shot up in the midst of a sugar cane field just above Kapoho. The main flow of liquid pahoehoe lava ran toward the ocean. A slower moving offshoot of aa lava crept toward the town, burying orchid farms in its path.

Earthen barricades were built and fire-hoses frantically pumped water onto the lava, but none of the attempts to harden or divert the flow worked.

On 28 January the lava entered Kapoho and buried the town. A hot springs resort and nearly 100 homes and businesses disappeared.

One bizarre phenomenon occurred when the river of lava approached the sea at Cape Kumukahi. Within a few feet of the cape's lighthouse the lava parted into two flows and circled around it, sparing the lighthouse from destruction. If you want to take a look, the lighthouse is 1¾ miles down the dirt road which continues beyond the intersection of Hwy 132 and Hwy 137. Cape Kumukahi, 'first beginning', is the easternmost point in the state.

The most dominant landscape feature in the Kapoho area is an ancient 420-foot cinder cone. The hill is lush green with thick vegetation and has a small crater lake on top of it.

One of the earliest legends of volcanic activity in Kapoho goes back to the 1300s. It seems Kahavari, a young Puna chief, was holding a holua (sledding) contest on this hill. One of the spectators was an attractive woman who stepped forward and challenged the chief to a race.

Kahavari tossed the woman an inferior sled and charged down the hill, daring her to overcome him. Halfway down he glanced over his shoulder and found her close behind, racing down atop a wave on a sea of molten lava. It was of course Pele, who chased Kahavari clear out to sea where he narrowly escaped in a canoe. Everyone and everything in Pele's path was buried in the flood of lava.

Highway 137

Hwy 137 (Kalapana-Kapoho Beach Rd) is barely above water level, bordered by invasive milo and hala trees that look as if they plan to reclaim the road. In places it's so overgrown there's almost a tunnel effect, with just a lacy bit of light filtering in through the trees. The road sometimes floods during winter storms and high surf.

Kapoho Tidepools

Kapoho Tidepools are in the Kapoho Vacationland subdivision, south of the lighthouse. To get there, turn left off Hwy 137 and take Vacationland Drive to the water.

Here you'll find a network of tidepools formed in lava basins. They're deep enough to swim in and it's Puna's best snorkelling spot.

Isaac Hale Beach Park

Isaac Hale Beach Park, which is on Pohoiki Bay on Hwy 137, has a shoreline of chunky lava rocks. This county park is small but on weekends there's usually a frenzy of local activity. Birthday picnics and fishing seem to be the biggest draws.

Puna's only boat ramp, which is somewhat protected by a breakwater, is here and the local kids swim near the ramp. There are sometimes surfers just south of the park. There are some warm freshwater springs nearby.

Camping is allowed, though you'll probably feel like you're in somebody's backyard as there's a fisherman's house right on the shore.

The park has restrooms, but no drinking water or showers.

MacKenzie State Recreation Area

There's no beach at MacKenzie State Recreation Area but rather 40-foot cliffs with a surging surf which sometimes breaks three-quarters of the way up. There's good fishing from the cliffs for ulua, a jack fish that favours turbulent waters.

This 13-acre park on Hwy 137 is quiet and secluded, in a grove of ironwood trees. There's a soft carpet of needles underfoot. Both tent and trailer camping are allowed. There are picnic tables, barbecue grills and pit toilets, but no drinking water. An old Hawaiian coastal trail passes through the park.

Places to Stay

Champagne Cove (Drs Keith & Norma Godfrey, 1714 Lei Lelua St, Hilo, HI 96720; tel 959-4487) is a new three-bedroom beachfront home on Kapoho Beach. The rate is $50 for two people, up to $70 for six and there's a three-day minimum stay.

Virginia Stein (280 Ponahawai St, Hilo, HI 96720; tel 961-2040) rents out a newish two-bedroom cottage in Kapoho, a short walk from the ocean. The cottage has a queen-sized bed in one room, two twin beds in another and space for two more people in the living room. There's a front porch, cooking facilities and a phone. It costs $50 a day, $775 a month, and has a three-day minimum stay.

Opihikao & Kalani Honua

The village of Opihikao is marked by a little Congregational church and a couple of houses.

Kalani Honua Culture Center and Retreat is 2½ miles south of Opihikao, before the 18-mile marker. Visitors are welcome to drive through and look around. There's a cafe and gift shop near the entrance.

The cafe has all-you-can-eat vegetarian meals. Breakfast for $4.50 includes granola, yoghurt, fruit, an egg dish, coffee and tea. Lunch at $5.50 and dinner at $9 generally include salad, a main dish and dessert.

Kehena Beach

Kehena Beach is a black sand beach, which is the result of a 1955 lava flow. It's a nude sunbathing spot and occasionally an unofficial camping site. Coconut and ironwood trees offer shade along the beach. Kehena is off Hwy 137 about three miles north of Kaimu Beach. Look for cars parked at a pull-off and follow the path down.

Kaimu Beach Park

Kaimu is the most visited of the black sand beaches. The curve of the cove lined with coconut trees looks good in photos but between adverse water conditions and all the tour buses that unload here Kaimu isn't appealing for beach activities.

Most visitors park at the Blacksand Beach Drive Inn & Gift Shop, directly across the road from the sandy part of the beach. For some reason the HVB puts their marker at the north end where there's neither parking nor beach. The Drive Inn sells sandwiches, ice cream and soft drinks.

Kaimu was once far bigger and very popular with surfers. During the big 1975 earthquake Kaimu sank a few feet, resulting in much of the beach eroding away. Not only is the beach not as broad as it once was but the breaks are now less favourable for surfing.

Kaimu is an unprotected beach with a seaward current and swimming is not recommended. Unsuspecting visitors often have to be rescued from the deep.

Harry K Brown Beach

This county park at the north-east end of Kalapana, which is a nice uncrowded walking beach, has sand just as black as Kaimu Beach but it's much bigger.

The park opposite the beach is an activity centre for local kids who play ball and hang out there. There's camping and full facilities.

The low platform between the volleyball court and the pond mauka of the road is the remains of a heiau.

A large enclosed tidepool that offers protected swimming is farther down, in town behind the painted church. It's a popular swimming hole on an otherwise rough and turbulent coast.

KALAPANA

The village of Kalapana sits precariously on the edge of Kilauea's active east rift zone.

For the past few years Kalapana has been one of the best vantage points to observe the billowy white steam clouds rising where molten lava hits the sea. At night, the lava draining down the hillsides from the active vents to the north-west glows red.

Kilauea, which erupted in January 1983, does not seem to show any signs of letting up.

In early 1990, the lava flows practically destroyed this coastal town, burning well over 130 houses. On top of this, about 1500 to 2200 metric tons of volcanic gases are poured into the air daily.

Painted Church

The Star of the Sea is a little white Catholic church noted for its interior murals painted in trompe l'oeil style to create the effect of being in a large cathedral. The illusion of depth is amazingly effective.

There's a nice stained glass window of Father Damien who was with this parish before he moved to the leper colony on Molokai.

In May 1990 the townspeople moved the church to safer ground, out of reach of Kilauea's lava flows.

Kau

The Kau district stretches from South Kona along the southern flanks of Mauna Loa, taking in the entire southern tip of the island all the way up to Hawaii Volcanoes National Park.

Kau is sparsely populated, with only about 5000 people and three real towns. Much of it is dry and desert-like. The highest temperature ever recorded in the state was in Kau in the town of Pahala: 100°F in April 1931. However Kau also has some lush areas in the foothills where sugar cane, macadamia nuts and most of Hawaii's oranges are grown.

Kau was the centre of devastation in the massive 1868 earthquake, the worst Hawaii has ever recorded. For five full days from 27 March, the earth was rattled almost continuously by a series of tremors and quakes. Then in the afternoon of 2 April the earth shook violently in every direction and an inferno broke loose from beneath the surface.

Those fortunate enough to be uphill watched as a rapidly moving river of lava poured down the hillsides and swallowed up everything in its path, including people, homes and cattle. Within minutes the coast

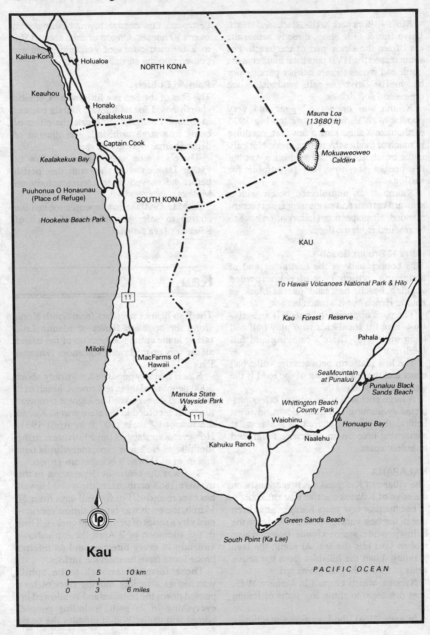

North Kona

Kailua-Kona
Holualoa

Keauhou

Honalo
Kealakekua

Captain Cook

Kealakekua Bay

Puuhonua O Honaunau
(Place of Refuge)

Hookena Beach Park

South Kona

Mauna Loa
(13680 ft)

Mokuaweoweo
Caldera

Kau

To Hawaii Volcanoes National Park & Hilo

Kau Forest Reserve

Pahala

SeaMountain
at Punaluu

Punaluu Black
Sands Beach

Milolii

MacFarms
of Hawaii

Manuka State
Wayside Park

Whittington Beach
County Park

Waiohinu

Honuapu Bay

Kahuku Ranch

Naalehu

Green Sands Beach

South Point (Ka Lae)

PACIFIC OCEAN

Kau

0   5   10 km
0   3   6 miles

was inundated by tidal waves and villages near the shore were swept away.

This deadly triple combination of earthquakes, lava flows and tidal waves permanently changed Kau's landscape. Huge cinder cones came crashing down the slopes and there was one landslide which covered an entire village. You can see the 1868 lava flow along the highway two miles east of the South Point turn-off. The old village of Kahuku lies beneath it.

MANUKA STATE WAYSIDE PARK
Manuka State Wayside Park is an eight-acre arboretum along Hwy 11. The trees and bushes planted here between the mid-1930s and the 1950s include 48 native Hawaiian species and 130 introduced species. Many are labelled, some with both Latin and common names.

Camping is allowed in the three-sided covered shelter which has space for about five sleeping bags. It might be fine for an overnight break between Hilo and Kona, though it's close to the road. Camping under the trees looks tempting but is prohibited. There are restrooms and picnic tables.

The park is in the midst of a natural area reserve which covers 25,550 acres and reaches from the slopes of Mauna Loa down to the sea where it takes in a couple of heiaus and other ruins.

A few miles east of Manuka there's a general store with a contract post office, a Texaco station and a hardware store. This is the commercial centre, such as it is, for Hawaiian Ocean View Estates and other struggling southside subdivisions.

SOUTH POINT
South Point is the southernmost spot in the USA. In Hawaiian it's called Ka Lae, which means simply 'the point'.

South Point has coastal cliffs and a turbulent ocean. It was the site of one of the earliest Hawaiian settlements and may have been where the first Polynesians landed. Much of the area is now under the jurisdiction of Hawaiian Home Lands.

The marked turn-off to South Point is between the 69 and 70-mile markers. South Point is 11 miles south of Hwy 11, at the end of a well-paved one-lane road. There are packed shoulders most of the way allowing cross-traffic to pass without having to stop.

South Point Rd starts out in house sites and macadamia nut farms which soon give way to grassy pastures. The winds are strong here, as evidenced by the trees, some bent almost horizontally with their branches trailing along the ground.

Ten miles down from the highway, South Point Rd forks and the road to the left goes to Kaulana boat ramp and a small cove. The old concrete foundations along the way were WW II military barracks.

The road to the right leads to the rugged coastal cliffs of South Point. The confluence of ocean currents here makes this one of Hawaii's most bountiful fishing grounds. Locals can be seen fishing from the cliffs, many precariously hanging out over the edge of steep lava ledges. Ulua, a jack fish, is particularly plentiful.

There are ruins here, including those of a heiau and a well-preserved fishing shrine. There are also numerous canoe mooring holes drilled into the rock ledges. Ancient Hawaiians used to anchor one end of a rope through the holes and tie the other end to their canoes. The strong currents would pull the canoes straight out to deep turbulent waters where they could fish without getting swept out to sea.

The wooden platforms built on the edge of the cliffs have hoists and ladders which are used to get things to and from the small boats that anchor below.

There's a large unprotected and unmarked hole in the lava directly behind the platforms where you can watch water rise and fall as the waves rush in. Keep an eye out for it, particularly if you have kids with you, as it's not obvious until you're almost on top of it.

Walk down past the beacon and continue along the wall to get to the southernmost point in the USA. There are no markers here, and no souvenirs to take home, just crashing surf and lots of wind.

You can also walk or drive down the other side of the wall where there's a 4WD coastal road. Here you might find a bit of green sand sparkling in the sun at the first spot where the beach is close to the road. These are olivine crystals worn from the lava cliffs by a relentless and pounding surf. The highest concentration of green sand in Hawaii is at Green Sands Beach, about three miles along this dirt road.

Kamaoa Wind Farms

The most surprising thing along this country drive are the rows of huge high-tech windmills lined up in a pasture beside the road. With cattle grazing beneath, it's a surreal scene, and the unearthly whirring sound is just what you'd expect an alien invasion to sound like.

Each of these Mitsubishi wind turbine generators can produce enough electricity for 100 families. Presently there are 37 up and running, with plans to double that number. It's thought, theoretically at least, that by using wind energy conversion the state could produce more than enough electricity to meet its needs.

South of the windmills, the electric poles stop at a few abandoned buildings which are wasting away. Until 1965 this was a Pacific Missile Range Station that tracked missiles shot from California to the Marshall Islands.

WAIOHINU

After South Point, Hwy 11 winds down into a pretty valley and the sleepy village of Waiohinu, nestled beneath green hills. First up on the right is the little wooden Kauahaao Church, white with green trim, dating from 1841.

Shirakawa Motel is 500 feet ahead on the left and there's a monkeypod tree planted by Mark Twain in 1866 just past the hotel, on the same side of the road. It has an HVB marker. The original tree fell in a typhoon in 1957 but hardy new trunks have sprung up and it's once again full-grown.

County camping permits are issued at Kau Base Yard (tel 929-7189) from 7 am to 3.30

pm Monday to Friday. To get there, turn onto the road between Kauahaao Church and Wong Yuen's Chevron gas station, at the sign for Discovery Harbor. The base yard is just a little way down on the right. The gas station is open until 7 pm.

From Waiohinu the road runs beneath the lower slopes of Mauna Loa through sugar cane fields, cattle ranchland and macadamia groves. Inland beyond the sugar cane fields is Kau Forest Reserve, which runs all the way up to Hawaii Volcanoes National Park.

Places to Stay

Shirakawa Motel (Box 467, Naalehu, HI 96772; tel 929-7462) is a green weatherbeaten motel with 13 basic units. The motel is plain, but the setting beneath the green hills is lovely. Rooms cost $25. The manager is friendly though the two dobermans who greet you may at first give you a scare. At dusk, flocks of myna birds fly through squawking.

NAALEHU

Naalehu's claim to fame is being the southernmost town in the USA. It's two miles east of Waiohinu and a few inches to the south.

Modest as it is, Naalehu is the region's shopping centre. It has three grocery markets, a couple of restaurants, a gas station, a movie theatre, an elementary school and the Kau police station. If you happen to be around between 1 and 5 pm on Tuesday or Thursday you can catch the tiny public library while it's open. It adjoins Naalehu Fruit Stand.

Naalehu closes up early, so you can't count on getting food or gas here if you're driving back to Kona from the Hawaii Volcanoes National Park at night.

Places to Eat

Naalehu Fruit Stand on Hwy 11 is a reasonably priced produce stand, health food store and sandwich shop all in one. The ovens out the back bake bread in the morning and pizzas to order from 11 am. They have prepared sandwiches such as teri-tofu on homemade whole wheat bread for $1.95 or you can get a sub with the works for a bit more. Macadamia nut cream cheese bars and other pastries cost about 75 cents. It's open from 9 am to 6.30 pm.

Naalehu Coffee Shop looks touristy with its gift shop and large dining room, but it's essentially a family-run local diner serving three meals a day. At breakfast, two thick slices of banana bread with homemade pineapple-papaya jam are $2.50. Gift shop trinkets include little bags of green or black sand for 40 cents. If you're coming from Kona, turn right just past the theatre.

Across the parking lot from the coffee shop, next to the grocery store, *Green Sands Shoppe* is quite literally a hole in the wall selling inexpensive sandwiches and $4 plate lunches.

WHITTINGTON BEACH COUNTY PARK

Two miles beyond Naalehu there's a pull-off with a scenic lookout above Honuapo Bay which has a view of the cement pilings of the old Honuapo Pier that was once used for shipping sugar and hemp.

Honuapo Bay is the site of Whittington Beach County Park and the turn-off is one mile from the lookout. Whittington has sheltered picnic tables, restrooms and showers.

There's really no beach at Whittington though there are tidepools to explore. The ocean is usually too rough and dangerous for swimming. The endangered green sea turtles are sometimes seen offshore. Apparently they've been hanging around here for a long time, as Honuapo means 'caught turtle'.

You're allowed to camp here and it's far enough from the highway to offer a little privacy. Overall, it's a pretty good choice for a county camping ground but avoid setting up near the street light by the parking lot. It's on all night and illuminates much of the lawn where tenting is allowed.

PUNALUU

Punaluu is a small bay with a black sand beach. The most visited section of the beach is the area in front of Punaluu Black Sands Restaurant. The beach is lined with coconut trees and backed by a duck pond.

Punaluu was once a good-sized port. Ruins of the Pahala Sugar Company's old warehouse and pier can be seen at the north end of the beach. Above it is the site of Kaneeleele Heiau.

There's a small museum on the grounds; admission is free. Take a quick look at the beach and then take a few minutes to check out the detailed mural by Hawaiiana painter Herb Kane to get a sense of what it was like in the 18th century before Westerners arrived. The mural shows the heiau on the point overlooking the bay and a village around the pond. After going back out to the beach it's easy to visualise the settlement which was once there.

The rest of the museum is only mildly interesting. It tells the story of the C Brewer Co, the 'diversified multinational agribusiness company' which owns the complex, then plugs their SeaMountain condo development before funnelling you into their restaurant.

Punaluu Beach County Park, just to the south, has restrooms, showers, drinking water, a picnic pavilion and camping. It's a flat, grassy area right on the beach and a nice place to camp though it's very open. At night the crashing surf works like a lullaby.

To get to the park or restaurant take the turn-off marked Punaluu Park.

SeaMountain, less than a mile south-west along Hwy 11, is Kau's only condo complex. It has a pool, restaurant and tennis courts and a golf course as well as a branch of the Aspen Institute for Humanistic Studies.

Places to Stay

SeaMountain at Punaluu (Box 70, Pahala, HI 96777; tel 928-8301; 800-367-8047 ext 145) is a comfortable condo complex with all the amenities you'd expect to find in Kona, but with none of the crowding. The studios are big and almost as large as one-bedroom units. Some one-bedroom units are two-level with cathedral ceilings. Garden view rates are $73 for studios, $94 for one-bedroom units, $121 for two-bedroom units. Ocean views cost about $10 more. There's a two-day minimum stay. Some units have phones.

Places to Eat

On the Tee is at the golf course at Sea-Mountain. Hot roast beef sandwiches or burgers cost $5.25 and come with salad, onion rings or fries and most of the dishes are moderately priced.

The *Punaluu Black Sands Restaurant* has a rather mundane lunch buffet from 10.30 am to 2 pm daily for $8.95. Tour buses start pouring in around 11.30 am. Á la carte lunch is served until 5 pm, and dinner from 5.30 to 8.30 pm.

PAHALA

Pahala is really two little towns side by side. Down by the mill it's still a working sugar town with old dusty shacks, cars rusting in the yards and 'Beware of Dog' signs. This part of town has a 1920s movie theatre, a little general store and big banyan trees.

The north side of town has tract homes, a hospital, bank, gas stations, a community centre and a modern grocery mart.

Kau Agribusiness which runs the mill has 15,000 acres of sugar cane planted for about 15 miles in either direction from Pahala. The production of sugar is in a gradual decline in these parts and they are diversifying with macadamia nut trees and oranges.

WOOD VALLEY RETREAT CENTRE

About four miles up the slopes from Pahala is remote Wood Valley and the Nechung Dorje Drayang Ling which is a Buddhist temple and retreat centre. The temple was built in the early 1900s by Japanese sugar cane labourers who lived in the valley.

In 1975 a Tibetan lama, Nechung Rinpoche, took up residence at the temple and in 1980 the Dalai Lama paid a visit and declared the temple sacred. Since that time lamas of many Tibetan lineage have visited and conducted programmes here. In addition to teachings of all aspects of Buddhism, the centre is also used by groups conducting Vipassana and Zen meditation, yoga classes and other New Age and spiritual programmes. If you're interested, the centre can send you a list of workshops for the coming year.

The retreat centre (Box 250, Pahala, HI 96777; tel 928-8539) is a two-storey building with a meditation hall and private rooms on the upper floor and guests are free to join in the morning service. The ground floor has two dormitories, a kitchen/dining area and a library of books and videos on Buddhist culture. There's also a small store with books, incense and items from the East.

At times when there are no programmes going on, the centre is open to individual guests. Room rates are $20/30 for singles/doubles and dormitory beds cost $18. Weekly rates are six times the daily. For those seeking a peaceful retreat, the temple is a special place.

TO HAWAII VOLCANOES NATIONAL PARK

Hawaii Volcanoes National Park begins 12 miles from Pahala. Hwy 11 crosses an 11-mile stretch of the park. There are no fees to drive through on the highway nor to explore the Mauna Loa side of the park.

Kilauea's south-west rift zone runs through this part of the Kau Desert, makai of the road. The rift runs for 20 miles, all the way from the summit of Kilauea down to the coast.

The Footprints Trail starts a quarter of a mile beyond the 38-mile marker. This three-quarter mile trail leads to the cast footprints of a group of Hawaiians killed when a cloud of volcanic ash rained down over them in 1790.

Further down Hwy 11, past Namakani Paio Campground, is Mauna Loa Rd. There are tree moulds near the turn-off, a hiking trail through a native forest and bird park a mile further up, and the trailhead to the Mauna Loa summit at the end of the road.

You'll know you're getting closer to Hawaii Volcanoes National Park when the signs start reading 'Caution, Fault Zones. Watch for Cracks in Road'.

Hawaii Volcanoes National Park

Hawaii Volcanoes National Park is hands down the most unique park in the US National Parks system. It's a huge area which not only contains two active volcanoes, but terrain ranging from tropical black sand beaches to the sub-arctic summit of Mauna Loa.

The centerpiece of the park is Kilauea Caldera, the sunken centre of Kilauea Volcano. This still-steaming crater, where molten lava boils just a few feet beneath the surface, is said to be the home of Madame Pele, goddess of volcanoes. Both a foot trail and a paved road circle the caldera's rim.

The park's landscape is geologically awesome with dozens of craters and cinder cones, hills piled high with pumice, and hardened rivers of lava which have frozen rock-solid on the hillsides complete with ripples and waves. There are also native bird reserves, rainforests and fern groves which have either been spared by lava flows or grown over them.

The park is one of Hawaii's best places for camping and hiking. It has three free drive-up camping grounds as well as backcountry camping, and 140 miles of amazingly varied hiking trails.

The park encompasses about a quarter of a million acres of land – more than the entire island of Molokai – and is growing. It even has a wonderful new black sand beach, courtesy of Kilauea's most recent series of eruptions.

Kilauea's south-east rift has been actively flowing since 1983, taking everything in its path with it. In 1989 the Wahaula Visitor Center on the south coast went under. Nearby, the 13th century Wahaula Heiau, the first temple to introduce human sacrifices to Hawaii, sits precariously between active flows.

Kilauea's current flow shows up best after dark, when the lava tubes on the mountainside and the steam clouds at the ocean glow red in the night sky.

Though many visitors expect to see lava fountains spurting up into the air, this is the exception rather than the rule. But whenever Pele does put on one of her spectacular firework displays, cars stream in from all directions. In Hawaii, people generally run *to* volcanoes, not away *from* them.

Volcanic Formations Hawaii's volcanoes are shield volcanoes, formed by repeated gentle eruptions, building up over time as thin layers of lava are deposited one on top of another. As the mountains get higher and wider, long cracks break open down their gently stretched slopes. These are called fault zones, or rift zones and lava eruptions may come from these cracks (as is currently the case with Kilauea) as well as from the summit crater.

The craters are formed when volcanic hills release their lava and collapse back into themselves.

'Pahoehoe' and 'aa' are Hawaiian words which are now used worldwide to describe the earth's two major types of lava. Pahoehoe is the rivers of lava which flow smooth and unbroken. When pahoehoe hardens it often twists into rope-like coils and swirls as the outer skin cools and stiffens while the hotter lava underneath continues to move a little.

Aa is rough and jumbled lava which moves so slowly that the tip of the flow hardens. It's only the molten lava pushing from behind that keeps the flow moving, with the lava at the front piling up and falling over itself, slowing rolling and clunking its way along.

Orientation

The park's main road is Crater Rim Rd which circles the moonscape sights of Kilauea Caldera. It's possible to take in the drive-up sites in an hour – and if that's all the time you have it's unquestionably worth it. Still, it's far better to give yourself a good three hours to allow time for a few short walks, and stops at the visitor centre and museum.

The park's other scenic drive is the Chain of Craters Rd which leads south 24 miles to the coast, ending at the site of the most recent

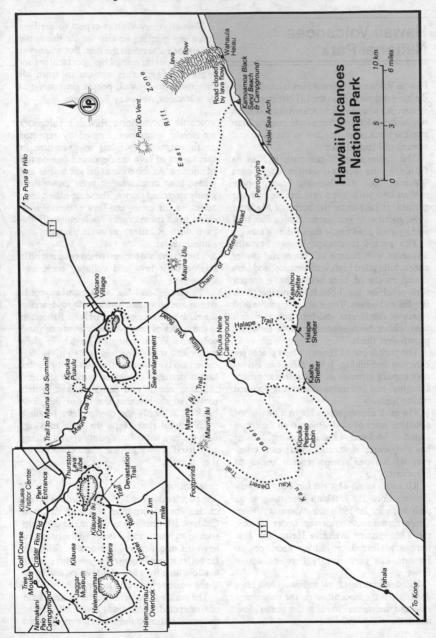

Hawaii Volcanoes National Park

To Puna & Hilo

11

Volcano Village

See enlargement

Trail to Mauna Loa Summit

Mauna Loa Rd

Kipuka Puaulu

Chain of Craters Road

Mauna Ulu

Puu Oo Vent

East Rift Zone

lava flow

Wahaula Heiau

Road closed by lava flow

Kamoamoa Black Sand Beach & Campground

Holei Sea Arch

Petroglyphs

Keauhou Shelter

Halape Trail

Halape Shelter

Kaaha Shelter

Kipuka Nene Campground

Hilina Pali Road

Mauna Iki Trail

Mauna Iki

Kipuka Pepeiao Cabin

Footprints

Kau Desert Trail

Kau Desert

To Kona

11

Pahala

To Kona

10 km
6 miles

5
3

0
0

See enlargement

Tree Moulds

Golf Course

Namakani Paio Campground

Crater Rim Rd

Kilauea Visitor Center

Park Entrance

Thurston Lava Tube

Devastation Trail

Kilauea Iki Crater

Kilauea Caldera

Jaggar Museum

Halemaumau

Halemaumau Overlook

Crater Rim Rd

2 km
1 mile

0
0

1

lava activity. Allow about three hours down and back to stop at all the lookouts along the way.

While you can get a good idea of the place in one full day, it would be easy to spend days, if not weeks, exploring this vast and varied park.

Information

The park's 24-hour hotline (tel 967-7977) has recorded information on current volcanic activity and directions to the best viewing sites.

Park entrance fees are $5 per vehicle per day, or $15 for an annual permit which also includes the Place of Refuge on the Kona Coast. Visitors entering on foot or bicycle through the check station are charged $2 each. The check station is open from 8.30 am to 4.30 pm daily, though the park is open 24 hours.

National park passes are sold here, including an annual pass for $25 which covers Haleakala on Maui, Kilauea Point on Kauai and all other US National Park sites. US citizens who are disabled or age 62 or older can get passes allowing free entry.

The park has a wide range of climatic conditions which vary with elevation and the weather can be moody as well. Rain and fog move in quickly and on any given day it can change from hot and dry to cool and damp. Near Kilauea Crater, temperatures average about 15°F cooler than in Kona. It's a good idea to wear clothing in layers.

Safety Precautions Hawaiian volcanoes are seldom violent as most of the lava that flows from cracks in the rift zones is slow moving. The eruptions don't spew out a lot of ash or poisonous gases either, which is what accounts for most volcano-related deaths in other parts of the world.

There have been only two known violent explosions of Hawaiian volcanoes – both from Kilauea, in 1790 and in 1924. The only direct fatality from a volcanic eruption in this century was during the 1924 explosion which tossed a boulder onto the leg of a photographer who bled to death.

The park service maintains that the presence of unhealthy gases in the volcano area is lower than in the smoggy air of most urban centres. Still, people with respiratory and heart conditions should avoid the areas where sulphur fumes are most highly concentrated.

Other potential hazards include deep cracks in the earth and thin lava crust which may mask hollows and lava tubes. Stay on marked trails and you shouldn't have any problems.

Getting There & Away

The park is 29 miles from Hilo and 97 miles from Kona.

The public bus which runs between Hilo and Waiohinu stops at the visitor centre once in each direction Monday to Friday. It leaves the visitor centre for Hilo at 8 am and returns from Hilo at 2.30 pm. The ride takes about one hour.

Crater Rim Road

Crater Rim Rd is a field trip in vulcanology. This amazing 11-mile loop road skirts the rim of Kilauea Caldera with marked stops at steam vents and crater lookouts. There are running off it short trails through a lava tube, a native rainforest and a forest devastated by pumice and it also passes trailheads for longer hikes into and around the caldera.

Natural forces have re-routed Crater Rim Rd on a few occasions. Earthquakes in both 1975 and 1983 rattled it hard enough to knock sections down into the caldera.

The most interesting stops are at Jaggar Museum, Halemaumau Overlook, Devastation Trail and Thurston Lava Tube. If you take Crater Rim Rd in a counter-clockwise direction you'll start off at the visitor centre.

Crater Rim Rd is a good road for cyclists and unlike the Chain of Craters Rd it's relatively level.

Kilauea Visitor Center The visitor centre is a good place to get oriented to the park. Rangers here have the latest information on volcanic activity, interpretive programmes, guided walks, backcountry trail conditions and the like. They have free hand-outs on a few of the park trails and sell books on volcanoes, hiking and park flora.

The centre contains a small theatre where a 10-minute film showing older eruptions of Kilauea and Mauna Loa is played on the hour. It includes footage of rivers of lava flowing 20 miles an hour, a 13-mile-long curtain of fire and a 1900-foot fountain of lava.

Commercial videos of the most recent eruptions run continuously in the centre's tiny museum. There are also several volcano-related exhibits. The centre (tel 967-7311) is open from 7.45 am to 5 pm daily.

Volcano Art Center The Volcano Art Center (tel 967-7511), which is next door to the visitor centre, sells island pottery, paintings, weavings, woodwork and other arts and crafts. The work is high-quality, with many one-of-a-kind items.

The centre is in a former Volcano House lodge, built in 1877. The non-profit organisation which runs the place offers workshops on painting, crafts, poetry, vulcanology, music, dance and more. It's open from 9 am to 6 pm daily.

Sulphur Banks The first stop beyond the art centre is the Sulphur Banks, where the day-glo colours and piles of steaming rocks look like a landscape from another planet.

This is one of many areas where Kilauea lets off steam, releasing hundreds of tons of sulphuric gases daily. As the steam reaches the surface, it deposits sulphur around the mouths of the vents, giving them a froth of fluorescent yellow crystals. The putrid smell of rotten eggs is hydrogen sulphide.

Steam Vents There are a couple of open non-sulphuric steam vents at the next pull-off, though they're nothing special to look at. Rain which sinks into the earth is heated by the hot rocks below and rises back up as steam.

More interesting is the three-minute walk out to a part of the crater rim called Steaming Bluff. The cooler it is, the more steam there'll be. A plaque on the rim has an interesting

legend about the struggles between Pele and the pig-god Kamapuaa.

Jaggar Museum This museum is worth stopping at both for its displays and for the fine view of Halemaumau Crater. Halemaumau sits within Kilauea Crater and is sometimes referred to as the 'crater within the crater'. Detailed interpretive plaques explain the geological workings of volcanoes. There's a good view of Mauna Loa in the opposite direction, 20 miles away.

The museum is named after Thomas A Jaggar, head geologist at the Massachusetts Institute of Technology, who began the first detailed studies of Kilauea in 1909. Scientists lowered their first thermometer into Halemaumau's lava lake in the summer of 1911. It registered 1832°F before melting. Today the observatory has Kilauea completely wired and it's the most studied volcano anywhere in the world.

The museum is open from 8.30 am to 5 pm daily. It has photo displays, a section on Pele, seismographs, tiltmeters and printed updates showing the current status of volcanic activity. The museum also sells video tapes and books.

The observatory is at Uwekahuna Bluff, the site of an infamous hut which once sat right on the ledge. Local kahunas are said to have tricked people into entering the building where they slipped through a false-bottomed floor to the crater pit below.

Halemaumau Overlook The next attraction is Halemaumau Overlook, where there's a 10-minute walk to the crater rim. For at least 100 years (from 1823, when missionary William Ellis first recorded the sight in writing) Halemaumau was a boiling lake of lava which alternately rose and fell, over-flowing and then receding.

This fiery lake attracted people from all over the world, some of whom compared it to the fires of hell while others saw primeval creation. Mark Twain wrote about staring down at:

...circles and serpents and streaks of lightning all twined and wreathed and tied together...I have seen

Halemaumau Trail

Vesuvius since, but it was a mere toy, a child's volcano, a soup kettle, compared to this.

In 1924 seeping water touched off a massive steam explosion, causing huge boulders and mud to rain down and setting off a lightning storm. When it was over the crater had doubled in size and the lava activity ceased. The crust has since cooled, though the crater still steams. The area is pungent with the smell of sulphur.

All of the Big Island is Pele's territory, but Halemaumau is her home. During special ceremonies the hula is performed in her honour here and throughout the year those wishing to appease Pele leave flowers, coins and bottles of gin at the crater rim.

Ohelo, a bush about two feet high with clusters of bright red berries, is one of the early takers to lava and grows here. It's thought to personify Pele's sister Hiiaka. Before eating any of the tart berries, some should first be offered to Pele.

Beyond Halemaumau Overlook

The Halemaumau Overlook is at the start of Halemaumau Trail which runs three miles across Kilauea Caldera to the visitor centre.

Though few people continue past the overlook it's an easy half-mile walk to the site of a 1982 lava flow. This is one of the most interesting parts of the Halemaumau Trail and even if you weren't planning on hiking it's worth coming this far (see Hiking Trails in this section).

The spewed lava here has amazing textures and colours and there's an eerie sense of the earth's raw power.

Devastation Trail

After the Halemaumau Overlook, Crater Rim Rd continues across the barren Kau Desert and then through the fallout area of the 1959 eruption of Kilauea Iki Crater. Ash and pumice blown south-west of the crater buried a mile of Crater Rim Rd eight feet deep. The road had to be ploughed by tractors, much like clearing snow after a blizzard.

Devastation Trail is a walk of just over half a mile across a former rainforest devastated by cinder and pumice from that eruption. Everything green was wiped out. What remains today are dead ohia trees, stripped bare and sunbleached white, standing stark against the black landscape. It's so barren and desolate it could be the movie set for a post-nuclear scene.

The trail follows a wooden boardwalk, with parking lots on each end. The prominent cinder cone along the way is Puu Puai, 'gushing hill', formed during the 1959 eruption. The north-east end of the trail looks down into Kilauea Iki Crater.

The Chain of Craters Rd intersects with Crater Rim Rd near Devastation Trail.

Thurston Lava Tube

On the east side of the Chain of Craters Rd intersection, Crater Rim Rd passes through the rainforest of native tree ferns and ohia which covers Kilauea's windward slope.

The speed limits are set low not only because the road is winding, but also because cars cruising through are taking a toll on native forest birds.

The Thurston Lava Tube Trail is an enjoyable 15-minute loop walk which starts out in ohia forest, goes through an impressive lava tube and then through a fern grove. The cibotium tree ferns here grow to 20 feet high.

Lava tubes are formed when the outer crust of a river of lava starts to harden but the liquid lava beneath the surface continues to flow on through. After the flow has drained out, the hard shell remains. Thurston Lava Tube is a grand example – it's tunnel-like, and almost big enough to run a train through.

You'll probably hear a lot of birdsong along this walk. The apapane, a native honeycreeper, is easy to spot here. It has a red body and silvery-white underside and flies from flower to flower drinking from the yellow blossoms of the mamane tree and the red pompom flowers of the ohia tree.

Kilauea Iki Crater When Kilauea Iki burst open in a fiery inferno in November 1959 the whole crater floor turned into a bubbling pool of molten lava. Its fountains reached record heights of 1900 feet, lighting the evening sky with a bright orange glow for miles around. At its peak it gushed out two million tons of lava an hour.

Today a trail runs across the crater floor. The hike is not dissimilar to walking on ice – here too there's a lake below the hardened surface, though in this case it's of molten lava not water.

From Kilauea Iki Overlook there's a good view of the mile-wide crater below.

Chain of Craters Road
The Chain of Craters Rd winds 24 miles down the southern slopes of Kilauea Volcano to the ruins of Wahaula Visitor Center on the Puna Coast. It's a paved two-lane road with no gas, water or other services along the way.

There are striking vistas of the coastline far below and for miles the predominant view is of long fingers of lava reaching down to the sea.

In some places the road slices through lava and in other places it's paved over it. You'll see both aa lava, which is crusty and rough, and pahoehoe lava, which is shiny and black as fresh tar. You can sometimes find thin filaments of volcanic glass known as Pele's hair in the cracks and crevices.

In addition to endless lava expanses, the road takes in an impressive collection of sights, including a handful of craters that you can literally pull up to the rims of and peer into. Some of the craters are so new there's no sign of life, while others are thickly forested with ohia lehua, wild orchids and ferns.

The Chain of Craters Rd once connected through to Hwy 130 and Hwy 137 and you could drive between the volcano and Hilo via Puna. Lava flows closed the road in 1969 but by 1979 it was back in service, re-routed slightly. Over the past few years flows from Kilauea's active east rift have again flowed over the road and cut the link.

Hilina Pali Road Hilina Pali Rd starts 2¼ miles down Chain of Craters Rd and leads five miles in to Kipuka Nene camping ground. It's another 3½ miles to Hilina Pali, a lookout at 2283 feet with a view of the south-east coast. The end of the road is the trailhead for the Kau Desert Trail and for the Kaaha and Hilina Pali trails which lead down to the coast. They are all hot, dry backcountry trails.

Mauna Ulu In 1969, eruptions from Kilauea's east rift began building a new lava shield which eventually rose 400 feet above its surroundings. It was named Mauna Ulu, 'growing mountain'.

By the time the flow stopped in 1974 it had covered 10,000 acres of parkland and added 200 acres of new land to the coast.

It also buried 12 miles of the Chain of Craters Rd in lava as deep as 100 metres. There's still a small portion of the old road left. You can drive up to the lava flow by taking the turn-off on the left 3¾ miles down Chain of Craters Rd. Just beyond this is Mauna Ulu itself.

As you continue down the Chain of Craters Rd you'll be passing over Mauna Ulu's massive flows.

Ke Ala Koma About halfway along the road is Ke Ala Koma, a covered shelter with picnic tables and a superb ocean view. This would be a great place to unpack a lunch.

From there the road begins to descend along a series of winding switchbacks, some deeply cut through lava flows.

Puu Loa Petroglyphs Puu Loa Trail leads about a mile to petroglyphs carved into the lava by early Hawaiians. The site is along an ancient trail between Kau and Puna and has one of the largest concentration of petroglyphs in Hawaii. Puu Loa, 'long hill', was also a place where Hawaiians brought the umbilical cords of their babies in the hope that burying them there would bring their children long lives.

The marked trailhead begins on the Chain of Craters Rd about a mile up from the coast.

Holei Sea Arch About 2½ miles after the petroglyphs, look for the sign marking the Holei Sea Arch. This rugged section of the coast has sharply eroded lava cliffs, called Holei Pali, which are constantly being pounded by crashing surf.

The high rock arch carved out of one of the cliffs is impressive, though the wave action has numbered its days. The ocean here is a deep rich blue.

Kamoamoa Black Sand Beach Kamoamoa is Hawaii's newest and most impressive black sand beach. It was formed when Kilauea's hot lava hit the ocean, exploded into a zillion tiny fragments and washed up here. The grains of sand are so new that they are still unrounded and cling together.

The white waves washing up on the beach create a striking contrast against the deep, radiantly black sand. The waves can be huge and break high. This is not a beach for swimming; there are strong and dangerous currents.

Kamoamoa is one of the park's three drive-up camping grounds. It is also the site of an old Hawaiian village where the ruins of Moa Heiau as well as stone walls built by cattle ranchers in the 1880s can be found.

End of the Road The road ends near the former Wahaula Visitor Center which was destroyed by lava flows in the summer of 1989.

If lava is still pouring into the ocean here, you may be able to see the billowing clouds of steam coming up from the shoreline and smoke rising from the lava tubes on the mountainside. At night it all glows in shades of orange and red.

Wahaula Heiau Wahaula Heiau was the first luakini heiau built in Hawaii. Its construction is credited to Paao, a Tahitian high priest who migrated here in the 12th century. Paao not only introduced human sacrifice into temple ceremonies, but also the concept of mana, a divine power which could be held within temple grounds as well as by the royal chiefs who worshipped there.

A strict social system of kapus (taboos) followed to protect that mana. Commoners were forbidden to eat the same foods or walk the same grounds as chiefs for fear they would absorb the chiefs' mana. Those who broke the kapus were put to death.

Mana was an elusive element that could be lost. When a temple no longer had its mana, it was abandoned and a new one built elsewhere. Wahaula Heiau never lost it – it was the last luakini temple where royalty worshipped before the Hawaiian gods were abandoned.

The heiau once had altars, idols and an oracle tower, though only the stone platform remains. The recent lava flows that swept away the visitor centre skirted around the heiau, 150 feet away. Apparently it still has some mana left!

Mauna Loa Road

Mauna Loa Rd leads off Hwy 11 about 2¼ miles west of the visitor centre. Kipuka Puaulu, a unique sanctuary for native birds and plants, is about 1½ miles up the road. The Mauna Loa Trail begins at the end of the road, 13½ miles from Hwy 11. (For more details, see the Hiking Trails section.)

Lava Tree Moulds Near the start of Mauna Loa Rd, there's a turn-off to some lava tree moulds. These tube-like holes were formed when a lava flow engulfed the rainforest that stood here. Because the trees were so waterlogged the lava hardened around them instead of burning them on contact. As the trees disintegrated, deep holes were left in the ground.

The first of the moulds are very close to the parking lot, making it easy to get a quick glimpse.

Hiking Trails

The park has an extensive network of hiking trails, from sea level to over 13,000 feet. The hikes range from many short and easy ones to serious backcountry treks. Trails strike out in a number of directions – across crater floors, down to secluded beaches, across the Kau Desert, through native forests and up to snow-capped Mauna Loa.

Crater Rim Trail Crater Rim Trail is an 11-mile hiking trail which roughly parallels Crater Rim Rd. On the north side the trail is along the crater rim, while on the south side it runs outside the paved road.

Because the vehicle road is designed to take in the main sights, you'll actually miss a few of them by hiking. If you have wheels of some sort, you might want to consider riding around the crater rim and saving your hiking legs for trails into areas inaccessible by car or bike.

Kipuka Puaulu The trail through Kipuka Puaulu is a mile-long loop through a 100 acre oasis of native forest. There's a free nature trail guide available at the visitor centre.

About 400 years ago a major lava flow from Mauna Loa's north-east rift covered most of the surrounding area. Pele spared this bit of land when the flow parted, creating an island forest in a sea of lava. In Hawaiian, it's known as a *kipuka*.

Kipuka Puaulu is a tiny and unique ecopreserve of rare endemic plants, insects and birds. The lava that surrounds the kipuka has served as a protective barrier against intruding species.

Koa is the largest of the trees here. The younger trees have fern-like leaves which are replaced with flat crescent-shaped leaf stalks as the koa matures and rises above the forest floor. The tree provides habitat for ferns and climbing peperomia that take root in its moist bark.

Kipuka Puaulu is quiet, except for the sounds of birds. The natives include the inquisitive elepaio and three honeycreepers – the amakihi, apapane and iiwi. The birds are sparrow size and brightly coloured. The honeycreepers have slender curved beaks that enable them to drink nectar from the flowers of native trees.

Also along the trail is a lava tube in whose dark depths a unique big-eyed spider was discovered only a few years back.

Mauna Loa Trail Mauna Loa Trail begins at the end of Mauna Loa Rd, 13½ miles north of Hwy 11. It's about an hour's drive between the trailhead and the visitor centre where overnight hikers are required to register (and where you can get more information on the trail).

This is a rugged 18-mile trail that ascends 6600 feet. The ascent is gradual but the elevation makes it a serious hike and it takes a minimum of three days.

There are two simple cabins available on a first-come, first- served basis. Red Hill cabin has eight bunks and Mauna Loa summit cabin has 12. The cabins have catchment water, though treatment is recommended.

The trail rises out of an ohia forest and above the treeline seven miles to Red Hill at 10,035 feet. This leg of the hike takes four to five hours. From Red Hill there are fine views of Mauna Kea to the north and Haleakala on Maui to the north-west.

It's 11 miles and a full day's hike from Red Hill to the summit cabin at 13,250 feet. The summit has a sub-arctic climate and temperatures normally drop to freezing point at night all year round. Winter snow storms can last a few days and bring snow packs as deep as nine feet. Occasionally snow falls as low as Red Hill and covers the upper end of the trail.

Acclimatising is important, as altitude

sickness is not uncommon. Common symptoms are headache, nausea and shortness of breath. For minor symptoms, deep breathing brings some relief as does lying down with your head lower than your feet. If the symptoms are serious get to a lower elevation immediately. Hypothermia from the cold and wind is another hazard. A good windproof jacket, wool sweater, winter-rated sleeping bag and rain gear are all essential.

Halemaumau Trail Diagonally across the road from the visitor centre there are signs marking the way to a number of trailheads, including Halemaumau Trail which starts a few minutes' walk from there.

The first section of Halemaumau Trail passes briefly through a moist ohia forest, with tall ferns and flowering ginger. It then descends about 500 feet to the floor of Kilauea Caldera and continues for three miles across the surface of this still- active volcano. This is the trippiest hike of all in a park full of extraordinary trails.

In ancient times the caldera was much deeper, but in the past 100 years overflows from Halemaumau Crater as well as eruptions from the caldera floor have built it up.

The process is easy to visualise as the trail crosses flow after flow, beginning with one from 1974. It continues over flows from 1971, 1885, 1954, 1982 and 1894, each distinguished by a different shade of black. The trail is marked with ahu, or piles of lava rocks.

Shortly after breakfast on 30 April 1982, at the Hawaiian Volcano Observatory geologists watched as their seismographs and tiltmeters unexpectedly warned of an imminent eruption. The park service quickly closed off Halemaumau Trail and cleared hikers from the crater floor. Before noon a half-mile fissure began to spew a million cubic metres of lava!

This 1982 flow created a landscape which is both very barren and richly beautiful. Some of the spatter formed high brittle mounds, many with small hollow areas. They have incredible textures, unusual shapes and deep shades of black accented

with rich shades of orange, rust and ochre. Sunlight glitters on tiny iridescent bubbles which have cooled in the lava. Ferns have already taken hold inside the cracks of steam vents which act like little terrariums.

The trail ends about 3½ miles from the visitor centre at Halemaumau Overlook. Needless to say there's no shade on the trail and it can be hot. Take water along with you as there's none at the lookout.

Kilauea Iki Trail When Kilauea Iki Crater exploded in 1959, its lava fountains set a new height record of 1900 feet. When the ash finally settled, it covered the whole area south-west of the crater.

Kilauea Iki Trail begins near the parking lot of Thurston Lava Tube and descends 400 feet to the crater floor. From there it goes clear across the mile-long crater, passing the main vent on the way. The crater floor is still steaming and there's molten lava beneath the hardened surface.

After you ascend the crater wall on the far side, you'll be on Byron Ledge, the ledge which separates Kilauea Iki from Kilauea Caldera. By looping around to the right, you can get back to the parking lot via Crater Rim Trail which skirts the north rim of Kilauea Iki. Altogether this loop is about 3½ miles long.

If you want to check it out before hiking, there's a drive-up lookout about half a mile north of the Thurston Lava Tube.

Footprints Trail The Footprints Trail is the beginning of the Mauna Iki Trail which leads to a network of trails through the Kau Desert. The trailhead, marked by an interpretive plaque, is between the 37 and 38-mile markers on Hwy 11, nine miles south of park headquarters. The footprints are an easy three-quarter mile hike in from the highway.

In 1790 a violent and massive explosion at Kilauea wiped out a regiment of soldiers retreating to Kau after attacking Kamehameha's sacred Waipio Valley. They were literally stopped in their tracks, suffocated by a rare cloud of poisonous gases. A shower of hot mud and ashes hardened

Kilauea Iki trail

around them, leaving a permanent cast of their footprints. Two hundred years later you can still count the toes.

Halape Trail The 7.2-mile trail to Halape starts from Kipuka Nene camping ground off Hilina Pali Rd. Halape was an idyllic beachfront camping ground bordered by coconut trees until 29 November 1975 when the strongest earthquake in 100 years shook the Big Island just before dawn. Rock slides from the upper slopes sent most of the 36 campers running toward the sea, where the coastline suddenly sank. As the beach submerged beneath their feet a series of tsunamis swept the campers up, carrying them first out to sea and then tossing them back up on shore. Miraculously only two people died.

The earthquake left a fine sandy cove inland of the former beach. There are strong currents in the open ocean beyond the cove. Halape has catchment water, a pit toilet and a three-walled shelter.

Volcano
The village of Volcano, about a mile east of the park, has two general stores with gas

pumps, a post office, a takeaway diner, a restaurant and a couple of places to stay.

Places to Stay
My Island B&B (Gordon & Joann Morse, Box 100, Volcano, HI 96785; tel 967-7216) has three bedrooms, with shared bathroom, in the Morses' home for $25/40 for singles/doubles, including breakfast. The living room is full of books on volcanoes, from photo essays to geological tomes, a few written by former guests. There are also three units separate from the house, each with a private entrance and bathroom, for $50. The two newest units have small refrigerators. The older unit is not quite as spiffy but it's larger and has a full kitchen.

During the annual Kilauea Volcano Marathon in January the Morses rent out beds (not rooms) for $10 and manage to squeeze in 21 runners. Gordon is very outgoing and can pile you high with information on the Big Island which he proclaims is 'the ONLY Hawaiian Island worth visiting'. The B&B is a quarter of a mile past Kilauea Lodge, on the left after Wright Rd. Nootka, their big white Samoyed, is trained to bark when a car pulls into the yard, but Gordon says he's gentle as a pussycat.

Kilauea Lodge (Box 116, Volcano, HI 96785; tel 967-7366), which is on the main road in Volcano village has four newly renovated rooms in what was formerly a YMCA dormitory. These are delightful rooms, with the sort of country comfort you'd find in a fine inn. They have working fireplaces, high ceilings, electric blankets, quilts and private bathrooms with tubs. The cost of $75 includes full breakfast served in the lodge's restaurant. There's also a two-room cottage for $95. Owner Albert Jeyte is an Emmy-winning make-up artist who worked with the Magnum PI series.

Places to Eat

The *Volcano Country Club Restaurant* at Volcano Golf Course serves continental breakfast from 7 am to 10.30 am and lunch from 11 am to 3 pm daily. Main dishes at lunch time range from chilli or Hawaiian stew for $4 to teriyaki steak for $6. All are served with soup or salad and rice or fries. Sandwiches or burgers with fries are $2.50 to $4.50.

Volcano Store & Diner at the Chevron station in Volcano has fairly inexpensive breakfasts, sandwiches and plate lunches around $3 to $5.

Kilauea Lodge (tel 967-7366) is only open for Sunday brunch (10.30 am to 2.30 pm) and for dinner (5.30 to 9 pm daily except Mondays). The Sunday brunch is off the menu with items such as French toast, seafood crepes and steak sandwiches averaging around $7 to $9. Complete dinners with beef, seafood, chicken and lamb dishes range from $13 to $18. For dessert there's ohelo berry, lilikoi chiffon or macnut pie for $2.95.

The dining room has high wooden ceilings, island artwork and window tables looking out on a fern forest. The big stone fireplace, built in 1938 when this was a YMCA camp, is embedded with an international collection of stones and coins.

Places to Stay – Volcanoes National Park

Namakani Paio Cabins (Box 53, Hawaii National Park, HI 96713; tel 967-7321) is a charmless place. The 10 windowless plywood cabins each have one double bed and two single bunk beds. There are electric lights but no power outlets or heating. The cabins are booked through Volcano House where you pay and pick up your bag of linen. The rate of $24 is for up to four people and there's a $15 deposit for keys and linen. There are communal showers and restrooms. It can get cold at night so if you have a sleeping bag, bring it along. (Or bring a tent as well and you can stay in the adjacent camping ground for free.)

Volcano House (Box 53, Hawaii National Park, HI 96713; tel 967-7321), which is right in the park, is walking distance from the visitor centre. Though it's perched on the rim of Kilauea Caldera, most of the room views are disappointing. The lower-level rooms look out onto the walkway and some of those on the upper floor have only a partial view of the crater. The current hotel dates from 1941. The rooms are plain and tired and noise carries through the louvred windows which open onto the hallway. Rates are $57 to $102.

Camping The park has three drive-in camping grounds. All have picnic pavilions and fireplaces, though wood is not provided.

Camping is free and the camping grounds are seldom crowded. There's no registration or reservation system, though camping is officially limited to seven days per camping ground per year. Rangers patrol the grounds and they're quite helpful and friendly.

Nights are crisp and cool at Namakani Paio (4000 feet) and Kipuka Nene (3000 feet).

Namakani Paio is the most frequented of the three camping sites. It's about three miles west of the visitor centre, just off Hwy 11. If you're on your way between Hilo and Kona it's a convenient place to stop for the night.

The open tent sites are in a small meadow with little privacy though it's surrounded by fragrant eucalyptus trees. This place is quite popular and it's a good place to meet other campers.

It's about a one mile hike to the Volcano

Observatory and Crater Rim Trail from the camping ground.

Kipuka Nene Campground is about five miles down Hilina Pali Rd, off Chain of Craters Rd. It's the least developed of the camping sites, though there's a water catchment system, toilets and a large shelter with picnic tables. Sites aren't marked, so you just pull off the road and look for a place to set up.

The area is bushy and grassy. True to the camping ground's name, a few friendly nene often hang out there.

The sea-level *Kamoamoa Campground* is at the new black sand beach of the same name. The camping sites are in a circle, with trees between sites to give a little privacy, and there are primitive toilets but no water.

If volcanic activity continues along recent patterns, you'll be able to look up the side of the mountain at night and watch the red glow where lava tubes are broken and the molten lava radiates out.

Down the coast you can see steam clouds where the lava pours into the ocean. Once in a while the spatter flies up and illuminates the steam cloud. It's visible with the naked eye, but with binoculars it's a spectacular sight.

Nights are warmer here than in the other camping grounds and you can hear the surf.

Cabins & Backcountry Camping Hiking shelters and simple cabins are available along some of the longer backcountry trails. There's no fee to use them.

There are coastal area shelters at Keauhou, Halape and Kalue. Kipuka Pepeiao cabin is along the Kau Desert Trail and there are two other cabins are along the Mauna Loa Trail. All have limited water catchment, which should be treated. The visitor centre keeps track of current water supplies and trail conditions.

All overnight hikers are required to register at the visitor centre before heading out and upon returning. Because of Mauna Loa's history of overdue or lost hikers, you need to list the colour of your backpacks and other equipment. This aids rangers in searching for lost or injured hikers as well as keeping track of hikers if there's an earthquake or eruption.

Essential backpacking equipment that the park recommends for any of the backcountry trails includes a first aid kit, a flashlight with extra batteries, a minimum of two quarts of water, emergency food, a compass, broken-in boots, complete rain gear, cooking stove with fuel, sunscreen and a hat. For a more comprehensive checklist write to Hawaii Volcanoes National Park, HI 96718.

The state maintains *Niaulani Cabin*, a housekeeping cabin, half a mile east of the national park. At 3700 feet, this secluded cabin sits all by itself in the seven-acre ohia forest of Kilauea State Recreation Area. It's on Kalanikoa Rd near Volcano village.

The cabin has two bedrooms, a living room, hot showers, a stove and refrigerator.

Rates are $10/14 for singles/doubles, and up to $30 for six people, but it's a long shot getting in. For reservations contact the Division of State Parks (tel 961-7200), Box 936, 75 Aupuni St, Hilo, HI 96721, where you also pick up the key.

Places to Eat – Volcanoes National Park
If you're trying to see the park in a day, you can save time by bringing a lunch and having a picnic wherever you are at noon. If you don't happen to be near the park entrance, it's a long haul from most points in the park out to a restaurant.

Volcano House serves up a cafeteria-quality lunch time buffet for $9.75. The dining room view overlooking Kilauea Caldera is magnificent though it can be matched over in the snack shop where they serve sandwiches for $2.95 and cookies, juice and coffee. Dining room hours are: breakfast 7 to 10.30 am, lunch 10.30 am to 2 pm and dinner 5.30 to 8.30 pm. The snack shop is open from 10.30 am to 4 pm.

Saddle Road/Mauna Kea

The Saddle Road, true to its name, runs between the two highest points on the island, with Mauna Kea to the north and Mauna Loa to the south.

The road passes over large lava flows and climbs through a variety of terrains and climates. At sunrise and sunset there's a gentle glow on the mountains and a light show on the clouds. In the early morning it's crisp enough to see your breath and if you take the spur road up to Mauna Kea you'll reach permafrost.

Though most car rental contracts prohibit travel on the Saddle Rd, it's a fine paved road straight across. There's a section on the Hilo side where the pavement is a bit crumbly and potholed, but it's no big deal – particularly by island standards.

Locals looking for the rationale behind the car rental ban come up with things like military convoys or evening fog. The crux of the matter seems to be that the rental agencies just don't want to be responsible if your car breaks down on Hawaii's most remote road.

The Saddle Rd is 50 miles long and has no gas stations or other facilities along the way. (Neither are there any gas stations on the 33-mile stretch of Hwy 190 between the Saddle Rd and Kona.)

Crossing the island on the Saddle Rd is a bit shorter than on the northern route of the Belt Rd, but it's also a slower road and timewise there isn't much difference either way.

On the western side, the Saddle Rd starts out in cattle ranchland with rolling grassy hills and planted stands of eucalyptus trees. It's beautiful, but like the rest of the western side it's changing. A new subdivision called Waikii Ranch has recently divided 3000 acres of the area's ranchland into half a million dollar house lots and is marketing them to wealthy urban cowboys.

After about 10 miles the land starts getting rougher and the pastures and fences fewer. The military takes over where the cows leave off. Bradshaw Army Airfield comes up first, then the quonset huts of the Pohakuloa Military Camp. Most of the vehicles on the road here are playing army, though in hunting season you'll come across a fair number of pick-up trucks and Broncos.

MAUNA KEA

Mauna Kea is Hawaii's highest mountain

and its 13,796-foot summit has a cluster of important astronomical observatory domes.

The unmarked Summit Rd which climbs up Mauna Kea is at the 28- mile marker, opposite a hunter's check station. It's a well-paved 6¼ miles to the visitor centre. The road winds up a few thousand feet in elevation. If you've got a small car it's probably going to labour a bit, but it shouldn't be a problem making it up as far as the visitor centre. A standard transmission is preferable.

Surprisingly, you don't really get closer views of Mauna Kea's peaks by driving up to the visitor centre. The peaks actually look higher and the views are broader from the Saddle Rd. But you'll find nice vistas from the Summit Rd and you can often drive up above the clouds. Mauna Kea doesn't appear as a single main peak, but rather a jumble of peaks, some black, some red- brown, some seasonally snow-capped.

The Summit Rd passes through open range of grazing cattle. It's easy to spot Eurasian skylarks in the grass and if you're lucky you might see the endangered *io* (Hawaiian hawk) hovering overhead. Both make their home on the grassy mountain slopes. The *io* is found only on the Big Island. Mauna Kea is also home to the *nene* goose, as well as the *palila*, a small yellow honeycreeper which lives no where else in the world.

One of the more predominant plants here is mullen, which has soft woolly leaves and shoots up a tall stalk. In the spring the stalks get so loaded down with flowers they bend over from the weight of what looks like big yellow helmets. Mullen was brought in by ranchers as a free-loading weed in grass seed.

Visitor Centre

The visitor centre, officially the Onizuka Center for International Astronomy, was named for Ellison Onizuka, a Big Island native and one of the astronauts who died in the 1986 Challenger disaster.

The centre shows an interesting 10-minute video on Mauna Kea's observatories. There are photo displays of the observatories and telescope viewings and information on discoveries made from the summit. Note the astronomers aren't peering through little eyepieces or looking at the sky directly but rather are watching images relayed on computer monitors.

The centre also has exhibits of the mountain's history, ecology and geology.

If you're planning to go up to the summit, stop here first to check road conditions and pick up brochures.

The visitor centre is open from 1 to 6 pm Fridays, 9 am to 2 pm Saturdays, 9 am to 2 pm and 4.30 to 6 pm Sundays and 1 to 5 pm Mondays. The outdoor restrooms are always open and have running water.

Summit Observatories

The summit of Mauna Kea has the greatest collection of state-of-the-art telescopes on earth and superior conditions for viewing the heavens. Nearing 14,000 feet, the summit is above 40% of the earth's atmosphere and 90% of its water vapour. The air is typically clear, dry and stable.

Not only is Hawaii itself isolated but Mauna Kea is one of the most secluded places in Hawaii. The air is relatively free from dust and smog. Nights are dark and free from city light interference. To further the cause, island streetlights have been converted to low-impact sodium. Rather than using the full iridescent spectrum, these orange lights use only a few wavelengths which the telescopes can be adjusted to remove.

Eight out of 10 nights are good for viewing. Only the Andes Mountains match Mauna Kea for cloudless nights, though air turbulence in the Andes makes viewing more difficult there.

The University of Hawaii holds the lease on Mauna Kea from the 12,000-foot level to the summit and UH receives observing time at each telescope as one of the lease provisions. Currently eight telescopes are in operation and two new massive ones are under construction.

UH built the first telescope in 1968 with a 24-inch mirror. In comparison, the Maxwell telescope built in 1987 by the UK, Netherlands and Canada has a 590-inch mirror.

The UK Infrared Telescope (UKIRT) with its 150-inch mirror, currently the world's largest infrared telescope, can be operated via computers and satellite relays from the Royal Observatory in England. In 1988 UKIRT and the Canada-France-Hawaii Telescope jointly identified the most distant galaxy yet discovered. Its light is 12 billion years old.

NASA's Infrared Telescope has measured the heat of volcanoes on Io, one of Jupiter's moons. The most active of Io's volcanoes is now named after Pele.

Scheduled to become operational in 1991 is the Keck Observatory, a project of Caltech and the University of California. It will be the world's largest and most powerful infrared and optical telescope. A price tag of $85 million makes it the world's most expensive as well.

Previously the sheer weight of the glass mirrors was a limiting factor in telescope design. The Keck telescope has a new honeycomb design with 36 hexagonal segments, each six feet across, that will function as a single piece of glass. Its capacity to receive light will be greater than twice that of all Mauna Kea's present telescopes combined.

On 11 July 1991 a rare total solar eclipse will pass over the entire Big Island. Quite amazingly, the centre of the path will pass almost directly over the astronomical observatories atop Mauna Kea.

The eclipse will begin at 6.30 am. Totality will occur at approximately 7.28 am and will last just over four minutes in the centre of the path. An eclipse of this duration is not expected again for another 140 years.

Viewing should be excellent anywhere on the Big Island where the weather is clear. Unless a *kona* storm blows in, the Kona Coast is expected to be the prime viewing area.

Most hotels are already booked solid. Parker Ranch, which is directly under the centre of the eclipse plans to create 20,000 camping spaces for the event, which it's billing as 'Summer Solar Festival '91'. Camping on the eve of the eclipse will be a whopping $60 to $75 per person. They plan to have viewing screens to transmit eclipse images, telescope views and lectures from scientists from Mauna Kea. For information contact Parker Ranch Visitor Center (tel 885-7655, Box 458, Kamuela, HI 96743).

Other than the Big Island, only parts of Kahoolawe and the Kaupo area of southern Maui will experience the total eclipse.

Copies of the brochure *The Total Solar Eclipse of July 11, 1991, over Hawaii* are available by writing to Karen Rehbock, Institute for Astronomy, 2680 Woodlawn Drive, Honolulu, HI 96822.

Driving to the Summit

Visitors are welcome to go up to the summit in daytime, but vehicle headlights are not allowed between sunset and sunrise because they interfere with observation. The Canada-France-Hawaii Telescope and the UH 88-inch Telescope have visitor galleries.

The pavement ends above the visitor centre near Hale Pohaku, the stone buildings where scientists stay during the day. The road from here to the summit is accessible by 4WD only. Harper Car & Truck Rentals in Hilo is the only car rental company that allows its jeeps to be driven to the summit.

The drive takes about half an hour. You should drive in the low range and loosen the gas cap to prevent vapour lock. The upper road can get iced over during winter. Be particularly careful on the way down and watch out for loose cinder.

About 4½ miles up is an area called Moon Valley where the Apollo astronauts rehearsed with their lunar rover before their journey to the real moonscape.

At 5½ miles up, look to the left for a narrow ridge with two caves and black stones. That's Keanakakoi, 'cave of the adze', an ancient adze quarry. From there high-quality basalt was quarried to make adze and other tools and weapons which were traded throughout the islands. For people interested in archaeology it's an impressive site. This is a protected area and nothing should be removed.

Lake Waiau

Lake Waiau is a unique alpine lake which, at 13,020 feet, is the third highest lake in the USA. It's inside the Puu Waiau cinder cone in a barren and treeless setting.

Lake Waiau is rather mysterious. It's a small lake, no more than 10 feet deep and set on porous cinder in desert conditions of less than 15 inches of rainfall per year. It's fed by melting winter snows and permafrost, which elsewhere on Mauna Kea quickly evaporates. Lake Waiau has no freshwater springs and yet it's never dry.

Hawaiians used to bring the umbilical cords of their babies and throw them in the lake to give their children the strength of the mountain.

Puu Poliahu

Just below the summit is Puu Poliahu, the home of Poliahu, goddess of snow.

Poliahu is said to be more beautiful than her sister Pele. In the legendary past during conflicts over men, Pele would get miffed and erupt Mauna Kea, Poliahu would cover it over with ice and snow, then Pele would erupt again. Back and forth they went. The legend is metaphorically correct. As recent as 10,000 years ago there were eruptions through glacial ice caps here.

Because of its spiritual significance, astronomical domes have not been built on Puu Poliahu.

Warnings

The summit air has only about 60% of the oxygen available at sea level and altitude sickness is not uncommon. The problem is not only the height itself but also the fact that people don't take the time to properly acclimatise.

Unlike Nepal, for instance, where great heights are generally reached only after days of trekking, here you can zip up from sea level to nearly 14,000 feet by car in two hours.

Scuba divers who have been diving within the past 24 hours risk getting the bends by going to the summit. It's recommended that children under 16, pregnant women and those with a respiratory condition, or even a cold for that matter, do not go beyond the visitor centre.

Even the astronomers who work up here never fully acclimatise and are always working oxygen-deprived in the summit's thin air. Anyone who gets a headache or feels faint or nauseous should head back down the mountain.

Mauna Kea can have snow flurries all year round and winter storms can dump a couple of feet of snow overnight.

Mauna Kea Summit Trail

There's a six-mile trail to the top of Mauna Kea which starts near the end of the paved road above the visitor centre. Instead of continuing on the main 4WD road, take the road to the left. The trail begins up through wooden posts and more or less parallels the summit road. It's marked with posts and stone cairns.

The trail starts at 9200 feet and climbs almost 4600 feet. Because of the altitude it's quite strenuous and it's also easy to get sunburned. Take sunscreen and plenty of water along with you. Give yourself a full day for this hike – most people take four to five hours to get to the summit.

It's a difficult hike as you're walking on cinders, but there are incredible vistas and strange moonlike landscapes. You may see feral goats, mouflon sheep or chukar partridge on the way up.

The trail passes through the Mauna Kea Ice Age Natural Area Reserve. There was once a Pleistocene glacier here and scratchings on rocks from the glacial moraine can still be seen.

The ancient adze quarry Keanakakoi, at 12,400 feet, is two-thirds of the way up. Lake Waiau is a mile farther.

You might be tempted to hitch a ride from someone at the visitor centre who's going to the summit and then walk down. But if you haven't spent the previous night in the mountains, there's a danger in doing this as you won't have as much time to acclimatise.

Visitor Centre Programmes

The visitor centre (tel 935-7606; 961-2180 for recorded information) has summit tours at 2.30 pm on Saturdays and Sundays beginning at the University of Hawaii's 88-inch telescope. Most of the time is spent at the observatory's refrigerated dome, control room and catwalk.

From 6 to 10 pm Saturdays the night sky is viewed through one of UH's 24-inch telescopes on the summit.

Both programmes are free but you need to provide your own 4WD transportation to the summit. If you're lucky, you might be able to catch a ride up with someone from the visitor centre, but you can't count on it. Children under 16 are not allowed because of altitude health hazards.

For the afternoon tours, check in at the visitor centre before 1.45 pm. The evening programme requires reservations (tel 935-3371) and is limited to 30 people.

In addition, right at the visitor centre, there's a free astronomy programme each Friday. It starts with a lecture or video at 7 pm, followed by stargazing using an 11-inch telescope until 9 pm. Children are encouraged to come to this one.

Tours

Pat Wright of Paradise Safaris (Box AD, Kailua-Kona, HI 96745; tel 322-2366) does tours of Mauna Kea summit for $80. The tour includes pick-up at West Hawaii hotels and stargazing from their own little telescope. It sometimes includes a tour of one of the observatories, so if that's important to you ask before signing up.

Waipio Valley Shuttle (tel 775-7121) does daytime tours of Mauna Kea for $65, leaving from Waimea.

Mauna Kea Astronomical Society makes a trip to Mauna Kea once a month, normally close to the new moon. The observation area is outside the visitor centre where the group maintains permanent mounts and members bring their own telescopes. It's open to the public and meeting times are posted in local newspapers.

For information on snow skiing, see the Activities section.

Places to Stay

Mauna Kea State Park In the *Mauna Kea State Park* (Pohakuloa area), near the 35-

mile marker, there are picnic tables, restrooms and a pay phone. The park is mostly shrubland with some wildflowers. At an elevation of 6500 feet, the days are commonly cool and the nights cold.

There are seven housekeeping cabins there which are mostly used by hunters who hunt pig, sheep, goats and game birds on the slopes of Mauna Kea. The cabins are fairly modern with basic kitchens, electric heating, bathrooms, hot showers and beds with the standard saggy mattresses. As most hunting is restricted to weekends, it's the most difficult time to book the cabins.

There are also two large barracks rented out to groups, including skiers when there's snow on the mountain. For reservations, contact the Division of State Parks (tel 961-7200, Box 936, Hilo, HI 96721). Rates are the same as for other park cabins: $10 for one person, $14 for two, up to $30 for six.

Nearby military manoeuvres can be noisy, but otherwise it's a good base for those planning to hike Mauna Kea or Mauna Loa.

MAUNA LOA'S NORTHERN FLANK

The road to Mauna Loa starts just east of the Summit Rd and climbs 18 miles up the northern flank of Mauna Loa to a weather station at 11,150 feet. The road is gently sloping, not paved but oil-packed, and passable in a standard car. It takes about 40 minutes to drive up. It might be wise to loosen your gas cap before you start in order to avoid vapour lock problems. Park in the lot below the weather station. The equipment used to measure atmospheric conditions is highly sensitive to exhaust.

The summit and domes of Mauna Kea are visible from here and when conditions are right you can see the 'Mauna Kea shadow' at sunset. Mauna Kea sometimes casts a blue-purple shadow behind itself in the sky. It's a strange and striking phenomenon.

Observatory Trail

The weather station is the trailhead for the Observatory Trail which connects up with the Mauna Loa Trail after three miles. From here it's 2½ miles around the western side of Mauna Loa's caldera, Mokuaweoweo, to the summit at 13,677 feet, or two miles along the eastern side of Mokuaweoweo Caldera to Mauna Loa cabin at 13,250 feet. The cabin marks the end of the 18-mile Mauna Loa Trail which starts down in the main section of Hawaii Volcanoes National Park.

The Observatory Trail is very steep and difficult. If you haven't been staying in the mountains, altitude sickness is very likely. The hike to the cabin takes four to six hours for strong hikers. Anyone who is not in top shape shouldn't even consider it.

Overnight hikers must register with the Kilauea Visitor Center in Hawaii Volcanoes National Park. For details, see the Hiking Trails section.

Continuing on to Hilo

Heading eastward from the hunter's check station below Mauna Kea's visitor centre, the terrain along the Saddle Rd gradually becomes *ohia*-fern forest, shrubby at first, but getting thicker and taller as Hilo gets closer.

Red *ohelo* berries are fairly common in this area. These low shrubs are from the heath family, related to blueberries and cranberries. They're tart but edible.

Though most of the road is fine there's one stretch that has some deep potholes and the road winds a bit. It's worthy of note as oncoming drivers often cut the curves and swerve to avoid the holes.

The last 11 miles of the highway is newly paved. As the road re-enters civilisation you can see Hilo Bay in the distance.

About four miles outside Hilo, Akolea Rd leads off to the left and connects in two miles to Waianuenue Ave, with Boiling Pots and Rainbow Falls (see Hilo section). Or, stay on the Saddle Rd and you'll soon come to Kaumana Caves, a small county park on the left.

Maui

Maui has much to lure the visitor, including superb scenery and diverse landscapes. Most of the sunny west coast is lined with beautiful white sand beaches and the island has world-class windsurfing and excellent conditions for most water sports. The shallow coastal waters around Maui are central wintering grounds for North Pacific humpback whales, making it prime whale watch country.

In the 1960s, Hawaii's first major development outside Waikiki was built on Maui. Since that time, Maui has become the most visited, the most developed and the most expensive of Oahu's neighbouring islands. As might be expected, it all centres around the beaches of West Maui.

The main tourist destinations – Lahaina, the Kaanapali area and the Kihei strip – are urbanised experiences. You have to be ready for highrises, traffic and crowds.

Maui does have another side. It's quite easy to escape the West Maui scene by heading to the east coast or the uplands. Making a base in the small towns of Paia, Kula or Hana is a totally different experience.

Haleakala is the massive mountain which provides the scenic backdrop to all of East Maui. Its slopes hold native rainforests, eucalyptus groves and open pastures with large cattle ranches.

Haleakala Crater, with a summit of 10,023 feet, is the centrepiece of Haleakala National Park. The crater is an extraordinary landscape of spewed red cinders and grey lava hills. Haleakala is the world's largest dormant volcano, its crater so big that an entire city could fit inside. There are some incredible hiking trails across the crater floor. Sunrise at the summit is awe-inspiring.

Kula, at a cool 3000-foot elevation on Haleakala's western slopes, is Maui's gardenland. Flowers and vegetables which ordinarily don't have a chance in the tropics thrive up there. Upcountry is Hawaii's only winery, with a tasting room in a century-old jail. It's a lovely area for country drives.

The windward side of Haleakala is lush, wet and rugged. The famous Hana Highway runs down the full length of it, winding its way above the coast through tropical jungle and past roadside waterfalls. It's the most beautiful coastal road in Hawaii.

Artists and craftspeople have long been drawn to Maui, and Hawaii's New Age activities are centred here.

Orientation

Most visitors to Maui land at the main airport in Kahului.

From Kahului, it's five miles to Paia down Hwy 36 and another 45 miles to Hana.

Upcountry (Kula) is 15 miles from Kahului on Hwy 37; though it's another 20 miles up to the summit of Haleakala.

It's about 10 miles to Kihei from Kahului along Hwy 350.

It's 25 miles from Kahului to Lahaina along Hwy 380 and Hwy 30. It's four miles more to Kaanapali.

Because of its figure eight shape and the level of development, Maui has a more extensive road network than the other outer islands.

Islanders refer to highways by name, rarely by number. If you ask someone where Hwy 36 is, chances are they won't know – ask about the Hana Highway instead.

Most main roads are called highways whether they're a busy four lanes or just a paved country road.

Facts

HISTORY

According to legend, the Polynesian demigod Maui was wandering the Pacific on a fishing expedition when his fish hook snagged the sea floor. He tugged with such a powerful force that the islands of Hawaii

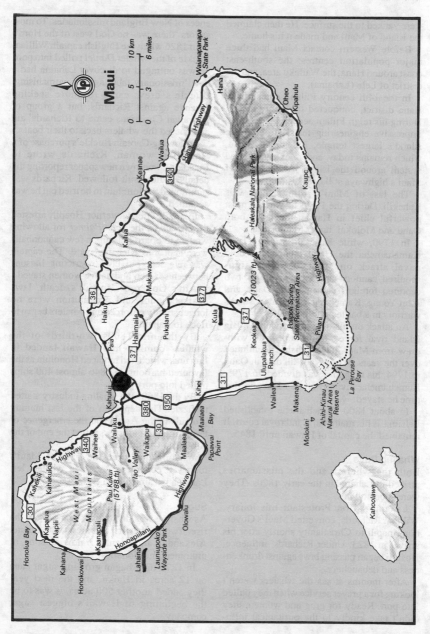

were yanked to the surface. He then claimed the island of Maui and made it his home.

Before Western contact Maui had three major population centres: the south-east coast around Hana, the Wailuku area, and the district of Lele (Lahaina).

In the 14th century Piilani, chief of the Hana district, conquered the entire island. During his reign Piilani accomplished some impressive engineering feats. He built the island's largest temple, Piilanihale Heiau, which remains today, and an extensive road system around the island. Almost half of Maui's highways still bear his name.

The last of Maui's ruling chiefs was Kahekili. During the 1780s he was the most powerful chief in Hawaii, bringing both Oahu and Molokai under Maui's rule.

In 1790, while Kahekili was in Oahu, Kamehameha the Great launched a bold naval attack on Maui. Using foreign-acquired cannons and the aid of his two captured foreign seamen, Isaac Davis and John Young, Kamehameha defeated Maui's warriors in a battle up in Iao Valley.

An attack on his own homeland by a Big Island rival forced Kamehameha to withdraw from Maui, but the battles continued over the years. When Kahekili died in Oahu in 1794, his kingdom was divided. In 1795, Kamehameha invaded all of Maui and that time he stayed.

In about 1800 Kamehameha established Lahaina as his main home and royal court. It remained the capital of Hawaii until 1845.

Whaling Days

Both the whalers and the missionaries arrived in Lahaina in the early 1820s. They were soon at odds.

Lahaina's first Protestant missionary, William Richards, converted Maui's Governor Hoapili to Christianity shortly after his arrival in 1823. Under Richards' influence, Hoapili began passing laws against drunkenness and debauchery.

After months at sea the whalers weren't looking for a prayer service when they pulled into port. Ready for grog and women, they didn't take kindly to the puritanical influ-

ences of New England missionaries. To most sailors 'there was no God west of the Horn'.

In 1826 when the English captain William Buckle of the whaler *Daniel* pulled into port, he was outraged to discover Lahaina had a new 'missionary tabu' against womanising. Buckle's crew came to shore seeking revenge against Richards, but a group of Hawaiian Christians came to Richards' aid and chased the whalers back to their boat.

Following Captain Buckle's purchase of a Hawaiian woman, Richards wrote to Buckle's hometown newspaper reporting the details. A libel suit followed. Richards was summoned to Honolulu to be tried but he was acquitted.

In 1827, after Governor Hoapili arrested the captain of the *John Palmer* for allowing women to board his ship, a few cannonballs were shot into Richards' yard. The captain was released, but laws restricting liaisons between seamen and native women stayed.

After Governor Hoapili's death, laws against liquor and prostitution were no longer strictly enforced and whalers began to flock to Lahaina.

By the mid-1800s two-thirds of the whalers coming into Hawaii landed in Lahaina, which had replaced Honolulu as the favoured harbour. In 1846 almost 400 ships pulled into port.

By the 1860s the whaling industry started to fizzle. The depletion of the last hunting grounds in the Arctic and the emergence of the petroleum industry spelled the end of the American whaling era.

Whaling had been the base of Maui's moneyed economy. After the whalers left Lahaina became all but a ghost town.

Sugar

As whaling was declining, sugar was on the rise. Two of the first planters were Samuel Alexander and Henry Baldwin, sons of prominent missionaries.

In 1870 they began growing sugar cane on 12 acres in Haiku, and the next year they added another 500 acres. It was to be the beginning of Hawaii's biggest sugar company.

In 1876 Alexander & Baldwin began construction of the Hamakua Ditch to service the Haiku plantations 17 miles away. This extensive irrigation system turned Wailuku's dry central plains into green sugar land. Sugar remained the strength of the economy until tourism took over in the 1960s.

GEOGRAPHY

Maui, the second largest Hawaiian island, arose from the ocean floor as two separate volcanoes. Eventually lava flows and soil erosion built up a valley-like isthmus between the two, linking them in their present form. The flat isthmus provides a fertile setting for fields of sugar cane and has given Maui the nickname 'The Valley Island'.

The eastern side of Maui, the larger and younger of the two, is dominated by Haleakala which has a summit elevation of 10,023 feet. This dormant volcano has a massive crater-like valley containing numerous cinder cones and vents. Haleakala last erupted in 1790, which on the geological clock means it could just be snoozing.

The West Maui Mountains dominate West Maui, with Puu Kukui, at 5778 feet, the highest point.

Both mountain masses are cut with deep ravines and valleys which lead down to the coast, most prominent on their rainy northeast sides. White sand beaches run along much of the western shoreline.

The largely submerged volcanic crater of Molokini lies midway between Maui and Kahoolawe. The crater rim has half eroded away, leaving a crescent moon shape which rises 160 feet above the ocean surface. Its land area is about 18 acres.

Molokini has transparent waters with abundant fish and coral, making it a popular snorkel and dive spot.

The US Navy used to shell Molokini for target practice and bombs are still found on the crater floor. In 1988 demolition experts removed three which were in just 20 feet of water.

Maui's total land area is 728 square miles.

CLIMATE

Maui's west coast is largely dry and sunny.

The south-east coast and the Kula uplands has intermittent clouds and receives more rain.

Temperatures vary more with elevation than season. The variance between winter and summer is only about 7° F in most places. The average August temperatures (over a 24-hour period) are 77°F in Hana, 78°F in Lahaina and Kihei, 79°F in Kahului and 50°F at Haleakala summit.

The lowest temperature ever recorded at the summit of Haleakala was 14°F and temperatures hovering around freezing are the norm on winter nights. It even gets an occasional winter snow cap.

Average annual rainfall is 69 inches in Hana, 13 in Kihei, 15 in Lahaina, 19 in Kahului and 44 at Haleakala summit.

Puu Kukui, the highest peak of the West Maui Mountains, gets 400 inches of rain a year. This is Maui's wettest spot, just five miles from the dry Wailuku plains.

FLORA & FAUNA

Maui is the island where you are most likely to see the endangered nene goose and the rare silversword plant. Haleakala is the habitat for both. Maui is also the best island for viewing humpback whales.

At least six birds native to Maui are found nowhere else in the world. They include the Maui parrotbill, Maui nukupuu, Maui creeper, Maui akepa, the crested honeycreeper and the poouli, all of which are endangered. The poouli was only discovered in 1973 by a group of University of Hawaii students working in the Hana rainforests.

Maui also has wild pigs, goats and game birds which are hunted.

Humpback Whales

After spending their summers up in Alaska, more than half of all humpback whales in the North Pacific come to Hawaii for the winter. The largest numbers are found in the shallow waters between Maui, Lanai and Kahoolawe.

Humpbacks have tail flukes with very distinctive individual markings, making them easy to identify. The Pacific Whale

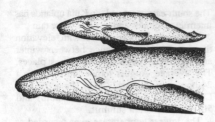

Humpback Whales

Foundation counted 674 humpback whales off Maui in the 1988 season.

The Peak season for humpbacks in Hawaii is the same as for tourists from other cold-weather climates. Some arrive as early as November and a few stay as late as May, with most in residence from January to March.

The western coastline of Maui from Olowalu to Makena (and the eastern shore of Lanai) are prime birthing and nursing grounds for mothers and newborns. Federal law protects these cow/calf waters, and prohibits boats and swimmers from approaching within 300 yards of the whales.

Humpbacks like to stay in shallow water when they have newborn calves, apparently as a safeguard against shark attacks. Maalaea Bay is a favourite nursing ground.

Humpbacks are highly sensitive to human disturbance and noise. Around Lahaina and Kaanapali where the waters are buzzing with activity, they stay well offshore.

Because whales abandon waters where jet skiing occurs, it's one tourist activity which wears particularly thin on Mauians. 'Save the Whales – Harpoon a Jet Ski' is a common bumper sticker on the island.

The best bet for whale spotting if you're in the Lahaina area is to go south at least as far as Launiupoko Wayside Park. The stretches from Olowalu to Maalaea Bay and from Keawakapu Beach to Makena Beach are prime whale watching spots.

GOVERNMENT
Maui County consists of the islands of Maui, Molokai, Lanai and uninhabited Kahoolawe. The county seat is in Wailuku.

ECONOMY
Maui's 1988 unemployment rate was 3.1%. The major industries are tourism, sugar cane, pineapple, cattle, and diversified agriculture, in that order.

Surprisingly, more land on Maui is used for grazing dairy and beef cattle than for any other purpose. For every acre of sugar, there are three acres of ranch land.

With sugar on the decline, experiments are under way with other replacement crops. Amfac, working with Hershey Foods, is harvesting its first cocoa from plots above Kaanapali. If it's successful they plan to eventually plant 6000 acres in cocoa.

Kula is one of the state's major flower and vegetable producing regions, accounting for more than half of the cabbage, lettuce, onions and potatoes grown in Hawaii, and most of the proteas and carnations.

After Oahu, Maui captures the lion's share of the tourist industry, accounting for roughly half the visitor accommodation on all the outer islands combined. Numbers, however, don't equate to bargains here. Maui has the highest room rates in Hawaii, averaging $140 a night, which is 50% higher than the state average.

PEOPLE
Maui has a population of a little over 81,000. The Wailuku district, which includes the sister towns of Wailuku and Kahului, accommodates half of the island's people.

Ethnically, 25% of the population is Caucasian, 20% Japanese, 16% Filipino and 2% Hawaiian. About one-third of Maui's residents consider themselves to be

of 'mixed blood', with two-thirds of these having some Hawaiian ancestry.

TOURIST INFORMATION

The Hawaii Visitors Bureau (tel 871-8691) has its office at 380 Dairy Rd (Box 1738), Kahului, HI 96732. Kahului Airport has a visitor information service. State and county offices are in Wailuku.

For information on Kaanapali, contact the Kaanapali Beach Operators Association (tel 661-3271), 2530 Kekaa Drive, Kaanapali, HI 96761. For info on Wailea, contact the Wailea Destination Association (tel 879-4258), 161 Wailea Ike Place, Wailea, HI 96753.

GENERAL INFORMATION
Official Maui

Maui's nickname is 'The Valley Island'. Its official colour is pink; its flower is the lokelani, which is a type of rose; and the unofficial slogan is *Maui no ka oi* – 'Maui is the best'.

Media

Maui's main newspaper, *The Maui News* (Box 550, Wailuku, HI 96793; tel 244-3981) comes out daily except Saturdays. The Friday edition, which includes the weekly activity guide, can be mailed to the US mainland for $1.62 each (or three months worth for $12). It can be ordered by calling 800-367-8047 ext 460.

Free tourist magazines such as *This Week Maui, Maui Gold, Maui Beach Press* and pocket-sized beach guides are full of ads, discount coupons, simple maps and general sightseeing information. They're everywhere – at the airport and in shopping malls, hotels and restaurants.

Lahaina News and *The Gold Coast News* are free local newspapers.

Books & Maps

The public library at Kahului is the best on Maui. There are others in Wailuku, Lahaina, Hana, Kihei and Makawao.

For books on Hawaii, try Whalers Book Shoppe at The Wharf shopping centre in Lahaina or Waldenbooks in Kahului, Kihei, Lahaina and Kaanapali.

The best map to buy for getting around the island is the University of Hawaii's map of Maui. It has all the main roads and includes beaches and major sights.

Weather

For recorded weather forecasts call 877-5111. For a more recreational forecast, including conditions at Haleakala and the road to Hana, sunrise and sunset times, tides and a marine forecast, call 871-5054.

Haleakala National Park (tel 572-7749) has a recorded forecast. For surf and marine conditions call 877-3477.

Emergency

Dial 911 for police, ambulance or fire emergencies. The county crisis and help line is 244-7407.

Maui Memorial Hospital (tel 244-9056) on Mahalani St in Wailuku has a 24-hour emergency service. The smaller Hana Medical Center (tel 248-8294) also has 24-hour service.

ACCOMMODATION

Other than camping the cheapest places to stay on Maui are at Happy Valley Inn in Wailuku and Pioneer Inn in Lahaina, both cost from about $20 for a very basic room. Studio units (often converted garages) and B&Bs in the Paia/Haiku area start around $40. Maui's only youth hostel is on the road to Hana.

Kihei has the highest concentration of middle range accommodation. Others can be found in Kahului, Honokowai and Napili. The lower end of the mid-range is about $45 to $70, but it's easy to spend $100 a night and not be in anything exclusive.

Maui's biggest resort development is Kaanapali Beach Resort, with a dozen hotels and condos. Prices at Kaanapali's cheapest condos start around $100, with most of the beachfront hotels starting closer to $200.

Wailea is Maui's most exclusive development. It's less congested, more tasteful and has better beaches than Kaanapali, with similar rates. For those with the means, it's the in place these days.

Rates can be substantially lower during low season (mid-April to mid-December) and you get to pick and choose. During high season, the better condo deals usually require reservations far in advance.

Paia works on a different calendar. High season in Paia is in the summer when the windsurfing peaks. Some of Paia's studios are just as nice as West Maui's $100 hotel rooms, but at half the price.

Condominiums

Maui has many more condo units than hotel rooms. Some condo complexes are booked only through rental agents, while others operate more like a hotel with a front desk, though even some of the latter are handled by agents.

Overall the best rates are through the agents, though you usually have to deal with security deposits and they sometimes slip in cleaning fees. For a short stay it may not be worth the hassle.

Most agents require deposits within one to two weeks of booking, with full payment within 30 days prior to arrival. Cancellation policies vary, but there will be a hefty charge (or no refund at all) for cancelling within the last month. The minimum stay is usually four to 14 days, depending on the place and season.

Each of the agents listed here handles a number of condo complexes and will send listings with rates so you can compare.

Maui Accommodations, 34 N Church St, Suite 203, Wailuku, HI 96793; tel 244-9551, 800-252-6284 from the USA, 800-445-6284 from Canada.

Kihei Maui Vacations, Box 1055, 1325 S Kihei Rd 213, Kihei, HI 96753; tel 879-7581, 800-367-8047 from the USA and 800-423-8733 from Canada, both ext 4000.

Kumulani Rentals, Box 1190, Kihei, HI 96753; tel 879-9272, 800-367-2954.

Bello Realty, Box 1776, Kihei, HI 96753; tel 879-3328, 800-541-3060.

Hawaiian Apartment Leasing Enterprises, 479 Ocean Ave No B, Laguna Beach, CA 92651; tel 714-497-4253, 800-472-8449 from California, 800-854-8843 from the rest of the USA, and 800-824-8968 from Canada.

Maalaea Bay Rentals, RR1 Box 389, Wailuku, HI 96793; tel 242-6553, 800-367-8047 ext 421. They handle six condo complexes in the Maalaea area with rates starting around $75.

Hawaiian Island Windsurfing, 460 Dairy Rd, Kahului, HI 96732; tel 572-5601, Cathy at 800-367-8047 ext 170.

Maui Windsurf Company, 520 Keolani Place, Kahului, HI 96732; tel 877-4816, 800-872-0999. These last two book studios and condos for as little as $40. Hawaiian Island Windsurfing has most of its units in Kihei, Maui Windsurf Company mostly in Paia.

Camping

Maui has fewer camping options than the other islands. Waianapanapa State Park and Haleakala National Park are good choices.

State Parks Polipoli and Waianapanapa, the only state parks with camping areas, both have tent sites and cabins. Permits are required and tent camping is free.

Polipoli, in Upcountry, has one primitive cabin and a primitive road into it, which often requires a 4WD. Waianapanapa, near Hana has 12 housekeeping cabins which must be reserved well in advance. They're great value at $10/14 for singles/doubles.

Cabins can be reserved through the Maui Division of State Parks (tel 244-4354) in the State Office Building, 54 High St, Wailuku; or Box 1049, Wailuku, HI 96793. Hours are 8 to 11 am and noon to 4.15 pm, weekdays.

County Parks On Maui there are only two county parks that allow camping, Baldwin and Rainbow. They're both in the Paia area and neither's a prize.

Permits cost $3 per per day (50 cents for children), limited to three consecutive nights at each camping ground. Tents are required.

Permits are available by mail or in person from the Department of Parks & Recreation (tel 243-7383), County of Maui, Wailuku, HI 96793. The office is in the Wailuku War Memorial Center at Baldwin High School, just off Kaahumanu Ave.

Haleakala National Park Tent camping is allowed at Hosmer's Grove, which is at the upper end of the park, and at Oheo Gulch on the coast south of Hana. They are both fine though Oheo has no drinking water. There are no fees or permits required. For camping inside the crater, see the Haleakala section.

ENTERTAINMENT

Maui's entertainment scene is second only to Oahu's, with a wide variety of music from rock, jazz and disco to mellow Hawaiian guitar. Maui has its own symphony orchestra, and there are occasional concerts by Windham Hill and New Age musicians. If you're into jazz, saxophonist Gabe Baltazar is not to be missed if he's doing a gig.

For an updated entertainment listing, check out Jon Woodhouse's 'Night Beat' column in Friday's issue of *The Maui News*.

Luaus

There are plenty of luaus happening around Maui so you'll have no trouble finding one. Most cost $35 to $40 (half price for children) and generally include a buffet dinner, drinks and a show with Polynesian dances.

ACTIVITIES
Beaches

Maui has lots of fine beaches and some of Hawaii's best windsurfing and board surfing. There are plenty of swimming, snorkelling and bodysurfing spots as well.

The north-west coast from Kaanapali up to Honolua Bay and the south-west coast from Maalaea down through Kihei to Makena are largely fringed with white sand beaches. This western side is dry and sunny and water conditions are generally calmer than on the windward northern and eastern coasts.

Most of the west coast beaches are backed by hotel and condo developments – good if you're looking to stay right at the beach, not so good if you prefer seclusion. Some fine exceptions are the secluded Slaughterhouse Beach and Honolua Bay in the north and Makena's Big and Little beaches in the south.

Swimming

The county has a large free public swimming pool at the War Memorial Center at Baldwin High School in Wailuku. It's open from 9 am to 4.30 pm daily, except Thursdays when it opens at 10.30 am and Sundays when it opens at 1 pm. On Saturdays it's closed between 11.45 am and 1 pm. In summer it's also open from 6.30 to 9.30 pm Wednesdays and Fridays.

There's also a pool at Kepaniwai Park up in Iao Valley, open from 9 to 11.45 am and 1 to 4.30 pm daily.

Surfing

For surfing, Honolua Bay is tops in winter. Maalaea Bay has a very fast break, best during south swells. Hookipa Beach near Paia has incredible winter waves and surfing almost year round.

Windsurfing

Maui is a mecca for windsurfers. Kihei and Kanaha are good spots for beginners, Spreckelsville and Hookipa for advanced.

The peak windsurfing season is May to October when the winds are most consistent. Though tradewinds can blow at any time of the year and flat spells can hit anytime, generally the windiest time is June to September and the flattest from December to February.

Some of the world's best windsurfing is at Hookipa, though it's for experts only. Other good windsurfing beaches are Kanaha Beach in Kahului, Spreckelsville Beach north of Paia, and Maalaea south through Kihei.

The Maui Boardsailing Association has developed a 'sail safe' programme with windsurfing guidelines. Brochures are available at the windsurf shops. You can receive their newsletter by becoming a member for $10 (MBA, Box 356, Paia, HI 96779).

Kahului has two large centres: Maui Windsurf Company (520 Keolani Place, Kahului, HI 96732; tel 877-4816; 800-872-0999) and Hawaiian Island Windsurfing (460 Dairy Rd, Kahului, HI 96732; tel 871-4981; 800-231-6958). They sell gear, rent boards for $40/200 a day/week, let you swap to try out equipment and they book accommodation.

They also hold two hour beginners classes for about $55, including equipment, usually at Kanaha Beach, daily except Sundays.

Instructors booked through Maui Windsurf use a one-way radio on the harness to direct you from the beach so they don't have to shout instructions.

Hawaiian Island puts together package tours including airfare from the US west coast, condo, car and equipment from about $800 ($700 May, June and July) a week. Call Cathy (tel 800-367-8047 ext 170).

Hi-Tech Sailboards (230 Hana Highway, Kahului; tel 877-2111; 800-367-8047) also rents boards for $40/200 a day/week, has lessons for beginners and arranges vacation packages.

Diving & Snorkelling

Some dive and snorkel boat tours go along the Maui shoreline, but the most popular by far are to the sunken volcanic crater of Molokini and to the island of Lanai. Although some dive boats take snorkellers, and vice versa, in general you're better off going out on a tour that's geared for the activity you're doing.

For snorkellers there's Black Rock at the Sheraton in Kaanapali; Olowalu, south of Lahaina; around the rocky points of Wailea and Makena beaches; and in summer only, Honolua Bay and Slaughterhouse Beach on the north-west shore. Kapalua Bay is calm for snorkelling year round.

Molokini Molokini is Maui's most popular snorkelling tour. The fish are tame and numerous and the water is clear.

Though the snorkelling is great, about 25 tour boats crowd the islet everyday. All of this activity has taken a toll on the reef, sections of which are dying, partly from dropped and dragged anchors which have carved swaths in the coral.

Morning is the best time to snorkel Molokini as winds pick up in the afternoon. The fish are given their breakfast call by boat captains who drop in loaves of bread to start the action.

For divers, Molokini has walls, ledges, white-tipped reef sharks, manta rays, turtles and a wide variety of other marine life.

Black coral was once prolific in Molokini's deeper waters. Most of it, however, made its way into Lahaina jewellery shops before Molokini was declared a conservation district in 1977.

Lanai Lanai also has clear waters, but without the crowds. The most common destination is Hulopoe Bay.

Hulopoe is a big beautiful beach which was once secluded but now has a luxury hotel at its north end. The reef on the left side harbours large schools of fish and is good snorkelling.

The Cathedrals, nearby, has caves, arches and connecting passageways for divers.

Dive Shops & Boat Dives Lahaina Divers (710 Front St, Lahaina, HI 96761; tel 667-7496; 800-367-8047) offers two-tank dives for $75 (Lanai or Molokini), introductory or night dives for $65 and training dives from $150. They book dive vacations as well.

Dive Maui (Lahaina Marketplace, Lahainaluna Rd, Lahaina, HI 96761; tel 667-2080) has two-tank dives along the Maui coast for $49, off Lanai for $69 and at Molokini for $75. Its four-day certification course costs $295.

Central Pacific Divers (780 Front St, Lahaina, HI 96761; tel 661-8718; 800-551-6767) has two-tank dives for $71, introductory dives for $57 and certification courses from $250. Dive packages are available with accommodation at Plantation Inn in Lahaina.

Maui Dive Shop (Box 1018, Kihei, HI 96753; tel 879-3388) has branches at Lahaina Cannery, Lahaina; Azeka Place, Kamaole Center and Rainbow Mall, Kihei; and 279 Wakea Ave, Kahului. They offer intro dives for $55; two-tank dives from $55 off Maui, $75 at Molokini, $85 off Lanai; and five-day certification courses for $295.

Underwater photographer Ed Robinson has a dive company called Hawaiian

Watercolors (Box 616, Kihei, HI 6753; tel 879-3584).

Maui has many other dive operations.

Snorkelling Tours & Rentals

A few dozen snorkelling cruises leave for Molokini daily from Maalaea Harbor. Boats are usually out from about 7 am to noon and cost about $45 to $60 including lunch or snacks and snorkelling gear.

Competition is heavy so deals and discount coupons can be found. Tickets are sold at activity booths around the island.

Lahaina Divers, Dive Maui and Central Pacific Divers have free snorkelling maps.

Snorkelling gear can be rented from most dive and windsurfing shops, hotel beach huts and some activity centres in the beach towns. Dive Maui in Lahaina rents snorkel sets for $5 per 24 hours.

Snorkel Bob's rents full snorkel sets for just $15 a week, with locations behind Paradise Fruit in Kihei (tel 879-7449) and at Napili Village Hotel in Napili (tel 669-9603). It's a great deal – this is close to the daily rate at many hotel beach huts.

Whale Watching

January to March is the peak humpback whale watching season, though there are whales around a month or so on either side.

There are lots of whale watch cruises in the $25 range, from double-hulled sailboats to 92-foot cruise vessels. They leave from Maalaea Bay, Lahaina and Kaanapali. Some companies claim to donate a portion of the ticket price to whale conservation groups. In season, there are advertisments everywhere. You'll have no trouble finding a cruise.

Many of the boats which take snorkellers to Molokini in the morning go out whale watching in the afternoon. During the season there's a good chance of spotting whales on the snorkelling trip to Molokini.

The Pacific Whale Foundation (tel 879-8811) has 2½-hour cruises leaving a few times daily from both Maalaea and Lahaina harbours. Rates are $25 for adults, $12 for children. They guarantee whale sightings or

you get another free trip. All profits go to their marine conservation projects.

Hiking

Haleakala National Park has some extraordinary trails across the 'lunar' landscape of Haleakala Crater. The Oheo section, south of Hana, has a trail to two impressive waterfalls.

Polipoli Spring State Recreation Area in Upcountry has an extensive trail system in cloudforest. One, the Skyline Trail, goes between Haleakala summit and Polipoli.

Several pull-offs along the Hana Highway lead to short nature walks. There's a coastal trail between Waianapanapa State Park and Hana Bay. The scenic Waihee Ridge Trail branches off the Kahekili Highway north of Wailuku, and from Makena there's a hardy hike over lava south along the coastline. And, of course, Maui has many white sand beaches perfect for strolls.

Sierra Club

The Maui branch of the Sierra Club (Box 2000, Kahului, HI 96732) leads a hike or two each month. A 50-cent donation is requested.

Service trips to help eradicate the invasive banana poka, a relative of the edible passion fruit vine, are held most weekends. Though banana poka has run rampant over native forests on the Big Island and Kauai, on Maui it's found only in a 250-acre area in Kula. Eradication tactics include bagging fruit and seedlings, pulling up vines and spraying herbicide on the roots.

Service trips are also made to Haleakala to help with fence maintenance and exotic plant control.

The club has a presentation and meeting at 7 pm on the fourth Thursday of each month in the Cameron Center auditorium, 95 Mahalani St, Wailuku.

Cycling

Each morning groups of cyclists gather at the top of Haleakala for the thrill of coasting 38 miles and 10,000 feet down.

Cruiser Bob's (tel 667-7717; 800-654-7717) is the original group (he started in 1982). Maui Downhill (tel 871-2155) and

Maui Mountain Cruisers (tel 572-0195) are newer.

Generally it's an all-day affair starting with a hotel pick-up around 3 am, a van ride up the mountain for the sunrise, about 3½ hours of biking down the mountain, followed by brunch and a ride back to the hotel. It's not a non-stop cruise as cyclists must pull over for cars following behind. The going rate is around $90 all inclusive.

All bikes are said to be special models with safety brakes and each group is followed by an escort van.

Horse Riding

Pony Express (tel 667-2200) is in a eucalyptus grove on Haleakala Crater Rd, 2½ miles up from Hwy 377. One and two-hour rides across the rolling meadows of Haleakala Ranch, with views from 4000 feet down to the ocean, cost $20 an hour.

Their most extraordinary ride meanders down into the moonscape of Haleakala Crater. It leaves at 9.30 am, takes four hours, covers 7½ miles, is open to novice riders and costs $90 including a picnic lunch on the crater floor. A full-day version goes to Kapalaoa Cabin for $120. Crater rides go via Sliding Sands Trail, are limited to 10 riders and require reservations.

Charley Aki Jr (c/o Kaupo Store, Kaupo, HI 96713; tel 248-8209) arranges day rides and pack trips from his home in Kaupo into Haleakala Crater. Overnight trips into the crater cost $150 to $200 each, depending on the number of people (two to six), including camping equipment or cabin fees and meals. It costs $25 less if you bring and fix your own food. As Charley is a working cowboy, trips require advance notice and payment.

Hotel Hana Maui Stable (tel 248-8268) has guided trail rides across Hana Ranch pasture, up to forests or along the shoreline for $25 an hour.

Holo Lio Stables (tel 879-1085) in Makena, just south of Maui Prince Hotel on the lower road, has hourly and full-day rides, some going to La Perouse Bay.

Kaanapali Kau Lio Stables (tel 667-7896) in Kaanapali has guided trail rides into the uplands of the West Maui Mountains.

Rainbow Ranch (tel 669-4991) in Napili offers canters along the beach and other rides.

Adventures on Horseback (tel 242-7445) has a five-hour 'waterfall adventure ride' for $110. Rides are limited to six people. The meeting place is near Haiku and the rides cross a variety of terrains and include a picnic lunch and break for swimming.

Tennis

The county maintains two tennis courts at each of these places: Kahului Community Center, Kahului; Kalama Park, Kihei; Hana Ball Park, Hana; Eddie Tam Memorial Center, Makawao; Pukalani Community Center, Pukalani.

In Lahaina the county has two courts at the civic centre and four at Maluuolele Park. In Wailuku there are seven courts at the Wailuku Community Center and four at the Wailuku War Memorial. All county courts are free to the public and lit for night play.

Maui Community College in Wailuku has four courts open after school hours. Maui Sunset, 1032 S Kihei Rd, Kihei, has two courts open to the public.

Makena Tennis Club (tel 879-8777) in Makena, Napili Kai Beach Club (tel 669-6271) in Napili, Kapalua Tennis Gardens (tel 669-5677) in Kapalua and Royal Lahaina Tennis Ranch (tel 661-3611) and Maui Marriott (tel 667-1200) in Kaanapali charge $8 to $10 per person per day.

Wailea Tennis Club (tel 879-1958) has hard courts for $12 per person per day, grass courts for $3 more. The resort likes to call the club 'Wimbledon West' as it has grass courts, a stadium court for exhibitions and a cafe serving strawberries and cream.

Though all rates listed here are daily, most places guarantee only the first hour and are subject to space availability after that.

Hyatt Regency Maui (tel 667-7474) charges $12 per hour for singles and $15 for doubles.

Golf

Maui has 11 golf courses and more in the making.

Waiehu Municipal Golf Course (tel 244-5433) in Waiehu, north of Wailuku, charges green fees of $15 to $20 plus $12 per cart.

Kapalua Golf Club (tel 669-8044) in Kapalua has two courses, Bay and Village. Green fees are $40 for resort guests, $70 for non-guests, with carts $15 extra. Fees are lower after 2 pm.

Kaanapali Beach Resort has two courses, the Royal Kaanapali North and South (tel 661-3691). Fees are $70 for greens and cart.

Wailea Golf Club (tel 879-2966) in Wailea has two courses, Blue and Orange. Fees vary from $25 to $90 depending on the season and whether players are residents, guests or neither.

Makena Golf Course (tel 879-3344) in Makena charges $40 to $50, including carts and clubs.

Silversword Golf Course (tel 874-0777) in Kihei charges $40 for greens and cart, $10 less after 2 pm. Pukalani Country Club (tel 572-1314) in Pukalani charges $10 per nine holes plus $10 for a cart. Maui Country Club (tel 877-0616) in Spreckelsville is open to the public on Mondays only.

All Maui golf courses are 18-hole par 72 or 71 courses except Maui Country Club which is 9-hole, par 74.

THINGS TO BUY
Maui Blanc, Maui's own pineapple wine, is a quality wine which makes a good gift. It sells for about $6 a bottle at liquor and grocery stores around the island.

Proteas are a Maui speciality. The best deal is to buy direct from the Upcountry farms.

There are a couple of businesses which sell food and flowers, including leis, Maui onions, papayas, pineapples and proteas, which are agriculturally pre-inspected and delivered to the airport for you to pick up on your way out. Two places are Airport Flower & Fruit (tel 877-6131) or Take Home Maui (tel 661-8067).

GETTING THERE & AWAY
Air
The main airport is in Kahului. There are two commuter airports: Kapalua/Kaanapali (also

called Kapalua-West Maui Airport) and Hana Airport.

Airline phone numbers are given in the Getting Around chapter. All fares listed here are one way; the return fares are double.

Kahului Airport Hawaiian Airlines and Aloha Airlines fly directly to Kahului from Honolulu, Lihue (Kauai), and Hilo and Kona (Big Island). Fares are about $50, except for the first and last flights out of Honolulu which are about $35.

Aloha IslandAir flies to Kahului from Princeville (Kauai), Honolulu, Molokai, Lanai and Kamuela (Big Island).

Panorama Air flies nine-passenger Piper Chieftans to Kahului daily from Honolulu, $60/105 one-way/return, and Molokai, $40/60.

From the US mainland, Kahului Airport is served by United, American and Delta.

Kahului's bustling main terminal has car rental booths, hotel/condo reservation phones, a snack bar, information booth, lei stand, gift shop and a newsstand that carries the University of Hawaii map of Maui.

Kapalua/Kaanapali Airport This is a small airfield with a single 3000-foot runway. Hawaiian Airlines services Kapalua from Honolulu with about 25 daily shuttle flights in 50-passenger Dash 7s, the largest plane the airport can handle. The first one leaves Honolulu about 6.10 am and the last one at 4.50 pm. Hawaiian also has a daily flight from Molokai. Fares are $40 from Molokai, $50 from Honolulu. You can also fly from the other islands via Honolulu for $50.

Aloha IslandAir has daily flights from Honolulu, Princeville, Kamuela, Kahului and Molokai. It costs $39 from Molokai, $47 from Honolulu and $50 from Princeville.

Panorama Air has daily flights from Honolulu, $60/105 one-way/return, and Molokai $40/60.

The airport is between Kapalua and Kaanapali, each about two miles away.

Hana Airport Aloha IslandAir flies to Hana from Princeville, Honolulu, Molokai, Kahului, Kapalua and Kamuela daily and from Lanai twice weekly. The fare from Honolulu is $50 and from Kahului is $30.

Air Hana offers customised non-scheduled flight transfers between Kahului and Hana in a six-passenger Twin Cessna 421. There must be at least two passengers and it costs $70.

Air Hana also offers services from Kapalua and Kamuela. Reservations are made through Hotel Hana-Maui (tel 248-8211; 800-321-4262).

Ferry

The *Maui Princess* runs twice daily between Molokai and Maui. The one-way fare is $21 for adults, $10.50 for children. For information call Sea Link of Hawaii (553-5736 on Molokai, 661-8397 on Maui, 533-6899 on Oahu).

Expeditions on Maui (tel 661-3756) has twice-daily service between Lanai and Maui. The one-way fare is $25 for adults and $20 for chiildren.

GETTING AROUND
Airport Transport

From Kahului Airport, Grayline-Maui has a shuttle bus which leaves on the hour between 7 am and 5 pm daily and goes to Lahaina and Kaanapali hotels. Tickets are $9.50 and are available from the shuttle counter by the car rental booths. Their service to the airport is slightly less frequent and reservations (tel 877-5507) are required. Robert's Hawaii (tel 871-6226) has a similar service.

Akina Bus Service (tel 879-2828) serves the Kihei-Wailea area with an airport shuttle bus from Kahului Airport. It's $7 one way ($9.50 to the Maui Prince Hotel). The bus leaves Kihei on the hour, the airport on the half hour, between 8 am and 4.30 pm. Reservations are required.

The Kaanapali Beach Resort (tel 667-7411) has a free airport shuttle bus between its hotels and the Kapalua-West Maui Airport. The shuttle runs about once an hour, the earliest leaving Kaanapali at 8.25 am. The latest leaves the airport at 5.15 pm.

Bus

There's no full-island bus service, but there are a couple of services providing shuttle runs. If you just want to hang around the west coast beaches it's possible to get by without renting a car.

Akina Bus Service (tel 879-2828) operates daily up and down South Kihei Rd with 15 stops from the Maui Inter-Continental in Wailea to Suda's store at the north end of Kihei. The fare is 50 cents.

There are also a couple of shuttles free to the public. The Lahaina Express (tel 661-8748) makes numerous runs daily between Kaanapali Beach Resort and Lahaina. Both Kaanapali and Wailea have shuttle services around their resorts.

Taxi

Taxi fares are regulated by the county. Including the minimum flagdown of $1.40 the first mile totals $2.40. Each additional mile is $1.20.

Approximate one-way fares from the airport are $5 to Kahului, $12 to $20 to Kihei, $30 to Lahaina and $35 to Kaanapali. Baggage costs 25 cents per bag, and surfboards or bicycles cost $3.

Car

Avis (tel 871-7575), Budget (tel 871-8811), National (tel 871-8851), Sunshine (tel 871-6221), Dollar (tel 877-2731) and Hertz (tel 877-5167) all have booths at Kahului Airport. Toll free numbers are in the Getting Around chapter.

Rental booths at the Kapalua/Kaanapali Airport include Hertz (tel 669-9042), Budget (tel 669-7044) and Dollar (tel 669-7400). National has a courtesy phone to an office outside the airport.

Budget also has offices at the Hyatt Regency Maui in Kaanapali and at the Maui Inter-Continental in Wailea.

In Lahaina, Rainbow Rent-a-Car (741 Wainee St; tel 661-8734) sometimes has older cars without air-con from $17.50 a day or $95 a week. Sunshine (tel 661-5646) has an office at 256 Papalaua in Lahaina and has small cars for $24.95 a day and $99 a week.

Dollar is the only rental agent for the Hana Airport.

Moped

Scooters for Rent has Honda scooters at two locations: on Lahainaluna St in downtown Lahaina (tel 661-8898) and at 1975 S Kihei Rd (tel 879-3858) in Kihei.

Go Go Bikes (tel 661-3063) rents mopeds and bicycles in Kaanapali.

Hitching

Hitching is illegal in Maui County, but if you want to give it a go, then do what most hitchhikers in these parts do: just stand at the side of the road and 'look' like you want a ride. The correct stance should be enough; there's no need for a thumb.

Tours

Maui has many sightseeing tour companies. Tours to Hana and Haleakala are most popular, followed by Iao Valley, Lahaina and full-island tours.

Grayline-Maui (tel 877-5507; 800-367-2420), one of the largest companies, is also one of the cheapest. Unlike most other companies which keep one rate per tour, Grayline's prices depend on pick-up location. Its rates are lowest from Kahului ($18.25 to Haleakala, $36.50 to Hana) and most expensive from Kapalua ($31.25 to Haleakala, $50 to Hana). It also has a $23 tour to Upcountry, Haleakala, Lahaina and Iao Valley which leaves Kahului Airport at 8.30 am daily.

A few of the other tour companies include Akamai (tel 871-8551; 800-922-6485), Polynesian Adventure Tours (tel 877-4242), No Ka Oi Scenic Tours (tel 871-9008) and Gentle Island Holidays (tel 879-0053; 800-367-8047).

Most companies charge about $45 to $55 for the trip to Hana, $27 to $35 to Haleakala. The fare for children is usually half to two-thirds the adult fare.

Helicopter Most of the helicopters that buzz Maui leave from Kahului.

Sunshine Helicopters (tel 871-0722) has a $49 20-minute tour over the waterfalls of Waihee Valley and a $99 45-minute Haleakala tour. It claims to 'fly neighbourly' providing 'noise abatement'.

Horizon Helicopters (tel 871-9143) has similar prices and tours.

These are about the lowest prices, but there are several other companies and deals constantly change. Some have discount coupons in the tourist magazines. Most offer free use of video cameras.

Papillon (tel 669-4884; 800-367-7095) leaves from both Kahului and Kapalua. Prices range from $95 for a 30-minute tour of West Maui to $325 for a full-day circle-island tour with a land tour of Hana.

Cruises

Maui has enough dinner cruises, sunset sails, deep sea fishing and charter sailboats to fill a book. Most leave from Lahaina or Maalaea, a few from Kihei and Kaanapali.

You can get current rates and information from activity booths all around Maui or from the tourist magazines – or just go down to Lahaina Harbor where the booths and the boats are lined up and check out the scene for yourself.

To Neighbouring Islands Club Lanai (333 Dairy Rd, Suite 201-A, Kahului, HI 96732; tel 871-1144, 536-3663 from Oahu) has a day-long tour to a secluded white sand beach (Halepalaoa Landing) on the east coast of Lanai. The ride takes 35 minutes aboard a 70-foot catamaran which leaves Lahaina at 7.45 am daily and returns at 4 pm. The club takes hammocks, to laze in once you get there, as well as bicycles, snorkelling gear and kayaks. It costs $69 which includes barbecue lunch, open bar and all activities.

Trilogy Excursions (tel 661-4743; 800-874-2666) sail from Lahaina to Lanai's Hulopoe Bay. It leaves early in the morning and returns around 4 pm. It costs $125, which includes a land tour, snorkelling and a barbecue.

Island Marine Activities (505 Front St 225, Lahaina, HI 96761; tel 661-8397) has day tours to Molokai for $79 ($58 for children) which includes passage aboard the *Maui Princess*, the Maui-Molokai ferry. Essentially it links up with the Molokai Wagon Ride for a visit to an ancient *heiau*, a barbecue and a few other activities.

Lahaina

Lahaina was a royal court for Maui chiefs and the bread basket, or more accurately the breadfruit basket, of West Maui. After Kamehameha I unified the islands he set up his base in Lahaina and the capital remained there until 1845. Hawaii's first stone church, first missionary school and first printing press were all in place in Lahaina by the early 1830s.

The whaling years reached their height in Lahaina in the 1840s with hundreds of ships pulling into port each year. The town took on the whalers' boisterous nature, with dance halls, bars and brothels. Hundreds of sick or derelict sailors, who had either been abandoned or jumped ship, roamed the streets. Herman Melville was among the multitudes that landed there.

These days Lahaina's streets are jammed with tourists. The wooden storefronts that once housed saloons and provision shops are full of slick boutiques and galleries.

Lahaina has become far too commercial and overdeveloped. If you're expecting something quaint and romantic you will be disappointed. The coastal setting with the mountain backdrop *is* pretty, however, and it's easy to see why people have been drawn here. There are soft breezes off the water and fine sunset views of Lanai.

Orientation
The focal point of Lahaina is its bustling small boat harbour backed by the historic Pioneer Inn and a huge banyan tree. Half the historic sights are clustered around this area.

The main drag and tourist strip is Front St, which runs along the shoreline.

If Front St seems too hectic, walk up a block or two to the residential streets. This is Lahaina's quieter and more Hawaiian side.

Most of Lahaina's major attractions are historical sites. Sightseeing spots include homes of missionaries, prisons for sailors and graveyards for both.

Information
Lahaina is best explored on foot though, because the town is long and narrow, you may end up walking a fair distance. The Lahaina Restoration Foundation puts out a free walking tour map.

Money There's a Bank of Hawaii in the Lahaina Shopping Center, and a branch of the First Hawaiian Bank on Wainee and Papalaua streets.

Post The post office sub-station in the Lahaina Shopping Center is open from 8.15 am to 4.15 pm Monday to Friday. There's often a long wait for a parking space and a long queue inside.

The main post office where you pick up mail sent general delivery (poste restante) to Lahaina is less crowded. It's near the civic centre, on Hwy 30 between Lahaina and Kaanapali. Hours are 8 am to 4 pm Monday to Friday, 10 am to noon Saturdays.

There's also a little contract post office at the Wharf Shopping Center which opens from 9 am to 5 pm Monday to Friday and 9 am to 1 pm Saturday.

Shopping The Wharf, a shopping center on Front St near Pioneer Inn, has over 50 shops and restaurants, as well as a triple movie theatre. Whalers Book Shoppe & Coffee House, upstairs, is a pretty good bookstore with cafe tables out the front. They sell Kona coffee and pastries. A few doors down, The Way of Nature has a large selection of save-the-whale paraphernalia. A percentage of the proceeds goes to Greenpeace.

Lahaina Shopping Center, bordering Front, Wainee and Papalaua streets, has a post office, Thai and Japanese restaurants, McDonald's, Bank of Hawaii, Nagasako

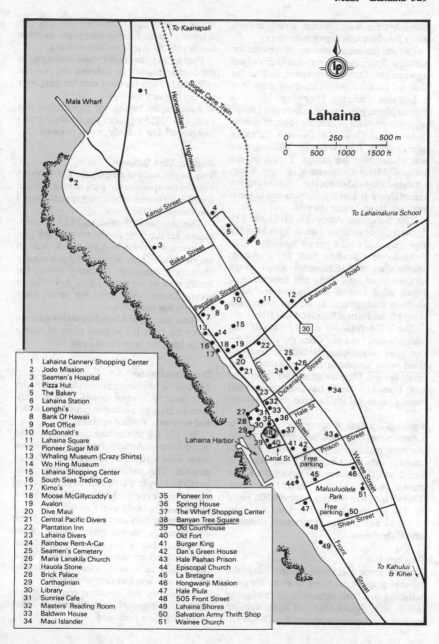

Lahaina

0   250   500 m
0   500   1000   1500 ft

1   Lahaina Cannery Shopping Center
2   Jodo Mission
3   Seamen's Hospital
4   Pizza Hut
5   The Bakery
6   Lahaina Station
7   Longhi's
8   Bank Of Hawaii
9   Post Office
10 McDonald's
11 Lahaina Square
12 Pioneer Sugar Mill
13 Whaling Museum (Crazy Shirts)
14 Wo Hing Museum
15 Lahaina Shopping Center
16 South Seas Trading Co
17 Kimo's
18 Moose McGillycuddy's
19 Avalon
20 Dive Maui
21 Central Pacific Divers
22 Plantation Inn
23 Lahaina Divers
24 Rainbow Rent-A-Car
25 Seamen's Cemetery
26 Maria Lanakila Church
27 Hauola Stone
28 Brick Palace
29 Carthaginian
30 Library
31 Sunrise Cafe
32 Masters' Reading Room
33 Baldwin House
34 Maui Islander
35 Pioneer Inn
36 Spring House
37 The Wharf Shopping Center
38 Banyan Tree Square
39 Old Courthouse
40 Old Fort
41 Burger King
42 Dan's Green House
43 Hale Paahao Prison
44 Episcopal Church
45 La Bretagne
46 Hongwanji Mission
47 Hale Piula
48 505 Front Street
49 Lahaina Shores
50 Salvation Army Thrift Shop
51 Wainee Church

Super Market, a laundromat, a camera store and a Ben Franklin department store.

Lahaina Square, off Wainee St opposite the Lahaina Shopping Center, has a Foodland supermarket, Denny's restaurant, Jack in the Box and Baskin-Robbins ice cream store.

Lahaina Cannery Shopping Center, a former pineapple cannery, is a massive shopping centre with absolutely bizarre traffic congestion. There's a 24-hour Safeway supermarket, Longs Drugs, Waldenbooks and about 50 other shops. Eating places include Marie Callender's, Burger King, Orange Julius and chocolate, yoghurt and ice cream shops. It's on the northern side of town between Front St and Hwy 30.

The Salvation Army Thrift Shop, 135 Shaw St, is open from 9 am to 5 pm Monday to Friday, and until 4 pm on Saturdays.

South Seas Trading Post, 851 Front St, stands apart from all the gaudy tourist shops in the central area. They sell Samoan tapa, Papua New Guinea face masks and Marshallese stick charts, as well as interesting things from Burma, Thailand and Bali.

Dan's Green House at 133 Prison St sells 'fuku-bonsai', created when the roots of the common house plant *schefflera* (octopus tree) wrap around a lava rock becoming quasi-bonsai. They are treated for export and cost from $15. Dan's has live macaws and monkeys too and is a hangout for local kids.

Parking Finding a space for your car in Lahaina can be a real hassle. Front St has on-street parking but there's always a line of cruising cars. Your best bet is the corner of Front and Prison streets where there's free public parking with a three hour limit. There's also free parking opposite 505 Front St. The best deal for paid parking is $1.50 a day in a lot off Wainee St between Dickenson and Hale streets.

Pioneer Inn

The old green and white Pioneer Inn is the most prominent landmark in town. It's got a whaling-era atmosphere with swinging doors, ship figureheads and signs warning against womanising in the rooms. The down-stairs saloon is Lahaina's most popular watering hole. Lively bluegrass or rock bands play all afternoon and evening.

Pioneer Inn has creaky stairs leading up to the cheapest rooms in Lahaina and you can still find brawny tattooed men hanging over the top balcony railings.

Actually, the two-storey Pioneer Inn was built in 1901, long after the whaling boom had passed, but nobody seems to care.

Banyan Tree Square

The largest banyan tree in the USA covers most of the space in the park next to Pioneer Inn. It even seems to be trying to push the old courthouse off the block.

The tree was planted in 1873 to commemorate the 50th anniversary of the first missionary arrival in Lahaina. It has 16 major trunks and scores of horizontally stretching branches reaching across the better part of an acre. Local kids like to swing Tarzan-style from the aerial roots through the branches.

There are shaded benches and walkways under the tree. It's a good place to take a break from the crowds on Front St.

Old Courthouse

Beyond the banyan tree is the old courthouse, built in 1859. It once served as the government centre with a customs house, post office and governor's office upstairs.

The old jail in the basement is now used by the Lahaina Arts Society and the cells that once held drunken sailors now display artwork. The society is a collective with artists kicking in a 20% commission to cover operating expenses. The gallery show changes completely every month.

All the exhibits are by island artists. There are paintings, blown glass, pottery, wood carvings and some native basketwork. Some of the baskets are composed entirely of Maui fibres such as wattle, watsonia, philodendron, draco, ape and fishtail palm.

The society also sponsors community art classes. A number of well-known Maui artists got their start here.

Old Fort

The Canal St corner of Banyan Tree Square has a reconstructed section of coral wall from a fort built in 1832 to keep rowdy whalers in line.

Each day at dusk a sentinel beat a drum to alert sailors to return to their ships. Those that didn't make it back in time ended up imprisoned in the fort. In 1854 the fort was dismantled and its coral blocks used as building materials for the new prison.

At one point the fort had 47 cannons, most of them salvaged from ships which sank in Hawaiian waters.

Canal St

Canal St, bordering Banyan Tree Square, used to be part of a canal system which ran through Lahaina. An enterprising American consul officer built this initial section of the canal in the 1840s to allow whalers easier access to fresh water supplies – for a fee of course.

Because of problems with mosquitoes most of the canal system was filled in long ago. Hawaii had no mosquitoes at all until the whalers brought them in from North America in their water barrels.

Lahaina Harbor

The four cannons on the waterfront directly in front of the old courthouse were raised from the wreck of a Russian ship which went down in Honolulu Harbor in 1816.

They point directly at Lahaina's crowded small boat harbour which is filled with glass-bottom boats, windjammers, sport fishing boats, whale watchers and sunset sailboats. Booths lining the edge of the harbour sell tickets for most of the cruises, as do activity booths around town.

The Carthaginian

In 1972, the 960-ton *Carthaginian*, one of the last square-riggers in Hawaii, was on its way from Maui to Honolulu for repairs when it hit a reef outside Lahaina Harbor and sank. The wooden-hulled *Carthaginian* belonged to the class of swift brigantines which made

freight runs between New England, Hawaii and China in the 19th century.

The *Carthaginian* which now sits in Lahaina Harbor is a replica, with a steel hull, built in Kiel, Germany in 1920. After being brought to Lahaina in 1973, the 97-foot brig had to be completely restored and all the masts and yards handcrafted – a process which took seven years.

It's now a maritime museum with films and displays of whales and the whaling days. It's open from 9 am to 4.30 pm Monday to Saturday, 11 am to 4 pm Sundays and is well worth the $2 admission.

Masters' Reading Room

The Masters' Reading Room, at the corner of Front and Dickenson streets, is the headquarters of the Lahaina Restoration Foundation (tel 661-3262), the group most instrumental in preserving Lahaina's past. They restored the Baldwin Home, Wo Hing Temple and Hale Pai and have been involved in a number of other historical projects.

During the whaling years the building was a reading room for sea captains. From here they could keep an eye on happenings in the harbour across the road. The original construction of coral and stone blocks has been preserved.

Baldwin House

The Baldwin House, next door to the Masters' Reading Room, is the oldest building in Lahaina, built in 1834. It was home to the Reverend Dwight Baldwin, a missionary doctor. The exterior of the coral and rock building once resembled the Reading Room but it's been plastered over. The walls are 24 inches thick, which keeps the house cool.

It took the Baldwins 161 days to get to Hawaii from their native Connecticut. The house still holds the china and chairs they brought with them around the Horn, as well as other period furnishings.

The entrance fee of $2 includes a brief tour. It's open from 9.30 am to 5 pm daily.

Around the Library

The first Western-style building in Hawaii was the Brick Palace, from where King Kamehameha I kept a watch on arriving ships. The modest two-storey structure built around 1800 by two Botany Bay convicts. All that remains is the excavated foundation on the ocean side of the Lahaina Library.

Hauola Stone is a water-worn lava stone on the shoreline to the right as you face the ocean. The Hawaiians believed this flat seat-shaped stone contained healing powers for those who sat on it.

All the grounds around the library were once planted with taro. The library is open from noon to 8 pm Mondays and 9 am to 5 pm Tuesdays to Thursdays.

If you walk north down Front St past the library there's a row of interesting turn-of-the-century buildings, best appreciated from the sea wall sidewalk.

Spring House

A small building off Front St, on the northern side of The Wharf Shopping Center, was the site of a freshwater spring in the 1800s. It now contains a Fresnel lens of lead crystal and bronze taken from the lighthouse in Kalaupapa on Molokai.

The lens has concentric grooves that operate as a prism and is capable of magnifying a 1000 watt bulb so that the beacon can be seen 21 miles across the sea. The exhibit uses a small light bulb to make its point.

Wo Hing Temple

The Wo Hing Temple, which is now a museum, was built in 1912 by the Chinese community in Lahaina. The two-storey building, on Front St, functioned largely as a meeting hall, though for a period after WW II it was also used as a home for elderly Chinese men.

As Lahaina's ethnic Chinese population declined, so too did the building. It was restored and turned into a museum by the Lahaina Restoration Foundation in 1983. There are cultural artefacts and old photos of the Chinese community downstairs and a Taoist shrine upstairs.

The tin-roofed cookhouse next door (built detached because of the danger of fire) has been set up as a little theatre which shows fascinating films taken in Hawaii by Thomas Edison in 1898 and 1905.

Against the wall there's a collection of little opium bottles found when cleaning up the grounds.

Entrance to both the temple and theatre is $1 – the best bargain in town.

Lahaina Whaling Museum

Lahaina Whaling Museum is a display of whaling era artefacts along one wall of the Crazy Shirts store at 865 Front St. It's authentic and free.

The collection includes antique harpoons, harpoon guns, ship logs, scrimshaw and photos of shipwrecks, including pictures of the Carthaginian sinking outside Lahaina Harbor in 1972. The figurehead hanging from the ceiling in the front of the store was salvaged from the Carthaginian. It was carved in 1965 for the ship when she was used in the filming of James Michener's novel Hawaii.

Outside on the back porch there's a rusty old cannon and anchor and a whaler's trypot used for boiling down blubber.

Holy Innocents' Episcopal Church

The interior of Holy Innocents' Episcopal Church, 561 Front St, is colourfully decorated with a Hawaiiana influence.

Paintings on the front of the koa altar depict a fisherman in an outrigger canoe and Hawaiian farmers harvesting taro and breadfruit. Above the altar is a Hawaiian madonna and child. A Lahaina mother and infant were the models for the painting.

The church site used to be the vacation home of Queen Liliuokalani, Hawaii's last reigning monarch.

Hale Piula

A couple of steps and a grassy building foundation between the Episcopal Church and the 505 Front St shopping centre is all that remains of Hale Piula, Lahaina's attempt at a royal palace.

Kamehameha III moved the capital to Honolulu before it was ever completed. Most of the stones used in the construction were later used to build the harbourside courthouse.

Maluuluolele Park

Maluuluolele Park, opposite Hale Piula, was once the site of a large pond with a legendary *moo* (water dragon). An island in the centre of the pond was home to Maui chiefs and at times to King Kamehamehas I, II and III. It held an ornate burial chamber for royalty.

The park's name is literally 'the breadfruit shade of Lele'. Lele was the ancient name for Lahaina.

In 1918 the island was levelled and the pond filled in. The park has basketball courts, tennis courts, a baseball field and not a hint of its fascinating past.

Wainee Church

Wainee Church, 535 Wainee St, was built in 1832. It was the first stone church in Hawaii, though it had problems standing.

The steeple and bell collapsed in 1858. In 1894 the church was torched by royalists because its minister supported the annexation of Hawaii. A second version burned to the ground in 1947, and the third was blown away in a storm a couple of years later. One could get the impression that the old Hawaiian gods didn't take kindly to the house and comgregation of this foreign god.

The fourth version has been standing since 1953. It's now called Waiola Congregational Church and holds regular Sunday services.

The cemetery next door is more interesting than the church. Here lies Governor Hoapili, who ordered the original church built; Queen Keopuolani, once the highest ranking woman in Hawaii and wife of Kamehameha I; and William Richards, Lahaina's first missionary. The old tombstones are quite interesting, both for their inscriptions and photo cameos.

Hongwanji Mission

The Lahaina Hongwanji Mission, 551 Wainee St, was built in 1927. It's usually locked but the front doors are glass so you can glance in. Unlike Buddhist temples in Japan, this one has rows of wooden pews. Services are held each Sunday in English and once a month in Japanese.

Hale Paahao

Hale Paahao, or 'stuck-in-irons house', Lahaina's old prison, was built in 1852. The old harbourside fort was dismantled by convicts who carried the blocks here to construct the eight-foot-high prison walls.

Inside, one of the whitewashed cells has an authentic-looking 'old seadog' mannequin with a recorded story about 'life in this here calaboose'.

In another cell you'll find a list of offences and arrests for the year 1855. The top three offences were drunkenness (330 arrests), adultery and fornication (111) and 'furious riding' (89). Others include profanity, aiding deserted sailors, drinking awa and giving birth to bastard children. Hawaiians could collect bounties by turning in sailors that jumped ship or fooled around with local women. There's also a copy of a seaman's diary describing his time spent in the prison.

Admission is free and you can pick up a historical walking map here. The whole thing is nicely done.

Seamen's Cemetery

The Seamen's Cemetery on Wainee St is next to Maria Lanakila Church, the first Catholic church on Maui.

It's basically a local cemetery, with only one seaman's tombstone actually identified. However, old records show that numerous sailors were buried here, including a shipmate of Herman Melville's from the *Acushnet* .

Pioneer Mill

It's hard to think of Lahaina as a sugar town, but it is. The Pioneer Sugar Mill has been a prominent part of Lahaina for 130 years and its cane fields stretch for 17 miles along the coast.

The mill sits on both sides of Lahainaluna Rd on the slopes above the town centre. It's part of the Amfac Corporation.

This is still an operating mill where people work hard to make a living. Their dusty work-place contrasts sharply with the tourist playground below.

Lahainaluna Seminary

Lahainaluna Seminary, established by the missionaries in 1831, was the first American educational institution west of the Rockies.

One of the school's early graduates was David Malo, a respected Hawaiian philosopher. He became Hawaii's first native rights spokesperson, warning in his early writings in 1837 that Hawaii was about to be swallowed up by the masses of foreigners arriving on its shores. His book *Hawaiian Antiquities* is today one of the best accounts of ancient Hawaiian history and culture.

Lahainaluna is now Lahaina's public high school, considered one of the best in the state.

The school is at the end of Lahainaluna Rd, above the mill. You get a nice view of Lahaina with Lanai in the background from the school parking lot.

Hale Pai

Hale Pai, the printing house in Lahainaluna's grounds, held the first printing press in Hawaii.

Though the main purpose of printing was to make the Bible available to Hawaiians, the press also produced the first botany book of the islands and Hawaii's first newspaper (in 1834).

Examples of early books are on display at Hale Pai. You can use a replica of the original Ramage press to hand print your own copy of a page from the first Hawaiian primer.

Admission is free though donations are appreciated. It's open from 10 am to 4 pm Monday to Friday.

Seamen's Hospital

In 1844, the building at 1024 Front St was leased by the US Government and turned into a hospital for sick and abandoned seamen.

Officials at the hospital were notorious for embezzlement. Sailors who weren't sick and others long since dead were signed onto the hospital books. A US warship with a board of inquiry sent to investigate the corruption disappeared at sea on the return home.

The seamen's hospital has been completely restored and Lahaina Printsellers (tel 667-7843) now sells antique maps and engravings inside. The framed and matted prints look as if they were meant to be hung inside this old stone block building. Their collection includes authentic Old World maps, some dating back to the days of Captain Cook.

There's a huge anchor outside on the lawn.

Lahaina Jodo Mission

A large bronze statue of Buddha overlooks the compound of Lahaina Jodo Mission, on Ala Moana, off Front St at the north end of town. The statue was put up in 1968 in celebration of the centennial of Japanese immigration to Hawaii. With its back to the mountains, the statue looks out over the Pacific toward Japan.

In the cemetery along the beach here, the county is in the process of moving graves disinterred by high surf.

Just to the north is the long Mala Wharf, constructed in the 1920s to allow inter-island ferries to land passengers directly ashore. It never passed the test. Rough seas prevented the ferries from pulling up alongside the pier, forcing them to continue shuttling passengers across the shallows of Lahaina Harbor in small boats.

The wharf is now crumbling and closed, though Mala does have a new launch ramp for small boats nearby.

Lahaina Beaches

Lahaina is not known for its beaches and wins no prizes for swimming areas. For the most part, the beaches are shallow and rocky. Your best bet is to go north to Hanakaoo Beach County Park or Kaanapali. If you don't have a car use the free trolley.

Places to Stay

You couldn't be more in the middle of the action than at the *Pioneer Inn* (658 Wharf St,

Lahaina, HI 96761; tel 661-3636, 800-657-7890). It can be noisy from the traffic, the throngs of tourists and the raucous bar and band, but this two-storey turn-of-the-century hotel is loaded with character. There are 48 rooms, all on the second floor surrounded by a porch-like lanai. Rooms in the original building face the harbour and are the cheapest and noisiest. They're very basic, with slanting floors and old beds. Rates are $21/24 for singles/doubles with a shared bath, $6 more with a private bath. Rooms in the newer wing have air-con and private baths and start at $42/45 for singles/doubles.

Lahaina Roads (1403 Front St, Lahaina, HI 96761; tel 661-3166; 800-624-8203) is a 42-room condo just north of Lahaina. All units are on the beachfront with full kitchens, lanais, TVs and phones with free local calls. It has a swimming pool. One-bedroom units cost from $60 in the low season, $85 in the high season. The minimum stay is one week in winter, three days in summer.

The *Plantation Inn* (174 Lahainaluna Rd, Lahaina, HI 96761; tel 667-9225; 800-433-6815) in downtown Lahaina, is an elegant two-storey Victorian-style B&B. It has hardwood floors, antique furnishings, stained glass, a tiled pool and spa. The nine rooms start at $78 a single, and $95 a double. Gerard's, the French restaurant downstairs, provides the breakfasts. Central Pacific Divers organise dive packages there.

Maui Islander (660 Wainee St, Lahaina, HI 96761; tel 667-9766; 800-367-5226) is a sprawling 372-unit hotel set back a few blocks from Front St. Rooms have cable TV, air-con and ceiling fans. There's a pool and tennis court. Rates are $89 for a room with a refrigerator and $102 (for up to three people) for a studio with kitchen. It's standard middle-class fare.

Lahaina Shores (475 Front St, Lahaina, HI 96761; tel 661-4835; 800-642-6284) is a 155-room beachfront condo run like a hotel by Classic Resorts. It's on the beach next to the 505 Front St shopping centre, on the south side of town. Studios cost from $99, one-bedroom units from $130, and it's about 10% cheaper in the low season.

Places to Eat
Lahaina has a few really good places to eat, most of them expensive, and lots of schlock tourist restaurants.

Places to Eat – bottom end
The *Sunrise Cafe*, just off Front St near the library, is a relief from all the mediocrity. It's friendly and casual with high-quality food catered by the upscale La Bretagne. Lunch specials change daily. We had marlin with tomato-herb sauce, linguini, fresh broccoli and French bread for $6. Quiche starts at $3 and there are whole-wheat croissants, bagels, good-looking pastries, cappuccino, espresso and herbal teas. It's open daily from 5.30 am to midnight.

Moose McGillycuddy's, 844 Front St, looks touristy but you'll find lots of locals here too. Breakfast is from 7.30 to 11 am with 17 different omelette plates at $5.50. The early bird special served until 9 am is two eggs, bacon, toast and orange juice for under $3. At lunch time, burgers and sandwiches range from $5 to $6. Dinners are from 5 to 10 pm, with dishes averaging about $10.

Pancho and Lefty's at The Wharf is OK for Mexican food. Two tacos cost around $6 and two enchiladas are $7; both with rice and beans. Meals come with homemade chips and salsa. The dinner salad ($1.50) with papaya seed dressing is excellent. Avoid the shredded beef which is tasteless and watery. Happy hour is from 3 to 6 pm with $1 beers and $2.25 margaritas.

Musashi in Lahaina Shopping Center has Japanese food. At lunch time, oyako domburi costs $4.50, chicken katsu or teriyaki are $5.25 and tempura is $6.50. They come with miso soup, pickles and rice. Dinners range from $9 to $25.

The Pioneer Inn has two dining rooms. Breakfast ($4 to $6) and lunch (sandwiches from $3 to $6) are served in the *Old Whaler's Saloon*. In the afternoon and evenings there's often live music and it gets more saloon-like. Dinner, which is served in the *Snug Harbor* restaurant just off the lobby, includes a simple salad bar. Prices range from around $7 for a burger to $20 for a T-bone steak.

Kimo's, 845 Front St, is on the beachfront with a sunset view. The bar is downstairs, the restaurant upstairs. Lunch is mainly sandwiches in the $6 to $10 range; dinner is mostly steak, chicken and seafood. Meals prices range from $10 to $20 and include salad, fresh warm carrot muffins, rolls and rice.

Sam's Beachside Grill, 505 Front St, has an ocean view and good food. At lunch time, you can get a papaya with curried shrimp salad for $8.50. Fish & chips or a chicken burrito with beans and rice cost about $7. Dinner is a bit more expensive. It's open for lunch from 11 am to 4 pm Monday to Saturday, for dinner from 5 to 10 pm daily.

In the same complex is the *Old Lahaina Cafe* with lunch specials around $5.50.

The Bakery, on Limahana Rd on the northern side of town, is a pretty good bakery with cheeses, fresh baked breads, pastries and cakes. The heavy cracked wheat bread is good. To get there, turn mauka at the Pizza Hut off Hwy 30.

Pizza Hut has a lunch time pizza special for around $2. *Denny's*, in Lahaina Square, is a family restaurant open 24 hours a day. Lahaina has several fast food restaurants, including *Burger King* at 632 Front St, not far from the banyan tree.

Places to Eat – top end

Avalon (tel 667-5559) at 844 Front St serves 'Pacific basin cuisine' outdoors on a covered patio. It's considered one of Maui's top restaurants. Although most dishes are expensive, with dinners up to $30, for around $9 you can get a good Chinese chicken salad with macadamia nuts and ginger-sesame dressing or gado-gado on brown rice. Their steamed clams in black bean sauce or Indonesian chicken stir-fry cost $17. There are 'twilight dinner specials' for around $10 and some dishes are available in half serves. It's open from 11 am to midnight daily.

La Bretagne (tel 661-8966) has a reputation for fine French food with fine French prices to match. Dishes range from chicken breast stuffed with mushroom and basil sauce for $17.50, to prawns with Maui onions and rack of lamb for $22 to $25. It's in a nice setting in an older house on Mokuhina Place, billed as 'casual elegance'. It's open from 6 to 10 pm daily.

Gerard's (tel 661-8939) serves French food in the Victorian-style Plantation Inn, 174 Lahainaluna Rd. It's open for breakfast, lunch and dinner. The chef has an excellent reputation. There's classical guitar music from 7 to 10 pm nightly.

Longhi's (tel 667-2288) at 888 Front St has made such a name for itself that it's hard to get in the front door. Dishes of homemade pasta average $15 and seafood, meat and poultry dishes about $20. The menu is extensive and ever-changing with such items as prawns amaretto, fresh ahi and pasta with pesto. It has an incredible wine list. It's open from 7.30 am to 10 pm.

Entertainment

The *Pioneer Inn* has live music daily from 3.30 to 6.30 pm and then again from 8.30 pm until midnight or 2 am. The music varies but is usually bluegrass, country, blues, rock or contemporary pop.

The *Old Lahaina Cafe*, 505 Front St, has upbeat music, usually Hawaiian, from 8.30 pm nightly.

Longhi's, 888 Front St, has rock bands from 10 pm to 1 am Fridays and Saturdays.

Moose McGillycuddy's, 844 Front St, has rock bands from 9.30 pm on Fridays and Saturdays and video disco from Sunday to Thursday.

A free Polynesian show is held at 6.30 pm Fridays at The Wharf. The *Lahaina Cannery* has a hula show at 7 pm Thursdays and a keiki hula show at 1 pm Sundays, both free.

'Art Night' in Lahaina is held from 6.30 to 9 pm on Fridays, with more than a dozen galleries along Front St providing entertainment, food, museum tours (Baldwin House and Wo Hing Temple) and artist appearances. It's a good night to walk the streets.

Luaus The Old Lahaina Luau (tel 667-1998), 505 Front St in Lahaina, is relatively small and the food is pretty good. Still, there's enough of a crowd that a lot of time is spent just waiting for the food to be served.

Movies & Theatre Lahaina Cinemas (tel 661-3347) has three screens at The Wharf shopping center.

The Omni Theater in Lahaina shows a 40-minute film about Hawaii, on a giant domed screen, on the hour from 10 am to 10 pm daily. It costs $5.95 for adults, $3.95 for children.

Things to Buy

Lahaina has numerous arts and crafts galleries, some with high quality collections and others which are mediocre. Lahaina Arts Society is a members' collective with a gallery in the old harbourside courthouse selling arts and crafts at good prices.

Getting Around

The Lahaina Express (tel 661-8748) is a bright green trolley bus which gives free rides daily between Lahaina and Kaanapali. It makes a run about every 40 minutes, stopping at each hotel in the Kaanapali Beach Resort beginning at 9 am and running down to Banyan Tree Square. The last bus leaves Lahaina at 10 pm.

LAHAINA TO MAALAEA

The stretch between Lahaina and Maalaea has pretty mountain scenery, but during winter most people are craning their necks to look seaward as they drive along. This is a whale watch road.

Launiupoko State Wayside Park

Launiupoko State Wayside Park is most popular as a picnic spot and as a place to watch the sun set behind Lanai. There are showers, toilets, picnic tables and changing rooms. It's 2½ miles south of Lahaina.

Olowalu

There's little to mark Olowalu other than Olowalu General Store and a seemingly mis-placed expensive French restaurant named Chez Paul.

Olowalu Beach was the site of an infamous massacre in 1790. After a skiff was stolen from the American ship *Eleanora* and burned for its iron nails and fittings, Captain Simon Metcalfe retaliated by tricking the Hawaiians into sailing out in their canoes to trade. He then gunned them down with his cannons, killing an estimated 100 people.

When the water is calm, there's good snorkelling around the 14-mile marker, south of the general store. The coral reef here is large and shallow. It's a pretty setting with cane fields backed by the West Maui Mountains. Olowalu means 'many hills.'

The whole area between Olowalu and Makena are humpback cow/calf waters, and whale watching from the shore here can be fantastic.

Papawai Point

There are a couple of inconspicuous roadside lookouts just south of the 10-mile marker, but they are unmarked and difficult to pull into and out of when there's heavy traffic. Your best bet is to drive a little further to Papawai Point, which is a clearly marked scenic lookout with a big parking lot.

Because the point juts into the waters at the western edge of Maalaea Bay, a favoured humpback nursing ground, it's a good sighting spot. Papawai Point is also good for sunsets, with Lanai, Kahoolawe and Molokini visible.

That popular bumper sticker 'I Brake For Whales' has particular significance around this stretch of road. Though they are usually spotted further offshore, humpbacks occasionally breach as close as 100 yards to the coast. Forty tons of whale suddenly exploding straight up through the water can be a real show stopper! Unfortunately, some of the drivers whose heads are jerked oceanward by the sight slam on their brakes and others don't, with rear-ender potential.

LAHAINA TO KAANAPALI

On the stretch from Lahaina to Kaanapali the driving is aggressive and there are often traffic jams up, sometimes to a standstill. The worst times are morning and late afternoon rush hours, but it can be bumper to bumper at other times as well. Plans for a new Lahaina bypass road are under way.

Wahikuli State Wayside Beach Park

The state has a wayside park on a narrow strip between the highway and the ocean, two miles north of Lahaina. With a gift for prophecy, the Hawaiians aptly named this coastal stretch Wahikuli, 'noisy place'.

The beach is mostly backed by a black rock retaining wall, though there's a small sandy area. If you don't mind the traffic noise, the swimming conditions are fine. There are showers and restrooms.

Across the street is Lahaina's civic centre, police and fire stations and main post office.

Hanakaoo County Beach Park

Hanakaoo County Beach Park is just south of Kaanapali Beach Resort.

It's a long sandy beach and like all public beaches there's free parking. The Hyatt is just a few minutes walk to the north.

The park has full facilities and a lifeguard on duty daily. The beach has a sandy bottom and water conditions that are usually quite safe for swimming.

Southerly swells, which sometimes develop in the summer, can create powerful waves with a brutal shorebreak.

You can snorkel down by the second clump of rocks on the south side of the beach park or, better yet, walk up to the Hyatt and snorkel out by the green buoy. A sort of exchange programme goes on, with Hyatt guests walking down to the beach to swim and snorkellers heading up to the Hyatt.

Hanakaoo Beach is also called Canoe Beach, as the Lahaina, Kahana and Napili canoe clubs all store their canoes there. You can see them paddling up and down in the early mornings and late afternoons. It's a pretty scene.

Kaanapali

Kaanapali is a highrise resort community. Despite the opulence of some of its hotels, the overall development is quite ordinary – there's as much LA influence as Hawaiian.

In the late 1950s Amfac, owner of the Pioneer Sugar Mill, earmarked 600 acres of relatively barren sugar cane land for development as the first resort outside Waikiki. The first hotels, the Royal Lahaina and the Sheraton Maui, opened in 1962.

Now Kaanapali Beach is lined with six luxury hotels, each with their own shops and restaurants, and the resort includes six condominiums, two 18-hole golf courses, about 40 tennis courts and the Whalers Village shopping centre.

Kaanapali has three miles of white sand beach and there are views across the Auau Channel to Lanai and Molokai.

Kaanapali is definitely not a 'getaway' in the sense of avoiding the crowds. In fact, this may be similar to the city scene that some people are trying to escape.

The north side of Black Rock and the condos up around the golf course are less bustling.

Information

Parking All Hawaii beaches are public and most resort developments are required to provide free beach access parking. Kaanapali, with all its space, could be more generous, particularly at its north end.

The Sheraton, fronting the most desirable beach, provides only five spaces for beach access. If they're taken (as they usually are), they'll hit you for $1 per half hour.

There are a dozen free beach access spaces between the Westin and the Whaler and 11 between Maui Marriott and Kaanapali Alii.

For the 11 spaces in front of the gate to the Marriott's pay-parking area, you may need to persuade the attendant that you plan to use the beach and not the hotel.

The Hyatt has 10 free beach access spaces. They also have free 'self parking' for hotel visitors on the south side of the hotel.

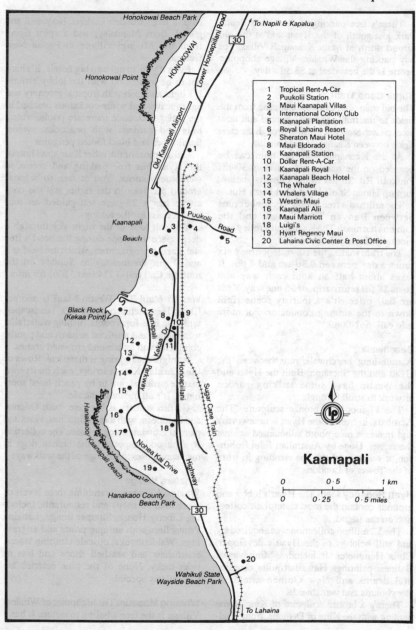

1 Tropical Rent-A-Car
2 Puukolii Station
3 Maui Kaanapali Villas
4 International Colony Club
5 Kaanapali Plantation
6 Royal Lahaina Resort
7 Sheraton Maui Hotel
8 Maui Eldorado
9 Kaanapali Station
10 Dollar Rent-A-Car
11 Kaanapali Royal
12 Kaanapali Beach Hotel
13 The Whaler
14 Whalers Village
15 Westin Maui
16 Kaanapali Alii
17 Maui Marriott
18 Luigi's
19 Hyatt Regency Maui
20 Lahaina Civic Center & Post Office

Kaanapali

0   0·5   1 km

0   0·25   0·5 miles

There's free parking at Hanakaoo Beach Park just south of the Hyatt and at the old airport north of Maui Kaanapali Villas. For pay parking the Whalers Village shopping centre is the best deal at $3.50 a day.

Sugar Cane Train

The old train that carried sugar cane from the fields to the mill has been restored and now takes passengers on a joy ride through the cane fields between Kaanapali and Lahaina.

At the Kaanapali end, the train can be boarded on the mauka side of Hwy 30 off Puukolii Rd. To get to the Lahaina station, turn up Hinau St off Hwy 30 at Pizza Hut.

The railroad's free double-decker bus runs between Banyan Tree Square and the Lahaina terminal. The Kaanapali Trolley services the Kaanapali station.

The train makes the six-mile journey six times a day between 9.30 am and 4 pm. It takes about half an hour each way and costs $8 for return trip, or $5 one way. Kids are half price. It's a touristy scene right down to the singing conductor. For more info call 661-0089.

Beachwalk

A mile-long beachwalk runs between the Hyatt and the Sheraton. Both the Hyatt and the Westin have some striking garden artwork to stroll through.

The 17-foot-high bronze sculpture 'The Acrobats' in front of the Hyatt is noteworthy and makes a nice photo silhouetted against the sunset. Done by Australian John Robinson, it's a copy of the one standing in front of the Tower of London.

Hyatt Regency Maui

The Hyatt's lobby and grounds contain the most tasteful art collection on the island.

The $2 million collection was acquired by and still belongs to the Hyatt's developer, Chris Hemmeter. It includes Ming vases, Balinese paintings, Hawaiian quilts, ceremonial drums and New Guinea artefacts, storyboards and war shields.

There's a bronze sculpture of King Rama battling with the King of Demons, from Thailand; a large wooden Buddha, lacquered and gilded, from Mandalay; and a spirit figure from the Misingi village in Papua New Guinea.

Even if you're not into big hotels, it's hard not to be impressed with the lobby atrium. It's light and lush with tropical greenery and has macaws and white cockatoos perched in the foliage. Outside there are pools, waterfalls and gardens with peacocks, swans, flamingoes and blackfooted penguins.

Unlike most of the other Kaanapali hotels, the Hyatt has free parking and seems to welcome visitors. You're free to wander around and take in the sights and the concierge has a 25-page self-guided art tour booklet just for the asking.

You can look at the night sky through a deep-space telescope during the hotel's free star-gazing programmes, which are held at 8 and 9 pm Wednesday to Sunday on the rooftop. Call 661-1234 (ext 3206) for info.

Westin Maui The Westin Maui is another Chris Hemmeter project. It's landscaped with five free-form pools, rushing waterfalls, waterslides and artificial streams and ponds, complete with swans and crowned cranes.

At night the lighting is theatrical. Rows of life-size clay Xian warriors, each on its own marble pedestal, are lit by peach-hued spotlights. It's all meant to dazzle.

Garden statuary is big here, both Oriental and European, with lots of Buddhas, vases and pairs of growling stone animals. The collection is a bit odd, especially the bronze dogs in menacing poses at the edge of the walkways.

Whalers Village

Whalers Village is a rambling three levels of more than 50 shops and restaurants, including Liberty House, Sharper Image, Lahaina Printsellers with antique prints and engravings, Waldenbooks, upscale clothing stores, scrimshaw and seashell shops and lots of ticky-tacky. None of the nine eateries are particularly special.

Whaling Museum

The highpoint of Whalers Village is the free whaling museum. It has a good collection of period photos and detailed interpretive boards explaining whaling history – from how whales were hunted to the uses of whale oil.

A lot of the character of the whalers comes through and you'll get a feel for how rough and dirty the work was. Wages were so low that sailors sometimes owed the ship money by the time they got home and had to sign up for another four-year stint just to pay off the debt.

There are harpoons, logs from whaling ships, all sorts of scrimshaw, a model of a whaling barque and a film on whaling history. The museum is on the 3rd level of Building G and is open from 9.30 am to 1 pm and 1.30 to 9.30 pm daily.

The separate open-air Whale Pavilion, at the entrance to Whalers Village, has the full skeleton of a sperm whale, earbone, blubber and baleen and a display on other marine mammals.

Kaanapali Beaches

Kaanapali can be divided into two beaches, with Black Rock the dividing mark. The stretch south of Black Rock down to the Hyatt (and beyond to Hanakaoo Beach County Park) is officially Hanakaoo Beach. The stretch from Black Rock north to Honokowai is Kaanapali Beach. Since the resort was built, however, the whole thing is generally called Kaanapali Beach.

Kaanapali/Hanakaoo Beach The Hyatt has a shallow reef which makes for good snorkelling but poor swimming. Snorkel out by the green buoy where the catamaran ties up. The fish hang out here because the catamaran crew dump bread overboard. Sea turtles are occasionally spotted here.

Much of the stretch in between the Sheraton and the Hyatt can be dangerous, particularly on the point in front of the Marriott where strong currents are sometimes created. At times the current is strong enough to see the ripple moving across the water.

As a general rule, waters are rougher in winter, though actually the worst conditions can occur in early summer if there's a south

swell. Be careful in rough surf as the waves can pick you up and bounce you onto the coral reef which runs from the south end of the Westin down to the Hyatt. Check with the hotel beach huts for present water conditions.

Black Rock Black Rock (Kekaa Point) is the rocky lava promontory which protects the beach in front of the Sheraton. This is Kaanapali's safest and best swimming and snorkelling spot. According to traditional Hawaiian beliefs, Kekaa Point, the western-most point of Maui, is a place where the spirits of the dead leap into the unknown and are carried to their ancestral home.

You can snorkel alongside the southern side of Black Rock where the fish are used to being fed and will swarm around you. But the real prize is the horseshoe cove cut into the tip of the rock, where there's beautiful coral and abundant tropical fish.

There's often a current to contend with off the point which can make getting to the cove a little risky, but when it's calm you can swim right around into the horseshoe and it's a delight. Check with the Sheraton beach hut or snorkellers in the water regarding current conditions. Black Rock is also a popular shore dive spot.

North of Black Rock To get to the north section of Kaanapali Beach, take the road makai of Puukolii Rd, just north of the main Kaanapali Beach Resort turn-offs. Then instead of turning left to Maui Kaanapali Villas, turn right to the old airport, where there's plenty of parking.

This is the quieter end of Kaanapali and a nice beach, known locally as Prindle Beach. It's open ocean but inshore it's usually calm and good for swimming distances. In earlier days, Pioneer Mill maintained a landing on this side of Black Rock for the shipping of sugar.

This is a good walking beach. If you walk north for about 15 minutes there's a big beautiful reef around Honokowai Point with clear waters and good snorkelling.

Places to Stay – top end

All Kaanapali accommodation is either on the beach or in walking distance of it.

Maui Eldorado (2661 Kekaa Drive, Lahaina, HI 96761; tel 661-0021; 800-367-2967) is a lowrise complex up the hill from the beach. There's a slower pace and a friendlier atmosphere here than at the big resort hotels. This is Kaanapali's best value. The studios are big with kitchens completely set apart from the bedrooms. The units are individually owned so they vary, but some are quite nicely furnished with wallpapered bathrooms, wicker furniture and the like. Ask if you can check out a few units before moving in. In high season, studios start at $105 and one-bedroom units at $137. Everything is $15 less in low season and a bit cheaper by the week.

International Colony Club (2750 Kalapu Drive, Lahaina, HI 96761; tel 661-4070) has 49 free-standing cottages spread over 10 acres. They are nice and spacious with big lanais, and all have phones (free local calls) and cable TV. Only 11 of the units are in the rental pool and they're mostly filled by repeat guests. The complex is about 25 years old and was one of the first in Kaanapali, back then when tastes were simpler and things weren't as crowded. It's pretty sedate up here. There are two heated swimming pools. One-bedroom units are $90, two-bedroom units are $105.

The *Kaanapali Beach Hotel* (2525 Kaanapali Parkway, Lahaina, HI 96761; tel 661-0011; 800-367-5170) is a 431-room midrise hotel on the beach. It has all the standard amenities but none of the pizzazz of the nearby resorts. At $115 (garden view) it's the beachfront bargain here. If you stay five nights or more, you can get a package with a free car rental. If you've got a Hawaii driver's licence, the kamaaina rate for the room alone is $68 whenever they're below 90% occupancy.

Royal Lahaina Resort (2780 Kekaa Drive, Lahaina, HI 96761; tel 661-3611; 800-621-2151) has 521 rooms on a broad beach on the north side of Black Rock. Standard rooms in the highrise section cost from $130. Rooms in cottages which are nicely clustered and spread out down to the beach are $165 to $210. The resort has 11 tennis courts and three pools.

The *Maui Kaanapali Villas* (2805 Honoapiilani Highway, Lahaina, HI 96761; tel 667-7791; 800-922-7866) is an Aston property between Royal Lahaina Resort and the old airport. Hotel rooms cost from $139 and studios are $159; all are $30 less in the low season.

The *Kaanapali Royal* (tel 667-7200; 800-367-7040) is a condo run by Hawaiiana Resorts. The units are very large. It's up the hill a few minutes from the beach and things don't seem as busy. During the high season, one-bedroom units start at $150 for up to four people, two-bedroom units from $175. In the low season it's $25 less.

The Whaler (2481 Kaanapali Parkway, Lahaina, HI 96791; tel 661-4861; 800-367-7052) is a 360-unit highrise condo that looks like a boxy apartment complex. Studios with garden views cost $160 high season, $145 low. Ocean views are $20 more.

The *Westin Maui* (2365 Kaanapali Parkway, Lahaina, HI 96761; tel 667-2525; 800-228-3000) has 762 rooms. It has waterfalls flowing into free-form pools and a garden full of statues and vases. The hotel itself is not as special as the grounds, but then the Westin wasn't built from scratch but is a remake of the old Maui Surf. Rates start at $175 for rooms in the old wing, $245 in the new.

The *Sheraton Maui Hotel* (2605 Kaanapali Parkway, Lahaina, HI 96761; tel 661-0031; 800-325-3535) got the prime beach spot, atop and alongside Black Rock. The 503-room hotel is large, sprawling and not very interesting. Garden rooms start at $185. The beachfront cottages on the rocky point are $275.

The 815-room *Hyatt Regency Maui* (200 Nohea Kai Drive, Lahaina, HI 96761; tel 661-1234; 800-228-9000) is the premier hotel on Kaanapali Beach. It's loaded with artwork and there's a massive meandering swimming pool with a swim-through grotto and a 130-foot waterslide. Rates start at $195 for a standard Hyatt room, with rooms overlooking the ocean from $265.

The *Maui Marriott* (100 Nohea Kai Drive, Lahaina, HI 96761; tel 667-1200; 800-228-9290) has 720 guest rooms in two long highrises connected by walkways. Rates start at $195. It's not special for the money.

Places to Eat
All of the hotels have restaurants, some formal and expensive, others casual poolside cafes.

The Marriott's *Moana Terrace* (tel 667-1200) has an early bird dinner from 5 to 6 pm with prime rib for $12.50 and catch of the day for around $9, both including beverage and soup and salad bar. It also has a nightly theme buffet. Dinners other than early bird cost around $20.

Nikko (tel 667-1200) is a Japanese teppanyaki restaurant at the Marriott, open for dinner only. Complete dinners include an appetiser of shrimp in ginger sauce, miso soup, salad, rice and teppanyaki vegetables, with main dishes like shrimp and chicken ($19) and lobster tail ($28.50). The best deal is one of the half dozen Samurai Sunset specials, served only from 6 to 6.30 pm daily. Complete dinners without the appetiser, but with green tea ice cream, range from about $12 for chicken to $16 for shrimp.

The *Lahaina Provision Company* at the Hyatt has a Chocoholic Bar, an all-you-can-indulge sugar rush of white and dark chocolate goodies served from 6.30 to 11.30 pm nightly. It's $3.50 with a meal, $5.50 alone.

Luigi's, at the main entrance to Kaanapali, has pasta dishes with bread and soup or salad from $8 to $14. It also has calzones, pizza, and meat and fish dishes.

Whalers Village
The *Rusty Harpoon, Leilani's* and *El Crab Catcher* all face the beach and all have burgers with fries for around $6, chicken dinners for $11 and fresh seafood, priced daily, that's likely to be double that. The Rusty Harpoon has happy hour from 3 to 5 pm daily with $1 draft beer and $1.50 margaritas. The *mahimahi* sandwich served at El Crab Catcher's poolside cafe has a generous portion of fish and comes with pasta salad for $7.

Ricco's is an uninspired deli with $5 sandwiches and pizza and pasta dishes moderately overpriced.

Yami is the cheapest place to eat around here. Sliced-bread sandwiches are $3 and they have yoghurts, salads and fruit as well.

Chico's has Mexican food and is one of the busier places here. A tostada, a burrito or two enchiladas cost around $9 with rice and beans. At lunch time combo plates are $7.

Breakfast Buffets
The breakfast buffet at the *Sheraton Maui Hotel* has traditional fare like bacon, eggs, hash browns, croissants, pastries, fruits and juices. There's a Belgian waffle bar with cherries, coconut, macadamia nuts and other toppings. It's all good food, nicely prepared, and is served from 6 to 10.30 am in the 8th floor Discovery Room atop Black Rock. It costs $12.50. Be sure to ask for a table with a view of the ocean.

The *Hyatt Regency Maui* has an average breakfast buffet in a superior setting at Swan Court for $13. One side is open air and overlooks a large swan pond, waterfalls and a Japanese garden.

The *Maui Marriott* has a breakfast buffet from 6.30 to 11 am at its Moana Terrace. There's an outside patio but no real view. They have fresh fruits and juices, strawberry blintzes, scrambled eggs, pastries, banana bread, yoghurt and cereals for around $11.

The *Kaanapali Beach Hotel* has an adequate but not exciting champagne brunch on Sundays from 9 am to 2 pm for $16. There are Belgian waffle and shrimp stir-fry stations, a roast beef round and good marinated salads. The guitar duo playing Hawaiian music is a nice touch.

Entertainment
Kapalua Bay Hotel and the Kaanapali hotels have dance bands, pianists, Hawaiian music,

Polynesian revues and the like in their various lounges and restaurants.

For disco with Gucci dance shoes, *Spats* at the Hyatt Regency Maui rocks nightly from 10 pm to the wee hours of the morning.

Banana Moon, the disco at Maui Marriott, is a little more casual (any shoes, no jeans). It's open from 8 pm to 2 am nightly (from 9 pm Saturdays).

The Shops at Kapalua has a free hula show at 10 am Thursdays.

The Sheraton's *Sundowner* bar atop Black Rock has a good sunset view and a Hawaiian duo from 4 to 6 pm.

El Crab Catcher at Whalers Village has Hawaiian music from 5 to 7 pm nightly.

Napili Kai Beach Club in Napili has Hawaiian music from 6 pm nightly except Fridays and Sundays. A hula show by children aged six to 16 is presented from 7 pm Fridays for $30, including a drink, dinner and the show. Reservations are required (tel 669- 6271).

Luaus The Aloha Luau held nightly at the Sheraton is popular and large scale. The Royal Lahaina Resort also has a luau and you'll see ads for other Polynesian shows.

Getting There & Around

The Kapalua-West Maui Airport is a 10 minute drive from Kaanapali Beach Resort. A free shuttle runs between Kaanapali and the airport.

The free Kaanapali Trolley (tel 667-7411) runs from 7 am to 11 pm daily around the resort, stopping at all the hotels, Whalers Village shopping centre, the golf courses, and the sugar cane train's Kaanapali station. It makes one complete loop about every 30 minutes.

The free Lahaina Express (tel 661-8748) makes runs between Kaanapali and Lahaina from 9 am to 10 pm daily. It stops in Kaanapali at the Sheraton, Kaanapali Beach Hotel, Whalers Village, the Marriott and then in Lahaina at Banyan Tree Square.

Go Go Bikes (tel 661-3063) rents bicycles and mopeds.

North-West Maui

North of Kaanapali the road forks. The main road is Honoapiilani Highway (Hwy 30) and the parallel shoreline road is Lower Honoapiilani Rd.

If you just want to zip up to the north shore beaches, stick to Hwy 30. Napili Bay, Kapalua Beach, Slaughterhouse Beach and Honolua Bay are all fine beaches.

The highway has a wide shoulder lane marked as a bike route. It's likely to have as many joggers as cyclists.

HONOKOWAI

To the degree that Kaanapali is a planned community, Honokowai is unplanned. It's basically a long stretch of condos squeezed between the shoreline and Lower Honoapiilani Rd.

Many of the condos were intended to be year-round housing for island residents but the growth in tourism makes daily and weekly rentals far more profitable.

For the most part, Honokowai lacks any sense of aesthetics. Though most of the condos are by the water, the sound of the surf isn't always strong enough to drown out the sound of the traffic.

Honokowai has fine views of Lanai and Molokai but most of the shoreline is rocky with mediocre swimming conditions.

Honokowai Beach Park

Honokowai Beach Park, largely lined with a submerged shelf of rock, has poor swimming conditions with shallow water and a rocky bottom. Most people staying here head to Kaanapali Beach. For snorkelling you can walk south to Honokowai Point (towards the pink Embassy Suites) where there's a good reef.

Places to Stay

Honokowai Palms (3666 Lower Honoapiilani Rd, Honokowai, HI 96761; tel 669-6130; 800-843-1633) is a 30-unit two-storey cinder block building. There's a little

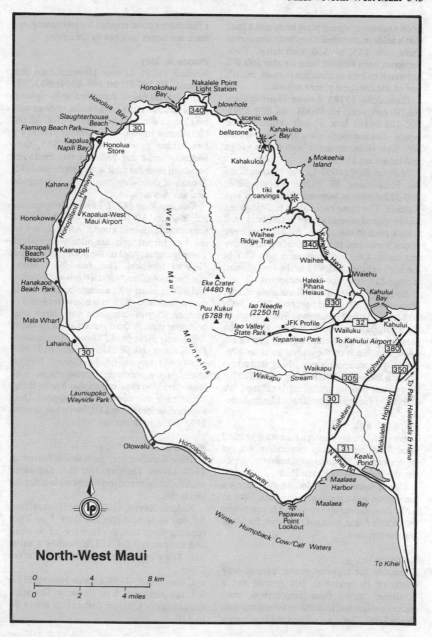

North-West Maui

book exchange, a ping pong table and a pool that's seldom crowded. One-bedroom condo units cost $55, or $60 with lanai. Two-bedroom units without lanai are also $60. It's not much to look at from the outside, but it's one of the cheapest places around.

Kaleialoha (3785 Lower Honoapiilani Rd, Honokowai, HI 96761; tel 669-8197; 800-222-8688) is a 67-unit condo on the beach. Studios with mountain views cost $59. One-bedroom units with ocean views and lanais are $69 to $79.

Mahina Surf (4057 Lower Honoapiilani Rd, Honokowai, HI 96761; tel 669-6068; 800-367-6086) is between Honokowai and Kahana. The three two-storey buildings are nicely spaced around a large grassy backyard with a pool in the centre. All 56 units have ocean views and lanais. There's a three-day minimum. One-bedroom units cost $85 in the high season, and $75 in the low season. It costs $15 more for two bedrooms.

Embassy Suites (104 Kaanapali Place, Honokowai, HI 96761; tel 661-2000; 800-362-2779) is on Honokowai Point, north of the Kaanapali resorts. From the highway, the massive pink giant catches your eye like a neon sign. Each of the 413 units is an 820-square-foot suite with everything down to a 35-inch TV with VCR. Rates start at $225 for up to four people, including breakfast. It's owned by Japanese pop singer Masao Sen.

Places to Eat

There aren't many choices for eating around here. Most people stay in condos and get groceries from Honokowai Superette, opposite the Honokowai Beach Park.

On the south end of Honokowai there's a gas station and a small grocery mart. Next to it *Fat Boys* serves up fast food. Or you might try *Ricco's Pizza*, north of Fat Boys, for pizza and sandwiches.

KAHANA

Kahana is the highrise stretch immediately north of Honokowai. It's geared for a wealthier crowd than Honokowai, with slicker condos and room rates averaging well above $100. There's a white sand beach with a few places good enough for swimming, but there are better beaches to the north.

Places to Stay

Noelani (4095 Lower Honoapiilani Rd, Kahana, HI 96761; tel 669-8374; 800-367-6030) has 50 nicely furnished units right on the beach. All units have lanais, phones with free local calls, sofa beds and VCRs. All but the studios have a washer/dryer. There's a beachfront pool. Studios are $65, one-bedroom units are $85 and two-bedroom, two-bath units for up to four people are $115. There's a three-day minimum. It's a good deal for this area.

Kahana Reef (4471 Lower Honoapiilani Rd, Kahana, HI 96761; tel 669-6491) is a four-storey, 88-unit condo. All units are on the beachfront and are nicely furnished. There's a small pool on the ocean with a great view of Molokai. The studios are almost one-bedroom size, with two roll-out couches and a little room with a single bed, for $87 in the high season, $77 in the low season. For another $5 you can get a very large one-bedroom unit. A third person costs $8 extra.

Kahana Villa (4242 Lower Honoapiilani Rd, Kahana, HI 96761; tel 669-5613; 800-367-6046) is part of the Colony Resorts chain. It's a modern highrise condo with lanais, microwaves and all that sort of thing. There's a tennis court, sauna and pool. One-bedroom units start at $110 in the low season, $125 in the high season.

Places to Eat

Dollie's Sandwiches, in Kahana Manor at 4310 Lower Honoapiilani Rd, has sandwiches, lasagne and teriyaki plate lunches for about $6.

Kahana Keyes, 4327 Lower Honoapiilani Rd, has early bird specials from 5 to 7 pm ranging from fish & chips for $8 to steak and lobster tail for $13, including a salad bar. They cost a few dollars more after 7 pm.

China Boat, 4474 Lower Honoapiilani Rd, is open from 5 to 10 daily. The standard range of Chinese dishes cost about $7 to $10.

NAPILI

Napili is more appealing than the resorts to the south. Though the beach is lined with condos, they're small, lowrise and less congested.

Napili Beach is a beautiful, curving white sand beach, with excellent swimming and snorkelling when it's calm. Big waves sometimes make it into the bay in the winter, attracting bodysurfers but also creating a strong riptide. To get to the beach turn down Hui Drive off Lower Honoapiilani Rd.

Napili Kai Beach Club, at the north end of the bay, opened in 1962 with $10 rooms. It was the first hotel north of Kaanapali. To protect the bay and their investment, Napili Kai organised area landowners and petitioned the county to create a zoning bylaw restricting all Napili Bay buildings to the height of a coconut tree and limiting them to 25% of the property.

The law was passed in 1964, long before the condo explosion took over the rest of West Maui. It worked. Napili is the most relaxed niche on the whole coast. A fair number of retired people spend winter here.

Most of Napili's condos are on the beach and for the most part away from the road and the sound of traffic.

Snorkel Bob's, in the Napili Village complex, rents full snorkel gear for $15 a week.

Places to Stay

Hale Napili (65 Hui Road N, Napili, HI 96761; tel 669-6184) is an 18-unit condo on Napili Beach. The management is friendly and the rooms have phones, microwaves and lanais. Garden studios cost $65, beachfront studios are $85. There's a three-day minimum and they don't accept credit cards. There's no pool.

The *Coconut Inn* (181 Hui Rd F, Napili, HI 96761; tel 669-5712; 800-367-8006) has elements of both a condo and a B&B. The two-storey inn has 40 units, each with their own kitchen, TV and phone. The grounds are lush with little gardens. Complimentary breakfast by the free-form swimming pool includes fruits, juices, Kona coffee and

banana bread. It's a 15 minute walk to the beach. Studios cost $69; and one-bedroom units are $99 with lofts, or $89 without. The latter can accommodate up to four people; third and fourth people cost $10 extra.

Napili Surf (50 Napili Place, Napili, HI 96761; tel 669-8002; 800-541-0638) is a motel-style, painted cinder block construction, at the south end of Napili Bay. All 53 units are pretty spiffy, the grounds are well kept and there's a pool. Studios cost $78 for a view of the garden, or $88 for a view of the ocean. One-bedroom units with views of the ocean are $120. There's a four-day minimum. It's a nice place.

Napili Sunset (46 Hui Drive, Napili, HI 96761; tel 669- 8083; 800-447-9229) has studios with garden views for $77 and one-bedroom beachfront units for $132. Local calls are free. There's a three-day minimum.

Napili Bay (33 Hui Drive, Napili, HI 96761; tel 669-6044; 800-367-8042) is booked through Hawaiian Islands Resorts. Studios cost from $85 in the high season, and $75 during the low season. It's $15 more to be by the ocean. The weekly rate is six times the daily rate. There's no minimum stay.

The *Napili Kai Beach Club* (5900 Honoapiilani Rd, Napili, HI 96761; tel 669-6271; 800-367-5030) is a 180-unit hotel at the north end of Napili Bay. The staff are friendly, almost pampering. The units all face the ocean and it's tasteful and low-key, with Polynesian decor and touches like shoji doors. Their Napili Kai Foundation works to preserve Hawaiian culture, mainly through teaching local children hula, history and Hawaiian arts and crafts. The children dance Fridays at the hotel restaurant. The catch here is the price: studios start at $140.

Places to Eat

The *Sea House Restaurant* at Napili Kai Beach Club is open air above the bay, with a fine sunset view and good food. Orchids grow out of lava rocks on an inside wall. Breakfasts are $4 to $8. Lunches such as burgers and fries, fish & chips and papaya stuffed with shrimp salad are $4.50 to $8. Dinners are in the $10 to $20 range with steaks, fish, scampi and the like. Spotlights on the breaking surf provide a kaleidoscopic show. On Sundays there's a champagne brunch from 8 am to 3 pm.

Napili General Store in the Napili Village complex sells groceries. There's a deli/pizza place next door.

KAPALUA

Kapalua Bay resort development has the Kapalua Bay Hotel, luxury condo developments, restaurants and a golf course. The Shops at Kapalua are a cluster of slick, pricey boutiques and gift shops in front of the hotel. There's free parking under the shops.

Kapalua marks the end of development on the West Maui coast. From there on it's rural Hawaii. Golf carts give way to pick-up trucks and old cars with surfboards tied on top. The coast gets more lush, green and rugged as you go along.

Kapalua Beach

Kapalua Beach is a pretty white sand crescent beach with a fine view of Molokai across the channel. The long rocky outcrops at both ends of the beach make it the safest year-round swimming spot on this coast.

There's good snorkelling on the right side. You'll find lots of large tangs, butterfly fish, wrasses and orange slate pencil sea urchins.

Take the paved drive marked 'shoreline access' just north of Napili Kai Beach Club. There are about 25 beach access parking spaces, restrooms and showers here. A tunnel leads under the Bay Club restaurant to the beach.

Places to Stay

The *Kapalua Bay Hotel & Villas* (1 Bay Drive, Kapalua, HI 96761; tel 669-5656; 800-367-8000) is a luxury complex with hotel rooms from $205 up and one-bedroom condos from $275.

One-bedroom condos in the same resort development can be rented from Ridge Rentals (888 Wainee St, Suite 207, Lahaina, HI 96761; tel 667-2851; 800-367-8047) for $100 in the low season, $150 in the high season.

Places to Eat

The *Bay Club* (tel 669-8008) is perched atop a promontory at the south end of Kapalua Bay with a beautiful view in an open-air setting. It specialises in seafood and has a good reputation. At lunch time (11.30 am to 2 pm) sandwiches cost around $7, specials like bay scallops with tarragon are $9 the salad bar costs $9.50. Get there early to avoid a wait. At dinner time, 6 to 9 pm, meals will cost around $25 to $40; there's a dress code and reservations are required.

The *Grill & Bar* (tel 669-5653) up on the golf course has a casual atmosphere and ocean view across the fairway. Lunch costs about $10, burgers a few dollars cheaper. Dinners are $12 to $20 for dishes like scampi, mixed grill or blackened seafood.

The *Pineapple Hill* is the former plantation home of David Fleming, the pineapple plantation manager after whom Fleming Beach is named. It's on a hill above a little pineapple patch and the golf course. There's a great view down to the ocean especially at sunset. The menu includes chopped steak for $10, shrimp Tahitian for $20 and fresh catch of the day. It's open from 4.30 pm for cocktails, 5.30 pm for dinner. To get there take Kapalua Drive up a mile-long drive through Norfolk pines. Reservations are requested (tel 669-6129).

HONOKAHUA

Honokahua's commercial centre – modest as it is – is set amidst the Kapalua Golf Course. It's comprised of Honolua Store and a gas station with an old church out the back. To get there turn up Office Rd, half a mile north of Kapalua Bay Hotel.

Fleming Beach Park

D T Fleming Beach Park on Honokahua Bay, about a mile north of Kapalua, is a developed park with restrooms, picnic facilities, showers, drinking water and a pay phone.

The long sandy beach is backed by ironwood trees. There's good surfing and bodysurfing, with winter providing the biggest waves. The shorebreaks can be tough and this beach is second only to Hookipa for injuries.

A sign warns of dangerous currents as there have been four or five drownings here in the last few years. The reef out on the right is good for snorkelling when it's very calm.

The Honokahua sand dunes just south of Fleming Beach were excavated in 1988 to build a new Ritz-Carlton hotel. After skeletal remains were found, the construction was halted, the bodies were reinterred and the hotel agreed to move its site to the inland side of the road. The Honokahua burial site is thought to contain the remains of over 1000 Hawaiians who were buried between 950 AD and the 1700s.

Places to Eat

The *Honolua Store* is an authentic old general store with high ceilings, old wooden shelves and a big ice chest full of beer. They have a cafeteria-style deli with dishes like stew, beef tomato and chicken. Plate lunches are served from 9 am to 4.30 pm, either 'hobo' style (a dish and rice for $2.75) or a full plate for $4.50. They have sandwiches for under $3 and all sorts of salads.

HONOLUA & MOKULEIA BAYS

About a mile north of Fleming Beach are Mokuleia Bay (Slaughterhouse Beach) and Honolua Bay. The two are separated by the narrow Kalaepiha Point and together form the Honolua-Mokuleia Bay Marine Life Conservation District. Fishing is prohibited as is collecting shells, coral, rock or sand. In the winter both bays see heavy surf and sand erosion.

In winter Honolua Bay has perfect waves, often making the cover of surfer magazines. The bay faces north-west and when it catches the winter swells it has some of the best surfing in the world.

Slaughterhouse is a hot bodysurfing spot during the summer when the rocks aren't exposed. It's also a popular nude beach.

In summer there's excellent snorkelling in both bays. Both sides of Honolua Bay have good reefs with lots of different coral formations, though the mid-section of the bay is just sand. Honolua Stream empties into the bay and it can get murky after heavy rains.

When it's calm you can snorkel around Kalaepiha Point from one bay to the other. In addition to the coral and reef fish, you might get lucky and spot a sea turtle.

There are a few pull-offs along the road and paths down the cliffs to the beaches. The paths are clay and can be slick when wet. Don't leave valuables in the car.

Sometimes a food van called RV Deli pulls up on weekends.

Kahekili Highway

Farther north the road climbs, offering some nice coastal views. The beaches beyond here are open ocean with rough water conditions.

It's possible to continue around on the coastal road to Wailuku (see Kahekili Highway). The last stop for gas and provisions on this side of Wailuku is at the Honolua Store in Honokahua.

Kihei

Kihei extends six miles along Maui's southwest coast, on the leeward side of Haleakala. Maalaca Bay is to the north, the more exclusive Wailea resort to the south.

Kihei is fringed with white sand beaches its entire length and has near-constant sunshine. It has long attracted sunbathers, boogie boarders, windsurfers and Kahului families on weekend picnics.

The beaches have views of Lanai and Kahoolawe as well as West Maui, which because of the deep cut of Maalaea Bay looks like a separate island from here.

Twenty years ago Kihei was a long stretch of undeveloped beach with kiawe trees, a scattering of homes and a church or two. Now it's Maui's fastest growing community with development continuing non-stop.

South Kihei Rd, which runs the full length of Kihei, is lined with condos, gas stations shopping centres and fast food places in such congested and haphazard disarray that it's the example most cited by anti-development

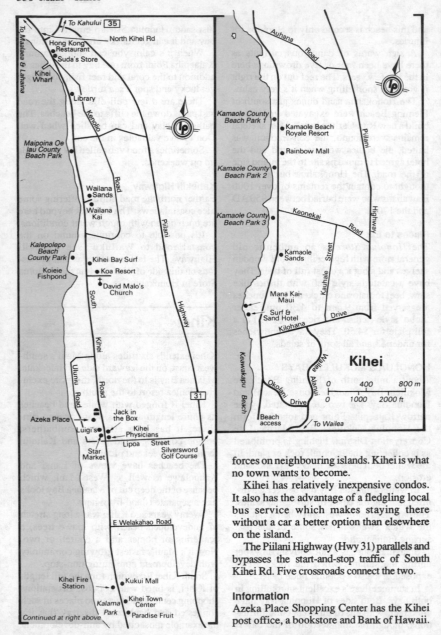

forces on neighbouring islands. Kihei is what no town wants to become.

Kihei has relatively inexpensive condos. It also has the advantage of a fledgling local bus service which makes staying there without a car a better option than elsewhere on the island.

The Piilani Highway (Hwy 31) parallels and bypasses the start-and-stop traffic of South Kihei Rd. Five crossroads connect the two.

Information

Azeka Place Shopping Center has the Kihei post office, a bookstore and Bank of Hawaii.

Kukui Mall has Waldenbooks and a laundromat.

Kihei library (tel 879-1141), 131 S Kihei Rd, is open from noon to 8 pm Mondays and Wednesdays, 8.30 am to 4.30 pm Tuesdays, Thursdays and Saturdays. Keolahou Congregational Church, next to the library, has services in Tongan at 5 pm on Sundays.

Kihei Physicians (tel 879-7781) is open daily in the Kihei Professional Plaza, 1325 South Kihei Rd, opposite the Star Market.

Maalaea Bay

Maalaea Bay runs along the south side of the isthmus between the two mountain masses of west and east Maui. Prevailing winds blow from the north funnelling between the mountains straight out toward Kahaloowe, creating midday gusts and some of Maui's best windsurfing conditions.

These are the strongest winds on the island. In winter, when the wind dies down elsewhere, windsurfers still fly along in Maalaea Bay.

The bay also has a couple of hot surfing spots. The Maalaea break, south of the boat harbour, freight trains right and is the fastest break on Maui. Summer south swells produce huge tubes.

Maalaea Bay is fronted by a continuous three-mile stretch of sandy beach which runs from Maalaea Small Boat Harbor south to Kihei. There's beach access at several places along North Kihei Rd (Hwy 31).

Maalaea has a handful of condo complexes and some notoriety for ripoffs.

Kealia Pond

Kealia Pond, on North Kihei Rd two miles south of the intersection of Hwys 31 and 30, is a saltwater marsh and bird sanctuary. From the side of the road you can see Hawaiian stilts (an endangered species) wading in the water. It's also a habitat for the Hawaiian coot.

Maipoina Oe Iau County Beach Park

Maipoina Oe Iau County Beach Park, at the north end of Kihei, has a long white sand beach. Swimming and sunbathing is best in the morning before the wind picks up. Windsurfing is best in the afternoon. Some of the windsurf shops give lessons here.

The park name means 'forget me not' and is dedicated to Maui's war veterans. It has full facilities.

Kalepolepo County Beach Park

The waters off Kalepolepo County Beach Park offer only mediocre swimming but this is one of the few places in Maui where you can see the stone wall remains of a fishpond.

Koieie Fishpond was built in the 16th century by King Umi of the Big Island. It was used to raise mullet for the alii.

In a story with an unusual menehune twist, Koieie Fishpond was said to have been built by regular-sized Hawaiians. After the workers protested that the work couldn't be done properly without the help of the menehune, the chief in charge angrily ordered that when the job was over the workers were to be cooked in an imu. The night before the last stone was to be placed, the menehune came down from the mountains and carried all the stones away. Only after the threats were withdrawn did the menehune return with the stones and rebuild the fishpond.

The park has restrooms, picnic tables and drinking water.

Across the road, near Koa Resort, is the site where Hawaiian philosopher and minister David Malo used to preach. Services are still held outdoors amongst the church ruins each Sunday morning.

Kalama County Park

Kalama County Park, opposite the Kihei Town Center, is a local park with ball fields, tennis courts, volleyball, a playground, picnic pavilions and restrooms. It's a long grassy park but the beach is shallow and unappealing for swimming.

Kamaole County Beach Parks

Kamaole County Beach Park is one long beach divided by rocky points into three sections. All three are pretty white sand beaches, though sometimes powerful *kona* storms temporarily wipe out much of the sand.

Each section is along the roadside opposite the condos and shopping centres, with full beach facilities and a lifeguard.

Water conditions vary greatly with the weather, but there's usually good swimming. Genreally the beaches have sandy bottoms with a fairly steep drop which tends to create good conditions for bodysurfing as well.

For snorkelling, Kamaole No 3 is the best bet, though the Wailea beaches are far better.

Keawakapu Beach

Keawakapu Beach is a long white sand beach bordered on the north end by the southernmost Kihei hotels and on the south end by Mokapu Beach and the Wailea resort. It's more scenic and less crowded than the roadside Kihei beaches. This is the ritzier and more attractive end of town.

Keawakapu is a sandy beach with a sandy bottom. Snorkelling is fairly good at the rocky outcropping at the south end of the beach.

As there's no reef off Keawakapu, the state has been working to develop an artificial reef here for the past 30 years. The original drop was piles of car bodies, the latest additions were old tyres embedded in concrete. About 1000 of these 'fish shelters' were dropped some 500 yards offshore in 1989.

There's a great view here and during the winter whales cavort offshore – sometimes quite close.

For public access to Keawakapu, instead of continuing along the main road as it curves up to the left to Wailea, go straight ahead on S Kihei Rd until it ends. There are 25 parking spaces and an outdoor shower.

Places to Stay

Kihei is packed with condos, but there are few hotels. In many places along South Kihei Rd, the traffic will challenge you to get a good night's sleep, so it's best to avoid units on the road.

Wailana Sands (25 Wailana Place, Kihei, HI 96753; tel 879-2026) is an older two-storey cinder block building on a quiet cul de sac a block back from the beach. Though it looks like a motel, all 10 units have kitchens and those on the second floor have lanais. There's a pool. Many Canadians return here each winter. Studios cost $40, one-bedroom units $55 and two-bedroom units $90 and the minimum stay is four nights.

Wailana Kai (34 Wailana Place; mailing address: Mary Caravalho, 255-E Alamaha St, Kahului, HI 96732; tel 877-5796) is next to Wailana Sands. It's a sparkling new place with 10 units. They have cable TV, full kitchens (including a dishwasher), a pool and everything you'd expect in a pricey condo except the price. It's great value if you can get in. One-bedroom units cost $50 in the low season and $60 in the high season. Two-bedroom units for up to four people cost $70/80 low/high. Credit cards are not accepted.

Kihei Bay Surf (715 S Kihei Rd, Kihei, HI 96753) is a condo complex directly opposite the Kalepolepo Park with 118 studio units. Units are individually owned and furnished, some with queen-size beds, others with old-fashioned Murphy beds. Rates vary, hovering around $45/$60 low/high, and they're handled through Kihei Maui Vacations, Maui Network or Hawaiian Apartment Leasing (see the general Maui Accommodation section). There's a pool, tennis court, jacuzzi and laundry facilities. If you get a good unit it's a good value.

Nani Kai Hale (73 N Kihei Rd, Kihei, HI 96753; tel 879-9120; 800-367-6032) is a six-storey condo at a busy intersection. There's not much atmosphere but it's on the beach. Two-bedroom, two-bath apartments cost $95/$125 low/high; one-bedroom apartments are from $65/$90 low/high; and studios are $48/$74 low/high. Rooms without kitchens cost $33/$43 low/high. There's a three-day minimum during the low season, seven days during the high season. Credit cards are not accepted.

The *Kamaole Beach Royale* (2385 S Kihei Rd, Kihei, HI 96753; tel 879-3131) is a seven-storey condo opposite Kamaole Beach No 1. It's quiet with open range behind and an ocean view from the top floors. Units are spacious and well-furnished with lanais, modern kitchens, washer/dryers, TVs, and phones with free local calls. It's particularly good value during the low season and the management is friendly. One-bedroom units cost $55/$90 low/high; two-bedroom units are $65/100 low/high. There's a cleaning charge ($35 minimum) for stays of four nights or less. They don't take credit cards.

The *Surf & Sand Hotel* (2980 S Kihei Rd, Kihei, HI 96753; tel 879-7744) has basic, well-worn rooms but a fabulous location on the north end of Keawakapu Beach. It has 100 units in two storeys. Some of the first floor units are a bit musty. Rates are $55 for garden views to $75 for beachfront. There's a room/car package for $69.

The *Kihei Alii Kai* (2387 S Kihei Rd, Kihei, HI 96753; tel 879-6770; 800-888-6284), opposite the Kamaole Beach No 1, is a 127-unit complex with a pool, sauna and tennis courts. All units have washer/dryers and cable TV. One-bedroom units cost $60/$80 low/high, and two-bedroom units are $10 more for up to four people. The minimum stay is three days.

The *Koa Resort* (811 S Kihei Rd, Kihei, HI 96753; tel 879-1161; 800-367-8047) has 54 very large units spread out over 5½ acres. All are fully equipped with washer/dryers, lanais, cable TVs etc. There are two tennis courts, a putting green, jacuzzi and large swimming pool. The friendly manager has a green thumb with tropical plants – check out the orange trumpet vines by the office. One-bedroom units cost $80/$90 low/high and two-bedroom units are $95/105 low/high. For this price category it's a good choice. The minimum stay is five days. Credit cards are not accepted.

Mana Kai-Maui (2960 S Kihei Rd, Kihei, HI 96753; tel 879-1561; 800-525-2025) is a highrise hotel/condo on the north end of scenic Keawakapu Beach. Hotel rooms include breakfast for $85/$90 low/high. One-bedroom apartments (without breakfast but with kitchen) cost $136/152 low/high and have lanais with ocean views. All these rates include a car from Tropical, picked up

at the airport, though there's a one-time 'handling fee' of $10. There's a pool.

Kamaole Sands (2695 S Kihei Rd, Kihei, HI 96753; tel 879-0666; 800-367-6046) is its own condo city with 440 units in 10 buildings. The units are very large, quite nice and have all the modern amenities, but the complex is big and impersonal with lots of concrete and parking lots. There's a pool, jacuzzi, tennis courts and many scheduled activities. It's directly opposite the Kamaole Beach No 3. Aston, which books many of the units, has one-bedroom units for $110/$125 low/high. Other agents may be cheaper.

Places to Eat

These Kihei restaurants are listed in order from north to south.

Polli's, a Mexican restaurant in Kealia Beach Shopping Plaza, 101 North Kihei Rd, has a daily lunch special for around $5 and an uninspired all-you-can-eat tostada bar for $7. There's a deck overlooking the beach. Happy hour is 2.30 to 5 pm and there's music and dancing from 9 pm to midnight Fridays and Saturdays.

Sara 'N Dipity in Kealia Beach Shopping Plaza is open from 8 am to 8 pm with inexpensive sandwiches, bagels, Dreyer's ice cream, yoghurt and pastries.

The snack shop adjacent to *Suda's store*, 61 South Kihei Rd, has cheeseburgers and saimin for under $2 and plate lunches for $4. Pizza is available from 5 to 9 pm. The 'Local Boy' version (medium $9) adds char siu to the cheese, green pepper, tomato and black olives.

The *Hong Kong Restaurant*, on the other side of Suda's, serves Cantonese and Sichuan food.

Azeka Snack Shop next to the grocery store in Azeka Place has plate lunches for under $4, saimin or hamburgers for $1.30. It's open from 9.30 am to 4 pm daily. There's a deli, *Baskin-Robbins* ice cream and *International House of Pancakes* here too.

Luigi's next to Azeka Place has moderately priced pizzas, calzones and pasta dishes.

Opposite the Azeka Place there's a classy *Jack-in-the-Box* with art deco decor and

Pegge Hopper prints on the walls. Its fajita pita sandwich with chunks of white chicken meat, tomatoes and lettuce on pita bread is surprisingly good for fast food. There's sometimes a two-for-one coupon in the free magazines.

The *Chuck's Steak House* in Kihei Town Center, 1847 S Kihei Rd, has a salad bar for $5.25 at lunch, sandwiches for $5 to $7 and standard steakhouse meals for $10 to $14. Early bird dinners cost around $9.

The Kihei Town Center also has a *McDonald's, Kentucky Fried Chicken* and a *Foodland* supermarket which are open 24 hours.

Paradise Fruit, next to Kihei Town Center, is an alternative food store with health foods, whole wheat bread and organic produce. The snack bar whips up smoothies, frozen yoghurt, salads and sandwiches such as the pita melt with cheese and vegetables for $3.25. Homemade pastries include such goodies as oatmeal raisin cookies with white chocolate chunks. There's a place to sit and eat and good bulletin boards. It's open 24 hours a day – only the kitchen closes from 2 to 5 am. The front counter displays Aloha condoms ('Share the Aloha Spirit') next to the vitamin gum.

Senor Gecko's is in the Rainbow Mall, 2439 S Kihei Rd. From 11 am to 3 pm, you can get a taco or enchilada for $4 or chile relleno or tamale for $6. They come with rice, refried beans, chips and salsa. They cost $2 more after 3 pm. It's pretty good food, though not spicy. If you ask for it hot they have the right stuff in the kitchen and they also serve Italian food.

The *Ocean Terrace* (tel 879-2607) at the Mana Kai-Maui has great ocean views. Dinners range from $13 for chicken teriyaki to $18 for steak & scampi and come with chowder or salad, fettucine and homemade bread.They sometimes have early bird specials, between 5 and 6 pm, costing from $10. It also serves breakfast from 7 to 11 am; lunch from 11.30 am to 2 pm; and Sunday brunch from 7 am to 1.30 pm.

Outrigger Maui (tel 879-1581), next to Surf & Sand Hotel, is right out on the beach with an unbeatable view. At lunch time, 11 am to 2.30 pm, sandwiches with fries cost $4 to $6. The chef's special of the day is a full meal for $6. At dinner time, there's a $10 buffet as well as more expensive dishes and an early bird special which includes a salad bar (limited but fresh) for $9.

Entertainment

Polli's On The Beach, 101 N Kihei Rd in Kihei, has music most nights, with rock bands from 9 pm to midnight Fridays and Saturdays.

Getting Around

Akina Bus Service (tel 879-2828) has one bus which runs daily along S Kihei Rd. It starts at 11 am at the Inter-Continental in Wailea, ending about 30 minutes later at Suda's store at the north end of Kihei. It makes 13 stops in between. Most hotels and condos have printed schedules and they're also listed at the bus stops.

The bus heads back to the Inter-Continental at 11.30 am, continuing up and down the road until 5 pm. The fare is 50 cents each time you board. They may have monthly passes so check it out if you're staying awhile.

Wailea & Makena

WAILEA

As soon as you enter Wailea you'll be struck by the contrast to the cluttery commercialism of Kihei. It has the feel of driving into a very exclusive suburb. Everything is green, manicured and precise.

Wailea is the most upscale development on Maui. It has a few swank hotels on the beach, lowrise condo villas, two golf courses, a shopping centre and a tennis club nicknamed 'Wimbledon West'.

Wailea is fronted by two miles of attractive white sand beaches. From Wailea and neighbouring Makena there are good views of Lanai, Kahoolawe and Molokini.

Information

If you're heading to Wailea beaches from Lahaina or Kahului, be sure to take Piilani Highway (Hwy 31) and not S Kihei Rd. It's less than 10 minutes this way whereas the Kihei strip can be a tedious 30 minutes through congested traffic.

Wailea's main road is Wailea Alanui which after Polo Beach changes its name to Makena Alanui and eventually just Makena.

A free shuttle bus runs around Wailea resort connecting the hotels, shopping centre, golf courses and tennis club.

Wailea Shopping Village has a few boutiques, gift shops, a First Hawaiian Bank, two restaurants and a little grocery store. It's in front of the Inter-Continental.

Wailea Beaches

Wailea's beaches begin with the south end of Keawakapu Beach and continue south with Mokapu, Ulua, Wailea and Polo beaches. They all have beautiful white sand, free parking and facilities.

Wailea's beaches can be hit by large surf and *kona* storms at which time they can have dangerous water conditions.

Ulua Beach Ulua Beach is between Stouffer Wailea Beach Resort and Maui Inter-Continental Wailea. The first road south of the Stouffer leads to beach parking.

When it's calm, Ulua Beach has the area's best snorkelling. There's coral at the rocky outcropping on the right side of the beach and you can usually spot long needlefish, large schools of goatfish and other tropicals. The water is very clear and it's best in the morning before the winds pick up.

When the surf's up there's usually good bodysurfing.

During WW II, US Marines trained for the invasion of Tarawa off this beach. Until Wailea resort moved in and named the beach Ulua, it was known as Tarawa Beach.

Wailea Beach Wailea is the largest and widest of Wailea's beaches. There's good snorkelling around the rocky point on the left side when the water is calm. Divers can

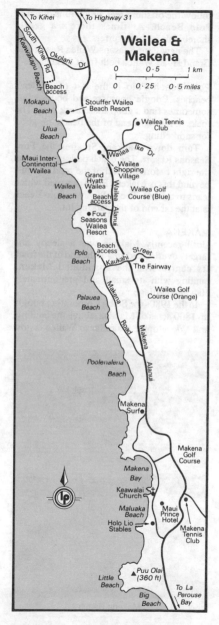

Wailea & Makena

To Kihei
To Highway 31
South Kihei Rd
Keawakapu Beach
Okolani Dr
Beach access
Mokapu Beach
Stouffer Wailea Beach Resort
Ulua Beach
Wailea Tennis Club
Wailea Ike Dr
Maui Inter-Continental Wailea
Wailea Shopping Village
Grand Hyatt Wailea
Wailea Beach
Beach access
Wailea Golf Course (Blue)
Four Seasons Wailea Resort
Wailea Alanui
Polo Beach
Beach access
Kaukahi Street
The Fairway
Palauea Beach
Wailea Golf Course (Orange)
Poolenalena Beach
Makena Alanui
Makena Surf
Makena Golf Course
Makena Bay
Keawalai Church
Maui Prince Hotel
Maluaka Beach
Holo Lio Stables
Makena Tennis Club
Puu Olai (360 ft)
Little Beach
To La Perouse Bay
Big Beach

0   0·5   1 km
0   0·25   0·5 miles

follow the offshore reef which runs down to Polo Beach. At times there's a gentle shorebreak for bodysurfers.

The new Four Seasons Wailea Resort and Grand Hyatt Wailea both front this beach.

Polo Beach Polo is the last of Wailea's beaches. Boogie boarders and bodysurfers sometimes find a good shorebreak here. The rocks at the right end of the beach are good for snorkelling.

Turn down Kaukahi St after the Four Seasons Resort. The beach parking lot is on the right before the end of the road and just beyond this is Makena Rd, a dirt road which leads to the left. The walkway to Polo Beach is at the far end of the parking lot.

MAKENA

Until recently Makena was a sleepy and largely overlooked area at the end of the road. Its centre was the abandoned Makena landing with its small and predominately Hawaiian village.

In the 1980s the Seibu Corporation bought up 1800 acres of Makena, above the landing, and a development similar to Wailea is now

Makena Beach

in the making. So far there's a golf course, a tennis centre, the Maui Prince Hotel and a new bypass road to it all.

Makena's dominant shoreline feature is Puu Olai, a 360-foot cinder hill a mile south of the landing.

Just beyond Puu Olai, Makena has two knock-out beaches adjoining each other. They are commonly called Big and Little beaches or, together, Makena Beach.

These are the finest undeveloped beaches on Maui. Big Beach is a huge sweep of white sand and a prime sunset-viewing locale. Little Beach is a secluded cove, Maui's most popular nudist beach.

In the late 1960s Makena was the site of an alternative-lifestyle free camping area, and took on the nickname 'Hippie Beach'. The tent city lasted until 1972 when police finally evicted everyone on health code violations. More than a few of Maui's residents can trace their roots on the island to the camp at Makena Beach.

Long-term plans call for developing Big Beach into a state park with full facilities.

Palauea Beach

Palauea Beach is along Makena Rd, a dirt road a quarter of a mile south of Polo Beach. The kiawe brushland between the beach and the road is marked private property, though a fair number of people use the beach for surfing and bodysurfing. It's a little more secluded than Polo Beach, but otherwise much the same. You can walk to it from Polo Beach.

Makena Bay

Turn right down Makena Rd after Makena Surf condos and go about a mile to get to Makena Bay.

In the 1800s Makena was the busiest landing on this side of Maui. Cattle from Ulupalakua and other ranches were shipped to market in Honolulu from Makena landing. By the 1920s inter-island boat traffic had shifted to other ports on the island and Makena lost its economic base.

Keawalai Congregational Church was built here in 1855 with three-foot-thick walls made of burnt coral rock. A congregation of over 100 still meets for Sunday services held in a mix of Hawaiian and English. The church graveyard has a fine bayside view and the tombstones have interesting cameo photographs.

The sheltered cove is protected by two rocky outcrops and its waters are almost always calm. The showers and restrooms opposite the church are the nearest facilities to Big Beach.

Makena Rd loops around the Maui Prince Hotel and the Holo Lio Stables before reconnecting with the main road near Makena Golf Course.

Maluaka Beach

Maluaka Beach, at the south end of Makena Bay, is the white sand beach fronting the Maui Prince Hotel. The beach slopes down from a grass-covered sand dune. Rocky formations at each end of Maluaka might provide decent snorkelling. Off the centre of the beach there's a sandy bottom.

Big Beach

This is the type of tropical island paradise people imagine when they dream of a Hawaiian beach. It's very big, uncrowded, and there's absolutely no development on the horizon – not even a lifeguard tower.

This white sand beach is well over half a mile long and as broad as they come, with clear turquoise waters. At least for the time being, Big Beach remains in a natural state. It's barely visible from the road through a line of kiawe trees.

The beach is about a mile past the Maui Prince Hotel (look for cars parked along the roadside). Either pull in at the small sign marking Shoreline Access No 101 (three-quarters of a mile from the intersection of Makena and Makena Alanui roads) and take the dirt drive leading to the beach, or park alongside the road a bit further down and hike a short way through the woods. There are no facilities.

The Hawaiian name for Big Beach is Oneloa (long sand) Beach. It's open ocean and when there's heavy surf there are powerful rip currents and dangerous shorebreaks.

Little Beach

Little Beach is hidden on the other side of a rocky outcropping jutting out from Puu Olai, the cinder cone which marks the north end of Big Beach.

A trail over the outcropping links the two and it's just a few minutes walk across. From the top there's a good view of both beaches.

Little Beach is a sandy cove with good conditions for bodysurfing and boogie boarding. Snorkelling along the rocky point is good when the water is calm. There can be dangerous currents when the surf is high.

A trail continues a few minutes beyond Little Beach to an area where lava outcrops stick out into the clear deep water like giant fingers. When it's very calm divers and confident snorkellers sometimes explore these formations, which include some caves and abundant marine life.

Little Beach, also known as Puu Olai Beach, is a nudist beach despite posted signs to the contrary. From time to time, police make an appearance.

Beyond Makena

Makena Rd turns into a dirt road about half a mile after Big Beach. The rough road continues a couple of miles more to La Perouse Bay before ending at the old King's Highway footpath.

Ahihi-Kinau The Ahihi-Kinau Natural Area Reserve covers 2045 acres and includes sections of Ahihi Bay and Cape Kinau.

Maui's most recent lava flow created most of the cape on its way to the sea in 1790. There are lava tidepools, coastal lava tubes and all the *aa* lava you could ever want to see.

It has been designated a natural area reserve because of its distinctive marine life habitat and its unique geological features, such as the *kipukas* in the midst of the flow and anchialine pools. The removal of any flora, fauna, lava or anything else is prohibited.

There are remains of a coastal Hawaiian village between lava flows at Ahihi Bay. The sites are marked by walled and terraced platforms.

La Perouse Bay In 1786 French explorer Jean Francois de Galaup La Perouse became the first Westerner to land on Maui. He sailed into the bay which now bears his name. Scores of Hawaiian canoes came out to greet him and trade.

After leaving Hawaii, however, La Perouse disappeared in the Pacific. There is speculation that he and his crew may have been eaten by cannibals in New Hebrides.

King's Highway Coastal Trail From La Perouse Bay it's possible to continue on foot along the old King's Highway. This ancient trail follows the coastline across jagged barren lava flows, so hiking boots are a good idea. It's a dry area with no water and little vegetation. It can be very hot.

The first part of the trail is along the sandy beach at La Perouse Bay. Right after the beach it's possible to take a three-quarter mile spur trail down to the lighthouse at the tip of Cape Hanamanioa.

Alternatively you can continue on King's Highway as it climbs up through rough *aa* lava inland for the next two miles before coming back to the coast at an older lava flow. Here there are old Hawaiian house foundations and pebble and coral beaches.

PLACES TO STAY
The *Stouffer Wailea Beach Resort* (3550 Wailea Alanui Drive, Wailea, HI 96753; tel 879-4900; 800-992-4532) is very much a luxury hotel, without being ostentatious. The grounds are lush, the 350 rooms are tastefully furnished with rattan and wicker and it's on a quiet beach. Rates range from $185 for mountain views to $1200 for the Aloha Suite.

The *Maui Inter-Continental Wailea* (3700 Wailea Alanui Drive, Wailea, HI 96753; tel 879-1922; 800-332-4246) has 600 rooms in two-storey buildings and a high-rise complex. It's larger, more rambling and not as polished as the Stouffer. Garden-view rooms cost $145/$175 low/high. An ocean view costs an extra $25. They sometimes have specials, up to half price, during the off-season.

The new *Maui Prince Hotel* (5400 Makena Alanui, Wailea, HI 96753; tel 874-1111; 800-321-6248) turns inward in typical Japanese fashion. From the outside it looks like a fortress but the interior incorporates a fine sense of Japanese aesthetics. The staff are welcoming. The five-storey hotel surrounds a courtyard with waterfalls and streams, carp ponds, raked rock gardens, orchids in planters and bougainvillea draped from the balconies. All 300 rooms have at least partial ocean views, from $180.

Wailea Villas (3750 Wailea Alanui Place, Wailea, HI 96753; tel 879-1595; 800-367-5246) books about 200 units in the Wailea and Makena area. Studio condos in Wailea begin at about $110/$130, low/high season. Makena Surf's two-bedroom condos start at $325.

PLACES TO EAT
If you're heading to the beach, the best bet is to pack a picnic lunch and something to drink.

Ed & Don's at Wailea Shopping Village has a variety of sliced bread sandwiches for around $4, as well as ice cream.

Sandcastle (tel 879-0606) at Wailea Shopping Village has sandwiches, salads and omelettes for around $5 to $7 from 11 am to 3 pm. It often has early bird specials from 4 to 6 pm for $12, but otherwise dinners range from $15 to $22.

Set Point Cafe (tel 879-3244) is at the Wailea Tennis Club overlooking the exhibition court. Breakfast is the likes of muffins, waffles and omelettes. At lunch time, it's soups, salads, sandwiches and quiche. Prices are moderate. It's open from 7 am to 2.30 pm Monday to Friday, 8 am to 2 pm Saturdays and Sundays.

The Fairway, up Kaukahi St amidst Wailea Golf Course, has outdoor tables and a fine ocean view. Breakfast fare and sandwiches, salads and burgers are moderately priced. The bar serves tropical drinks at Wailea prices. There's a salad bar at dinner.

The hotels have fine dining as well as less-formal cafes serving breakfast, lunch and dinner. For the more formal restaurants, reservations are required.

Hakone (tel 874-1111) at the Maui Prince Hotel has full Japanese meals in the $25 range. It's a rather elegant setting with kimono-clad waitresses and shoji screens and the food's said to be good. There's also a sushi bar.

Prince Court (tel 874-1111) at the Maui Prince has 'new American cuisine' and live classical string music from 6 to 10 pm. There's a Sunday champagne brunch from 10 am to 2 pm.

Raffles' (tel 879-4900) at Stouffer Wailea Beach Resort has a rich colonial decor with oak doors, chandeliers and Oriental rugs and vases. Main dishes range from $20 to $30. *Opakapaka* wrapped in taro leaf with grilled orange and Napoleon brandy sauce is $24.50.

La Perouse (tel 879-1922) at the Maui Inter-Continental Wailea has an extensive wine list and is considered one of the best restaurants in Maui. Its callaloo (crabmeat) soup is a speciality, as are the fresh fish dishes in the $20 to $30 range. It's an elegant dark wood setting. The Inter-Continental has champagne brunch with ocean views on Sundays from 9 am to 1 pm.

ENTERTAINMENT
The Wailea/Makena hotels have Hawaiian and contemporary music.

Entertainers like Leo Kottke and Windham Hill artists William Ackerman and Liz Story sometimes play on the lawn at the Stouffer Wailea Beach Resort. Stouffer's also has a disco from 9 pm to 1 am Tuesdays to Saturdays.

The Wailea Shopping Village presents a free Polynesian show at 1.30 pm every Tuesday.

Movies & Theatre Free movies are shown outdoors at 8 pm Wednesdays at Wailea Shopping Village (tel 879- 4465). Bring your own beach mat or chair.

Kahului-Wailuku Area

Kahului and Wailuku are Maui's two largest communities and flow together to form the island's largest urban sprawl. This is where regular folks live, work and shop.

Kahului is the commercial centre. The main road, Kaahumanu Ave, is a collection of stores, banks and office buildings and a mile-long strip of shopping centres.

Kahului Harbor, Maui's deepwater commercial port, services barges, cargo ships and the occasional cruise liner. This one's geared for work – there are no charming wharfs or sailboats.

Kaahumanu Ave continues into Wailuku where it becomes Main St. Wailuku, the county seat, is the more distinctive and less hurried end of it all. It's an older town with back streets of small grocery shops, hole-in-the-wall ethnic restaurants and curio shops.

Maui's main airport is in Kahului. After landing, most people drive right out and don't come back until they're ready to leave. Unless you're up for mall shopping there's really not much in Kahului for visitors. Wailuku, on the way to Iao Valley State Park, has a few historic places of interest and makes for a good lunch break and stroll.

Information
The county and state office buildings and Wailuku Post Office are next to each other on High St in downtown Wailuku. Kahului's post office is on Puunene Ave.

Money The Bank of Hawaii has branches at 2105 Main St in Wailuku and 27 Puunene Ave in Kahului.

Libraries Kahului has the best public library on the island. It's at 90 School St and is open from noon to 8 pm Tuesdays and Wednesdays and 10.30 am to 4.30 pm Thursdays, Fridays and Saturdays.

The Wailuku library at 251 High St is open from 9 am to 5 pm weekdays, and until 8 pm Mondays and Thursdays.

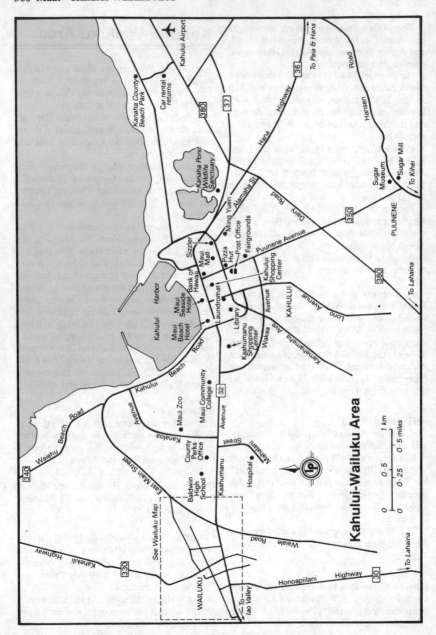

Kahului-Wailuku Area

Emergency The Maui Memorial Hospital (tel 244-9056) is on Mahalani St in Wailuku.

Laundry The Washhouse laundromat is at 74 Lono Ave, Kahului, next to Dairy Queen. It's open from 5 am to 10 pm daily.

Shopping Kaahumanu Shopping Center, Kaahumanu Ave, Kahului has a Liberty House and Sears department stores, Waldenbooks, Foodland, Holiday Theatres, McDonald's, pizza and taco stands and about 50 other shops and eateries.

Maui Mall on Kaahumanu Ave in Kahului has Longs Drugs, Woolworth, a one-hour photo processing and, Waldenbooks, Star Market supermarket and Maui Natural Foods, a standard mall-style health food store. Sizzler Steak House and Safeway supermarket are out the back.

Maui Swap Meet is held from 8 am to noon Saturdays and Sundays at Kahului Fairgrounds. It's on Puunene Ave, just a little south opposite the post office.

KAHULUI

The community which had grown up around the harbour at Kahului was burned to the ground in 1900 in an attempt to wipe out an outbreak of bubonic plague.

The new Kahului is a planned community developed in 1948 by Alexander & Baldwin. It was called Dream City by sugar cane workers who dreamed of moving away from the nearby mill camps to a home of their own. Their tract homes are at the south end of town.

Kanaha Pond Wildlife Sanctuary

Kanaha Pond is a sanctuary for the endangered black-necked stilt, a wading bird which feeds along the marshy edges of the pond. It's a graceful bird in flight with long orange legs which trail behind. The total stilt population in all Hawaii is estimated at 1500.

Access to the pond is on Hwy 396, near the junction of Hwy 36. The parking lot is marked with an HVB warrior. There's an observation deck you can walk out to, from where you can see coots, ducks and black-crowned night herons.

Close the gate behind you and walk in quietly as some of the best sightings are along the shoreline. The pond is a respite in the midst of suburbia, right in the flight path for the airport next door and just beyond the highway where trucks go barrelling along.

Kanaha County Beach Park

If you're stuck in Kahului, Kanaha County Beach Park is OK , though most locals head for the cleaner, clearer waters of Kihei.

Most of the windsurfing shops give their lessons here. When the wind is right, it gets crowded.

Kanaha has a long white sand beach and a nice view of the West Maui Mountains all the way up the coast to Hakuhee Point. There's a little roped-off swimming area, restrooms, showers, phones and lots of picnic tables and barbecue grills under the shade of kukui, ironwood and kiawe trees. The airport noise can be annoying.

The beach access sign is down by the car rentals near the airport. Or from downtown Kahului take Amala Rd, the coastal road which runs makai of the Chevron storage tanks near the end of Kaahumanu Ave.

Maui Zoological & Botanical Garden

This is basically a weary little children's zoo with animals in small, confined cages. There are goats, pygmy burros, peacocks, swans, monkeys, ocelots and ostriches – even a flock of *nene* with goslings.

The 'botanical garden' part has a few labelled plants, but don't expect much.

Maui Zoo is between Kahului and Wailuku, one third of a mile down Kanaloa Ave off Kaahumanu Ave. It's open from 9 am to 4 pm daily and admission is free.

Places to Stay

Maui Seaside Hotel (100 Kaahumanu Ave, Kahului, HI 96732; tel 877-3311; 800-367-7000) has two wings. The older wing, which used to be called the Hukilau Hotel, has rooms from $65. The newer wing is a modern, air-conditioned building that has comfortable, larger rooms with mini-refrigerators for $78. Rates are $10 less in the low season. With this chain, you often get better rates if you book within Hawaii. They have packages which add on a car for $16 more a day and advertise specials in the Sunday Honolulu papers. Both this and the Maui Beach are on the main commercial strip.

Maui Beach Hotel (170 Kaahumanu Ave, Kahului, HI 96732; tel 877-0051; 800-367-5004) is part of Hawaiian Pacific Resorts. This two-storey hotel with 154 rooms is older and lacklustre. Rates range from $69 in the low season to $79 in the high season. It'd be a good deal at half the price. They do have free airport transfers.

Hawaiian Pacific Resorts is planning a new highrise hotel next door at the old Maui Palms location.

Places to Eat

CD Rush's in Kaahumanu Shopping Center is a cafe, deli and bar. Large slices of quiche with salad cost $6. Pasta dishes start at $6.50 and include the salad bar and garlic bread. The salads are fresh and sulphide-free. There's a nice relaxed atmosphere and occasional entertainment.

The *Coffee Store*, a casual place with a few cafe tables in Kaahumanu Shopping Center, roasts its own coffee right in the store and serves it straight or as espresso or cappuccino. Croissant sandwiches or quiche cost $2.50 and lasagne is $4. It has lots of good-looking pastries such as white chocolate and raspberry cheesecake.

The *Ming Yuen* (tel 871-7787), behind Maui Mall at 162 Alamaha St, has good Cantonese and Sichuan food. It has a daily lunch special with a main dish, rice and vegetable for $5 (with two dishes for $6), but ordering from the menu isn't much more. It's open from 11.30 am to 9 pm.

Sir Wilfred's Espresso Cafe is the best place to have lunch in the Maui Mall. Sandwiches such as vegie-tofu burger or hot pastrami with pesto salad are in the $5 range. It has a variety of steamed coffees and serves breakfasts of bagels, croissants and egg dishes.

There's a *Taco Bell* and *Pizza Hut* on Kamehameha Ave and *McDonald's* is nearby, on Puunene Ave.

Entertainment

The *Red Dragon Room* in the Maui Beach Hotel has a disco from 10 pm to 2 am on Fridays and Saturdays.

The *Koho Grill & Bar* at the Kaahumanu Shopping Center has easy listening jazz or Hawaiian music Tuesday to Saturday.

CD Rush's in the Kaahumanu Shopping Center has music from 8 to 11 pm Thursdays and Fridays.

Movies & Theatre Kahului has Holiday Theatres (tel 877-6622) at Kaahumanu Shopping Center and Maui Theatre (tel 877-3560) at Kahului Shopping Center.

PUUNENE

Puunene is a working plantation village surrounded by sugar cane fields, with a mill run by the Hawaiian Commercial & Sugar Company. When the mill is in operation the air hangs heavy with the sweet smell of sugar.

The power plant next to the mill burns residue sugar cane fibres called bagasse to run the mill machinery which extracts and refines the sugar. With a capacity of 37,000 kilowatts, it's one of the world's largest biomass power plants. Excess electricity is sold to Maui Electric.

Puunene's main attraction is the sugar museum opposite the mill.

Sugar Museum

The Alexander & Baldwin Sugar Museum tells the history of sugar in Hawaii. It explains how sugar cane grows and is harvested, complete with an elaborate working scale model of a cane crushing plant.

What's most interesting here, however, are the images of people. The museum traces how Samuel Alexander and Henry Baldwin gobbled up vast chunks of Hawaiian land and fought tooth-and-nail with an ambitious Claus Spreckels to gain access to upcountry water. They dug extensive irrigation systems which made large-scale sugar cane plantations a possibility.

Representing the other end of the scale is a turn-of-the-century labour contract from the Japanese Emigration Company stating that the labourer shall be paid $15 a month for working 10 hours a day in the field, 26 days a month (minus $2.50 banked for return passage to Japan). There are interesting period photos and artefacts of plantation life.

The museum (tel 871-8058), originally the home of the mill's superintendent, is near the intersection of Puunene Ave (Hwy 311) and Hansen Rd. It's open from 9.30 am to 4 pm Monday to Saturday and admission is $2 for adults, $1 for children.

WAILUKU

Wailuku sits beneath the eastern flank of the West Maui Mountains.

The town's streets are lined with a hodge-podge of older shops. The end of Market St closest to the town centre has the pawn shops. Farther down Market St, opposite the Siam Thai restaurant, there's a row of antique

shops. The most interesting of these is Traders of the Lost Art with ancestral carvings and primitive ritual art from Papua New Guinea, Oceania and the Antipodes.

Kaahumanu Church

Kaahumanu Church, on the corner of West Main and High streets, dates from 1837, making it the oldest Congregational church in Maui. The present building was built in 1876 by missionary Edward Bailey.

The church was named in honour of Queen Kaahumanu who cast aside the old gods and burned temple idols, allowing Christianity to flourish. She visited Wailuku in 1832 and in her ever-humble manner requested that the first church be named after her.

The old clock in the steeple was brought around the Horn and it still keeps accurate time. Hymns are sung in Hawaiian at Sunday morning services.

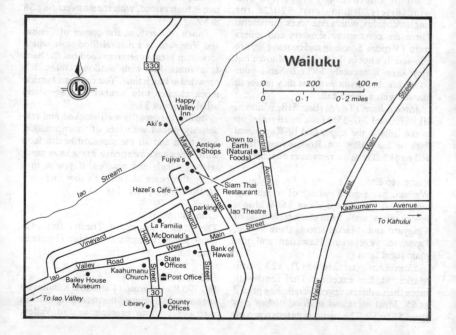

Bailey House Museum

The Bailey House, a five-minute walk up Iao Valley Rd from Kaahumanu Church, was home to the family of missionary Edward Bailey who came to Wailuku from Boston in 1837.

The building, also called Hale Hoikeike, is the headquarters of the Maui Historical Society which has turned the former mission house into a little museum.

There's a Hawaiiana section with tapa, bottle gourds, calabashes and the like, as well as period furnishings from the missionary days. Bailey was a painter and engraver and many of his works are on display. One of Olympian Duke Kahanamoku's redwood surfboards is outside. Admission is by donation, with $2 suggested.

Places to Stay

The *Happy Valley Inn* (310 Lower Market St, Wailuku, HI 96793; tel 244-4786) is a very modest hostel, but it's clean and cheap. It gets a lot of international travellers and windsurfers. Rooms cost $20/28 for singles/doubles, with a one-week minimum. There are community showers and toilets and a TV room. Smoking and cooking are not allowed. It's not in the best part of town but they keep it securely locked. Send your phone number if you write, as they prefer to answer with a phone call.

Mark Edison's Lodge (Box 518, Wailuku, HI 96793; tel 242-5555) is a small motel up in the hills at the upper end of Kapaniwai Park on Iao Valley Rd. Rooms range from $65 to $85. There's a restaurant attached.

Places to Eat

Wailuku has a good variety of restaurants where you can eat for about $5. Within a few minutes walk from the intersection of Vineyard and Market streets there's Thai, Japanese, vegetarian, Hawaiian and just plain local food.

Siam Thai (tel 244-3817), 123 North Market St, has excellent Thai food with more than a dozen vegetarian dishes priced at $5. Most meat and seafood dishes cost from $6 to $9. The menu is extensive with everything from green papaya salad to Pad-Thai noodles and curries. Dishes are spiced hot, medium or mild (mild has no heat at all!). Lunch is served from 11 am to 3 pm weekdays, and dinner from 5 to 10 pm daily. The menu is the same at both.

People who work around here think *Hazel's Cafe*, 2080 Vineyard St, is the place to go. It's local food with generous portions, from hamburgers to fresh fish for $4 to $6. It's open from 6 am to 9 pm, closed Sundays.

Fujiya's, next to Siam Thai, has a wide variety of Japanese dishes in the $4 to $5 range.

Aki's, a five-minute walk north from Fujiya's on Market St, serves Hawaiian food. Kalua pig with cabbage, rice and salad costs $5, a small octopus with coconut milk is $3.35 and a side of poi is 80 cents. It's a local experience and is open from 11 am to midnight.

La Familia is on Vineyard between Church and High streets. It has two dining rooms, one open air. For Mexican food it's rather high priced, with meals averaging $8 to $9.

Down to Earth, at the corner of Central and Vineyard, is a natural food store which serves up great vegetarian food out the back at a snack bar with outdoor tables. It's crowded at lunch time. You can get a burrito, mock chicken tofu sandwich or soup and salad for about $3.

Inside, the store is well stocked and reasonably priced with lots of fresh produce, bulk food and all the standard health food stuff. They have inexpensive takeaway sandwiches, salads and pastries. If you're in a hurry, this beats McDonald's (but there is a *McDonald's* on Main St).

Entertainment

The Maui Community Theater (tel 242-6969) presents plays at the old Iao Theatre in Wailuku.

IAO VALLEY ROAD

In 1790 Kamehameha I attacked Kahului by sea and quickly routed the defending Mauian warriors up into precipitous Iao Valley.

Those unable to escape over the mountains were slaughtered along the stream. The waters of Iao Stream were so choked with bodies that the area was called Kepaniwai, 'dammed waters'.

The scenic Iao Valley State Park is at the end of Iao Valley Rd, with a few sights on the way up starting with the Bailey House Museum.

Tropical Gardens of Maui

If you're looking for a botany lesson, Tropical Gardens of Maui has in-depth interpretive plaques explaining the background of many of the plants. Otherwise it's not a spectacular garden and not very natural. It's open from 9 am to 5 pm daily and admission is $3.

Kepaniwai County Park

Kepaniwai County Park is dedicated to Hawaii's varied ethnic heritage.

Like Hawaii itself, there's a little bit of everything mixed in here. There's a Hawaiian hale with a pili grass roof, a Filipino thatched house, a little New England missionary home and a Portuguese garden with a statue of the Virgin Mary overlooking a bubbling fountain and outdoor bread oven.

The manicured Oriental gardens with their pavilions, stone pagodas and miniature bridges over flowing water are the most prominent. The Chinese pavilion, bright red and white with a green ceramic tile roof, has the requisite statue of Sun Yat-Sen. A bronze statue of Japanese sugar cane workers in traditional garb commemorates the centennial of Japanese immigration.

Iao Stream runs through this large park. It's bordered by many long picnic pavilions with fireplaces and is a popular place for barbecues and parties.

JFK Profile

After Kepaniwai Park there's a bend in the road where there's often a few cars pulled over and a bunch of people staring off into a gorge on the right. One of the rock formations looks surprisingly like John F Kennedy's profile. There's a pipe set up as a scope to help you find the obvious.

Iao Valley State Park

Iao Valley State Park is tucked up in the mountains three miles out of central Wailuku. The valley is named for Iao, the beautiful daughter of Maui and Hina.

Iao Needle, a rock pinnacle which rises 1200 feet from the valley floor, is said to be Iao's clandestine lover whom Maui captured and turned to stone.

Clouds often rise up the valley, forming a shroud around the top of Iao Needle. A stream meanders below and the steep cliffs of the West Maui Mountains form a backdrop.

Just before the bridge there's a walkway looping downhill by the stream. For photography, this is one of the nicest angles – capturing the stream, bridge and Iao Needle together. There are some Job's-tears bushes here. The dried grey bracts are often strung as beads.

Over the bridge, a short walkway leads up to a sheltered lookout with a fine view of Iao Needle. If you go a little bit further along the trail that begins beyond the lookout rail you'll see it from a closer and completely different angle.

Coming down from the lookout, you can turn to the right and follow a well-beaten path 10 to 15 minutes upstream over rocks and tree roots and through yellow ginger. There are some pools deep enough for a dip – though the mosquitoes can be thick.

The park gate is open from 7 am to 7 pm.

HALEKII & PIHANA HEIAUS

Halekii-Pihana Heiaus State Monument marks one of Maui's most important pre-contact historical sites.

Kahekili, the last ruling chief of Maui, lived here; and Keopuolani, wife of Kamehameha I and mother of Kamehamehas II and III, was born here. After the decisive battle of Iao in 1790, Kamehameha I came here to worship his war god.

The two adjoining heiaus are atop a knoll and have a commanding view of the entire region, clear across the plains of central Maui and up the slopes of Haleakala. The temples were built with stones carried up from Iao Stream.

Halekii (house of the idol), the first heiau, has stepped stone walls and a flat grassy top. (Watch out for bullhead thorns if you're wearing flip-flops.) The pyramid-like mound of Pihana Heiau is directly ahead, a five-minute walk away.

Pihana is fairly overgrown with kiawe, wildflowers and weeds. Few people come this way and it's very peaceful. Doves fly up from the bushes as you approach, and the only sounds are bird calls and the rushing waters of Iao Stream below.

This is a powerful place and a certain spiritual essence still emanates from the site. Ignore the industrial warehouses and tract homes which have grown up around the base of the hill and concentrate instead on the vistas and the stones to imagine it all through the eyes of the Hawaiians 200 years back. It must have been an incredible scene.

The heiaus are less than half a mile from Hwy 340 (Waiehu Beach Rd). Turn mauka onto Kuhio St (about three-quarters of a mile south of the intersection of Hwy 340 and Hwy 330) and then take the first left onto Hea Place and drive up through the gates.

WAIKAPU

Honoapiilani Highway (Hwy 30) runs along the east side of the West Maui Mountains between Wailuku and Maalaea. Maui Tropical Plantation is along the way in Waikapu, a couple of miles south of Wailuku.

The main attraction is a touristy narrated tram ride past fields of sugar cane, pineapple and tropical fruit trees. It takes around 30 minutes and costs $8.

If you're driving by you might want to make a quick stop, but it's not worth going out of your way. The free admission section includes shops, small gardens, a nursery, a taro patch and some exhibits, most fairly shallow in content. The poi factory exhibit is one of the better ones, with nice photos from the Bishop Museum.

The on-site restaurant has a daily buffet from 10.30 am to 2 pm with a reasonably good salad bar with fruit, a few dishes, soup, dessert and drink for $9.

KAHEKILI HIGHWAY

Kahekili Highway (Hwy 340) curves around the undeveloped north-east side of the West Maui Mountains. It's ruggedly scenic, with deep ravines, eroded red hills and rock-strewn pastures. The coastline is rocky lava sea cliffs and open ocean.

It's pastoral and quiet with a couple of waterfalls, blowholes and one-lane bridges. You may spot cowboys on horseback and egrets riding the backs of lazy cows.

As a coastal drive, it's second only to the road to Hana.

The north end of the road is at Honokohau, the south at Wailuku, a distance of about 22 miles.

Road Conditions Like its counterpart to the south (the Piilani Highway around the southern flank of Haleakala), Hwy 340 is shown as a black hole on most tourist maps and car rental agencies forbid use of their cars on it.

Much of the Wailuku side is winding and narrow, almost one lane, with some blind curves and 15 mph signs. But taking it slowly is the whole point anyway.

The only part that's unpaved is a two-mile stretch around Kahakuloa. You'll have to slow down to avoid hitting bottom, but it's no big deal. The last five miles to Honokohau is a regular two-lane road. It's all passable in a car with no real challenge.

Waiehu & Waihee

Waiehu Beach Rd turns into Kahekili Highway at the north end of Wailuku and heads through pineapple fields and the little towns of Waiehu and Waihee. Waihee Country Store is the last store until Kapalua.

Waiehu Municipal Golf Course is down near the shore, bordered by two county beach parks which have poor swimming conditions and little appeal.

Rock Arch

From the direction of Wailuku, the road climbs out of ticky-tacky houses and up into the mountains. From here on it just gets better.

There's a natural rock arch on the coastline below a little dirt turn-off, midway between the five and six-mile markers.

Waihee Ridge Trail

A side road up to the Boy Scouts' Camp Mahulia is a pretty winding drive through open pasture which leads to the start of the Waihee Ridge Trail.

Turn mauka just before the seven-mile marker and go up almost a mile. It's a good one-lane paved road, but be prepared to stop for cattle in the road.

The trailhead is on the left just before the camp, marked with a sign and a rusting turnstile. Another sign announces a $1000 reward for information leading to the arrest of cattle rustlers!

The trail is three miles one way. It's a rather steep, well-defined trail which crosses forest reserve land. Starting at an elevation of 1000 feet, the trail climbs a ridge, passing from pasture to damp forest, with a view south to the green cliffs of Waihee Gorge and then north into Makamakaole Gulch. The trail ends at the 2563-foot peak of Lanilili where there are great views in all directions, including Eke Crater at 4480 feet to the south-west.

Waterfalls & Tikis

Back on the highway, you'll pass a gentle waterfall on the left. Then at the pull-off just past the eight-mile marker a big waterfall flows into a pool in the ravine below.

Halfway between the nine and 10-mile markers, keep an eye out for a metal gate mauka of the road. There are two mysterious carved wooden tiki images with saplings growing out of their heads.

Kahakuloa

The village of Kahakuloa is at the base of a small green valley. Though there are only a few dozen simple homes, the village has two churches. The little tin-roofed Catholic mission sits up a hill at the south end of town,

just off the road. The green wooden Protestant church is on the valley floor.

Up out of the valley at the north edge of town there's a good view of the village and its boulder beach. The rise on the south side of Kahakuloa Bay is Kahakuloa Head, 636 feet high.

Bellstone

A rusting HVB warrior marks Pohaku Kani, a large bellstone on the side of the road just past the 16-mile marker.

If you hit the bellstone with a rock on the Kahakuloa side where the deepest indentations are you might be able to get a hollow sound. It's pretty resonant if you hit it right, but it takes some imagination to hear it ring like a bell.

Pastures & Cliffs

The wide turn-off half a mile beyond the 16-mile marker looks down over a clifftop plateau with a rugged coastline and crashing surf. The stretch of green turf practically invites you to walk from the road down along the coastline. It would be a great place to break out a bottle of wine and a picnic lunch.

This is hilly country, with rocky cattle pastures and tall sisal plants. There are a number of viewpoints and pull-offs where you can stop and explore.

Stone cairns are piled everywhere. They look like religious offerings, but most are just the creations of sightseers and are of no significance.

There's a blowhole at the wide turn-off just past the 20-mile marker. Look down to the left.

Nakalele Point Light Station

There's a walk out to the light station at the end of Nakalele Point, midway between the 21 and 22-mile markers. The coastline has interesting pools, arches and other formations worn out of the rocks by the pounding of the surf.

Molokai comes into view around the bend north of here. The scenery is very lush on the way to Honokohau Bay.

Paia

Paia is an old sugar town with a fresh coat of paint.

As part of the original Alexander & Baldwin sugar cane plantation, Paia had about 8000 residents in the early 1900s, which was four times its present size. Most of the plantation camps were located up the slopes above the mill.

The mill is still open though its heyday is past. During the 1950s many Paia residents moved to Kahului, shops closed and Paia began to collect cobwebs.

In the early 1980s windsurfers discovered nearby Hookipa Beach and Paia was dubbed the 'Windsurfing Capital of the World'.

Today Paia has as many windsurfers as sugar cane workers. They come from all over the world, including Germany, Switzerland, Australia and Japan, giving Paia more of an international feeling than any other small town in Hawaii.

This is the last real town before Hana. Some of Paia's small businesses, such as a picnic lunch deli and the last gas station, cater to people heading south.

Paia is our first choice of places to stay on Maui. It's relatively cheap (you can stay in a home rather than a condo) and it's central to Upcountry, Wailuku and the road to Hana. It has an earthy alternative character and comes closer than any other place in Maui to being a laid-back travellers' hangout.

Information

Officially Paia is the area up Baldwin Ave around the sugar mill and Lower Paia is the section down on the Hana Highway. Most people call it all Paia.

There's a Bank of Hawaii and a laundromat on Baldwin Ave.

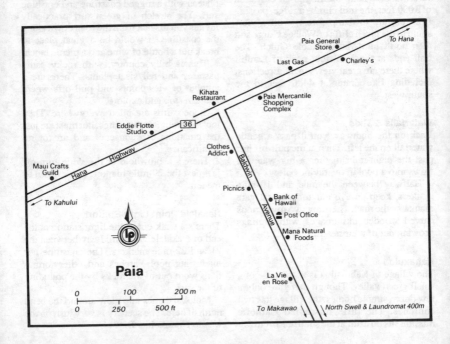

Paia

The post office, also on Baldwin Ave, is open from 8 am to 4.30 pm Monday to Friday, 10.30 am to 12.30 pm Saturdays.

Both Mana Foods and La Vie en Rose have good bulletin boards, with rooms for rent tacked up amid notices of such things as used mountain bikes, windsurfing lessons, massage workshops and dharma dances.

Hunt Hawaii, in the Paia Mercantile Shopping Complex on the Hana Highway, and North Swell, up on Baldwin Ave, sell and rent boards and equipment. Most of the larger windsurfing shops are in Kahului.

Spreckelsville Beach

Spreckelsville Beach, by the golf course between Kahului Airport and Paia, is a hot windsurfing spot. It's one of the windiest places on the north shore. The best wind conditions are in summer.

This is a long stretch of beach, similar to adjacent Kanaha Beach in Kahului. It has a few spots good enough for swimming.

Baldwin Beach Park

Baldwin Beach Park is a big county park about a mile west of Paia. It has a long sandy beach with good bodysurfing. There are showers, restrooms, picnic tables and camping. The park also has baseball and soccer fields, which tends to make it a rather congested and local scene.

The tent spaces are on a flat grassy spot by the road, surrounded by a chain link fence. Even with the high visibility it's not a particularly secure place to stay and there have been some serious assaults on campers here.

Downtown Paia

Paia has small grocery stores which have been in the same families for generations, good restaurants and offbeat boutiques selling antique aloha shirts and bikinis. Many of the old wooden storefronts are painted in bright tones of rose pink, sunshine yellow and sky blue, adding to the town's unique character.

The Hana Highway (Hwy 36) runs straight through downtown Paia. Baldwin Ave leads from the centre of town up to Makawao and the upcountry.

Maui Crafts Guild

Maui Crafts Guild, on the left as you come into town, is a collective of Maui artists and craftspeople.

This is the island's best crafts shop with dyed cloth, woodwork, pottery, baskets, beadwork, shakuhachi flutes and more. Prices are much lower than in Lahaina. Guild members take turns staffing the store once a month.

Even if you're not looking to buy, it's worth a stop – it's almost a crafts museum. There's a view of the surrounding sugar cane fields from the top floor. It's open from 9 am to 6 pm daily.

Eddie Flotte Studio

Eddie Flotte is a watercolourist who paints scenes of Paia: ageing sugar cane workers, wooden storefronts and old pick-up trucks. He does nice work.

His studio and gallery (tel 579-9641) is at 83 Hana Highway (behind Exotic Maui Woods) in the middle of town. It's usually open daily into the early evening.

Paia Mill

The century-old Paia Mill sits above town, less than a mile up Baldwin Ave. The power plant adjacent to the mill burns bagasse, the fibre residue of the sugar cane plant, producing steam power to run the mill.

The mill operates 24 hours a day, shutting down only four days a month. It's a whole little world of its own. It's odd driving by at night with all the lights glowing and a buzz of activity.

Rather than the more usual process of squeezing sugar cane by rollers, the Paia Mill flushes juice out of shredded sugar cane in a process resembling a drip coffee maker.

Mantokuji Buddhist Mission

Mantokuji is a Buddhist temple with an ocean view and a big gong in the yard. It's on the Hana side of town. The graves here are decorated with colourful proteas, birds of paradise and anthuriums.

Hookipa County Beach Park

Hookipa, which has long been one of Maui's prime surfing spots, has recently become

Hawaii's premier windsurfing spot. It has good year-round action for both. Winter has the biggest waves for board surfers and summer has the most consistent winds for windsurfers.

Hookipa Beach attracts some of the world's top windsurfers, especially for the Marui/O'Neill Invitational in April and the Aloha Classic in October.

Between the strong currents, dangerous shorebreak and razor-sharp coral, it's definitely an area for experts. As a spectator sport, it's great – you're watching some of the best.

Hookipa is just before the nine-mile marker. There's usually a line of cars on the lookout above the beach. This is a county park with restrooms, showers and picnic pavilions.

Places to Stay

Paia has no hotels, but with the surge of windsurfers (and others escaping the West Maui scene) lots of people in the Paia/Haiku area are converting garages into studios. Rates average $40 to $50 a day. Check 'Vacation Rentals' in *The Maui News* classifieds or bulletin boards in Paia and the windsurf shops.

Salty Towers (Drawer E, Paia, HI 96779; tel 579-9669) is at 237 Baldwin Ave, a few minutes walk from downtown. Claire Christen rents out three rooms with queen-size beds and cable TV in an older house furnished with antiques and mementos. There's a place to store sailboards and bikes. The small room with shared bath is $40 a day, $225 a week. Two larger upstairs rooms with private baths and little refrigerators cost $50 a day, $275 a week. Long-term guests have access to the kitchen. Smoking is not allowed.

Kaiholo Places (Murray & Georgie Hunter, 10 Kaiholo Place, Paia, HI 96779; tel 579-9925), opposite the Kuau Plaza, has a large studio in a converted garage with tile bath, fold-down bed, full kitchen and use of the washer/dryer. It rents for $50 a day and is attached to a three-bedroom house that rents for $140 a day for up to six people. A

deposit is required; be sure you get the conditions before clear you move in.

Steve Smeltzer (270 Kahiapo Rd, Haiku, HI 96708; tel 575-2406) rents three rooms in a new house near Hookipa. Steve lives behind the house where he makes menehune sculptures and other fantasy creatures. He gets a fairly international crowd of windsurfers. The upstairs has a bedroom with its own bathroom and kitchen for $45. Two downstairs rooms share a bathroom and kitchen; each is $28/35 for singles/doubles. The weekly and monthly rates are a bit cheaper.

The *Kuau Plaza* (777 Hana Highway, 106, Paia, HI 96779; tel 579-8080), near the eight-mile marker, is a run-down 30-unit condo with one-bedroom units for $54/315/1080 a day/week/month, for up to three people.

At *Maui Windsurf Company* (520 Keolani Place, Kahului, HI 96732; tel 877-4816; 800-872-0999), Tom Corso books accommodation in the Paia area. He has B&Bs from around $40. He might be able to help you out with a room in a 'windsurf hotel', a large house shared by lots of people, for $100 to $150 a week.

If you're staying any length of time, you might be able to get a room on your own in a shared house for as little as $200 to $300 a month. Mana Natural Foods and La Vie en Rose are good places to ask around.

Places to Stay – alternatives

Old Maui Zendo (915 Kaupakalua Rd, Haiku, HI 96708; tel 572-8795) is a small secluded upcountry retreat centre on the 55-acre Akahi Farm in Haiku. They have individualised packages which include room, vegetarian meals, hot tub, massage and other activities for $1000 a week. They sometimes hold 10-day Vipassana retreats and yoga and tai chi workshops. There's also an octagonal redwood cottage on the property that costs $850 a week or $350 a weekend.

Aikido Week Maui (Box 830, Paia, HI 96779; tel 575-2568) holds training seminars in Shin-Shin Toitsu Aikido. Accommodation is at Akahi Farm, though most of the classes are held at the aikido dojo in Wailuku. The five-day package, including a trip to Haleakala, costs $490 with meals, $340 without. Sessions are once a month and advance reservations are required.

Places to Eat

La Vie en Rose (tel 579-9820), 62 Baldwin Ave, is *the* scene. It's painted bright pink and has the carefree atmosphere of a large beach shack. It feels more like Jamaica or Kuta Beach than anywhere in the USA. The owner, who whips up great French food, is a Basque surfer named Michel Larronde (he's on the cover of the surfing magazine above the counter). You can get duck confit for $6.25, fresh fish for $8 and vegie tofu lasagne for $5 – a fraction of what they'd cost on the western side of Maui. They also make good French pastries and bread. Breakfast of a freshly baked croissant, half a papaya and coffee is $4. It's open from 10.30 am to 8.30 pm.

Picnics, 30 Baldwin Ave, is a deli with takeaway or eat-in service. Its hearty sandwiches include all the usual selections, as well as more creative stuff like a good vegetarian spinach nut burger for $4. The Plantation Breakfast is cheddar cheese melted over scrambled eggs on toast, papaya-pineapple jam and Kona coffee for $3. The macnut sticky buns and carrot cake are good and their menu has a guide to the Hana Highway on the back. They also prepare picnic box lunches. It's open from 7.30 am to 3.30 pm daily.

Charley's on the Hana Highway has good pizza. Pasta and meatballs with salad and garlic rolls cost $5.50. They open at 7 am for breakfast and again at 4 pm for dinner.

Mama's Fish House (tel 579-9672) is fine dining overlooking the ocean. The speciality is fish dinners, mostly in the $20 to $25 range. At lunch time meals range from $12 to $15. The food is good, but overrated. You're welcomed by a signed photo of Frank Sinatra. Those who like Frankie will probably like the atmosphere at Mama's. It's on the Hana Highway, 1½ miles south of Lower

Paia; look for their antique cars parked at the turn-off. It's open from 11 am to 10 pm daily.

The *Kihata Restaurant* on the Hana Highway has acceptable Japanese food. Domburis in the $5 range are the best value. Teishoku meals are a pricey $9.50 to $11.50.

Mana Natural Foods on Baldwin Ave is a large down-to-earth health food store. They have a wide variety of yoghurts, kefir, bulk nuts, granola, organic and commercial produce, eggs, cheeses, vitamins, teas and whole wheat French bread from La Vie en Rose. It's open from 9 am to 7 pm Sundays, 8 am to 8 pm on other days.

Things to Buy

Maui Crafts Guild in Paia is a co-op with a wide range of quality island-made arts and crafts at the best prices on the island.

The Road to Hana

The Hana Highway runs from central Maui to the village of Hana and beyond to the pools of Oheo Gulch. In a place where there are so many candidates for the most incredible scenery award, the Hana Highway ranks as *the* most spectacular coastal drive in Hawaii. The road was built in 1927 using convict labour.

The cliffside road winds deep into lush valleys and back out above a rugged coastline, snaking its way around more than 600 twists and turns.

One-lane bridges mark dozens of waterfalls. Some are tiny and Zen-like, others sheer and lacy. The 54 bridges to Hana have 54 poetic Hawaiian names taken from the streams and ravines they cross – names like Heavenly Mist, Prayer Blossoms and Reawakening.

The valleys drip with vegetation. There are dense rainforests, bamboo groves and fern-covered hillsides. African tulip trees add bright splashes of orange.

It would take about two hours to drive straight through from Kahului to Hana. But this is not a drive to rush. If you're not staying

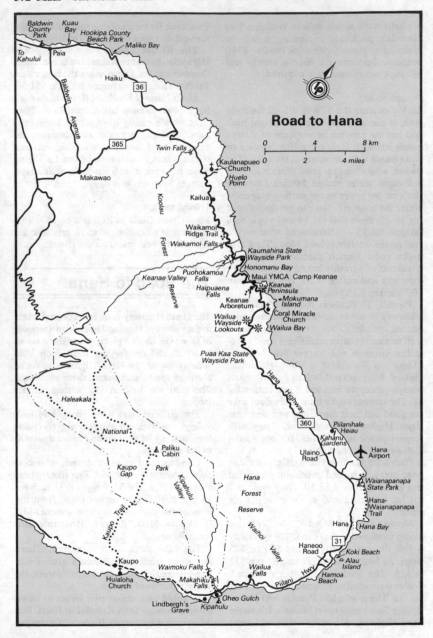

Road to Hana

0   4   8 km

0   2   4 miles

over in Hana, get an early start to give yourself a full day. There are short trails to hike, mountain pools to dip in and a couple of historic sites to check out, all just a few minutes beyond the road for those with time to explore.

Remember to pull over if local drivers are behind you. They move at a different pace.

Paia to Hwy 360

A couple of miles past Paia the road passes Hookipa Beach, where there's a clifftop vantage point looking down onto some of Hawaii's top windsurfers in action.

From there, fields of sugar cane are replaced by rows of pineapple. You'll pass through Haiku, but there's not much to see. It's a spread-out little town, most of it up the slopes.

Hwy 365, which leads up to Makawao and other upcountry towns, comes in just after the 16-mile marker. At this point the Hana Highway changes from No 36 to No 360 and the mile markers begin again at zero.

The road then changes dramatically, slicing through cliffs and becoming more of a mountain road than a highway. Hana is 35 scenic miles away.

Twin Falls

The trail to Twin Falls starts at the first bridge after the two-mile marker. Park on the shoulder after crossing the bridge and walk up along the side of the stream. It's about a five-minute walk to these double waterfalls. They're not terribly high, but when the water's rushing they're quite broad and it's a pleasant enough scene.

If you're going all the way down to Hana or Oheo you'll see better waterfalls, but if you're hanging around Paia these are worth checking out.

Huelo

Huelo Rd, half a mile past the three-mile marker, is a passable dirt road which leads a short way down to Kaulanapueo Church, a coral and stone church built in 1853. It's likely to be locked and if you're short on time this one can be easily bypassed.

Koolau Forest Reserve

After Huelo, the road winds and the vegetation becomes increasingly lush as the highway runs along the edge of the Koolau Forest Reserve.

Koolau, which means 'windward', is the windward side of Haleakala and catches the rain clouds. Most of this coast gets 60 to 80 inches of rain a year, while a few miles up on the slopes there are annual falls of 200 to 300 inches.

The reserve is heavily forested and cut with numerous ravines and streams. From here there seems to be a one-lane bridge and a waterfall around every other bend.

Kailua

Kailua is home to many of the people who work for the East Maui Irrigation Company. They maintain the 75 miles of ditches and tunnels that bring water from the rainforests to the sugar cane fields of dry central Maui. The century-old system is capable of carrying 450 million gallons of water a day.

Many of the dirt roads leading mauka from the highway are the maintenance roads for the Koolau Ditch which roughly parallels the highway about two miles inland.

Leaving town, you'll notice Norfolk pines up on the hillside, followed by a grove of painted eucalyptus trees with rainbow-coloured bark, then a long stretch of bamboo and more painted eucalyptus.

Waikamoi Ridge Trail

Waikamoi Ridge Trail is a peaceful loop trail through tall trees with wonderful, fresh scents. You're welcomed by a sign: 'Quiet. Trees at Work'.

Pull off at the unmarked turnoff half a mile after the nine-mile marker. The trailhead is up to the left near the covered picnic table.

This is an easy trail, three-quarters of a mile long. The tall reddish trees with the huge climbing vines are eucalyptus *robusta*. There are lots of hala, ferns and paper-bark eucalyptus as well. From the ridge at the top there's a good view of the winding Hana Highway.

Waikamoi Falls

Waikamoi Falls is at the bridge just before the 10-mile marker. There's a waterfall and pool near the road. You can walk up to a higher waterfall beyond this, but the rocks can be slippery and anyway the bottom waterfall is as pretty as they get.

If you need drinking water, there's good spring water flowing from a pipe on the other side of the bridge. Past Waikamoi, bamboo grows almost horizontally out from the cliffside creating a canopy effect over the road.

Puohokamoa Falls

Puohokamoa bridge and waterfalls is at the 11-mile marker. Because of its two picnic tables and parking space it's more visited than Waikamoi or Haipuaena waterfalls. It's also pretty and just a minutes walk from the road.

Haipuaena Falls

Haipuaena Falls, half a mile after the 11-mile marker, is another gentle little waterfall with a wonderful pool deep enough for swimming.

There's space for only one car on either side of the bridge. Most people don't know this one's here as you can't see the pool from the road. If you want to take a dip but don't have a bathing suit, this seems like a good choice.

Walk upstream for a couple of minutes, on the Hana side of the bridge, where wild ginger grows and ferns hang from the rock wall behind the waterfalls. It's an idyllic setting.

Kaumahina State Wayside Park

Kaumahina State Wayside Park is shortly after the 12-mile marker. There's a walk up the hill under the park's tall eucalyptus trees. The soil along the path is so eroded that the roots stand above the ground exposed. At the top there's a broad ocean vista with Keanae Peninsula to the south-east. There are picnic tables and restrooms.

Honomanu Bay

For the next several miles, the scenery is particularly magnificent. This is one of those places where you keep grasping for superlatives around each bend.

Just after crossing the bridge at the 14-mile marker an inconspicuous gravel road heads down to Honomanu Bay with its rocky black sand beach. The water's usually too rough for swimming and it's mostly used by surfers and fishermen, though on very calm days it's possible to snorkel and dive there.

Keanae

Keanae is about halfway to Hana. The Maui YMCA Camp Keanae is midway between the 16 and 17-mile marker (see Places to Stay – Hana). There's a pay phone at the road.

Keanae Arboretum, the road to Keanae Peninsula and the Keanae Peninsula Overlook come up in quick succession within the next half a mile.

Keanae Arboretum

Keanae Arboretum is three-quarters of a mile past the 16-mile marker. It has six acres of timber, ornamental and food plants displayed along a marked nature walk. One area is of introduced tropical plants, including painted eucalyptus and thickets of golden-stemmed bamboo with green stripes that look like the strokes of a Japanese shodo artist.

The trail then leads up past sections of heliconia, ti, banana, guava, breadfruit, ginger and other fragrant plants. The higher ground has dozens of varieties of Hawaiian taro in irrigated patches, separated by earthen walls which serve as footpaths. You can follow an unfrequented trail about a mile up the stream past the taro patches to a rainforest.

Keanae Valley sits beneath the Koolau Gap in Haleakala Crater. It averages 150 inches of rain a year.

Keanae Peninsula

The road down to Keanae Peninsula is just past the arboretum.

Lanakila Ihiihi O Iehova Ona Kaua (Keanae Congregational Church) is an attractive old (1860) stone church about half a mile down. This is one church made of lava rocks and coral mortar whose exterior hasn't been covered over with layers of whitewash. And rather than locked doors, there's a 'Visitors Welcome' sign.

Keanae is a quiet little village with colts and goats roaming freely, and taro patches. You can drive to the end of the road but there's no beach here, just jagged rock. The rock island down the coast is Mokumana Island, a seabird sanctuary.

Keanae Peninsula Lookout
Keanae Peninsula Lookout is at an unmarked pull-off just past the 17-mile marker. Look for the mailbox under the tsunami speaker.

There's a good view of the village below with its squares of planted taro, coconut trees, red ginger and Keanae Stream.

Keanae Peninsula was formed by a later eruption of Haleakala which flowed through Koolau Gap down Keanae Valley. Outlined with a black lava coastline, the peninsula still wears its birthmark around the edges. It's very flat, like a leaf floating on the water.

Fruit Stands
Waianu Fruit Stand, just past the lookout, is open 8.30 am to 4 pm daily. They have reasonably priced fresh fruit, banana bread, coffee and shave ice as well as a 24-hour drink machine out front.

A mile farther is Uncle Harry's snack shop. Harry Kunihi Mitchell is a woodworker and songwriter. He wrote 'Mele O Kahoolawe' (Song of Kahoolawe) and is a representative of the Hawaiian people in the Nuclear Free Pacific movement.

There's a little house here made of lashed-together pili grass which displays squid lures, poi pounders and other bits of Hawaiiana. Harry sells Hawaiian-made wood carvings, shell jewellery and baskets.

Muffins, fruit, taro chips, soda and the like are for sale from 9 am to 4 pm Monday to Saturday. There's a shaded picnic area above a stream.

Wailua
Wailua Rd heads makai after the 18-mile

marker. The main attraction is Our Lady of Fatima Shrine.

The shrine, built in 1860, is also known as the Coral Miracle Church. The coral used in the construction came from a freak storm which deposited coral rocks up onto the beach. Before this, men in the congregation had been diving quite deep but were only able to bring up a few pieces of coral each time. After the church was completed another storm washed all the leftover piles of coral back into the sea. Or so they say.

The church has just six little pews. The current congregation uses St Gabriel's Mission, the larger pink-shingled church next door.

From Wailua Rd you can get a view of the long cascade of Waikani Falls, just to the left of Wailua Lookout up on the Hana Highway.

Wailua Rd ends half a mile down, though you might not want to go that far as driveways blocked off with logs and milk crates prevent cars from turning around.

Wailua Wayside Lookout
Back on the Hana Highway, just before the 19-mile marker, Wailua Wayside Lookout comes up on the right. It has a broad view into Keanae Valley, which appears to be a hundred shades of green. There are a couple of waterfalls and you can look up toward Koolau Gap, a break in the rim of Haleakala Crater.

If you climb up the steps to the right you can get a good view of Wailua Peninsula, but there's a better view of it at a turn-off just down the road.

Puaa Kaa State Wayside Park
Puaa Kaa State Wayside Park is midway between the 22 and 23-mile markers. A tranquil waterfall empties into a pool and then flows downhill into a ravine. This one's a treasure.

There are picnic tables along the stream, pools that you can swim in, restrooms and a pay phone.

Kahanu Gardens
Kahanu Gardens (tel 248-8912) is run by Pacific Tropical Botanical Garden. To get

there, turn makai onto Ulaino Rd at the 31-mile marker.

The 120-acre botanical garden on Kalahu Point has medicinal plants and ethnobotanical collections of hala, breadfruit and coconut trees. On the grounds is Piilanihale Heiau, the largest heiau on Maui. It was built by Piilani, the 14th century Mauian chief who is also credited with building many of the coastal fishponds and taro terraces in the Hana area.

The garden is open from 10 am to 2 pm Tuesday to Friday. Admission is $5, or free for children under 12.

Waianapanapa State Park

The road into Waianapanapa State Park is half a mile south of the turn-off to Hana Airport. This 120-acre park has 12 cabins, tent camping, picnic pavilions, restrooms, showers and drinking water.

There's a scenic coastline of low rocky cliffs, including a natural lava arch on the right side of the bay. The small black sand beach is unprotected and there are usually strong rips. When it's very calm the area around the arch is said to be good for snorkelling. Check it out carefully, as people have drowned here.

Caves Some impressive lava-tube caves are just a few minutes walk from the parking lot along a loop path. On the outside the caves are covered with ferns and flowering impatiens. Inside they're dripping wet and cool on even the hottest days.

Waianapanapa means 'glistening waters' and you might be tempted to take a dip. The clear mineral waters leave you feeling squeaky clean.

On certain nights of the year, the waters in the cave turn red. Legend says it's the blood of a princess and her lover who were killed in a fit of rage by the princess' jealous husband after he found them hiding together here. Less romantic types account it to swarms of tiny bright red shrimp called opaeula which occasionally emerge from subterranean cracks in the lava.

Hana – Waianapanapa Trail A coastal trail which parallels an ancient 'King's Highway' leads south about two miles from the park to Kainalimu Bay at the north end of Hana Bay. Some of the original smooth lava stepping stones are still in place along the trail.

Past the cabins, the trail passes blowholes and the ruins of a heiau. There are gorgeous coastal views with cobalt blue water below craggy black lava outcrops. The most predominant vegetation is hala and beach naupaka, the latter with delicate white flowers which look as if they've been torn in half.

From the end of the trail it's about a mile farther to the centre of Hana.

Hana

Hana is separated from Kahului by 54 bridges and almost as many miles. Its isolation has protected it from development and though a line of traffic passes through each day not that many people stay on.

Hana sits beneath the rainy slopes of Haleakala, surrounded by green pasture and a black jagged coastline. In ancient times it was the heart of one of Maui's largest population centres. The village itself was thought to have been reserved for the alii.

In the late 1800s, Chinese, Japanese and Portuguese labourers were brought in to work the newly planted sugar cane fields and Hana became a booming plantation town. A narrow gauge railroad connected the fields to Hana Mill. In the 1940s Hana could no longer compete with larger sugar cane operations in central Maui and the mill shut down.

In 1943 Paul Fagan, a San Francisco businessman who owned Puu O Hoku Ranch on Molokai, purchased 14,000 acres in Hana. Starting with 300 Herefords, he converted the cane land into ranch land.

A few years later Fagan opened the six-room Hotel Hana Ranch as a getaway resort for his rich friends. Geographically and economically, Hana Ranch and the hotel became the hub of town.

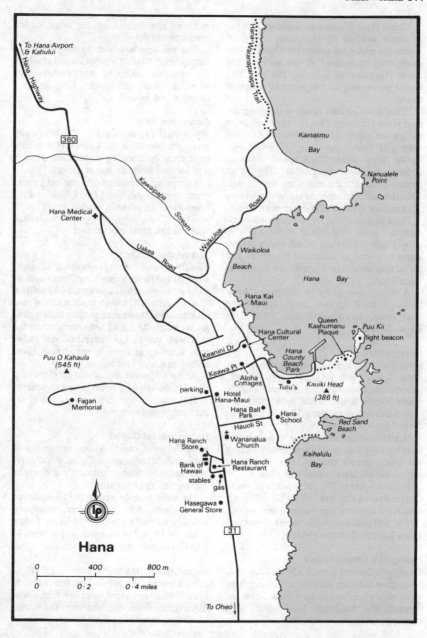

Hana

```
0          400          800 m
0        0·2        0·4 miles
```

To Hana Airport & Kahului

Hana Highway

360

Kawaipapa Stream

Hana Medical Center

Uakea Road

Waikoloa Road

Hana-Waianapanapa Trail

Kainalimu Bay

Nanualele Point

Waikoloa Beach

Hana Bay

Hana Kai Maui

Queen Kaahumanu Plaque

Puu Kii

light beacon

Hana Cultural Center

Puu O Kahaula (545 ft)

Keanini Dr

Keawa Pl

Hana County Beach Park

Aloha Cottages

parking

Hotel Hana-Maui

Tutu's

Kauiki Head (386 ft)

Fagan Memorial

Hana Ball Park

Hauoli St

Hana School

Red Sand Beach

Wananalua Church

Hana Ranch Store

Bank of Hawaii

Hana Ranch Restaurant

stables

gas

Hasegawa General Store

Kaihalulu Bay

31

To Oheo

Today Hana Ranch has about 4000 head of cattle worked by Hawaiian cowboys. When the cattle are ready for Oahu stockyards, they're trucked all the way up the Hana Highway to Kahului Harbor. The trucks leave early in the morning to avoid traffic.

Hana is not a grand finale to the magnificent Hana Highway. People expecting great things are often disappointed. While the setting is pretty, the town is simple and sedate. What makes Hana special is more apparent to those who stay on. There's an almost timeless rural character and though 'Old Hawaii' is an oft-used cliche elsewhere, it's hard not to think of Hana in such terms.

Hana is one of the most Hawaiian communities in the state. Many of Hana's 1800 people have Hawaiian blood and a strong sense of ohana, or extended family. If you spend time around here you'll hear the words 'auntie' and 'uncle' a lot.

A small community of celebrities have homes in the Hana area, including George Harrison, Richard Pryor and Kris Kristofferson.

Information

Hana Ranch Center is the commercial part of town. It has a post office, Bank of Hawaii, gas station, Hana Ranch Restaurant and the Hana Ranch Store which sells groceries, liquor and drugstore items. The store is open from 7 am to 6.30 pm daily.

Hana closes up early. If you're going to be heading back late, get gas in advance. During the week, there's nothing open for dinner except the exclusive Hotel Hana-Maui.

Hana Airport is 3½ miles north of town. Dollar Rent-A-Car (tel 248-8237) will meet you at the airport if you've got a reservation.

The ball park has public tennis courts and Hana Ranch offers horse riding.

Hasegawa General Store

Hasegawa General Store is a Hana landmark. Its narrow aisles are jammed with everything from bags of poi and aloha dolls to kerosene lanterns and machetes. Hasegawa's sells clothing, groceries, hardware, newspapers, gas and the record of the song which immortalised the store.

The business has been in the Hasegawa family since 1910. It's often crowded with a mix of locals picking up supplies, travellers stopping for gas and snacks, and sightseers taking a look around.

Fagan Memorial

When Paul Fagan died in 1959 his family erected a memorial on Lyon's Hill with a huge cross overlooking all of Hana. There's a good view from the top of the hill.

There's a trail, used by cyclists and joggers starts opposite the Hotel Hana-Maui, which takes about 15 minutes to walk up. It might also be OK to drive up, but you should check with the hotel bell captain first.

Wananalua Church

The Wananalua Congregational Church, south of the Hotel Hana-Maui, looks like an ancient Norman church in a park-like setting. It was built in 1838 with thick walls of lava rock and coral mortar to replace the original grass church. There's a little cemetery at the side with graves randomly laid out rather than lined up in rows. Even at rest, Hana folks like things casual.

About 50 people still attend services each Sunday, though they're no longer conducted in Hawaiian. The roof, tower and belfry are currently being restored.

Hana Cultural Center

Hana Cultural Center is a small museum with tapa quilts, Hawaiian artefacts, wood carvings and old photographs. It's a friendly community-run operation.

The same grounds has the old Hana district police station and a three-bench courthouse which operated for over 100 years before closing in 1978. The museum is open from 10 am to 4 pm daily and admission is $2.

Hana County Beach Park

Hana County Beach is at the south end of Hana Bay. It has a black sand beach, community centre, snack bar, showers, restrooms, small boat ramp and picnic tables.

Hana folks come down here with ukuleles, guitars and some beers for impromptu parties in the evenings. You may even find one of Hana's celebrities joining in.

When water conditions are favourable, snorkelling and diving are good out in the direction of the light beacon. Currents can be strong and snorkellers shouldn't go beyond the beacon. If there's any wave action forget it.

Waikoloa Beach, at the north end of the bay, is where the surfing's at.

Kauiki Head

Kauiki Head, the 386-foot cinder hill at the south side of Hana Bay, is said to have been the home of the demigod Maui and was the site of an ancient fort.

The islet at the tip of the point, which now holds a light beacon, is Puu Kii (image hill) and is where the great king Umi set up a huge wooden idol to scare invaders away. In 1780 the Mauian chief Kahekili successfully fought off a challenge by Big Island chiefs at Kauiki Head.

Queen Kaahumanu, the favourite wife of Kamehameha I and one of the most powerful women in Hawaiian history, was born in a cave here in 1768. It was Kaahumanu who destroyed the ancient kapu system and freed women from restrictive taboos.

A trail to a plaque noting her birth starts along the hill just before the wharf. It leads through ironwood trees toward the light beacon, passing by a tiny red sand beach. The walk to the rock where the plaque is mounted is only mildly interesting, but then again it's just five minutes. Watch where you step, as some of the trail is a bit crumbly.

Red Sand Beach

Red Sand Beach (Kaihalulu Beach), on the south side of Kauiki Head, is a local nudist beach. It's a gorgeous little cove with sand eroded from the red cinder hill and beautiful turquoise waters.

It's partly protected by a lava outcropping, though the currents can be dangerous if the surf is up. Water drains through a break on the left side which should be avoided.

The path to the beach is at the end of Uakea Rd beyond the ball park, below the Japanese cemetery. The red cinder can be loose underfoot.

Helani Gardens

Helani Gardens is a 70-acre drive-through botanical garden a mile north of town. It's a mature garden with clumps of bamboo, a fishpond and other nice things. It's pretty lush, but then again so is all of Hana. It's open from 10 am to 4 pm and admission is $2 for adults, $1 for children.

Places to Stay

The *Hana Plantation Houses* (Box 489, Hana, HI 96713; tel 248-7248) has six units, all different. A three-bedroom home with hardwood floors, redwood walls, ocean views, 25-inch TV, VCR, washer/dryer and full kitchen right down to the microwave costs $130.

There's a little Japanese-style studio with an efficiency kitchen, TV, stereo, fans and a jacuzzi on the deck for $65. The cheapest is a simple room on the beach with an outdoor bath for $45. Rates are for singles/doubles with $10 for each extra person. Two units are on Waikaloa Beach and the others are about 10 minutes out of town.

The *Aloha Cottages* (Zenzo & Fusae Nakamura, Box 205, Hana, HI 96713; tel 248-8420) has one studio for $52, three two-bedroom units for $62 and a house for $75. All have kitchens. Most of the units are on Keawa Place, opposite the Hotel Hana-Maui.

Heavenly Hana Inn (Box 146, Hana, HI 96713; tel 248-8442) is on Hwy 360, a mile north of town. It has four apartment-like units, each with two bedrooms, a lanai, bathroom and kitchenette. Everything's under one roof. From the outside it looks like a Japanese temple, with hanging paper lanterns and stone lions guarding the gate. Inside it's a hodgepodge of knick-knacks, antiques and Japanese touches. Rates are $65 a single and $10 for each additional person. It also has a studio for $45 with no cooking facilities.

The inn also books a beach cottage on Hana Bay for up to four adults for $75 single and a family cottage in town for up to six people for $60 single. For both cottages it's $10 for each additional person.

The *Hana Kai Maui* (Box 38, Hana, HI 96713; tel 248-8426, 800-346-2772), just north of town, is a modern but not fancy 19-unit condo. Studios cost $80, one-bedroom units are $95. It has lanais with fine ocean views of Hana Bay, in earshot of the breaking surf.

The *Hana Bay Vacation Rentals* (Box 318, Hana, HI 96713; tel 248-7727; 800-657-7970) manages about 10 cottages, cabins and homes in the Hana area. Prices range from $80 to $125.

Hotel Hana-Maui (Hana, HI 96713; tel 248-8211, 800-321-4262) is one of Hawaii's top getaway hotels. It's on 23 acres in the quiet centre of town. Hana-Maui is low profile, more like a plantation estate than a luxury hotel. Everything's very open air with a lot of wood and Hawaiian accents from local art to quilt bedspreads. The 61 rooms are in one-storey cottages. They have bleached hardwood floors, tiled baths, a view over a private garden and French doors to

trellised patios. You need a big wallet to stay here. Rates start at $360/445 for singles/doubles and include all meals.

The *Maui YMCA Camp Keanae* in Keanae, midway between Kahului and Hana, is on a knoll overlooking the coast. Maui's only youth hostel, it's affiliated with the AYH and IYH associations. Sometimes the whole place is rented to groups, but otherwise there's space for six women and six men at $8 each. It provides a mattress but you have to bring your own sleeping bag and food. There's a three-night limit, though the caretaker can sometimes extend it. The sign on the caretaker's door reads 'Check in Time 4 pm to 6 pm. Later? Forget it.' There's no pool, but there's a swimming hole nearby in Palauhulu Stream. Make reservations at the Maui YMCA office (tel 244-3253), 95 Mahalani St, Wailuku, HI 96793.

The *Waianapanapa State Park*, just north of Hana, has housekeeping cabins which can be reserved through the state park system for $10/$14 singles/doubles. Camping is free with permits issued from the State Parks office (tel 244-4354), 54 High St, Wailuku.

Camping is also possible at Oheo Gulch, 10 miles south of Hana. No permits are needed.

Places to Eat

Tutu's, right at the beach park at Hana Bay, is open from 9.30 am to 3.30 pm weekdays. It has hamburgers from $2, turkey sandwiches or teriyaki burgers for $3.25, plate lunches around $4.50, plus fruit and vegetable salads.

The *Hana Ranch Restaurant* is open for dinner on Fridays and Saturdays and daily from 8 am to 3.30 pm for breakfast and lunch. At lunch time, there's a salad bar for $6.50 or a one-trip buffet for around $8. There's also a takeaway counter. For dinner, dishes range from $13.50 for stir-fry to $16.50 for fresh fish and include the salad bar.

Hotel Hana-Maui (tel 248-8211) serves three meals a day. At lunch time (11.30 am to 2 pm), main dishes range from teriyaki chicken with soba for $12.50 to a steak sandwich with Maui onion rings for $19.50.

Dinner (from 6.30 to 8 pm) is prix fixe for $50, with main course dishes such as grey snapper with papaya basil relish. Meals are served in an open-air dining room with high beam ceilings and live orchids on the tables. Reservations are required.

HANA TO KIPAHULU

From Hana, the road continues on to Kipahulu, passing Oheo, the southern end of Haleakala National Park. It's an incredibly lush stretch, perhaps the most beautiful part of the entire drive. As it continues south from Hana, the road changes name to the Piilani Highway.

The road from Hana to Oheo is narrow, bumpy and winding. Between the hairpin turns, narrow bridges and drivers trying to take in all the sights, it's a slow-moving 10 miles.

You'll get extra coastal views by detouring along the 1½-mile Haneoo Rd loop which runs past Koki and Hamoa beaches and a couple of ancient shoreline fishponds. The turn-off is half a mile south of Hana Ranch headquarters.

Koki Beach is at the base of a red cinder hill less than half a mile from the start of the loop. Most of the sand washes away in winter, leaving a rocky shoreline. Local surfers know the coastline surf here, but rocks and strong currents make it hazardous for newcomers.

The offshore rock topped by two coconut trees is Alau Island, a seabird sanctuary. The trees were planted by a couple of Hana residents so they'd have coconuts to drink while fishing off the island.

A little further is Hamoa Beach, a nice silvery grey sand beach. It's used by the Hotel Hana-Maui which provides a lifeguard and maintains a shower and toilet. There's public access down steps below the hotel's bus stop sign. When the surf's up, there's good surfing and bodysurfing. When seas are calm, swimming in the cove is good.

Past this there are waterfalls down the cliffs, breadfruit and coconut trees, orchids growing out of rocks and even a statue of the Virgin Mary tucked into a rockface on the side of the road.

Wailua Falls, three miles before Oheo, is particularly attractive with its 100-foot drop visible from the road. There's usually a couple of people at the turn-off here selling handpainted T-shirts and the like.

OHEO GULCH

Oheo Stream dramatically cuts its way through Oheo Gulch as a lovely series of waterfalls and wide pools, each one tumbling into the next one below. In fair weather you can swim in them. A two-mile trail runs up the streambed.

There was once a large Hawaiian settlement spread throughout the Oheo area. The stone remains of more than 700 structures have been counted. These early villagers cultivated taro and sweet potatoes in terraced gardens.

One of the expressed purposes of the national park is to manage the Oheo area 'to perpetuate traditional Hawaiian farming and *hoonanea* – a Hawaiian word meaning to pass the time in ease, peace and pleasure'.

Not so long ago Oheo Gulch was dubbed Seven Sacred Pools, a tourism promotion

Oheo Gulch

idea. There are actually 24 pools from the ocean all the way up to Waimoku Falls and they were never sacred (although it was kapu for menstruating women to bathe in them). There's a display by the parking lot restrooms explaining how this inaccurate nickname got started.

Rangers hang out around the parking lot from 7.30 am to 4 pm daily to answer questions. There are no other services or drinking water at Oheo.

Kipahulu Valley

Oheo Gulch is part of the 11,000 acres of Kipahulu Valley which was jointly purchased by the Nature Conservancy and the state and added to Hakeakala National Park in 1969.

The upper Kipahulu Valley is pristine native rainforest and home to endangered native plants and birds. The Maui parrotbill, which lives only here, has a habitat range of just over eight miles. Fewer than 500 of the birds survive. The entire population (30) of the Maui *nuku-puu*, Hawaii's most endangered honeycreeper, also lives in Kipahulu Valley. The nuku-puu was last seen on Kauai in 1985 and is believed to be extinct on Oahu. The parrotbill and nuku-puu are both beautiful birds, about five inches long, with bright yellow underbellies.

The upper part of the valley gets up to 300 inches of rain a year and is swampy with dense vegetation. In an effort to protect the habitat, no public access is allowed.

Lower Pools

A path from the parking lot heads down to the lower pools. There's a broad grassy knoll here with a beautiful view of the Hana coast. On a clear day you can see the Big Island across the Alenuihaha Channel, 30 miles away. It would be a fine place to break out a picnic basket.

The large freshwater pools are almost terraced one atop the other, connected by gentle cascades. They're usually calm and great for swimming, though the water's brisk. The second big pool below the bridge is a favourite.

If it's been raining heavily and the water is flowing too high and fast, the pools are closed and signs are posted by the ranger. Still at any time heavy rains in the upper slopes can bring a sudden torrent of rising waters. If the water starts to rise, get out. People have been swept from the pools by flash floods. The ocean below is not inviting at all – it's quite rough and is populated by grey sharks!

Actually, the biggest cause of injury here is from falls on slippery rocks. Another hazard is the submerged rocks and ledges in some of the pools. Check them out before diving in.

Oheo is home to a rare goby fish. It spends the first part of its life in the ocean, but returns to breed in the upper stream. It works its way up the chain of pools and waterfalls by using its front fins as suction cups on the rocks.

The path makes a short loop from the coast up along the lower pools to the road and back to the parking lot. There are interpretive signs along the way.

Trail to Waterfalls

Opposite the parking lot is a trail leading up to Makahiku Falls (half a mile) and Waimoku Falls (two miles). The path passes large mango trees and plenty of guava, forking after about 10 minutes.

Makahiku Falls is just off to the right. This is a long bridal-veil waterfall which drops into a deep gorge. Thick green ferns cover the sides of the 200-foot basalt cliffs here. Hawaiians sometimes ride up to the overlook on horseback.

To the left of the overlook there's a path in a ditch which goes up to the top of the waterfalls where there's a popular skinny dipping pool. Rocks above the waterfalls protect the pool as long as the water level isn't high. A cut on one side lets the water fall over the cliff.

If the water starts to rise, get out immediately. Around midday the pool is great but by late afternoon the sun stops hitting it and the mosquitoes move in.

Waimoku Falls is a thin, lacy 400-foot waterfall dropping down a sheer rockface. The walk to the falls is made all the more special by three thick groves of bamboo. When you come out of the first grove, you'll see the waterfall in the distance. By the time you emerge from the third thicket, you're there.

It takes 45 minutes to hike to Waimoku Falls from the parking lot. There are a couple of stream crossings on the way. Don't attempt them if the water is high or rising.

The upper part of the trail is muddy with a boardwalk over sections of it. There are old abandoned taro patches along the way.

The pool under Waimoku used to be beautiful but in 1976 an earthquake caused a landslide and the pool's not very deep anymore. Anyway, swimming is not recommended due to the danger of falling rocks. There are concerns that heavy vibrations from helicopters hovering over the waterfalls are destabilising the rocks even more.

There are better pools to swim in along the way. About 100 yards before Waimoku Falls you'll cross a little stream. If you go left for 10 minutes up the stream there's a beautiful waterfall and a little pool. This one's about neck deep. There's not really a trail but you can walk along the side of the stream to get to it.

There's also a nice pool in the stream about halfway between Makahiku and Waimoku falls.

Rangers lead interpretive walks from the parking lot to the falls from 9 am to 1 pm on Saturdays.

Places to Stay

Camping There's an undeveloped camping ground on the south side of the park. This is Hawaiian style, free with no unnecessary structures – just a huge open coastal pasture. There are incredible places to pitch a tent on grassy cliffs right above the coast. All you will hear is the pounding surf.

With the stunning scenery and the ruins of an old Hawaiian village, this is a powerful place. In winter there are usually only a handful of tents here. It gets quite a few

campers in summer but apparently never fills to the point where people are turned away. There are pit toilets and a few picnic tables but *no* water. Permits aren't required though camping is officially limited to three nights each month.

KIPAHULU

The town of Kipahulu is less than a mile south of Oheo. Around the turn of the century Kipahulu was one of several sugar plantation villages in the Hana area. It had a working mill from 1890 to 1922. The mill closure was followed by some attempts to grow pineapple until ranching took hold in the late 1920s.

Today Kipahulu has both exclusive estates and more modest homes. A scattering of impromptu fruit stands are set up along the roadside, some attended by elderly women who string leis and sell bananas and woven lauhala hats. This is the end of the line for most day visitors who have pushed beyond Hana.

Lindbergh's Grave

The Hana area was home to aviator hero Charles Lindbergh during the last years of his life. He began visiting in the 1960s, built a cliffside home here in 1968 and died in Maui of cancer in 1974.

Lindbergh is buried in the graveyard of Palapala Hoomau Congregational Church. His simple grave is surrounded by a chain and marked with little US flags. Lindbergh's own words are carved in the gravestone: 'If I take the wings of the morning and dwell in the uttermost parts of the seas'.

People sometimes get the location mixed up with the green St Paul's Church, which sits on the highway three-quarters of a mile south of Oheo, but the dirt drive down to Palapala Hoomau Church is quarter of a mile beyond that. Look makai for the red roof and white walls of the church. Turn in left at the metal gate just past the wooden cistern at the end of the field. The short road in can get very rutted.

Palapala Hoomau Church, the walls of which are 26 inches thick, dates from 1864.

It's dusty, with simple wooden pews and wax candles melting in the candelabra. The church is known for its window painting of a Polynesian Christ dressed in the red and yellow feather capes worn only by Hawaii's highest chiefs.

The churchyard is a peaceful place, with sleepy cats lounging around waiting for a nice warm car hood to sprawl out on.

Getting There & Away

A lot of people leave Oheo in mid-afternoon to head back up the Hana Highway – some of them become impatient drivers.

Leaving a little later not only gives you more sightseeing time, but allows you to avoid the rush. Getting caught in the dark returning north on the Hana Highway does have certain advantages. You can see the headlights of oncoming cars around bends that would otherwise be blind and the traffic is almost nonexistent.

There are no short cuts, but there's sometimes another option.

From Kipahulu, the Piilani Highway (Don't be misled by the term 'highway' – there's barely a road in places!) heads west through Kaupo up to Keokea in Kula. It's usually passable, but not always, and it shouldn't be done in the dark.

The best way to find out current road conditions is to drive to the far end of Kipahulu and talk to people coming from the Kaupo direction. Most likely they've either just driven down from Kula or else have started up the road from Kipahulu, found road conditions bad and turned around.

For details on the drive, see the Piilani Highway section.

Upcountry

Upcountry refers to the highland area of East Maui on the western slopes of Haleakala. This is some of the finest countryside in all Hawaii, with rolling hills, grazing horses and green pastures.

Upcountry is uncrowded and dotted with small towns. Much of it is ranches, with Haleakala Ranch covering vast spreads to the north and Ulupalakua Ranch to the south.

Kula, in the centre of it all, has rich farmland where most of Maui's vegetables and flowers are grown. There are landscaped gardens and a winery tasting room to visit. Upcountry peaks above Kula in the cloudforests of Polipoli. You have to drive through Upcountry to get to Haleakala National Park, but it's well worth visiting for its own sake.

From Upcountry you can look across the central plains to the West Maui Mountains and get a good view of the Maui coastline and the neighbouring islands. Daytimes are cooler in the Upcountry and nights can be downright brisk.

Paia to Makawao

Baldwin Ave (Hwy 390) runs seven miles from Paia on the Hana Highway up to Makawao. It starts amid sugar cane, passes the Paia Mill and then runs on through pineapple fields interspersed with little open patches where cattle graze.

There are two churches up Baldwin Ave. The Holy Rosary Church, with its memorial statue of Father Damien, comes up first on the right and the Makawao Union Church, built in 1869 of dark stone with stained glass windows, is farther along on the left.

The roadside Rainbow County Park is exactly three miles up. It has covered picnic tables, restrooms and camping, but it's in a low area which can get a bit soggy when it rains.

Hui Noeau Visual Arts Center is on the left between the five and six-mile markers.

Hui Noeau Visual Arts Center Kaluanui, the former nine-acre plantation estate of sugar magnates Harry & Ethel Baldwin, now houses a classy gallery and arts centre. Hui Noeau (tel 572-6560) is a non-profit group offering community classes in printmaking, weaving, batik and dozens of other visual arts.

The two-storey pink plantation home with Spanish-style tile roof was designed by

Top: Kahakuloa, Maui
Left: Oheo Gulch, Maui
Right: Makena Beach, Maui

Top: Jodo Mission, Lahaina, Maui
Left: Nene, Haleakala National Park, Maui
Right: Kaupo, Maui

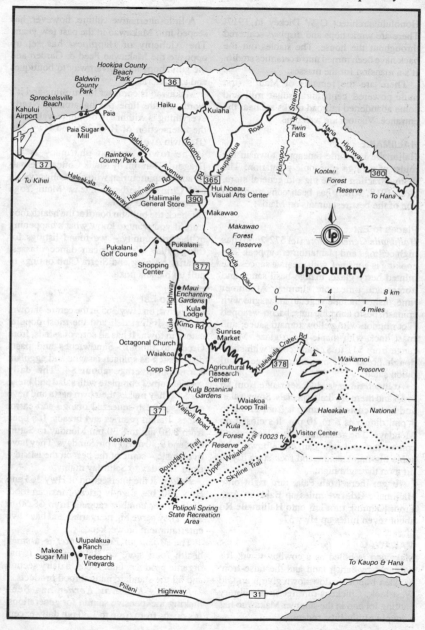

Upcountry

0   4   8 km

0   2   4 miles

Honolulu architect C W Dickey in 1917. There are workshops and displays scattered throughout the house. The stables out the back have been turned into a ceramics studio. It's a mansion for the masses.

There are the remains of Maui's first mule-powered centrifugal sugar mill and some abandoned railroad tracks are near the entrance. Visitors are welcome.

HALIIMAILE

Haliimaile is a little pineapple town in the midst of a large pineapple plantation. The main attraction is the big old general store, circa 1918, which has been converted into one of the best restaurants on Maui.

Places to Eat

Haliimaile General Store (tel 572-2666) has high ceilings and plantation-era appeal. The cooking is gourmet, with creative sauces like minted berry glaze, mango-basil sauce and homemade pineapple chutney. At dinner time, dishes include vegetarian lasagne with spinach, pesto and pine nuts; bacon-wrapped filet mignon with yellow tomato sauce; and roast duck with maple-pecan glaze. Meals range from $11 to $23 and come with sour-dough bread and mandarin orange Maui onion salad.

At lunch time, sandwiches range from $6 to $8 and there are daily specials. Soup, salad and bread costs $5. Lunch is from 11 am to 3 pm, dinner is 6 to 10 pm. It's closed on Mondays. The restaurant has a Hollywood connection and you can rub elbows with some big-name actors and rock stars if you hit it on the right night.

To get there from Paia, turn right onto Haliimaile Rd, five miles up Baldwin Ave. From Kahului, turn left onto Haliimaile Rd about seven miles up Hwy 37.

MAKAWAO

Makawao is billed as a cowboy town. It's bordered by ranch land and the false-front wooden buildings downtown give it an Old West look. Chickens run free in the library parking lot and in the summer Makawao has a couple of big-time rodeos.

A little alternative culture, however, has seeped into Makawao in the past few years. The Alchemy of Happiness has set up opposite the Makawao Feed & Garden and the gun shops have given way to boutiques and art galleries.

Makawao is compact for strolling and it's worth a little time poking around. Nearly everything is within a two-minute walk from the intersection of Hwy 365 and Hwy 390 (Baldwin Ave).

The town's newest pharmacy is the Dragon's Den run by Malik Cotter, a herbalist and acupuncturist, who also sells crystals and Chinese herbs and teas. Maui Yoga Therapy is next door.

Check the bulletin board at the health food store if you want to know what's happening in the community – we found listings for things like West African dance classes, polarity training and Sierra Club outings to pull up banana poka.

Places to Eat

Casanova, on Hwy 365 in the centre of town, is a fine Italian deli and the most popular eatery in town. It has all sorts of salads, from Greek to tabouli. Sandwiches and pasta dishes such as spinach lasagne and eggplant parmesan average about $4. The daily special comes complete with salad and bread for $5. They makes their own pasta and have espresso, fresh-squeezed orange and carrot juices, Italian pastries and breads. It's open from 8.30 am to 8.30 pm Monday to Saturday, and 9.30 am to 7 pm Sundays. They have live music – some of the best on the island – from Tuesday to Saturday nights.

Polli's, at the intersection of Hwy 365 and Hwy 390, has slightly pricey Mexican food, with dinner combos ranging from $8.50 to $12. They serve big margaritas and have live entertainment on weekends.

The *Mountain Fresh Market* is a small health food store on Baldwin Ave. It has organic produce, bulk foods, a dairy section and all the standard natural food products.

Kitada's Kau Kau Korner has been making inexpensive saimin for generations. It's opens from 6 am to 1.30 pm daily except

Sundays. It's on Baldwin Ave opposite the *Makawao Steak & Fish House*.

Entertainment

Casanova has rock, rhythm & blues, jazz, African disco and the like Tuesday to Saturday. This is the hot place on this side of the island, with big name Hawaiian rock bands such as Kalapana on Fridays and Saturdays.

Polli's also has live music on weekends.

MAKAWAO TO HANA HIGHWAY

Scenic back roads head out in all directions from Makawao and almost any one you choose to explore will make a prime country drive.

One route, which we enjoyed making, is to take Kaupakulua Rd (Hwy 365) downhill from Makawao toward the Hana Highway. After a mile, turn left onto Kokomo Rd and keep going for about two miles to a picnic stand at Camp Maui where the Fourth Marine Division was stationed during WW II. It's beneath a hill, shaded with eucalyptus trees.

Then it's through pineapples to Haiku, a modest two-store village. Alexander & Baldwin grew their first 12 acres of sugar cane near Haiku and there was once a mill here.

If you turn right at the crossroads, you'll be on a narrow winding road lined with old mango trees, passion fruit and viney tropical growth. It leads to the even tinier village of Kuiaha where Ohashi General Store looks like it's been sitting for a hundred years. The big building across the street was once a pineapple cannery. These days it's used by small companies making windsurfing equipment and cabinets.

PUKALANI

Pukalani, on the way to Haleakala, is the biggest Upcountry town. It's a residential community with a population of 4000.

Pukalani is two miles from Makawao along Hwy 365. Midway between the two towns is a picture-perfect ranch scene with rolling pastures, horses and cattle grazing and a mountain backdrop. Beyond this the rows of pineapple start up again.

If you're coming from Kahului, the Haleakala Highway (Hwy 37) climbs for five miles through cane fields before turning into green grassy pastures below Pukalani. If you've been to the Big Island, the prickly pear cactus in the fields might look familiar. The seeds were introduced by cattle shipped to Maui from a Big Island ranch.

Places to Eat

Pukalani Terrace Shopping Center is south of the intersection of Hwy 365 and Hwy 37. It has a *Dairy Queen* with fast food fare; *Christine's*, a mall-type diner with moderate prices and bright red and orange decor; and *Y's Okazu-Ya & Crack Seed Shop*. Y's is open from 5.30 am to 1 pm with cheap breakfasts, coffee and saimin. Two eggs, ham and toast cost $2.50. They also sell banzai mix, smoked ika and dried cuttlefish.

There's also a *McDonald's* a little farther up the highway, with a convenience store next to it that sells fried chicken and giant steak fries by the piece.

Pukalani Terrace Country Clubhouse (tel 572-1325) is where Pukalanians head when they want to go out. It's at the golf course, less than a mile past the shopping centre on Pukalani Rd. Standard Western fare, from hamburgers to steaks, ranges from $7 to $12; and a Hawaiian meal which includes kalua pig, lomi, poi, haupia and Maui onions costs $8. There's also a soup and salad bar for $2.50 with the meal or $6.50 alone. The dining room has a good view down to the ocean, but you might need a reservation to get a window seat. It's open from 10 am to 2 pm and 5 to 9 pm daily.

KULA

Kula is the agricultural heartland of Maui. The average elevation is 3000 feet. Crops such as lettuce, tomatoes, carrots, cauliflower and cabbage thrive in Kula's warm days, cool nights and rich volcanic soil. No gourmet cook in Hawaii would be without sweet Kula onions.

During the California Gold Rush in the mid-1800s, Hawaiian farmers in Kula shipped so many potatoes off to the miners that the area became known as Nu Kaleponi, the Hawaiian pronunciation for New California. In the late 1800s, Portuguese and Chinese immigrants moved in to farm the Kula area after they had worked off their contracts on the sugar plantations.

Kula grows most of Hawaii's proteas, large bright flowers with an unusual flair. Some, like the pincushion varieties, are very delicate and others have spine-like petals.

Almost 90% of the carnations used in *leis* throughout Hawaii are grown in Kula, as are many of the chrysanthemums.

Hwy 377 (Haleakala Highway) and Hwy 37 (Kula Highway) are both scenic. Take your pick, or go up one and down the other.

Gardens

All of Kula is a garden, but if you want to get a closer look there are established walk-through gardens.

Upcountry Protea, one mile up Upper Kimo Drive off Hwy 377, has a free protea garden open from 8 am to 4.30 pm daily. They sell protea on site and by mail order.

Sunrise Market, on Hwy 378 on the way to Haleakala, has a free garden with a small but select group of proteas.

Kula Botanical Gardens is a mature garden of tropical plants, pleasantly overgrown and shady. It's on Hwy 37, three-quarters of a mile up from the southern intersection of Hwy 377 and Hwy 37. It's open from 9 am to 4 pm daily and admission is $3. Check the freebie tourist magazines for discount coupons.

The more recently planted Maui Enchanting Gardens is open and sunny with both tropical and cool-weather garden flowers. Everything's labelled in both Japanese and English. It's on Hwy 37, just south of Omaopio Rd, and is open from 9 am to 5 pm daily and admission costs $3.50.

Agricultural Research Center The University of Hawaii maintains a 20-acre agricultural research station in Kula. It's here that Hawaii's first proteas, natives of Australia and South Africa, were established in 1965. You can walk through rows of their colourful descendants as well as dozens of new hybrids under development. The protea has more than 1400 varieties and is named after the Greek god Proteus noted for his ability to change form.

There are now over 50 protea farms in Hawaii supplying the cut flowers to florists on the US mainland, Japan and Europe. The nearest is just across the street from the research centre.

You can visit the garden until 3.30 pm weekdays after signing in at the office. It's free. Some sections of the garden are part of experiments in plant pathology and are closed to visitors. Avoid Fridays, which is the day they spray pesticides.

To get there, take Copp St (between the 12 and 13 mile markers on Hwy 37), turn left on Mauna Place; it's half a mile above town.

Octagonal Church

The distinctive octagonal Holy Ghost Church is a hillside landmark in Waiakoa. The white church with its pink trim has a roof that glints silver in the sun. Built in 1897 by Portuguese immigrants, the ornate interior of the church looks like it came right out of Portugal, and much of it did.

Places to Stay

Kula Lodge (RR1, Box 475, Kula, HI 96790; tel 878-1535), on Hwy 377 less than a mile before Hwy 378, has five rustic attached cottages with a view of the West Maui Mountains. Some of the units have fireplaces. Rates for one or two people range from $80 to $125 and include breakfast in Kula Lodge's restaurant.

Kilohana Elua (Jody Baldwin, 378 Kamehameiki Rd, Kula, HI 96790; tel 878-6086) is a B&B on three acres next to Haleakala Ranch. There are four rooms, two with private bathrooms, from $65 double. Rooms are furnished with antiques and a buffet-style breakfast of fruit, breads and Kona coffee is provided. There are fruit trees in the yard and you're free to pick the fruit.

Places to Eat

Kula Country Store, a quarter of a mile from

the Octagonal Church, is a grocery store with a deli counter. Sandwiches range from $3 to $5. It's open from 7 am to 9 pm daily.

The dining room at *Kula Lodge* is on a knoll with 180° wrap-around windows and a spectacular view of central and northern Maui and the ocean beyond. Breakfasts cost about $5. Lunch is a pretty good deal with soup and sandwich for $5.50 and a couple of specials for not much more. Dinner is more upscale, in the $10 to $20 range. The food is good and the lodge has some nice touches such as mellow music and stained glass windows. It's on Hwy 377, less than a mile before Haleakala Crater Rd (Hwy 378). It's open from 7 am to 9 pm.

Sunrise Market is a quarter of a mile up from the intersection of Hwy 378 and Hwy 377 on the way to Haleakala. You can pick up your morning coffee here along with homemade bakery items and a good selection of local fresh and dried fruit. Gigantic cookies cost 65 cents, shrimp and chef salads are $3.50 and sandwiches start around $2. The store is open from 7.30 am to 4 or 5 pm. There's a nice little protea garden on the side of the store.

POLIIPOLI

Polipoli Spring State Recreation Area is high up in the Kula Forest Reserve on the west slope of Haleakala. The park is in a coniferous forest with picnic tables, camping and a network of trails. It's not always possible to get all the way to the park without a 4WD, but it's worth driving even part way up for the view.

Waipoli Rd, the road to the park, is off Hwy 377 just under half a mile before its southern intersection with Hwy 37. The road is not marked, but it's the first real road north of the intersection.

Waipoli is a narrow switchbacking one-lane road. The drive is often through layers of clouds which drift in and out of groves of eucalyptus and past open rangeland. (Watch for cattle on the road.) When the clouds lift there are vast views across green rolling hills to the islands of Lanai and Kahoolawe.

Few people venture up this way. Except

for the symphony of bird calls, everything is still.

When the clouds are heaviest visibility is measured in feet. The road has some soft shoulders, but the first six miles are well paved. The road then enters the forest reserve and turns to dirt. When it's muddy, the next four miles up to the state park are not worth trying in a standard car.

The whole area was planted during the 1930s by the CCC (Civilian Conservation Corps), a Depression-era work programme. Several of the trails pass through old CCC camps. There are stands of redwood, ash, cypress, cedar and pines. It all looks somewhat like the northern California coast.

Waiakoa Loop Trail

The trailhead to the Waiakoa Loop Trail starts at the hunter check station five miles up Waipoli Rd. Walk three-quarters of a mile down the grassy spur road to the left to a gate marking the trail which starts out in pines.

Since a recent fire, the trail has not been marked or maintained and it's no longer possible to do the whole three-mile loop. However, you can start from the left side of the loop and walk about two miles to where it connects with Upper Waiakoa Trail.

Upper Waiakoa Trail

The Upper Waiakoa Trail is a maintained seven-mile trail which begins off Waiakoa Loop. The trail starts at an elevation of 6000 feet, climbs 1800 feet up switchbacks and then drops back down 1400 feet.

It's stony terrain, but high and open so it has a view. Bring a full canteen of water.

The trail ends on Waipoli Rd between the hunter check station and the camping ground. If you want to start at this end of the trail, keep an eye out for the trail marker for Waohuli Trail, as Upper Waiakoa begins across the road.

Boundary Trail

The four-mile Boundary Trail begins about 200 yards beyond the end of the pavement. Park to the right of the cattle grate which marks the boundary of the Kula Forest Reserve.

This is a steep downhill walk which crosses ravines and goes down deep into the trees where there's eucalyptus, pine and cedar as well as a bit of native forest. In the afternoon the fog rolls in. The trail is marked and maintained.

Skyline Trail

It's possible to hike 8½ miles from the summit of Haleakala to Polipoli campground at 6200 feet. At the end of Haleakala National Park, go past the summit and take the road to the left just before Science City. (Hang gliders sometimes soar from the cliffs here.)

The first 6½ miles is down Skyline Trail, a dirt road used to maintain the state park. It starts at the 9750-foot elevation in an open terrain of cinder and craters.

The tree line begins with a native mamane forest at 8500 feet, about three miles down. In the winter mamane is heavy with clusters of delicate yellow flowers which look like sweet pea blossoms.

Skyline Trail merges into Haleakala Ridge Trail and then Polipoli Trail which spurs half a mile to the camping ground.

There's solitude on this walk. If the clouds treat you kindly there are broad views as you pass from the barren summit to a dense cloudforest.

Places to Stay

Camping Besides tent camping, Polipoli has one housekeeping cabin at $14 for two people, reserved through the state park system. Unlike the other state cabins, this one has gas lanterns but no electricity or refrigerator.

This is cold country and in the winter the temperature drops below freezing at night. There's drinking water and restrooms. It's a popular spot for pig hunters.

KEOKEA

Around the turn of the century, Keokea was home mainly to Hakka Chinese who farmed the remote Kula region.

Keokea is the last real town before Hana if you're swinging around the southern part

of the island. It has two small stores with gas pumps (Fong Store/Shell and Ching Store/Chevron) and a great coffee shop.

The green and white St John's Episcopal Church was built in 1907 to serve the Chinese community. 'St John's House of Worship' is written in Chinese above the door.

On a clear day there are good views of West Maui and Lanai.

Places to Stay

Bloom Cottage (RR2 Box 229, Kula, HI 96790; tel 878-1425) is a two-bedroom free-standing cottage in Keokea. Nights are cool up there and there's a fireplace in the living room. There's also a TV and a front porch to catch the sunset from. The rate is $75 for doubles, $10 for each extra person, plus $10 more if you stay just one night. Smoking is not allowed. There are cooking facilities and breakfast fixings are provided.

Places to Eat

Upcountry folks gravitate to *Grandma's Coffee House* for homemade pastries and dark roasted Maui coffee. It's a sunny, light place, homely and friendly. Slabs of delicious zucchini bread cost 85 cents. You can also get espresso, cappuccino, saimin, sandwiches and frozen yoghurt.

Alfred Franco's family has grown coffee on the slopes of Haleakala since 1918. Alfred started selling at flea markets, packing his coffee in little brown paper bags with felt-penned labels. In 1988 he set up a 103-year-old roasting machine and opened Grandma's. Demand for Maui coffee is high – roasted beans sell for more than $2 an ounce. More Upcountry growers are beginning to get into planting. If you want to see coffee trees just walk out to the side porch.

ULUPALAKUA RANCH

From Keokea, Hwy 37 winds south through ranch country with good views of Kahoolawe and the little island of Molokini. Even on overcast days you can often see below the clouds to sunny Kihei on the coast.

MAUI BLANC

Maui Blanc is a wine made from the juice of fresh Hawaiian pineapples. Fermentation of the rich golden juice takes place in temperature controlled vats and is stopped at near dryness, resulting in a soft, fruity wine with an unmistakable pineapple bouquet. The taste is a pleasant surprise in that it is dry with only a subtle, fragrant hint of pineapple.

Served chilled, Maui Blanc is perfect by itself or will complement light foods such as fish, fowl, ham, and desserts.

The painting "Puu Olai" depicting a scene on the coast below the winery, was created especially for our Maui Blanc label by the noted Hawaiian artist, Curtis Wilson Cost.

You are invited to visit the winery and tasting room in rustic Ulupalakua on your next visit to Maui.

HAWAIIAN PINEAPPLE WINE

Tedeschi Vineyard Wine Label

Tedeschi Vineyards, in the middle of Ulupalakua Ranch, is 5½ miles south of Keokea.

In the mid-1800s Ulupalakua Ranch was a sugar plantation owned by whaling ship captain James Makee. The 25,000-acre ranch has been owned by Pardee Erdman and family since 1963. It's a working ranch with about 6000 cattle, 1500 sheep and 50 head of elk.

Tedeschi Vineyards

Tedeschi Vineyards (tel 878-6058) is the only winery in Hawaii. The first grapes were planted in 1976. While waiting for the vines to mature, they started producing Maui Blanc, a pineapple wine. It's surprisingly light and dry and sells for about $6 a bottle.

Tedeschi now makes three wines from grapes, including champagne and a blush zinfandel, which you can try out in the tasting room from 10 am to 5 pm daily. The little stone building is actually Captain Makee's old jail. Winery tours are given until an hour before closing.

Opposite the winery, you can see the remains of the three stacks of the Makee Sugar Mill, built in 1878.

Piilani Highway

The Piilani Highway (Hwy 31) curves along the southern flank of Haleakala. From Tedeschi Winery it's 25 rugged miles to the town of Kipahulu, near Oheo Gulch, the south end of Haleakala National Park.

Someday in an asphalt future this may well be a real highway with cars zipping along in both directions. For now, it's an unspoiled adventure.

In different sections the road is of broken pavement, gravel, dirt or stones. It takes a good two hours to drive it.

Signs such as 'Motorists Assume Risk of Damage Due to Presence of Cattle' and 'Narrow Winding Road, Safe Speed 15 mph' give clues that this is not your standard highway.

Road Conditions The hardest part is finding out if the road is currently open and passable. Tourist maps mark it impassable and signs at the road's beginning imply the same. Car rental agencies say just being on it is a violation of their contract.

Down around Kaupo, the road goes over three rocky creekbeds. These are usually dry and pose little problem. But after hard rains, streams flow over the roads making passage difficult, if not dangerous. Flash floods sometimes wash away portions of the road, making it impossible to get through until it's repaired.

The best way to approach the road is with an early morning start. Take something to munch, plenty to drink and check your oil and spare tyre. Go slow enough so you don't bottom out. If you break down it's a long haul to civilisation. The tow charge is said to be around $400. If all goes well it's possible to be soaking in one of Oheo's pools by early afternoon.

The road is pretty good for the first 10 miles after the winery. It's patchwork asphalt with a sprinkling of potholes. The next five miles is rougher. Around Kaupo there are some torturous climbs over rocky riverbeds. The strip between Kaupo and Kipahulu is the worst.

A 4WD is recommended, or at least a high riser with a standard (manual) transmission. Still, all said and done, we drove it in a low-slung small car and amazed ourselves by not scraping bottom even once. There were sections where we had to take it very slow, but other than being bounced and rattled, we had no problems.

Keokea is the last place on the Kula side to get food and gas. In the Oheo Gulch area you might find a fruit stand, but there's no drinking water or real services until Hana.

From Tedeschi Vineyards to Kaupo
South from Tedeschi Vineyards, groves of eucalyptus trees and green pastures soon give way to a drier and scrubbier terrain with pink-tipped grasses and wildflowers. It's open rangeland with cattle grazing alongside and moseying across the road.

A few miles south of the winery the road crosses an expansive lava flow dating from 1790, Haleakala's last eruption. This is the flow which covers the La Perouse area of the coast south of Makena. It's still black and barren all the way down to the sea.

Just offshore is the crescent island of Molokini with Kahoolawe beyond. The large grassy hills between here and the sea are volcanic cinder cones.

Painters sometimes set up their easels here to paint scenes of the grassy rock-strewn hillside and the distant ocean. There's such a wide-angle view that the ocean horizon is curved.

The road then runs in and out of numerous ravines and crosses a few bridges, gradually getting closer to the coast. Around the 28-mile marker keep an eye out for a natural lava sea arch. Beyond here there are a couple of black sand beaches.

Kaupo
Kaupo Gap is a deep and rugged valley with the only lowlands on this section of the coast. The village of Kaupo is around the 35-mile marker. Don't expect a developed village in any sense of the word.

Kaupo is spread out and there's not much to see. This is the scattered community of paniolos who work the Kaupo Ranch, many of them third generation ranch hands.

Kaupo General Store is on the east side of the gap. As the fading sign proclaims, it's the only store for 20 miles, though you can't count on it being open.

Kaupo was once heavily settled. It has three heiaus from the 1700s and two churches from the 1800s. Loaloa Heiau is the biggest and is a registered national historical monument. All three heiau sites are mauka of the church.

Huialoha Church, less than a mile from the store, is down on the rocky black sand Mokulau Beach. Mokulau means 'many small islands', named for the rocks just offshore. There's rough surf and strong currents here. It was an ancient surfing site.

The picturesque whitewashed church was built in 1859 and was restored in 1978. It's surrounded by a stone wall and a few windswept trees.

From here the road curves in and then out at which point it's well worth another stop for the view of the church across the bay. It's cool and forested here with sisal plants on the hillsides.

There used to be a landing in the bay for shipping Kaupo Ranch cattle. You can still see steps leading down into the water on a rock jutting out into the ocean.

The road winding into Kipahulu sometimes skirts the edge of rocky cliffs and the vegetation picks up, with hala and guava trees. The road surface is like heavy cobblestones in places and in other sections loose and sliding.

Kipahulu

The pavement begins again at Kipahulu. The road is now flat and shaded with big mango trees which drop fruit in season, banyans, bougainvillea and wiliwili trees with their red tiger claw blossoms.

For details, see the end of the Hana to Kipahulu section.

Haleakala

Haleakala Crater is an awesome geological wonder. It resembles the surface of the moon, with a seemingly lifeless crater floor dotted with high majestic cinder cones. Haleakala is the world's largest dormant volcano, 7½ miles long and 2½ miles wide. It last erupted 200 years ago.

Haleakala National Park centres around the crater, offering views from its rim and hikes across the crater floor.

Haleakala, 'House of the Sun', has long been considered Maui's soul. The summit is thought to be an energy vortex, a natural power point for magnetic and cosmic forces. In ancient times it was a spiritual centre for Hawaiian kahunas. When the planets aligned in 1987, Haleakala drew thousands of visitors observing the harmonic convergence.

Whether it's the lingering mana of the gods who once made their home here or the geological forces of the earth which still release an occasional tremor, Haleakala does emanate a sense of some omnipresent power.

The requisite pilgrimage to witness the sunrise at the rim of the crater can be an experience that borders on the mystical. Mark Twain called it 'the sublimest spectacle' he'd ever seen.

Morning is usually the best time for viewing the crater. Later in the day warm air generally forces clouds higher and higher until they pour through the two gaps and into the crater.

Though sunrises get top billing, sunsets can be impressive too. Sometimes there's a high thin layer of cirrus clouds and a lower layer of fluffier clouds with colours on both levels. At other times, however, it's completely clouded over.

Haleakala National Park stretches from Haleakala Crater down to the pools of Oheo Gulch on the coast south of Hana. There are separate entrances to both sections of the park, but no passage between them. For information on the Oheo area, see the Oheo Gulch section.

Legendary Past

Legend says that long ago the goddess Hina was having problems drying her tapa cloth because the days were too short. Her son Maui, the prankish demigod for whom the island is named, decided to take matters into his own hands.

One morning he went up to the mountain top and waited for the sun. As it came up over the mountain Maui lassoed the rays one by one and held on until the sun came to a halt. When the sun begged to be let go, Maui demanded that as a condition for its release it hereafter slow its path across the sky.

The sun gave its promise, the days are longer and the mountain is known as House of the Sun. There's about 15 more minutes of daylight here than on the coast.

Geology

In its prime, Haleakala probably reached a height of 12,000 feet before water erosion began to eke out two large river valleys. Eventually the valleys eroded into one another, forming what is known today as Haleakala Crater. The valley gaps, Koolau

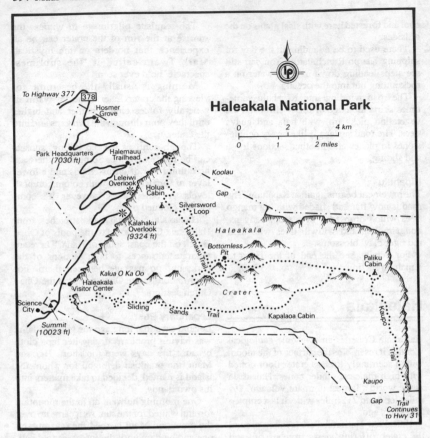

Haleakala National Park

To Highway 377

378

Hosmer Grove

Park Headquarters (7030 ft)

Halemauu Trailhead

Leleiwi Overlook

Holua Cabin

Koolau Gap

Silversword Loop

Kalahaku Overlook (9324 ft)

Haleakala

Halemauu Trail

Bottomless Pit

Paliku Cabin

Kalua O Ka Oo

Haleakala Visitor Center

Crater

Sliding Sands Trail

Kapalaoa Cabin

Kaupo Trail

Science City

Summit (10023 ft)

Kaupo Gap

Trail Continues to Hwy 31

0   2   4 km
0   1   2 miles

Gap on the north-west side and Kaupo Gap on the south-east, are dominant features in the crater wall.

Later eruptions have added numerous cinder cones to the floor of Haleakala. The yellow colours are from sulphur, the reds from iron oxide.

Information

It's a good idea to check out the weather conditions (tel 572-7749 for a recorded forecast) before driving up. It's not uncommon for it to be cloudy at Haleakala when it's clear on the coast. A drizzly sunrise is a particularly disappointing non-event after getting out of bed at 4 am. *The Maui News* prints a sunrise schedule.

You can call park headquarters (tel 572-9306) to talk to a ranger or check activity schedules.

The park never closes. The pay booth at the park entrance opens after dawn, but you can drive through before that. Entrance passes, good for seven days, cost $3 per car, $1 per bicycle and nothing for walk-ins and US citizens aged over 61. National park passes are valid.

There's no food for sale in the park. Bring

something to eat, particularly if you're going up for the sunrise, so that a growling stomach doesn't force you to rush all the way back down the mountain before you've had a chance to explore the sights.

Activities Park rangers lead a guided 2½-hour hike into the crater down Sliding Sands Trail from 10 am Tuesdays, Saturdays and Sundays, leaving from the visitor centre.

Guided hikes into Waikamoi Preserve leave from Hosmer Grove camping ground at 9 am Mondays, Thursdays and Fridays and last 2½ hours.

Nature talks are held at the summit for 15 minutes at 9.30, 10.30 and 11.30 am daily. Crater rim walks of varying lengths are held during the summer. Other walks and activities vary with the season.

You can hike or ride a horse down into Haleakala Crater and come back the same day, or camp on the crater floor in a tent or cabin.

Bicycle tours down Haleakala via the park road and horse rides into the crater are detailed in the Facts section at the start of this chapter.

Volunteer Programmes The national park service has a programme allowing volunteers to work at the park. Duties may be as varied as office work, leading hikes, fence construction, trapping predatory animals, propagating native plants and controlling invasive ones, or cleaning pit toilets.

There's a preference for volunteers with a background in natural sciences and a knowledge of practicalities like first aid. A three-month commitment is required. There's no salary though barracks-style housing is usually provided and occasionally there's a $6 to $9 daily stipend. For information write: Volunteers in Parks, Haleakala National Park, Box 369, Makawao, HI 96768.

Another group, the Student Conservation Association (Box 550C, Charlestown, NH 03603), is basically a clearinghouse which sends a couple of people each year to work for three months as volunteers at Haleakala. They provide the round-trip air fare to

Hawaii, a small weekly stipend and accommodation. Anyone over 18 may apply.

The Sunrise Experience

Sunrise at Haleakala is unforgettable. As you drive up in the dark, the only sights are lights: a skyful of stars, scattered city lights resembling a large connect-the-dots drawing and a distant fishing boat or two on the dark horizon.

About an hour before sunrise, the night sky begins to lighten and turn purple-blue and the stars fade away. Interesting silhouettes of the mountain ridges appear.

Plan to arrive 30 or 40 minutes before the actual sunrise. The gentlest colours show up in the fragile moments just before dawn. The undersides of the clouds lighten up first, accenting the night sky with pale silvery slivers and streaks of pink.

About 20 minutes before sunrise, the light intensifies on the horizon in bright oranges and reds, much like a sunset. Turn around for a look at Science City, whose domes turn pink.

Temperatures hovering around freezing and a cold wind are the norm at dawn. There's often a frosty ice in the top layer of cinders which crunches underfoot.

If you don't have a winter jacket or sleeping bag to wrap yourself in, take a warm blanket from your hotel. This will give you the option of sitting outside in a peaceful spot to take it all in rather than huddling for heat inside the crowded visitor centre.

Everyone comes out for the grand finale. The moment the sun appears, the earth awakens and everything glows.

Every morning is different, but once the sun is up the silvery lines and the subtleties disappear. The best photo opportunities are before the sun rises.

Park Headquarters

Park headquarters, less than a mile from the park boundary, is open from 7.30 am to 4 pm. This is where you get camping permits and brochures. They also sell books on geology, flora and fauna. There are a few silverswords planted out the front and occasionally a pair of nene walk around the parking lot.

Silversword

The strikingly beautiful silversword with its pointed silver leaves is a distant relative of the sunflower. The plant grows for four to 25 years before blooming just once.

In its final year, it shoots up a flowering stalk sometimes as high as nine feet. During the summer the stalk flowers with hundreds of maroon and yellow blossoms. When the flowers turn to seed in late autumn, the plant dies.

The silversword, found only in Hawaii, was nearly wiped out in the early 1900s by grazing feral goats and by people who took them for souvenirs. It's making a comeback due to efforts by the park service who have fenced in sections of the park to protect the plants.

Nene

The native nene, Hawaii's state bird, is related to and resembles the Canada Goose. It has been brought back from the verge of extinction (only 30 birds remained in 1951) by a captive breeding and release programme.

Currently the nene population at Haleakala is holding steady at about 150. The birds generally nest in high cliffs surrounded by rugged lava flows with sparse vegetation.

Nene are rather curious. Many hang out where people do, from the crater floor cabins to park head-

Nene

quarters. Unfortunately they don't do well in an asphalt habitat and many have been run over by cars.

Hosmer Grove

Hosmer Grove is three-quarters of a mile north of park headquarters. It has a pleasant half-mile loop trail that begins in the camping ground. The trail starts in a forest of introduced trees and then passes into Hawaiian shrubland.

The exotics in Hosmer Grove were introduced in 1910 in an effort to develop a lumber industry in Hawaii. They include incense cedar, Japanese sugi, Douglas fir, eucalyptus and various pines. Though the trees adapted well enough to grow, they didn't grow fast enough at these elevations to make tree harvesting practical. Thanks to this failure, there's a park instead.

Native plants include ohelo, pukiawe, mamane, pilo and sandalwood. There are wonderful scents along the trail and lots of bird calls.

Walking through either Hosmer Grove or the nearby Waikamoi Preserve, you might see the native iiwi and apapane, both fairly common sparrow-size bright-red birds. The iiwi has a very loud, squeaking call and a curved salmon-coloured bill. The apapane is a fast-moving bird with a white under-tail. It feeds on the nectar of ohia flowers.

You might also see the melodious laughing thrush, also called the spectacle bird for the circles around its eyes which extend back like a pair of glasses, and the greenish Japanese white-eye, also with eye circles. These two are foreign species.

Waikamoi Preserve

Waikamoi Preserve is a 5230-acre preserve adjoining the north-east area of the park. In 1983 Haleakala Ranch conveyed the management rights of the land to the Nature Conservancy.

The area contains native koa and *ohia* rainforest and is a habitat for Hawaiian forest birds, including a number of rare and endangered species. The yellow-green Maui creeper and the crested honeycreeper are both endangered but they're more common than some of the others. The beautiful crested honeycreeper is an aggressive bird which often dive-bombs apapane and chases them off branches.

The conservancy has hikes for members on the second Sunday of each month. Reservations are required and can be made by calling the preserve manager (tel 572-7849).

The national park service guides hike in from Hosmer Grove camping ground at 9 am Mondays, Thursdays and Fridays.

Leleiwi Overlook

Leleiwi Overlook is midway between park headquarters and the visitor centre. From the parking lot it's just a few minutes walk out to the overlook, from where you can see the West Maui Mountains and both sides of the isthmus connecting the two sides of Maui. You also get another angle on Haleakala Crater.

In the afternoon if weather conditions are right you might see the Brocken spectre, an optical phenomenon which occurs at high elevations. Essentially, by standing between the sun and the clouds your image is magnified and projected onto the clouds. The light reflects off tiny droplets of water in the clouds, creating a circular rainbow around your shadow.

Kalahaku Overlook

Kalahaku Overlook is about a mile above Leleiwi Overlook. The lower section has a fenced enclosure containing lots of silversword, from seedlings to mature plants.

The upper section has an observation deck looking down into Haleakala Crater. Using the display here, you can clearly identify seven cinder cones on the crater floor below.

For photography, afternoon light is best. In the early morning you can get more favourable light by walking a few minutes down an unmarked path to the left of the observation deck.

Haleakala Visitor Center

The visitor centre, on the rim of the crater, is the main sunrise-viewing spot. It's open daily from 30 minutes before sunrise until 3 pm.

The centre has good displays on geological and volcanic evolution and a recording explaining what you see looking out of the window into the crater floor 3000 feet below. Books on geology, plants and the national park are for sale here and there's usually a ranger on duty.

The Summit

The Puu Ulaula (Red Hill) Overlook, at 10,023 feet (3055 metres), is Maui's highest point. The octagon summit building at the overlook has wrap-around windows and interpretive displays explaining the surrounding sights.

On clear days you can see the Big Island, Lanai, Molokai and even Oahu. The summit building is half a mile uphill from the visitor centre.

The 37-mile drive from sea level to the summit of Haleakala is said to be the highest elevation gain in the shortest distance in the world. You can buy a certificate at the visitor centre saying you've made the trip. The dollar for the certificate goes to help exterminate pests in the park, including cats, rats and mongoose.

Science City

On the Big Island's Mauna Kea scientists study the moon. Here at Haleakala, appropriately enough, they study the sun.

Science City, just beyond the summit, is outside park headquarters and off limits to visitors. It's under the jurisdiction of the University of Hawaii which owns some of the domes and leases other land for a variety of private and government research projects.

In addition to UH's solar observatory, the university's Institute of Astronomy operates a lunar ranging facility. Purdue University and the University of Wisconsin jointly operate a gamma ray telescope.

The most ominous tenant is the Air Force which is involved in the beaming and catching of lasers. In the next phase of research the lasers will be beamed at a satellite orbiting in space. The beams will be bounced off the satellite's mirrors and aimed back down to an antenna farm planted above Kihei's Silversword Golf Course. It's all part of testing and research for the ill-conceived SDI 'Star Wars' project.

Two other defence-related facilities at Science City are a satellite tracking and identification facility and a deep-space surveillance system.

Places to Stay
Camping Free camping is allowed at three camping grounds in the upper park and one on the coast at Oheo Gulch.

Hosmer Grove is a drive-up camping ground immediately after the park entrance. It has a picnic shelter, toilets, water and grills. Permits are not required for this site or for Oheo Gulch. There's a three-day limit per month. It's busier in summer than in winter and is often full on holiday weekends. It tends to be cloudy and a bit wet.

There are two backpack camping grounds inside Haleakala Crater. One is at Holua cabin, four miles down Halemauu Trail, and the other is at Paliku at the trail's end. Both are below steep cliffs, though Holua is dry and barren while Paliku is lush and wet.

Permits are required for backpack camping. They can be picked up at park headquarters from 7.30 am to 4 pm daily and are issued on a first-come first-served basis only. Camping is limited to three nights a month, with no more than two consecutive nights at any camping ground. Each camping ground is limited to 25 people. Permits can go quickly if large groups show up, a situation more likely to occur in summer than at other times of the year.

The camping sites have pit toilets and water. Fires are prohibited and you'll need to carry all your rubbish out.

Cabins There are three trail cabins in the crater, one each at Holua, Kalalaoa and Paliku. Each has a wood-burning stove, some cooking utensils, 12 bunks and mattresses and water and pit toilets. Hiking distances from the crater rim range from four to 10 miles. Fees are $5 per person per night,

with a $15 minimum, plus $2.50 per person per night for firewood. There's a three-day limit per month.

The problem here is the demand. The park service actually holds a lottery to award reservations! To enter, you must send a reservation request to get there before the first of the month, two months prior to the proposed stay. (Requests for cabins in March are selected on 1 January.)

If you have alternative dates it increases your chances. You can send in your request with a letter or ask for a form. Don't send money until you're notified. The address is: Cabin Reservation Request, Box 369, Makawao, HI 96768.

Getting There & Away
Haleakala Crater Rd (Hwy 378) runs 11 miles from Hwy 377 up to the summit. It's a good paved road but it's steep and winding. You don't want to rush it.

The drive to the summit takes about 1¼ hours from Paia or Kahului, two hours from Lahaina.

As you wind back down the mountain much of Maui unfolds below, with fields of sugar cane and pineapple in patches on the valley floor. The highway snakes back and forth, with as many as four or five layers of switchbacks in view all at once.

Just south of the park there's a eucalyptus grove with Pony Express stables which has horse rides. Further on is Sunrise Market with its free protea garden and local produce for sale.

HIKING THE CRATER
Hiking the crater floor offers a completely different angle on Haleakala's lunar landscape. Instead of peering down from the rim you're looking up at the walls and towering cinder cones. It looks so much like a moonscape that US astronauts trained here before going to the moon.

The crater is a very still place to walk. Cinder crunching underfoot is often the only sound.

The trails inside the crater crisscross and each other. A popular full-day hike goes down the first four miles of Sliding Sands Trail and comes back along Halemauu Trail, taking in the short Silversword Loop. Trails are marked at junctions.

Weather Conditions The weather at Haleakala can change suddenly from dry hot conditions to a cold windswept rain. Though the general rule is sunny in the morning and cloudy in the afternoon, fog and clouds can blow in at any time.

No matter what the weather is like at the start of a hike, be prepared for temperatures which can drop into the 50s (F) during the day and the 30s at night, at any time of year. Hikers without proper clothing risk exposure to hypothermia.

The climate also changes radically as you walk across the crater floor. In the four miles between Kapalaoa and Paliku cabins, rainfall varies from an annual average of 12 inches to 300 inches. January to June is the wetter season.

With the average elevation on the crater floor at 7000 feet, the relatively thin air means that hiking can be quite tiring here. The higher elevation also means that sunburn is more likely. Take sunscreen, rain gear, a few layers of clothing and a full canteen of water.

Sliding Sands Trail

This trail is the summit trail into the crater. It starts at the south side of the visitor centre parking lot. The trail leads 9½ miles to Paliku camping site and cabin, passing Kapalaoa cabin at 5¾ miles. The first six miles of the trail follows the south wall of the crater.

From Kapalaoa to Paliku there's a gentle descent and the vegetation gradually increases. Paliku (6380 feet) is beneath a sheer cliff at the eastern end of the crater. It has heavy rainfall, in contrast to the crater's barren western end. Here there are ohia forests climbing the slopes and grassy camping sites.

Sliding Sands-Halemauu Trail

A popular hike for people in good shape is the 12-mile hike which starts down Sliding Sands Trail and returns via Halemauu Trail. It's a strenuous full-day hike.

Sliding Sands starts out at 9780 feet and descends over loose cinders down to the crater floor. If you hike it after catching the sunrise you'll walk directly into a gentle warmish wind and the rays of the sun. There are great views on the way down but, except for a few shrubs, there's no vegetation in sight.

Four miles down, after an elevation drop of 2500 feet, a spur trail leads north about a mile to Halemauu Trail.

Once on Halemauu Trail it's possible to take a short loop to the Bottomless Pit. Legends say the pit leads down to the sea, though the park service says it's just 65 feet deep. It's basically a large hole in the ground of limited interest.

About 1½ miles up the Halemauu Trail is the short Silversword Loop. It passes by silversword plants in various stages of development. If you're here in summer you should be able to see some in bloom.

About a mile further along Halemauu Trail is Holua cabin and camping ground. There's a large lava tube here that's worth exploring. At 6960 feet this is one of the lowest areas along this hike and there are impressive views of the crater walls rising a few thousand feet to the west. From the cabin it's four miles to the Halemauu trailhead.

Because of its descent, Sliding Sands Trail makes a better entry trail into the crater than a return trail. The Halemauu trailhead, at an elevation of 8000 feet, is an easier exit.

Halemauu trailhead is on Hwy 378, six miles below the visitor centre (and the trailhead to Sliding Sands) and 3½ miles above park headquarters. If you haven't arranged to be picked up, you might try hitching.

Halemauu Trail

This trail can be hiked part way. Even hiking in the first mile to the crater rim gives a fine view of the crater with Koolau Gap to the east. It's fairly level up to this point.

If you were to continue on the trail and hike down the switchback to Holua cabin and back it would make a fine hardy day hike of eight miles round trip. From the trailhead to the bottom of the pali the trail descends 1400 feet. Once on the floor of the crater the trail follows the west wall for about a mile to Holua cabin at 6960 feet. The trail continues another six miles to Paliku cabin.

Halemauu trailhead, 3½ miles above park headquarters, is marked. You might find nene in the parking lot here.

Kalua O Ka Oo Trail
The first two miles of this trail descends 1600 feet down Sliding Sands Trail, where there's a spur trail which leads up the Kalua O Ka Oo cinder cone, about half a mile to the north.

Silversword can be seen midway along Kalua O Ka Oo Trail. From the visitor centre to Kalua O Ka Oo and back it's a hardy three-hour hike.

Because of the uphill climb back, this is a good hike to do early in the morning to avoid the midday heat.

Kaupo Trail
From Paliku camping ground on the eastern edge of the crater floor, it's possible to continue another nine miles down to Kaupo on the southern coast. The first 3½ miles of the trail drops 2600 feet in elevation before reaching the park boundary. It's a rocky trail through rough lava and brushland. The last 5½ miles passes through Kaupo Ranch property on a rough jeep trail as it descends the Kaupo Gap. There are fine coastal views along the way.

The 'village' of Kaupo is a long way from anywhere, with little traffic. Still what traffic there is – largely sightseers braving the circle-island road – moves slow enough along Kaupo's rough road to start conversation. If you do have to walk the final stretch, it's seven miles to Oheo Gulch and what will seem like hordes of people and traffic.

This is a strenuous hike and because of the remoteness and the ankle-twisting conditions it's not advisable to hike it alone.

Molokai

Molokai is the last stronghold of rural Hawaii. It manages to hold out in a sort of time warp: no packaged Hawaiiana, no high-rises, more farmers than tourists. This is a place to get in touch with basics.

If you're looking for anything slick, Molokai isn't the place. Instead, you can walk along Hawaii's largest beach with not another soul in sight, or take the cliffside mule trail down to the old leprosy colony of Kalaupapa. This island has fine hikes and campgrounds, spectacular valleys, a wildlife park and a handful of historical sites.

Molokai is the most Hawaiian of the main islands, with almost 50% of its population of native Hawaiian ancestry. It's only sparsely populated, with but a handful of small towns.

According to ancient chants, Molokai is a child of Hina, goddess of the moon.

In the morning you can sit on the edge of an 800-year-old fishpond and watch the sun rise over distant Maui. In the evening you can watch the sun set behind the silhouette of Molokai's royal coconut grove.

Molokai retains so much small-town character that at times it seems more like an outpost in the South Pacific than the island between the highrises of Maui and Waikiki.

Orientation

Molokai lies midway in the Hawaiian chain, 26 miles south-east of Oahu and nine miles north-west of Maui. Lanai is nine miles directly south.

The airport is on the island's flat central plains, more or less in the centre of Molokai.

Take a right turn when you leave the airport to get to Hwy 460. At the highway, to the left it's seven miles to Kaunakakai, the main town; to the right it's 13 miles to the Kaluakoi Resort on the west coast.

This one highway is Molokai's main road, stretching from east to west. From Kaunakakai westward it's called Hwy 460 (Maunaloa Highway). From Kaunakakai eastward it's Hwy 450 (Kamehameha V Highway).

Exploring Molokai Molokai is not the place to explore dirt roads just to see what's there. People on Molokai spend a lot of time out-doors and their yards are extensions of their homes. Many dirt paths that seem like they could be roads are just driveways into someone's backyard. In addition, as on all the islands, there's a bit of pakalolo growing here and there as well. All in all, folks aren't keen on outsiders cruising their private turf.

On the other hand if there's a fishpond you want to see and someone's house is between the road and the water, it's usually easy to stop and strike up a conversation. Molokai people are generally receptive and friendly. If you ask permission first they'll usually let you cross their property. If you appear interested they might even share a little local lore and history – the old timers in particular can be fascinating to listen to.

Facts

HISTORY

Molokai had powerful sorcerers whose reputations were respected throughout the islands. Through carvings of poisonwood idols and other elaborate rituals, they were able to keep potential invaders at bay. For centuries, the battling armies of Maui and Oahu were careful to bypass Molokai.

By the 18th century, magic wasn't enough to keep things together. Internal dissent among the alii of Molokai, largely over access to valuable fishing grounds at Moomomi, led them to align with chiefs from other islands.

Oahu, Maui and the Big Island all got involved in the picture. Eventually Peleioholani, the ruler of Oahu, established his rule over Molokai. When the daughter he

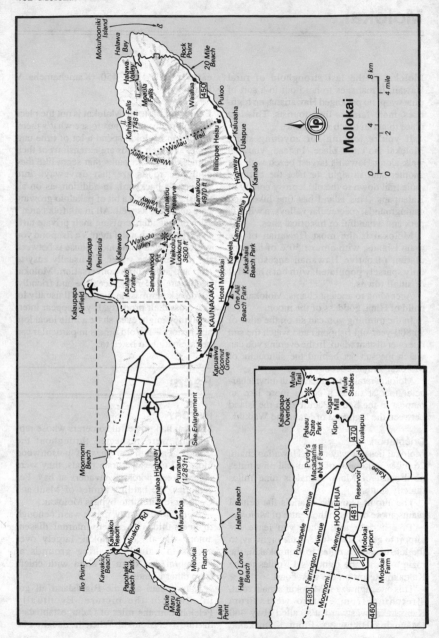

Molokai

left on Molokai was captured and killed by Molokai chiefs, Peleioholani hastily returned to the island and struck back with a vengeance. Molokai chiefs who were unable to flee to Maui were captured and roasted alive.

Oahu continued to rule over Molokai until 1785. From that time warring Maui and the Big Island took alternate turns in ruling Molokai until Kamehameha the Great united all the islands in 1795.

The first detailed description of the island was recorded by Captain George Vancouver, a British navigator, who anchored off Molokai in 1792. His guesstimate placed Molokai's population at around 10,000.

When the missionaries arrived in the 1830s they did a more detailed count, estimating Molokai's total population at 8700.

Molokai's largest settlements were on the rainy south coast of the eastern half of the island. The shallow waters and coastal indentations there were ideal for the construction of fishponds. In the valley wetlands, taro patches flourished.

The missionaries found the densest populations between Kamalo and Waialua. It is in this area that they established their first missions and some of the churches still stand today.

Kalaupapa Peninsula had the other major settlement, with about 2500 people. The north shore valleys of Halawa, Pelekunu, Wailau were also populated. Molokai's central plains and dry western half were only lightly settled.

GEOGRAPHY

Molokai is Hawaii's fifth largest island. It is 38 miles long, 10 miles wide and roughly rectangular in shape, with a land area of 264 square miles.

The western half of Molokai is dry and arid, with rolling hills and the gradually sloping range of Maunaloa (1381 feet). The island's highest point, Kamakou (4970 feet), is in the middle of the rugged eastern half.

Geologically Molokai is a union of two separate shield volcanoes which erupted to form two distinct islands. The rugged mountains of eastern Molokai captured the clouds, and heavy rainfall and stream erosion cut deep valleys into its towering north face. Western Molokai formed into more modest hills and tableland. Later eruptions spilled lava into the channel which separated the two, forming the Hoolehua Plains and creating present-day Molokai.

Kalaupapa, on the north shore of Molokai, seems to have been an afterthought by Madame Pele. An eruption from offshore Kauhako Crater created the flat lava peninsula long after the rest of Molokai had been formed. Kauhako Crater, at 400 feet, is Kalaupapa's highest point.

CLIMATE

At Kaunakakai, the average daily temperature is 70°F in winter, 78°F in summer. The average annual rainfall is 27 inches.

FLORA & FAUNA

The two most dominant forest types on Molokai are kiawe in the drier areas and ohia lehua in the wetter.

Along the banks of streams, once heavily cultivated with taro, forests of kukui and guava now dominate.

The axis deer which run free in Molokai are descendants of eight deer introduced from India in 1868 as a gift to King Kamehameha V. Feral pigs, introduced by the early Polynesian settlers, roam the upper wetland forests and feral goats inhabit the steep canyons and valley rims. All three cause havoc on the environment and are hunted game animals.

Native waterbirds include the common moorhen, Hawaiian coot and black-necked stilt, which are all endangered. Molokai has five native forest birds (mostly in the undisturbed upland forests) and the Hawaiian owl.

GOVERNMENT

Kalaupapa Peninsula is a county unto itself, called Kalawao, and is basically administered by the State Department of Health. The rest of Molokai, along with neighbouring Lanai, is swallowed up in the mire of Maui County.

In large part administrative decisions affecting Molokai are made on Maui. Since most community planning and development issues are decided at a county level, the island of Maui, with 12 times Molokai's population, has the clout.

ECONOMY

Cattle and sheep introduced in the mid-1800s had a major impact on Molokai's environment and economy. Grazing resulted in widespread destruction of native vegetation, causing upland soils to wash down into the coastal fishponds, destroying the extensive centuries-old system of aquaculture.

In the 1850s Kamehameha V acquired the bulk of Molokai's arable land, forming Molokai Ranch. After his death the ranch became part of the Bishop Estate, which sold it off to a group of Honolulu businessmen in 1897.

A year later the American Sugar Company, a division of Molokai Ranch, attempted to develop a major sugar plantation in Central Molokai. They built a railroad system to haul the cane, developed harbour facilities and installed a powerful pumping system to draw up water. By 1900 the well-water used to irrigate the fields had become so saline that the crops failed.

The company then got into honey production on such a scale that at one point Molokai was the world's largest honey exporter. In the mid-1930s an epidemic wiped out the hives and the industry.

In the meantime Molokai Ranch continued its efforts to find '*the* crop for Molokai'. Cotton, rice and numerous grain crops all took their turn biting the red dust of Molokai.

Finally pineapple took root as the crop most suitable for the island's dry, windy conditions. In 1920, plantation-scale production began in Hoolehua. Within 10 years Molokai's population tripled to over 5000 as immigrant labour was introduced to work the fields.

In the 1970s competition from overseas brought an end to pineapple's reign on Molokai. Dole closed down its operation in 1976 and the other island giant, Del Monte, later followed suit. It brought hard times and the highest unemployment levels in the state.

Then cattle raising, long a mainstay, suddenly collapsed. In a controversial decision in 1985 the state, after finding an incidence of bovine tuberculosis, ordered every head of cattle on Molokai to be destroyed. Molokai Ranch has recently begun to restock its herd, but the majority of the smaller 240 former cattle owners have given up.

Molokai Ranch still owns about one-third of Molokai, which is more than half of the island's privately held lands.

Homegrown Economy

With the collapse of the pineapple plantations, islanders are beginning to develop more small-scale farms and businesses.

Molokai has rich soil and there is talk that the island may have the potential to be Hawaii's 'breadbasket'. Recently, watermelon growers on Molokai have not only captured the Oahu market from mainland growers, but have begun to export to Canada as well.

The Kaunakakai area has one of the world's best growing conditions for seed corn. Hawaii's climate makes it possible to produce three generations of hybrids each year versus only one on the mainland. Corn for seed has been raised in Hawaii since the late 1960s and about half of the corn produced in the USA can now trace its roots to Molokai. Seed production is labour intensive – each ear of corn is bagged, tagged and eventually harvested by hand.

Development

In 1981 a Maui County Committee was appointed to create a community plan to address future development on Molokai. The committee conducted hearings and surveys on Molokai and much to the surprise of Molokai residents the recommendations put forth in the final plan were tuned in to their own feelings on growth.

The Molokai Plan calls for the preservation of Molokai's rural lifestyle and the maintenance of agriculture as the basis of the economy. It also calls for all resort development to be limited to the western side and to be lowrise. It recommends a number of environmental protection schemes, including conservation practices to reverse erosion, the maintenance of fishponds and the creation of marine conservation areas. The Molokai Plan has been widely accepted as the guiding code for land use on Molokai and is referred to whenever there are disputes over development – which is often.

You can pick up a lot of local antidevelopment sentiment walking around Kaunakakai. One faded poster in a shop window begins with the phrase, 'The thing about untouched beauty is that people want to instantly touch it...', while the hottest bumper sticker on pick-up trucks around town reads 'Molokai Is Too Small To Be Big'.

Biomass Plant
A controversial biomass plant now generates Molokai's electricity. The idea behind the plant was to burn pineapple stalk refuse, but it never worked out. Kiawe was tried, but it was too hard to chip and it broke the machines. Now they're harvesting softer woods and clearing hillsides around the island. It's a potentially good idea gone astray.

Trees from Molokai Ranch, state forest reserves and private lands are all being levelled to produce wood chips to fuel the power plant. The logging is often little more than clear-felling that has resulted in topsoil being reduced to inches of dry powder.

Concerned about the deforestation, Molokai environmental group Hoopakele Aina, which means Rescue the Land, is challenging the logging. The Sierra Club Legal Defense Fund has joined in with a lawsuit demanding an environmental impact statement on the harvesting of forest reserve lands. Other suits seem likely to follow.

Not only is Molokai losing its forests, but the islanders pay Hawaii's highest electricity rates.

The power plant, called Onsite Energy, is makai of the Seventh Day Adventist school, west of Kaunakakai. In the yard a huge stack of chipped wood is piled as high as the plant itself.

PEOPLE
Molokai's population is just under 7000. Molokai is the most Hawaiian of the islands

outside of Niihau. Almost 50% of its people are Hawaiian or part-Hawaiian. Filipino is the next largest ethnic group, followed by the usual mixture.

The large Hawaiian population is in part due to the Hawaiian Homes Act of 1921 which awarded 40-acre blocks of land to people with at least 50% Hawaiian ancestry. The purpose of the act was to encourage homesteading among native Hawaiians who had become the most landless ethnic group in Hawaii. The first settlements under the act were made on Molokai.

TOURIST INFORMATION
Destination Molokai (Box 233, Kualapuu, HI 96757; tel 567-6255 on Molokai; 941-0444 on Oahu; 800-367-4753 from the USA, 800-423-8733 from Canada, 0014-800-125-569 ext 447 from Australia) handles tourist information on Molokai. There's no staffed office, but they mail out brochures.

GENERAL INFORMATION
Official Molokai
Molokai's official flower is the white kukui

White Kukui Blossom

blossom, its official colour is green and Molokai's nickname is The Friendly Island.

Money

The Bank of Hawaii, in Kaunakakai, is the largest of half a dozen banks and credit unions on the island. Friendly Market has a Western Union office.

Post

The new post office in downtown Kaunakakai is open from 8 am to 4.30 pm, Monday to Friday. There are also post offices in Hoolehua, Kualapuu, Maunaloa and Kalaupapa.

Media

Newspapers Molokai has two newspapers, the *Molokai News* (Star Route, Box 329, Kaunakakai, HI 96748) and *Molokai Dispatch* (Box 440, Kaunakakai, HI 96748). Both are published twice monthly and distributed free around the island.

The *Maui News* and the *Honolulu Advertiser* are sold at the airport, Kaluakoi Hotel and at C Pascua Store in Kaunakakai.

Maps

The best map of Molokai is the Molokai-Lanai combination put out by the University of Hawaii and sold around town. A free island recreation map, especially useful for hikers and those who want to go off on jeep roads, is available from the Department of Land & Natural Resources, Division of State Parks, Box 1049, Wailuku, HI 96793.

Weather

For recorded weather and marine forecasts by the National Weather Service dial 552-2477.

Emergency

Dial 911 for police, ambulance and fire emergencies. Molokai General Hospital (tel 553-5331) in Kaunakakai has a 24-hour emergency service.

ACCOMMODATION

The Kaunakakai area has two hotels, Pau Hana Inn and Hotel Molokai, and one condo, Molokai Shores. All three front onto a beach with a good view of Lanai, but with waters too shallow and silty for swimming.

Molokai's only resort is Kaluakoi, on the west coast. It has one hotel, a golf club, two condo complexes and white sand beaches.

The Wavecrest condos are 13 miles east of Kaunakakai, on Molokai's wetter and lusher eastern side. There are a few B&Bs around this neck of the woods as well.

Unless otherwise specified, the rates given are the same for both singles and doubles.

Camping

Camping is allowed at Palaau State Park, in Kapuaiwa Coconut Grove, at the beach parks of Papohaku and One Alii, at Waikolu Lookout and at a couple of beaches owned by Molokai Ranch.

The Department of Public Works (Box 526, Kaunakakai, HI 96748; tel 553-3221) sells camping permits for Papohaku and One Alii county parks from 7 am to 3 pm Monday to Friday at Mitchell Pauole Center in Kaunakakai. Permits are $3 per adult and 50 cents per child per day. Camping is limited to three consecutive days. Both parks have restrooms, drinking water, showers and picnic areas.

ACTIVITIES

Beaches

Papohaku Beach on the west coast is the broadest and longest white sand beach in all of Hawaii. Though it's a great walking beach, it's not safe for swimming.

However, just a few miles south is Dixie Maru Beach. It's in a small protected bay and is the West End's most popular family beach.

For something less frequented there's Kawakiu Beach north of Kaluakoi Golf Course. It's a crescent beach with fine coastal views and good swimming when the seas are calm.

Moomomi Beach, on the north coast, is another secluded coastal stretch, this one backed by expansive dunes.

The coast around Kaunakakai has shallow waters and a silted bottom. The public swimming pool in town is the best spot for swimming there.

At the south-eastern end of the island, the beach around the 20-mile marker offers the best swimming and snorkelling. Rock Point, not far from there, and Halawa Bay, at the end of the road, are popular surfing spots.

There are other beaches in restricted places, such as the south-west coast on Molokai Ranch land, and a few remote beaches on the North Shore. But Molokai is the last place you'd need to torture yourself with washed-out roads or trips through jungles simply to get away from it all. For those who have ever fantasised about having a vast secluded beach to themselves, all that's needed is to drive up to the miles of white sands at Papohaku and start walking.

Snorkel sets and boogie boards can be rented from Kaluakoi Hotel or Molokai Fish & Dive. The *Molokai Dispatch* prints a tide chart.

Swimming
The Mitchell Pauole Center in Kaunakakai has a 25 metre pool open free to the public from 9 to 11.45 am daily except Thursdays and Sundays, and 1 to 4.30 pm daily (also from 6 to 8.30 pm Wednesdays and Fridays in the summer). The lifeguard is friendly and welcomes anyone to come in and use the pool. It's not uncommon to have it to yourself.

Sailing
Molokai Charters (Box 1207, Kaunakakai, HI 96748; tel 553-5852) has a $30 two-hour sunset sail and a $40 four-hour midday sail. There's also a full-day $75 trip to Lanai which includes four hours of sailing (and sailing lessons) plus three hours of anchoring off Lanai for snorkelling, swimming and lunch. The boats sail from Kaunakakai.

Whale-watching tours aboard the *Maui Princess* (tel 553-5736) go out at 10 am Wednesdays and Saturdays during the season - roughly from Christmas to Easter. The cruise lasts 2½ hours and costs $25 for adults, $12.50 for children.

Hiking
Molokai has a variety of hiking opportuni-

ties. The hike to Moaula Falls in Halawa Valley, on the eastern side of the island, is the most popular.

The Nature Conservancy's Kamakou Preserve offers unique rainforest hikes in the island's rugged interior.

From the Kalaupapa Overlook there's a pleasant hour-long hike through a forest of fragrant eucalyptus and ironwood. The hike down the mule trail to Kalaupapa not only offers fine views, but is a way to get to the peninsula without paying.

On the western side, there's the easy hike to Kawakiu Beach from the Kaluakoi Golf Club. The expansive white sands of Papohaku Beach and the coast of Moomomi Beach offer fine walks as well.

The only cross-island trail goes to Wailau Valley on the North Shore. It's a challenging trek that shouldn't be made alone. All trails are detailed in their respective sections.

Wagon Ride
Molokai Wagon Ride (Larry Helm, Box 56, Hoolehua, HI 96729; tel 558-8380 days, 567-6773 evenings) is a small business which combines a horse-drawn wagon ride from Hoolehua to Iliiliopae Heiau, coconut husking and net throwing demonstrations, hula lessons and lunch of barbecued fish or chicken on the beach at Mapulehu. It's touristy but quite pleasant and most people seem to enjoy themselves. The ride leaves at noon Monday to Saturday and the cost is $33 for adults, $16.50 for keikis. To get there look for a big mango grove, makai side, just past the 15-mile marker on Hwy 450. They also have 90-minute guided horseback rides that stop at the heiau for $35.

Tennis
The Mitchell Pauole Center has two good lighted tennis hardcourts just beyond the pool. Like everywhere else in Molokai, you're not likely to find a crowd waiting.

The Kaluakoi Hotel in Kaunakakai has four lighted tennis courts open to non-guests at $3 per hour.

Golf

The Kaluakoi Golf Club has an 18-hole par 72 course. The hours are from 7 am to 6 pm. The resort has a driving range, putting green and pro shop.

Other Activities

Kaluakoi Hotel has some activities free to the public, including nature walks, torchlighting ceremonies and evening movies.

THINGS TO BUY

Craft shows are held sporadically, usually a couple of times each month at Hotel Molokai in Kaunakakai or Kaluakoi Hotel in Maunaloa. It's a good way to meet local artists who sell their own silkscreen designs, lauhala weaving, coconut fibre crafts, pottery, woodwork and a few other handicrafts.

GETTING THERE & AWAY
Air

Hawaiian Airlines' 50-seat Dash 7s are the biggest passenger planes flying in to Molokai's little airport.

From Honolulu, Hawaiian Airlines charges $39.95 one way, $46.95 return. From its other destinations (Lihue, Kahului, Kapalua/Kaanapali, Kona, Hilo), most of which connect through Honolulu, the cost is $49.95 one way. There are occasional flights between Molokai and Lanai for $39.95.

Aloha IslandAir charges $38.94 each way between Honolulu and Molokai. They also have flights from Hana, Kahului and Kamuela.

Both airlines have about eight flights a day from Honolulu.

Molokai Airport Molokai Airport, sometimes called Hoolehua Airport, has car rental booths, a snack bar, a liquor lounge, a visitor information booth which is occasionally staffed, restrooms and pay phones.

Miriam's Leis has good-looking leis at cheap prices. The two free Molokai newspapers can be picked up here. The snack bar sells loaves of Molokai bread.

Ferry

The *Maui Princess* (Sea Link of Hawaii, 505 Front St, Suite 230, Lahaina, HI 96761; 553-5736 on Molokai, 661-5857 on Maui) runs between Maui and Molokai twice daily.

The boat leaves Kaunakakai at 5.45 am and 4 pm. It leaves Maui Slip 3, Lahaina, at 7.15 am and 5.30 pm. The ride takes 75 minutes. The one-way fare is $21 for adults, $10.50 for children. For Information contact Sea Link of Hawaii (tel 553-5736 on Molokai, 661-5857 on Maui).

Molokai is a sleepy isle but it wakes up early. In an effort to bring down unemployment rates on Molokai of more than double Hawaii's average, the state has chartered the *Maui Princess* for the 5.45 am and 5.30 pm runs. Some 200 Molokai residents commute to jobs on Maui, primarily in Kaanapali hotels. Paying passengers are accepted on those runs if the ship isn't full.

There are no tourist facilities where the boat pulls in at Kaunakakai Wharf and it's a mile to town.

GETTING AROUND
Airport Transport

Grayline-Molokai has an hourly shuttle service between the airport and Kaluakoi Resort. It costs $6 per person one way, with a minimum of two people.

Taxi

A couple of taxi services have recently started up on Molokai.

Molokai Taxi (tel 553-3979) seems to be the biggest, with three cars, and they plan to get a 4WD to do backwoods tours such as to Waikolu Lookout.

TEEM Cab Molokai (tel 553-3433 or 553-3786) has a 24-hour service with advance reservations. They accept collect calls from the neighbouring islands.

Alex Taxi & Tour (tel 553-3369) does 4WD mountain tours as well as standard tours and taxi service.

Car

There are gas stations in Kaunakakai, Maunaloa and Kualapuu.

Car Rentals Renting a car on Molokai is just about essential if you intend to explore the island.

The only car rentals are at the airport. Budget, Dollar, Tropical and Avis all have booths there. See the Getting Around chapter for toll free numbers.

If you rent a 4WD, check first to see if it's real or only decoration. And even with a 4WD, rental contracts officially 'prohibit' driving on dirt roads.

Hitching

Hitching is officially illegal in Maui County. It probably wouldn't be too difficult to get a ride between the airport and town, but hitching is fairly rare on Molokai and distant corners such as Halawa and the west coast beaches just don't get much traffic.

Tours

Robert's Hawaii (tel 552-2751; 800-843-5978) has a tour to the Kalaupapa Overlook from the airport for $12, from Kaluakoi Resort for $18. Another tour includes the overlook, Kaunakakai and the road to Halawa Valley for $25 from the airport, $32 from Kaluakoi.

Grayline-Molokai (tel 567-6177) also does tours.

Kaunakakai

Kaunakakai, Molokai's biggest town, takes much of its character from what it doesn't have. There's not a single traffic light, no shopping centres and no fast food stands.

Most of Molokai's businesses are lined up along Ala Malama St, the main street. Their wooden imitation storefronts give Kaunakakai the simple appearance of a frontier town. There are four restaurants, a bakery, post office, pharmacy and one of just about everything else a small town needs. The tallest point is still the church steeple.

This is a town that hasn't changed its face at all for tourism. It has a nice slow pace.

Information

Since Molokai doesn't have a daily newspaper, bulletin boards around Kaunakakai are the prime source of news and announcements. The board next to the Bank of Hawaii is the most extensive.

Kaunakakai has a good public library (tel 553-5483). It's open from noon to 8 pm Mondays and Wednesdays and from 9 am to 5 pm Tuesdays, Thursdays and Fridays.

The laundromat behind Outpost Natural Foods is open from 7 am to 9 pm.

The Mitchell Pauole Center contains the fire and police stations, a swimming pool, tennis courts and the county public works office where you pick up camping permits.

Kaunakakai Harbor

Gone are the days when pineapple was loaded from Kaunakakai Wharf, but a commercial inter-island barge still pulls into the harbour a couple of times a week and the commuter ferry to Maui shows up each day. There are also mooring facilities for small boats there.

Molokai was the favourite island and playground of King Kamehameha V, who built a large vacation house of thatched grass on the shores of Kaunakakai Harbor. The house was called Malama which today is the name of the main road leading from the harbour through town. All that remains of King Kamehameha V's home is the foundation, now overgrown with grass. It's on the right side of the road before the wharf, mauka of the canoe shed.

Walking on Water

If you're down at the beach at night you might spot what looks like ghosts walking out on the water. There's no need to be spooked – it's actually fishermen who walk far out onto the shallow coastal reef carrying lanterns. The fishing is good at night when the wind dies down and the lantern light stuns their prey.

You might also see something that looks like distant lightning or fireworks beyond Lanai. If so, it's probably flares from US

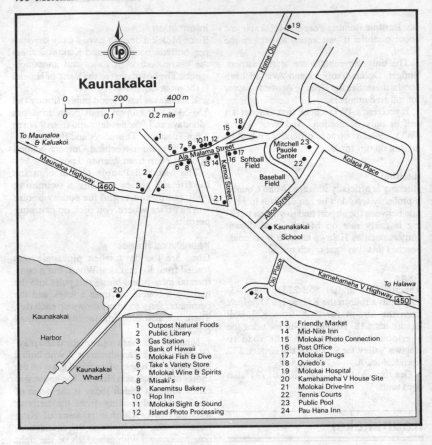

Kaunakakai

To Maunaloa & Kaluakoi

Maunaloa Highway 460

Ala Malama Street

Kamoi Street

Home Olu

Mitchell Pauole Center

Kolapa Place

Softball Field

Baseball Field

Ailoa Street

Kaunakakai School

Oki Place

Kamehameha V Highway 450

To Halawa

Kaunakakai Harbor

Kaunakakai Wharf

1	Outpost Natural Foods	13	Friendly Market
2	Public Library	14	Mid-Nite Inn
3	Gas Station	15	Molokai Photo Connection
4	Bank of Hawaii	16	Post Office
5	Molokai Fish & Dive	17	Molokai Drugs
6	Take's Variety Store	18	Oviedo's
7	Molokai Wine & Spirits	19	Molokai Hospital
8	Misaki's	20	Kamehameha V House Site
9	Kanemitsu Bakery	21	Molokai Drive-Inn
10	Hop Inn	22	Tennis Courts
11	Molokai Sight & Sound	23	Public Pool
12	Island Photo Processing	24	Pau Hana Inn

military manoeuvres on Kahoolawe, the island which lies south of Lanai.

Fishponds

Molokai's south-east coast is dotted with the largest concentration of ancient fishponds in Hawaii. Grazing by cattle and sheep introduced in the mid-1800s resulted in widespread erosion, and the clay that washed down from the mountains choked out the ponds. Efforts have been made to revive a few of the fishponds, though without much commercial success.

One of the most impressive and easily

visited is Kalokoeli Fishpond, behind Molokai Shores' condos.

Kapuaiwa Coconut Grove

The coconut grove one mile west of the main part of town has 10 oceanside acres of coconut palms planted by King Kamehameha V around 1860. It is today under the management of Hawaiian Home Lands.

Across the highway is Church Row where a quaint white church with green trim sits next to a quaint green church with white trim and so on down the line. Any denomination that gets a handful of Hawaiian members gets its own little tract of land to put up a church. Some of the more recent arrivals include Seventh Day Adventists and Mormons.

Half a mile up the road you might catch sight of a white horse that grazes in front of scarlet bougainvilleas, a visual treat.

One Alii Beach Park

One Alii, three miles from Kaunakakai, is the nearest beach park east of town and is used mainly for picnics, parties and ball games. Two memorials commemorate the first immigration of the Japanese in 1885. The park borders a nice coconut grove and Alii Fishpond.

Places to Stay

Pau Hana Inn (Box 546, Kaunakakai, HI 96748; tel 553-5342; 800-367-8047 ext 162 from the USA, 800-663-1118 from Canada) is the closest to town. The cheapest of its 39 rooms are those in the long house at $45. They are small and simple but sufficient, with two twin beds and a bathroom with shower. Try to get one of the end rooms on the ocean side – they're lighter and airier. There are four other room categories ranging from $69 for poolside units (which are no prize) to $125 for the beachfront suite. There's a small pool and a restaurant. Pau Hana means 'work's over' and its bar is a popular drinking hole. It gets noisy on weekends when a live band plays until 12.30 am. Between the bar and the beach is an impressive 100-year-old Bengalese banyan tree.

Molokai Shores (Box 1037, Kaunakakai, HI 96748; tel 553-5954; 800-367-7042), about 1½ miles east of town, has 102 condo units. Most rooms are decorated quite nicely. Each has a kitchen, sofa bed, wooden louvred windows, lanai and ceiling fans and they even throw in a little welcome basket. Ask for a unit on the top floor: they have cathedral ceilings and some have lofts. One-bedroom units hold up to four people, with rates for two at $70/80 in the low/high season. Two-bedroom units hold up to six people, with rates for four at $100/105 in the

low/high season. Additional persons are $8. If you stay a week, the seventh day is free and additional days are discounted by one-seventh. Though not the cheapest accommodation, it's the best value around Kaunakakai. There's a pool and coin-operated laundry.

Hotel Molokai (Box 546, Kaunakakai, HI 96748; tel 553-5347; 800-367-8047 ext 162 from the USA, 800-663-1118 from Canada), about two miles east of town, has 55 units with a Polynesian design of sorts. For a good night's sleep, avoid the rooms next to the road where the 5 am ferry traffic zooms by. The 1st floor of the two-storey units can get noisy as well, as sound travels right through the floor. The rooms have small refrigerators, portable fans, louvred windows and lots of wood – one interior wall is even covered with clapboards! There's no TV, but sunsets and stargazing on the beach here are more rewarding than the nightly news anyway. It's a bit funky, but overall the atmosphere is nice. It has a pool and a good restaurant. Rates range from $55 for standard rooms up to $115 for family units for up to five people.

Argyle Two B&B (Hannah & Will Johnstone, Box 295, Kaunakakai, HI 96748; tel 553-5048) is a studio 1½ miles east of Kaunakakai, in the Molokai Shores area. The cottage has twin beds, a kitchenette and cable TV, and is available from November to March only. The rate of $50/55 a single/double includes breakfast. Children are not allowed.

Camping Camping is permitted at One Alii Beach Park. It's a roadside park on a shallow, silty beach close to Kaunakakai. Though it doesn't have a great deal of appeal it tends to be more frequented than the one at Papohaku Beach.

Hawaiian Home Lands (tel 567-6104), on Puukapele Ave in Hoolehua, issues permits for only one group each night for camping at Kapuaiwa Coconut Grove just west of Kaunakakai. The cost is $5. The site has electricity, water, picnic tables, pavilion, restrooms and showers.

Places to Eat
Because lots of people head for work around 5.30 am getting a cup of coffee early in the morning is no problem.

Central Kaunakakai *Mid-Nite Inn* is the biggest eating and social spot on Molokai. The hot cakes at $1.50 are enormous. Most full dinners are under $5, burgers and sandwiches under $2. The fish dinner is whatever was biting for Molokai fishermen that day, cooked with green onions and a touch of soy sauce on a seasoned 50-year-old cast-iron grill. Not only is this some of the freshest fish you'll find in Hawaii, but at $6 it's probably the cheapest.

Mid-Nite Inn does not stay open until midnight like it used to in the 1930s when it was a small stand selling saimin to dockworkers who worked at Kaunakakai Harbor at night. These days it's open from 5.30 am to 1.30 pm and from 5.30 to 9 pm daily, except Sundays. It's OK to bring your own beer. The Mid-Nite Inn T-shirts have the best pun in town!

Hop Inn (tel 553-5465 for takeaway orders) has pretty good Chinese food and friendly service. Many of the dishes seem to have the same gravy-like sauce so if you want a little more flavour, ask them to spice it up. You can bring in your own beer. Most dishes are in the $5 to $6 range. Lunch plates are $4.50. It's open from 11 am to 9 pm daily.

Kanemitsu Bakery makes the famous Molokai bread which is shipped around the islands, plus other good breads, a variety of Danish pastries and doughnuts. The apple crisp (50 cents) is a favourite. The restaurant in the back serves three meals a day. A breakfast of eggs, toast, coffee and ham will cost you $3. Lunch and dinner are a few bucks more. It's open from 5.30 am to 8 pm every day but Tuesday.

Outpost Natural Foods has the standard collection of natural foods and vitamins as well as fresh produce, some of it marked organic. They make good burritos for $2 to $3, but they make them very slowly. Pre-made avocado and cheese sandwiches are $2.50 and they also sell salads. *Oasis Juice*

Bar in the back is open from 10 am to 2 pm and makes fresh-squeezed juices. The store and juice bar are closed on Saturdays.

Oviedo's sells Filipino plate meals for $6 at lunch and dinner, lumpia for under a $1 and ice cream cones for $1.

Molokai Drive Inn has inexpensive plate lunches and food to take away. This place used to be a Dairy Queen, but Molokai wasn't quite ready for fast food so the sign came down.

Hotel Restaurants *Hotel Molokai* has an open-air restaurant right on the beach. When people want to 'go out' for dinner they put on their muumuus and head there, though it's casual enough for you to feel equally at home in boots and jeans. There's a fine sunset view with Lanai across the channel and water lapping at the shore. It's also a nice place to watch the sun rise. Breakfast is from 7 to 10.30 am. You can get an order of hot cakes made with papaya batter and topped with diced macadamia nuts for $3. At lunch time, 11.30 to 3 pm, there's a good all-you-can-eat soup and salad bar with Molokai bread for $5. With a main dish it's $7. Sandwiches and salads are in the $4 to $7 range. Dinners are about double.

Pau Hana Inn serves three meals a day. Breakfast is from 6.30 to 10.30 am. They have a soup and salad bar similar to Hotel Molokai's, minus the Molokai bread, for $5.25 at lunch time. The daily lunch special (11.30 am to 2 pm) is $7 with the salad bar. Dinner is from 6 to 9 pm and features steaks and seafood with prices starting at $13. Their big dining room fireplace is sometimes lit on cool winter evenings.

Entertainment
The local band FIBRE (Friendly Isle Band Rhythmic Experience!) plays dance music from oldie standards and rock 'n' roll to Hawaiian, from 9 pm to 12.30 am Fridays and Saturdays at *Pau Hana Inn*. The cover charge is $1. The action is out on the patio, with the band setting up under the big banyan tree.

Kimo Paleka plays a mellow guitar at dinner time and through the early evening on

Thursdays, Fridays and Saturdays at *Hotel Molokai*'s restaurant. Kimo sings a little of everything, some in English, some in Hawaiian, running the gamut from folk music to Don Ho favourites. He'll even sing 'The Cock-Eyed Mayor of Kaunakakai' on request. Sometimes visiting musicians just walk on stage. If you're lucky Clyde Sproat might be on the island. His salt-of-the-earth singing and ukelele playing is authentic Hawaiian folk music at its best.

Hotels aside, the baseball field in Kaunakakai is about the most active spot on the island. For some local flavour, you could go down and cheer on the Molokai Farmers as they compete against their high school rivals, the Lanai Pinelads.

Things to Buy
Misaki's and Friendly Market are the island's major grocery stores. Both also sell booze, flip-flops and sundry goods. Molokai Wine & Spirits has lots of imported beers, a very good selection of wine at reasonable prices and occasionally local produce. Despite all the corn stalks around town you'll seldom see corn in the stores as it's all grown for seed.

Molokai Fish & Dive (tel 553-5926) no longer fills tanks and it doesn't do dive tours, but it does have fishing supplies, knives, tabis, snorkelling and sports equipment and every kind of ball except footballs. It's a pretty good place to pick up T- shirts: check the discount rack for some good cheapies. T-shirts with slogans proclaiming Molokai's rural pride make a good souvenir. They rent out snorkel sets for $7 and boogie boards for $6, though the most popular rentals there are the coolers filled with ice.

Molokai Photo Connection has a full line of film and camera accessories. It sends film to Honolulu for two-day service by Kodak or overnight processing by Fuji.

Island Photo Processing has an on-site same-day print service.

Molokai Drugs, besides being a pharmacy, is practically a department store. It has snorkels, hardware, magazines and the cheapest film in town. Photocopies are 10 cents.

Molokai Sight & Sound sells records, including Hawaiian music, and rents out videos for $3 and VCRs for $5.50.

And when nobody else has what you want, they'll generally point you toward Take's Variety Store.

Or you could take back the same stash islanders do when they leave Molokai: a homegrown watermelon and some Molokai bread from Kanemitsu Bakery.

East Molokai

The road from Kaunakakai to Halawa Valley edges alongside the ocean for much of the way with the mountains of East Molokai rising up to the north. The terrain starts out relatively dry and becomes greener and lusher as you head east. It's all quite pastoral, with small homes tucked into the valleys, horses grazing at the side of the road and silver waterfalls dropping down the mountainsides.

The beaches along this stretch are mostly shallow and silted and not good for swimming until about the 20-mile marker. The last part of the road is narrow, with lots of hairpin bends and scenic coastal views, winding up to a clifftop view of Halawa Valley. One of Molokai's best hikes starts from the valley floor, following Halawa Stream to Moaula Falls.

The 28-mile drive from town to Halawa Valley along Kamehameha V Highway (Hwy 450) takes about 1½ hours one way. It's a good paved road from start to finish. Check your gas gauge before starting off as there are no gas stations after Kaunakakai.

KAWELA
Kakahaia Beach Park is a grassy roadfront park in Kawela with a rather unappealing beach. The park is the only part of the Kakahaia National Wildlife Refuge open to the public. Most of the 40-acre refuge is mauka of the road. It includes marshland with a dense growth of bullrushes and an inland freshwater fishpond, which has been

expanded to provide a home for the endangered Hawaiian stilt and coot.

Inland from here is the Kawela puuhonua, a place of refuge which was used in ancient times by those running from the law or personal enemies. The stone ruins are on a high ridge separated by deep ravines and nearly impossible to get to.

Along four miles of this coast in 1795 Kamehameha the Great lined up his war canoes and quickly brought Molokai under his command. From here he went on to invade Oahu, the last battle in a campaign which united all the Hawaiian islands.

KAMALO

Kamalo is a village about 10 miles east of Kaunakakai.

St Joseph's Church

Two of the four churches Father Damien built outside the Kalaupapa Peninsula on Molokai are still standing, including St Joseph's in Kamalo. This simple one-room wooden church built in 1876 has a steeple and bell, plain wooden pews and some of the original wavy glass panes. A statue of Damien and a little cemetery are at the side. Only the yellow speaker for warning of tsunamis brings the scene into the 20th century.

Smith-Bronte Landing

About a mile from the church a small wooden sign makai of the road notes the site where pilot Ernest Smith and navigator Emory Bronte safely crash-landed their plane at the completion of the world's first civilian flight from the US mainland.

They left California on 14 July 1927, landing in Molokai 25½ hours later. A little memorial plaque is stuck among the kiawe trees and overgrown grasses, which look just as they must have then. Oahu was the intended destination.

Places to Stay

Herb & Marian Mueh (Star Route, Box 128, Kaunakakai, HI 96748; tel 558-8236) have a B&B cottage in Kamalo. The rate of $50 includes breakfast items for meals you fix yourself. The cottage is quiet and private, in the midst of five acres of lime trees and away from both the main house and the road. It's studio-style with twin beds which convert into daytime couches, a bathroom with stall shower and a kitchen. The minimum stay is three nights. Children are not allowed. The Muehs, moved here from Lahaina where Herb had a print shop and Marian was an accountant.

Things to Buy

Across the road from the B&B Herb Meuh has set up a self-service fruit hut selling limes from his orchard of 98 lime trees. A little signboard tells what produce is for sale each day. In addition to limes he sometimes sells coconuts, pomegranates and toy reef fish woven from coconut fronds.

UALAPUE

The Wavecrest condo development is at the 13-mile marker in Ualapue. The village has a small grocery store.

Kilohana School is across the street from the condos. Just beyond the school, on the ocean side, is Ualapue Fishpond. The state has plans to restore this fishpond and hopes in the process to bring back a part of traditional Hawaiian culture that has largely been lost.

Places to Stay

Wavecrest Resort (Star Route, Kaunakakai, HI 96748; tel 558-8101; 800-367-2980) has 126 condos. The friendly people at the front desk handle 26 of the units. Oceanview units are $61 for a one-bedroom unit, $81 for up to four people in a two-bedroom unit. Add $10 more for a beachfront room. There's a $15 charge on stays less than three nights. The condos are slightly faded, but fine. Each has a kitchen, sofa bed, TV and lanai. Even if you fold out the sofa bed, the living room is still large enough to move around. Breezes blow right through the beachfront units and there are great views of Maui and Lanai from the lanai. The resort has a pool, tennis courts and a little grocery store.

KALUAAHA

The village of Kaluaaha is about two miles past Wavecrest. The ruins of Molokai's first church are here, a bit off the road, mauka side, but visible if you keep an eye out. Kaluaaha Church was built in 1844 by Molokai's first missionary, Harvey R Hitchcock.

Our Lady of Sorrows Church is a little further. The current church is a 1966 reconstruction of the original wooden-frame building built in 1874 by Father Damien. Services are still held here. A little cemetery is around the back.

ILIILIOPAE HEIAU

Iliiliopae is the largest and best-known heiau on Molokai, and probably the oldest. Approximately 300 feet long and 100 feet wide, it is about 22 feet high on the east side and 11 feet high at the other end. It is strikingly level. It's believed the heiau may have originally been three times its current size, reaching out beyond Mapulehu Stream. Legend says it was built in one night by menehunes who brought stones over the mountains from Wailau Valley. In return for their efforts each was given one shrimp.

Lono, the god of harvest, and Ku, the war god, were both worshipped here. Human sacrifices were made at this heiau, always on the eve of a full moon. Drums were beaten to call all males to the temple where, upon the priest's direction, all fell prone and the victims to be sacrificed were brought to the platform. Amid chanting and rituals these victims, always male, were strangled to death and their bodies later burned.

One legend tells of a man, Umoekekaua, who lost nine of his 10 sons to sacrifice at Iliiliopae. He became so outraged that he went with his only remaining son to Pelekunu Valley to seek the aid of Kauhuhu, the Shark God. Kauhuhu sent a torrent of rain whose flood waters damaged the heiau and washed the priests responsible for the sacrifices into Pukoo Harbor where they were duly eaten by sharks.

The path to the heiau is mauka of the highway, nearly half a mile past the 15-mile marker, immediately after a little bridge. It starts on a dirt drive on the east side of the creek. After a 10-minute walk a footpath leads off to the left, just before reaching a house. The heiau is two minutes from here.

Today Iliiliopae is silent except for the chittering of birds. African tulip trees line the trail to the site, a peaceful place with stones that still seem to emanate vibrations of a powerful past. A good place to sit and take it all in is on the north side, up the steps to the right of the heiau.

WAILAU VALLEY & TRAIL

The Wailau Trail is a rugged cross-island ridgeline hike of about eight miles, running from the south-eastern end of the island to Wailau Valley on the north shore.

The trail begins at Iliiliopae Heiau. It offers great views of Molokai's south coast on the way up and mountains and valleys on the way in. It's strenuous, muddy and not well maintained. The descent into the valley from the 3200-foot summit is very steep. In places, a slip could be fatal.

Wailau Valley is the largest valley on the north coast. It has wild taro, thick rainforest and the remains of a village overgrown with Java plum and hau. The trail ends on Wailau Beach at the mouth of Wailau Stream. Kukui trees and mountain apples are found at the top of the valley.

The best way to hike into Wailau Valley is to take one of the Sierra Club's infrequent hikes. They also periodically go into the valley in an attempt to eradicate *Clidemia hirta*. This invasive weed was recently introduced to Molokai, most likely as a seed caught in the tread of someone's hiking boots. The work trips last five days. If you're interested, contact the Sierra Club's Honolulu office.

Because of the dangers involved and the fact that the trail is not well defined, it shouldn't be done as a solo hike. Contact the state Division of Forestry & Wildlife for more information.

PUKOO

Pukoo was once the seat of local government – complete with a courthouse, jail, wharf and post office – until the plantation folks built Kaunakakai and centered everything there.

Kapeke Fishpond, about a quarter of a mile beyond the 16-mile marker, is a large and rather well-preserved fishpond that's visible from the road and easy to explore.

Places to Stay

Honomuni House (Star Route 306, Kaunakakai, HI 96748; tel 558-8383) is a guest cottage 1½ km east of Pukoo. This is the nicest B&B on the island. There are lush gardens and old taro terraces behind the cottage, making it a good place for people who like to hike and explore. The cottage is spacious with a kitchen, bath, separate sleeping space and outdoor deck and shower. The living room has a sofa bed, TV and tables made of monkeypod wood from the grounds. Rates are $55 for two, or $10 for each additional adult. The rates for longer stays depend on the season, but are about $330 a week, $750 to $1000 a month. Fresh eggs, papayas, bananas and other fruits in season are free. Hosts Jan (a marine biologist) and Keaho (a teacher of Pacific studies) live in a large house on the same grounds.

Places to Eat

Neighborhood Store 'N' Counter in Pukoo is the only restaurant on the east side. You order at a window and eat at outdoor picnic tables. They have plate lunches for around $4, fries and sandwiches. There's a little grocery store next door. It's open from 7 am to 7 pm daily.

WAIALUA

Waialua Congregational Church was built of stone in 1855. Waialua Beach is the site of keiki surf meets.

SUGAR MILL REMAINS

The remains of a stone chimney and rusting metal boiler sit in the midst of overgrowth and papaya trees a quarter of a mile before the 20-mile marker, mauka of the highway. This is all that remains of the Moanui Sugar Mill which processed sugar from a nearby plantation until it burnt down in the late 1800s.

TWENTY-MILE BEACH

A stretch of white sand beach pops up right along the roadside at the 20-mile marker. During the winter, when other Molokai beaches are rough, this is the area everyone points you to for swimming and snorkelling.

However, when the tide is low the water is sometimes too shallow for snorkelling inside the reef. Snorkelling is much better beyond the reef, but unless it's very calm the currents can be dangerous.

ROCK POINT

The point of rocks sticking out as the road swings left just before the 21-mile marker is called, appropriately enough, Rock Point. It's a popular surfing spot and local competitions sometimes take place there.

ROAD TO HALAWA

Around the 22-mile marker the road winds upwards. Tall grasses just at the edge seem to be trying to reclaim the paved road. Ironwood trees and the tall spikes of sisal plants decorate the hillsides.

It's a good paved road – the only problem is there's not enough of it. In places, including some cliff-hugging curves, it's really only wide enough for one car and you'll need to do some serious horn tooting.

The road levels out just before the 24-mile marker where there's a view of the ocean with the offshore island of Mokuhooniki. Kanaha Rock is in front.

The fenced grassland here is part of Puu O Hoku Ranch, Molokai's second largest cattle ranch. A grove of sacred kukui trees on the ranch property marks the grave of Lanikaula, a famous kahuna of the late 16th century.

Once you see the sign for Halawa, the jungle begins to close in and the smell of the soil and eucalyptus fills the air. After about half a mile, just before the road descends, there's a lookout with a great panoramic view of Halawa Valley.

There are lots of 'beep as you go' hairpin bends on the way down to the valley, but the road is in good condition and the incline reasonably gradual.

Top: Molokai's north coast from Kalaupapa Peninsula
Bottom: Halawa Valley, Molokai

Top: Kaunakakai, Molokai
Left: Sunset at Kapuaiwa Coconut Grove, Molokai
Right: Saint Joseph's Church, Kamalo, Molokai

HALAWA VALLEY

Halawa Valley once had three heiaus, two of which are thought to have been used for human sacrifice. Little remains of the sites. In the mid-1800s the fertile valley had a population of about 500 people and produced most of Molokai's taro as well as many of its melons, gourds and fruits. Taro production declined over the years, coming to an abrupt end in 1946 when a massive tsunami swept up Halawa Valley, wiping out the farms and much of the community. A second tsunami washed the valley clean in 1957. Only seven families now remain in Halawa. Sunday services are still held in Hawaiian at the little church.

One elderly Hawaiian man manages to collect a little money from tourists who follow the 'security parking' signs onto his property and leave their cars there while they hike to the waterfall. If his $5 fee seems steep, ask him about the history of the valley and get your money's worth in stories. He also sells soft drinks, candy, chips and bananas.

There's no indication that parking off to the right after reaching the valley floor is not equally safe. You could also park at the beach at the road's end.

Moaula Falls Trail

The hike to the 250-foot Moaula Falls is Molokai's most-hiked trail, though it's not the easiest to follow. The one-hour walk up is neither steep nor particularly strenuous, but it is often muddy and slippery. It's more suited to old sneakers than new white Reeboks. A walking stick would make a good companion.

The trail goes through a forest of lush tropical vegetation: giant mango trees, wild taro, ti, papaya and bananas. On the ground you might see the warty yellow fruits of the noni whose pungent odour is favoured by swarms of fruit flies. Stopping too long to observe this – or anything else – is a sure way to find out what the voracious mosquitoes favour.

The trail starts on a dirt road in front of the church. Go straight ahead on this road for about 10 minutes. At the last house the road becomes a footpath. About 100 metres farther the path splits. This split is easy to miss so keep an eye out for a white PVC water pipe crossing the trail here and for some rocks on either side of the trail which heads down to the right. Take this trail down to the stream.

You'll have to cross Halawa Stream, either by walking across stones which can be deceptively slippery, or by stepping right into the water and walking on the streambed. If you wade across, choose your footing carefully. Water depth can go from ankle-high to knee-high in one step and if it's been raining heavily, water levels can rise to the point where it's impossible to cross the stream safely.

A few trees have orange trail markings painted on them, though not with much consistency. After crossing a narrow orange-bottomed brook (or mudflat, depending on water levels) the path will fork. Take the trail to the left which parallels the stream, usually within hearing of it, though not always within sight. Along most of the trail there's a water pipe going up toward the falls, but it does disappear in places. There are moss-covered stone walls along the way, most of which were built in the 1800s as cattle fences.

About halfway up you'll begin to hear the waterfall. Once it comes into sight there's another stream crossing, this one a little more challenging. Use the metal water pipes to help climb down to the stream and cross over the boulders to the other side. Moaula Falls is less than five minutes straight up from here. Under the waterfall is a good-sized pool, at least 40 feet wide. Partly because the pool is so deep in the centre, the water is shockingly cold. Moaula translates as 'red chicken' and fittingly the water appears reddish.

If you plan on taking a dip here, it's best to first place a ti leaf in the water. Legend has it that a moo, a giant lizard-like creature, resides in the pool. If the ti leaf floats she welcomes company and it's OK to swim. If it sinks, it's a warning she wants no visitors.

Halawa Beach Park

Halawa Beach was a favoured surfing spot for Molokai's chiefs and remains so today for local kids. When the water is calm it's good for swimming, particularly in the cove on the left which is more protected. In the centre of the bay there's a channel through the reef that's subject to dangerous rip currents when the surf is heavy.

Halawa Beach Park has restrooms and running water, though a sign warns that the water does not meet health standards and needs to be treated. The water is piped down from the upper valley.

PELEKUNU VALLEY

Pelekunu Valley is under the stewardship of the Nature Conservancy. Their 5729-acre Pelekunu Valley Preserve extends from sea level up to a height of almost 5000 feet at the valley's upper rim in Kamakou Preserve.

The valley has one of the last free-flowing streams in Hawaii. It's an important habitat for gobies and river shrimp which return from the ocean each year to swim up and lay their eggs in the fresh water of Pelekunu Stream.

Due to the wilderness conditions and safety concerns in the steep valley, public access is restricted. You can look down into the valley from a hike in Kamakou Preserve.

KAMAKOU

The mountains that form the spine of Molokai's east side include Kamakou, Molokai's highest peak (4970 feet). Over half of Molokai's water supply comes from the Kamakou rainforest.

Hawaiian women used to hike up to the top of Kamakou to bury the afterbirth of their babies to assure their children would reach great heights in life. These days islanders come to the forest to pick foliage for leis as well as to hunt pigs, deer and goats.

The Nature Conservancy's Kamakou Preserve is a near-pristine forest which is home to more than 250 native plants and some of Hawaii's rarest birds. Just before the preserve entrance, Waikolu Lookout offers a panoramic view of Waikolu Valley.

Kamakou is a treasure, but it doesn't come easy. It is wilderness and is protected in that state in part because the rutted dirt road leading to it makes it difficult to get to.

To Kamakou Preserve

Coming from Kaunakakai on Hwy 460 turn right three quarters of a mile after the three-mile marker, immediately before Manawainu Bridge. The paved road ends shortly at the Kalamaula hunter check box. The 10-mile drive from the highway to the lookout takes about 45 minutes, depending on road conditions. During the rainy season vehicles leave tracks and the road gets progressively more rutted until it's regraded in the summer.

A 4WD is best. In dry weather, some people do make it up to the lookout in a standard car. If it's been raining heavily it's not advisable to try. In places where it's narrow, if one person gets stuck the whole road is blocked. It's impossible to go beyond Waikolu Lookout without a 4WD.

From the hunter check box the road starts out fairly smoothly, but deteriorates as it goes along. Bear left at the first fork, about five minutes drive up the dirt road, and from there just follow the main road all the way in.

Though there's no visible evidence of it from the road, the Kalamaula area was once extensively settled. It was here that a grieving Kamehameha the Great knocked out his two front teeth over the death of a female high chief that he had come to visit.

The landscape starts off shrubby, dry and dusty, later turning to woods of eucalyptus with patches of cypress and Norfolk pines.

The Molokai Forest Reserve starts about 5½ miles in. A road to a boy scout camp loops off to the left, reconnecting after a short distance with the main road. After another 1½ miles there will be an old water tank and reservoir off to the left. Just past this a wooden sign marked 'Kakalahale' points to the right. (This is one of several 4WD roads used by hunters that lead south to the coast or to Kaunakakai. Once the roads leave forest reserve land they run across private property, often with closed gates along the way.) It's two miles more to the Sandalwood Pit and one mile past that to Waikolu Lookout and Kamakou Preserve.

The denuded parts of the forest along the drive are casualties of Molokai's biomass plant project.

Sandalwood Measuring Pit

Lua Moku Iliahi or Sandalwood Pit is a hull-shaped grassy depression on the left side of the road. It's marked with a sign. It takes a little imagination to get the whole picture as over the years water erosion has rounded the sides.

The sandalwood pit was dug in the early 1800s, shortly after the lucrative sandalwood trade began. In the frenzy to make a quick buck to pay for the foreign goods they craved, the alii forced the makaainana (commoners) to abandon their crops and work the forest.

The pit was dug out to the exact measurements of a 75-foot-long ship's hold and filled with fragrant sandalwood logs cleared from the nearby forest. When the pit was full, the wood was hauled down to the harbour for shipment to China. The sea captains made off like bandits and Hawaii lost its sandalwood forests.

After all the mature trees were taken, the makaainana pulled up virtually all the new saplings in order to spare their children the misery of another generation of forced harvesting.

Waikolu Lookout

Waikolu Lookout, at 3600 feet, provides a spectacular view into Waikolu Valley and out to the ocean beyond. Even if you're not able to spend time in Kamakou Preserve, the lookout is a fine destination in itself. If it's been raining recently you'll be rewarded with numerous waterfalls streaming down the sheer cliffsides. Morning is the best time for views as afternoon trade winds commonly carry clouds to the upper level of the canyon.

A grassy picnic and camping area is directly opposite the lookout. If you can bear the mist and cold winds that sometimes blow

up from the canyon, this could make a good base camp for hikes into the preserve.

The steep mountains here effectively prevent the rain clouds from entering Molokai's dry central plains. In 1960 a 5½-mile tunnel was bored into the western side of Waikolu Valley. It now carries up to 28 million gallons of water each day down to the Kualapuu Reservoir.

Kamakou Preserve

In 1982 Molokai Ranch conveyed rights to the Nature Conservancy of Hawaii to manage the Kamakou Preserve, which starts immediately beyond Waikolu Lookout. Its 2774 acres of native ecosystems include cloudforest, bogs, shrubland and habitat for many species of endangered plants and animals.

Much of the preserve is forest of ohia lehua, a native tree with fluffy red blossoms whose nectar is favoured by native birds. The forest is home to two rare birds which live only on Molokai (Molokai creeper and Molokai thrush) and to the bright red apapane, the yellow-green amakihi and the pueo (Hawaiian owl), all natives. Other treasures are tree ferns, native orchids and silvery lilies.

The road deteriorates rapidly from the preserve entrance. Even with a 4WD, if you're not used to driving in mud and on steep grades it can be challenging. There are a few spots where it would be easy to flip a vehicle.

The Nature Conservancy asks visitors to sign in and out at the preserve entrance. Check out the sign-up sheet: on it people have written such entries as 'We've abandoned our car in the mud', 'The hike was wonderful', or 'We found thimbleberries to eat along the way'.

Hiking As Kamakou is a rainforest, trails in the preserve can be very muddy.

The best hiking trail is the Pepeopae Trail, just over half a mile long. A raised wooden boardwalk built over Pepeopae Bog allows hikers access while protecting the fragile ecosystem from being trampled. Pepeopae is a nearly undisturbed Hawaiian montane bog, a mysterious miniature forest with stunted trees and dwarfed plants. The area gets about 180 inches of rain each year.

There are two ways to get to the Pepeopae Trail. The easiest is to walk from Waikolu Lookout about 2½ miles along the main jeep road to the trailhead. It's a nice forest walk that takes about an hour. There are some side roads along the way, but they're largely overgrown and it's obvious which is the main road. You'll eventually come to a beaten-up 'Pepeopae' sign marking the trail which branches to the left.

The second and far muddier way is to take the Hanalilolilo Trail. It begins about five minutes' walk past Waikolu Lookout, shortly after entering the preserve. The trailhead is marked, on the left side of the road.

The Hanalilolilo Trail climbs 500 feet through a rainforest of moss-covered ohia trees, connecting up with Pepeopae Trail after 1½ miles.

At the junction of Hanalilolilo and Pepeopae trails there is a half-mile trail which climbs to a summit overlooking Pelekunu Valley. You get a view of majestic cliffs and can see down the valley out to the ocean if it's not clouded over. This last trail has been in rough shape, though the Nature Conservancy had plans to extend the Pepeopae boardwalk trail to the Pelekunu Valley Overlook and it should be completed by the time you read this.

Occasionally portions of the preserve are closed to the public. Notices are posted at Kaunakakai post office, Kalamaula hunter check box and the preserve entrance.

A good way to see Kamakou Preserve is to take one of the Nature Conservancy's guided hikes. The hikes occur once a month, though the conservancy hopes to increase them. The cost is $5 for members and $10 for nonmembers and includes transport to and from the preserve. They'll even pick you up at the airport. Each hike is limited to 10 people and often fills up far in advance.

To get a hike schedule, make reservations or check road conditions contact Ed Misaki (tel 567-6680), Molokai Preserves Manager, Box 40, Kualapuu, HI 96757. If you're writing, include a stamped, self-addressed envelope.

Places to Stay

Camping Camping is permitted at Waikolu Lookout, just outside Komokou Preserve. There are pit toilets but there's no water supply.

There's supposed to be a ranger for the Division of Forestry & Wildlife on Molokai who issues camping permits, but we were unable to track him down. It seems like an unnecessary exercise. Contact the Division of Forestry & Wildlife (Box 1015, Wailuku, HI 96793) for information.

North Shore

It takes about 20 minutes to drive the 10 miles from Kaunakakai to the Kalaupapa Overlook in Palaau State Park from where you can take in one of the prettiest sights on Molokai.

Molokai's north coast, from Halawa all the way around to Kalaupapa, is entirely towering cliffs with deeply cut valleys.

They include the world's highest sea cliffs, listed in the *Guinness Book of World Records* to be 3300 feet with an average gradient of more than 55°.

The area is spectacular, but for the most part the steep slopes and rainforests are virtually inpenetrable. The main way to get into the valleys is by boat, though rough winter seas restrict that to the summer season.

Cruises

Glenn Davis does boat tours of the ruggedly scenic north shore during the summer months (about May to September) when seas are calm. Davis lives in Halawa Valley and the boat departs from there. He charges $70 per person, with a two-person minimum, for a four-hour cruise in his 25-foot twin-engine boat. Tours go as far as Kalaupapa Peninsula and back. You'll get a glimpse of the world's highest sea cliffs, Hawaii's highest waterfall (Kahiwa Falls, 1750 feet) and an incredible coastline. For information, write to Hokupaa Ocean Adventures, Box 350, Kaunakakai, HI 96748.

PALAAU STATE PARK

Palaau State Park is at the end of Hwy 470. The Kalaupapa Overlook is a few minutes' walk from the parking lot. A short trail in the opposite direction leads to a phallic stone. The park has restrooms, camping sites and picnic areas.

Kalaupapa Overlook

Kalaupapa Overlook has a scenic overview of the entire Kalaupapa Peninsula from 1600-foot cliffs. It's like an aerial view without the aeroplane.

Interpretive plaques identify the landmarks below and explain Kalaupapa's history as a leper colony. The village where all residents live now is visible, but Kalawao, the original settlement and site of Father Damien's church and grave, can not be seen from here.

The lighthouse at the northern end of the island once had the most powerful light beam in the Pacific. The 700,000-candlepower Fresnel crystal lens, which was taken down and replaced by an electric light beacon in 1986, is now on display in Lahaina, Maui.

Kalaupapa means 'flat leaf', an accurate description of the lava slab peninsula created when a low shield volcano poked up out of the sea, long after the rest of Molokai had been formed. The dormant Kauhako Crater, visible from the overlook, contains a little lake over 800 feet deep.

Kalaupapa residents use the term 'topside' to refer to all of Molokai outside their peninsula. From here it's obvious why.

Whether or not you get down to Kalaupapa itself, the overlook is a must. Because of the angle of the sun, the best light for photography is usually late morning to early afternoon.

Hiking There's an old trail which continues directly beyond the last plaque at the overlook. If you walk along it for a few minutes you'll come to a little offshoot path to the right, from where it's only about 50 metres to a spectacular clifftop view of the peninsula. You can see even more of the coast and get a peek into the valleys from there. Be

Kalaupapa Peninsula from Kalaupapa Overlook

careful approaching, as it drops off suddenly and the wind can be strong.

For one of Molokai's nicest forest walks, get back on the trail and follow it for another 30 minutes. Few people go this way and it's very peaceful. You walk on a carpet of soft ironwood needles through a thickly planted forest that goes from ironwood to eucalyptus, dotted here and there with Norfolk pine. These diagonal rows were planted during a 1930s reafforestation project. The trees create a canopy over the trail and, as is generally true under ironwood and eucalyptus trees, there's little undergrowth to obscure the way.

There's no destination – the joy here is the woods. Eventually the trail winds down into a gully and peters out a little after that.

Phallic Stone Kauleonanahoa, literally 'the penis of Nanahoa', is Hawaii's premier phallic stone, poking up in a little clearing in an ironwood grove. Nature has endowed it well but it's obviously been touched up by human hands.

Though it's said that women who spend the night here will return home pregnant, there apparently is no danger in just going to have a look.

Places to Stay
Camping Camping is free at Palaau State Park. Permits are required and may be picked up at the Department of Land & Natural Resources office in Hoolehua or from Scott, the caretaker, who lives at the house down the drive just north of the mule stables. If you can't get a permit during business hours, it's OK to just set up camp and let Scott find you.

The camping area is in a grove of ironwood trees which is cool and shady in the summer, but can feel a bit dark and damp when it's rainy in winter. In winter you may well have the place to yourself and even in the summer you're unlikely to find a crowd.

There are restrooms, ageing picnic tables and fireplaces, but no showers. Officially the water is not drinkable as it doesn't meet new health standards, though local people seem to feel it's the same water they've been drinking for years.

KALAUPAPA PENINSULA
Kalaupapa Peninsula has been a leprosy settlement for more than a century.

The trip to the peninsula – accessible only by mule, on foot or by small plane – is one of Molokai's major attractions. It's also a pilgrimage of sorts for admirers of Father Damien de Veuster, the Belgian priest who devoted the latter part of his life to helping people with leprosy, before dying of the disease himself.

Kalaupapa Peninsula is a national historical park jointly managed by the State Department of Health and the US National Park Service.

The rock island just offshore is the legendary home of a giant shark. From some angles it looks like a shark's head coming straight up out of the water, from other angles it looks like a dorsal fin.

Sometimes schools of dolphin come in to the beach back by the end of the mule trail. In winter, whales are sometimes seen off the point of the peninsula.

History
Ancient Hawaiians used Kalaupapa as a refuge when caught in storms at sea. The peninsula held a large settlement at the time of early Western contact and the area is rich in archaeological sites.

The first case of leprosy was diagnosed in Hawaii in 1835, one of many diseases introduced by foreigners, this one probably by Chinese labourers. Alarmed by the spread of the disease, in 1865 King Kamehameha V signed into law an act which banished people with leprosy to Kalaupapa Peninsula. Peninsula residents were relocated topside.

It was a one-way trip. Kalaupapa Peninsula is surrounded on three sides by some of Hawaii's roughest and most shark-infested waters and on the fourth by the world's highest sea cliffs. Once the afflicted arrived on Kalaupapa Peninsula there was no way out, not even in a casket. Hawaiians called leprosy *mai hookaawale*, which means separating sickness, a disease all the more dreaded because it tore families apart forever.

Father Damien arrived at Kalaupapa in 1873. He wasn't the first missionary to come, but he was the first to stay.

Damien nursed the sick, wrapped bandages on oozing sores, hammered coffins and dug graves. On the average he buried one person a day. He put up more than 300 houses – each little more than four walls, a door and a roof, but still a shelter to those cast here. He was a good carpenter. Some of the solid little churches he built earlier around the Big Island and Molokai are still standing.

The original settlement was in Kalawao, at the wetter eastern end of the peninsula. Some of the afflicted arrived in boats, whose captains were so terrified of the disease that they would not land and instead dropped patients overboard into the bay. Those who could, swam to shore.

Early conditions were unspeakably horrible. Before modern medicine, leprosy manifested itself in dripping, foul-smelling sores. Eventually there was loss of sensation and tissue degeneration which could lead to fingers, toes and noses becoming deformed or falling off altogether.

In 1888 Damien installed a water pipeline to the sunnier western side and the settlement moved to where it is today. Over the years, some 8000 people have come to Kalaupapa Peninsula to die. During Damien's time lifespans here were usually short.

Yet even in Damien's day leprosy was one of the least contagious of all communicable diseases. All in all more than 1100 volunteers have worked with patients at Kalaupapa, but only Damien contracted leprosy. He died in 1889 at the age of 49.

Damien's work inspired others. Brother Joseph Dutton arrived in 1886 and stayed 44 years. In addition to his work with the sick, he was a prolific writer who kept the outside world informed on what was happening in Molokai. Mother Marianne Cope arrived a year before Damien died. She stayed 30 years, helping to establish a girls' home and encouraging patients to live life to the fullest. Some consider her the mother of the hospice movement.

In 1909 a fancy medical facility called the US Leprosy Investigation Station opened at Kalawao. However, the hospital was so out of touch (requiring patients to sign themselves in for two years, live in seclusion and give up all Hawaiian-grown food) that even in the middle of a leprosy colony it attracted only a handful of patients. It closed four years later.

Although sulfone antibiotics have been used successfully to control leprosy since the 1940s, isolation policies in Kalaupapa weren't abandoned until 1969.

Kalaupapa Today

Today fewer than 100 patients live in Kalaupapa Peninsula. It's an old population, getting older, with only a few under 50. Some of the elderly have become blind or weakened. Others fish or tend gardens, though lots of people just stay glued to their TVs. As a matter of fact, most people have a spare TV because there's no repair shop here.

Current residents are free to leave, but Kalaupapa is the only home most of them know. They have been given guarantees that they can stay in Kalaupapa Peninsula throughout their lifetimes. To minimise the impact on residents, the park requires all visitors to join a guided tour.

The state of Hawaii officially uses the term 'Hansen's Disease' for leprosy.

Kalawao

The road to Kalawao was graded in 1989 when dignitaries flew in to commemorate the 100th anniversary of Damien's death, though it's likely to revert back soon to being very bumpy and neglected.

St Philomena Church (better known as 'Father Damien's Church') in Kalawao underwent a major restoration for the centenary. You can still see where Damien cut open holes in the floor so that the sick who needed to spit could attend church and not be ashamed. The graveyard at the side contains Damien's gravestone and original burial site. His body was exhumed in 1936 and returned to Belgium.

The view from Kalawao is one of the island's finest. It looks out on the pali of the north-east coast, each successive cliffside jutting out behind the one in front, each looking more like a shadow in the mist. The park boundaries include the Waihanau, Waialeia and Waikolu valleys, east of the peninsula.

Getting There & Around
Air Aloha IslandAir leaves Honolulu for Kalaupapa at 9.15 am, stopping first to pick up passengers at Molokai Airport at 9.50 am, and arriving in Kalaupapa around 10 am.

Flights leave Kalaupapa at 3.05 and 3.55 pm for Honolulu, stopping to drop passengers off at Molokai Airport. Flights are cancelled or added according to demand.

Molokai Airport to Kaluapapa is $12.95 one way. Honolulu to Kalaupapa is $77.90 return.

The 'airport' at Kalaupapa is just a runway on a grassy field and a covered waiting area with a few chairs, restrooms and a pay telephone.

Tours The switchback mule trail down the pali is the only land route to the peninsula. No matter how you get there, you cannot wander around Kaluapapa Peninsula by yourself, but must take a guided tour.

On typical tours the village looks semideserted. The sights are mainly cemeteries, churches and memorials. Places where residents go to talk story – the post office, store and hospital – are pointed out but no stops are made. Visitors are not allowed to photograph the patients. Kalaupapa is a tourist attraction but its people are not.

Stops are made in town at memorials for Father Damien and Mother Marianne and at a mini-museum where photographs of the original settlement are on display and books are for sale. The tours then go across the peninsula to Kalawao.

Damien Tours (Box 1, Kalaupapa, HI 96742; tel 567-6171/567-6675) does the tours for people who come to Kalaupapa on foot or by plane. Richard Marks, who runs Damien Tours, is a wonderful storyteller, an oral historian and the third generation of his family to be banished to Kalaupapa. He leads the best tour of Kalaupapa. The cost is $17.50.

Old state laws which require everyone who enters the settlement to have a 'permit' and which only allows entry to those 16 years of age and older are no longer required for medical reasons, but are kept on the books to protect the privacy of the patients.

There's no actual paper permit. A reservation with either Damien Tours or Molokai Mule Ride is considered a permit.

Only guests of Kalaupapa residents are allowed to stay overnight. Unless you're on the mule tour, bring your own food and beverages. There are no stores or other public facilities for visitors.

Hiking The hike along the mule trail takes about one hour going down, a bit longer going up. It's best to begin hiking by 8.30 or 9 am, before the mules start down, to avoid walking in fresh dung. The narrow trail is rutted in places and can be slippery and muddy if it's been raining, but otherwise it's not terribly strenuous.

The trail starts on the right side of Hwy 470 midway between the mule stables and Kalaupapa Overlook. Don't be intimidated by the sign at the start of the path. If you have tour reservations, this is the trail in.

Mule The mules move none too quickly – actually, hiking can be faster – but there's a certain thrill in trusting your life to a mule while descending 1600 feet on 26 narrow cliffside switchbacks.

In general, people on the mules tend to be more into the ride than the destination. Because the mule-ride starts back by midafternoon, the tour time is limited.

The ride costs $75, includes a box lunch and lasts from about 8.30 am to 3.30 pm. The stables are on Hwy 470. A half-hour minilesson in mule riding is given before starting off down the trail.

Make reservations with Molokai Mule Ride, Box 200, Kualapuu, HI 96757 (tel 567-6088; 537-1845 from Oahu, 800-843-5978 from the mainland).

MOOMOMI BEACH
Moomomi Beach, 10 miles west of the Kalaupapa Peninsula, is ecologically unique. It stands as one of the few undisturbed coastal

sand dune areas left in Hawaii. Among its native grasses and shrubs are at least five endangered plant species that exist nowhere else on earth. It is one of the few places in the populated islands where green sea turtles still find a habitat suitable for breeding.

Evidence of an adze quarry and the fossils of a variety of long-extinct Hawaiian birds have been unearthed here, preserved over time by Moomomi's arid sands. Moomomi is not lushly beautiful, but windswept, lonely and wild.

To get there turn off Hwy 460, east of the airport, onto Hwy 481. Then turn left onto Hwy 480 (Farrington Ave) and head west. The paved road ends after about three miles. From there it's 2½ miles futher along a red dirt road that is in some areas quite smooth and in others deeply rutted. In places you may have to skirt along the edge of the road and straddle a small gully. It could be difficult going if it's muddy. People do make it down in standard cars, though the higher the vehicle the better.

A little over two miles after the paved road ends the road forks. Bear to the right and follow this road half a mile down to the beach. If it gets too rough there's a spot halfway down this last stretch where you can pull off to the right and park.

At the end of the road is Moomomi Bay with a little sandy beach used by sunbathers. The rocky eastern point which protects the bay provides a perch for fishermen. There are no facilities here, just the foundations of a bathhouse that burned down years ago.

The beautiful beach that people refer to as Moomomi is not here, but at Kawaaloa Bay, a 20-minute walk to the west. Kawaaloa is a broad white sand beach. The wind, which picks up pretty steadily each afternoon, blows the sand into ripples and waves. The high hills running inland are actually massive sand dunes. The coastal cliffs sculptured into jagged abstract designs by wind and water are made of sand which has petrified because of the dry conditions.

The narrower right side of Kawaaloa Bay is partially sheltered, though the whole beach can be rough when the winter surf is up. A tattered old changing room and pavilion are at the east end of the bay. Kawaaloa collects a lot of drifting debris, some of it driftwood and some of it less romantic.

There's a fair chance you'll have Kawaaloa to yourself, but if you don't you can always walk farther on to one of the other sandy coves along the shore. Most of the area west of here is open ocean with strong currents.

In 1988 the Nature Conservancy bought 920 acres of Moomomi from Molokai Ranch and hopes to eventually put in a self-guided trail. Call Molokai Preserves manager, Ed Misaki (tel 567-6680), for current information.

Central Molokai

Turning north off Hwy 460 onto Hwy 470 (Kalae Highway), the road starts in dry grasslands and climbs, passing the town of Kualapuu, a golf course, a restored sugar mill, a community of single-rooster dwellings, hillsides of grazing brown sheep, a mule stable and the trail down to Kalaupapa Peninsula. The road ends near the overlook.

KUALAPUU

Kualapuu is the name of both a 1017-foot hill and the village which has grown up north of it.

At the base of the hill is the world's largest rubber-lined reservoir. It can hold up to 1.4 billion gallons of water, which is piped in from the rainforests in East Molokai for use on the island's dry western side.

Water use is a hot issue as both farmers and West End developers are concerned not only with the present supply, but also with who gets priority in the event of a drought. The reservoir is the sole source of water for Hoolehua Plains and the towns in the West End.

Del Monte set up headquarters here in the 1930s and Kualapuu developed into a plantation town. The centre of Del Monte's activities covered the spread between Kualapuu and the nearby Hoolehua homesteads.

In 1982 Del Monte decided to phase out its Molokai operations and the economy came tumbling down. Today old pineapple harvesting machinery sits rusting quietly in grassy, overgrown fields.

Kualapuu is a friendly village with a tiny post office and beauty salon tucked beside the general store. Gas pumps are out the front, the barber shop is in the back and a restaurant and laundromat are across the street. There's a little church up the hill, but otherwise that's pretty much it for the town.

Places to Eat

The *Kualapuu Cookhouse* (tel 567-6185) is bright and cheerful and serves up good inexpensive food. It's also the local ice-cream shop. The meal of the day costs $4, a cup of corn chowder is 50 cents and they make a mean teriburger for $1.65. They have great pies and cakes, as well as sundaes topped with homemade passion fruit extract. Owner Nannette Yamashita, a weaver who has one of her works hanging in the state capitol building, knows a lot about arts and crafts, herbal medicines and other holistic goings-on in the community. The restaurant is open from 7 am to 6 pm.

The pottery at the restaurant is made by Dan Bennett, a high school maths teacher who makes quality stoneware at his home studio in nearby Kipu. He has one major sale before Christmas and shows pieces by appointment (tel 567-6585) the rest of the year. The prices are reasonable.

KALAE
R W Meyer Sugar Mill

Four miles north of Hwy 460, in Kalae, is the sugar mill built by Rudolph W Meyer, an industrious German immigrant.

Meyer was on his way to the California gold rush when he dropped by Hawaii, married a member of Hawaiian royalty and in the process landed a tidy bit of property.

Meyer found his gold in potatoes which he grew and exported to the Californian miners. Other hats he wore were overseer of the Kalaupapa leprosy settlement and manager of King Kamehameha V's ranchlands.

In the 1850s Meyer established his own ranch and exported cattle from Palaau village. In one infamous incident, after finding his herd declining, he had all the men of Palaau charged with cattle rustling and sent off to a jailhouse in Honolulu.

Meyer later tried a number of crops including coffee, corn and wheat before settling on sugar. He built his sugar mill in 1878, around the time a reciprocity treaty gave Hawaiian sugar planters the privilege to export sugar free of duty to the USA. The mill operated for about 10 years.

A lot of time and money has gone into authentically restoring the mill, including the complete rebuilding of a 100-year-old steam engine and other rusting machinery abandoned a century ago. It's the last mill of its kind. If you're into sugar mills, antique steam engines and that sort of thing you'll probably find it interesting.

Soon after the restoration, two mules were harnessed and sent circling to demonstrate the working mechanisms of the cane crushers. One of the mules, who apparently wasn't used to travelling in such fine circles, fell into the pit. The mule wasn't hurt, but the story might make some people think twice about descending a steep cliffside on the back of one of these creatures!

The sugar mill (tel 567-6436) is open from 10 am to noon Monday to Saturday and from 1 to 5 pm Sundays. Admission is $2.50 for adults, $1 for children.

Meyer and his descendants are buried in a little family plot behind the mill. Plans are in the works to build a museum of Molokai's history and culture nearby.

Ironwood Hills Golf Course

There are no polo shirts with little alligators on them here. Ironwood Hills is a pretty casual golf course, with crabgrass growing in the sand pits and local golfers who actually look like they're having fun. Fees for nonresidents are $8 for nine holes, $10 for 18.

The course is a little way down an unmarked, red dirt road at the tree-lined edge of the pasture immediately south of Meyer Sugar Mill.

Originally built by Del Monte for its employees, it was maintained by Molokai residents after Del Monte left. The whole thing may be in for some changes as the management has recently been taken over by Molokai Golf, the people building the new exclusive Molokai Highlands Golf Club in nearby Kipu.

Sheep on the Hills

The sheep dotting the hillsides belong to a New Zealand company which in 1988 began leasing 1100 acres in Kalae from Meyer Ranch. They shipped in 2500 ewes from Niihau and some rams and sheepdogs from back home. The aim is to replace frozen lamb from New Zealand now on the Hawaii market with cheaper Molokai lamb.

HOOLEHUA

Hoolehua is the dry plains area which separates eastern and western Molokai. Here, in the 1790s, Kamehameha the Great trained his warriors in a year-long preparation for the invasion of Oahu.

Hoolehua was settled as an agricultural community in 1924 as part of the Hawaiian Homes Act, which made public lands available to native Hawaiians. The land was divided into 40-acre plots. By 1930 more than half of Molokai's ethnic Hawaiian population was living on Hawaiian homesteads.

The first homestead was attempted closer to the coast at Kalanianaole, but it failed when the well water pumped to irrigate crops turned brackish. Many of these people then moved up to Hoolehua where homesteaders were already planting pineapple, a crop which required little water. As the two giant pineapple companies established operations in Molokai, homesteaders found it increasingly difficult to market their own pineapples and were eventually compelled to lease their lands to the plantations.

These days there's a reliable water supply and crops, which are more diversified, include tomatoes, potatoes, papaya and fresh herbs.

Information & Orientation

Three paved roads run east to west, with dirt crossroads going north to south. The post office and the Department of Land & Natural Resources office are on Puupeelua Ave (Hwy 481), just south of where it intersects with Farrington Ave (Hwy 480). Farrington Ave is Hoolehua's main street with a fire station, Episcopal church and Molokai's high school. The Hawaiian Home Lands office is on Puukapele Ave.

Puukapele Ave leads westward to another paved road which deceptively appears to be a find, heading beachward, but the road ends at the Western Space & Missile Center. Here a bunch of odd metal towers and wire cables look for all the world as if grown-up kids have been playing with a giant Erector Set.

Purdy's Macadamia Nut Farm

Tuddie Purdy runs the best little macadamia nut farm tour in all of Hawaii. Everything is Molokai scale. You can crack open macadamia nuts on a stone with a hammer and sample macadamia blossom honey scooped up with slices of fresh coconut.

Unlike tours on the Big Island which focus on processing, Purdy takes you into his orchard and explains how the nuts grow. The

Purdy's Macadamia Nut Farm

macadamia trees can be in various stages of progression - some with flowers in blossom, others with tiny nuts just beginning, while some might have clusters of mature nuts. His 1½ acres of mature trees are over 60 years old and grow naturally: no pesticides, herbicides, fertilisers or even pruning.

Purdy, a Molokai native who left a job with Aloha Airlines to work his homestead, is as interesting as the orchard and can tell you a lot about the island.

Admission is free. Macadamia nuts (roasted or raw) and honey are for sale. To get to the farm (tel 567-6601), head north, turn left onto Farrington Ave from Hwy 470 and after one mile turn right onto Lihi Pali Ave. It's less than half a mile up, on the right.

The hours are from 9 am to 1 pm daily, but they sometimes close a bit early after the one daily tour bus leaves.

MOLOKAI FARM
On the way to the West End, you might take a drive down to Maui Community College's Molokai Farm to see what is potentially the biggest antidevelopment movement going – diversified agriculture.

The farm has greenhouses, classrooms and 28 acres of gardens. As well as training a new generation of farmers, they're doing innovative things to develop marketable crops. In a small macadamia nut orchard they graft trees, enabling them to produce by the fourth year instead of the usual seven. In one plot a group of Molokai elders are growing fresh herbs, which are snipped and shipped to mainland gourmet restaurants.

Molokai Farm is a mile down the road leading south from Hwy 460 at the eight-mile marker, one mile west of the airport. It's not a sightseeing attraction, but it's open to visitors interested in horticulture.

West End

The Maunaloa Highway (Hwy 460) heads west from Kaunakakai, passes Molokai Airport, and then climbs and winds into the high grassy rangeland of Molokai's arid western side. The land is dry and still scarred by the severe drought of the mid-1980s and related brush fires.

Hwy 460 is about 17 miles long and the drive takes about half an hour from its start in Kaunakakai to its end at Maunaloa. It's a good paved road all the way, as are the roads to and around Kaluakoi Resort and down to Papohaku and Dixie Maru beaches. Most other West End roads, however, are privately owned dirt roads which are locked off to the public.

Molokai Ranch owns most of the land on this side of the island. Access is at the whim of the ranch, but generally requires special permission.

From Molokai's West End beaches, the twinkling lights of Oahu are just 26 miles away. The view is of Diamond Head to the left, Makapuu Point to the right.

West End Development
In the 1970s Molokai Ranch joined with Louisiana Land & Exploration Co to form the Kaluakoi Corporation. They proposed developing western Molokai into a major dormitory suburb of Honolulu, complete with a ferry service to the capital. The plan called for 30,000 private homes on the heretofore uninhabited west coast. A vocal antigrowth movement boomed quicker than the buildings could, and the plan was scrapped.

In its place a somewhat more modest master plan was drawn up for the development of Kaluakoi Resort that called for 1100 hotel units, 1200 condo units, 1000 single-family homes and a 15-acre shopping centre.

Only 200 of the condo units, one golf course and one of the four planned hotels have thus far been built. The 290-room hotel has never really taken off and has only about a 35% occupancy rate. The houselots have been subdivided and roads and utilities installed, but few homes built. Apparently, there's not yet enough activity to make it a popular destination.

Tokyo Kosan purchased Kaluakoi Resort in 1988 and now has plans underway to build two more golf courses and a second hotel.

In 1989 Sekihyo Seibaku Co, another Japanese developer, bought the entire undeveloped south-western tip of Molokai, from the southern end of Kaluakoi Resort around to Hale O Lono Beach.

MAUNALOA

The long mountain range that comes into view on the left past the 10-mile marker is Maunaloa, which means Long Mountain. Its highest point is Puunana at 1381 feet. Maunaloa is also the name of the town at the end of the road.

Maunaloa was the site of Hawaii's first hula school, had one of the most important adze quarries in the Hawaiian islands and was once a centre of sorcery.

According to legend, fire gods who roamed the heavens as shooting stars landed on Maunaloa, where they inhabited a grove of trees. Unsuspecting men who tried to cut down the possessed trees were poisoned upon touching the wood, until at last one of the gods explained to a kahuna how to cut the trees down. The kahunas were then able to carve the poisoned wood into images which harnessed the force of the gods. During the 17th century it became a powerful sorcery which could be sent off into the night to avenge enemies. It was potent stuff and nobody messed with Molokai in those days.

The town of Maunaloa, with its line of uninspired houses, was built in the 1920s by Libby, McNeill & Libby. This little plantation town was the centre of their pineapple activities on Molokai. Dole, which acquired Libby, McNeill & Libby, closed down operations in Maunaloa in 1975.

Maunaloa now looks a bit abandoned, though there are plans to build public housing.

Maunaloa has a cemetery, a church, an elementary school, a few back streets and occasionally an unlocked road heading away from town which invites impromptu exploration, but basically that's it.

Currently about 600 people live in the area, many working for Molokai Ranch or at Kaluakoi Resort.

Information

Maunaloa Service, the only gas station in the West End ('Our view of Diamond Head is a gas'), is open from 7.30 am to 5.30 pm Monday to Saturday.

Maunaloa General Store, well-stocked with groceries and booze, is open daily to 8 pm. The little rural post office is open until 4.30 pm Monday to Friday.

The Molokai Ranch office, on the right as you enter town, is where you pick up camping permits for Halena and Kawakiu beaches.

Places to Eat

Jojo's Cafe (tel 552-2803) with its long wooden bar, stools in front and mirrors behind, looks like an old-time saloon. In fact that's what it was, but things got so rowdy that the last two owners never bothered to renew the liquor licence and these days it's a quiet small town diner. If you want beer or wine with your meal, you can pick it up at the general store across the way and bring it in. Fish dishes are in the $5 to $7 range, burgers are $1.50. You can get a bowl of Portuguese bean soup for $2. It's open from 11.30 am to 7.30 pm daily.

Things to Buy

Big Wind Kite Shop sells designer kites of all shapes and styles. Owner Jonathan Socher's kites have a reputation throughout the islands for their creative flair.

Many of the kites are made on site and if you're there at the right time you can watch the process. It's open from 8.30 am to 5 pm Monday to Saturday, 10 am to 2 pm Sundays.

An extension of the kite factory is the Plantation Gallery next door: a gift shop with imports from Bali, horn scrimshaw from Molokai deer, books on Molokai and the like.

Molokai Red Dirt Shirts specialises in T-shirts with Molokai designs.

There are also a couple of artsy shops in town worth browsing in.

HALENA BEACH

Halena Beach is a broad white sand beach with a protective reef. Molokai Ranch owns

Halena and keeps the gates locked. Halena Beach has water, but it should be treated, and restrooms.

About 1½ miles west of Halena is Hale O Lono Beach, the starting point of the Molokai-to-Oahu outrigger canoe race held each year during Aloha Week.

Two miles to the east of Halena is the abandoned Kolo Wharf. Libby, McNeill & Libby shipped Maunaloa pineapples from here until moving their operations to Kaunakakai Harbor in the 1950s.

Places to Stay

Camping Molokai Ranch (tel 552-2767) allows camping at Halena Beach on weekends only, wants a minimum of two weeks advance notice and recommends a 4WD. Permits are available weekdays at their office in Maunaloa. The ranch charges $5 for the gate key plus $5 per person per day.

MOLOKAI RANCH WILDLIFE PARK

In the late 1960s, Molokai Ranch began importing antelope in an effort to control the rapid spread of kiawe trees, which were encroaching onto their cattle pastureland. The antelope, which feed on kiawe in their native habitat, adapted so well to Molokai that the ranch later started importing other exotic animals to breed for game parks and zoos. When Kaluakoi Resort opened Molokai Ranch began providing tours for the resort's guests.

About 1000 animals from Africa, India, Asia and South America roam the park's 1000 acres. The more numerous animals are the eland, Indian blackbuck, oryx and greater kudu, all strikingly marked antelopes; Barbary sheep, with thick curved-back horns; and sika deer from Japan.

There are a few zebras (whose white stripes soon become red from Molokai's soil), giraffes, rheas and East African crowned cranes. Flocks of wild turkey, ring-necked pheasant, francolin, quail and other game birds have flown in on their own.

The park's grassy hillsides and scrubby kiawe trees look so convincingly like the Serengeti that both American and Japanese film companies have used it to fake African backdrops.

Van tours around the park's rutted dirt roads last about 1½ hours. The best tours are those led by park manager Pilipo Solatorio, who treats the animals almost as pets and keeps up a lively commentary. When Pilipo honks his horn the animals come running to be fed.

Lots of stops are made for animal sightings and feedings, and for photography. The sliding door gets opened several times, so the best seats for viewing are closest to that door and at the front of the van. The front-seat passenger is apt to get nuzzled by a friendly eland – a large African antelope weighing a good 1500 pounds – which sticks its head in the window to be fed.

Tours of the ranch begin at 8, 10 am, 1 and 3 pm daily, weather permitting. It's $25 for adults, $10 for children. Reservations can be made by calling 552-2767.

KALUAKOI RESORT

Off Hwy 460 at the 15-mile marker a road leads down to Kaluakoi Resort. The 6700-acre development includes Kaluakoi Hotel & Golf Club, the condominium complexes of Paniolo Hale and Ke Nani Kai, subdivided houselots and a beautiful windswept coast.

Kepuhi Beach

Kepuhi is the white sand beach in front of Kaluakoi Hotel. During the winter the surf breaks close to shore, carrying a tremendous amount of sand to and fro. Experienced surfers like the northern end of the beach.

Swimming conditions are often dangerous here. Not only can there be a tough shorebreak, but currents are often strong and can be present even on calmer days. The folks at the hotel beach hut maintain a daily chart on water conditions.

Kaiaka Rock, the promontory 110 feet high at one end of the beach, still has some bunkers from WW II. There have been on-again off-again plans for a luxury hotel there.

Watersports Rentals

Molokai Beach Rentals (tel 552-2555), the beach hut in front of the hotel, rents snorkel

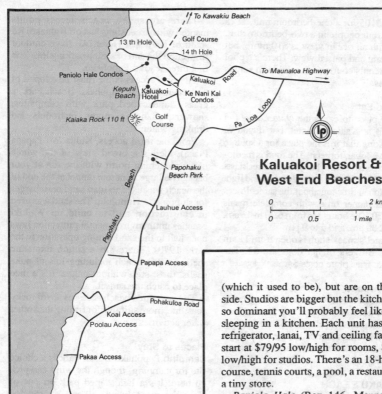

Kaluakoi Resort & West End Beaches

```
0          1          2 km
0      0.5      1 mile
```

sets or boogie boards for $10 a day, surfboards for $15 per four hours, 110 mm underwater cameras for $10, wave skis, fishing poles, coolers, kites and kayaks. There are no rentals on days when the seas are so rough they think they might lose the gear.

Places to Stay

Kaluakoi Hotel & Golf Club (Box 1977, Maunaloa, HI 96770; tel 552-2555; 800-367-6046 from the USA, 800-663-1118 from Canada) has 290 rooms and is run by Colony Hotels & Resorts. The cheapest rooms are fairly standard for a Sheraton-style hotel (which it used to be), but are on the small side. Studios are bigger but the kitchenette is so dominant you'll probably feel like you're sleeping in a kitchen. Each unit has a small refrigerator, lanai, TV and ceiling fan. Rates start at $79/95 low/high for rooms, $89/105 low/high for studios. There's an 18-hole golf course, tennis courts, a pool, a restaurant and a tiny store.

Paniolo Hale (Box 146, Maunaloa, HI 96770; tel 552-2731; 800-367-2984) is a 77-unit condo at Kaluakoi Resort. Each unit has a kitchen, ceiling fans, TV, washer/dryer and screened lanai. Studios start at $75. Up to four people in a one-bedroom unit costs from $95, in a two-bedroom unit from $115. The minimum stay is three nights. They discount 10% for weekly stays and 15% for monthly stays. There's a pool and barbecue grills. The office is open from 8 am to 4 pm Monday to Friday, 8 am to noon Saturdays.

Ke Nani Kai (Box 126, Maunaloa, HI 96770; tel 552-2761; 800-888-2791) is a 120-unit condo at Kaluakoi Resort, set back from the ocean. Each unit has a kitchen, lanai, washer/dryer and sofabed. Units on the 2nd floor have high exposed-beam ceilings and are probably the nicest on Molokai. The rates are $105 for a one-bedroom unit, $125 for up to four people in a two-bedroom unit. A unit with an ocean view is $10 more, but it's a distant and partial view. There's a pool and two tennis courts. The minimum stay is two nights.

Places to Eat

The only place to eat is the *Ohia Lodge* (tel 552-2555) at Kaluakoi Hotel, but if you've been thinking that it is the place for a splurge meal on Molokai, forget it. The food is mediocre and expensive for what you get. Breakfasts are in the $6 to $9 range. Sandwiches and light meals at lunch time are about the same. Prices step up at dinner time with complete meals around $20. The hours are from 6.30 to 11 am, noon to 2.30 pm, and 6 to 9 pm.

The hotel's snack shop is open from 11 am to 5 pm. Burgers or hot dogs are $3. The chicken & fries plate costs $4.50.

Getting Around

The Kaluakoi Hotel rents out Honda mopeds for $5 an hour or $15 per four hours. Tenspeed mountain bicycles are $3 an hour or $10 a day. Riding is limited to the paved road as kiawe thorns on the dirt roads give some mean flat tyres.

PAPOHAKU BEACH

Papohaku Beach lays claim to being Hawaii's largest white sand beach. It's 2½ miles long and vast enough to hold the entire population of Molokai without getting crowded, though that would be an unlikely scenario. Even on sunny days there's usually only a handful of beachgoers and you can often walk the shore without seeing another set of footprints.

It's a beautiful beach and easy to get to, so why is no-one there? Well, for one, it can be windy. But the main drawback is the water itself which is usually too treacherous for swimming.

Yet for barefoot strolling it's a gorgeous stretch, with soft white sand gleaming in the sun and wisps of rainbows tossed up in the crashing surf – 'a beach to die for' as one islander said.

There are seven beach access points marked with street signs just off Kaluakoi Rd south of Kaluakoi Hotel. All have outdoor showers at the end of sealed parking lots. The first three lead to Papohaku.

The first access is the most developed of the seven. This is Papohaku Beach Park, a grassy landscaped park with campsites, showers, changing rooms, restrooms and drinking water.

From the third access, Kulua (off Papapa Place), there's a broad view of the whole beach stretching north with the sun at your back. The large concrete tunnel at the end of the beach was used to load sand onto barges for shipping to Honolulu. The sand was used in construction and to build up Waikiki beaches until environmental protection laws put a halt to the sand mining operation in the early 1970s. There are a zillion miniature shells on this beach including lots of puka shells, most still without pukas. It's a nice place to catch the sunset.

The next three beach accesses are of rocky coastline, more suitable for fishing than other water activities.

Places to Stay

Camping Papohaku Beach Park is a choice site for camping, though the wind can pick up here. It's a landscaped park on one of Hawaii's most beautiful and uncrowded beaches. The surf will lull you to sleep and the birds will wake you up. Watch for thorns from the kiawe trees when you set up camp.

DIXIE MARU BEACH

The beach at the end of the road is called Dixie Maru after a ship that went down in the area long ago. The Hawaiian name for the beach is Kapukahehu.

Dixie Maru is the most protected cove on the west shore and the most popular swimming area. There are usually a fair number of families here. The waters are generally calm except when the surf is high enough to break over the mouth of the bay.

MAKE HORSE BEACH

Make (pronounced 'mah-kay') Horse Beach

Danger...falling coconuts

supposedly takes its name from days past when wild horses were run off the cliff north of here. *Make* means 'dead'. This pretty little white sand beach is a bit more secluded than the one in front of Kaluakoi Hotel. It's a good place for sunbathing but it's not safe for swimming.

To get there turn off Kaluakoi Rd onto the road to Paniolo Hale condos and then turn left as if going to the complex. Either park just beyond the condos and walk a quarter of a mile down to the golf course or drive the rutted dirt road to the end where there's a little spot to park. From there cross a narrow stretch of fairway and you're on the beach.

KAWAKIU BEACH

Kawakiu is a special place. It's a broad crescent beach of white sand and bright turquoise waters north of the Kaluakoi Resort complex.

In 1975 Kawakiu was a focus of Molokai activists who began demanding public access to private, and heretofore forbidden, beaches. The group, Hui Alaloa, marched to Kawakiu from Moomomi in a protest that convinced Molokai Ranch to grant public access to Kawakiu Beach.

To get there, turn off Kaluakoi Rd onto the road to Paniolo Hale, but instead of turning left down to the condos continue straight toward the golf course. Where the paved road ends, there's a place to pull over and park. There are restrooms and drinking water at the 14th hole. It's the last chance to get water.

The red dirt road which continues down to the beach should be OK with a 4WD and might also be passable in a standard car. However, it's quite rocky in places and if you did bottom out or brush one of the rocks on the side it could put a dent in things. Anyway, why hassle driving when it's a pleasant half-hour hike down to the beach?

After the golf course the road passes through ranchland with kiawe trees. Trees that died during the drought of the mid-1980s now stand bleached white by the sun, making interesting silhouettes against the blue sky.

You'll come first to a rocky point at the southern end of the bay. Scramble around up here before descending to the beach and you can find old rock foundations and get a scenic view of the coast south to the sands of Papohaku Beach and north to Ilio Point.

When seas are calm, Kawakiu is generally safe for swimming, though that's more common in summer than winter. When the surf is rough, there are still areas where you can at least get wet. On the southern side of the bay is a little sandy-bottomed wading pool in the rocks. The northern side has an area of flat rocks over which water slides to fill up a shallow shoreline pool. On weekends there's usually a few families picnicking under the kiawe trees.

Places to Stay

Camping Molokai Ranch (tel 552-2767) allows camping at Kawakiu Beach, but requires a permit. Permits are free and may be picked up weekdays during business hours at the Molokai Ranch office in Maunaloa.

Lanai

Lanai is a one-crop, one-company, one-town island.

Castle & Cooke owns 98% of Lanai and through its Dole subsidiary runs the island as its own private pineapple plantation. There are some 300 million of the spiked bushes planted row upon row in the red soil of Lanai's high central plateau, as far as the eye can see. One-fifth of the world's pineapples come from Lanai.

Lanai City – not a city at all, but a small plantation town – is home to all but two dozen of Lanai's 2200 residents, most of whom work for Castle & Cooke.

Yet despite the image of Lanai as one large pineapple field, only one-sixth of the island is planted in 'pine', as pineapple is called there.

Lanai also has forested ravines, dry and dusty gullies, white sand beaches and cool, foggy uplands. The island has some good archaeological sites and petroglyphs and the last native dryland forest in Hawaii.

Although Lanai is interesting to explore, many of the sights are a good distance from town, along rutted dirt roads that require a 4WD vehicle.

Until recently Lanai had but one hotel, with just 10 rooms. The few visitors were largely hunters, hikers and travellers trying to avoid the tourist scene on the other islands.

Lanai is undergoing some major changes. Castle & Cooke is promoting two new luxury hotels, gambling that enough wealthy visitors in search of seclusion will show up to make it pay off. The new hotels will be operated by Rockresorts, a company founded by Laurance Rockefeller.

The Lodge at Koele, just above Lanai City, has the lowest profile of the two. The lowrise hotel has the ambience of an overgrown plantation estate, with wrought-iron rails, garden paths, stone fireplaces, beam ceilings and guest rooms furnished with four-poster beds. The Lodge has a genteel image with lawn bowling, croquet and afternoon tea.

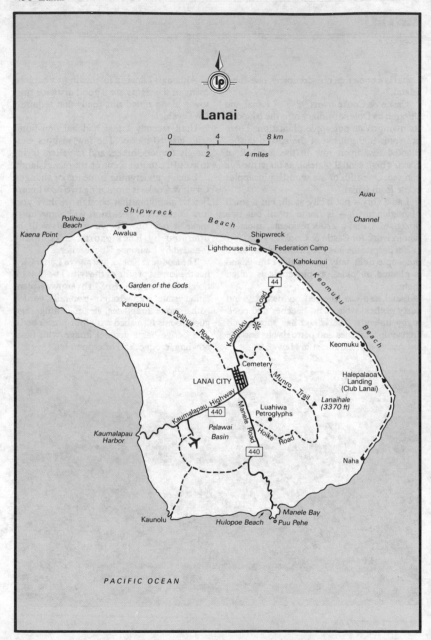

At $46 million in construction costs, each of the 102 rooms has cost around $450,000, far exceeding the cost of those of the new Hyatt Waikoloa mega-resort on the Big Island.

The more controversial Manele Bay Hotel has cost even more to build. It sits above the western end of Hulopoe Beach and is intended to be elegant and exclusive, with lobby boutiques, fountains, Italian marble and grand pianos.

Hulopoe is Lanai's best beach and has long been a popular weekend camping and picnicking spot. Lanaians are concerned that the new resort will restrict their access to the beach.

Orientation

Lanai has only one town, Lanai City, smack in the centre of the island. The town is laid out in a sensible grid pattern, which makes it easy to get around.

Outside Lanai City there are only three paved roads: Keomuku Rd (Hwy 44), which heads north-east toward Shipwreck Beach; Kaumalapau Highway, which heads west to Kaumalapau Harbor; and Manele Rd, which goes south to Manele and Hulopoe bays. Both Kaumalapau Highway and Manele Rd are marked Hwy 440, though they are two distinct roads.

The airport is on Kaumalapau Highway, 3½ miles from town.

Dirt Roads There are scores of dirt roads through the pineapple fields, with conditions varying from good to impassable. Castle & Cooke generally grades the roads in the spring or whenever they get so rutted that the pineapple trucks have difficulty passing.

Some dirt roads wash out during severe winter storms. Outside the pineapple fields, the common practice is not to regrade again until spring.

The car rental agencies can tell you the current best routes to out-of-the-way sights. Often there are a few alternatives and they know which roads are washed out and which are passable. Occasionally one of their 4WD vehicles bottoms out and has a transmission

case crack open. They have had a few flip over on washed-out roads as well. It can be a long walk back from the boonies on Lanai.

The routes we describe were the best at the time, but that may have changed.

Facts

HISTORY

According to legend, Lanai was a land of spirits, and spirits alone roamed until the 15th century.

It was at this time that Kaululaau, the young prince of Maui, lived in what is today the town of Lahaina. He was a troublesome kid. After he had torn out breadfruit trees that his father had just planted, it was decided to banish him to uninhabited Lanai, an almost certain death.

Not easily intimidated, Kaululaau got into tricking the evil akua (spirits) of Lanai. During the day the akua would see him on the beach and ask where he spent his nights. He convinced them he slept in the surf, though when darkness fell he slipped off to the shelter of a cave.

Night after night, the akua returned to the beach and rushed out to look for Kaululaau in the waves. The longer they searched, the more exhausted they got, until finally the pounding surf overcame them. Kaululaau continued his pranks until at last all 400 of Lanai's akua had either perished or fled to Kahoolawe.

Kaululaau's family had given him up for dead, when Mauians noticed a light from a fire across the Auau Channel, which separates Maui and Lanai. When they went over to check it out they found Kaululaau alive and well and the island rid of spirits. Kaululaau was brought back to Maui a hero.

Early Settlements

Archaeological studies indicate Lanai was never heavily settled. Villages were relatively small and scattered throughout the island.

Since ancient times, Lanai has been under the rule of Maui. In 1778, when the Big

Island chief Kalaniopuu was routed in a failed attempt to invade Maui, he decided to take his revenge on tiny Lanai and sent warriors under the command of Kamehameha.

Kamehameha's troops were brutal. They killed everyone they found and virtually depopulated Lanai. In 1792 when the Western explorer Vancouver sailed by Lanai he saw no villages and noted that the island might at best be only sparsely populated.

Visitors were largely dissuaded from landing on Lanai's shores by a tough ocean swell that by the 1820s had already claimed a few foreign ships. In 1823 the missionary William Ellis became the first Westerner to step ashore. He guessed the island's population to be 2000.

Though the early missionaries didn't spend much time on Lanai they still had an influence. They introduced the heretofore unknown crime of adultery to Hawaii and in the 1830s Maui women accused of the offence were banished to the barren northwestern side of Lanai as punishment.

Mormons

In the 1850s the Mormons moved in and set up a community at Palawai Basin, south of present-day Lanai City. Their intention was to establish a 'City of Joseph' in Hawaii.

The community floundered until 1861 when a new charismatic elder, Walter Gibson, arrived. Mormons from around the islands poured in, as did money to buy Palawai Basin. At the height of it all, there was one Mormon for every Lanaian.

Gibson, a shrewd businessman, handled the financial matters for the community. He was more concerned with land than preaching. Things got sticky when it was discovered that he had made the land purchases in his own name, rather than in the church's. In 1864, after refusing to turn over the title to his Lanai holdings to the mother church in Salt Lake City, he was excommunicated by church leader Brigham Young.

This didn't seem to faze Gibson. The Lanai congregation faded away and the 300 or so Mormons left for Laie on Oahu's north shore, where their church is centred today.

Gibson held onto the prime Lanai real estate he had cornered. In the early 1880s, Gibson became a friend and confidant to King Kalakaua and came to hold a number of positions in Kalakaua's cabinet, including that of premier.

Sugar

Gibson left the land to his daughter upon his death. In 1888 she and her husband, Frederick Hayselden, established the Maunalei Sugar Company and developed a landing at Halepalaoa on Lanai's east coast. A water pumping station went up at nearby Keomuku, the surrounding area was planted with sugar cane and the whole shebang was connected by a little railroad. Over 400 Japanese labourers were brought in to work the fields. The sugar days were short lived, however. By 1901 the pumps were drawing saltwater, the sugar cane had died and the whole thing folded.

This was not the first try at the sugar business on Lanai. In 1802 a Chinese man landed on Lanai with granite rollers to crush sugar cane and iron pots to boil down the syrup. He is credited with being the first to attempt sugar production in Hawaii. Though the enterprise was a failure, it was Chinese know-how that was the base for sugar mills on other islands.

Cattle

After the dismal failure with sugar, the land was sold off to ranching interests. In 1910 the newly formed Lanai Company consolidated most of the holdings and established cattle ranching on a larger scale. The following year George Munro was hired to manage the ranch and a cattle landing was established at Manele Bay.

In 1917 the Baldwin brothers, sons of missionaries from Maui, purchased the Lanai Company. With the exception of a small haole-held ranch and about 500 acres held by Lanaians, the Baldwins owned the entire island.

Pineapples

In 1922 Jim Dole paid $1.1 million for

Pineapple

Lanai – just enough for the Baldwins to buy the coveted Ulupalakua Ranch on Maui. Dole, who had already established pineapple production on Oahu, doubled his holdings of cultivable land by purchasing Lanai.

Dole's Hawaiian Pineapple Company poured $4 million into Lanai to turn it into a plantation island. It built the plantation town of Lanai City, dredged Kaumalapau to make it a deep-water harbour, put in roads and water systems, cleared the land and planted pineapples. By the end of the 1920s production was in full swing.

Dole had marketed his pineapples well, was producing bumper crops and the future looked rosy. Then sales plummeted as the Great Depression hit the mainland. The newly popular canned pineapples were suddenly seen as an exotic extra, one that most Americans could easily do without in hard times.

After an $8 million loss in 1932, a reorganisation took place. Castle & Cooke purchased much of the stock and eventually gained a controlling interest in Dole.

GEOGRAPHY

Lanai is the sixth largest Hawaiian island. It's 18 miles long, 13 miles wide and shaped like a teardrop. It has an area of 140 square miles.

Lanai lies nine miles south of Molokai and nine miles west of Maui. The name Lanai means 'hump'. When viewed from Maui it looks somewhat like the back of a whale rising out of the water.

The island was formed by a single volcano, Palawai, now long extinct. The large flat basin of Palawai crater is today covered with pineapples.

Lanai's terrain and climate are dominated by a ridge running from the north-west to the south-east. It reaches a height of 3370 feet at Lanaihale. From there, a series of ravines radiate down to the east coast, ending at a strip of coastal flats.

The western side of the ridge is a cool central plateau, containing the island's agricultural land. In the centre of it all is Lanai City at 1620 feet.

The south-west coast has sheer sea cliffs, some higher than 1000 feet. North-west Lanai is dry and barren and slopes gently down to the coast.

CLIMATE

Lanai City has a mild climate. The lowest temperature on record is 46°F, the highest 88°F. Average temperatures range from 73°F in the summer to 66°F in the winter. Evenings can be brisk, commonly dipping down to around 50°F in winter. There are more fireplaces than lanais in Lanai.

Lanai is rather dry. Molokai and Maui to the north and east draw much of the rain out of the moisture-laden trade winds before they reach Lanai.

Annual rainfall averages 37 inches in Lanai City and 10 to 15 inches along most of the coast. The difference is great enough that when it's overcast in Lanai City, chances are good that Shipwreck Beach or Manele Bay will be sunny.

As with the rest of Hawaii, October to April is the rainiest season. Even dry areas can get whacked with heavy rainfall during winter storms.

FLORA & FAUNA

Besides pineapples, the most noticeable types of vegetation are thorny kiawe trees and stately Norfolk Island pines. Lanai has a unique native dryland forest, under the protection of the Nature Conservancy.

Lanai has no mongoose, which on other islands eat the eggs of ground nesting birds, so introduced game birds thrive. Ringnecked pheasants, francolins, chukar partridges, quails, doves and wild turkeys are all hunted. The island has at least two endemic birds – the Hawaiian owl and the apapane – but they are scarce.

Lanai has about 6000 axis deer, descendants from a herd of eight brought to Molokai from India in 1868. The deer were introduced to Lanai in 1920 and are more prolific than on Molokai, the only other Hawaiian island where they roam free.

Mouflon sheep were introduced to Lanai in 1954 and inhabit the island's gullies and ridges.

GOVERNMENT

Lanai is part of Maui County. Historically Lanai has been treated as an extension of Maui, much as Niihau has been of Kauai. Lanai had at most only limited autonomy, with Maui kings maintaining suzerainty.

These days the control of the island is largely in the hands of Castle & Cooke. They own all but 2% of Lanai and thus the beaches, forests and most of the dirt roads around the island are on their property. Total county and state land accounts for just over 100 acres.

ECONOMY

Until recently Lanai's economy could be summed up in one word: pineapples.

About 15,000 of the island's 90,000 acres are planted with pine. Each plant takes 1½ to two years to produce a single fruit. After it's picked, ratoons may shoot up to produce an additional fruit or two, but that's it. One acre can hold 20,000 plants.

Because pineapples in the field do not ripen all at once, they must be picked by hand. Workers wear hats and heavy clothing to protect themselves from the thorny spikes.

Picked fruits are placed on a moving conveyer belt and dropped into huge bins which are then trucked down to Kaumalapau Harbor for shipping to Dole's Honolulu cannery.

Though pineapples are produced year-round, the height of the harvest season is from April to August. Dole hires about 100 off-island workers – mainly teenagers and college students – to help harvest the summer crop. Pay is $5 an hour. (Apply at Dole's personnel office, tel 565-6685.) Housing is in modular units with shared bath houses. In the past, they've used the long cabins on Lanai Ave down by Lanai City Service.

In 1989 Lanai had about 11% unemployment, the highest in the state.

Development

In addition to the 352 new hotel rooms, both hotels are part of project areas that include residential developments. Near Manele there will be a little commercial district as well. Some 700 new workers will be needed for the hotel industry. In addition, the wealthy and the second-homers who have bypassed Lanai up to now are beginning to show interest. If it all develops according to plan, Lanai's population will more than quadruple to 10,000.

Development raises mixed feelings on Lanai. Sentiments seem to be pretty evenly divided between those for it and those against it. Some people see it as an opportunity to break out of the pineapple fields, others see it as the end of Lanai's rural lifestyle. There are a lot of issues at stake.

The tiny Lanai branch of Maui Community College is gearing up for a changing economy by doubling its course offerings, adding Hotel Accounting and Supervisory Housekeeping.

PEOPLE

Lanai has seen some dramatic rises and falls in its population. It had dropped well below 200 when Dole arrived in 1922.

Lanai's population is 2200, about 1000 less than it had been in the 1950s. All but two dozen live in Lanai City. The largest ethnic group is Filipino (51%), followed by Japanese (18%), Caucasian (11%) and part-Hawaiian (9.2%).

Approximately a third of the people living on Lanai were born in the Philippines.

GENERAL INFORMATION

There's no local newspaper so community notices are posted on bulletin boards. There are boards outside the post office, Pine Isle Market and Dahang's Pastry Shop.

Official Lanai

Lanai's nickname is 'The Pineapple Island'. Its official flower is the kaunaoa. Its official colour is yellow.

Money

The first Hawaiian Bank is on Lanai Ave near 7th St.

Library

The library is on Fraser Ave, adjacent to the school. It's open from 8 am to 8 pm Mondays and Wednesdays, and from 8 am to 5 pm Tuesdays, Thursdays and Fridays.

Weather

For recorded weather forecasts and water conditions call 565-6033. For information on trails try the state's Department of Land & Natural Resources (tel 565-6688) on 8th St.

Emergency

For all emergencies call 911. Lanai Community Hospital (tel 565-6411) on 7th St has 24-hour emergency service.

ACTIVITIES

Castle & Cooke has built the new $3 million public recreation centre in Lanai City, next to the school, with a 75-foot-long pool, a playground and a couple of rubberised, lit tennis courts. Its construction has raised suspicions among some islanders that it may be intended as a trade-off for Hulopoe Beach.

The Cavendish Golf Course is a nine-hole course just above town. Green fees are either $5 or nothing, depending on who you ask.

New 18-hole designer golf courses are being planned for the two new hotels.

Lanai City Service rents snorkel sets for $10 a day.

Cockfighting, while not legal, is not uncommon on Lanai. The fights are private and you won't find them unless you're around for a while and make the right friends. It's not a bring-a-guest situation.

People go to bed early in Lanai and to speak of there's no night life.

THINGS TO BUY

Not pineapples. There aren't any in the stores. If you feel you must have some, sales can be arranged through Dole, but they'll need at least 24 hours notice. The minimum order is one dozen, but the best deal comes from buying a ton!

GETTING THERE & AWAY
Air

Aloha IslandAir flies daily to Lanai direct from Honolulu, Kahului, Kapalua/Kaanapali and Molokai. The most frequent service is from Honolulu, with five flights a day. The one-way fare is $39.

Hawaiian Airlines flies to Lanai direct from Honolulu once a day on Mondays, Thursdays, Saturdays and Sundays. Honolulu to Lanai and Molokai to Lanai fares are $40 one way. You can also get a connecting flight to Lanai through Honolulu from Hilo, Kona, Lihue or Kapalua/Kaanapali for $50.

Lanai Airport lacks the navigational equipment to allow instrument landings. When it's foggy, as it sometimes is for days on end in winter storms, planes are unable to land.

Airport Lanai Airport is not much more than a runway. Hawaiian Airlines and Aloha IslandAir share a small wooden building, which also houses the restrooms. There are no other services.

Dole's airport sign has long proclaimed Lanai to be the world's largest pineapple plantation. Now, apparently attempting to promote the image of Lanai as a classy destination, the word 'largest' has been replaced with 'premier'.

Ferry

Expeditions on Maui (tel 661-3756) has passenger ferry service between Lahaina on Maui and Manele Boat Harbor on Lanai. The 24-passenger boat runs twice daily, departing Lahaina at the public loading dock in front of Pioneer Inn at 8.30 am and 3 pm and departing Manele at 9.45 am and 4.15 pm. The trip takes about an hour and additional runs are sometimes made. One-way fares are $25 per adult and $20 per child (aged 2 to 11). 3.45 pm and departing Manele at 8 am and 5 pm. The trip takes about an hour. One-way fares are $20 for adults and $10 for children.

GETTING AROUND
Car

The directory board at the airport lists two companies in its U-Drive section: Oshiro Service and Lanai City Service. Move over to the Tours section and there are also two companies: Oshiro Service and Lanai City Service. This is a small island.

There are no car rental booths at the airport. Both agencies meet people with reservations and transfer them to their offices in town and both tack on a fee for the service.

Oshiro Service & U-Drive (Box 516, Lanai City, HI 96763; tel 565-6952) at 850 Fraser Ave rents older cars without air-con for $25 a day, newer ones with air-con from $32 a day and 4WD vehicles range from $75 to $85. All cars (except 4WDs) are limited to paved roads and the contract has two rate schedules, one tripling the rate 'if it is found that auto was taken ANYWHERE off paved road'.

The airport transfer for people renting cars is $5 return. Oshiro also has a taxi service for $6 per taxi one way between the airport and town. The station is open from 8 am to noon and from 1.30 to 5.30 pm Monday to Saturday, and Sundays by appointment.

Lanai City Service (Box N, Lanai City, HI 96763; tel 565-7227; toll free 533-3666 from

Oahu and 244-9538 from Maui) on Lanai Ave rents cars with air-con for $35 a day and 4WD vehicles for $60 on weekdays and $90 on weekends. Their shuttle service between the airport and town is $6 one way for the first person and $2 for each additional person. They'll meet boaters at the harbour for motor service and fuel. The station is open from 7.30 am to 5.30 pm daily except Sundays, when it's open until noon.

Dollar (800-342-7398 in Hawaii, 800-367-7006 from the mainland) has plans to start a service on Lanai once the hotels open and already books through Lanai City Service.

Around the Island

LANAI CITY

Lanai City is nestled among Norfolk pines on a cool central plateau. It's wrapped on three sides by pineapples and on the fourth by the slopes of Lanaihale Mountain.

Lanai City is fairly classy for a plantation town. Unlike Hawaii's working sugar towns, most of the homes in Lanai City are privately owned. Houses are brightly painted and have gardens with flowering trees and ornamental bromeliads.

Lanai City invites leisurely walking. The centre of town is Dole Park, a large grassy park lined with Norfolk pines. The park stretches six blocks from Fraser Ave to Lanai Ave, the two main roads in town.

Lanai's restaurants are on the north side of the park and the grocery stores are on the south side. To the west of the park are the post office, hospital and Hotel Lanai. To the east are the school and recreation centre with houses spread out five or six blocks on either side and that's about it.

The one 'sight' in town is Ito's Garden. This one-man beautification project is a little terraced roadside garden of flowering plants. It's gone downhill since Ito moved off the island, but if you're kicking around town it's worth a look. It's up on Queens Ave.

Lanai is the place to come to unwind the

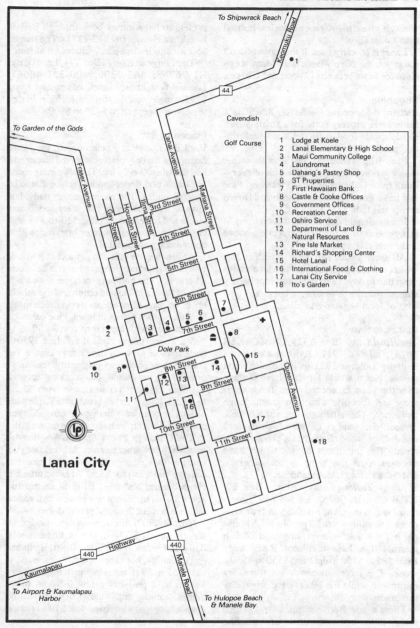

To Shipwreck Beach

Keomuku Road

1

44

Cavendish

Golf Course

To Garden of the Gods

Lanai Avenue

Fraser Avenue

Gay Street
Houston Street
Ilima Street

3rd Street

4th Street

5th Street

6th Street

7th Street

Dole Park

8th Street

9th Street

10th Street

11th Street

Mahana Street

Queens Avenue

1	Lodge at Koele
2	Lanai Elementary & High School
3	Maui Community College
4	Laundromat
5	Dahang's Pastry Shop
6	ST Properties
7	First Hawaiian Bank
8	Castle & Cooke Offices
9	Government Offices
10	Recreation Center
11	Oshiro Service
12	Department of Land & Natural Resources
13	Pine Isle Market
14	Richard's Shopping Center
15	Hotel Lanai
16	International Food & Clothing
17	Lanai City Service
18	Ito's Garden

2
3
4
5
6
7
8
15
9
10
14
12
13
16
11
17
18

Lanai City

440 Highway 440

Kaumalapau

To Airport & Kaumalapau Harbor

Manele Road

To Hulopoe Beach & Manele Bay

clock. It's hard to imagine a town less hurried than Lanai City.

Lanai is an early riser. If the roosters don't rouse you the 5 am whistle will. Many shops close for siesta between 12 noon and 1.30 pm.

Shopping

Richard's Shopping Center on 8th St is a fairly large grocery store for a small island. In addition to food, it also sells non-prescription medicines.

Pine Isle Market on 8th St is the other major grocery store. It carries a bit of everything from Coleman lamps to watches. Pine Isle has a good selection of fresh and frozen meats and fish.

International Food & Clothing on Ilima St is a general store that sells groceries, booze and some clothing.

All three stores sell fresh produce. Just which store has the freshest produce varies from day to day. They're mostly supplied by shipments from other islands, but there's also a bit of local vegetable farming.

Places to Stay

The *Hotel Lanai* (Box A 119, Lanai City, HI 96763; tel 565-7211; 800-624-8849) was built by Dole in 1923 to lodge plantation guests. Not a whole lot has changed there over the years except the rates. The hotel is cozy and friendly, with a mountain lodge ambience. The 10 rooms are simple: bed, dresser, desk and chair, with high ceilings and lots of wood. Each has a private bathroom. The four front rooms, which have porches, cost the same as the others – $51/58/65 a single/double/triple.

Lanai Realty (Kathy Oshiro, Box 67, Lanai City, HI 96763; tel 565-6597) rents four houses in town, from 2½ to four bedrooms, sleeping six to 10 people. Each house has a TV, a washer/dryer, linen and kitchen utensils. Two have fireplaces. Rates range from $85 to $150 a night and $550 to $950 a week. The largest house has a three-day minimum, while the others have a two-day minimum.

There's one B&B on the island – two rooms in the home of Lucille Graham. She prefers to have guests book through Bed & Breakfast Hawaii (tel 822-7771). The rate of $50 for singles/doubles includes breakfast.

The *Lodge at Koele* (Box 774, Lanai City, HI 96763; 565-7300; 800-321-4666), Lanai's first luxury hotel, has rooms from $275 single/double. Suites include butler service and cost from $425 to $900.

Places to Eat

Until the Lodge at Koele opened, the *Hotel Lanai* was the only place that served dinner and had the island's only bar. The big dining room has hardwood floors and a fireplace that is lit on cool nights. The menu changes daily, but always includes fresh fish, beef, pork and chicken. Dinners are around $10 to $14 and come with a baked potato or brown rice plus homemade soup or salad.

At lunch time you can get a chef's salad, fish & chips, sandwiches or burgers between $4 and $5. The hamburgers come with a big slab of fresh tomato and onion and the salads are crisp. Breakfast does not cost much more here than other places in town. Pine cakes or French toast with fresh fruit cost $3.50.

S T Properties is good if you like 1950s-style hamburgers – a little heavy on the fat and sodium, but unquestionably the most popular on the island. Burgers cost around $1.50 to $2. Lunch plates range from $3.50 to $4.50. It also serves breakfast. There's an old-style counter where you can sit over coffee and watch the bacon sizzle on the grill.

The *Dahang's Pastry Shop* makes doughnuts and a few other pastries. At breakfast you can get two eggs with Spam and rice (or sausage and toast) for $3.50. At lunch time it's cheeseburgers and fries, BLTs or saimin for about $2. It's an unassuming place with formica tables, a cement floor and plastic dishes.

The *Main Dining Room* at the Lodge at Koele (tel 565-7300) serves three meals daily. Breakfast (from 7 to 10 am) includes eggs, waffles, hot cakes and pastries, mostly in the $5 to $9 range. The lunch menu (from 11 am to 2 pm) has a few fish and meat dishes, salads, and sandwiches, including cheeseburgers with fries for $10. Dinner (served until 10 pm) includes fish and steak, as well as Lanai specialities such as pheasant and grilled venison. Main dishes at dinner time range from about $28 to $34.

SHIPWRECK BEACH & KEOMUKU

The highway that runs 8½ miles from town to the north-east coast – Hwy 44 – is narrow and well paved. To get to the highway, head north on Lanai Ave and bear right on Keomuku Rd (Hwy 44).

The road heads into hills of cattle country and pastures. The uplands here are often cool, with fog and cloud cover drifting in and out.

The new Lodge at Koele is on Hwy 44, a mile above town. A mile past the lodge is a paved road that leads off to the right to the Munro Trail.

The road into the trailhead makes a nice side drive. It's a pretty mountain road lined with Norfolk pines. It's only half a mile down to the end where there's a cemetery with gravestones in Japanese and Filipino. Sake offerings are placed at some of the graves. Pinwheels, bunny rabbits and pink flamingos adorn other sites where children are buried.

Back on Hwy 44, three miles out of town, there's a pull-off to the right with a beautiful view of the neighbouring islands. Straight ahead is the undeveloped south-east shore of Molokai and its tiny islet of Mokuhooniki. The view to the right is of Maui and the Kaanapali highrises.

From the lookout, the road starts down to the coast towards Molokai. There are no pineapples in this direction, just grasses and shrubs and interesting rock formations sticking up out of the eroded red earth. The formations are similar to those at Garden of the Gods. Later a shipwreck comes into view.

The paved road ends near the coast. The dirt road to the left leads to Shipwreck Beach and a former lighthouse. If you continue instead on the main road, it leads down the coast to Keomuku.

Shipwreck Beach

Shipwreck Beach is the name given to nine miles of Lanai's north-east shore. It starts at Kahokunui at the end of Hwy 44 and goes up to Polihua Beach. True to its name, there are a couple of shipwrecks as well as a shore good for beachcombing.

The dirt road that heads left from the highway ends at the site of a former lighthouse on a lava point 1¾ miles in. Only the cement foundations of the lighthouse remain.

When it's dry the road is usually passable by car, though you'll miss the beach walk. An alternative is to hike (or drive) in about half a mile from the end of the paved road, cut down to the beach and walk to the lighthouse from there. You can walk back by the road, which is quicker.

Lots of driftwood washes up on this wind-swept beach. Some of the pieces are identifiable sunbleached timbers from shipwrecks – hulls, side planks, perhaps even a gangplank if your imagination is active. There are also fishing nets, ropes and kukui nuts.

It's likely to be just you and the driftwood, though about 20 minutes up the beach there's a cluster of small wooden beach shacks called Federation Camp, sometimes used by Filipino fishermen. The lighthouse is 10 minutes farther.

The beach sand is a bit soft and sinks underfoot, making this a good walk for your calves. The sand gradually changes colours as you walk along. In some places it's a colourful, chunky mixture of rounded shells and bits of rock that look like a sort of beach confetti.

A low rock shelf lines much of the shore. It's shallow, murky water and not good for swimming or snorkelling.

Up on the slopes some of the beach morning glory (pohuehue) is entwined with an airplant that looks something like yellow-orange fishing line. This is kaunaoa, Lanai's official flower, a leafless parasitic vine.

Petroglyphs From the lighthouse, white-wash markings lead directly inland for about five minutes to some small petroglyphs. The simple figures are etched on large boulders on the right side of the path, down the slope past the 'Do Not Deface' sign.

The rocky path is through ground cover of

flowering golden ilima and pink and yellow lantana. The former is native, while the latter was introduced to Hawaii just 30 years ago and has escaped from cultivation to become a major pest throughout the islands.

Keep your eyes open for animals. Up on the hill across the way we saw mouflon sheep – one male with curled-back horns and a harem of light brown females.

Up the Beach It's about 15 minutes farther up the beach to a rusting WW II Liberty ship that has washed up on the reef. You can see the shipwreck clearly from the lighthouse.

This is the point where most people turn around and head back but it's possible to walk another six miles down to Awalua, which long ago was the location of a north shore landing. There's another shipwreck at Awalua but not much else. The beach is generally windy and it's a hot dry hike, though the farther down the beach you go, the prettier it gets.

Keomuku Beach
Keomuku Beach is the stretch of shore from Kahokunui, at the end of Hwy 44, south to Halepalaoa Landing where Club Lanai has set up shop.

The dirt road is likely to be either dusty or muddy, with deep ruts. This is 4WD material. The coast is not particularly attractive and there's not much to see though there are several historical sites. Maui is visible across the Auau Channel. There are scattered groves of coconuts along the way and lots and lots of kiawe.

Real diehards can go the full 12 miles down to Naha, at the end of the road. It may take as long as two hours one way, depending on road conditions.

Less than a mile down the road is Maunalei. An ancient heiau that once sat there was taken apart and its stones used to build a cattle fence by Frederick Hayselden, who later lost his shirt in the ill-fated Maunalei Sugar Company. Islanders believed the temple desecration was what caused the wells to turn salty and kill off the sugar cane he had planted.

Keomuku, 5¾ miles down, was the centre of the short-lived sugar cane plantation. There's little left to see other than the old abandoned Ka Lanakila O Ka Malamalama Church, built in 1903 after Maunalei Sugar collapsed. The ruins of a couple of fishponds are along the coast, but not easily visible.

Another heiau at Kahea, 1½ miles south of Keomuku, was also dismantled by Maunalei Sugar Co, this time to build a railroad to transport the sugar to Halepalaoa Landing. Kahea, meaning 'red stains', was a luakini heiau where human sacrifices were made.

Club Lanai Halepalaoa Landing, just south of Kahea, is now Club Lanai. This is one of the few places on Lanai not owned by Castle & Cooke. It's the destination of a tour boat that leaves from Maui for day outings. They've set up their own private getaway with kayaks, snorkelling, bicycles, hammocks and a little bar.

If you're not expecting it, Club Lanai suddenly appears like a totally incongruous mirage! Halepalaoa is on a long white sand beach, the best on this end of the island.

MANELE BAY & HULOPOE BAY
Lanai's best beach, Hulopoe, is reached by a 20-minute drive down Manele Rd, a good paved road that starts just south of town. The beach is 7½ miles south of the intersection of Manele Rd and Kaumalapau Highway.

Rows of pineapples line both sides of the road most of the way down. Pheasants, quails and other colourful game birds hang out in this southern half of the island, where hunting's prohibited.

About 1½ miles down Manele Rd, a very wide dirt road comes in diagonally to the left. This is Hoike Rd, which leads to the Munro Trail and the Luahiwa Petroglyphs.

After four miles Manele Rd veers to the left and a mile farther there's a small pull-off with a pretty coastal view of both Manele Bay to the left and Hulopoe Bay to the right. The island beyond is Kahoolawe.

Manele Boat Harbor
Manele Harbor is a scenic, crescent-shaped

natural harbour backed by sheer cliffs. Lanai folks like to fish from the stone breakwater that sticks out into the mouth of the bay.

Manele is a very protected harbour and a popular sailboat anchorage. Lanai is one of the easier islands to sail to from Honolulu (though 'easy' is a relative term and the water can be rough).

In the early 20th century, cattle were herded down to Manele Bay for shipment to Honolulu. The remains of a cattle chute used to load them directly onto the ships can be seen by walking around the point to the right at the end of the parking lot.

Stone ruins from a Hawaiian fishing village and concrete slabs from the days of cattle ranching are up on the hill above the parking lot. The ruins are largely overgrown with kiawe and ilima.

There are restrooms and drinking water here.

Hulopoe Beach

Hulopoe Beach is a gently curving white sand beach. It's long and broad and protected by a rocky point to the left. On the right side of the bay there's a low terraced area topped by the new Manele Bay Hotel.

Lanai's best snorkelling is found on the left side of the bay, where there are lots of colourful coral and reef fish.

Also on that side, just beyond the sandy beach, there's a low lava shelf with tidepools worth exploring. One area has been blasted out, making a protected pool for children. Cement steps lead down to the pool from the rocks. It looks like every kid on Lanai rushed down to scrawl their name in the cement when it was poured in August 1951.

Hulopoe Beach has showers, restrooms, drinking water and camping sites. There are game birds and deer in the kiawe woods above the beach, though with the activity from the hotel they're likely to move farther back into the woods.

Both Manele and Hulopoe bays are part of a marine-life conservation district in which the removal of coral and rocks is prohibited and many fishing activities are restricted.

Puu Pehe Cove

There's a short path to the rocky point that juts out beyond Hulopoe Beach. The lava forming the point has rich rust-red colours with swirls of grey and black in fascinating patterns. The texture is bubbly and brittle – so brittle that huge chunks of the point have broken off and fallen onto the coastal shelf below. There's a small sea arch below the point.

Puu Pehe is the name of the cove to the left of the point as well as the islet. The islet, also called Sweetheart's Rock, has a tomb-like formation on top.

Legend says an island girl, Puupehe, was so beautiful that her lover decided that they should make their home in a secluded coastal cave, lest any other young men in the village set eyes on her. One day the lover was up in the mountains fetching water when a kona storm suddenly blew in. He rushed down the mountain but by the time he arrived the waves had swept into the cave, drowning Puupehe.

The islanders brought a tapa cloth and prepared to bury the girl in the village. But Puupehe's lover slipped off with her body at night and carried it out to the rock where he built her a tomb. When he was finished, he jumped into the surging waters below and was dashed back onto the rock. The islanders recovered his body, wrapped it in the tapa they had prepared for Puupehe and buried him in the village.

Places to Stay

Until the hotel loomed on the horizon, camping was allowed in three camping sites right on Hulopoe Beach. The expectation of hundreds of tourists using that same beach may not bode well for campers.

If the Koele Company (Box L, Lanai City, HI 96763; tel 565-6661) is still issuing permits, here's how it goes. There's a $5 registration fee per camping site plus $5 per person per night. The maximum length of stay is seven days. Fees must be paid within five days of confirmation of the reservation.

Sometimes you can get permits without notice if the camping ground's not full. The Koele Company is in the Castle & Cooke offices opposite the post office.

Campfires and stoves are permitted and water is available.

For information on the *Manele Bay Hotel* contact Rockresorts (30 Rockefeller Plaza, New York, NY 10112; tel 212-765-5950 or 800-223-7637). The tentative opening date is summer 1991.

KAUNOLU

Kaunolu was the site of an early Hawaiian fishing village abandoned in the mid-1800s. It has the greatest concentration of ruins on Lanai.

It was a vacation spot for Kamehameha the Great, who went there to fish the prolific waters of Kaunolu Bay. He also held tournaments and sporting events there. His house site was up on the bluff on the eastern side of the bay.

Kaunolu Gulch separates the two sides of the bay. Most of the house sites sit on the eastern side. Halulu Heiau, on the western side, dominates the whole scene. Beyond the ruins the Palikaholo sea cliffs rise more than 1000 feet.

The heiau included a puuhonua, a place of refuge where kapu breakers could find absolution and escape the punishment of death. There are a number of petroglyph sites around, some on the southern side of the heiau.

North-west of the heiau there's a high natural stone wall along the perimeter of the cliff. Look for a break in the wall at the cliff's edge where there's a sheer 90-foot drop. This is Kahekili's Jump, named after a Lanaian chief. There's a ledge below it that makes diving a bit death-defying. Apparently Kamehameha used to amuse himself by making upstart warriors jump from the cliff.

Dr Kenneth Emory of the Bishop Museum did an extensive survey of Kaunolu in 1921 and counted 86 house sites, 35 stone shelters and a number of grave markings, pens and gardens. These days many of the sites are overgrown with kiawe.

To get there, drive parallel to the airport runway until you come to the edge of the pineapple fields and then turn left so that bushes are on your right and pineapples are on your left. Drive until you see the Kaunolu marker. From there, look down and you'll see a white lighthouse. That's the road down to Kaunolu.

None of these roads are paved. Travel time depends on road conditions, but it usually takes about 45 minutes from town.

KAUMALAPAU HARBOR

Kaumalapau, Lanai's commercial harbour, is about seven miles west of town. Once past the airport, the main traffic on Kaumalapau Highway is from the big trucks that haul pineapples down to the harbour, where the containers are loaded onto barges and shipped to the Dole cannery in Honolulu. It's fairly interesting to watch, though the harbour is not set up for visitors.

Local fishing boats also moor there. You'll sometimes find people fishing from the pier for awa (milkfish), a good-eating fish and a common catch in the bay.

The deep waters at Kaumalapau are extremely clear, and scuba divers use the bay as well.

As along most of the south-west coast, Kaumalapau has sheer coastal cliffs.

NORTH-WEST LANAI

Polihua Rd (Awalua Highway) is a dirt road that leads from Lanai City to Garden of the Gods and beyond to Polihua Beach. The section of the road leading up to Garden of the Gods is a fairly well-maintained pineapple road. From town, it usually takes about 20 minutes.

To get from Garden of the Gods to Polihua Beach is another matter. If it's been graded recently it can take 20 minutes. If it's the middle of the rainy season it might take an hour. The turn-off to Polihua Beach is marked.

Kanepuu

The Nature Conservancy is taking over management of 462 acres at Kanepuu, a diverse native dryland forest that is the last of its kind.

Native plants include iliahi (Hawaiian sandalwood), olopua (an olive), lama (in the persimmon family), a morning glory, a native gardenia and fragrant vines of maile and huehue.

Top: Pineapple field, Lanai
Bottom: Shipwreck Beach, Lanai

Top: Hanalei Bay, Kauai
Left: Kalokoeli Fishpond, Molokai
Right: Makahiki Festival, Kaunakakai, Molokai

Dryland forests were once common on the leeward slopes of other Hawaiian islands, but feral goats and cattle did them in. Only this one remains. Credit goes to the naturalist and former ranch manager George Munro, who realised the need to protect this ecosystem and fenced hoofed animals out in the 1920s.

The Kanepuu Preserve is about six miles north-west of Lanai City. Castle & Cooke retains title to the land, but has given the Nature Conservancy an easement to the forest in perpetuity.

Garden of the Gods

There's no garden at Garden of the Gods but rather a dry and barren landscape of strange wind-sculptured rocks in rich shades of ochre, pinks and browns. The colours change with the light and are much nicer and gentler in the early morning and late afternoon.

How godly they appear depends on what you're looking for. Some people just see rocks, others find the formations hauntingly beautiful.

Polihua Beach

Polihua Beach, on the north-western tip of the island, is a broad, 1½-mile-long white sand beach. It has a great view of the entire south coast of Molokai. Though it's a gorgeous beach, strong winds kicking up the sand often make it uncomfortable. Water conditions are treacherous all year round.

Polihua means 'eggs in the bosom' and refers to the green sea turtles that used to nest there en masse. Now endangered, the turtles no longer lay their eggs on Polihua.

MUNRO TRAIL

Munro Trail is an 8½-mile jeep road that can either be hiked or driven in a 4WD vehicle. Driving it takes about one to 1½ hours. On foot, it's a full day's hike. If you're driving, watch out for sheer drops. The road can be dangerous when wet.

To start, head north on Hwy 44, the road to Shipwreck Beach. About a mile past the Lodge at Koele turn right onto the paved road that leads to a cemetery half a mile down.

Munro Trail starts at the left of the ceme-

tery. It goes through sections planted with eucalyptus and up along the ridge where it's fern-draped and studded with Norfolk pines.

The trail is named after the naturalist George Munro, who planted the trees along this trail and around the island to provide a watershed. He selected species that draw moisture from the clouds and fog, both of which are fairly common in the high country (more so in the afternoon than in the morning).

Before the Munro Trail was upgraded to a jeep road it was a footpath. It's along this trail that islanders tried to hide from Kamehameha when he went on a rampage in 1778. Hookio Battleground, where Lanaians made their last stand, is just above Hookio Gulch, about 2½ miles in.

The trail passes a series of deep ravines that run down the eastern flank of the mountain. To the west are the endless pineapple fields, in tidy ribbon-like rows.

The trail passes Lanaihale – at 3370 feet, the highest point on Lanai. On a clear day you can see all the inhabited Hawaiian islands except Kauai and Niihau from various points along the trail. The trail ends in a pineapple field on Hoike Rd.

Hoike Rd is a little more than 1½ miles south of the intersection of Manele Rd and Kaumalapau Highway. Though it's not marked, it's obviously one of the big daddies of the pineapple roads.

Luahiwa Petroglyphs

The Luahiwa Petroglyphs are carved onto about two dozen boulders spread over three acres. This is Lanai's highest concentration of petroglyphs and includes a wide variety of forms thought to have been carved during different eras. There are lots of dogs in various poses, linear and triangular human figures and a canoe or two. Unfortunately many of the petroglyphs are quite weathered.

It's a little challenging to get there, but basically you turn onto Hoike Rd and then head for the water tower on the ridge. The boulders are near the head of a ravine north of the road, below the trees.

Kahoolawe

Kahoolawe, the uninhabited island seven miles off the south-west coast of Maui, is used by the US military as a bombing target.

The channel between Lanai and Kahoolawe, as well as the westernmost point of Kahoolawe itself, is named Kealaikahiki, meaning 'pathway to Tahiti'. When ancient voyagers made the journey between Hawaii and Tahiti they lined up their canoes at this departure point.

Hundreds of ancient sites have been identified on Kahoolawe. They include several heiaus and many koa shrines and kuula stones dedicated to the gods of fishermen. Puu Moiwi, in the centre of the island, has one of Hawaii's largest ancient adze quarries.

In 1981 Kahoolawe was added to the National Register of Historic Places as an archaeological area. The island has the distinction of being the only such historic area being bombed.

The island has become a symbol of the separation of Hawaiians from their land and a focal point in the growing Hawaiian rights movement. Protect Kahoolawe Ohana is the leading force in the effort to have Kahoolawe returned to the Hawaiian people.

GEOGRAPHY

Kahoolawe is 11 miles by six miles, with a land area of 45 square miles. With the help of a vivid imagination, its shape can be seen as a crouching lion facing eastward.

A ridge runs diagonally across the island. The highest point is Lua Makika at 1477 feet.

Because of the windblown red dust on the island, Kahoolawe often appears to have a pink tinge when viewed from Maui, particularly in the afternoons when the winds pick up. At night it's pitch black, devoid of any light.

HISTORY
Prisoners & Opium

Since ancient times Kahoolawe has been under the rule of Maui.

From 1830 to 1848 Kaulana Bay, on the island's northern side, was used as a place of exile for Mauian men accused of petty crimes. (Women outcasts were sent to Kaena Point on the north-western tip of Lanai.)

Kahoolawe proved to be less of a 'Prison Isle' than intended. In 1841 some of the prisoners managed to swim to the Makena area of Maui where they stole food and canoes and paddled back with their booty. Later raids included one to Lanai where they picked up women prisoners and brought them back to Kahoolawe.

Kahoolawe's secluded south-western side was used for decades by smugglers bringing in illegal Chinese opium. To avoid detection, they'd unload their caches at Hanakanaea Bay (commonly known as Smugglers Bay) on arrival from China and come back later in small fishing boats to pick them up.

Smugglers Bay is today the site of the US military base camp.

Overgrazing

Kahoolawe was once green and forested. It is now largely barren. Pili grass and kiawe trees are the main forces in keeping the dry red soil from blowing away completely.

The first attempt at ranching was in 1858 by R C Wyllie, the same Scotsman who developed a sugar plantation at Princeville on Kauai. Wyllie leased the entire island of Kahoolawe from the Territory of Hawaii, but the sheep he brought over were diseased and the venture failed. Those sheep that survived were left to roam freely, causing serious damage to native plants.

Over the years, the territory granted a series of leases to other ranchers. Cattle were first brought over around 1880 and sheep were also tried again. Land mismanagement was the order of the day.

By the early 1900s, feral goats, pigs and sheep had dug up, rooted out and chewed off so much of the vegetation that Kahoolawe was largely a dust bowl.

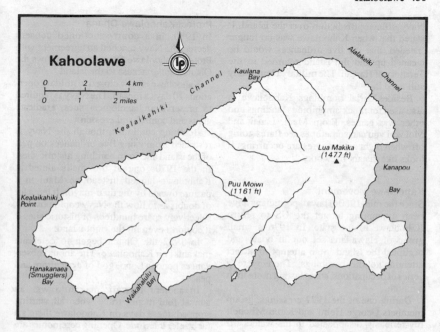

Kahoolawe Ranch

The most successful ranching operation on Kahoolawe was run from 1918 to 1941 by Angus MacPhee, former manager of Maui's Ulupalakua Ranch.

When MacPhee got his lease from the territory in 1918, Kahoolawe was overrun with goats and looked like a wasteland. MacPhee rounded up 13,000 goats which he sold on Maui and built a fence across the width of the entire island to keep the remaining goats at one end. He then brought in large redwood tanks to store water and planted grasses and groundcover.

Once the land was again green, MacPhee created Kahoolawe Ranch Company in partnership with Harry Baldwin, a sugar plantation owner. Cattle were brought over and raised for the Honolulu market. Ranching Kahoolawe was not easy, but MacPhee was the only one to make it profitable.

Inez MacPhee Ashdown, Angus' daughter, has written her story in *Kahoolawe*

(Topgallant Publishing Co, 1979). The book includes legends of Kahoolawe, as told to her by native Hawaiians, as well as ranch history.

A Bombing Target

In 1939, Kahoolawe Ranch subleased part of the island to the US Army for bombing practice and moved their cattle and ranchhands over to Maui.

After the bombing of Pearl Harbor in 1941, the military took all of Kahoolawe and began bombing the entire island. Ranch buildings and water cisterns were reduced to rubble.

Of all the fighting that took place during WW II, Kahoolawe was the most bombed island in the Pacific – even though the 'enemy' never fired upon it.

After the war, civilians were forbidden from returning to Kahoolawe. MacPhee was never compensated for his losses.

In 1953 a presidential decree gave the

Navy official jurisdiction over the island. It stated that when Kahoolawe was no longer 'needed' that the live ordnances would be cleaned up and the island returned to the Territory of Hawaii. The military claims they still need it.

Besides aerial bombings Kahoolawe is also used for mock amphibious landings and other war games. From Maui, Lanai and Molokai you can sometimes see flares going off when night manoeuvres are occurring. It looks like distant fireworks.

Kahoolawe Movement

Since the mid-1960s Hawaii politicians have been attempting to get the US to return Kahoolawe to the state. In 1976 a small group of Hawaiians set out in boats and occupied the island in an attempt to attract attention to the bombings. There were a series of occupations, some lasting more than a month.

During one of the 1977 crossings, group members George Helm and Kimo Mitchell mysteriously disappeared in the waters off Kahoolawe. Helm had been a key inspirational figure and with his death the Hawaiian-rights movement Protect Kahoolawe Ohana sprang up. Helm's vision of turning Kahoolawe into a sanctuary of Hawaiian culture and identity became widespread.

In June 1977 two group members, Walter Ritte Jr and Richard Sawyer, were tried for trespassing on Kahoolawe and sentenced to six months in jail.

In a letter to President Jimmy Carter asking that the two men be pardoned, Daniel Inouye, US Senator from Hawaii, wrote:

...it was a form of protest against, what was to them, the unconscionable desecration of the land by the Navy's continued bombing of Kahoolawe. Aloha aina, love for the land, is an important part of the Native Hawaiian religion and culture...Kahoolawe has become a symbol of the resurgence of the Hawaiian people, a movement formulating for many Hawaiians a renewed respect for their culture and their history.

Protect Kahoolawe Ohana

In 1980, in a court-sanctioned consent decree, the Navy reached an agreement with Protect Kahoolawe Ohana which allows the Ohana regular access to the island.

Kahoolawe is now closed to military operations 10 days a month. The Navy is required to preserve archaeological sites, eradicate goats and control soil erosion.

Bombing continues, though the Navy is restricted from using live ordnances on part of the island and from bombing historic sites. In the 1970s one of the shells aimed at Kahoolawe landed instead on Maui in a pasture owned by the then-mayor. It left a lot of doubts as to how the Navy could possibly selectively spare hundreds of historic sites if it couldn't even hit the right island.

In 1982 the Ohana began to celebrate makahiki on Kahoolawe. The annual observances honour Lono, god of agriculture and peace.

In ancient Hawaii, makahiki was an annual four-month truce when all warring stopped; these days on Kahoolawe there's a far briefer interlude. Opening ceremonies are held during their October visit, and the closing ceremonies in January.

The Ohana has begun construction of traditional houses and hula mounds. They picture Kahoolawe restored to its original condition – minus the goats, cleaned of dangerous live ordnances, reforested with native plants and with the ancient sites restored.

Maui County, of which Kahoolawe is a part, adopted a planning document in 1982 calling for a 20-year phase-out of the military and development of Kahoolawe as an historical and cultural site, with Protect Kahoolawe Ohana as the stewards of the land. The Navy refuses to recognise the document.

Hawaii's first Hawaiian governor, John Waihee, and other state politicans have again petitioned to have Kahoolawe returned to Hawaiians. A recent state proposal called for the building of a floating island which the Navy could use as a replacement target, with the state paying $10 million of the cost. So far the Navy has shrugged it off.

Stopping the Bombing

In what some see as the ultimate insult to Hawaiian heritage, the US military offers Kahoolawe as a bombing target to foreign nations. Since 1971 the Navy has conducted biennial exercises with Pacific Rim nations that include a coordinated bombardment of Kahoolawe.

An international movement against the bombing has had partial success. Protests by peace and/or union groups in New Zealand, Australia, Japan and Britain have resulted in those countries withdrawing from the Kahoolawe exercises. Canada is currently the only country continuing to join the USA in the bombing of the island.

A letter-writing campaign to stop attacks on Kahoolawe is supported by the mayor of Maui and by groups in places as distant as Canada, Vanuatu and Micronesia. For more information contact the South Pacific Peoples Foundation of Canada (409-620 View St, Victoria, BC V8W 1J6, Canada).

GETTING THERE & AWAY

There's no public access to the island. Unless you're a member of the Ohana, or a GI on a mission, it is nearly impossible for you to get to Kahoolawe.

Occasionally on weekends the Navy opens the offshore waters surrounding Kahoolawe for fishing, boating and diving. The announcement is always accompanied by a statement that 'the US government will not be responsible for property damage, personal injury or death resulting from exploding ordnance in those waters'.

Kauai

Kauai is so richly green that it's nicknamed 'The Garden Island'. It's the oldest of the main Hawaiian land masses and arose from the sea as a high, smooth island. Over time heavy rains have eroded deep valleys, while pounding waves and falling sea levels have cut steep cliffs.

Kauai's central volcanic peak, Mt Waialeale, acts like a magnet drawing rain. The water flows down, feeding seven rivers, including Hawaii's only navigable one.

An impressive north-to-south rift slices the western end of the island, creating the Waimea Canyon.

The North Shore is lush and mountainous, with waterfalls, beautiful beaches and stream-fed valleys planted with taro. The north-west coast is lined by the steeply fluted Na Pali sea cliffs.

Movie makers looking for scenery bordering on fantasy have often found it in Kauai. *South Pacific* and *Raiders of the Lost Ark* were both filmed on Kauai's North Shore. Honopu Valley on the Na Pali Coast was the jungle home of King Kong.

Kauai is the least developed of the four major islands and most of its interior is mountainous forest reserve.

The Alakai Swamp is poised on a high, cliff-bound plateau, about 1000 feet below Mt Waialeale. There, clouds and mist that rarely lift promote a unique ecosystem where trees grow knee high.

Kauai is dry and sunny on its southern and western sides, with long stretches of white sand beaches. Sugar cane fields cover large portions of the island just inland from the coast in a semicircle from the north-east to the west.

Kauai's main attraction is its scenery. There are hiking trails into some incredible places.

Orientation

Kauai is roughly circular. A belt road runs three-quarters of the way around the island, ending at Haena in the north and Polihale in the west.

Most travellers arrive at the main airport in Lihue, the county capital, on the east coast. From Lihue the road runs north past the heiaus and waterfalls of Wailua, a mountain shaped like a sleeping giant, and the town of Kapaa. It continues up to the sea-bird sanctuary of Kilauea, Princeville resort and the scenic North Shore communities of Hanalei and Haena. The road ends at the eastern edge of the Na Pali cliffs.

South of Lihue the road detours down to the winter resort beaches of Poipu before continuing west to Waimea. There, one road goes west to the arid Barking Sands region and another heads north along the Waimea Canyon into Kokee State Park.

Facts

HISTORY

Kauai was probably settled between 500 and 700 AD by Polynesians who migrated from the Marquesas Islands. Archaeological finds, including identical ring-shaped poi pounding stones found both in Kauai and the Marquesas support the connection.

While in Hawaiian lore there are no direct references to the Marquesan culture, Kauai is often referred to as the home of a race of little people called menehunes. Legend after legend tells of happy Disneyland-type elves coming down from the mountains to produce great engineering works in stone.

It seems likely that when the first wave of Tahitians arrived in about 1000 AD they conquered and subjugated the Marquesans, forcing them into slavery to build the temples, irrigation ditches and fishponds now attributed to the menehunes.

The Tahitian term for 'outcast' is *manahune*. And the diminutive social status the Marquesans had in the eyes of their

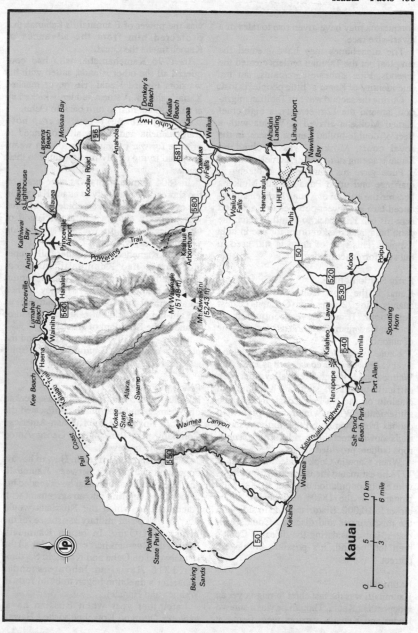

Kauai

conquerors may have given rise to tales of a dwarf-size race.

The menehunes may have created the temples, but the Tahitian settlers created the legends. Fine stonework remains, but the true identity of Kauai's 'little people' is lost.

During the second wave of Tahitian migration, around the 12th century, a high chief named Moikeha arrived at Wailua with a fleet of double-hulled canoes. There, in the royal court, Moikeha was received by Kauai's ageing *alii-nui* (high chief), Puna.

Puna gave his daughter to Moikeha in marriage and upon Puna's death Moikeha became the alii-nui of Kauai. Moikeha introduced taro and sweet potatoes to Kauai and sent his son Kila back to Tahiti to fetch the pahu hula, a sharkskin drum for use in hula temples. This type of drum is still used in hula performances today.

Early Settlements

Kauai is the most isolated of the major islands, lying 72 miles from Oahu, its nearest neighbour. It was never conquered by another Hawaiian island and its history is one of autonomy.

Kauai was settled most intensively along river valleys near the coast, such as at Wailua, Waimea and Hanalei. Even valleys that were difficult to reach, such as Kalalau and Nualolo on the Na Pali Coast, had sizable settlements. When winter seas prevented canoes from landing on the northern shore, trails down precipitous ridges and sennit-rope ladders provided access.

When Captain Cook landed on Kauai in 1778 he estimated the island had 50 villages with a total population of about 30,000. Missionaries in the 1820s estimated it to be closer to 10,000. Historians tend to side with the missionaries and discredit Cook's estimates, but considering the diseases Cook's men left behind, it's possible both were correct.

Kaumualii

Kaumualii was the last chief to reign over an independent Kauai. Though he was a shrewd leader and Kauai's warriors were fierce, it was the power of Kaumualii's kahunas that protected him from the advances of Kamehameha the Great.

In 1796 Kamehameha, who had conquered all the other islands, sailed with his warriors toward Kauai. He never reached Kauai's shores. A storm suddenly kicked up at sea, forcing him to turn back to Oahu.

During the next few years, both Kamehameha and Kaumualii continued to prepare for war by gathering foreign weaponry and trying to ally foreign ships to their cause.

In 1804 Kamehameha was once again on the shores of Oahu ready to attack Kauai. On the eve of the invasion an epidemic of what was probably cholera struck the island of Oahu, decimating his warriors and forcing yet another delay.

While Kamehameha's numerically superior forces had Kaumualii unnerved, Kaumualii's uncanny luck had a similar effect on Kamehameha. In 1810 they reached an agreement that recognised Kaumualii as the alii-nui of Kauai but ceded the island of Kauai to the Kingdom of Hawaii.

It was essentially merely a truce, and the plotting continued. Kaumualii never fully accepted Kamehameha's authority.

Russian Presence

In January 1815 a Russian ship was wrecked off Waimea, and Kaumualii confiscated the cargo. In November, the Russian-American Company sent their agent, Georg Anton Schaeffer, to retrieve it.

When Schaeffer arrived in Hawaii he saw opportunity in the rift between Kaumualii and Kamehameha. In Kauai he exceeded his authority by entering into an agreement with Kaumualii in which the Russians would provide a ship and military assistance for the invasion of Oahu. In return Kaumualii offered the Russians half of Oahu plus all the sandalwood on Oahu and Kauai. In September 1816 Hawaiian labourers under Schaeffer's direction began to build forts in Waimea and Hanalei.

Later that year when Russian naval explorer Otto von Kotzebue visited Hawaii he informed Kamehameha that the Russian government did not endorse Schaeffer's alliance. Kamehameha, tired of all the scheming, ordered Kaumualii to kick the Russians out. In May 1817 Schaeffer was escorted to his ship and forced to leave Kauai.

The End of a Kingdom

When Kamehameha died in 1819 he was succeeded by his son Liholiho, who didn't trust Kaumualii's loyalties any more than his father had. In 1822 Liholiho set off for Kauai in an 83-foot luxury schooner he had purchased in exchange for sandalwood.

In Kauai he tricked Kaumualii into going out for a cruise. He then kidnapped him and took him to Oahu where Kaumualii was forced to marry Kamehameha's widow, Kaahumanu. In the grand scheme of royal design this served to bring Kaumualii into the fold. When Kaumualii passed away in 1824, so too did the kingdom of Kauai.

GEOGRAPHY

Kauai is shaped like a slightly compressed ball. It is 33 miles wide and 25 miles from north to south. The highest elevation is Mt Kawaikini at 5243 feet.

The fourth largest of the islands, Kauai has an area of 558 sq miles.

Kauai arose as a single volcano of which Mt Waialeale is the eastern rim. Moisture-laden trade winds blow into the deep North Shore valleys which channel the winds up to the top of Mt Waialeale. Near its 5148-foot summit cooler temperatures cause the moisture to condense, creating the heaviest rainfall on earth.

CLIMATE

Kauai's temperature varies more with location than season. Average coastal temperatures are 70°F in February and 77°F in August. At Kalalau Beach the temperature seldom drops below 60°F, while a few thousand feet above at Kokee State Park it dips into the 30s during winter nights. Kokee averages a crisp 55°F in February and 65°F in August.

Kauai's average annual rainfall is about 40 inches but variances are extreme. Waimea in the south averages 21 inches while Princeville in the north averages 85 inches. And Mt Waialeale in the swampy interior averages a whopping 486 inches, a world record.

Summer trade winds keep humidity from becoming oppressive and bring in showers.

Winter is far less predictable. It's quite possible to have fairly continuous downpours for a week at a time in midwinter. Then again, it might be all blue skies and calm seas. We've experienced both.

Hurricane Iwa

Hurricane Iwa tore into Kauai on 24 November 1982. It struck with gusts of up to 117 miles per hour, the highest ever recorded in Hawaii. When it was over, Kauai looked like a war zone.

Many of the corrugated metal roofs that had peeled off and flown like Frisbees over the streets, ended their flight wrapped around telephone poles. Snapped power lines and trees littered the roads.

In Poipu the basements of some of the big beachside hotels became instant aquariums, one complete with a shark. Marbled lobbies were piled high with sand. Some places had literally blown away, including a two-storey wing of the Sheraton.

When the storm was over, stranded tourists had to be transported out of Poipu by small boat.

Iwa damaged 50% of the island's homes, about 500 of them beyond repair. Though people were injured by flying debris, quite amazingly no-one on Kauai was killed.

The next day was Thanksgiving, America's traditional 'turkey day'. Without electricity it took on an unusual air, as turkeys were barbecued on backyard hibachis.

It took a few weeks to restore electricity, a few months to finish clearing the roads and a few years to finish rebuilding. Tourism hit a lull. It was a boon for construction workers, but overall the times were hard for Kauai.

FLORA & FAUNA

Kauai has the largest number of native bird species in Hawaii. It is the only major island free of mongoose, which prey upon the eggs of ground-nesting birds.

The greatest concentration of Kauai's native forest bird species is found in the remote Alakai Swamp. Many of those species are endangered, some having fewer than 100 birds remaining.

The Kauai oo, the last of four remaining species of Hawaiian honeyeaters, was thought to be extinct when a nest with two chicks was discovered in Alakai Swamp in 1971. The call of the oo was last heard in 1987.

Alakai Swamp is unique in that it has 10 times as many native birds as introduced. (Elsewhere in Hawaii introduced birds outnumber the natives many times over.) Not only is the swamp inhospitable to exotic bird species, but due to its high elevation it is one of the few places in Hawaii where mosquitoes that transmit avian diseases do not flourish.

The ao, or Newell's shearwater, is an endangered sea bird that once nested on all the major Hawaiian islands; today its only known nests are in the mountains of Kauai. The ao digs an earthen burrow and lays just one egg each year. It has a call that sounds like a donkey braying.

The ao is attracted to bright urban lights and often flies into buildings and utility wires, falling stunned onto highways. Through a successful forestry programme, more than 90% of the 1500 ao that crash-land each year are recovered by islanders and released.

GOVERNMENT

Kauai County is composed of the islands of Kauai and Niihau.

In the last county mayoral election, a string of good ol' boys were finally ousted by JoAnn Yukimura, who had been running for the office for years on a pro-environment, controlled-growth policy.

ECONOMY

Kauai's 1988 unemployment rate was 3.8%; the registered labour force was 25,650. The service industry, including hotels, accounted for about 25% of all workers. It was followed by retail trade at 21%, government at 12%, then agriculture, manufacturing and real estate.

The sugar industry still cultivates 43,000 acres on Kauai, but mechanisation has streamlined its labour force to 1000 employees.

Development

Kauai, the least developed of the four major islands, is in the midst of a building boom. During the past couple of years the island has seen a 25% increase in the number of hotel rooms. To keep them full, hoteliers now want the airport runway lengthened to accommodate direct flights from Japan.

On the other side, a strong voice is being raised against runaway growth by islanders determined to prevent Kauai from becoming 'another Maui'. A lot of Kauaians are weary of off-island developers dictating the island's future. With unemployment rates negligible and traffic jams on the rise, it's hard to sell the benefits of boom to the islanders.

PEOPLE

According to the state's latest statistics, the population of Kauai is about 47,600. People of Filipino ethnicity make up 23% of Kauai's population. They are followed by Japanese (22%), part-Hawaiian (22%) and Caucasian (19%).

TOURIST INFORMATION

The Hawaii Visitors Bureau (3016 Umi St, Lihue, HI 96766; tel 245-3971; 800-AH-KAUAI) is open from 8 am to 4.30 pm Monday to Friday.

The county and state government offices are in Lihue.

GENERAL INFORMATION
Official Kauai

Kauai's flower is the mokihana, from a small tree of the citrus family found only on Kauai.

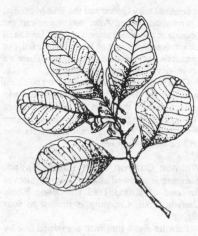

Mokihana

Tiny anise-scented mokihana berries are commonly combined with twists of fragrant maile leaves as a ceremonial lei. Kauai's colour is purple.

Media

Kauai's main newspaper, the *Garden Island* (Box 231, Lihue, HI 96766; tel 245-3681), is published daily except Tuesdays and Saturdays. *Kauai Times* (3133B Oihana St, Lihue, HI 96766; tel 245-8825) is a weekly paper.

Free tourist magazines such as *This Week Kauai*, *Spotlight Kauai* and *Kauai Beach Press* are loaded with ads and discount coupons for everything from cheeseburgers to helicopter tours. You can find them at the airport and at hotels.

Libraries

There are public libraries in Lihue, Hanapepe, Kapaa, Koloa and Waimea.

Weather

The National Weather Service has recorded local weather information (tel 245-6001) and marine forecasts (tel 245-3564). KAUAI radio (720 AM) has beach and surf reports and at 7.35 and 8.25 am reports weather conditions at Kokee State Park. To find out where the surf's up, dial 335-3611.

Emergency

Dial 911 for police, ambulance and fire department.

The main hospital is Wilcox Memorial Hospital (3420 Kuhio Highway, Lihue; tel 245-1100). Kauai Veterans Memorial Hospital (4643 Waimea Canyon Drive, Waimea; tel 338-9431) is smaller but does have a hyperbaric chamber for divers who get the bends. Both hospitals have 24-hour emergency room services.

The local help-line (tel 245-3411) provides crisis intervention, counselling and referrals.

ACCOMMODATION

Local regulations limiting hotel heights to that of a coconut tree have saved Kauai's hotels from themselves. Hotels tend to be smaller and more appealing there than on the other islands. The rates given are the same for singles and doubles, unless noted otherwise.

Three areas – Poipu, Princeville, and Lihue to Kapaa – have almost all the hotels and condos. Of these, Poipu is the most difficult area in which to find a moderately priced place to stay.

For the most part, the beach hotels are expensive. Condos tend to be a better deal, particularly if you're travelling in a group.

Other than camping grounds, the cheapest places are the dormitories at the YMCA in Haena at $10 per person and the cabinettes at Kahili Mountain Park at $20 for up to four people. Lihue has some local in-town hotels beginning at $18 but don't expect much.

Overall, B&Bs are the best deals. Although there aren't that many on the island, more are beginning to spring up. Wailua has the most, with prices averaging about $40/50 a single/double.

Rooms in private homes, particularly in the Princeville area, are sometimes advertised in the classifieds or posted on bulletin boards. They're typically about $40 a day.

Camping

Kauai has some fine camping spots. Camping is allowed at three state parks (Kokee, Na Pali Coast and Polihale), seven county parks (Haena, Hanalei, Anini, Hanamaulu, Niumalu, Salt Pond and Lucy Wright) and at forest reserve trailside camps in Waimea Canyon.

Some are drive-up beach parks, some are in dense forest and others are at the end of day-long hikes into remote valleys. For more details, see the appropriate beach or park listing.

State Parks Camping at state parks requires a permit. They are issued free from 8 am to 4 pm Monday to Friday in the State Office Building, Room 306 (tel 245-4444), 3060 Eiwa St, Lihue, and at state park offices on other islands.

Up to 10 people may be listed on each permit, but the person applying for the permit must show an ID for each person. Permits may be obtained by mail (Box 1671, Lihue, HI 96766) if a photocopy of each camper's ID is sent. Without copies of IDs only the reservation will be issued by mail and you'll need to pick up the permit in person upon arrival. Permits need to be applied for seven days in advance.

Camping is allowed for five nights at each state park. The Milolii Valley section of Na Pali Coast State Park is accessible only by boat and has a three-day limit.

County Beach Parks As for the county parks, Haena, Anini and Salt Pond are all on nice beaches and are good choices. Niumalu, near the commercial harbour, isn't really a tourist area and isn't recommended for camping.

All have showers and restrooms, and most have covered picnic pavilions and barbecue grills, though there's a typically Hawaiian free style to them. Don't expect to find numbered sites or caretakers.

Permits cost $3 per person per day and are issued from 7.45 am to 4.30 pm at the Parks & Recreation Department (tel 245-8821), 4193 Hardy St, Lihue, HI 96766. The office is behind Dairy Queen and the War Memorial Convention Center. After hours, you can get permits at the police station at 3060 Umi St in Lihue. Reservations can be made by mail, but permits must be picked up in person. There's a seven-day limit at each camping site.

Campers without permits may set up camp and wait for the ranger to come around and collect, but in that case it's $5 per person. Also, if the ranger decides the camping area is too full, it's campers without permits who will be asked to move.

Waimea Canyon In Waimea Canyon, camping is allowed at four camping sites at the end of Kukui Trail and along Koaie Canyon Trail. Camping is limited to four nights.

Permits and a trail map are issued free by mail or in person from the Division of Forestry (Box 1671, Lihue, HI 96766; tel 245-4433), in the same office as the state parks.

Cabins Cabins run by a private concessionaire are available in Kokee State Park; in Kahili Mountain Park, north of Koloa; and at the YMCA camp in Haena. See the relevant sections for more information.

Camping Supplies Hanalei Camping & Backpacking (Ching Young Village, Hanalei; tel 826-6664) and Kekaha Camping & Backpacking (Kekaha Rd, Kekaha; tel 337-9331) are sister stores open daily. They rent three-person dome tents for $12 the first night and $8 for each additional night. Backpacks are $3 to $6 per day. They also rent camping stoves, child carriers, sleeping pads and poncho liner blankets. They sell the same supplies they rent and have a wide selection of books, maps, snorkelling gear, freeze-dried foods and backpacking items.

Outfitters Kauai (Kiahuna Shopping Village, Box 1149, Poipu, HI 96756; tel 742-9667) rents tents for $10 a day, backpacks for $8 and stoves and cooking sets for $3. Weekly rates are charged as five days. It also sells topographical maps for Kauai, and other camping and hiking supplies.

ENTERTAINMENT
Luaus
At all luaus you can expect standard Hawaiian dishes – kalua pig, lomi salmon and poi – as well as some Western dishes and probably an open bar or at least watered down mai tais.

The luau at Tahiti Nui (tel 826-6277) is Hanalei's version of what a luau should be – funky, down-to-earth and personal. The show is presided over by Aunty Louise, who always lets out a few tunes in her native Tahitian as well as French and Hawaiian. It's essentially a family affair, with cousins, uncles and daughter-in-law Haunani, a former Miss Hawaii, joining in. The whole thing has the feel of a neighbourhood party. The food's OK, but the high point is the aloha. The luau is held at 6.30 pm on Wednesdays and Fridays and costs $30.

The Sheraton Coconut Beach Hotel (tel 822-3455) has the island's most popular luau. They do the real imu-oven pig, and post the time when the porker is filled with hot rocks and covered with ti leaves. If you're around at 11 am or so, you can take a look, but don't expect a great photo opportunity. The show is accompanied by electric guitar and begins around 9 pm. You can glimpse it from the Sheraton parking lot. There's an open bar from 7 pm and dinner begins at 7.30 pm. It costs $40.

Aston Kauai Resort in Lihue, the Stouffer Waiohai in Poipu and Smith's Tropical Paradise at Wailua Marina also have luaus in the same price range.

ACTIVITIES
Swimming
There are respectable beaches all around Kauai. For most water activities except surfing, the northern shore area is tops in summer, the southern shore in winter.

Hanalei Bay has calm swimming in summer, and Poipu, on the south shore, has a string of beautiful white sand beaches.

To the west, Salt Pond Beach is a family beach with protected swimming. Farther west, Kekaha, Barking Sands and Polihale have expansive white sand beaches, though with open ocean and often treacherous water conditions.

The beaches around Lihue and Kapaa are not great. The biggest draw is Lydgate Beach in Wailua, a large family park with a retaining wall creating a protected year-round swimming pool.

Donkey's, north of Kapaa, is a fine secluded beach hidden beyond a sugar cane field. It and the more spectacular Secret Beach in Kilauea are unofficial nudist beaches.

Surfing
Generally the best surfing is on the north coast in winter, the south in summer and the east during transitional swells.

Hanalei Bay is a very good spot for North Shore surfing, as well as boogie boarding and bodysurfing. Tunnels and Cannons are two other popular North Shore surf spots.

The area around the Sheraton at Poipu Beach is a top summer surf spot. Brennecke's is popular for boogie boarding and bodysurfing.

Pakalas and Major's Bay are two West Side favourites. Pakalas can be good in both summer and winter.

When the breaks are on the east coast, Kealia and the Coco Palms area can be good.

Aquatics Kauai in Kapaa rents surfboards for $11 per 24 hours and Brennecke's in Poipu rents them for $15 a day. In Hanalei, Sand People rents boards for $12.

Windsurfing
Beginners at windsurfing usually start off at Anini Beach on the North Shore or Nawiliwili Bay near the Westin. Tunnels Beach in Haena and Salt Pond Beach in Hanapepe are for the more advanced.

Hanalei Sailboards (Hanalei Trader Building, Hwy 560, Box 496, Hanalei, HI 96714; tel 826-9732) offers three-hour beginner classes daily at Anini Beach for $55, including equipment. After two classes you can be certified. Standard boards and rigs cost $38 a day, $175 a week.

Sailboards Kauai (3470 Paena Loop, Lihue, HI 96766; tel 245-5955), near the

Westin Kauai, has windsurfing lessons, rentals and sales.

Diving

Popular summer diving spots on the North Shore include Kee Beach, Tunnels and Cannons, all shore dives in Haena. Cannons is a wall dive near the shore. It has crevices and lava tubes sheltering all sorts of marine life.

Koloa Landing and Poipu Beach Park in Poipu are easy beach dives. On those rare days when kona winds blow from the south, east-side diving is good and Ahukini Landing becomes a favoured site. There are a number of offshore boat dives as well.

Dive shops sometimes give a free scuba lesson in hotel pools at the Sheratons in Poipu and Coconut Plantation, and at Kiahuna Plantation Resort in Poipu, amongst others.

This is just a partial listing of Kauai dive shops. Most shops charge about $75 for introductory dives, $90 for two-tank boat dives and $350 for certificate courses. Sea Sage has been around the longest – since 1973.

Sea Sage Dive Center, Kapaa Trade Center, 4-1378 Kuhio Highway, Kapaa, HI 96746 (tel 822-3841)
Fathom Five Divers, Box 907, Koloa, HI 96756 (tel 742-6991)
Aquatics Kauai, 733 Kuhio Highway, Kapaa, HI 96746 (tel 822-9213; 800-822-9422)
Brennecke Ocean Sports, 2100 Hoone Rd, Box 638, Poipu, HI 96756 (tel 742-6570)
Ocean Odyssey, Box 807, Kapaa, HI 96746 (tel 822-9680)

Snorkelling & Boogie Boarding

On the North Shore, Tunnels Beach and Hanalei Bay have good summer snorkelling, while Kee Beach is fine most of the year.

Poipu Beach Park on the south shore is protected year round and is one of Kauai's best snorkelling spots for novices.

Snorkel sets and boogie boards can be rented at lots of places, including at most resort beaches.

Sand People in Hanalei rents snorkel sets or boogie boards for $7 per day. Sea Sage in Kapaa rents snorkel sets for $8 a day, boogie boards for $6. Aquatics Kauai in Kapaa is just a bit more expensive. Most places right on the beach tend to charge about $15 a day.

Kayaking

Kayak Kauai (Hwy 560, Hanalei; tel 826-9844) rents two-person kayaks for $35 to $48. Two popular trips are up the Hanalei River through the wildlife refuge and up the Wailua River to the Fern Grotto. Each takes three to four hours. You pay when you pick up the kayak, but there's no need for credit cards or deposits and they even take personal cheques. They also lead guided kayaking trips along the Na Pali Coast for $85. The shop is open from 8 am to 5.30 pm daily.

Outfitters Kauai (Kiahuna Shopping Village, Box 1149, Poipu, HI 96756; tel 742-9667) rents two-person river kayaks for $45. It has half-day guided ocean kayaking trips to Lawai Kai, including snorkelling or paddle surfing, for $44. Guided trips along the Na Pali Coast are $95 for one day, $260 for two days and $390 for three days. The longer trips include camping in Kalalau and Milolii valleys.

Pedal & Paddle (Ching Young Village, Hanalei; tel 826-9069) rents kayaks for $45 to $55.

Hiking

Kauai has some excellent hikes. The best known is the 11-mile Kalalau Trail along the rugged Na Pali Coast.

Kokee State Park is a hiker's paradise with the largest concentration of trails on Kauai. Some lead to spectacular views of the Na Pali Coast. Others include short nature walks, mountain stream trails and a muddy trek through the unique Alakai Swamp.

South of Kokee, trails lead deep into Waimea Canyon, forking into abandoned river valleys.

In the Kapaa-Wailua area there's a trail that goes across the chest of the Sleeping Giant mountain. A couple of ridge trails start at Keahua Arboretum in Wailua, including the Powerline Trail, which goes all the way to Princeville.

Hanalei Valley has a hot and dry ridge trail and a cool and muddy river trail.

These hikes are all detailed in their respective sections.

The Kauai division of the Sierra Club (Box 3412, Lihue, HI 96766) offers guided hikes for $2.

Horse Riding

CJM Country Stables (tel 245-6666) has one-hour rides with mountain and ocean views for $25, a two-hour afternoon ride along the beach for $44 and a three-hour morning ride to secluded Mahaulepu Beach for $55. The stables are in Poipu, 1¾ miles down the dirt road past the new Hyatt. They're closed on Sundays.

Pooku Stables (tel 826-6777), just past Princeville Airport, has trail rides on Princeville Ranch lands. The cost is $23 for one hour, $44 for two hours and $70 for a three-hour picnic ride to a waterfall. They're closed on Sundays.

Tennis

County courts are free and open to the public in these places: near the convention centre in Lihue; Wailua Park, Wailua; Kapaa New Park, Kapaa; near the fire station, Koloa; Waimea High School, Waimea; on the corner of Hwy 550 and Hwy 50, Kekaha; Kalawai Park, Kalaheo; and near Hanapepe Stadium, Hanapepe.

Guests are charged $6 a day for hard-surface courts and $8 for clay courts at Coco Palms Resort in Wailua, $6 a day at Stouffer's Poipu Beach and Waiohai hotels in Poipu, and $4 an hour at Sheraton Coconut Beach Hotel in Kapaa. Non-guests are charged $4 more at Coconut Beach, $2 more at the others.

Courts cost $5 a day at Hanalei Bay Resort in Princeville and $9 per person per hour at Kiahuna Tennis Club (tel 742-9533) in Poipu for non-guests. Both are free to guests.

All players are charged $3 a day at Kauai Hilton in Lihue and $5 an hour at Princeville Tennis Garden (tel 826-9823). All places that charge fees have pro shops and rentals and most offer lighting and lessons.

Golf

Kauai has one municipal, one private and five resort golf courses.

Princeville resort has two courses, the nine-hole par 36 Prince and the 27-hole par 36 Makai. The LPGA Women's Kemper Open is held there each February. Green fees are $68.

Kiahuna Golf Club (tel 742-9595) is an 18-hole par 70 course at $50. Westin Kauai has two 18-hole par 72 courses at $100 and $125.

Wailua Municipal Golf Course (tel 245-8092) is a county-owned 18-hole par 72 course. It's a highly rated public course and very heavily played. Reservations for two people or more are taken up to a week in advance. Green fees are $10 on weekdays and $11 on weekends.

Kukuiolono Golf Course (tel 332-9151) in Kalaheo is a nine-hole par 36 private course on an old estate with a grand hilltop view and a more earthy appeal. Green fees are just $5.

THINGS TO BUY

Island pottery, paintings and Niihau shell leis are sold at the collection of galleries in Kilohana in Puhi and at shops at Ching Young Village in Hanalei.

Kenichi Tasaka, a Hanalei resident in his 90s, makes handwoven sandals using bulrushes he gathers from Hanalei Marsh. They would make a unique gift. They're sold at Stones Gallery in Kukui Grove Shopping Center in Lihue, or you could try the handicraft shops at Ching Young Village.

GETTING THERE & AWAY

Air

Kauai's main airport is in Lihue. Both Aloha Airlines and Hawaiian Airlines serve Lihue from Honolulu, Hilo and Kona on the Big Island, and Kahului on Maui.

The most frequent service is from Honolulu, with each airline flying about once an hour between 6 am and 8 pm. One-way fares are $50.

Aloha IslandAir flies to Princeville Airport on Kauai's North Shore from Honolulu,

Molokai, Lanai, Kamuela on the Big Island and from the Maui airports of Kapalua/Kaanapali,KahuluiandHana.Most fares are $50.

United Airlines has flights to Lihue from Seattle, Los Angeles and San Francisco.

Lihue Airport Until 1987, inter-island flights touched down in a Lihue sugar cane field. Now there's a big modern terminal, an airstrip that can handle direct flights from the US mainland and agricultural inspection for passengers leaving the state. There are car rental booths in front and an information booth inside.

Princeville Airport This little airport on the North Shore is serviced by Aloha IslandAir and Avis and Hertz car rentals, and has a cafe/lounge.

GETTING AROUND
Kauai has no public transport. Renting a car is almost essential for exploring the island in depth.

Surprisingly, Kauai has rush hour traffic jams, especially between Lihue and Kapaa. It can be an inconvenience but it's not unbearable.

Shuttle Bus
Shoppe Hoppers (tel 332-7272) provides a shuttle van service between Kapaa, Lihue, Koloa and Poipu. Scheduled stops are made at the Sheraton Coconut Beach, Coco Palms, Kauai Hilton, Sheraton Kauai and Stouffer Waiohai hotels, with on-call service available at points in between.

If it's letting someone off or has a request for a pick-up, it stops at the airport every 90 minutes between 9.30 am and 3.30 pm from both directions. The service operates Monday to Saturday.

One-way rates from Kapaa are $1 to Wailua, $5 to Lihue and $9 to Poipu. From Poipu it costs $1.50 to Koloa and $6 to the airport. Children under 13 are half-price. Reservations are recommended. Trans Hawaiian (tel 245-5108) also provides an airport shuttle to Wailua and Poipu four or five times a day for similar prices.

Taxi
Taxis average about $1.80 per mile. The fare from Lihue Airport to Coco Palms Resort in Wailua is about $10.40.

Car
Car Rental Budget (tel 245-4021); Hertz (tel 245-3356); Avis (tel 245-3512); Sunshine (tel 245-9541); Alamo (tel 245-8953); United (tel 245-8894); Dollar (tel 245-3651); National (tel 245-3502) and Rent-A-Wreck have car rental booths at the airport.

Rent-A-Wreck (tel 245-4755) is a local company. It doesn't offer the best deal by the week, but it has one of the cheaper rates by the day, from $19. Toll-free numbers for the other agencies are in the Getting Around chapter.

Jeep Rental Adventures Four Wheel Drive (3145 Oihana St, Lihue; tel 245-9622; 800-356-1207) rents newish 4WD Wrangler jeeps for about $50 to $60 a day.

Insurance is optional, but unlike the major car rental agencies it covers your travel off paved roads. However, there's still an amount you're liable for. Insurance is $5 a day with $500 deductible, $8 a day with $250 deductible.

Bicycle & Moped
Pedal & Paddle in Hanalei rents 10-speed bikes as well as five-speed beach cruisers with wide tyres and padded seats. The rates are $4 per hour, $20 per 24 hours and $52.50 per week. A credit card or a $100 deposit is required.

North Shore Bike Cruise & Snorkel (Box 1192, Kapaa, HI 96746; tel 822-1582) has full-day guided trips with six miles of cycling, snorkelling on the North Shore and a barbecue lunch for $65.

South Shore Activities (2230 Kapili Rd, Poipu; tel 742-6873), down by the Sheraton, rents bicycles by the hour, day or week at prices comparable to Pedal & Paddle. Mopeds are $28 a day.

Outfitters Kauai at the Kiahuna Shopping Village in Poipu rents mountain bikes from $15 to $25 a day and from $75 to $125 a week.

Hitching

Hitching is officially illegal, but the law is seldom enforced. Overall, Kauai tends to be hit and miss for hitching; folks on the North Shore being the most sympathetic. Some drivers will go out of their way to take hikers to trailheads.

A friend of ours who commutes between Hanalei and Princeville by hitching says that unlike on the mainland she doesn't find it scary on Kauai. Still, the usual precautions apply.

Tours

Polynesian Adventure Tours (tel 246-0122) has full-day tours which include Wailua, Fern Grotto, Waimea, Koloa, Poipu and Waimea Canyon for about $50.

Trans Hawaiian (tel 245-5108) does half-day North Shore tours for about $25 and Waimea Canyon tours for about $30.

Kauai Mountain Tours (Box 3069, Lihue, HI 96766; tel 245-7224) has 4WD vehicles for trips that go down backroads from Kokee State Park. Seven-hour tours are $75.

Other tour companies include Kauai Island Tours (tel 245-4777), Robert's Hawaii Tours (tel 245-9101) and Gray Line-Kauai (tel 245-3344).

Glider Tradewinds Glider Rides (tel 335-5086; 800-245-4337) has 20-minute rides over Hanapepe for $75 for one person and $90 for two. A mile-high 35-minute ride along the coast and into Hanapepe Valley is $125/150. For an expensive twirl, aerobatic rides cost $175. The gliders leave from Burns Field near Port Allen; its office is on Hana Rd in Hanapepe.

Helicopter Many wilderness hikers resent the intrusiveness of helicopters, and local environmentalists have successfully stopped their landings on Na Pali Coast beaches. However these 'Kauai mosquitoes' that are an irritant to people on the ground no doubt offer some pretty spectacular views as they swoop deep into Waimea Canyon, run along the Na Pali Coast and seek out hidden waterfalls.

Around-the-island tours begin at about $115. There's usually some sort of 'ultimate splendour' or 'delight' tour that can run up another $50. The freebie magazines often have discount coupons. Many of the offices are in Lihue near the corner of Hwy 56 and Ahukini Rd.

Nuisance low buzzes are supposedly controlled. There's a helicopter hotline (tel 826-1182) to take complaints, run by Kauai helicopter owners and operators.

Cruises More than a dozen boat companies have cruises down the Na Pali Coast. Most use Zodiac rafts, catamarans or other small boats that can hug the coast and enter sea caves. The typical tour is narrated, lasts 3½ to 4½ hours, goes down the coast as far as Nualolo, includes snorkelling and costs $55 to $80.

Snorkelling and sea cave exploration require suitable weather and surf. If it's important to you, ask about current conditions before you book.

The smoothest rides are usually in summer. At times in winter, the seas get too rough for the boats even to go out. Many of these companies then take to the calmer southern shore for snorkelling cruises and whale watching tours.

The companies listed here are all within a few minutes walk of one another around Hwy 560 and Aku Rd in Hanalei, making it easy to shop and compare.

If you just want to go down and see the coast, Hanalei Sea Tours (tel 826-7254; 800-367-8047 ext 155) does a three-hour mini-tour without snorkelling for $50. It has longer tours as well, uses both Zodiac rafts and power catamarans and is one of two companies allowed to drop off and pick up backpackers along the Na Pali Coast. This summer-only service costs $60 one way and $110 return to Kalalau, $130 return to Milolii.

Captain Zodiac (tel 826-9371) uses Zodiac rafts. You pay a bit more there, but Captain Zodiac has a good reputation and apparently some clout, as this is the only company allowed to leave from Tunnels Beach, instead of the more usual (and further) Hanalei Beach Park. Its backpacker drop-off service is about the same price as Hanalei Sea Tours.

Paradise Adventure Cruises (tel 826-9999) has a four-hour snorkelling trip on a Boston Whaler, limited to six passengers plus one 'singing captain'.

Na Pali Adventures (tel 826-6804) uses power catamarans.

East Side

LIHUE

Lihue is the county capital, the commercial centre and the arrival point of most visitors to Kauai. Though it's the largest town on the island, its population is only 5000 and it's essentially a grown-up plantation town. It has inexpensive hotels and restaurants and the island's main shopping centre. There are a few sights of interest, but Lihue itself is ordinary, with no special charm.

Information

The Hawaii Visitors Bureau (3016 Umi St; tel 245-3971) is open from 8 am to 4.30 pm Monday to Friday.

The government offices are centred around Rice, Umi and Hardy streets.

Post & Money The post office is opposite the museum on Rice St, next to the Bank of Hawaii.

Library The Lihue Public Library (4344 Hardy St, tel 245-3617) is open from 8 am to 8 pm Mondays and Tuesdays, from 8 am to 4.30 pm Wednesdays, Thursdays and Fridays and from 8 am till noon Saturdays.

Laundry Lihue Washerette is behind the Lihue Shopping Center on the corner of Rice St and Hwy 56.

Kauai Museum

A few hours at the Kauai Museum (4428 Rice St; tel 245-6931) will give you a good overview of the island's history.

The displays begin with Kauai's volcanic genesis from the ocean floor, then move on to natural history and ecosystems. The first floor is Hawaiian history, with the likes of hula instruments, a hand-carved wooden canoe and a section on the short-lived Russian presence in Kauai.

Upstairs the sugar cane workers and missionaries arrive on the scene. A replica of a plantation worker's spartan shack sits opposite the spacious bedroom of an early missionary's house furnished with a four-poster koa bed and Hawaiian quilts. It is to these folks that Hawaii traces its multi-ethnic roots and vastly unequal distribution of land and wealth. The displays are accompanied by well-written interpretive presentations of life in old Kauai.

At the 'please touch' section visitors can tap a piece of tapa, pick up a stone poi pounder and shake gourd rattles. In another room a video about Kauai runs continuously and includes aerial views of the Na Pali Coast and Kauai's rugged, inaccessible interior. The gift shop has an excellent selection of books on Hawaiiana, including some esoteric research books on Hawaiian culture and history.

The museum is open from 9 am to 4.30 pm Monday to Friday and from 9 am to 1 pm Saturdays. Admission is $3 for adults and free for children under 18. If you run out of time, ask for a free re-entry pass when you leave.

Lihue Sugar Mill

The conveyer belt crossing over Hwy 50 just south of its intersection with Hwy 56 transports crushed sugar cane to the Lihue Sugar Mill. The mill produces raw sugar crystals that are shipped to California to be refined. Molasses is also made there and on those days the air has an extremely sweet smell.

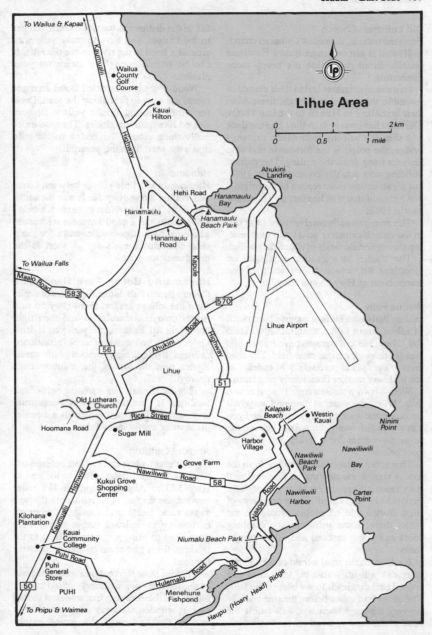

Lihue Area

To Wailua & Kapaa

Kaumualii Highway

Wailua County Golf Course

Kauai Hilton

Hanamaulu

Hanamaulu Road

To Wailua Falls

Maalo Road 583

Hehi Road

Hanamaulu Bay

Hanamaulu Beach Park

Ahukini Landing

Kapule Highway

570

Lihue Airport

56

Ahukini Road

Lihue

51

Old Lutheran Church

Hoomana Road

Rice Street

Sugar Mill

Grove Farm

Kukui Grove Shopping Center

Nawiliwili Road

58

Kilohana Plantation

Kaumualii Highway

Kauai Community College

Puhi General Store

PUHI

Puhi Road

50

To Poipu & Waimea

Hulemalu Road

Menehune Fishpond

Kalapaki Beach

Westin Kauai

Ninini Point

Nawiliwili Bay

Nawiliwili Beach Park

Nawiliwili Harbor

Harbor Village

Niumalu Beach Park

Wapaa Road

Carter Point

Haupu (Hoary Head) Ridge

Old Lutheran Church

From the outside, the oldest Lutheran church in Hawaii is just one more quaint Hawaiian church. From the inside it's much more interesting.

German immigrants styled their church to resemble the boat that brought them from their homeland to Hawaii in the late 1800s. The floor has been built to slant like the deck of a ship, the balcony resembles a captain's bridge, the pulpit is the forecastle and ship lanterns hang from the ceiling. The current building was actually constructed in 1983, but it's an almost exact replica of the original 1885 church that was levelled by Hurricane Iwa in 1982.

The immigrants themselves now lie at rest in the church cemetery on a knoll overlooking the sugar cane fields in which they toiled.

The church is a quarter of a mile up Hoomana Rd, which is just south of the intersection of Hwy 56 and Hwy 50.

Wailua Falls

Wailua Falls is an 80-foot waterfall just north of Lihue. From Lihue, turn left onto Maalo Rd (Hwy 583), a narrow paved road that weaves through a sugar cane field. The road ends at the falls at precisely 3.94 miles - as the highway marker fastidiously proclaims.

Wailua (two waters) is usually seen as two falls. When the water is running strongly it becomes one wide rushing waterfall and you can watch fish being thrown out beyond the powerful waters for a flying dive into the pool below.

This is not a waterfall to explore from the top. A sign at the parking lot near a closed path reads, 'Slippery rocks at top of falls. People have been killed'. There are plenty of local stories told of people sliding on the rocks there, some miraculously grabbing roots and being rescued and others not so lucky.

Back down the road a third of a mile, at a large dirt pull-off with a big tree, there's an eroded trail that leads to the base of the falls. The steep trail starts below the tree and can be very slippery when wet. Just below the head of this trail you can see another water-fall in the distance to the right. Once you get to the bottom, you have to make your way around a bend in the river to see the falls. It can be humid enough to steam up your glasses.

Wood roses used in dried floral arrangements are easy to find along the road. Look for vines bearing bright yellow flowers shaped like morning glories. They are especially thick around the bridge half a mile down the road from the waterfall.

Hanamaulu

Hanamaulu is a little village between Lihue and Wailua along Hwy 56. It was the birthplace of the legendary hero Kawelo. Hanamaulu has a good Japanese restaurant, a hole-in-the-wall post office and a doughnut shop that closes each day as soon as the doughnuts are gone.

Hanamaulu Beach Park Hanamaulu County Beach Park is three-quarters of a mile from the village centre. From Hwy 56 turn makai onto Hanamaulu Rd and then right onto Hehi Rd. Entering the park you'll drive under the arched trestle of an old abandoned railroad bridge, now topped with grass. Egrets nest on top of the shrubby trees nearby.

This local park has camping with full facilities. It's on the inside of Hanamaulu Bay, a deep protected bay with a boulder breakwater across its mouth.

Ahukini Landing

If you've got some time to kill before your flight, you could drive down to the end of Hwy 570 to Ahukini Landing, 1½ miles beyond the airport. The road runs through sugar cane fields and crosses a series of narrow-gauge railroad tracks which were once used to bring sugar cane down to the landing. Ilima and chain of love grow along the road.

Ahukini State Recreation Pier is at the end of the road. It consists largely of old cement pillars and the decaying framework of the old pier. A wooden walkway runs out across it and at the end over the water, rather inexplicably, is a picnic table. The pier is now used mostly by old-timers for pole fishing. At the head of the bay is Hanamaulu Beach.

Ninini Point

The lighthouse on Ninini Point stands 100 feet above the shore, marking the northern entrance to Nawiliwili Bay. The road down to the lighthouse begins off Hwy 51, half a mile south of Hwy 570. Access is through a gate on the Westin Kauai Hotel's property and visitors are allowed to pass to the lighthouse 2½ miles in.

There are plans to develop this whole area, from Ninini Point north to Ahukini Point, into the Westin's third 18-hole golf course. As the plans proceed, no doubt the road will change with the landscape.

Just how the landscape changes is the centre of much controversy. This is one of the last sections of accessible shore in the area where Hawaiians can still fish, pick opihi and gather limu as they've done for generations. Plans for building the course on coastal conservation land and restricting local beach access have been hotly contested by local fishermen, the Sierra Club and Mayor Yukimura.

The Westin Kauai Hotel

The Westin Kauai is mammoth, with huge Chinese cloisonné vases, squawking parrots and fat pillars of pink faux marble. Art and antiques are everywhere, even on the men's restroom wall, where a distinguished Chinese gentleman of another century peers sideways across the row of urinals. Past the front desk are balconies looking onto a gigantic swimming pool with fountains spurting from the mouths of sculptured beasts.

The Westin offers rides around its manicured grounds in carriages pulled by Clydesdale horses (for $42 an hour!) and boat rides around little islands stocked with exotic birds and monkeys.

The Westin is the old Kauai Surf Hotel refurbished. As the island's only high-rise, its very construction led to a successful campaign that limited the height of all future hotels to that of a coconut tree.

The hotel is still controversial. Many islanders feel the Westin's bedazzling opulence is more befitting Las Vegas than Kauai. With all its natural beauty, Kauai is just about the oddest place to build artificial lagoons and electric waterfalls.

The Westin is off Hwy 51 at Nawiliwili Harbor. It's on Kalapaki Beach, a white sand beach sheltered by points and breakwaters. Swimming is usually good, even in the winter unless storms kick the surf up.

Nawiliwili Bay

Nawiliwili Bay is a deep-water port with a commercial harbour. The adjacent small boat harbour is picturesque, backed by the edge of the Haupu (Hoary Head) Ridge which ends at Carter Point. The kayak company Island Adventures and several deep-sea fishing boats are based there.

Waapa Rd runs south from the Westin past the harbour and a couple of unexciting beach parks. It then connects with Hulemalu Rd, which leads up to an overview of the Menehune Fishpond.

You could continue about a mile past the fishpond, turn right onto Puhi Rd and come out to Hwy 50 at Puhi General Store.

Nawiliwili Beach Park Nawiliwili Beach Park is largely a parking lot facing an ocean retaining wall. From there you can look over at the Westin, the light beacon on Kukui Point and a long breakwater. The park is a local hangout and drinking spot.

There's no beach there, but if the waters in Nawiliwili Stream are not running strongly you could cross over to Kalapaki Beach in front of the Westin.

Right at the mouth of the stream is an old shelter under ironwood trees with a wooden sign reading 'Pine Tree Inn'. It's an impromptu neighbourhood open-air bar of sorts. Old-timers gather there during the day with little ice chests to talk story. Sometimes someone has food to throw on the grill, but mostly they bring a few beers and drink until they're gone.

Niumalu Beach Park This county beach park is in a less affluent residential area and has been partly settled by people who have set up tents and lean-tos. The park has a boat ramp used mainly for launching outrigger canoes. Camping is officially allowed, though it's not an area recommended for most visitors.

Menehune Fishpond Overlook

Half a mile up Hulemalu Rd there's a lookout on the left with a view of the Alakoko Fishpond, more commonly called the Menehune Fishpond. In the background is the misty Haupu Ridge.

The fishpond, created by a stone wall that runs along a bend in the river, was said to have been built in one night by menehunes. The stone wall is covered by a thick green line of mangrove trees. Morning is a good time for viewing as in the afternoon you look into the sun.

Huleai National Wildlife Refuge lies between the road and the fishpond. Once planted with taro and rice, the area now provides breeding and feeding grounds for endemic water birds. The refuge is not open to the public.

Grove Farm Homestead

Grove Farm Homestead Plantation Museum (tel 245-3202) is up Nawiliwili Rd (Hwy 58), 1¾ mile from Waapa Rd. It was built in 1864 by George Wilcox, son of the missionaries Abner and Lucy Wilcox. It's a bit like the house of an old aunt, rather musty and filled with memories. Rocking chairs sit on a covered porch. One room is lined with bookshelves stuffed with a home library, with koa calabashes and a model ship on top. In one corner a card table is set up, waiting for a foursome to sit down to a wild game of cribbage.

Tours are given at 10 am and 1 pm

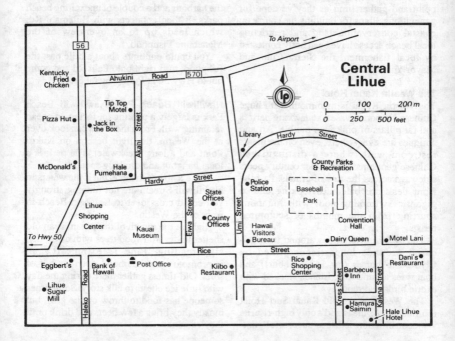

Mondays, Wednesdays and Thursdays. Reservations are required and must sometimes be made a couple of weeks in advance. The cost is $3.

Kukui Grove Shopping Center

Kukui Grove Shopping Center, at the intersection of Hwy 50 and Hwy 58, is Kauai's largest shopping centre. The major department stores are Liberty House, J C Penney, Sears, Woolworth and Longs Drugs. It also has Kukui Grove Cinema, Star Market, Bank of Hawaii, Waldenbooks, an art gallery and a video arcade. Kauai Cinnamons sells large hot cinnamon rolls for $1.50. Other food places include a coffee and dessert cafe, Rosita's Mexican restaurant, Brick Oven Pizza, Burger King and other fast-food joints.

Kilohana

Kilohana , 1½ miles south of Lihue on Hwy 50, is the 1930s sugar plantation estate of Gaylord Parke Wilcox, once head of Grove Farm Plantation. It was the most distinguished house on Kauai at the time.

The home has been restored, with most of the rooms turned into shops that sell artwork, antiques and handicrafts. It was a nice way to preserve the old estate and you get to look around without being hit for an admission fee.

Visitors are free to wander through rooms full of antiques or even plop down in one of the overstuffed couches and read a book. The hallways hold cases of Hawaiian artefacts such as stone poi pounders and ornaments made of dog teeth. Oriental rugs litter the hardwood floors. There's also a restaurant, Gaylord's, in a U-shaped courtyard setting around the lawn.

Many island galleries rent space there, giving Kilohana the widest collection of arts and crafts on Kauai. A former cloakroom is now the Hawaiian Collection Room, which sells finely strung Niihau shell leis and scrimshaw. Island Memories has shadow puppets from Bali, and war clubs and masks from Papua New Guinea.

The upstairs bedrooms have been turned

into still more shops, with displays laid out even in the bathrooms and closets. Sea Reflections sells mangrove and monkeypod carvings of dolphins and sharks hand crafted by the Kapingamarangi people of Pohnpei. Kilohana Galleries has quality contemporary paintings and crafts by Hawaiian artists, including some Kauai-made pottery swirled with abstract mountain and wave designs. There's a jewellery shop, one-of-a-kind clothing, a greenhouse and Japanese antiques and prints. Stones, out the back in a former guest house, has Hawaiiana prints, clothing and some interesting ceramic fish.

Kilohana (tel 245-5608) is open from 9 am to 9.30 pm daily. The 35-acre grounds have gardens, a working farm and a little plantation village which you can explore. Turn-of-the-century carriages pulled by Clydesdale horses give 20-minute tours at $5 for adults and $3 for children. It's a bit touristy but cheaper and more in tune with historical Kauai than the Westin's Clydesdale rides.

Places to Stay – bottom end

Central Lihue has some of Kauai's cheapest hotels. They are generally drab places and except for Motel Lani are filled more with local residents than visitors. You'll get a place to sleep but by no means are these vacation spots. People down on their luck tend to end up on Akahi St.

The *Motel Lani* (4240 Rice St, Box 1836, Lihue, HI 96766; tel 245-2965) seems the best of the lot. It has 10 rooms for $20 to $28, and one room for three people at $30. All have mini-refrigerators and are very basic but clean. There's a two-day minimum or a $2 surcharge.

The *Hale Lihue Hotel* (2931 Kalena St, Lihue, HI 96766; tel 245-3151) has 20 rooms for $18/20 a single/double. Rooms are basic with twin beds, private showers and toilets but not much atmosphere.

The *Tip Top Motel* (3173 Akahi St, Box 1231, Lihue, HI 96766; tel 245-2333) has two simple two-storey cinder block buildings. Rates are $20/26 for singles/doubles. Rooms have twin beds with passable mattresses, air-con, louvred windows and perhaps a collapsing chest of drawers.

If you're desperate you might try the *Hale Pumehana* (3083 Akahi St, Lihue, HI 96766; tel 245-2106). It's attached to a liquor store. Its rates are $20/24 for singles/doubles.

The *Elima Hale Apartments* (3352B Elima St, Lihue, HI 96766; tel 245-9950) offers mostly long-term rentals, but between residents it sometimes has something to rent by the day. Rates vary according to whether the room has a private bathroom, kitchen, etc, but generally cost $30 to $40 a night.

Places to Stay – top end

The *Kauai Hilton & Beach Villas* (4331 Kauai Beach Drive, Lihue, HI 96766; tel 245-1955; 800-445-8667) has 350 hotel rooms and 150 villa units with kitchens. The hotel is a standard Hilton and could easily be anywhere. Rates for rooms without ocean views start from $125 for hotel rooms and $140 for one-bedroom villas.

The *Westin Kauai* (Kalapaki Beach, Lihue, HI 96766; tel 245-5050; 800-228-3000) is one of the 'fantasy hotels' designed by developer Chris Hemmeter. Rates begin at $185 for a courtyard view and climb to $295 for a beachfront unit, with suites up to $1500.

Places to Eat

The *Hanamaulu Restaurant & Tea House* (tel 245-2511) on Hwy 56 in Hanamaulu has many faces. It has a sushi bar with a little carp pond, individual tatami-matted tea rooms, a robatayaki and a dining area. Japanese plate lunches of miso soup and rice with teriyaki or sukiyaki cost $5 at lunch and $5.70 at dinner. Chinese plate lunches are similarly priced. Saimin costs $1.75. Call in advance to reserve one of the tea rooms – they really set the mood. It's open from 9 am to 1 pm and from 4.30 to 9.30 pm daily except Mondays.

At *Hamura Saimin*, 2956 Kress St in Lihue, you can get a bowl of freshly made saimin cooked by Mrs Hamura herself for $2. There are no tables there, just a winding saimin bar where visitors and locals rub elbows as they slurp bowls of steaming hot saimin. The one rule of etiquette is written on the menu – 'Please do not stick gum under counter'!

You could drop *Kiibo Restaurant*, 2991 Umi St in Lihue, into the foothills of Mt Fuji and not a thing would need to be changed. From the elderly Japanese waitresses to the indigo cushions, it's authentic Japanese country decor. A lunch bento of shrimp tempura, chicken katsu, beef teriyaki, rice and miso is a great deal at $3.85. Sukiyaki is $5.50. The sushi bar and dinner prices are higher. Kirin beer is $1.60. Ice cream or shave ice comes in green tea and azuki bean flavours. It's open from 11 am to 1.30 pm and from 5.30 to 9 pm daily except Sundays and holidays.

Gaylord's (tel 245-9593) at Kilohana has a pleasant open-air estate setting and draws a crowd. We were disappointed with the food, however, after trying one of their specialities, the 'famous baby back ribs' ($8 only at Saturday lunch, $14 at early-bird dinner) at lunch time; the portions were small and the sauce ordinary. Lunch is served from 11 am to 3.30 pm daily except Sundays, with sandwiches and salads from $6 to $8. Dinner is served from 5 to 9 pm nightly with main courses from $18 to $22. The early-bird dinner served from 5 to 6.30 pm is slightly cheaper. On Sundays, there's a brunch from 10 am to 3 pm.

The *Kauai Chop Suey*, in Harbor Village opposite the Westin, has plate lunches for $4.90 and plate dinners for $5.40 plus lots of standard Cantonese dishes in the $5 to $6 range. Kauai doesn't have any really great Chinese restaurants, but this is one of the better ones.

Eggbert's, 4483 Rice St, Lihue, is popular for omelettes and eggs benedict. Expect to pay $5 to $7 with coffee. It has burgers and other food too, but you're best off sticking with eggs. Breakfast is served from 7 am to 3 pm daily.

Lots of working people start their day at *Dani's Restaurant*, at 4201 Rice St in Lihue. Omelettes, from cheese for $2.70 to kalua pig for $4.25, come with rice or toast. The waitress plops down a thermos of coffee as soon as you sit down – no extra charge. The restaurant has Hawaiian, American and Japanese lunch dishes. The most expensive Western dish is New York steak for $4.50. Breakfast is served from 5 to 11 am daily. Lunch is served from 11 am to 2 pm Monday to Saturday.

Rosita's in Kukui Grove Center has rather standard Mexican dishes at moderate prices. Some of the cheaper items are burritos with rice or beans for $6.50, and two tacos for $4.50. It also has American and Italian food and a reasonably priced kiddie menu.

The *Hale O' Health* in Lihue's Rice Shopping Center is a typical shopping centre health food store. It does have Alta-dena yoghurt, kefir, Hains products, packaged granola and other standard items, though no bulk food.

The *Oroweat Thrift Shop* next to the Dairy Queen on Rice St in Lihue has day-old bakery products at discounted prices.

At the **Westin Kauai** *Cooks on the Beach* is a pool-side cafe serving three meals a day. The spinach ravioli with pesto sauce and vegetables is good at lunch time for $8.25. Toasted sandwiches with fries cost from $7.50. The dinner menu is similar, with most items about $1 more.

For a splurge, *Inn on the Cliffs* has elegant dining with crystal and white linen, French doors all around, views of Nawiliwili Bay and good food. It's pleasant, not stuffy. Seafood pasta dishes are the best deal. At lunch time they cost about $10 to $13 and at dinner they're $5 to $6 more. Crispy mini-loaves of warm French bread come with the meal. Reservations may be necessary for dinner, though lunch usually isn't a problem. Ask for a window table. You can also have pupus around the lounge fireplace or catch the sunset from the verandah. Lunch is 11.30 am to 2 pm. The lounge is open and dinner is served from 5.30 to 9.45 pm. You can get there by the boat launch from the lagoon. The cost of the ride is deducted from the tab for diners.

Entertainment

The Westin Kauai's high-tech *Paddling Club* is Kauai's number one disco. There's no cover charge but there is an age limit of 21 and a 'strict' dress code, which in Kauai means no shorts, no tank tops and no sandals.

Westin's *Inn on the Cliffs* is more romantic and sophisticated, with both an outdoor deck and indoor fireplace. A pianist plays at 7 pm, and there's a jazz quartet and dancing from 8 pm. Westin's *Colonnade Lounge* features solo Hawaiian musicians from 6 to 11 pm nightly.

Winter sees a local crowd at *Gilligan's*, a nightclub and disco at the Kauai Hilton. In the summer it's more of a tourist crowd. It's open until 4 am on Fridays and Saturdays and until 2 am other nights. The dress code is the same as the Paddling Club's.

The *Club Jetty* at Nawiliwili Harbor has live rock 'n' roll music on Thursdays, Fridays and Saturdays and a bar with karaoke singing. This used to be a popular local pick-up bar. Not many tourists come here and the place can be a bit rowdy.

The *Park Place* is an art deco disco with a dress code and a minimum entry age of 21. It's in the Harbor Village complex across from the Westin Kauai.

WAILUA

The three-mile stretch of Kuhio Highway (Hwy 56) from Wailua to Waipouli to Kapaa is largely a scattering of stores, restaurants, hotels and condos. There are a number of sights clustered around the Wailua River area. Neither Wailua nor Waipouli have anything that resembles a town centre.

Wailua was the site of Kauai's royal court. There are 'Seven Sacred Heiaus' running from the mouth of the Wailua River up to the top of Mt Waialeale.

Six of the sites are within a mile of the river mouth. Five are visible. The sixth is abandoned in a sugar cane field on the northern side of the Wailua River. All date back to the early period of Tahitian settlement and are considered to be typical menehune construction.

Wailua State Park is a hodgepodge that includes Lydgate and Wailua beaches, sections of the Wailua River bank, the Fern Grotto, and most of the heiau sites. It also includes the riverboat basin and a public boat ramp.

Wailua River, 11.8 miles long, is the only navigable river in Hawaii. Though most people travel the river on packaged riverboat tours, the more adventurous use a kayak or water ski on it.

Lydgate Beach Park

Lydgate is a popular family beach with protected swimming in a large seawater pool created with stone walls. It's great for kids but deep enough for adults to swim in too. In the open ocean beyond there can be strong currents and there have been many drownings on both sides of the river's mouth. The park has changing rooms, restrooms, showers, large picnic pavilions and drinking water.

Lydgate is makai of the Aston Kauai, down Leho Drive.

Hikina A Ka La Heiau

Hikina A Ka La (Rising of the Sun) Heiau is the long, narrow heiau aligned directly north to south at the far end of the Lydgate Beach parking lot.

The heiau is thought to have been built around 1200 AD. Boulders still outline the shape but most of the stones have long since been removed.

At the northern end of the heiau, a bronze plaque on a large stone reads 'Hauola, City of Refuge'. The mounded grassy area behind the plaque is all that remains of this former refuge for kapu breakers. The lucky ones who managed to reach Hauola had their lives spared.

The stone with bowl-shaped depressions 10 feet to the left of the plaque is an adze grinding stone. The stone hasn't always been in this upright position since to grind a correct edge it would have needed to be flat. There are also a couple of flat stone saltpans on the grounds.

If you look straight out across the river's mouth you can see the remains of Aa Kukui Heiau on the point in front of the Lae Nani condos. You can make out the foundation stones but the heiau site is landscaped over in a carpet of condo grass now. In ancient times torches were lit on this point at night to help guide outrigger canoes.

If you walk straight down to the beach while looking toward Aa Kukui Heiau you may find stones with petroglyphs on them, though they're hidden under shifting sands from time to time.

Malae Heiau

Malae Heiau is in a thick clump of trees growing on the edge of a sugar cane field, a mere 40 feet in from the highway across from the Aston Kauai Resort. Though this is the largest heiau on Kauai it's thickly overgrown with grasses and Java plum trees and almost impossible to explore. Trust us.

In the 1830s the missionaries converted Deborah Kapule, the last Kauaian queen, to Christianity and she converted the interior of Malae into a cattle pen. Except for these alterations it's relatively well-preserved, thanks largely to its impenetrable overgrowth.

The whole area is state property and there are plans eventually to incorporate the heiau into the Wailua parks system. In the meantime the caretakers who have cleaned up Hikina A Ka La Heiau are interested in clearing Malae as well. Java plums, by the way, are used in making wine. But should you be tempted to try the fresh fruit you'll find they're bitter enough to dry out your mouth!

Highway 580

This highway, also known as Kuamoo Rd begins at the traffic light off Hwy 56 at Coco Palms Resort. It passes heiaus, historical sites, Opaekaa Falls, Wailua Homesteads and the University of Hawaii's agricultural experiment station before reaching hiking trails and Keahua Arboretum.

Holoholoku Heiau

Holoholoku Heiau is a quarter of a mile up Hwy 580. Like all the Wailua heiaus, this was

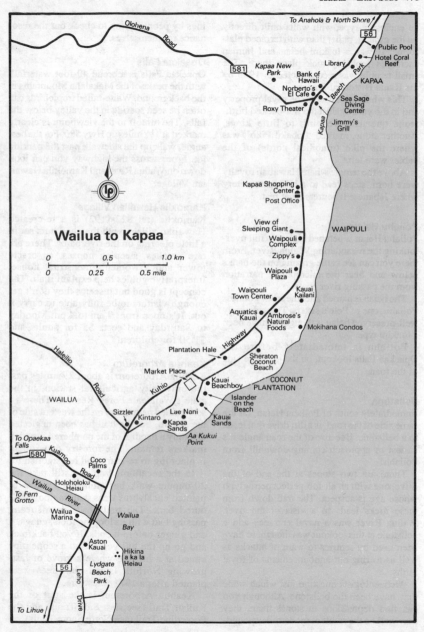

Wailua to Kapaa

To Anahola & North Shore

56

Public Pool
Hotel Coral Reef
Library

Kapaa New Park
581
Bank of Hawaii
Norberto's
El Cafe
KAPAA

Beach Park

Roxy Theater
Sea Sage Diving Center

Jimmy's Grill

Kapaa River

Olohena Road

Kapaa Shopping Center
Post Office

View of Sleeping Giant
WAIPOULI
Waipouli Complex
Zippy's
Waipouli Plaza
Kauai Kailani
Waipouli Town Center
Aquatics Kauai
Ambrose's Natural Foods
Mokihana Condos

Highway

Plantation Hale
Sheraton Coconut Beach
COCONUT PLANTATION
Market Place
Kauai Beachboy
Islander on the Beach
Kauai Sands

Kuhio

Haleilio Road

WAILUA
Sizzler
Kintaro
Lae Nani
Kapaa Sands
Aa Kukui Point

To Opaekaa Falls
580
Kuamoo Road
Coco Palms

Holoholoku Heiau

To Fern Grotto
Wailua River
Wailua Marina

Wailua Bay

Aston Kauai
Hikina a ka la Heiau

Lydgate Beach Park

56
Leho Drive

To Lihue

0   0.5   1.0 km
0   0.25   0.5 mile

an enclosure-type, with walls built directly on the ground, rather than with terraced platforms. It was a luakini heiau and human sacrifices probably took place there. The small temple was reconstructed in 1933 by the Kauai Historical Society.

This whole area used to be royal property and in the yard against the flat-backed birthstone queens gave birth to little kings. Another stone, marked 'Pohaku Piko', was where the piko (umbilical cords) of the babies were left.

Above the temple where Hawaiian royalty were born, steps lead to a hilltop cemetery where Japanese labourers lie at rest.

Poliahu Heiau

Poliahu Heiau is perched high on a hill overlooking the meandering Wailua River. From there you can see cattle grazing on the banks below and hear the microphone narration from the passing river boats.

The heiau is named after the snow goddess Poliahu, one of Pele's sisters. This relatively well-preserved heiau is thought to have been a luakini type.

Poliahu is immediately before the Opaekaa Falls lookout, on the opposite side of the road.

Bellstone

Immediately south of Poliahu Heiau, on the same side of the road, is a dirt drive that leads to a bellstone. Because of the road angle it's easiest to approach coming downhill from Poliahu.

There are two stones at the end of the drive, one with an all-too-perfect petroglyph whose age is suspect. The trail down from these rocks leads to a vista of the river. Wailua River was a naval entrance and a bellstone at this lookout was thought to have been used by sentries to warn of attacks as well as to ring out announcements of royal births.

Archaeologists question just which stone may have been the bellstone. Although you can find depressions in stones there, they may well be the result of modern-day pound-

ings by people trying to check out the resonance for themselves.

Opaekaa Falls

Opaekaa Falls is a broad 40-foot waterfall, with the peaks of the Makaleha Mountains in the background. White-tailed tropicbirds can often be seen soaring in the valley below the falls. The turnoff to the viewpoint is clearly marked at 1½ miles up Hwy 580. For the best angle, walk up the sidewalk past the parking lot. From across the highway you can look down on Wailua River and Kamokila Hawaiian Village.

Kamokila Hawaiian Village

Kamokila (tel 822-1192) is a re-created Hawaiian village with thatched huts set in a little clearing on the riverbank. There are taro patches, sleeping houses, an oracle tower and a women's menstrual house. Interpretive guides help explain it all. The concept is good but it seems they don't get enough visitors to be fully able to carry it out. It's open from 9 am to 4 pm Monday to Saturday and costs $5 for adults and $1.50 for children.

Keahua Arboretum

Keahua Arboretum is about 2¼ miles past the university agricultural station, in the state's Waialeale Forest Reserve. There's a self-guided nature trail on the western side of the stream, but the trail has been neglected and only a handful of the numbered wooden markers remain. The forestry department is planning to re-mark and re-establish it.

In the meantime you can still take the 20-minute walk beginning in a grove of painted eucalyptus trees with rainbow-coloured bark. The trail heads downstream, passing hau with its looping roots, guava, ti and ginger before it ends. If you backtrack and go up the hill you'll find a scope pipe aimed at a hillside where a grove of fast-growing Norfolk Island pine trees were planted after a 1971 forest fire.

Keahua Arboretum is the start of the Kuilau Trail (see East Side Trails) and the Powerline Trail (see North Shore Trails).

Coco Palms

The Coco Palms Resort was built on the site of Kauai's ancient royal court, in the midst of a large coconut grove.

There's a Hawaiian design to it all, with thatched cottages and lagoons, and it looks a bit like a movie set. Like movie sets, the closer you get, the less authentic it appears – you begin to notice that the coconut palm pillars are made of cement and that sort of thing.

The chapel there was originally built in 1954 for the movie *Sadie Thompson* with Rita Hayworth. The highest-profile wedding that took place at Coco Palms was between Elvis Presley and Joan Blackman in *Blue Hawaii*. A few faded decades later, about 700 people each year still come to the little chapel in the palms to be married.

Near the chapel is a small free museum with some Hawaiian artefacts. The hotel leads free walking tours of the grounds at 9.30 am daily and there are a few peacocks, gibbons and a donkey in cages out the back that they call a zoo. However, the best time to look around the grounds is just before dusk, so you can also catch the free torchlighting ceremony.

Fern Grotto

Fern Grotto is Kauai's busiest tourist attraction. It's a riverboat tour complete with corny jokes and packaged sentimentality to the tune of Elvis' 'Hawaiian Wedding Song'.

The riverboats are big with wide flat bottoms – very simple, like covered barges. Some people compare them to cattle boats even before they pack the tourists on. The grotto itself is a large musty cave beneath a fern-covered rock face. It's pretty, but overrated.

Smith's Motor Boat Service (tel 822-4111) and Waialeale Boat Tours (tel 822-4909) both charge $9 for adults and $4.50 for children and leave every half hour from 9 am to 4 pm from Wailua Marina.

Smith's Tropical Paradise

Smith's Tropical Paradise (tel 822-4654) at Wailua Marina has a mile-long loop trail

through 30 acres of theme gardens and artificial 'villages'. It's open from 8.30 am to 4.30 pm daily. Admission is $4, with guided tram tours $3 more; it's half-price for children. In the evening there's a luau and Polynesian show.

Coconut Plantation

Coconut Plantation has four hotels, one condo and a shopping centre. The large grassy field between the Beachboy and Sheraton hotels is popular with egrets and the occasional kite flyer. A line of ironwoods shades the half-mile-long beach.

The calmest section for swimming seems to be down between the Islander and Kauai Sands hotels where there's a break in the low lava shelf that fronts much of the rest of the beach. It's said that the currents can be tricky all along there, though it was calm when we were in the water. There's a shower in front of Al & Don Restaurant at Kauai Sands. Snorkelling is rather average though you can see unicorn tangs, wrasse and Moorish idols. The beach has unique sand, each little piece polished to a high gloss.

The Sheraton rents boogie boards and snorkel sets for $5 an hour and $15 a day. They do a reef snorkel tour for $30 and have surfing and introductory diving lessons.

Market Place The Market Place at Coconut Plantation is open from 9 am to 9 pm daily. It has 70 different shops, including Liberty House, a kite shop, a movie theatre, Hawaiian Airlines office, Waldenbooks, an art gallery, T-shirt shops, clothing stores with big pink signs announcing perpetual 50%-off sales and shops with names like 'Nik-Nak Shak' and 'Return to Paradise'. Food places include a couple of steak restaurants, a bakery, a bar, ice cream and fast-food kiosks and a convenience store.

Free Polynesian-style hula shows take place at 4 pm Thursdays, Fridays and Saturdays.

Places to Stay

In the Wailua Homesteads area, off Hwy 581, on the other side of the Sleeping Giant, the government once gave 160-acre parcels to people willing to work the land. This mostly meant cattle grazing. Later Dole grew pineapples in the area. Today it has largely spacious residential lots mixed with pastoral countryside reminiscent of Pennsylvania Quaker farmland.

Many of Kauai's B&Bs are in Wailua Homesteads. They are all more intimate and better value than the nearby hotels. The area is scenic rural country with fine mountain views.

The *House of Aleva* (Ernest and Anita Perry, 5509 Kuamoo Rd, Kapaa, HI 96746; tel 822-4606) is a B&B two miles up Kuamoo Rd (Hwy 580) from Coco Palms. Ernest is a former seaman and Anita reads tarot cards. Rooms cost $35/50 for singles/doubles.

The *Cloud 9 Holiday B&B* (5876 Ohe St, Kapaa, HI 96746; tel 822-7371) is a very large modern unit with a private entrance, cable TV, a phone, a tub and a tiled sink. You wake up to a lush garden view with the Sleeping Giant as a backdrop. There's a microwave and a little refrigerator stocked with healthy breakfast fixings. The rate is $60. Karol and Paul Kyno are transplanted Texans who are interested in scuba diving. They occasionally rent an upstairs room in their home for $50. They keep the place very neat and don't allow smoking.

The *Rosewood B&B* (Rosemary & Norbert Smith, 872 Kamalu Rd, Kapaa, HI 96746; tel 822-5216) has one bedroom in an 80-year-old restored plantation home. It's very much a wholesome family scene, with two dogs, two cats and five friendly kids. Rosemary runs Rosewood Real Estate and Norbert runs Rosewood Landscaping. Presently a bathroom is shared with three children but they're working on a private bath. Breakfast is served in the kitchen. Smoking is not allowed. The rate is $35.

The *Makana Inn* (6485 Makana Rd, Kapaa, HI 96746; tel 822-1075) is tucked into rolling pasture at the end of a quiet road. A modern one-bedroom unit is separate from the house, with a king-size bed, a kitchen and a splendid country view for $60. A second

unit, under the main house, with a kitchenette and a queen-size bed, costs $50. Both have private entrances, fold-out futons in the living room, cable TV and a telephone. They share a washer and a dryer. Breakfast food items are provided. A third guest can stay for $10 extra.

Kay Barker's B&B (Box 740, Kapaa, HI 96746; tel 822-3073) is run by Kay, who is in her 80s, and her son Gordon. There are four rooms, each with a private bathroom. The backyard looks out onto a field with grazing horses and is just below the trailhead to Sleeping Giant. The house is not as polished as the other B&Bs around there, but it's a reasonable $25 to $40 for singles, $30 to $40 for doubles.

The *Kapaa Sands* (380 Papaloa Rd, Kapaa, HI 96746; tel 822-4901; 800-222-4901) has 24 condo units set up in fourplexes. All have kitchens, fans and louvred windows to catch the breeze. They are simple but adequate and relatively good value at $59 for studios and $79 for two-bedroom units for up to four people. There's a three to seven-day minimum stay.

The *Aston Kauai Resort* (3-5920 Kuhio Hwy, Kapaa, HI 96746; tel 245-3931; 800-92-7866) is directly above Lydgate Beach Park and next to the Wailua Golf Course. The grounds are lacklustre and the pool is really small. Standard rooms cost $89 to $139, while studios cost $129 to $149.

The *Coco Palms Resort* (Box 631, Lihue, HI 96766; tel 822-4921; 800-542-2626) has a dated South Pacific motif, with old thatched-roof cottages and giant clam shell washbasins. Hotel rooms are $110 to $150, cottages (not recommended) are $180 to $240, suites are $155 to $250. You pay for the resort's reputation, and honeymoon packages are big.

Places to Stay – Coconut Plantation

Coconut Plantation has four hotels and a condo, all fairly modern, with lanais, pools and the usual standard facilities. It also has a long stretch of uncrowded beach but it's not great for water activities nor is it gorgeous like Poipu or North Shore beaches.

The *Sheraton Coconut Beach Hotel* (Box 830, Kapaa, HI 96746; tel 822-3455; 800-325-3535 from the USA and Canada, 008-222229 from Australia) is a 309-room secluded hotel at one end of Coconut Plantation. It's quite appealing for a chain hotel. The rooms are nicely decorated and the 4th floor rooms have high ceilings, though the hotel is stingy with lanai space. Rooms cost $105 to $155, depending on the view. This is the nicest hotel in the Wailua to Kapaa area.

The *Kauai Beachboy* (484 Kuhio Highway, Kapaa, HI 96746; tel 822-3441; 800-367-8047 from the USA, 800-423-8733 from Canada) is a standard beach hotel with 243 rooms from $88 to $103.

The *Islander on the Beach* (484 Kuhio Hwy, Kapaa, HI 96746; tel 822-7417; 800-367-7052) has 200 rooms in half a dozen three-storey buildings. Rooms have refrigerators and are $88 to $109. There's a poolside bar.

The *Kauai Sands Hotel* (420 Papaloa Rd, Kapaa, HI 96746; tel 822-4951; 800-367-7000 from the USA, 800-654-7020 from Canada) is one of the Sand & Seaside Hotels. The rooms have recently been renovated, although the bright striped wallpaper and turquoise and green decor give the overall ambience of a budget chain motel. Rates are $64 to $80 ($87 with kitchenettes).

The *Plantation Hale* (484 Kuhio Hwy, Kapaa, HI 96746; tel 822-4941; 800-367-6046) is on the highway, not the beach. It has 160 one-bedroom units with kitchens and separate living rooms for $105 for up to four people.

Places to Eat

The *Sizzler* steak house (4361 Kuhio Hwy) is a real surprise. It has a great salad bar with fresh fruits rivalling those at any hotel buffet. It costs $6.80 and includes a taco and pasta bar. It's classy-looking for a Sizzler, with lots of skylights.

The *Lagoon Dining Room* at Coco Palms Resort has a buffet lunch from 11.15 am to 2 pm for $11. It has a fair variety of fruits and vegies. The main dishes are average buffet fare. The open-air restaurant looks out over the lagoon and coconut grove. Tour groups stop there and you could find yourself in the midst of 100 hungry rushing groupies.

Perry's Smorgy in Kauai Beachboy Hotel is cafeteria style and quality, but at $4 for an all-you-can-eat breakfast you can't beat the price. There's fresh fruit like papaya, pineapple and watermelon. Lunch is from 11 am to 2.30 pm and costs $5.50; dinner is from 5 to 9 pm and costs $8. The large open-air dining room looks out towards the beach.

Buzz's Steak & Lobster in the Market Place at Coconut Plantation has one of the island's freshest salad bars with nice touches like avocados and seaweed salad. The salad bar alone is $6.25, though sometimes they do an early-bird dinner that includes the salad bar, for not much more. Otherwise, most dinner main courses cost from $11 to $15. At lunch there's a soup, salad and sandwich bar for $6.75.

JJ's Boiler Room, on the other side of the Market Place, has prices similar to Buzz's but a skimpy salad bar.

The Market Place's *Cafe Espresso* is a takeaway bakery and cafe with a variety of coffees from $1 and croissants, muffins, pies, cakes and other pastries. It's open daily from 7.30 am, closing at 3 pm Sundays and 9 pm other days.

The *Kintaro* (tel 822-3341), opposite the Sizzler, has Japanese dinners in the $12 to $15 range. The sushi is good but the tempura is mediocre. There's also a teppanyaki room where the chef prepares food at your table with 'flying' knives for a few bucks more. It's open from 5.30 to 9.30 pm daily.

Entertainment

The *Aston Kauai Resort* draws names like Jesse Colin Young, the Peter Moon Band and Windham Hill for concerts with seating around tables and no dancing.

Buzz's in the Market Place at Coconut Plantation has live music from 9 pm till midnight Wednesday to Saturday.

The *Coco Palms Resort* has a torchlighting ceremony nightly at 7.30 pm. It's theatrical but fun, with young men in malos running around the grounds lighting torches to the beating of drums. Best of all, this one's a freebie.

WAIPOULI

Waipouli is the name given to the area between Coconut Plantation and Kapaa. Its biggest draw is its little shopping centres. Waipouli Town Center has a Foodland supermarket (open 24 hours a day), a McDonald's and a Pizza Hut. Kapaa Shopping Center has Kapaa's post office, Big Save supermarket, Laser Ready Copies (nine-cent photocopies) and a video shop.

Sleeping Giant

The Sleeping Giant is taking his eternal rest stretched out atop the Nonou Ridge with his head in Wailua and his feet in Kapaa. There's a marked viewpoint just north of the Waipouli Complex.

Legend says a friendly giant fell asleep there after eating too much poi at a luau. When his menehune friends needed his help they tried to awaken him by throwing stones at him, but the stones bounced from his full belly into his open mouth. As the giant swallowed the stones, he died and turned to rock.

A hiking trail runs across the ridge connecting Wailua Homesteads and Wailua Houselots (see East Side Trails). The giant's forehead, the highest point on the ridge, is 1241 feet .

Wailua Houselots, east of the ridge, was the first subdivision on Kauai. It was originally divided into two-acre lots and had some spacious Hawaiian-style homes. Most of the lots have since been subdivided and the homes are now more typical standardised tract development.

Places to Stay

The *Mokihana of Kauai* (796 Kuhio Hwy, Kapaa, HI 96746; tel 822-3971) has 79 studio units on the beach. Each has twin beds, a hot plate, a refrigerator and a lanai with an ocean view for $45. There's a laundry room and a large pool too. This is a time-share complex that rents to people without bookings if space is available. Not many people know about it. When we came in at the height of the season and every other hotel was full, two rooms were available there. It has a three-night minimum stay. The rooms are rather plain but around this area an ocean view for $45 is a bargain!

The front desk at Mokihana also handles the 57 one-bedroom time-share units at nearby *Kauai Kailani I & II* . The units have full kitchens and cost $55. Ask for Kauai Kailani I as it's on the ocean.

These three properties are the best-value condos around. For reservations contact Hawaii Kailani, 119 N Commercial, Bellingham, WA 98225; tel 206-676-1434.

Places to Eat

The *King & I* (tel 822-1642) in Waipouli Plaza is our favourite Kauai restaurant. It's casual and friendly and has fantastic Thai food. The spring rolls served with fresh mint, cucumber and peanut sauce are not to be missed. The green curry gets its colour from fresh basil, lime leaves and lemongrass. They grow their own herbs. Many dishes cost between $5 and $6 and can be prepared mild, medium or hot. They have brown rice and a whole page of vegie dishes. The owner used to cook at Keo's, Honolulu's premier Thai restaurant. It's open from 11 am to 2 pm Mondays, Tuesdays, Thursdays and Fridays and from 5 to 9 pm nightly.

The *Bull Shed* (tel 822-3791) at Mokihana condos is a busy steak and seafood place. It's known for its prime rib at $16. Other dishes are from $10. There's another Bull Shed (tel 245-4551) in Nawiliwili at Harbor Village, opposite the entrance to the Westin Kauai.

The *Aloha Diner* in Waipouli Complex is the place to try real Hawaiian food. You can order à la carte or get complete lunches from about $6. Dinner costs $7.50 to $9.50. It's open from 10.30 am to 3 pm and from 5.30 to 9 pm.

The *Dragon Inn* in Waipouli Plaza is Kapaa's most popular Chinese restaurant, though the food's mediocre. Many main dishes are in the $5 range. Local people like to go there for the chow mein with cake noodles. It's open from 11 am to 2 pm

Top: Taro fields, Hanalei Valley, Kauai
Left: Waipoo Falls, Waimea Canyon, Kauai
Right: Na Pali cliffs, Kauai

Top: Haena Beach, Kauai
Left: Kilauea Lighthouse, Kauai
Right: Kalalau Valley, Kauai

Tuesday to Saturday and from 4.30 to 9.30 pm nightly.

Zippy's, next to Waipouli Plaza, has a large menu, including lots of plate lunches from $4.30 to $5.70. It's very much fast-food quality, but it is open 24 hours a day.

The *Waipouli Restaurant* in Waipouli Town Center has a breakfast special of egg, pancakes and bacon for $2. They have lots of diner-quality dinners from salad to coffee for $6. Lunch is a bit cheaper and it has inexpensive saimin.

Ambrose's Natural Foods (tel 822-7112), opposite Waipouli Town Center, sells local produce and other island-produced foods. Ambrose opens up whenever he feels like it and generally stays open until 6 pm. Otherwise he says to look for him in the yard or telephone him. It's closed on Sundays.

Tropical Taco in Kapaa Shopping Center has unexciting Mexican food at moderate prices. Their speciality is fresh fish fried in beer batter and served in a taco for $8 with rice and beans.

KAPAA

Kapaa is an old plantation town with a centre geared more towards local needs than tourism. It has a small hotel, a few restaurants and an old theatre on the comeback.

Kapaa, as unimposing as it appears, is Kauai's second largest town. You can walk the main drag in 10 minutes. Most of the residential area is mauka of there.

The Kapaa Beach Park, off Niu St behind the ball field, has a beach, picnic tables and a public swimming pool.

The Kapaa Public Library (1464 Kuhio Hwy; tel 822-5041) is open from 9 am to 5 pm Mondays, Wednesdays, Thursdays and Fridays and from noon to 8 pm Tuesdays.

The Roxy Theater, recently reopened, was originally built in the 1930s with the help of Honolulu architect C W Dickey. It first opened with *Lady of the Tropics* starring Heddy Lamar and Robert Taylor: the tickets were 25 cents.

Places to Stay

The *Hotel Coral Reef* (1516 Kuhio Hwy,

Kapaa, HI 96746; tel 822-4481; 800-843-4659) has two sections. The older part has nine rooms for $35 and a room without windows for $25. Rooms are basic but clean with standing fans and painted cinder block walls. The louvred doors and windows don't act as much of a barrier to the traffic noise. There's almost a boarding house atmosphere, with a communal TV downstairs. The newer wing has 16 rooms with ocean views for $65. There's no pool.

Places to Eat

All these restaurants are in central Kapaa, within a few minutes walk of each other.

Norberto's El Cafe (tel 822-3362) on Hwy 56 has been in the neighbourhood a long time, a sure sign that it's doing something right. You can get an enchilada or chilli rellenos plate with soup, vegies, rice and beans for $10. Or order à la carte, where a taco costs $2.25. It has margaritas and beer to wash it all down. It's open from 5.30 to 9.30 pm daily.

The *Decko Gecko*, on Hwy 56 next to Sea Sage, has curry dishes and fresh tamales (tofu and pumpkin, green chilli and cheese, as well as the more standard beef and pork). It also has a different quiche each day, along with sandwiches, salads, great pastries and whole-grain breads.

Marilyn Monroe smiles down from a movie poster above the tables at *Roxy Diner*, adjacent to the Roxy Theater on Kukui Rd. Omelettes with toast and hash browns are $5 to $6. The servings are large. Eggs Seattle is a good choice. At lunch time it's burgers or sandwiches with fries at similar prices.

Jimmy's Grill on Hwy 56 is where the crowd goes to have a few beers and watch the game on TV. It has burgers and sandwiches for $4.75 to $6.75 as well as soups and salads.

Entertainment

The *Roxy Theater* has something for everyone. It hosts some decent rock groups (UB40 played there), mellow Hawaiian guitarists and local bands as well as such oddities as female wrestling. Most Friday and Saturday nights there's a DJ, a dance contest and videos.

KAPAA TO KILAUEA

The drive from Kapaa to Kilauea is through fields of sugar cane in varying stages of growth, from newly planted seed cane to mature stalk. Beyond the fields, the jagged edges of the Anahola mountain peaks cut their way through the clouds. In the other direction there are glimpses of bright blue ocean and distant bays.

A couple of scenic lookouts just north of Kapaa are worth pulling over for. Sunsets can be particularly nice if there's a low tide with waves breaking over the shallows and fishermen out with their throw nets.

Kealia Beach

The long, pretty beach at the 10-mile marker is Kealia Beach. During transitional swells, Kealia can be a good place for surfing. There are no facilities here.

Donkey's Beach

Donkey's Beach is best known as a nudist beach, though it's used by both clad and unclad sunbathers. This windswept sandy beach is completely hidden from the road. All the ironwood trees there lean away from the shore and those right at the beach are so blown over they almost look like shrubs. Naupaka and ilima grow in the sand.

The trail to Donkey's begins about half a mile past the 11-mile marker, just before the guard rail starts. It's 10 minutes down a well-worn path beside a sugar cane field. Cross the barbed wire fence that holds in a few mules (not donkeys, but what the heck) to get to the beach. It's down to the right. There are no facilities.

Anahola

Anahola Beach Park, a county park on Hawaiian Home Lands, has an encampment of indigenous Hawaiians who have built a little shanty town of tents, plywood and plastic sheeting and are determined to take back the land.

Anahola is a wide bay and was an ancient surfing site. To get there, turn off Hwy 56 onto Kukuihale Rd at the 13-mile marker, and just less than a mile down, turn onto the dirt beach road.

Places to Stay The *Mahina Kai* (Box 699, 4933 Aliomanu Rd, Anahola, HI 96703; tel 822-9451) is a B&B on Anahola Bay that caters mainly for the gay community. Hosts Dale and Rick are well-travelled former Californians whose home has lots of Asian-Pacific aesthetics such as shoji doors, meditating buddhas, Oriental carpets and a little fountain courtyard. It's a nice place to relax. There are four nice rooms at $70/95 for singles/doubles and a studio apartment for $130.

Places to Eat *Duane's Ono Burger* on Hwy 56 sells burgers and teri sandwiches for $3.65 to $6. It's just a window with picnic tables outside, very popular with local beachgoers. It's open from 10 am to 6 pm Monday to Saturday. You may have to wait in line at lunch time.

Anahola's post office and the Whaler's General Store are next door. Just past Duane's, fresh flower leis are sold from a pick-up truck parked at the side of the road.

Hole in the Mountain

The Hole in the Mountain can't presently be seen from the HVB marker as the hole closed during a landslide at the time of Hurricane Iwa. But just slightly north of the 15-mile marker, look back at the mountain down to the right of the tallest pinnacle and you might be able to see the small hole that has started to re-open.

Legend says the original hole was created when a giant threw his spear through the mountain causing the water stored within to gush forth as waterfalls. After the hole closed, Hawaii began to experience one of the worst droughts in its history.

Koolau Road

The paved but bumpy Koolau Rd is a peaceful drive through rich green pastures with white egrets and bright wildflowers. Take it as a scenic loop off the highway or to get to Moloaa Beach or Larsens Beach. Both the road and the beaches are off the tourist track. Neither beach has any facilities.

Koolau Rd connects with Hwy 56 half a mile past the 16-mile marker (at Sunrise Fruit Stand) and again three-quarters of a mile past the 19-mile marker.

To get to Moloaa Beach coming from the south, turn right onto Koolau Rd at the fruit stand and after 1¼ miles turn right onto Moloaa Rd. The road ends three-quarters of a mile down at a few beach houses.

Moloaa is very rural, with horses grazing on the hills above the crescent-shaped bay. Because it's not heavily frequented it's a pretty good beach for shelling. Sometimes people unofficially camp under the trees fronting the beach.

The northern end of the beach before the rocky outcrop is somewhat protected for swimming though it's not all that deep. The whole bay can have strong currents when the surf is rough.

On the grassy hill north of the bay a trail leads to a point offering peeks into the coastal hills and valleys to the south. The trail is through flowering groundcover of pink and yellow lantana; sensitive plants whose leaves close when touched; and pau-o-Hiiaka, a trailing vine with small tulip-like blue flowers, related to the morning glory.

The turnoff to Larsens Beach is a little more than a mile down from the north intersection of Koolau Rd and Hwy 56, or just over a mile north of the intersection of Moloaa and Koolau roads. Turn makai on the dirt road there and then take the immediate left. It's about a mile in. Larsens is a long golden sand beach but it has dangerous currents, especially during winter. Riptides at either end of the beach can be very strong.

EAST SIDE TRAILS
Kuilau Trail
For the effort, the Kuilau Trail is one of the most visually rewarding trails on the island. The marked trailhead is on the right, just before Hwy 580 crosses the stream at the Keahua Arboretum.

The maintained trail starts up a wide dirt path that is also used by horses and the occasional dirt bike and four-wheeler. The trail rises out of eucalyptus trees to hillsides covered with lush ferns. There are broad vistas of the mountains all along and plenty of guava to pick.

The hike up is along a broad ridge that offers views into valleys on both sides, right down to the coast. You can see Kapaa to the right. It takes about half an hour to walk the 1¼ miles up to a grassy clearing with a great view and a picnic table.

Beyond there, Kuilau Trail continues as a narrow footpath offering even more spectacular views. It ends in about a mile at the Moalepe Trail. If you don't want to go that far, some of the best vistas are just a few minutes past the picnic area.

At the connection with the Moalepe Trail, if you go left you'll come to a viewpoint after about 10 minutes. If you go right on Moalepe you'll come out on Olohena Rd in Wailua Homesteads about 2¼ miles down.

Nonou Ridge (Sleeping Giant) Trail
The Nonou Ridge Trail goes up the Sleeping Giant to a summit point on his upper chest that affords views of the Wailua to Kapaa coast and the highland valleys inland. It's a well-maintained trail that takes 1½ to two hours for the round trip.

It has two trailheads. The trail on the western side is a shaded forest trail of tall trees and moss-covered stones. The trail on the eastern side is a little more open and a bit longer. The eastern trail begins at the water pump site a mile up Haleilio Rd in Wailua Houselots.

The western trail starts on Hwy 581 (Kamalu Rd), near mailbox 1068. Walk through a metal gate marked as a forestry right of way and up along a small cattle pasture to the trailhead.

It's a wonderful trail to do early in the morning when it's relatively cool and you can watch the light slowly spread across the valley below. The eucalyptus at the trailhead soon gives way to a tall thick forest of Norfolk pines. These were planted in a

Civilian Conservation Corps (CCC) reforestation programme during the 1930s.

A few minutes up the trail there's a fork. Veer left up the path with the large rock beside it. The packed trail can get slippery when wet so look for a walking stick. Hikers sometimes leave them near the trailhead.

The trail passes through thick strawberry guava bushes that can grow up to 15 feet high. In places they create a canopied tunnel-like effect. The small red fruit is eaten whole: the sweetest of the guavas, it is considered a delicacy.

A few minutes below the summit, the eastern and western trails merge on the ridge. Continue up to the right past some hala trees. On the summit is a picnic table shelter that offers protection from the rain. Passing showers can give some incredible valley rainbows. To the west there's a 180° view of Wailua Valley and the Makaleha Mountains.

Below to the east you can see Kapaa, sugar cane fields, Wailua Houselots, Coco Palms and the Wailua River. To the right of the riverboat docks and mauka of the Kauai Aston Hotel there's a square dark-green area in the sugar cane field. This is Malae Heiau, now overgrown with Java plums.

If you go south across the picnic area the trail continues. About five minutes up there's a rocky area where you can sit and enjoy the view. The ridge continues up the giant's head. Should it tempt you, size it up carefully. It's sharp, and loose rocks and slides are visible.

North Shore

Kauai's North Shore has an unhurried pace and incredible scenery. It has deep mountain valleys, ancient taro fields, one-lane bridges, white sand beaches and the rugged Na Pali Coast.

It's lush and often wet. In winter that can mean days of rain on end, but in summer it usually means brief showers followed by rainbows. On bright full-moon nights you might even see a moonbow – a rainbow coloured with moonbeams.

Rainy days are almost dream-like. The tops of the mountains become shrouded in clouds that alternately drift and lift revealing a series of waterfalls that plunge down the face of the mountains.

The North Shore takes in the sea-bird sanctuary at Kilauea and a couple of small coastal villages before reaching the resort community of Princeville with its condos and golf courses.

But it's the area beyond, from Hanalei Bridge to Kee Beach at road's end, that best embodies the North Shore spirit. This is a part of Hawaii that has resisted mass tourism and stalled development. Its appeal is not in creature comforts but in stunning natural beauty. It attracts people tuned in to the environment. Over the years musicians like Graham Nash and Buffy Sainte-Marie and all sorts of artists have called Kauai's North Shore home.

KILAUEA

Kilauea is an old sugar plantation town whose main attraction these days is its picturesque lighthouse and sea-bird sanctuary at Kilauea Point.

Kolo Rd, the turnoff into Kilauea, is just past the 23-mile marker on Hwy 56. You pass a gas station, a post office with a mini-mart and an Episcopal church in quick succession. Kilauea Rd starts opposite the church and ends two miles on at Kilauea Point.

The famed Kilauea Slippery Slide, built for the movie *South Pacific*, is on private property and is no longer accessible to the public due to concerns about liability.

Episcopal Church

The Christ Memorial Episcopal Church attracts attention because of its striking lava rock architecture. It was built in 1941. The interesting lava rock headstones in the churchyard are older, dating back to when the original Hawaiian Congregational church stood on this site.

'Birds only beyond this sign'

Shops
Aloha International runs the Hawaiian Art Museum & Bookstore near the corner of Kolo and Kilauea roads. It's not really a museum, but rather a shop with a pretty good selection of Hawaiiana books and paintings.

Kong Lung Center, half a mile up Kilauea Rd, has shops and a few places to eat.

Quarry Beach
If you're looking for somewhere new to explore, you might try Quarry Beach at Kilauea Bay. Take the second dirt road to the right after Kong Lung Center and go down about 1½ miles. The road, which starts off through a sugar cane field, is bumpy and rutted but usually passable if it hasn't been raining a lot. You have to wade across Kilauea Stream to get to the beach. It's nice enough, but Secret Beach is the real prize in these parts.

Secret Beach
Secret Beach is a gorgeous golden sand beach with a view of Kilauea Lighthouse. The beach can't be seen from the road so few tourists discover it, making it a private hideaway for people who know the island.

This long broad beach is Kauai's premier nudist beach – though surfers and suited people frequent it as well. There are apt to be a few tents, as it's a popular unofficial camping spot.

Coming from Kilauea, turn left onto Kauapea Rd, the last paved road before reaching the lighthouse. About a quarter of a mile down the road there's a beach access sign. (If the sign's gone, look for cars parked along the side of the road).

The beach is a five-minute walk down a fairly steep trail. If you have sandals on you might want to kick them off and go barefoot as the ironwood needles covering the trail are slippery. Just before landing on the beach it's lush and jungle-like. In fact the vegetation is so dense that it can be a little challenging finding the trail when you leave!

A more idyllic setting would be hard to find. You can walk along the beach in either direction for still more seclusion.

Kilauea Point
Kilauea Point, a national wildlife refuge, is the northernmost point of the inhabited Hawaiian islands. Its lighthouse, built in 1913, is picture postcard material.

Four species of birds come to Kilauea to nest, leaving after their young have been hatched and reared.

Red-footed boobies are the most visible. They are abundant on the cliffs to the east where they build nests of sticks and leaves in the trees. Sea turtles can sometimes be seen swimming in the cove at the base of these cliffs. During winter, whales pass by off the point.

Wedge-tailed shearwaters arrive by April and stay through the summer. They nest in burrows which they dig right into Kilauea Point. Another species of birds here is the red-tailed tropicbird, which nests along the cliff edges.

Laysan albatross are here from about November to July. Some nest on Mokuaeae Rock, straight off the tip of the point. Inland, the grassy area to the west was cleared specifically to attract more albatross. Some now nest there on the ground at the base of the trees. Below this is Secret Beach, divided into three scalloped coves by lava fingers.

Great frigate birds nest on the northwestern Hawaiian islands, not Kauai, though these aerial pirates do visit Kilauea Point during the winter to steal food from other birds. You won't see the distinctive red throat balloon that the male puffs out to attract females, however, as they're not here for courtship. Frigate birds have a distinctive forked tail and are beautiful when they soar.

The visitor centre loans binoculars at no charge, has a telescope set up for bird-watching and sells books.

The cost for a single entry permit is $2, which includes an accompanying spouse, children and parents.

The refuge (tel 828-1414) is open from 10 am to 4 pm Monday to Friday. Even outside those hours it's worth driving to the end of Kilauea Rd for the view of the lighthouse and the point.

Crater Hill

Crater Hill, a recent 100-acre addition to the refuge, is east of Kilauea Point. This 568-foot cliff is geologically younger than the rest of the area by a few million years. It's a nesting site for sea birds and until acquired by the refuge was a favourite local spot for catching the sunset.

In due time about three miles of rugged hiking trails will be open to naturalists. Visitors will have to be accompanied by trained guides who know how to steer clear of the ground nests.

Guava Plantation

The Guava Kai Plantation has 480 acres of guava trees which produce juice for Ocean Spray. There are tours of its operations and the visitor centre doles out free samples of guava juice. There's a little deli with sandwiches and salads and you can even pick up guava souvenirs. The plantation is open from 9 am to 5 pm daily.

It's on Kuawa Rd, which is mauka of Hwy 56, about a mile south of the main turnoff to Kilauea.

Places to Eat

Jacques' Bakery is in an old sugar mill Quonset (Nissen) hut on Oka St off Kilauea Rd. It's a good place to stop for breakfast on your way to the lighthouse. You can get a croissant and coffee for a mere $1 and eat it outside at one of the rickety old tables. Breakfast is from 6.30 to 10 am Monday to Friday. Two eggs, meat and rice cost $3.

The *Casa di Amici*, an up-market Italian restaurant in the Kong Lung Center, has an open-air setting and waiters with an annoying patter. Submarine sandwiches cost $4 to $5 at lunch time. Dinner main courses cost from $7.50 to $22. It's open from 11 am to 3 pm and from 5 to 9.30 pm Monday to Saturday.

The Bread Also Rises, a bakery tucked behind Casa di Amici, sells bread, cookies and great cinnamon rolls. Its speciality is a flat seven-grain bread with garlic for $3. With a slab of cheese and a bottle of wine you'd have a gourmet picnic lunch. It's open from 7 am to 5 pm daily.

The *Farmer's Market*, a grocery store with a deli, is in the Kong Lung Center. The deli has such things as chocolate truffles, turkey swiss sandwiches on whole-wheat bread and

Mexi salad with brown rice, vegies and herbs. Shave ice and ice cream are sold from a little window at the side of the market.

Banana Joe's is that bright yellow shack on the left side of Hwy 56 just beyond the turnoff to Kilauea. Banana Joe and his sister Alex dish up a mean frozen fruit frosty. It's made solely of frozen fruit squeezed through a processor, coming out as smooth as ice cream. The papaya and pineapple flavours are the best. A bowl of this ($1.50) and a granola bar make a good light breakfast. They also dry their own banana strips and sell fresh fruit from their 6½-acre plot of bananas, citrus and guava. It's open from 9 am to 6 pm daily.

KALIHIWAI

Kalihiwai Rd was a loop road going down past Kalihiwai Beach, connecting with the highway at two points, until the tidal wave of 1957 washed out the bridge over Kalihiwai River. Now there are two Kalihiwai roads, one on each side of the river.

The Kalihiwai Rd on the Lihue side, half a mile beyond Kilauea, leads down a mile to Kalihiwai Beach. At the very end of the road you can still see the pillars that once supported the bridge. The river empties out into a wide, deep bay. The broad sandy beach is a popular spot for all kinds of activities including swimming, bodysurfing, boogie boarding and picnicking. The river is popular with kayakers.

From Kalihiwai Beach, it's possible to hike to Kalihiwai Falls by walking straight along the dirt 4WD road which starts at the very end of the paved road. The road, which follows the river up, at times may look like little more than tyre tracks. The road goes through a pasture area of scrub where cattle graze and ends at the first set of falls and a pool. On the other side of the river a little trail goes uphill to the second set of falls and an even nicer pool. It's about an hour's walk up from the beach and it can be muddy.

On your way back up to the highway along Kalihiwai Rd, look to the left just before going over the tiny white bridge with the 10-ton weight limit sign. A picturesque waterfall is almost hidden in a lush little gully full of hanging vines.

Waterfalls

Back on Hwy 56 there's a pull-off on the right immediately before the sweeping Kalihiwai Bridge, about one mile past Kalihiwai Rd. Views of three waterfalls are nearby.

The most scenic is Kalihiwai Falls, seen by walking a third of the way onto the bridge ahead and looking up into the valley. Below the bridge you can see the dirt road that leads up to the falls.

You can see a bit of another falls by walking to the eastern side of the pull-off and looking down over the edge. For the third you must walk back along the road a minute or two toward Lihue. The falls is just above the road.

Kauai's native roosters – moa – hang out here. Like pigeons surrounding a park bench, they stare arrogantly with beady little eyes at those who fail to offer a hand-out.

Places to Stay

At *Hale Ho'o Maha* (Box 422, Kilauea, HI 96754; tel 828-1330), Kirby Guyer rents one room in her house on the beach at Kalihiwai Bay. Kirby is very personable with lots of aloha. If you're a people person this is a great alternative to the hotel scene. The rate of $40 includes continental breakfast. Smokers and social drinkers are welcome. There's even a little boat that guests are free to take upriver.

ANINI

Anini has a long beach and vast reef flats. To get there take the Kalihiwai Rd on the Hanalei side of the bridge and then bear left onto Anini Rd. It's about 1½ miles from the highway to the beach.

There has been talk of connecting Princeville and Anini by a direct coastal road. A grassroots group, Concerned Citizens to Save Anini, has managed to keep the road at bay. For now, Anini's dead-end street means little traffic, keeping the area unhurried and quiet.

Still, Anini is growing, with some expensive private homes going up. A group of investors, including Sylvester Stallone, has recently bought a large chunk of Anini from Princeville. Stallone can sometimes be seen playing polo on the field across from the beach.

Anini Beach

Anini Beach County Park (marked Wanini, the old spelling) is a long beach park divided into day-use, windsurfing and camping areas. It has gentle breezes and tropical almond shade trees. There are showers, changing rooms, drinking water, picnic pavilions and a pay phone.

Anini has a good camping ground right on the water. It's spacious for a beach park and the camping sites are shaded by trees. It gets a little more crowded on weekends when locals, mostly families, come down.

In addition to the day-use area, you can also swim and snorkel in front of the camping area, though it's best when the tide is high. A pretty good spot here is opposite the midpoint of Kauai Polo Club's fence.

Half a mile past the camping area you can watch people walking way out onto the shallow reef of Anini Flats picking opihi, net fishing for bait fish and catching octopuses.

PRINCEVILLE

Princeville seems a bit too orderly, too manicured and too large for Kauai's free-spirited North Shore.

Princeville, Kauai's biggest development, has a couple of championship golf courses, 10 condo complexes, 22 tennis courts, hundreds of private homes, a luxury hotel, restaurants and a shopping centre. It's all spread over 11,000 acres on a promontory between Hanalei Bay and Anini Beach. Princeville even has its own little airport.

Princeville traces its haole roots to Robert Wyllie, a Scottish doctor who later became foreign minister to Kamehameha IV. In the mid-1800s Wyllie bought a large coffee plantation in Hanalei and began planting sugar.

When Queen Emma and Kamehameha IV came to visit in 1860, Wyllie named his plantation and surrounding lands Princeville in honour of their young son, Prince Albert. The plantation later became a cattle ranch and in 1968 ground was broken for the Princeville Resort.

Princeville Resort is currently in the midst of a building boom. Its growth has given the North Shore the distinction of being the fastest growing district in the state.

Future plans call for the development of light industry, expansion of the airport runway, a sports complex and two more resort hotels. There are also plans for a controversial movie museum, the centrepiece of a huge addition which will almost triple the size of the current shopping centre.

The Sheraton Princeville hotel is on one of Hawaii's prime locations, overlooking Hanalei Bay and the Bali Hai mountains. It's the site of an old Russian fort built in 1817.

Developers got around height restrictions by terracing the sprawling hotel down the hillside. Instead of designing the lobby to take in the scenery, it is enclosed and dark. The atmosphere is more African safari than Hawaiian.

Islanders, who lost one of their best sunset viewpoints to the hotel, nicknamed the fortress-like building 'The Prison'.

Information

Princeville Shopping Center has a gas station, a supermarket, a kite shop, a camera shop, a Bank of Hawaii, a Western Union office and several restaurants and boutiques. Foodland supermarket is open from 7 am to 11 pm daily.

Princeville Chevron is open from 7 am to 8 pm daily. If you're heading toward Kee Beach at the end of the road, this is the last place to fill your car with gas.

Kuhio Highway changes from Hwy 56 to Hwy 560 at the 28-mile marker in front of Princeville Shopping Center. The 10-mile stretch from there to Kee Beach at the end of the road is one of the most scenic drives in all of Hawaii.

Places to Stay

You can frequently find someone in Princeville renting out a bedroom in their condo or home, often for about $40 a day. Look for ads in the paper or on the bulletin board at Foodland in the Princeville Shopping Center.

Princeville has 10 condo complexes, some perched on cliffs, others by the golf course. A fair number of the condo units are for year-round housing.

Most complexes are represented by a number of different rental agents. Two of these agents are: Blue Water Vacation Rentals, Princeville Shopping Center, Box 366, Princeville, HI 96714 (tel 826-9229; 800-367-8047 ext 311); and Kauai 800, Box 640, Poipu Beach, HI 96756 (tel 742-7502; 800-443-9180).

The *Hanalei Bay Resort* (Box 220, Hanalei, HI 96714; tel 826-6522; 800-367-7040) was recently bought out by a New Zealand company which is remodelling and standardising the former condos. Some of the 176 units have good views of Hanalei Bay. Not all have kitchenettes. It has a front desk and is run as a hotel. Rooms are $80 to $180. There are pools and tennis courts.

Hawaiian Islands Resorts (Box 212, Honolulu, HI 96810; tel 531-7595; 800-367-7042) manages the following three Princeville properties: the *Hale Moi* which has hotel rooms for $55/$65 low/high season, and studios for $75/85 low/high; the *Pali Ke Kua* which has hotel rooms for $55/65 low/high season and one-bedroom units from $95/105 low/high; and the *Puu Poa* which has two-bedroom units from $150. Weekly rates are six times the daily rate.

Sealodge is an older complex, but it's high on a cliff and many of the 86 units have great sunrise views looking across the expansive coral reef of Anini. If you leave the windows open the surf is guaranteed to give you nautical dreams. One-bedroom units generally cost from $75 to $100.

Paliuli Cottages (Box 351, Hanalei, HI 96714; tel 826-6264) has eight separate cottages on the golf course. Each has beam ceilings, two bedrooms, a kitchen, a gas fireplace and its own tiny pool for $105 to $125.

The *Sheraton Princeville* (Box 3069, Princeville, HI 96722; tel 826-9644) is currently being refurbished.

Places to Eat

Cafe Zelo's in the Princeville Shopping Center is a casual cafe with creative, reasonably priced food. It's open for breakfast and lunch daily. The spinach lasagne with garlic bread is $5.50. Sandwiches and salads are similarly priced. From 5 to 10 pm Thursdays, Fridays and Saturdays it serves dinners with a Mediterranean flavour.

Chuck's Steak House in the Princeville Shopping Center has a pretty good all-you-can-eat salad bar for $8. Full dinners which include the salad bar range from $11.50 to $30. It's open from 6 to 10 pm nightly. Lunch is served on weekdays only, featuring the salad bar and sandwiches.

The *Pizza Burger* in the Princeville Shopping Center is the closest the North Shore comes to fast food. In addition to pizza, you can get a Hanalei buffalo burger there.

The *Bali Hai Restaurant* in the Hanalei Bay Resort has open-air dining with a fine view of Hanalei Bay and the Bali Hai mountains. At breakfast, macadamia nut waffles with coffee cost $5.50. At lunch, sandwiches with fries cost from $6 to $8. Dinners are in the $15 to $20 range. The food's good, but the view's the real attraction.

The *Beamreach* (tel 826-9131) is considered one of Princeville's best restaurants. Steak, seafood and chicken dinners with salad and baked potato cost from $9 to $20. Beamreach is at Pali Ke Kua, off to the right on the way to the Sheraton. It's open from 6 to 10 pm nightly.

If the locations of the *Sheraton Princeville's* restaurants don't change with the renovations, there are a few worth checking out for the view alone. The cafe one level below the lobby has a fantastic view of Hanalei Bay. It used to put on a great, though not inexpensive, breakfast buffet. There is also a fine view from the corridor in front of the 8th floor restaurants.

Entertainment

Scott Moulton sometimes plays at the *Bali*

Hai Restaurant in Princeville. He's an accomplished local guitarist worth seeing.

HANALEI VALLEY

Just beyond Princeville, Hanalei Valley Lookout has a spectacular overview of the patchwork taro fields spread across the valley floor. Don't miss it.

The Hanalei National Wildlife Refuge encompasses 917 acres of the valley, stretching up both sides of Hanalei River. The private taro farms in the refuge provide most of Hawaii's commercially grown taro as well as habitat for endangered water birds.

In the mid-1800s rice farming was introduced into Hanalei Valley to feed the Chinese labourers who worked the sugar cane fields. The rice grew so well that by the 1880s it became a major export crop. Now taro once again predominates and the old Hariguchi Rice Mill that stands along the river road is closed.

From the lookout, to the lower right, you can glimpse the North Shore's first one-lane bridge, opened in 1912. The road leading into the valley along the western bank of the river is Ohiki Rd. From Ohiki there's a trail that runs deep into the upper valley and another that climbs the first ridge on the right, going up to the twin peaks (see the North Shore Trails section later).

Hanalei Bridge

The seven one-lane bridges between Hanalei River and the end of the road not only link this part of the North Shore to the rest of the island, they also protect it from runaway development.

Big cement trucks and heavy construction equipment are beyond their limits. Even large package-tour buses are kept at bay.

Over the years North Shore residents have successfully beaten down proposals to build a two-lane bridge over Hanalei River. For the moment they seem to have won. In 1989 the old one-lane Hanalei Bridge underwent long-needed repairs instead and received a fresh coat of paint.

During unusually heavy rains the road between the taro fields and the river can flood and the Hanalei Bridge closes until it subsides.

The rules of the road on the North Shore dictate that when two cars approach an empty one-lane bridge, the car that reaches the

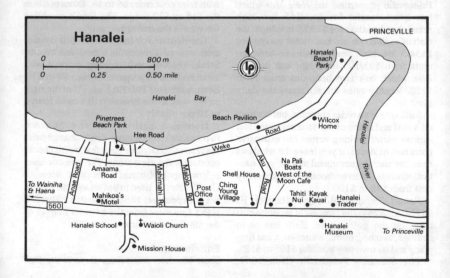

bridge last yields to the entire line-up of approaching cars, rather than alternating one car in each direction.

After the bridge, the valley widens. Buffalo belonging to Hanalei Garden Farms graze in the pastures to the right. They have shed their thick woolly fur for a short tropical coat. Buffalo burgers and teriyaki buffalo kebabs have begun to find their way onto Kauai menus. There is talk of doing tours of the ranch in the future.

Ohiki Road

If you want to go into Hanalei Valley, turn left onto Ohiki Rd immediately after Hanalei Bridge. The drive is along the river and taro fields.

Snow-white egrets are common alongside the road. Night herons and endangered Hawaiian water birds live there too, including coots, stilts, the Hawaiian duck and the coot-like Hawaiian gallinule with its bright red bill.

On the latter part of the drive you pass banana trees, bamboo thickets, hau trees and ferns. Ohiki Rd ends in two miles at the Halalea Forest Reserve where a trail leading deep into the valley starts along a dirt road.

HANALEI

After the Hanalei Bridge, Hwy 560 runs parallel to the Hanalei River. The mile before Hanalei village is a very pastoral scene of taro patches and grassland. There's no development of any kind and no buildings in sight. Take away the telephone poles and asphalt and this is how it's looked for centuries.

Hanalei has one museum depicting the modest lives of rural labourers and another of the more affluent missionary lifestyle. There are a growing number of small businesses. Hanalei's three best restaurants are still in weatherbeaten wooden buildings – it's that kind of town. The beaches are just off the main drag.

Hanalei is friendly, casual and slow. If you're in a hurry, you're in the wrong place.

Hanalei Trader

The first sign of town is Hanalei Trader, a green building on the right. It has the Hanalei Dolphin restaurant, Hanalei Sailboards, Bali Hai Realty, Sand People and Ola's.

Sand People (tel 826-6981) sells beach clothing and rents boogie boards and snorkel sets for $7 a day and surfboards for $12.

Ola's (tel 826-6937) has beautiful works in glass, wood, ceramic and other media by craftspeople from Hawaii and the mainland.

Hanalei Museum

Hanalei Museum is in a simple green wooden building built in the 1860s by Ho Pak Yet, a Chinese immigrant who began work at the age of 14 as an indentured labourer on the Big Island. Four generations of Hos lived in this house. It's appropriate that this typical Hawaiian home of the late 1800s is today a down-home museum, as it fits both the Hanalei of yesterday and today. The house retains its old sloping floors but has a new corrugated roof.

The museum walls are covered with interesting turn-of-the-century photos of rural Hanalei. The most striking thing about the photos is just how familiar it still looks. The museum also has poi boards and glass bottles, exhibits on taro and rice growing and photos of the 1946 tsunami, Hawaii's worst. Admission is free, though there's a donation box.

Ching Young Village

The old Ching Young Store, since the turn of the century the North Shore's main general store, has evolved to become the Ching Young Village Shopping Center. It has a Big Save supermarket open from 7 am to 9 pm daily, a Bank of Hawaii, a camping and backpacking store, Na Pali Coast boat tour companies, a health food store, several restaurants and other shops. Across the street the old Hanalei School is being turned into another shopping centre.

The former Ching Young Store is now a collection of nine different shops selling flowers, hand-dyed clothing and Hawaiian crafts as well as standard tourist garb. The Artisans' Guild of Kauai is upstairs.

Waioli Church

Hanalei's first missionaries, the Reverend

and Mrs William Alexander, arrived in 1834 in a double-hulled canoe. Their church, hall and mission house are in the middle of town, set on a huge manicured lawn with a beautiful mountain backdrop. These folks knew how to pick property.

The picturesque Waioli Huiia Church is a favourite subject of area watercolourists. The green wooden church retains an airy Pacific feel with large stained-glass windows that open outwards and high ceilings. A Bible printed in Hawaiian in 1868 is on display on the old organ in the back corner of the room.

Waioli Mission Hall, to the right of the church, was built in 1836. The hall was formerly the church and was built of coral lime and plaster with a distinctive high-pitched roof to handle Hanalei's heavy rains. The church graveyard is beside the hall.

Waioli Mission House Museum

The Waioli Mission House is behind the church and hall. As they tell it there, the Alexanders spent their first three years living in a grass hut on these grounds, but couldn't handle living Hawaiian-style and put up this big New England house. It was home to other missionaries over the years, most notably Abner and Lucy Wilcox.

The main part of the house was built in 1837. It has all period furnishings, including braided rugs, lanterns, a spinning wheel and simple straight-backed chairs.

A large bookcase in the living room contains the original collection of Alexander's books. Of the two melodeon cases in this room only one contains a melodeon. The other came back empty after having been sent off to San Francisco in the late 1800s to be repaired. Such were the hardships of missionary life.

The house has old wavy glass panes, some nice simple woodwork and other interesting architectural features. For instance, the upstairs porch slopes, not from settling but because it was built that way to let water run down during the valley's frequent torrential rains. The boy's bedroom on the 2nd floor has a central post that carries the weight of the 1st floor ceiling beneath it.

The original cookhouse was separate so if the cookhouse burned down there'd still be a house. With the advent of electricity it was linked to the main house. One corner still has the original fireplace with hanging iron pots. The fireplace was made of sandstone blocks cut in Waipa Valley, three miles away.

The museum's inconspicuous parking lot is just past the church. Turn left before the school and then again at the second yellow hydrant. It's open from 9 am to 3 pm Tuesdays, Thursdays and Saturdays. Admission is free, though donations are welcomed. You're free to explore the garden area and taro patch out the back.

Hanalei Bay

Hanalei means 'crescent bay', and that it is – a large, perfectly shaped bay, one of the most scenic in all Hawaii. Weke Rd, which runs a mile along the bay between Waioli Stream and Hanalei River, can be reached by turning off Hwy 560 at Aku Rd.

Just after turning right onto Weke from Aku there's a public beach with a pavilion that serves as a local drinking hangout. Hanalei Beach Park is about half a mile farther, at the end of Weke Rd. Pinetrees Beach Park is in the opposite direction.

All three beaches have restrooms, showers, drinking water, picnic tables and grills. Hanalei Beach Park is the best place for catching the sunset as you can see Bali Hai from there. It's a popular summer anchorage for sailboats.

The big brown house with the wraparound porch mauka of the road midway between the pavilion and Hanalei Beach Park is the old Wilcox estate, home to descendants of early Hanalei missionaries Abner and Lucy Wilcox.

If the road names have a familiar sound, it means you're beginning to learn the names of Hawaiian fish – each road along the beach is named after a different one.

Hanalei Beach County Park

Hanalei Beach County Park is one of the North Shore's most popular beach parks. It has a grassy area and a long beach shaded by ironwood trees. The beach has a sandy bottom and a gentle slope. Swimming and snorkelling are good in summer, surfing in winter.

The remains of a narrow-gauge railroad track still lead up to the long weatherbeaten pier that sticks out into the bay. A lifeguard sits there all through the summer and on weekends the rest of the year.

The Hanalei River's mouth and a small boat ramp are at the eastern end of the park. That part of the beach is sometimes called Black Pot after the big iron pot that was once hung there by local fishermen for impromptu cook-outs. Camping is allowed on Fridays, Saturdays and holidays.

A snack truck arrives before noon every day but Monday, leaving when the sun hits the mountains. Drinking coconuts are $2, sold to the tune of classical music.

The bluff north of the Hanalei River's mouth was once the site of the Hanalei Plantation Hotel. It was followed by Club Med which, despite the spectacular angle on Hanalei Bay, was unable to make a go of it there. More recently a Honolulu developer went bankrupt in the midst of building million-dollar condos. They now sit on the bluff unfinished. The Princeville owners have purchased the property.

Pinetrees Beach Park

Pinetrees Beach Park, named by surfers, is actually shaded by ironwood trees.

From Weke Rd, turn either onto Hee Rd, which has the bigger parking lot, or Amaama Rd, which has the restrooms. This end of the bay is lined with little beach houses with rusty tin roofs.

Pinetrees, with its slow and gradually sloping break, draws surfers on longboards, the old-style nine-foot boards that are making a comeback. The annual Pinetrees Longboard Surf Classic is held there around the last weekend in February.

Places to Stay

Mahikoa's Motel (Hwy 560, Hanalei; tel 826-9333) has five simple units, four of them

with kitchenettes. It's $55 for one night and $45 a night for three nights or more.

Places to Eat – bottom end

The *West of the Moon Cafe* on Aku Rd has giant homemade muffins such as wholewheat carrot or chocolate cream cheese. With butter and jam, they're a meal in themselves for $2. Or try scrambled tofu with an Irish scone for $4. The cafe makes its own salsa and often has some sort of special Mexican dish. It's a nice place to start the day. It opens from 7 am to noon only.

The *Pizza Hanalei* (tel 826-9494) in Ching Young Village has Kauai's best pizza. A cheese pizza with crisp whole-wheat crust topped with sesame seeds is $5.85. Its calzone-style pizzarittos are loaded with cheese and vegies, and make a good meal for $3.75. It delivers as far as Princeville and is open from 11 am to 9 pm daily.

Next door, *Hanalei Natural Foods* sells freshly squeezed juices, fruit, organic produce, sandwiches, deli items and all the health food standards. It's open from 8.30 am to 8.30 pm daily.

The *Papagayo Azul* in Ching Young Village has inexpensive Mexican food. You order from a window and eat at a table on the porch. The food's rather ordinary but they don't use lard and will substitute vegetables for meat.

The *Village Snack & Bake Shop* in Ching Young Village sells deli and bakery goods, breakfasts, wrapped sandwiches, doughnuts and coffee. It's open from 6 am to 5 pm daily.

The *Foong Wong* in Ching Young Village has Sichuan and Cantonese dishes, but the food's awful.

At the Hanalei Trader building, Saturdays and Sundays are *Tropical Taco* days, when a big ol' funky green van parks in front and dishes out Mexican food. The other days belong to the *Menehune Hut*, a sterile Coney Island-style stand that dispenses hot dogs and lemonade. It's open from 10 am to 4 pm.

A counter at the side of the Hanalei Museum sells standard plate lunches at around $4, sandwiches and cold drinks. It's open from 10 am to 4 pm daily.

Places to Eat – top end

The *Shell House* (tel 826-7977), on the corner of Hwy 560 and Aku Rd, serves breakfast from 8 to 11 am. Macadamia nut pancakes or Mexican omelettes are $5. Lunch, from 11 am to 4 pm, features hamburgers, sandwiches, salads and quesadillas in the $5 to $8 range. The dinner menu is varied, with some Thai and Cajun influences. The cheapest seafood dish is prawns in macadamia nut pesto at $15 though you can get a hamburger with a salad, chowder and steak fries for $9. You might have to wait for a table at dinner time (from 4.30 to 10 pm) but the crowd is upbeat and there's a bar. The food is good and the Shell House is open daily.

The *Hanalei Dolphin* (tel 826-6113) at Hanalei Trader has a reputation for consistently good fresh fish. Main dishes with salad cost from $12 to $20. North Shore people go there for special occasions. It's open from 6 to 10 pm daily.

The food is pretty good at the *Tahiti Nui* (tel 826-6277), on Hwy 560 near Aku Rd, though service can be slow. (OK, so it was Valentine's Day when we were there and this is Hanalei, but 1½ hours between seating and salad?!) Kilauea freshwater prawns or a big serving of fresh fish cost $15, including salad and a glump of white rice. Soup and salad alone is $6.50. At lunch time, burgers and sandwiches cost from about $4. Every Wednesday and Friday it has a luau.

Entertainment

The *Tahiti Nui* (tel 826-6277) usually has Hawaiian or rock music on Fridays and Saturdays and country music with R J Mossman and the Rexall Rangers on Sundays and Mondays. It also has community-oriented entertainment such as ballroom dancing or the local school production of *South Pacific*.

HANALEI TO WAINIHA
Waikoko Beach

The western part of Hanalei Bay, called Waikoko Beach, has a sandy bottom, is protected by a reef and is shallower and calmer than the middle of the bay. There are places to park under ironwood trees around the four-mile marker, but no facilities.

Winter surfing is sometimes good off Makahoa Point, the western point of the bay, called Waikokos by surfers.

Lumahai Beach

Lumahai is the gorgeous mile-long stretch of beach where Mitzi Gaynor promised to wash that man right out of her hair in the 1958 musical *South Pacific*. It's a broad white sand beach with lush jungle growth on one side and tempestuous open ocean on the other.

There are two ways onto Lumahai. The first is a hike down that begins at a pull-off along a stone retaining wall three-quarters of a mile past the four-mile marker. Park in the direction of the traffic flow to avoid a ticket. The trail to the beach starts at an inconspicuous 'No Lifeguard' sign and goes down to the left.

It's a good beach for walking and exploring. Around some of the lava outcrops you can find green sand made of olivine.

The lava point at the eastern end of the beach offers protection from the winds which often blow from the Princeville direction. These rocks are a rather popular place for sunbathing, but size it up carefully as people have been washed off by high surf and rogue waves. Lumahai has dangerous shorebreaks and is not a beach to turn your back on. It's particularly treacherous in winter, though there are strong currents year round. Lumahai has been nicknamed Luma*die* by locals.

Back on the road, there are three lookouts, the first at the five-mile marker, all with good views of Lumahai below.

The other access to Lumahai is along the road at sea level at the western end of the beach. It's just before crossing the Lumahai River Bridge. The beach there is lined with ironwood trees. Across the road is Lumahai Valley, open and flat with ranchland.

WAINIHA

Wainiha has the oldest general store in these parts and it's the last store on the North Shore that sells groceries and beer. It is open until

7 pm. There's a little sandwich shop at the side.

Ancient house sites, heiau sites and old taro patches reach deep into the Wainiha Valley. The valley is said to have been the last hideout of the menehunes. In fact as late as the mid-1800s 65 people in the valley were officially listed as menehune on the government census!

Wainiha Powerhouse Road

Wainiha Powerhouse Rd begins shortly before the seven-mile marker. It leads up into Wainiha Valley, a narrow valley with steep walls. It's a ride into an older Hawaii.

The road is lined with simple tin-roofed homes, old rusting cars and sleeping dogs. At 1½ miles up there's suddenly a manicured estate with a cool blue stream meandering through it. Shortly after this you arrive at the Wainiha hydroelectric plant. It was built in 1906 by McBryde Sugar Company and still pumps out juice today. Beyond the powerhouse the road turns to dirt and begins to feel more private.

HAENA

Haena has houses on stilts, little beachfront cottages, a few vacation homes, the YMCA camp, Hanalei Colony Resort condos, large caves, camping sites and beautiful sandy beaches.

Tunnels Reef

Tunnels is a big horseshoe-shaped reef that has great diving and snorkelling when the water is calm, which is generally in the summer. There's a current as you head into deeper water. When conditions are right, you can start snorkelling near the east point and let the current carry you westward. It's more adventurous than Kee Beach. The coral is beautiful.

Tunnels was not named after the caves and other crevices in the underwater walls but by surfers for its winter surf break.

To get there, turn makai on the dirt road a third of a mile past the eight-mile marker, at a tree painted with an orange stripe. If you

miss it there's another beach access a quarter of a mile ahead.

Haena Beach Park

Haena Beach is a beautiful curve of white sand. To the right, you can see the horseshoe shape of Tunnels outlined by breaking waves. To the far left is Cannons, another good dive spot. Haena itself has a strong riptide.

Shell collectors will find a large number of tiny polished white opercula (the dome-shaped trap doors that are sucked closed by the shell's inhabitant).

The county beach park has camping sites, restrooms, showers and grills. There are usually a few hikers from the Kalalau Trail camping there. It's a bit over a mile to the trailhead and this is a safer place to park a car if you're going on to Kalalau.

Snack trucks usually park there during the day serving up plate lunches, chilli, soft drinks and shave ice.

Maniniholo Dry Cave

Three large sea caves, which were part of the coast thousands of years back, are mauka of the road between Haena and Kee Beach. One is dry and two are wet. According to legend they were created when the goddess Pele dug into the mountains looking for a place on Kauai's North Shore to call home.

Maniniholo Dry Cave, across the road from Haena Beach Park, is a big broad cave that you can walk deep into. Dry is a relative term there. Water drips down from the top and is absorbed by the sandy floor.

Limahuli

Limahuli is the last valley before the start of the Na Pali Coast. Much of it is still virgin forest with rare native Hawaiian plants.

The Pacific Tropical Botanical Garden owns 1000 acres of the valley. Sections are being developed into collections of ethno-botanical and medicinal plants. The garden starts at the highway just before the stream that skims over the dip in the road marking the Haena State Park boundary. It's open for self-guided tours to members.

Wet Caves

Haena State Park includes the two wet caves and Kee Beach. The caves are near each other, less than a quarter of a mile from the end of the road, marked with HVB warrior signs. The first, Waikapalae Wet Cave, is just a few minutes walk uphill from the road. The second, Waikanaloa Wet Cave, is at the side of the road.

Both are big, deep, dark and dripping with pools of very cold water. Divers sometimes explore them, but the caves can be dangerous and it's best to go with a local diver the first time.

Kee Beach

Kee Beach is commonly called 'the beach at the end of the road', which it is.

On the left side of the beach is the distinctive 1280-foot cliff that marks the start of the Na Pali Coast. Almost everyone calls it Bali Hai, its name in *South Pacific*. The Hawaiian name is Makana, which means 'gift'. A heiau and ancient hula school site is at its base.

Snorkelling is very good at Kee Beach, which has a variety of tropical fish. A reef protects the right side of the cove and it's usually fairly calm. The left side is open and can have a strong current, particularly in winter.

When it's really calm – generally only in summer – snorkellers cross the reef to the open ocean where there's great visibility, big fish, large coral heads and the occasional sea turtle. It makes the inside of the bay look like kid's stuff, but check it out carefully because breaking surf and strong currents can create some pretty dangerous conditions.

When the tide's at its lowest you can actually walk a great distance out on the reef without getting your feet wet and peer down into tidepools.

Showers, changing rooms, drinking water and restrooms are tucked back in the woods behind the parking lot.

There are several ways to get views down the Na Pali Coast from there. One way is to walk the first 30 minutes of the Kalalau Trail. Another is to walk out around the point at the left of the beach.

Or, walk down the beach to the right and look back as the cliffs open up. About 15 minutes down this way you'll come to a stream and the site of the former Taylor Camp.

In the late 1960s, a little free-style village of tents and tree houses sprang up on property owned by Elizabeth Taylor's brother. Reports of drugs, orgies and pipe organ music in the middle of the night eventually got the authorities down on their case. When the state tried to evict everyone on public health grounds, the campers challenged them in court claiming squatters rights. The 'squatters' eventually lost and the property was incorporated into the state park system. Taylor Camp remains part of North Shore folklore, though there's nothing left to see.

Kaulu Paoa Heiau

To walk out to Kaulu Paoa Heiau, take the dirt path on the western side of the beach. Go past the private Allerton house and then follow the stone wall as it curves uphill. You can see the heiau almost immediately.

The section at the foot of the hill is one of the more intact parts of the heiau, but don't stop there. Walk up the terraces toward the cliff face. Surf pounding below, vertical cliffs above – what a spectacular site to worship the gods from!

Beneath the cliff face large stones retain a long flat grassy platform. A thatched-roofed halau, a long house used as a hula school, once ran the whole length of the terrace. Dances to Laka, the goddess of hula, were performed there. This was Kauai's most sacred hula school and students aspiring to learn hula came to Kaulu Paoa from all the islands.

Offerings to Laka are still placed into the crevices of the cliff face: rocks wrapped in ti leaves, fern wreaths, leis, anklets and flowers. The area should be treated with respect. Night hula dances are still performed on special occasions.

Lohiau's House Site

Lohiau's house site is just a minute's walk

Na Pali Coast

above the parking lot at Kee Beach. At the Kalalau Trail sign, go left along a dirt path to a vine-covered rock wall. This overgrown level terrace runs back 54 feet to the bluff and is said to have been the home of Lohiau, a 16th-century prince.

Legend says that the volcano goddess Pele was napping one day under a hala tree in Puna on the Big Island when her spirit was awakened by the sound of distant drums. Her spirit rode the wind in the direction of the sound, searching each island in turn until she finally arrived at Kee Beach. There she found Lohiau above the heiau beating a hula drum, surrounded by graceful hula dancers.

Pele took the form of a beautiful woman and captured Lohiau's heart. They became lovers and moved into this house. In time Pele had to go back to the Big Island, leaving a lovesick Lohiau behind. His longing quickly got the better of him and on this site he died from his grief.

Places to Stay

The *Kauai YMCA-Camp Naue* (Box 1786, Lihue, HI 96766; tel 246-9090) charges $10 for a bunk bed in a rustic dormitory on the beach. If it's not full, couples can get a dormitory to themselves for $20. To pitch a tent it's $8 for the first person and $5 for each extra person. Check in is by 6 pm. This is a nice place to meet people and unless there's a large group, the camp can usually take everyone who shows up. Reservations are taken from groups only. From May to mid-September it's a kiddies summer camp only. The camp is in Haena just before the eight-mile marker on Hwy 560. It's a 15-minute walk to Tunnels Beach.

The *Hanalei Colony Resort* (Box 206, Hanalei, HI 96714; tel 826-6235; 800-367-8047 from the USA, 800-423-8733 from Canada) is a 20-year-old condo that's none too spiffy but right on the beach. Each of the 49 units has two bedrooms, a kitchen and a lanai. Rates are $100 to $155. Charo's restaurant is next door.

Entertainment

Charo's has a 'Tropical Fiesta' Las Vegas revue of latin and flamenco dancers. Dinner begins at 6 pm. The show is at 8.30 pm, with a cover charge of $5. There's a piano bar and dancing until 11 pm.

NA PALI COAST

Na Pali means simply 'the cliffs', and these are Hawaii's grandest example.

The Na Pali Coast is the rugged 22-mile stretch between the end of the road at Kee Beach in the north and the road's opposite end at Polihale State Park in the west. It has the most sharply fluted coastal cliffs in Hawaii.

Kalalau, Honopu, Awaawapuhi, Nualolo and Milolii are the five major valleys on the Na Pali Coast. These deep river valleys once contained sizable settlements.

In the mid-1800s missionaries established a school in Kalalau, the largest valley, and registered the valley population at about 200. Influenced by Western ways, people began to move to towns and by the end of the century the valleys were largely abandoned.

Koolau the Leper

The Na Pali valleys, with limited accessibility and abundant fertility, have long served as a natural refuge for people wanting to escape one scene or another. Koolau the Leper is the best known.

Koolau was a paniolo who contracted leprosy in 1893. Rather than accept separation from his family and banishment to Molokai's leper colony, Koolau, his wife and young son hiked down into Kalalau Valley. Shortly after, a sheriff and deputy showed up to clear the valley of renegade lepers. Koolau was the only resister. That night, in the light of a full moon, the sheriff snuck up the valley hoping to take Koolau in his sleep. In self-defence Koolau shot the sheriff.

When word reached Honolulu, a shipload of soldiers was sent to land on Kalalau Beach. As they marched up the valley they met Koolau's gunfire. After two of the soldiers were shot off the ridge, and a third accidentally killed himself, they switched strategies. Before dawn they blasted Koolau's hideaway with cannon fire, not knowing he had slipped through their lines the night before. From a nearby waterfall he watched as the soldiers loaded up and set sail. They never returned. Koolau lived the rest of his days there undisturbed.

Eventually the son, and then Koolau, died of leprosy. They are buried on a valley hillside. When his wife, Piilani, left the valley she found Koolau had largely been forgotten. A decade later a visiting reporter, John Sheldon, recorded her story. Jack London later wrote *Koolau the Leper*, a more fictionalised account.

Getting There & Away

Precarious trails once led from the Kokee area to the valley floors below. In some places footholds were gouged into cliffsides and in others rope ladders were used. These trails no longer exist.

Only Hanakapiai, Hanakoa and Kalalau valleys can still be entered on foot, solely along the 11-mile Kalalau coastal trail.

The only other access is by boat. Landings are limited to Kalalau, Nualolo and Milolii valleys and are largely restricted to summer when the seas are calm. Milolii, part of Na Pali Coast State Park, has primitive camping. Currently, Hanalei Sea Tours and Captain Zodiac are the only companies licensed to drop off or pick up backpackers along the Na Pali Coast.

Kokee State Park has a drive-up lookout right on Kalalau's rim, it is the only Na Pali valley you can look into without a hike or a helicopter. Kokee has hardy hikes out to cliff tops with gorgeous views of Honopu, Awaawapuhi and Nualolo valleys (see the Kokee State Park section later).

NORTH SHORE TRAILS

Kalalau Trail

Kalalau is Hawaii's premier trail. It's common to come across hikers here who have trekked in Nepal or climbed to Machu Picchu. The Na Pali Coast is similarly spectacular, a place of singular beauty.

The trail runs along high sea cliffs and winds up and down across lush valleys before it finally ends below the steep fluted pali of Kalalau. The scenery is breathtaking, with sheer green cliffs dropping into brilliant turquoise waters.

While hikers in good shape can walk the 11-mile trail in about six hours, it's less

Hanakapiai Falls

strenuous to break it up and spend a night camping in one of the two valleys along the way. The first two miles of the hike makes a popular day trip.

This is largely the ancient trail used by Hawaiians who lived in Kalalau and other remote north coast valleys.

The hike can be divided into three parts: Kee Beach to Hanakapiai Valley (two miles); Hanakapiai to Hanakoa Valley (four miles); and Hanakoa to Kalalau Valley (five miles).

The trail is part of Na Pali Coast State Park. Camping is allowed in all three valleys, but is limited to five nights total, with no two consecutive nights in Hanakapiai or Hanakoa. Permits are required.

Kee Beach to Hanakapiai The two-mile trail to Hanakapiai has some excellent views of the coast. Morning is a good time to be going west, and the afternoon to be going east, because you have both the sun at your back and good light for photos. This part of the hike can get a bit muddy.

The trail weaves through kukui and ohia trees and then back out to clearings with coastal views. There are purple orchids, wildflowers and tiny Zen-like waterfalls.

The black nuts half buried in the clay are kukui, polished smooth by the scuffing of hundreds of hiking shoes.

Just a few minutes up the trail you can look back at Kee Beach. After 30 minutes you get your first view of the Na Pali Coast. Even if you weren't planning on a hike, it's well worth coming this far.

Hanakapiai has a sandy beach in the summer. In the winter the sand washes out and it becomes a beach of boulders, some of them sparkling with tiny olivine crystals. The western side of the beach has a small cave with dripping water and a miniature fern grotto.

There's a guide rope for crossing the stream. Pit toilets and garbage cans are on the western side.

The ocean is dangerous here, with unpredictable riptides year round. It's particularly treacherous during winter high surf conditions. There have been many drownings at Hanakapiai Beach.

If you're just doing a day hike, it makes more sense to head up the valley to Hanakapiai Falls than it does to continue another couple of miles on the coastal trail.

Hanakapiai Falls The two-mile hike to Hanakapiai Falls takes about 2½ hours for the round trip. Because of some tricky rock crossings, this trail is rougher than the walk from Kee to Hanakapiai Beach, but it's fairly easy to follow and marked along the way wherever there's any doubt. There are a few trees down over the trail but they are only a minor inconvenience. Because of the possibility of flash floods in the narrow valley, this is a fair-weather hike.

The trail starts on the western side of Hanakapiai Stream above the pit toilets. About 50 yards up there's a picnic table, old stone walls and guava trees. If the guava is ripe it's a good place to stock up. There are also some big old mango trees along the way.

Ten minutes up from the trailhead you'll find thickets of green bamboo, interspersed with eucalyptus. Off to the left there's a picnic table shaded by horizontally leaning bamboo with ginger behind. It's Eden-like.

Along the trail is the site of an old coffee mill. All that remains is a little of the stack.

The first of four or five stream crossings is about 25 minutes up at a sign which warns: 'Hazardous. Keep away from stream during heavy rainfall. Stream floods suddenly.'

Be particularly careful of your footing on the rocky upper part of the trail. Some of the rocks are covered with a barely visible film of slick algae. It's like walking on glass.

The waterfall is spectacular, with a wide pool gentle enough to swim in. Directly under the falls the cascading water forces you back from the rock face, a warning from nature as rocks can fall from the top.

This is a really peaceful place to spend a little time meditating. It's a beautiful lush valley though it's not terribly sunny near the falls because of the incredible steepness.

Hanakapiai to Hanakoa Just 10 minutes up the trail from Hanakapiai to Hanakoa there's a nice view of Hanakapiai Beach, but then the trail goes into bush and the next coastal view is not for another mile. This is the least scenic part of the trail.

The camping site at Hanakoa is tucked in the valley about half a mile inland. Of the three camping areas, Hanakoa is the wettest.

Hanakoa Stream has pools perfect for swimming. There's a waterfall about a third of a mile up the valley, but it's rough getting up there. The valley was formerly settled by farmers who grew taro and coffee, both of which still grow wild there.

Hanakoa to Kalalau This is the most difficult part of the trail, although without question the most beautiful. Make sure you have at least three hours of daylight left.

About a mile out of Hanakoa Valley you'll reach the coast again and begin to get fantastic views of Na Pali's jagged edges. A little past the halfway mark you'll get your first view into Kalalau Valley.

The large valley has a beach, a little waterfall, a heiau site, some ancient house sites and some interesting caves that are sometimes dry enough to sleep in during the summer.

A two-mile trail leads back into the valley

to a pool in Kalalau Stream where there's a natural water slide. Terraces where Hawaiians cultivated taro until 1920 are now largely overgrown with Java plum and guava. Feral goats scurry up and down the crumbly cliffsides and drink from the stream.

Kalalau Valley has fruit trees, including mango, papaya, orange, banana, guava and mountain apple. In the 1960s pakalolo was also introduced. During the 1960s and 1970s people wanting to get away from it all tried to settle in Kalalau, but forestry rangers eventually routed them out. It's still common to find a few folks hanging out in the valley, making flutes or otherwise whiling away the time. Clothing is optional.

Warnings & Information This is rugged wilderness and accidents do occur. Most casualties are the result of trying to ford swollen streams, walking in the dark on cliffside trails or swimming in treacherous surf. For someone who's cautious and in tune, it can be paradise.

There's no shortage of water sources along the trail, but all water must be boiled or treated.

Bring what you need but travel light. You won't want to have extra shifting weight on stream crossings or along cliff edges. Shoes should have good traction; it's not a trail for flip-flops. If you bring a sleeping bag make it a light one.

Break-ins to cars left overnight at Kee Beach are common. Some people advise leaving cars empty and unlocked. It might be safer to park at the camping ground at Haena Beach Park. Or get a lift to the end of the road.

Hanalei Area Trails
Powerline Trail In the 1930s electric transmission lines were run along the mountains and a 13-mile maintenance route now known as the Powerline Trail was created. There is occasional talk of turning it into a real inland road connecting Princeville to Wailua.

The trail starts at the paved road running up from Pooku Stables, soon after the 27-mile marker on Hwy 56. The paved road ends at a water tank 1¾ miles up and even if you don't plan to hike it's a pretty drive to here. The road goes past large contemporary homes with grazing horses. There are fine mountain views and glimpses of Hanalei Bay.

The trail continues as a 4WD dirt road used mainly by hunters and the power company, passing a hunter check box and continuing all the way to the Keahua Arboretum. Wild orchids and hibiscus bloom along the trail.

Hanalei River Trail The Hanalei River Trail begins at the end of Ohiki Rd at a 4WD road in Halalea Forest Reserve. The trail goes deep into Hanalei Valley where taro fields and rice paddies once flourished. The area is rich in both native and introduced plants and there are large bamboo groves and big old mango trees along the way. After about 1½ miles the trail crosses Hanalei River. If the water is running swiftly it's not wise to cross. The trail continues along the opposite river bank and into the interior. It's a muddy hike but there are places to wash off and swim.

Okolehau Trail The Okolehau Trail offers ridge-top views of Hanalei and Waioli valleys. Take Ohiki Rd about half a mile and turn right onto the unmarked paved road.

The hike starts up the 4WD power-line maintenance road to the left of the cemetery. It goes up through fragrant eucalyptus trees and past wild orchids. When you reach the Norfolk pines you can continue up the ridge top to Mt Kaukaopua, 1272 feet high. It's a little more than two miles to this point.

The trail becomes more strenuous as it rises. It's possible to continue through the Puu Ki area, following the ridge to the twin peaks of Hihimanu at 2262 feet. Give yourself an early start if you intend to go this far in and carry plenty of water.

Moonshiners who distilled a liquor called okolehao from the roots of ti plants established this trail during the Prohibition era of the 1920s. The ti they planted is still plentiful along the trail.

The literal translation of okolehao comes from *okole*, meaning 'buttocks', and *hao*, meaning 'iron', referring to the iron-bottomed still that was used. As the old-timers say, 'It'll knock you on your okole and how!'

South Coast

Poipu is Kauai's main beach resort area. It's typically sunny and for the larger part of the year, including the winter, it has calm waters for swimming and snorkelling. During the summer the surf kicks up and the surfers move in.

The village of Koloa, three miles inland from Poipu, was the site of Hawaii's first sugar plantation. This sleepy town could have doubled for Dodge City before it got caught up in Poipu's boom. Now most of its shops are geared for tourists and it catches the overflow from Poipu.

Poipu and Koloa are about 10 miles south of Lihue. To get there take Hwy 520 (Maluhia Rd) from Hwy 50 (Kaumualii Hwy).

Tree Tunnel

Immediately after turning down Maluhia Rd you enter the Tree Tunnel, a mile-long stretch of road canopied by swamp mahogany trees, a type of eucalyptus. Originally the tree tunnel was more than double this length but when Hwy 50 was re-routed south most of the tunnel was lopped off.

Hurricane Iwa brought down many of the branches, temporarily destroying the tunnel effect. It's filling back in nicely.

The cinder hill to the right about two miles down Maluhia Rd is Puu O Hewa. Here the ancient Hawaiians raced wooden holua sleds down paths covered with oiled pili grass. To add even more excitement to this popular spectator sport the Hawaiians crossed two sled paths near the middle of the hill. The paths were about five feet wide and if you strain your eyes you might be able to see the X on the hill where they crossed.

Hewa means 'wrong' or 'mistake'. The hill's original name was lost when a surveyor jotted 'Puu O Hewa' (wrong hill) on a map he was making and it mistakenly went off to the printer like that.

The two grassy hills to the left of the road are Mauna Kalika, or Silk Mountain. Two American entrepreneurs introduced Chinese silkworms there in the 1830s in an attempt to develop a Hawaiian silk industry. The climate proved unsuitable.

KOLOA

Hawaii's first sugar plantation was started in Koloa in 1835. The raw materials had arrived long before: sugar cane with the original Polynesian settlers and small-scale refinery know-how with the earliest Chinese immigrants.

Plantations got their start when William Hooper, a 24-year-old Bostonian, arrived in Kauai and made inroads with the alii and Honolulu businessmen. With financial backing from Ladd & Company, he leased land in Koloa from the king and paid the alii a stipend to free commoners from their traditional work obligations. He was then free to hire them as wage labourers and Koloa became Hawaii's first plantation town.

Koloa Rd (Hwy 530) runs between Koloa and Lawai and if you're heading west it's the best way out of Koloa. It's a rural road through sugar cane fields, pasture and tree-covered hills.

Sugar Exhibits

Any sugarologists in the crowd? The field at the intersection of Hwy 520 and Koloa Rd is for you.

In a tiny garden a dozen varieties of sugar cane have been labelled with interpretive markers. Some are noted for their high tonnage, others for high sucrose and some for their good ratooning (their ability to grow new roots), though the different varieties have all grown to twist and clump together.

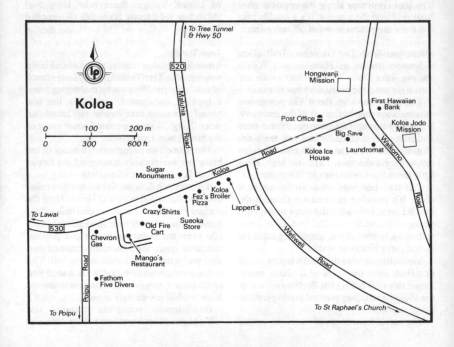

Who knows, maybe there's a great new hybrid right there.

The stone stack in another corner of the field is a relic from one of Koloa's early mills. It dates back to 1841.

The eight principal ethnic groups that worked the plantations are immortalised in a sculpture there. The Hawaiian wears a malo and has a poi dog by his side. The Chinese, Korean, Japanese, Portuguese, Filipino and Puerto Rican groups are likewise in native field dress. Noticeably missing is the Caucasian overseer, who on a high horse once dominated the sculpture. Somebody has taken the liberty of removing him from the picture.

If you want to learn more about the history of sugar, there are informative plaques here.

Old Koloa

Koloa looks like an Old West town of wooden buildings with false storefronts. It was a thriving plantation town and commercial centre that largely went bust after WW II.

Its history is sugar but its present is tourism. The former fish markets, tailor shops, barber shops, Japanese bath houses and beer halls are now boutiques, galleries and pizzerias.

The building that houses Crazy Shirts was until recently the Yamamoto General Store. Moviegoers would line up at Yamamoto's for crack seed and soft drinks before the theatre across the street burned down. On the sidewalk in front of the store a lifelike sculpture of a craggy mechanic stands next to an ancient Texaco gas pump. The courtyard behind the store looks onto the former town hotel. Back there you'll find an old horse-drawn fire cart and a little display on Koloa's history.

Though it's pretty touristy it's still a pleasant town to walk around. The 'newly quaint' shops are in stark contrast to a handful of old sugar shacks that still house cane workers farther down the street. The town is beginning to boom beyond its old wooden buildings, with a couple of new construction projects underway.

Koloa Jodo Mission

Koloa Jodo Mission dates back to 1910. The temple on the left is the original. Next to it is a newer and larger one where services are now held. During services the smell of incense and the sound of beating drums fills the air. It's still very Japanese but grass tatami mats and cushions have been replaced by wooden floors and folding chairs.

St Raphael's Catholic Church

St Raphael's is the oldest Catholic church on Kauai. Some of the first Portuguese immigrants to Hawaii are buried in the churchyard cemetery. The original building, built in 1856, was of lava rock and coral mortar with walls three feet thick. When the church was enlarged in 1936 it was all plastered over and it's less interesting now. To get there from Koloa Rd, turn into Weliweli Rd then right onto Hapa Rd. It's half a mile to the church.

Places to Stay

The *Kahili Mountain Park* (Box 298, Koloa, HI 96756; tel 742-9921) is just beyond the seven-mile marker on Hwy 50 and then a mile up a sugar cane field. This is a semi-camping set-up run by the Seventh Day Adventist church in a beautiful setting beneath Mt Kahili. Its cabinettes are very simple structures on cement slabs and are rather dark and dank. It also has cabins that are spread out for privacy, off the ground and nicer. Each has a two-burner gas stove, a sink and a refrigerator. Cabinettes are $20 and cabins are $35 for singles or doubles. Each extra person is $4. Cabinettes hold four people, cabins hold up to seven. It's only about 20 minutes from the beaches in Poipu.

Places to Eat

Sueoka Store, *Fez's Pizza*, *Koloa Broiler* and *Lappert's* ice cream store are in a row on Koloa Rd near its intersection with Maluhia Rd.

The snack shop at the side of Sueoka Store sells burgers, cheese sandwiches and saimin, for just $1 each. Plate lunches are in the $3 range. It's open from 10 am to 3 pm.

Koloa Broiler (tel 742-9122) is in a funky

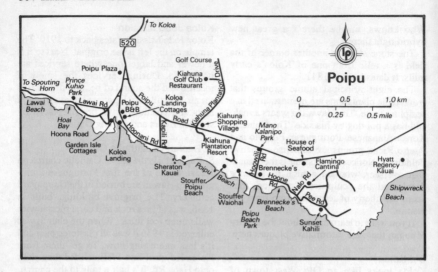

old wooden building with a tin roof – a former soft drink bottling plant. The 'menu' is a display case of raw meat and fish. You cook your choice over a communal gas grill. Sirloin steak is $9.45, mahimahi or barbecued chicken $8.50, burgers $6. A simple buffet of rice, beans and salad is included. It's open from 11 am to 10 pm daily.

Fez's Pizza has sandwiches, pizza and pasta – standard stuff at standard prices.

Mango's Tropical Restaurant (tel 742-7377), behind the Chevron station, is a trendy place. At lunch, sandwiches and burgers with fruit salad are $5.50 to $7.50. Dinners cost about double that and include some interesting house specialities such as the $17 seafood combination of grilled prawns with honey mustard, fish with macadamia nut butter and sweet & sour scallops. During happy hour, 3 to 5.30 pm, draught beer is $1 and mai tais are $2.50.

POIPU

Poipu is about three miles south of Koloa down Poipu Rd. Other than its beaches, Poipu's most popular attraction is the Spouting Horn blowhole. To get to Spouting Horn,

turn right off Poipu Rd onto Lawai Rd, just past Poipu Plaza.

Prince Kuhio Park

Prince Kuhio Park is about half a mile down Lawai Rd, across from tiny Hoai Bay. Here you'll find Hoai Heiau and a monument honouring Jonah Kuhio Kalanianaole, the Territory of Hawaii's first delegate to the US Congress. It was Prince Kuhio who spearheaded the Hawaiian Homes Commission Act, which provided homesteads for native Hawaiians. The remains of a fishpond and an ancient Hawaiian house platform are also on the grounds.

Between the monument and heiau are two puu kalaunu (crown flower) bushes, one lavender and one white. The crown-shaped centres of the flowers are used to make leis and they also dry well.

Baby Beach

There's a protected swimming area just deep enough for children off Hoona Rd, east of Prince Kuhio Park. Look for the beach access post at a little clearing between the road and the beach. Adults may want to walk west down the beach and swim out in front of the white house where there's a sandy break with fewer rocks and deeper water.

Lawai Beach

Lawai Beach is west of Prince Kuhio Park, just after Kuhio Shores apartments and the Beach House restaurant. It's a little rocky but during winter the water is usually quite clear and snorkellers can hand-feed the fish. When the surf's up in summer, the beach is inundated with surfers.

Lawai Beach Recreation Center, opposite the beach, rents boogie boards or snorkel sets for $6 for four hours or $15 per day. It's open from 8.30 am to 5 pm daily.

Kukuiula Bay

Kukuiula Bay is a small boat harbour maintained by the state. It's mostly used by fishing and diving boats. The beach is rocky and more suitable for pole fishing than other water activities. There are showers, restrooms, picnic tables, a launch ramp, nine mooring spaces and a concrete wharf.

Spouting Horn Beach Park

Spouting Horn is a blowhole that has its days. Sometimes it has a pretty good spout, other times it's not impressive at all. The waves, the tides, and the overall force of the sea rushing into the lava tube decide how much water surges through the spout. The low whooshing of the rushing water sounds like a whale breathing. The late afternoon sun sometimes makes rainbows in the spray.

All of Kauai's tour buses pull up here and there's often a small crowd with cameras clicking away. Jewellery and trinket stalls line the walkway down to the viewing area.

The road ends about a third of a mile past Spouting Horn at the locked gate to the Allerton Estate. You can sometimes get a free look into Lawai Valley and the Allerton Gardens by walking up the cane road that runs along the ridge. About five minutes up, it's possible to catch a glimpse of the valley and the sands of Lawai Bay. The views get even better a little farther on.

Koloa Landing

Koloa Landing, at the mouth of Waikomo Stream, was once Kauai's largest port. Whalers put in there for provisions and local farmers shipped out oranges and sweet potatoes to California gold miners in the 1850s. Sugar was also shipped from there. Other than a county boat ramp there's not much left.

Beneath the water it's another story. Koloa Landing is a popular snorkelling and diving spot. Its protected waters reach depths of about 30 feet and it's generally calm all year. It has a good variety of coral and fish, which are a bit better on the right side.

The landing is off the western end of Hoonani Rd. A highway marker reading 5.08 (miles) marks the drive down to the landing.

Poipu Beach

The long stretch of white sand fronting the Sheraton, Kiahuna Plantation and the two Stouffer hotels is referred to as Poipu Beach. It's actually three attractive crescent beaches with narrow points or outcrops in between. The water is turquoise and good for swimming, bodysurfing, surfing and snorkelling. You can rent gear and get information on current water conditions at the hotel beach huts.

On the beach in front of the Stouffer Waiohai a tiny section of Kihahouna Heiau has been rebuilt, but there's not much to see.

Moir Gardens

Moir Gardens were part of the Moir Estate before it was turned into Kiahuna Plantation Resort.

The plantation house, now Plantation Gardens Restaurant, was a wedding gift to Hector and Alexandra Knudsen Moir when they married in 1933. It had previously been part of Hawaii's first sugar plantation, owned by Alexandra's father. The Moirs were avid gardeners and created large flowering cactus gardens and water lily ponds. The garden paths are open to the public and make for wonderful strolling.

Kiahuna Plantation Drive

African flame trees have been planted along Kiahuna Plantation Drive, the road leading to Kiahuna Golf Course and the club restaurant.

Kiahuna Shopping Center, on the corner of Poipu Rd and Kiahuna Plantation Drive, has a couple of places to eat and some art and craft shops worth browsing through. A few of the shops have fine Hawaiian and Pacific handicrafts, though don't expect to find bargains.

Mano Kalanipo

Mano Kalanipo is a new county park being developed on the corner of Poipu and Hoowili roads. It will be dedicated to Hawaiian culture.

Poipu Beach Park

Poipu Beach Park, at the end of Hoowili Rd, has good swimming and snorkelling. If you've never snorkelled before this is a good place to try. The cove is protected and has calm waters and the fish, almost tame from being fed constantly, will swarm around you. Dive shops often hold lessons for beginners at this beach park.

One section of the cove is a shallow swimming area for children, and has a lifeguard all year round. The park has some fun playground equipment for kids as well.

Snorkelling sets can be rented across the street at Brennecke Ocean Sports at $6 for two hours or $15 a day.

Brennecke's Beach

Brennecke's was once one of the south shore's main beaches. After Hurricane Iwa hit, the beach hadn't a grain of sand left − it was all in the 1st floors of nearby condos. Now it's a tiny sandy beach about 50 feet long, slowly making a comeback. It's a popular bodysurfing spot. Brennecke's is off Hoone Rd, just down from Poipu Beach Park.

Shipwreck Beach

Shipwreck Beach is a beige sand beach particularly popular with surfers and boogie boarders. The new Hyatt will front Shipwreck Beach, giving it a new road and new clientele. For now, temporary beach access has been set up around the construction.

Mahaulepu Beach

Secluded Mahaulepu Beach, a couple of miles beyond Shipwreck Beach, has some nice white sand sections, tidal pools and coves. There's a cinder cone with an interesting cave you can walk deep into and find an opening looking straight up to the heavens. It feels like sitting in a little volcano. At various times of the year the area is good for surfing, windsurfing, boogie boarding and snorkelling. Ghost marchers are said to come in from the sea at night along the coast here.

Places to Stay − bottom end

Since the YMCA next to Brennecke's closed down, Poipu hasn't had anything in the budget range. It's an expensive tourist area. Unlike Princeville, it's difficult to find a room in a private home.

Places to Stay − middle

Koloa Landing Cottages (2704B Hoonani Rd, Poipu, HI 96756; tel 742-1470) is a friendly family-run place. There are four cottages with full kitchens, TV and free local phone calls. The two studios are $50. The other cottages have a living room, two bedrooms and two bathrooms for $70 singles or doubles, $85 for up to four people. A four-night deposit is required and winter is often booked up a year ahead.

Garden Isle Cottages (2666 Puuholo Rd, Poipu, HI 96756; tel 742-6717) has seven cottages above Koloa Landing and two houses nearby. Studios are $47 to $70. One-bedroom units are $78 to $108. Two-bedroom units are $108 to $140. The rooms are decorated with abstract paintings and sculpture by owner/artist Robert Flynn. The studios have refrigerators. The others have kitchens. One of the houses is opposite the ocean, the other has a tiled lap swimming pool.

Gloria's Spouting Horn Bed & Breakfast (4464 Lawai Beach Rd, Poipu, HI 96756; tel

742-6995) is a beach house right on the ocean's edge, on the road to Spouting Horn. The rooms are light and breezy, four of which have sliding glass doors leading onto oceanfront balconies. The rates are from $55 to $95.

The *Poipu Bed & Breakfast Inn* (2720 Hoonani Rd, Poipu, HI 96756; tel 742-1146; 800-552-0095) has four bedrooms, each with a private bathroom. It's formally chic with white wicker, antique pine, chintz fabrics and an antique carousel horse in each room. Two rooms are $65. The other two have large whirlpool tubs and cost $85 and $100.

Sunset Kahili (1763 Pee Rd, Poipu, HI 96756; tel 742-1691; 800-367-8047 from the USA, 800-423-8733 from Canada) is a well-maintained 20-year-old condo with a friendly manager. Each of the 35 units has an ocean view, a washer/dryer and a cable TV. It's good value for Poipu. Rates are $75 for two people in a one-bedroom unit and $105 for up to four people in the two-bedroom units. The top floors are $5 more. Prices drop gradually the longer you stay. The minimum stay is three nights. The condo gets a lot of return traffic in the winter.

Places to Stay – top end

The *Stouffer Poipu Beach Hotel* (2251 Poipu Rd, Poipu, HI 96756; tel 742-1681; 800-426-4122) has 142 rooms, each with a kitchenette and little lanai. The rates are $85 to $140.

The *Stouffer Waiohai Beach Hotel* (2249 Poipu Rd, Poipu, HI 96756; tel 742-9511; 800-468-3571) is quite ordinary yet a bit snooty. The cheapest of the 430 rooms are $135 and they're small with almost no view. Oceanfront rooms jump to $230. Prices go up to $1200 for two-bedroom suites.

The *Sheraton Kauai Hotel* (2440 Hoonani Rd, Poipu, HI 96756; tel 742-1661; 800-325-3535 from the USA and Canada, 008-222229 from Australia) has 456 rooms. The buildings tend to ramble but there are gardens and carp ponds in between. It's cheerier and more casual than the Waiohai but rates start at a steep $140.

The *Hyatt Regency Kauai* hadn't been completed when we were there, but should be open by the time you read this.

The *Kiahuna Plantation Resort* (2253 Poipu Rd, Koloa, HI 96756; tel 742-6411) is a 333-unit condo complex managed by Village Resorts. The rooms are rather average, but pleasant with big private balconies. The lush surroundings include the Moir Gardens. Prices for one-bedroom units are $130 to $295 for up to four people. Two-bedroom units are $220 to $390 for up to six people.

Places to Stay – vacation rentals

The Poipu Beach Resort Association (Box 730, Koloa, HI 96756; tel 742-7444) has a brochure of members; and the following companies each handle about 100 vacation rentals in condos and private homes in the Poipu area:

Suite Paradise
    4480 Ahukini Rd, Lihue, HI 96766 (tel 245-6600; 800-367-8020)
R&R Realty & Rentals
    RR1, Box 70, Koloa, HI 96756 (tel 742-7555; 800-367- 8022)
Grantham Resorts
    Box 983, Koloa, HI 96756 (tel 742-7220; 800-325-5701)

Places to Eat – bottom end & middle

The *Taqueria Nortenos* in Poipu Plaza has cheap Mexican food. It's essentially a takeaway place with some indoor picnic tables. The meatless burrito is good value at $2. An enchilada with brown rice and beans is $4. It's fine for the price.

Brennecke's, opposite Poipu Beach Park, is a touristy beachfront restaurant crowded with would-be surfers and enthusiastic staff. A fresh fish sandwich costs $8, a fish dinner about double that.

It's more fun to get the Surfer's Special of an ahi burger with fries and soft drink for $5 from the sidewalk snack shop below the restaurant and take it across the street for a beach picnic. The ahi is good and fresh. The snack shop is open from 10.30 am to 4 pm daily.

The *Flamingo Cantina* (tel 742-9505), halfway up Nalo Rd, serves generous portions of good Mexican food. At happy hour, 3.30 to 5.30 pm, margaritas are $1.50. Dinner is from 5 to 9.30 pm daily with prices ranging from $8 for a taco salad to $10 for fajitas.

The *Pizza Bella* (Kiahuna Shopping Village; tel 742-9571) has pizzas from $9, lasagne, sandwiches and salads. Pizza is sold by the slice until 4.30 pm for $2. It's open from 11.30 am to 10 pm daily. They also home deliver.

A few shops down, *Shipwreck Subs* has takeaway vegetarian or meat submarine sandwiches at moderate prices.

The *Kiahuna Golf Club Restaurant* has a view of the course. Sandwiches served with fries and coleslaw cost from $5 to $7. Breakfasts such as Mexican omelettes, banana pancakes or mahimahi and eggs are in the same price range. Lunch is served until 3.30 pm. There's no dinner.

Keoki's Paradise (Kiahuna Shopping Village; tel 742-7534) doesn't look like much from the outside but inside it's open-air with seven waterfalls, lit torches, bamboo and hanging vines. Somehow it all works. The ginger chicken at $10 is good. The catch of the day is about double that price. Dinners include good homemade muffins and Caesar-style salad. Dinner is from 5.30 to 10 pm daily.

Places to Eat – top end

Plantation Gardens (tel 742-1695) at Kiahuna Plantation condos is in a former plantation home with a garden setting. Dinners cost from $18 for shrimp scampi to $27 for fruits de mer. If you're up for a treat this is a good choice for Poipu. Request a verandah or gardenside table. It's open from 5.30 pm daily.

The open-air *Tropical Garden Cafe* at the side of Plantation Gardens doesn't have the same elegance but is still pleasant. A cheeseburger or ahi sandwich with fries is $7. It has light meals, salads and tropical drinks as well. It's open from 5 to 10 pm daily.

The Sunday champagne brunch at the Stouffer Waiohai is widely considered Kauai's best. If you can deal with paying $21.50 the only problem is the wait. Brunch is from 10 am to 2 pm but the line starts forming around 9 am. Either go early or wait

until noon. It has everything from sashimi to an incredible dessert bar.

The Waiohai's *Tamarind* restaurant (tel 742-9511) has a fixed meal each evening for $42.50 in an elegant setting. Formal dress is required.

The *House of Seafood* (tel 742-6433) in Poipu Kai Resort is a seafood restaurant with a good reputation. Meals cost from $15.50 for shrimp pasta to $35 for abalone. It has a keiki menu for children with dinners from salad to dessert for $5.50 to $9. It's open, for dinner only, from 5.30 pm.

Entertainment

Most Poipu entertainment is at the hotel nightclubs. Occasionally they get big names in.

The *Sheraton Kauai Hotel* has contemporary or Hawaiian duos from 6 to 10 pm Tuesday to Saturday and live dance bands from 8 pm to midnight nightly. The Sheraton also has a Polynesian-style dinner show.

The *Stouffer Poipu Beach Hotel* has contemporary Hawaiian music on Mondays and Tuesdays and top-40 bands from 8 pm till midnight Wednesday to Sunday. Shorts and tank tops are OK there.

The *Stouffer Waiohai* has pianist Kimo Garner nightly in its Tamarind lounge.

West Side

The top destinations on Kauai's West Side are Waimea Canyon and Kokee State Park, both with ruggedly spectacular scenery.

It's 38 miles along Kaumualii Rd (Hwy 50) from Lihue to Polihale State Park. This is sugar country, with sugar cane lining the roadside most of the way.

PUHI

Puhi, two miles south of Lihue, is small enough to have an old-fashioned general store, complete with rural post office. The clerk still gets your groceries one item at a time from the shelves behind the counter,

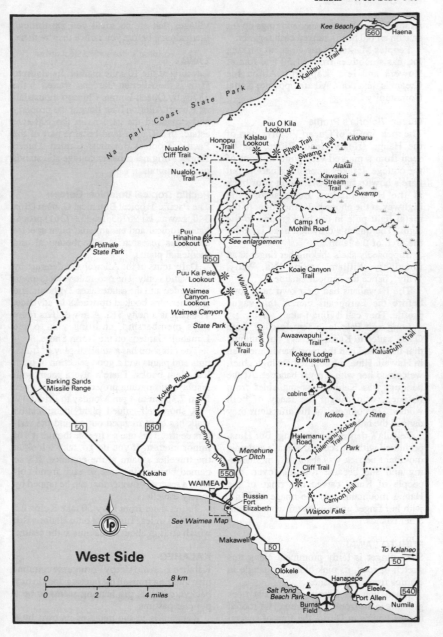

West Side

Kee Beach
Haena
560
Kalalau Trail

Na Pali Coast State Park

Puu O Kila Lookout
Honopu Trail
Kalalau Lookout
Nualolo Cliff Trail
Pihea Trail
Kilohana
Alakai
Swamp Trail
Nualolo Trail
Alakai
Kawaikoi Stream Trail
Swamp
Polihale State Park
Puu Hinahina Lookout
See enlargement
Camp 10-Mohihi Road
550
Puu Ka Pele Lookout
Koaie Canyon Trail
Waimea Canyon Lookout
Waimea Canyon
State Park
Waimea Canyon
Kukui Trail
Kokee Road

Barking Sands Missile Range

50
550

Menehune Ditch
Waimea Canyon Drive
550

Kekaha
WAIMEA
Russian Fort Elizabeth
See Waimea Map

0   4   8 km
0   2   4 miles

Makaweli
50
Olokele
Salt Pond Beach Park
Burns Field
Hanapepe
Eleele
Port Allen
Numila
540
To Kalaheo

Enlargement

Awaawapuhi Trail
Kaluapuhi Trail
Kokee Lodge & Museum
cabines
Kokoo
State
Halemanu Road
Halemanu-Kokee Trail
Cliff Trail
Park
Canyon Trail
Waipoo Falls

wraps them in brown paper and rings up the sale on an old hand-cranked cash register.

Peoples Market, in the adjacent parking lot, has smoothies from $1.50 and lots of flowers and leis. Lappert's Aloha Ice Cream is next door. All are opposite Kauai Community College.

Queen Victoria's Profile

The rock profile of Queen Victoria, part of the Haupu (Hoary Head) Ridge, can be seen from a marked viewpoint in front of the college. It takes some imagination, but here's how to find it. Start with your back at the HVB marker. Look across the highway at the phone pole, then over to the metal light pole in the background to the right. The queen's crowned head is under the arch of the lamp.

Supposedly she's shaking her finger at an imaginary William, saying 'Na, Willy, Willy', hence the harbour's name.

The Hawaiians had their own story long before the Europeans named this vague profile. They call it Hina-i-uka.

Long ago Peleula, a female chief from Oahu, sailed to Kauai to check out rumours that the island had the most handsome men in Hawaii. Hina, a Kauai female high chief, welcomed her with a royal banquet. At the banquet was Kahili, a young chief from Kilauea, who caught the fancy of both women. To compete for his affections they danced the hula.

Peleula's dance was stunning. But Hina, perfumed with the scent of Kauai's endemic mokihana berries, was absolutely mesmerising and she became Kahili's lover. The people of Kauai carved one ridge of the Haupu mountains into the image of Hina, with her finger up to warn off women from other islands.

PUHI TO LAWAI

Shell ginger is fairly prominent along this stretch of road, its pink blossoms dangle in clumps from large bushes.

When you see banana and guava trees growing in the front yards of small tin-roofed homes you're in Omao, the first of several villages that are so small you zip through them almost before you notice they're there.

LAWAI

Lawai is at the 10-mile marker. Its claim to fame is the Allerton Gardens, started in the 1870s by Queen Emma. Chicago industrialist Robert Allerton later bought the property and expanded the gardens in the 100-acre estate. In 1971 the land became part of the Pacific Tropical Botanical Garden. Queen Emma's original summer cottage still stands on the grounds.

Pacific Tropical Botanical Garden

The Pacific Tropical Botanical Garden (Box 340, Lawai, HI 96765; tel 332-7361) propagates tropical and endangered plant species and does research in ethnobotanical and medicinal plants.

Daily tours of the Allerton Gardens are by reservation only. The two-mile walk through the garden and the estate takes 2½ hours and is sometimes booked up weeks in advance. The cost is a hefty $15. A few dollars more buys membership, entitling you to see Limahuli Gardens on the North Shore.

The gift shop has a small display of fruits, nuts and plants and a good selection of tropical plant books. There's also a room with displays of ongoing projects. Both are open from 7.30 am to 4 pm Monday to Friday.

A short self-guided plant identification walk has been mapped out around the visitors centre. This one's a freebie though it's of minor interest. If you do go, take a look at the traveller's palm at the entrance. It's so named because the base of each frond collects a reserve of water that can be tapped by thirsty travellers.

To get there from Hwy 50 take Koloa Rd south 1¼ miles. Turn right onto Hailima Rd, which ends in about half a mile at the centre.

KALAHEO

Kalaheo is an old sleepy Portuguese community. Judging from all the hunting dogs in tiny backyard cages, pig hunting seems to be a popular pastime.

Kalaheo is in the midst of its own little

development boom, not of hotels and condos but of private homes. Doctors and other highly paid professionals are buying up the cliffside oceanview lots below the golf course.

The town's main shops are clustered around the intersection of Hwy 50 and Papalina Rd. There's a laundromat behind the Pineapple Hut.

Kukuiolono Park

Kukuiolono Park (tel 332-9151) is a golf course with gardens and a scenic viewpoint. Kukuiolono means 'light of Lono', referring to the torches that were once placed on this hill to help guide canoes safely to shore.

From Hwy 50, turn left onto Papalina Rd in Kalaheo. Just short of a mile turn right onto Puu Rd and then make an immediate right turn up through an old stone archway into the park. A neat little Japanese garden is at the right end of the parking lot.

The green pavilion on the knoll south-west of here looks down on a wide expanse of the south coast. To get there look for the satellite dish and head for the Norfolk pines. It's a 10-minute walk on a paved road across the golf course.

The ominous-looking gismo on the flat hill directly south of the pavilion is a navy signal beacon. Poipu is at the point on the left. To your back is Mt Kahili at 3089 feet.

The park gates are open from 6.30 am to 6.30 pm. The nine-hole golf course is open to the public on a first-come, first-served basis. Green fees are $5. The little clubhouse has a snack shop.

Puu Road Scenic Drive

Puu Rd is a scenic side loop with small ranches, sugar cane fields, bamboo clumps, grand mango trees and coastal views. It's a winding road, only one lane in places, with some blind curves, but nothing tricky if you drive slowly. This is a quiet country road and it's quite possible you won't even encounter another car.

After leaving Kukuiolono Park, turn right onto Puu Rd. It's just over three miles back to Hwy 50 this way. About halfway along

you'll look down on Port Allen's oil tanks and the Numila sugar mill smokestack.

Around another bend macadamia trees march in rows up the distant hills ahead. Down the slope to the left of the road are coffee trees, part of a total of 400 acres planted near Kalaheo. Both the coffee and nuts belong to the McBryde Sugar Company and are an attempt to diversify crops on land that has formerly been planted only with sugar cane. The coffee is a joint venture with Hills Bros Coffee. McBryde is also experimenting with tea and patchouli.

Olu Pua Botanical Garden

The Olu Pua estate home was built in 1931 by Honolulu architect C W Dickey. It was the headquarters of Alexander & Baldwin's Kauai Pineapple Plantation. US presidents Reagan, Carter, Ford and Nixon have all been guests. It's still a private home though the 12-acre gardens are open to the public for guided tours. It was recently for sale at $5½ million. Any takers?

Olu Pua (tel 332-8182) claims to have Hawaii's finest collection of tropical flowers. One section is of edible and useful plants, others are of palms, hibiscus and orchids. The front lawn has flowering shade trees.

Olu Pua is at the end of a long driveway mauka of the road immediately after the intersection of Hwy 50 and Hwy 540. Tours are at 9.30, 11.30 am, 1.30 and 3.00 pm daily and cost $10.

Places to Stay

Classic Vacation Cottages (Dick and Wynnis Grow, Box 901, Kalaheo, HI 96741; tel 332-9201) has three units in Kalaheo, half a mile up from Hwy 50 and about 20 minutes from the beaches at Poipu. The studio is a great bargain at $35, with a queen-size bed, a skylight and French doors to a little porch. The one-bedroom unit has high ceilings, a lanai and a peek at the ocean for $50. The third unit is $45. It's a friendly place and the rooms are cheery. All have kitchens and TVs. Breakfast for two is $5 more.

Places to Eat

The *Brick Oven Pizza* (tel 332-8561) on Hwy 50 in Kalaheo can be crowded, particularly at dinner time. There's a choice of whole wheat or white crusts and garlic oil around the rim on request. The cheese pizza is $6 for a small one and $12 for large. The small salad at $1.25 is good and not so small. It also serves sandwiches, wine and beer. It's open daily.

The *Bread Box*, just down Papalina Rd in the centre of town, makes good breads such as whole-wheat, French and wheat germ sourbread. Cinnamon rolls cost $1, coffee 25 cents. It's open from 6 am to 4 pm Monday to Saturday.

The *Sugar Shack*, across the street, has good-looking pies, cakes, pastries and muffins at reasonable prices. The *Pineapple Hut* next door is open for three meals. Kalbi rib lunch costs $5, spam and cabbage $3.50 and omelettes around $3. The interior is worth a look.

KALAHEO TO HANAPEPE

The scenic lookout that comes up soon after the 14-mile marker gives a view deep into Hanapepe Valley. The red clay walls of the cliffs are topped by bright green cane like a sugar frosting.

The same Robinson family that owns Niihau owns a lot of land around these parts and has a hideaway estate up in the valley.

Eleele Shopping Center, at the 16-mile marker, has a doughnut shop, a deli, a Dairy Queen, a Big Save supermarket, a post office, a laundromat and a gas station. Other than the shopping centre there's not much to the town.

Hwy 540 is an alternate route which leads off Hwy 50 just after Kalaheo and connects back to Hwy 50 at Eleele. It passes Numila, a small cane town with little wooden houses and deep red earth. Numila centres around McBryde Sugar Company and mill. However, if you take this route you'll miss the Hanapepe Valley Lookout.

Port Allen on Hanapepe Bay is both a commercial harbour and Kauai's most active recreational boat harbour. The state-run small craft harbour is protected by break-

waters and has launch ramps, berthing and mooring spaces. US Navy activities sometimes restrict harbour use.

HANAPEPE

Hanapepe is a step back in time, moving along at its own slow pace. The main street is lined with old wooden buildings, some with fading signs, a few recently smartened up. With its dusty feed store, boarded-up theatre and ageing laundry called Up-to-Date Cleaners, this town is full of character.

Parts of *The Thorn Birds* was filmed here, because it bears a resemblance to the dusty Australian outback of earlier days.

A new sign reads 'Welcome to Hanapepe, Kauai's Biggest Little Town', and a recent grant to spiff up Main St may change the town's face. Time will tell.

Salt Pond Beach

Kauai has long been known for its red alae salt, made by adding a little of its iron-rich earth to sea salt. The salt is made by letting seawater into shallow basins called salt pans and allowing it to evaporate. When dry, the salt crystals are scraped off. Native Hawaiians still make salt down on the coast south of Hanapepe.

Salt Pond Beach County Park is just beyond the salt ponds. It has a sandy beach, camping sites, picnic tables, showers and a lifeguard on duty daily. Water in the cove gets up to 10 feet deep and is good for swimming laps. Four times across equals half a mile. Both ends of the cove are shallow and good for kids.

To get to the beach, turn left just past the 17-mile marker onto Lele Rd at the sign for the refuse transfer station, then right onto Lokokai Rd.

Places to Eat

The *Green Garden Restaurant* (Hwy 50, Hanapepe; tel 335-5422) is a large restaurant with a varied, if not overly exciting menu. Tours pull up here by the busload. Sandwiches are $4 to $5 and there are usually a few lunch specials around $5. Dinners begin at a few dollars more. Green Garden sells

Taro Ko Chips, made from Hanapepe-grown taro, which is sliced thin and then fried into chips. Green Garden is open daily for three meals, except dinner on Tuesdays.

The other choice in Hanapepe is *Conrad Wong's*. The last time we went through we stopped there and picked up Chinese food and headed down to the beach with it. When we broke out the food we found it to be so inedible we ended up throwing half of it away.

OLOKELE

Olokele exists for the Olokele Sugar Company. Of the 260 employees, mostly field labourers, 230 live in Olokele.

The road to the sugar mill, immediately after the 19-mile marker, is shaded by tall trees and lined with turn-of-the-century electric post lights. For a glance at real plantation life, take a drive down this road. Everything is red, covered with a layer of dust from the sugar cane fields which completely surround the town. Rather than fight it, most of the houses are painted in beige-red tones.

MAKAWELI

Makaweli is headquarters for Gay & Robinson, Niihau Ranch and Niihau Helicopters; all enterprises of the same Robinson family who owns Niihau. Quite a few native Niihauans live in this area, many of them working for the Robinsons. Once or twice a week an old military landing craft makes the 17-mile trip between Niihau and Makaweli Landing.

Nearby Pakalas break at Pakala Point is a popular surfing spot. When the surf hits, it can be quite good.

RUSSIAN FORT ELIZABETH

The remains of Russian Fort Elizabeth stand above the east bank of the Waimea River. Hawaiian labourers started building the fort in 1816 under the direction of Georg Anton Schaeffer, an agent of the Russian-American Company. The alliance between the Russians and Kauai's King Kaumualii was short-lived and the Russians were tossed out in 1817, the same year the fort was completed.

You can take a short walk through this curious period of Kauai's history using a self-guiding map found at the trailhead. The most intact part of the fort is the exterior lava rock wall. It's eight to 10 feet high in places and largely overgrown with scrub and colourful wildflowers. The seaward side was designed like the points of a star, but it takes some close observation to get the effect. A dozen markers point out where things used to be, such as the trading house, armoury and barracks.

The fort has a good view of the western bank of Waimea River where Captain Cook landed. Down the dirt road from the fort parking lot there's a sandy area above the river mouth with a view of Waimea Pier.

The trees in the parking lot are kukui. There are restrooms there.

WAIMEA

Waimea (which means 'reddish water') was the site of an ancient Hawaiian settlement. It was there that Captain Cook made his first Hawaiian landing on 19 January 1778. In 1820 the first wave of missionaries to Hawaii landed at Waimea. In 1884 Waimea Sugar moved in and Waimea developed into a plantation town.

Today Waimea is the biggest town on this side of the island. It has lots of small wooden buildings, some with false fronts, each with its own little history. The dominant building by the square is the First Hawaiian Bank, built in 1929 in the neo-classical style.

If you're on your way up to Waimea Canyon or out to the beaches, it probably doesn't make sense to give Waimea too much time. Most people just eat and move on.

If you do want to explore, Waimea Library, at the 23-mile marker, has a map of historical sights that can be photocopied and used for a self-guided walking tour. The library (tel 338-1738) is open from noon to 8 pm Mondays and Wednesdays and from 8.30 am to 4.30 pm Tuesdays, Thursdays and Fridays.

Waimea has an annual Captain Cook fair on the last weekend in February with

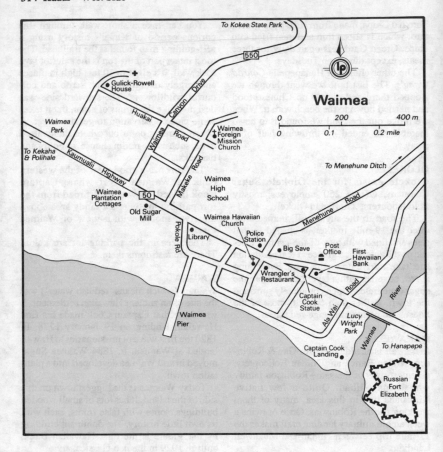

Waimea

0   200   400 m

0   0.1   0.2 mile

carnival games, live music, pig-on-a-spit, cotton candy and lots of beer.

Waimea Canyon Drive heads north from town to Kokee State Park.

Lucy Wright Park
The Cook landing site is noted with a simple plaque on a nondescript rock on the western side of Waimea Bay. A well-worn trail has been made by tourists who pull in and out like pilgrims.

The plaque is in Lucy Wright Park, on Ala Wai Rd, just over the Waimea Bridge. The park has a ball field, picnic tables, restrooms

and showers. Camping is allowed on a flat grassy area, but it's at the side of the road in town and doesn't have much appeal.

Captain Cook Statue
The statue of Captain Cook in the centre of town is a replica of the original statue by Sir John Tweed that stands in Whitby, England. The Pacific's greatest navigator is all decked out in his best captaining finery with maps in hand.

Waimea State Recreation Pier
Until Port Allen was built, Waimea was the

region's main harbour. It was a major port of call for whalers and traders during the mid-1800s. Later in the century plantations started exporting sugar from here.

Waimea Pier is now used primarily for pole fishing, crabbing and picnicking. It's off Pokole Rd.

Waimea Churches

Waimea Foreign Mission Church was originally a thatched structure built in 1826 by the Reverend Samuel Whitney, the first missionary to Waimea. Whitney and his wife are buried in the churchyard. The present church was built of sandstone blocks and coral mortar in 1858 by the Reverend George Rowell.

In 1865 Reverend Rowell had a spat with some folks in the congregation and went off and built the Waimea Hawaiian Church, the wooden frame church opposite Wrangler's Restaurant.

It was Rowell who finished building what is now called the Gulick-Rowell House, at the end of Huakai Rd. Construction began in 1829, making it the oldest house still standing in Kauai. The two-storey stone block house is now privately owned and not open to the public.

Menehune Ditch

Menehune Ditch is a stone and earthen aqueduct built prior to Western contact. Kauai's legendary little people, the menehunes, are said to have built the ditch in one night. The ditch was an engineering masterpiece with rocks carefully squared and jointed to fit close together.

When Captain Vancouver visited Waimea at the end of the 18th century he walked up the river valley atop the wall of the ditch which also served as a footpath. He estimated the walls to be 24 feet high. These days most of the ancient waterway lies buried beneath the road, but one section about two feet high can still be seen. The ditch still diverts water from the Waimea River along and through the cliff to irrigate the taro patches below.

To get there, turn at the police station onto Menehune Rd and go about 1⅓ miles up

Waimea River. The ditch is along the left side of the road after a small parking lot, just before the swinging bridge.

On the drive up to the ditch, notice the scattered holes in the cliffs to the left. They are Hawaiian burial caves. One group of seven caves behind the Japanese temple was explored by Wendell Bennett of the Bishop Museum in the 1920s. At that time each of the caves held a number of skeletal remains, some in canoe-shaped coffins and others in hollowed-out logs.

Places to Stay

The only place to stay in the town of Waimea is at *Waimea Plantation Cottages* (Box 367, Waimea, HI 96796; tel 338-1625; 800-992-4632). Here's the concept: bring in tired wooden plantation workers' homes from the early 1900s, 'yuppify' them and hope for a nostalgia boom. The cottages are clustered in a coconut grove and are cutely rustic with little porches. Once they're painted and polished they rent for $65 to $175. They look pleasant enough though there's some irony in having placed them next to a neighbourhood of real workers' cottages. Then there's the two- storey five-bedroom manager's estate for $2100 a week. Up in Hanalei they have a second estate at the same price and a one- bedroom cottage for $80 for up to three people.

Places to Eat

Wrangler's Restaurant (tel 338-1218) in Waimea is the place to eat in these parts. It serves up generous portions of good food. The teri beef sandwich with fries and salad is $4.50. The chilli rellenos with rice, beans, chips and salad is $5.50. Seafood and steak dishes are $7.50 to $17. This is a good place to try lilikoi pie, made daily by the manager's mother. The building was originally the Ako Store, built by Chinese shopkeeper Ah Go in 1909. It's open from 11 am to 9 pm Monday to Thursday, and until 10 pm Fridays and Saturdays.

Next door to Wrangler's there's a little shop that sells wrapped sandwiches for about $2 to $4.

The *Kauai Kitchen*, next to Big Save, has lacklustre plate lunches for about $4 and other diner fare.

KEKAHA

Kekaha has great beaches, or rather it has one long glorious stretch. The road follows the beach for about two miles, with roadside parking all along the way. It's open ocean and when there's no swell there are usually people swimming. Niihau and its offshore island, Lehua, are visible from there.

There's a very inconspicuous shower just mauka of the highway between Alae Rd (Hwy 550) and Amakihi Rd, and restrooms and picnic tables farther in. Nearby are tennis courts and a county swimming pool.

A few blocks up Kekaha Rd, the main street, runs parallel to the highway. It has a couple of grocery stores, a post office, gas station, Thai restaurant and a camping and backpacking store. Kekaha's sugar mill is visible from the highway.

On its eastern end, Kekaha Rd comes out to Hwy 50 near the Kikiaola Small Boat Harbor. This state harbour has one launch ramp and eight mooring spaces.

Kekaha is the last town before the end of the highway. As you head towards Polihale, the inland cliffs get higher and the ravines deeper. Corn and sunflowers planted for their seed grow in farms along the road. Cattle and cattle egrets feed in the pastures.

Places to Eat

Toi's Thai Kitchen (tel 337-9922) in the Traveler's Den on Kekaha Road serves both Thai and American food. Thai saimin or sandwiches are $2 to $4. Chicken with coconut milk costs $7, buttered garlic shrimp $9. It's open from 10.30 am to 2 pm and from 5 to 8.30 pm daily except Saturdays.

BARKING SANDS

Barking Sands Pacific Missile Range, a US Navy base, usually has one stretch of its beach open to the public. For a recorded message on current access, dial 335-4229.

The road in is at the 'Pacific Missile Range Facility' sign, less than half a mile after the 32-mile marker. At the gate they ask to see your driver's licence and rental car keys. They give you a map and explain where you can go, which is usually the beach about two miles south of the gate, which locals call Major's Bay and the military calls RecArea No 3.

This broad sweep of fine golden sand is a good sunbathing and walking beach, though open and hot. The bush behind the beach offers no shade, but it hardly matters as the vegetation line is the DMZ line and you're forbidden to go beyond it anyway.

Major's Bay is a popular winter surfing spot. Like all West Side beaches the waters can be dangerous. There are no facilities. The purple-tinged island of Niihau can be seen on the horizon.

On very sunny days, when the wind is blowing off the water just right, the moving sands make sounds similar to dogs barking.

The missile range facility provides the above-ground link to a sophisticated sonar network that tracks more than 1000 square miles of the Pacific. Established during WW II, it's been developed into the world's largest underwater listening device. The equipment is sensitive enough to pick up the songs of wintering humpback whales. The base probably has the most comprehensive collection of humpback whale soundtracks recorded anywhere.

POLIHALE

Polihale is near-desert. When it's raining everywhere else, beachgoers head this way.

Polihale has a beautiful long white sand beach with aqua-coloured water that often comes to shore in huge explosive waves. Expert surfers occasionally give Polihale a try, but strong riptides make the waters dangerous for swimming.

Polihale State Park is about five miles from the military base. Turn left three-quarters of a mile north of the base entrance onto a wide dirt road that runs through sugar cane fields. The road is bumpy but passable. Set your odometer at zero here.

At about three and a quarter miles, at a large tree in the middle of the road, a turnoff leads to the only safe swimming spot in the area. To get there turn left at the tree and then after a quarter of a mile follow the road up the hill to the right to the base of the dunes. Walk a couple of minutes to the north along the shore and you'll come to Queen's Pond. This large semicircle of reef comes almost to shore creating a year-round protected swimming pool. Along the rest of the beach is open sea.

To get to Polihale State Park go back to the tree at the main road that runs through the sugar cane fields, turn left and continue down a mile. A turnoff on the left leads to a camping area with restrooms, outdoor showers, drinking water and a picnic pavilion. Farther down, other camping areas are in the dunes just above the beach amidst thorny kiawe trees.

At the very end of the beach is Polihale Cliff, the western end of the Na Pali Coast. There's a terraced heiau towards the base of the cliff. It was originally on the seashore but shifting sands have since added about 300 feet of beach to the shore. It's so overgrown that even after you tramp through the bushes and find it, it's really hard to get a perspective on it. Wasps are another obstacle. If you're allergic to stings, forget about exploring this one.

WAIMEA CANYON

Waimea Canyon is nicknamed the 'Grand Canyon of the Pacific'. This may sound like promotional hype but it's not a bad description. It's smaller and 200 million years younger than the famed Arizona canyon, but Waimea Canyon is certainly grand.

The colourful river-cut gorge is 2785 feet deep. The river that runs through it, the Waimea-Poomau, is 19½ miles long, and is Kauai's longest. It seems incredible that such an immense canyon could be tucked inside such a small island.

The view of the canyon is usually a bit hazy. The best time to be there is a sunny day after it's been raining heavily. At such times, the earth's a deeper red and waterfalls cascade throughout the canyon. You can't beat it.

Waimea Canyon Drive

Waimea Canyon Drive (Hwy 550) starts in Waimea. The road is about 19 miles long, ending at lookouts with terrific views into Kalalau Valley on the Na Pali Coast.

The views start about a mile up from Waimea and get better and better as the road climbs. There are plenty of little looks where you can stop to take it all in. The one at 1¾ miles looks down on the road to Menehune Ditch and the taro patches it irrigates. From there on in it's all canyon views.

WAIMEA CANYON STATE PARK

The southern boundary of Waimea Canyon State Park is about six miles up. Waimea Canyon Drive and Kokee Rd, both labelled Hwy 550, merge nearby. Kokee Rd connects with Hwy 50 at Kekaha. It has views, but not of the canyon. From there north the road is called Kokee Rd.

Iliau Nature Loop

The trailhead for the Iliau Nature Loop is shortly before the nine-mile marker. Just a short walk up the trail there's a bench with a good view of Waimea and Waialae canyons. After heavy rainfall waterfalls explode down the sheer rock walls across the gorge.

Iliau Loop starts to the right of the bench and takes about 15 minutes to walk. Iliau, a plant endemic to western Kauai, grows along the trail. Like its cousin the silversword, iliau grows to a ripe old age. Then for a grand finale it bursts open with blossoms and dies. The stalks are up to 10 feet high.

In 1989 a sandalwood replanting project was started along this trail to commemorate the bicentenary of Chinese immigration to Hawaii.

Lookouts

Waimea Canyon Lookout is a big turnoff where all the tour buses stop. The lookout offers a sweeping view of the canyon from a perch of 3100 feet.

Waipoo Falls can be seen from a couple of small unmarked lookouts before the 12-mile marker and then at the marked Puu Ka Pele Viewpoint. Sometimes a rainbow shows up in the spray of the 800-foot falls. The east-running canyon most prominent from this point is Koaie Canyon. Across the road is a picnic area with barbecue pits, restrooms and water, as well as Camp Hale Koa, a Seventh Day Adventist camp.

Puu Hinahina Lookout, at 3640 feet, is a major turnoff between the 13 and 14-mile markers. There are two lookouts. One looks down Waimea Canyon clear out to the coast. The other has a view of Niihau.

Waimea Canyon Trails

The trailhead for the Kukui Trail is shortly before the nine-mile marker up Hwy 550 on the way to Kokee State Park. Kukui Trail continues from the Iliau Nature Loop at a sign-in box and picnic table. It's a steep 2000-foot descent down the western side of Waimea Canyon, 2½ miles to the Waimea River. Wiliwili Camp is at the end of the trail.

Koaie Canyon Trail begins at Kaluahaulu Camp, half a mile up the Waimea River from the end of Kukui Trail. From there it runs east for three miles along the southern side of Koaie Canyon. There are some good swimming holes in the stream along the way and at the end of the trail. This trail should be avoided during stormy weather due to the danger of flash flooding.

The canyon's fertile soil once supported a Hawaiian settlement, long abandoned. The remains of a heiau and some house sites are still discernible.

The trail passes Hipalau Camp and ends at Lonomea Camp. All four camping sites are part of the forest reserve system. Although all have simple open-air shelters, there are no facilities and the water needs to be treated before drinking.

During the hunting season, mainly weekends and holidays from October to February, the trails are fairly heavily used by pig hunters.

KOKEE STATE PARK

The Kokee State Park boundary starts after Puu Hinahina Lookout.

You may still see signs for NASA (National Aeronautics and Space Adminis-

tration). The space-flight tracking station they opened here in 1960 was closed in 1989 after a new satellite network rendered this ground station obsolete.

From about the 15-mile marker, you pass park cabins, a ranger station, Kokee Lodge, a museum and a camping ground one after the other. Kokee Lodge is not an overnight lodge but a restaurant and is where the concessionaire for the nearby cabins can be found.

Information

The ranger station in Kokee is currently not staffed. People at the museum or store can usually give you a little assistance. The museum sells a map of park trails and may have some pamphlets as well.

Camping permits, trail maps and park information are available at the state parks office in Lihue (tel 245-4444). For cabin rentals, see Places to Stay.

At 7.35 and 8.25 am KUAI radio station (720AM) announces the weather conditions at Kokee State Park.

Kokee Museum

The Kokee Natural History Museum (tel 335-9975) is a good place to learn about Kauai's ecology. It has topographical maps and displays of local plants, birds, petroglyphs and geology. Check out the landslide photos showing how a 3000-foot side of Mt Waialeale collapsed, filling Olokele Canyon in 1981. Koa bowls, books and maps are sold at the museum. It's open from 10 am to 4 pm daily and admission is free.

According to legend the meadow opposite the museum was once a forested hang-out for an evil akua (spirit) who enjoyed harassing people passing through on their way to Kalalau Valley. Distraught travellers appealed to the great god Kanaloa to protect them from the akua. Kanaloa responded by ripping out all the trees and declaring that they were never again to grow here, thus destroying the akua's hiding place. These days the meadow is full of good vibes and a perfect place for throwing a frisbee.

A very short nature trail that should

probably be taken off the map starts between the museum and the lodge. It's mostly overgrown and eroded, with a few plaques hanging on the sides of fallen trees. Kauai sandalwood trees are identified just to the right of the lodge's back door.

Those chickens running around the park are not the common garden variety, but moa, or jungle fowl. Early Polynesian settlers brought moa to Hawaii and they were once common on all the main islands. Now they remain solely on Kauai, the only island free from mongoose, who eat the eggs of ground-nesting birds.

Kalalau Lookouts

The two Kalalau Valley lookouts at the end of the road are not to be missed. From a height of 4000 feet you can see deep into the green depths of the valley straight out to the sea. Late afternoon rainbows sweep so deeply into Kalalau Valley that the bottom part of the bows curve back inward. Bright red apapane birds feed from the flowers of the ohia lehua trees near the lookout railings.

Kalalau Valley was once the site of a large settlement and was joined to Kokee by a very steep trail that ran down the cliffside. These days the only way into the valley is along the coastal trail from Haena.

The cone-shaped pinnacles along the valley walls look rather like a row of sentinels standing at attention. One legend says that rain has sculptured the cliffsides into the shape of the proud chiefs who are buried in the mountains.

The mushroom-shaped white dome and satellite dishes visible on the hill as you walk back to the parking lot are part of the Kokee Air Force station. There's drinking water at this first lookout.

Puu O Kila Lookout

The paved road continues another mile to Puu O Kila Lookout. This is the last leg of the aborted Kokee-Haena Highway, which would have linked Kokee with the North Shore, thus creating an island circuit road. When you look at the cliffs at the end of the road it's easy to see why the plan was dropped.

The Pihea Trail that climbs the ridge straight ahead runs along what was to be the road.

From this lookout you get another view into Kalalau Valley and a glance inland toward the Alakai Swamp Preserve. A sign here points to Waialeale, the wettest spot on earth.

Kokee State Park Trails

Kokee State Park is the starting point for about 45 miles of trails, some maintained by the park service, others by the forestry. Pig and goat hunters use some of these trails during the hunting season.

Four of the trails – Nualolo, Awaawapuhi, Honopu and Pihea – offer cliff-top views into valleys on the Na Pali Coast. Honopu Trail is not well maintained. Other trails go into the bogs of Alakai Swamp but the rest are easy nature trails.

Halemanu Road Trails Halemanu Rd is just north of the 14-mile marker. Whether or not it's passable in a standard car often depends on whether it's been raining recently. It's the starting point for several scenic hikes.

The first is Cliff Trail, a five-minute walk to an overlook into Waimea Canyon. From there you can continue along Canyon Trail, a rather strenuous 1¾ miles one way that follows the canyon rim, passes Waipoo Falls and ends at Kumuwela Lookout with views down the canyon to the ocean beyond.

A little farther down Halemanu Rd is the start of Halemanu-Kokee Trail. This easy 1¼-mile (one way) nature trail passes through a native forest of koa and ohia trees that provide habitat to native birds. One of the common plants found on this trail is banana poka, a member of the passion fruit family and a serious invasive pest. It has pretty pink flowers but it drapes the forest with its vines and chokes out less aggressive native plants.

Nualolo & Awaawapuhi Trails The Nualolo and Awaawapuhi trails each go out to the very edge of sheer cliffs, peering down into valleys accessible only by boat. They connect via the recently opened Nualolo Cliff Trail. If you combine all three it makes for a hardy day hike. The valley views are extraordinarily beautiful. This is our favourite hike in Kokee.

The whole hike is about 10 miles of trails. Then you'll have to either hitch a ride or walk an additional two miles back down the road to where you started.

If you're only going to do one of the trails, we recommend Awaawapuhi, though it's more strenuous than the Nualolo Trail. There are interpretive markers along the way and the views at the end are unbeatable.

The trails are marked at quarter-mile intervals. There's no water along the way. Edible plants along the trail include blackberries, thimbleberries, guava and passion fruit (lilikoi), the latter recognisable by its vine and beautiful pink flowers.

These days the only valley settlers are goats, easily spotted along the cliff walls. The goats have no natural predators in Hawaii and are prolific in the North Shore valleys. They are capable of breeding at five months of age. The goats are interesting to watch but they've caused a fair amount of ecological damage.

The 3.8-mile Nualolo Trail starts between the cabins and Kokee Lodge. The trail begins in cool upland forest and descends 1500 feet, ending down a narrow ridge at a lookout on the rim of Nualolo Valley.

The Awaawapuhi Trail begins near the 17-mile marker and descends 1600 feet, ending just over three miles at a steep and spectacular pali overlooking Awaawapuhi and Nualolo valleys.

The trail starts in ohia forest. About half a mile down the trail, the forest becomes drier and koa begins to mix in with the ohia. A fair number of the koa trees are dead, with some of the dead trees still standing. It's all a result of Hurricane Iwa's wrath in 1982.

About 50 of the trees and plants along the trail are marked. An interpretive nature guide for this trail is available free from the forestry office. Awaawapuhi means 'valley of ginger'. Kahili, a yellow ginger, is seen at marker number nine.

The 2.1-mile Nualolo Cliff Trail is very scenic and offers numerous viewpoints into Nualolo Valley. There's even a picnic table where you can break for lunch along the way. The Nualolo Cliff Trail connects at the Nualolo Trail near the 3¼-mile mark and at the Awaawapuhi Trail near the 2¾-mile mark.

Camp 10-Mohihi Rd Trails A number of hikes start off Camp 10-Mohihi Rd which is up past the museum on the right. This road is typical of many of the dirt roads in Kokee. When it's dry, standard cars usually make it down. Occasionally when it's really wet and rutted even 4WD vehicles can't make it down.

The Kawaikoi Stream Trail begins between Sugi Grove and Kawaikoi camping grounds. It's a scenic mountain stream trail and the round trip is about 2½ miles. It starts out following the southern side of Kawaikoi Stream, then heads away from the stream and makes a loop, coming down the northern side of the stream before reconnecting with the southern side. If the stream is running high, don't make the crossings.

The Pihea Trail starts from the Puu O Kila Lookout. The first mile runs along the ridge with views into Kalalau Valley. The beginning of the trail was graded in the 1950s, before plans to make this the last leg of the circle-island road were abandoned.

The Pihea Trail eventually turns inland and at about 1¾ miles crosses the Alakai Swamp Trail. If you turn left here you can continue on for about two miles through the Alakai Swamp to Kilohana Lookout. If you go straight instead, you will connect with Kawaikoi Stream Trail in about two miles.

The 3½-mile Alakai Swamp Trail starts off Camp 10-Mohihi Rd. The trail goes through rainforest and bogs before reaching Kilohana Lookout on Wainiha Pali. If it's not overcast there will be a sweeping view of Wainiha and Hanalei valleys. This is an extremely muddy trail and there are plenty of stories of people slogging knee-deep in it.

If your car can't make it down Camp 10-Mohihi Rd, parking at Puu O Kila Lookout and approaching Alakai Swamp Trail via the Pihea Trail is probably your best bet.

Alakai Swamp is inaccessible enough that even invasive plants haven't been able to choke out the endemic swamp vegetation. Native bird species still have a stronghold there.

There are parts of the swamp that receive sunlight so sparingly that the moss grows thick and fat on all sides of the trees. Most people that see this swamp see it from a helicopter. The Alakai Swamp Trail passes through a corner of it.

Kauapuhi Trail

The Kaluapuhi Trail is a forest trail leading to a plum grove. It's about two miles long. The marked trailhead starts at the highway a quarter of a mile past the 17-mile marker. This is a busy trail during midsummer when lots of people come up to pick the wild plums.

Places to Stay

Kokee Lodge (Box 819, Waimea, HI 96796; tel 335-6061) manages the 12 cabins in Kokee State Park. The older cabins are a little tired and have just one large room with three beds for $35. Newer two-bedroom cedar cabins are $45 for up to six people. All have basic kitchens, linens, hot showers and fireplaces. State park rules limit stays to five days. The cabins are often booked up well in advance. However, cancellations do occur and you can sometimes get in if you're flexible.

Kokee has one camping ground just past Kokee Lodge, above the meadow in a fairly uncrowded grassy area. Three other camping sites are along Camp 10-Mohihi Rd; they're at *Kawaikoi*, *Sugi Grove* and *Camp 10*. There are restrooms, showers, water and picnic tables. Camping is free and allowed up to five nights, but permits are required.

The camping grounds are at almost 4000 feet and nights are crisp and cool. This is sleeping bag and warm clothing country. The nearest store and gas station are in Waimea, 15 miles away.

Places to Eat

The *Kokee Lodge* (tel 335-6061) has pretty good food and it's quite reasonable considering there's no competition. At breakfast French toast and coffee will cost about $5. At lunch time, burgers with fries are about the same. Dinners are in the $10 to $12 range. It's open from 8.30 am to 3.30 pm daily, and for dinner from 6 to 9 pm Fridays and Saturdays.

Niihau

Niihau has long been closed to outsiders, earning it the nickname 'The Forbidden Island'.

No other place in Hawaii has more successfully turned its back on change than Niihau, which has no paved roads, no airport, no island-wide electricity and no telephones.

Niihau is a native Hawaiian preserve and the only island in the state where Hawaiian is still the primary language. The entire island, right down to the church, belongs to the Niihau Ranch, which is privately owned by the non-Hawaiian Robinson family who are highly protective of Niihau's isolation.

Most of Niihau's 202 residents live in Puuwai, a settlement on the dry western shore. They make a living working the Robinson's ranch. Each house in the village is surrounded by a stone wall to keep grazing animals out of the gardens. It's a simple life. Water is collected in catchments; toilets are in outhouses.

Niihauans speak their own melodic dialect of Hawaiian. Business is conducted in Hawaiian, as are Sunday church services. Both of the Robinson brothers who manage the ranch speak Hawaiian fluently.

Children learn English as a second language when they go to school. Niihau has a two-room school with about 25 students, and two teachers instructing the children from kindergarten through to 12th grade. Courses are taught solely in Hawaiian up to the fourth grade.

The economy of the island is based on sheep and cattle ranching. It's a windswept, marginal grazing operation. Major droughts of the 1970s and '80s have taken a toll on the herds, and Niihau has been through some hard times.

A secondary and growing income comes from the production of mesquite charcoal from the kiawe that flourishes in the dry, dusty environment. The mesquite is shipped off to restaurants both in Hawaii and on the mainland.

Niihau is 17 miles from Kauai by a weekly supply boat that plies between the two islands. The boat, an old WW II military landing craft, docks in Kauai at Makaweli, headquarters of Niihau Ranch and the Robinson family. Makaweli is also home to a settlement of Niihauans who prefer to live on Kauai, though many of them still work for the Robinsons.

Niihau is by no means a living history museum of Hawaiians stuck in time. Though it's got a foot in the past it takes what it wants from the present. The supply boat brings Cokes as well as poi, and the island has more dirt bikes than outrigger canoes.

Niihau residents are free to go to Kauai to shop, have a few beers (Niihau itself is dry) or just hang out. What they are not free to do is bring friends from other islands back home with them. Those Niihauans who marry people from other islands, as well as those whom the Robinsons come to see as undesirable, are rarely allowed to return.

Still, for the most part, Niihauans seem to accept that that's the way things are. Some who leave are critical, but those who stay don't appear to be looking for any changes.

To outsiders, Niihau is an enigma. Some romanticise it as a pristine preserve of Hawaiian culture. Others liken its lifestyle to slavery.

The Robinsons see Niihau as a private sanctuary and themselves the protectors of it all. It's that paternalism that sometimes rubs outside native Hawaiian groups the wrong way, though for the most part Niihauans don't seem to share those sentiments and resist interference.

HISTORY
Niihau's First Visitors
Captain Cook anchored off Niihau on 29 January 1778, two weeks after 'discovering' Hawaii. Cook noted in his log that the island was lightly populated and largely barren, a

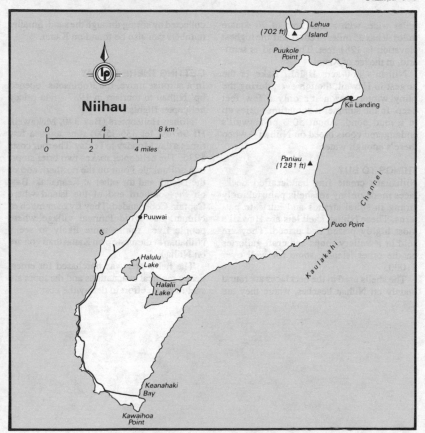

Niihau

Lehua Island (702 ft)

Puukole Point

Kii Landing

Paniau (1281 ft)

Puuwai

Halulu Lake

Halalii Lake

Puoo Point

Kaulakahi Channel

Keanahaki Bay

Kawaihoa Point

0   4   8 km
0   2   4 miles

description still true today. His visit was short, but it had a lasting impact.

It was on little Niihau that Cook first introduced two things that would quickly change the face of Hawaii. He left two goats, the first of the grazing animals that would devastate the native flora and fauna. And his men introduced syphilis, the first of the Western diseases that would decimate the Hawaiian people.

In 1864 Elizabeth Sinclair, a Scottish widow who was moving from New Zealand to Vancouver when she got sidetracked in Hawaii, bought Niihau from Kamehameha V for $10,000. He originally tried to sell her the 'swampland' of Waikiki, but she passed it up for the 'desert island'. Interestingly, no two places in Hawaii today could be further apart, either culturally or in land value.

Mrs Sinclair brought the first sheep to Niihau from New Zealand and started the ranching operation that her great-grandsons continue today.

GEOGRAPHY

Niihau is the smallest of the inhabited Hawaiian islands. It is 18 miles long and six miles wide, with a total area of 70 square miles. It has 45 miles of coast and the highest elevation is 1281 feet. The island is semi-arid, in the lee of Kauai.

Niihau's 860-acre Halalii Lake is the largest in Hawaii, though even during the rainy winter season it's only a few feet deep. In the summer it sometimes dries up to a mud pond. About 50% of Hawaii's endangered coots breed on Niihau – when there's enough water.

THINGS TO BUY

Niihauans create fine handcrafted necklaces made of tiny seashells painstakingly strung in spiral strands and intricate patterns. These Niihau shell leis are Hawaii's most highly prized and priced. They are sold in jewellery shops and craft galleries on the other islands, some for well over $1000.

The shells used in the necklaces are found mainly on Niihau beaches, where they are collected by sifting through the sand. Smaller numbers can also be found on Kauai.

GETTING THERE & AWAY

In a surprise move, the Robinsons 'opened up' Niihau to tourism in 1987 – via pricey helicopter flights.

Niihau Helicopters (Box 370, Makaweli, HI 96769; tel 335-3500) runs tours a few times a day Monday to Friday. The tour costs $235. The helicopter makes two brief stops, one at Puukole Point on the northern end of the island, and the other at Keanahaki Bay, on the southern end of the island where Captain Cook landed. They fly over much of Niihau, but avoid Puuwai village where people live. You're more likely to see a Niihauan at the airstrip on Kauai than you are on Niihau.

The helicopter was purchased for emergency medical evacuations and the tours are said to be an effort to defray the cost.

Northwestern Hawaiian Islands

The Northwestern Hawaiian Islands stretch nearly 1300 miles across the Pacific from Kauai in an almost straight north-westerly line. They are also called the Leeward Islands.

There are 10 island clusters in all. They include atolls, each with a number of low sand islands formed on top of coral reefs, as well as some single rock islands and a reef that is mostly submerged.

Listed according to their order from Kauai, the clusters are Nihoa, Necker Island, French Frigate Shoals, Gardner Pinnacles, Maro Reef, Laysan Island, Lisianski Island, Pearl and Hermes Atoll, Midway Islands and Kure Island.

Together the 10 clusters have 34 named islands, all of which are small. Excluding Midway, the total land area is just under three square miles, though the atoll lagoon areas are a hundred times that.

All the groups except Kure Atoll (a state sea bird sanctuary) and the Midway Islands are part of the Hawaiian Islands National Wildlife Refuge. The refuge, established in 1909 by US president Theodore Roosevelt, is the oldest and largest of the national wildlife refuges.

Visitors are not allowed on the islands unless they have permits, and these are granted only in the rarest of circumstances. Human activities are simply too disturbing to the fragile ecosystem. The only human habitation in the refuge is at Tern Island, and that is for wildlife researchers.

The Midway Islands, though geographically in the Hawaiian archipelago, are under the control of the US Navy and not part of the state of Hawaii. There are five islands, with a total land area of two square miles, supporting a population of about 2000. Midway gained notoriety in WW II when the USA secured a major victory over Japan in a naval battle there in June 1942.

The other islands come under the political, though not the practical, jurisdiction of the City and County of Honolulu.

The Northwestern Hawaiian Islands, volcanic in origin, once jutted up high above sea level as the main Hawaiian islands do now. They are slowly slipping back into the sea, however, as a result of a sagging of the ocean floor and the forces of erosion.

The coral reefs appear like flower leis left floating on the water where the mountains once raised their heads.

FAUNA

The Northwestern Hawaiian Islands are home to around 15 million sea birds, who each find room for at least a foothold. Endangered Hawaiian monk seals, green sea turtles and four endemic land birds also live there.

Sea Birds

Eighteen sea bird species nest on these islands, feeding on the abundant fish that live around the submerged reefs. They include frigate birds, boobies, albatrosses, terns, shearwaters, petrels, tropicbirds and noddies.

The sooty terns are the most abundant, numbering in the several millions. These screeching black and white birds also nest on the offshore islets of Oahu's windward coast.

Shearwaters and petrels lay their eggs in burrows that they dig in the sandy soil. The roofs of the burrows can easily collapse under the feet of non-observant walkers, which is one reason why visitors are discouraged.

Land Birds

The Laysan duck, Laysan finch, Nihoa finch and Nihoa millerbird, endemic to Laysan and Nihoa islands respectively, are all listed as endangered or threatened species.

This is not because their numbers are declining but because these species exist in only one place on earth and are therefore susceptible to the introduction of new diseases and predators or the disruption of their habitat. One rat from a shipwrecked boat, weed seed from a hiker's boot or an oil slick washing ashore could mean the end of the species.

Monk Seals

The endangered Hawaiian monk seal, which exists only in Hawaii, uses Kure Atoll, the French Frigate Shoals and Laysan, Lisianski, Nihoa and Necker islands for pupping grounds. The seals are easily disturbed by human contact.

In the 19th century the seals were nearly hunted to extinction. Military operations in the area during and after WW II also resulted in a decline.

Fewer than 200 seal pups are born each year, many of which die from shark attacks. The total species population is around 1000.

FRENCH FRIGATE SHOALS

The French Frigate Shoals consist of 13 sand islands and a 135-foot rock, La Perouse Pinnacle, which was named after the French explorer who was almost wrecked on the reef. One of the sand islands, 37-acre Tern Island, is the field headquarters for the Hawaiian Islands National Wildlife Refuge.

Most of Tern Island is covered by an airfield left over from the days when the US Coast Guard had a loran (radio navigation system) station there. The old coast guard barracks now house two refuge managers, who work for the US Fish & Wildlife Service, and up to a dozen volunteers.

Tern Island is home to 17 species of sea bird and a lot of Hawaiian monk seals. Ninety percent of the green sea turtles that nest in the Hawaiian Islands nest at French Frigate Shoals.

LAYSAN ISLAND

Laysan Island is a classic example of how human interference can wreak havoc on island ecology.

Laysan is 1.45 square miles in size, which is small although it's actually the largest of the Northwestern Hawaiian Islands. From 1890 to 1904 Laysan was mined for guano – the phosphate-rich bird droppings used for fertiliser. Houses were built, mules brought ashore and ships docked to take the guano away.

There were once millions of birds on Laysan – mostly Laysan albatrosses, otherwise known as gooney birds. In addition to guano mining, albatross eggs were collected by the hundreds of thousands to be sold for their albumen, a substance used in photo processing.

As each albatross lays just one egg a year, an 'egging' sweep could destroy an entire year's hatch. Hunters also ravaged the islands. In one six-month period alone, 300,000 birds were killed for their feathers, which were used by milliners to make hats for fashionable ladies.

Rabbits were introduced to Laysan, first as pets for the workers' children and later for breeding. They virtually destroyed the island's vegetation, and where they left off sandstorms took over. The loss of native food plants spelt the end of the Laysan flightless rail, Laysan honeycreeper and Laysan millerbird – all endemic land birds. The rabbits were finally exterminated in 1923.

There are now about 160,000 pairs of Laysan albatrosses on the island, still the world's largest colony. Albatrosses sometimes court and dance for five annual mating seasons before actually mating. Once they do mate, pairs stay together for life and sometimes live for 30 years.

The Laysan duck reached the brink of extinction as a result of the activities of rabbits and hunters. Their numbers were reduced to just six by 1911, but they're making a modest comeback. Laysan ducks swim in the brackish lagoon in the centre of the island, their only habitat. With a current population of about 300, they are one of the rarest ducks in the world.

The Laysan finch, the population of which was once as low as 100, thanks to the rabbits, is now common on Laysan Island and has also been introduced to Pearl and Hermes Reef. Unlike its cousin the honeycreeper on the main Hawaiian islands, which feeds on nectar, the Laysan finch has become carnivorous and feeds on sea-bird eggs as well as the carcasses of dead sea birds.

There are also more than one million sooty terns nesting on Laysan.

NECKER & NIHOA

Necker and Nihoa, closest to the main Hawaiian islands, were probably settled more than a thousand years ago. Remains of stone temple platforms, numerous house sites, terraces and carved stone images have been found on the islands. Archaeological remains suggest that the early settlers were from the Marquesas.

Necker and Nihoa are not coral atolls but rugged rocky islands, each less than a quarter of a square mile. Nihoa is the highest of the Northwestern Hawaiian Islands, with sheer sea cliffs and a peak elevation of 910 feet.

Two land bird species live only on tiny Nihoa.

The Nihoa finch, which like the Laysan finch is a raider of other birds' eggs, is hanging in there with a population of a few thousand. Attempts were made in 1967 to develop a back-up colony in case something happened to the birds on Nihoa. It failed when all 42 finches sent to the French Frigate Shoals died.

The grey Nihoa millerbird, related to the old world warbler family, is rare and secretive. It wasn't even discovered until 1923 and was so named because it eats miller moths. Approximately 400 birds remain.

Glossary

aa – lava which is rough and jagged

ahi – albacore (yellowfin) tuna

ahu – stone cairns used to mark a trail; or an altar or shrine

ahupuaa – a traditional land division, usually in a wedge shape from the mountains to the sea

aku – skipjack tuna

akua – god, spirit, idol

akule – mackerel bigeye scad

alii – chief, or royalty

aloha – the traditional greeting meaning love, welcome, goodbye.

amakihi – small yellow-green bird, one of the more common of the native birds

apapane – bright red native Hawaiian honeycreeper

au – marlin

awa – kava (*piper methysticum*), made into an intoxicating brew

bento – the Japanese word for a fixed box lunch

elepaio – a brownish forest bird with a white rump

hala – pandanus; the leaves are used in weaving mats and baskets

hale – house

haole – Caucasian; literally 'without breath', it was formerly applied to any foreigner

hau – common indigenous lowland tree with spreading tangled branches; the flower resembles a hibiscus, the wood is often used for outrigger canoes

haupia – coconut pudding

heiau – ancient stone temple, a place of worship in Hawaii before Western contact

holua – sled, or sled course

hukilau – net fishing, with a seine, which involves a group of people; the word can also refer to the feast that follows

hula – traditional Hawaiian dance

hula halau – hula school or troupe

iiwi – a bright vermillion forest bird with a curved salmon-coloured beak

ilima – native groundcover with a delicate yellow-orange flower

imu – underground earthen oven used in traditional luau cooking

kahuna – wise person in any field, commonly a priest, healer or sorcerer

kahili – a feather standard, used as a symbol of royalty

kalua pig – pig baked in an *imu*; this is a traditional luau dish

kamaaina – native-born Hawaiian or a long-time resident; literally 'child of the land'.

kapu – taboo, part of strict ancient Hawaiian social system

keiki – child, children

kiawe – a relative of the mesquite tree introduced to Hawaii in the 1820s, now very common; its branches are covered with sharp thorns

kipuka – an area of land spared when lava flows around it; an oasis

koa – native hardwood tree often used in woodworking of native crafts

kona – leeward, or a leeward wind

konane – ancient Hawaiian board game similar to checkers

koolau – windward side

Ku – Polynesian god of war

kukui – the candlenut tree; this is the official state tree and a native to Hawaii; the oil from the nuts was once used in lamps

kuula – fishing shrine

lanai – veranda

lauhala – leaves of the *hala* plant used in weaving

laulau – wrapped package; pork or beef with salted fish and taro leaves wrapped in leaves and steamed

lei – garland, usually of flowers, but also of leaves or shells

lilikoi – passion fruit

limu – seaweed

528

lomi – raw, diced salmon marinated with tomatoes and onions

Lono – Polynesian god of harvest, agriculture and peace

loulu – native fan palms

luakini – a type of *heiau* dedicated to the war god Ku and used for human sacrifices

luau – traditional Hawaiian feast

mahalo – thank you

mahimahi – this means a 'dolphin', but this fish is unrelated to the mammal

maile – native twining plant with fragrant leaves often used in leis

makaainana – common people; literally 'people who tend the land'

makahiki – ancient annual four-month winter festival dedicated to Lono when sports and celebrations replaced all warfare

makai – towards the sea

malo – loincloth

mana – spiritual power

mauka – towards the mountains; inland

menehune – 'little people' who according to legend built many of Hawaii's fishponds, *heiaus* and other stonework

milo – a native shade tree with beautiful hardwood

moo – water spirit, water lizard or dragon

muumuu – a long, loose-fitting dress introduced by the missionaries

naupaka – a native shrub, the delicate white flower of which looks like it's torn in half

nene – a native goose; Hawaii's state bird

noni – Indian mulberry; a small tree with yellow, warty, smelly fruit, used medicinally

ohana – family, extended family

ohia lehua – native Hawaiian tree; the flowers, which are most often red, are tufted feathery pompoms

ohelo – low-growing native shrub with edible red berries related to cranberries, said to be sacred to Pele

okole – buttocks

ono – delicious; also the name of the wahoo fish

opakapaka – pink snapper fish

opihi – edible limpet

pahoehoe – type of lava which flows quickly and smoothly

pakalolo – marijuana; literally 'crazy smoke'

pali – cliff

paniolo – a Hawaiian cowboy; the word is derived from 'espanole', as Hawaii's first cowboys were Mexican and Spanish

Pele – goddess of fire and volcanoes, whose home is in Kilauea volcano

piko – navel, umbilical cord

pili – a bunch grass, commonly used for thatching houses

pilikia – trouble

poha – gooseberry

poi – a staple food of the Hawaiian diet, poi is a gooey paste made from taro roots

puka – any kind of hole or opening

pupu – snack food, hors d'oeuvres; shells

puu – hill, cinder cone

puuhonua – place of refuge

saimin – a Japanese noodle soup

tabi – Japanese reef-walking shoes

tapa – cloth made by pounding and mashing the bark of the paper mulberry tree; used for early Hawaiian clothing

taro – a plant, with green heart-shaped leaves, cultivated in Hawaii for its edible rootstock. The root is mashed to make *poi*.

teishoku – Japanese word for fixed-plate meal

ti – common native plant; its long shiny 'multi-purpose' leaves are used for a variety of things, including plates and *hula* skirts

ukelele – a stringed musical instrument derived from the 'braginha', which was introduced to Hawaii in the 1800s by Portuguese immigrants

ulu – breadfruit

wahine – woman

Index

MAPS

Temperature

To convert °C to °F multiply by 1.8 and add 32
To convert °F to °C subtract 32 and multiply by .55

Length, Distance & Area

	multiply by
inches to centimetres	2.54
centimetres to inches	0.39
feet to metres	0.30
metres to feet	3.28
yards to metres	0.91
metres to yards	1.09
miles to kilometres	1.61
kilometres to miles	0.62
acres to hectares	0.40
hectares to acres	2.47

Weight

	multiply by
ounces to grams	28.35
grams to ounces	0.035
pounds to kilograms	0.45
kilograms to pounds	2.21
British tons to kilograms	1016
US tons to kilograms	907

A British ton is 2240 lbs, a US ton is 2000 lbs

Volume

	multiply by
imperial gallons to litres	4.55
litres to imperial gallons	0.22
US gallons to litres	3.79
litres to US gallons	0.26

5 imperial gallons equals 6 US gallons
a litre is slightly more than a US quart, slightly less than a British one

Guides to North America & Mexico

Alaska - a travel survival kit
Jim DuFresne has travelled extensively through Alaska by foot, road, rail, ferry and kayak, and tells how to make the most of the enormous possibilities offered in one of the world's great wilderness areas.

Canada - a travel survival kit
This comprehensive guidebook has all the travel facts on the USA's huge neighbour — the Rocky Mountains, Niagara Falls, ultra-modern Toronto, remote villages in Nova Scotia, and much more.

Mexico - a travel survival kit
A unique blend of Indian and Spanish culture, fascinating history, and hospitable people, make Mexico a travellers' paradise.

Baja California - a travel survival kit
For centuries, Mexico's Baja peninsula — with its beautiful coastline, raucous border towns, and crumbling Spanish missions — has been a land of escapes and escapades. This book tells you how and where to escape in Baja.

Lonely Planet Guidebooks

Lonely Planet guidebooks cover virtually every accessible part of Asia as well as Australia, the Pacific, Central and South America, Africa, the Middle East and parts of North America. There are four main series: 'travel survival kits', covering a single country for a range of budgets; 'shoestring' guides with compact information for low-budget travel in a major region; trekking guides; and 'phrasebooks'.

Mail Order

Lonely Planet guidebooks are distributed worldwide and are sold by good bookshops everywhere. They are also available by mail order from Lonely Planet, so if you have difficulty finding a title please write to us. US and Canadian residents should write to Embarcadero West, 112 Linden St, Oakland CA 94607, USA and residents of other countries to PO Box 617, Hawthorn, Victoria 3122, Australia.

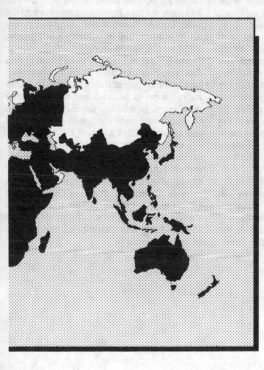

Lonely Planet

Lonely Planet published its first book in 1973. Tony and Maureen Wheeler had made an overland trip from England to Australia and, in response to numerous 'how do you do it?' questions, Tony wrote and they published *Across Asia on the Cheap*. It became an instant local best seller and inspired thoughts of a second travel guide. A year and a half in South-East Asia resulted in their second book, *South-East Asia on a Shoestring*, which they put together in a backstreet Chinese hotel in Singapore in 1975. The 'yellow book', as it quickly became known, soon became the guide to the region and has gone through six editions, always with its familiar yellow cover.

Soon other writers came to them with ideas for similar books - books that went off the beaten track, books that 'assumed you knew how to get your luggage off the carousel' as one reviewer put it. Lonely Planet grew from a kitchen table operation to a spare room and then to its own office. Its international reputation began to grow as the Lonely Planet logo began to appear in more and more countries. In 1982 *India - a travel survival kit* won the Thomas Cook award for the best guidebook of the year.

These days there are over 70 Lonely Planet titles. Over 40 people work at our office in Melbourne and another half dozen at our US office in Oakland, California.

At first Lonely Planet specialised in the Asia region but these days we are also developing major ranges of guidebooks to the Pacific region, to South America and to Africa. The list of walking guides is growing and Lonely Planet now has a unique series of phrasebooks to 'unusual' languages. The emphasis continues to be on travel for travellers and Tony and Maureen still manage to fit in a number of trips each year and play a very active part in the writing and updating of Lonely Planet's guides.

Keeping guidebooks up to date is a constant battle which requires an ear to the ground and lots of walking, but technology also plays its part. All Lonely Planet guidebooks are now stored on computer, and some authors even take lap-top computers into the field. Lonely Planet is also using computers to draw maps and eventually many of the maps will be stored on disc.

The people at Lonely Planet strongly feel that travellers can make a positive contribution to the countries they visit both by better appreciation of cultures and by the money they spend. In addition the company tries to make a direct contribution to the countries and regions it covers. Since 1986 a percentage of the income from each book has gone to aid groups and associations. This has included donations to famine relief in Africa, to aid projects in India, to agricultural projects in Central America, to Greenpeace's efforts to halt French nuclear testing in the Pacific and to Amnesty International. In 1989 $41,000 was donated by Lonely Planet to these projects.